AA004034

IARIA Congress 2023

The 2023 IARIA Annual Congress on Frontiers in Science, Technology, Services, and Applications

November 13th – 17th, 2023

Valencia, Spain

IARIA Congress 2023 Editors

Hans-Werner Sehring, Nordakademie – University of Applied Sciences, Hamburg, Germany

Steve Chan, Decision Engineering Analysis Laboratory, VTIRL, VT, USA

Isaac Caicedo-Castro, Universidad de Córdoba, Colombia

Arcady Zhukov, University of Basque Country, UPV/EHU, Spain

Roy Sterritt, Ulster University, UK

Printed from e-media with permission by:

Curran Associates, Inc.
57 Morehouse Lane
Red Hook, NY 12571

Some format issues inherent in the e-media version may also appear in this print version.

Printed with permission by Curran Associates, Inc. (2024)

International Academy, Research, and Industry Association (IARIA)
412 Derby Way
Wilmington, DE 19810

Phone: (408) 893-6407
Fax: (408) 527-6351

petre@iaria.org

Additional copies of this publication are available from:

Curran Associates, Inc.
57 Morehouse Lane
Red Hook, NY 12571 USA
Phone: 845-758-0400
Fax: 845-758-2633
Email: curran@proceedings.com
Web: www.proceedings.com

Table of Contents

Fostering Trust on Machine Learning Inferences 1
Dalmo Cirne

Social Requirements for Designing Self-Adaptive Privacy Schemes in Cloud: The Interrelation of Social Identity with Self Disclosure Practices 5
Angeliki Kitsiou, Maria Sideri, Aikaterini – Georgia Mavroeidi, Katerina Vgena, Eleni Tzortzaki, Michail Pantelelis, Stavros Simou, and Christos Kalloniatis

Utilization of Ozone Water Generators for Preventing Infection in Home Care 11
Koichi Umimoto, Shinichi Iguchi, Yoshimasa Shimamoto, Kastunori Tachibana, Syunji Nagata, and Yuki Nakamura

Satellite Selection Algorithm to Optimize a Solution for Autonomous Driving Applications 14
Tiago Goncalves, Gianmarco Fedeli, Clara Lazaro, Helder Silva, and Telmo Vieira

The Screen is not Flat 20
Luciane Maria Fadel

Exploring the Temperature Dependent Magnetic Properties and Magnetoimpedance Effect in Fe-rich Microwires for Temperature Monitoring 26
Paula Corte-Leon, Ivan Skorvanek, Frantisek Andrejka, Valentina Zhukova, Mihail Ipatov, and Arcady Zhukov

SLAM-based Mapping in Truck-and-Robot System for Last-Mile Delivery Automation 31
Ryo Nakamura, Masafumi Hashimoto, and Kazuhiko Takahashi

A Tool for Automating Sizing in Agile Development Using the COSMIC Method 38
Bruel Gerancon and Sylvie Trudel

Towards Hypothesis-driven Forensic Text Exploration System 42
Jenny Felser, Dirk Labudde, and Michael Spranger

Comparison of 2D Virtual Learning Environments with Classic Video Conferencing Systems for Tertiary Education 48
Gerhard Hube, Kevin Pfeffel, and Nicholas Mueller

Development and Application of a New Ontology in the Context of Hybrid AC/DC Grids 58
Alessandro Rossi, Marzia Mammina, Jawad Kazmi, Zhiyu Pan, Charles Emehel, Bharath Varsh Rao, and Antonello Monti

An Autonomic Approach to Security Incident Response and Prevention in Cloud Computing 65
Glenn Russell and Roy Sterritt

AC/DC: Autonomic Computing to Maintain Drone Fleet Continuity 73
Fiachra Merwick and Roy Sterritt

Autonomic Computing in the Cloud: An Overview of Past, Present and Future Trends 77
Alistair McLean and Roy Sterritt

Autonomic Computing for Autonomous Vehicles 83
Alastair Martin and Roy Sterritt

Development of Free Space Microwave Sensing of Carbon Fiber Composites with Ferromagnetic Microwire Inclusions 88
Valentina Zhukova, Mihail Ipatov, Paula Corte-Leon, Alvaro Gonzalez, Alfonso Garcia-Gomez, Francisco Javier Vallejo, Peio Olaskoaga, Johan Malm, Christer Johansson, Rafael Garcia-Etxabe, and Arcady Zhukov

Electric Network Frequency Optical Sensing Devices 94
Christos Moysiadis, Georgios Karantaidis, and Constantine Kotropoulos

Physical Demonstrator of Medical Imaging Unit: Threat Analysis and Protection Strategies in Cybersecurity 100
Marina Galiano Botella

Towards a Secure City: The Contribution of the Smart City Physical Demonstrator in Threat Assessment 104
Marina Galiano Botella, Eduardo Ortega Serrano, and Elvira Lara Maudos

Hybrid Networking Platform for Minority Groups in Accessing Labour Market 108
Cecilia Olivieri, Agathe Semlali, Davide Carminati, and Lorenzo Maggio Laquidara

Verification Tasks through Deep Learning in a Semantic Information Extraction System 111
Angel Luis Garrido, Norman U. Bellorin, Alvaro Peiro, and Eduardo Mena

Model-supported Software Creation: Towards Holistic Model-driven Software Engineering 113
Hans-Werner Sehring

Improvement of Fatty Acids Composition of a Microalga Isolated from the Moroccan Seawater for Biodiesel Production 119
Salima Ouled Hajja, Miloudia Slaoui, and Houria El Bakraoui

Sensorization and Optimization of Industrial Graphic Arts Machinery Using Artificial Intelligence Techniques 121
Angel Luis Garrido, Jonathan Rodriguez, Mariano Sanchez, Jose Manuel Anton, Roberto Castan, Susana Sangiao, Carlos Bobed, and Eduardo Mena

Cod Catch Forecasting through Machine Learning Algorithms at the Haul Level 123
Huamin Ren, Yajie Liu, and Keshav Prasad Paudel

Non-deterministic Operation Profiles Based on Multi-Layer Interest Landscapes for Autonomous Robotic Teams 128
Florian Segor, Igor Tchouchenkov, Aleksej Buller, and Matthias Kollmann

Applying Multimodal Data to Meta Learning for Time-Series Analysis in CPS 136
Philipp Ruf, Christoph Reich, and Djaffar Ould-Abdeslam

A Multivocal Review on Derivation Games 144
Diego Castro and Claudia Werner

Exploring Product Line Concepts in Game Building 150
Diego Castro and Claudia Werner

Application of Three-Phase Methodology for Retrofit 4.0 in Legacy Industrial Plants 153
Andrei Tchepurnoy Machado, Renan Yamaguti, Raphael Montali Assumpcao, Omar Carvalho Branquinho, and Paulo Cardieri

BCI-based Game Control to Boost Focus and Attention in Students 160
Komalpreet Kaur and Manish Wadhwa

Commute Tracking Mentor Tool for Automobile to Decrease Car Accidents 164
Mario Ervin and Kanwalinderjit Kaur

Direct Democracy System Architecture for Sustainable Community Participation 170
Aderonke Thompson, Nikolaos Papakonstantinou, and Dharmendra Sharma

Forecasting Failure Risk in Early Mathematics and Physical Science Courses in the Bachelor's Degree in Engineering 177
Isaac Caicedo-Castro, Mario Macea-Anaya, and Samir Castano-Rivera

An Exercise Recommendation System While Performing Daily Activities Based on Contextual Information 188
Mizuki Kobayashi and Kaori Fujinami

The Triumvirate of Bespoke Diverse Hybridized Activation Functions, Adaptive Momentum, and Enhanced Entropic Wavelet Energy Spectrum Discernment for Higher Efficacy Detection of Artificial Intelligence-centric Attacks 196
Steve Chan

Moment Generating Function Based Calculation of Average Bit Error Probability in an ?-μ Fading Environment with Selection Diversity Receiver 203
Dragana Krstic, Suad Suljovic, Devendra S. Gurjar, and Suneel Yadav

Estimating Text Similarity based on Semantic Concept Embeddings 208
Tim vor der Bruck and Marc Pouly

IARIA Congress 2023

Forward

The 2023 IARIA Annual Congress on Frontiers in Science, Technology, Services, and Applications (IARIA Congress 2023), held between November 13th and November 17th, 2023, continued a series of international events keeping pace with the achievements and challenges our society is facing in science, technologies, services, and applications.

The annual event was a multidomain assembly of scientists, specialists, and decision makers from all economical, educational, and governmental entities, on Social Systems, Software, Data Science Analytics, Communications, Technology, and Networked Services. Apart from classical topics, the congress targeted frontier achievements on Knowledge Science, Data Science, Artificial Intelligence / Machine Learning (AI/ML)-based systems, Self-managing systems, Human-centric technologies, Advanced robotics, Virtual Worlds, Mobility, Sensing, Energy, Electric Vehicles, Green Energy, etc.

The IARIA Congress had a special scientific format where outstanding former IARIA scientists delivered dedicated speeches (Keynote speeches, Tutorial lectures) along with peer-reviewed contributions on the themes of achievements and challenges in science, technologies, services, and applications.

We take here the opportunity to warmly thank all the members of the IARIA Congress 2023 technical program committee, as well as all the reviewers. The creation of such a high-quality conference program would not have been possible without their involvement. We also kindly thank all the authors who dedicated much of their time and effort to contribute to IARIA Congress 2023. We truly believe that, thanks to all these efforts, the final conference program consisted of top-quality contributions. We also thank the members of the IARIA Congress 2023 organizing committee for their help in handling the logistics of this event.

We hope that IARIA Congress 2023 was a successful international forum for the exchange of ideas and results between academia and industry and for the promotion of progress in our society.

IARIA Congress 2023 Chairs

IARIA Congress 2023 Steering Committee

Carlos Becker Westphall, Federal University of Santa Catarina, Brazil
Luigi Lavazza, Università dell'Insubria – Varese, Italy
Timothy T. Pham, Jet Propulsion Laboratory - California Institute of Technology, USA
Hermann Kaindl, TU Wien, Vienna, Austria
Arcady Zhukov, University of Basque Country (UPV/EHU), San Sebastian / Ikerbasque, Basque Foundation for Science, Bilbao, Spain
Lasse Berntzen, University of South-Eastern Norway, Norway
Bob Duncan, University of Aberdeen, UK
Yasushi Kambayashi, Sanyo-Onoda City University, Japan

IARIA Congress 2023 Publicity Chairs

Lorena Parra Boronat, Universitat Politecnica de Valencia, Spain
Sandra Viciano Tudela, Universitat Politecnica de Valencia, Spain
Jose Miguel Jimenez, Universitat Politecnica de Valencia, Spain

IARIA Congress 2023
Committee

IARIA Congress 2023 Steering Committee

Carlos Becker Westphall, Federal University of Santa Catarina, Brazil
Luigi Lavazza, Università dell'Insubria – Varese, Italy
Timothy T. Pham, Jet Propulsion Laboratory - California Institute of Technology, USA
Hermann Kaindl, TU Wien, Vienna, Austria
Arcady Zhukov, University of Basque Country (UPV/EHU), San Sebastian / Ikerbasque, Basque Foundation for Science, Bilbao, Spain
Lasse Berntzen, University of South-Eastern Norway, Norway
Bob Duncan, University of Aberdeen, UK
Yasushi Kambayashi, Sanyo-Onoda City University, Japan

IARIA Congress 2023 Publicity Chairs

Lorena Parra Boronat, Universitat Politecnica de Valencia, Spain
Sandra Viciano Tudela, Universitat Politecnica de Valencia, Spain
Jose Miguel Jimenez, Universitat Politecnica de Valencia, Spain

IARIA Congress 2023 Technical Program Committee

Tamer Abdou, Ryerson University, Canada
Nitin Agarwal, COSMOS Research Center | University of Arkansas at Little Rock, USA
Abiola Akinnubi, Infinity Ward (Activision Publishing) Woodland Hill / COSMOS Research Center Little Rock, Arkansas, USA
Sedat Akleylek, Ondokuz Mayis University, Samsun, Turkey
Murat Akpinar, ASELSAN A.Ş., Ankara, Turkey
Raid Rafi Omar Al-Nima, Northern Technical University, Iraq
Hesham Ali, University of Nebraska Omaha , USA
Ali T. Alouani, Tennessee Technological University, USA
Mohammad Alsulami, University of Connecticut, USA
Lasse Berntzen, University of South-Eastern Norway, Norway
Ayush Bhargava, Meta, USA
Sandjai Bhulai, Vrije Universiteit Amsterdam, Netherlands
John Blake, University of Aizu, Japan
Oleksandr Blazhko, National University «Odessa Polytechnic», Ukraine
Natalia Bogach, Peter the Great St. Petersburg Polytechnic University, Russia
Abdelmadjid Bouabdallah, University of Technology of Compiegne, France
Christian Bourret, Université Gustave Eiffel (Paris Est Marne-la-Vallée), France
Isaac Caicedo-Castro, University of Córdoba, Colombia
Dirceu Cavendish, Kyushu Institute of Technology, Japan
Steve Chan, Decision Engineering Analysis Laboratory, USA
André Constantino da Silva, Federal Institute of São Paulo - IFSP, Brazil
Toon De Pessemier, Imec - WAVES - Ghent University, Belgium
Lizette De Wet, University of the Free State, South Africa

Michael Spranger, Hochschule Mittweida | University of Applied Sciences, Germany
Christos Troussas, University of West Attica, Greece
Jos van Rooyen, Huis voor software kwaliteit, The Netherlands
Eric MSP Veith, OFFIS e.V. - Institut für Informatik, Oldenburg, Germany
Zhijie Xu, University of Huddersfield, UK
Nanmiao Wu, Center for Computation and Technology of Louisiana State University, USA
Maram Bani Younes, Philadelphia University, Jordan
Elena Zaitseva, University of Zilina, Slovakia
Xingyu Zhou, Dow Inc., USA
Arkady Zhukov, University of Basque Country - UPV/EHU | IKERBASQUE - Basque Foundation for Science, Spain

Copyright Information

Fostering Trust on Machine Learning Inferences

Dalmo Cirne
Machine Learning for Financials
Workday
Boulder, USA
email: dalmo.cirne@workday.com

***Abstract*—Artificial Intelligence (AI) and Machine Learning (ML) providers have a tremendous responsibility to develop valid and reliable systems. Much is discussed about trusting AI and ML inferences, but little has been done to define what that means. Those who work in the space of ML-based products, have familiarity with the topics of transparency, explainability, safety, bias, and so forth, yet there are no frameworks to quantify and measure such items. Producing ever more trustworthy machine learning inferences is a path to increase the value of products (i.e., increased trust in the results) and to engage in conversations with users to gather feedback to further improve products. In this paper, we begin by examining the dynamic of trust between a provider (Trustor) and users (Trustees). Trustors are required to be trusting and trustworthy, whereas trustees need not be trusting nor trustworthy. The challenge for trustors is to provide results that are good enough to make a trustee increase their level of trust above a minimum threshold for: 1- doing business together; 2- continuation of service. Then, we conclude by proposing a framework to capture quantitative metrics to be used to objectively understand how trustworthy an AI and ML system can claim to be, and their trend over time.**

***Index Terms*—artificial intelligence, game theory, machine learning, trust.**

I. Introduction

The emergence of a new technology has always been accompanied by the challenge of earning the trust of the public in general. This has happened during the Industrial Revolution—with the mechanization of processes—and in numerous other occasions. Today, our problem is to establish a framework for increasing trust on systems powered by machine learning.

Much talk has taken place, but not much has been done to establishing a framework to measure trust.

In this paper, a step is taken in the direction of defining a framework for quantifying and measuring trust on machine learning inferences. This, however, has its own challenges, such as: defining a starting point, measuring qualitative aspects, and tracking the trust level over time.

The paradigm explored here assumes that trust is built by an initial *altruistic* act by the trustor, signaling that the actor is trustworthy. More specifically, the trustor's altruistic act would be to invest in building a product and offer it to customers with the promise that it will generate value to them; more value than what is paid in return for the service. The trustor decides how much to invest, and the trustee decides whether to reciprocate and give continuity to the business relationship.

The objective is to make customers trust—above a minimum threshold T—as to incentivize them to engage in the *Trust Game* [1]. These games are extensions built on top of the foundation of *Game Theory* [2].

In addition, trust has a temporal element to it. Once established, there are no guarantees that there will be a continuation; therefore, this is an extensive form of the interactions, where both actors collaborate and observe each other, reacting to historical actions from one another.

Models are representations that aspire to approximate reality, and like other models, the framework proposed here is subject to the noise in its variables, and the gap between what is captured versus what actually happens. The fewer distortions, the better the framework becomes.

In the *Trust Games* section, we establish the flow of how the value of a product is transferred to trustees, and how trustors receive a portion of that value back. Then, we propose a numeric framework to measure the trust level in the *Quantifying Trust* section. Next, we define the criteria for obtaining a minimum level of trust in the *Threshold* section, and last, in the *Simulated Experiments* section, we conclude by presenting the results from the simulations [3].

II. Trust Games

The motion of a *Trust Game* is developed around two actors: a trustor and a trustee. The trustor has a service of value V to offer to a trustee. The value in question is *quality machine learning inferences*. ML is implemented as a software service and, by its nature, software can be replicated to any number n of customers without physical constraints, thus V can be offered independently and concurrently to all customers.

Note that the nature of concurrency allows for independent actors (trustees) to observe and react to the actions of other actors.

It could be the case that the value V of inferences may be only partially absorbed by a trustee. The limited, portioned, consumption could be due to a variety of reasons, including, but not limited to, eligibility or capacity to use all the features (i.e., satisfies all requirements), service subscription tiers, users have yet to be trained.

In order to represent the range of scenarios where the trustor may transfer the entirety of value V or a smaller portion of it, we introduce a multiplier p, where $\{p \in \mathbb{R} \mid 0 \leq p \leq 1\}$. Therefore, the initial remittance sent by trustor u is:

$$R_u = pV \tag{1}$$

Depending on the quality of the results delivered by the trustor, the perception of value by trustees may be magnified or reduced by a factor K, where $\{K \in \mathbb{R}\}$. For $K > 1$, it means that the trustor improved the efficiency of operations for the trustee (they do better than operating on their own). For $K = 1$ the trustee is operating at the same efficiency, and for $K < 1$ (negative values are also possible) the trustee is less efficient than before they started using the service.

The initial perceived gain received by trustee v is:

$$\begin{aligned} G_v &= KR_u \\ &= KpV \end{aligned} \tag{2}$$

A trustee is free to reciprocate or not. They may decline continuing the trial or decline a contract renewal. On the other hand, assuming that the value received from ML inferences improved their efficiency, the incentive is to continue to engage. In either case, a trustee will give back a portion q of the gain received, where $\{q \in \mathbb{R} \mid 0 \leq q < 1\}$. The value sent back may take the form of monetary payment for the service, interviews, usability feedback, labeling of transactions, or a combination of those. The repayment B expected by trustor u is, therefore:

$$\begin{aligned} B_u &= qG_v \\ &= qKpV \end{aligned} \tag{3}$$

There could be a consideration to introduce a magnification factor on the repayment from trustee v. That, however, is not necessary in the scope of this paper, since trustees do not need to be trustworthy; trustor u is not evaluating whether to trust them or not.

Fig. 1 represents the flow of the initial step in this trust game. The blue line segment represents the range of possible values delivered to trustees by the trustor, the large blue circle is the magnification factor applied to the value delivered, and the orange line segment represents the range of possible values reciprocated to the trustor by a trustee.

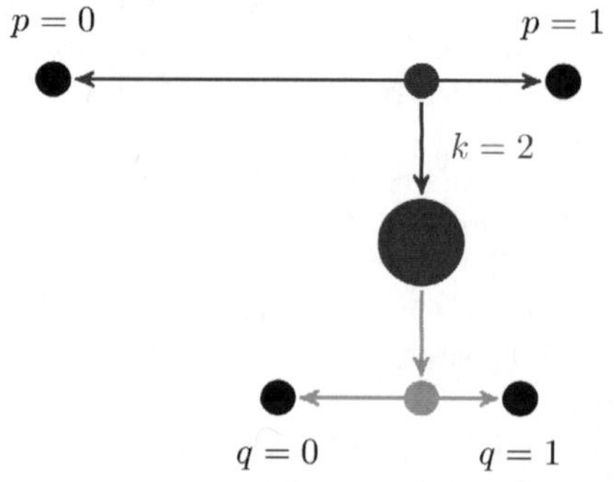

Fig. 1: Trust Game payoffs.

Regarding the magnification factor, for the cases where $K > 1$, the value received back by trustor u is positive and enables the necessary conditions for an extensive form of the trust game (long-term engagement). It becomes a strong indicator that trustee v trustiness towards trustor u is equal or above the minimum threshold T, where $\{T \in \mathbb{R} \mid 0 \leq T \leq 1\}$.

When $0 \leq K < 1$, the service is causing the trustee some form of disruption (in the sense that efficiency has dropped below the level prior to using the service). This would be acceptable during the development phase of a product where the trustee takes part in a beta test program. In such situation, the trustee sees a benefit in participating, assuming future value in adopting the service and the ability to harvest the benefits early on.

The worst-case scenario happens when $K < 0$. This could lead to rapid erosion of trustor u trustworthiness, customer churn, and other negative outcomes.

III. QUANTIFYING TRUST

The aim of this trust game is to create the circumstances necessary for continuous and repeated interactions between trustor and trustee that take place over long periods of time, with no specified temporal upper boundary.

After the initial remittance R_u (1), there may be residual value r on the trustor's side that a trustee did not take advantage of. For instance, maybe not all product features are being used, inference happens in batches and data is yet to be sent through the pipeline, or some other reason. That residual value is what is left from V:

$$\begin{aligned} r_u &= V - R_u \\ &= V - pV \\ &= (1 - p)V \end{aligned} \tag{4}$$

The accumulated value A for trustor u upon completing the first cycle is the residual value r_u (4) plus the repayment B_u (3) received from the trustee:

$$\begin{aligned} A_u^{\text{1st cycle}} &= r_u^1 + B_u^1 \\ &= (1 - p_1)V + q_1K_1p_1V \\ &= V(1 - p_1 + q_1K_1p_1) \end{aligned} \tag{5}$$

On the trustee's side, they will have received a value of G_v (2) and given back a portion q of it. The net gain N for trustee v at the end of the first cycle is:

$$\begin{aligned} N_v^{\text{1st cycle}} &= G_v^1 - q_1G_v^1 \\ &= (1 - q_1)K_1p_1V \end{aligned} \tag{6}$$

Generalizing the gains for trustor and trustee for n cycles of the trust game, we have equations for trustor:

$$A_u = V\left(1 - \sum_{i=1}^{n} p_i + \sum_{i=1}^{n}(q_i)\sum_{i=1}^{n}(K_i)\sum_{i=1}^{n}(p_i)\right) \tag{7}$$

and trustee:

$$N_v = V\left(1 - \sum_{i=1}^{n} q_i\right) \sum_{i=1}^{n}(K_i) \sum_{i=1}^{n}(p_i) \quad (8)$$

The objective is to maximize the payoff to trustee and trustor, establishing a region where the exchange of values is considered fair trade. As such, trust must be repaid [4] (i.e., $q > 0$). The trustor benefits from economies of scale by the aggregate of payoffs from all trustees.

IV. THRESHOLD

For a trustor to increase its trustworthiness (W_u) in the eyes of a trustee, the gains delivered by the service must be higher than if the trustee was operating on their own. Such condition is satisfied by the following system of inequalities:

$$W_u \subseteq \begin{cases} pV \geq T \\ K \geq 1 \end{cases} \quad (9)$$

That happens when the value of the remittance R_u is equal or greater than the threshold T (the value sent is at a minimum equal to the perceived value received), and the magnification factor K greater or equal to one.

Being a system of inequalities, it is also possible to have a lower remittance ($pV < T$) and increase trustworthiness, as long as the magnification factor is large enough ($K \gg 1$) to make up for the shortfall. Although plausible, this would be uncommon.

V. SIMULATED EXPERIMENTS

The following are a set of four experiments that simulate scenarios from fostering to eroding trust as a result of the quality of machine learning inference.

All the experiments begin from the same exact starting point, where it is assumed that the potential value of a product being offered to customers is of one million points (1,000,000). The starting number is an arbitrary value and could have been any positive number: forty-two, nine thousand, or seventy-three billion. What we want to observe is the shape of the curve formed from plotting interaction cycle after interaction cycle.

The hypothesis is that, by providing good machine learning inferences, a trustee would increase their trustiness level towards the trustor. Conversely, less than good enough results would have the opposite effect (i.e., erode trust).

In each of the experiments, we observe the shape of the curves and their accumulated trend iteration after iteration. Also, throughout all four simulations, all parameters are kept the same, varying only the magnification factor K.

A. Simulation 1: Machine Learning Inferences Add Value

For this experiment, we will go step-by-step in the first interaction. For subsequent experiments, only the final graph plots will be shown. Irrespective of the experiment, they all can be reproduced using the source code [3] that accompanies this paper.

Here, the assumption is that machine learning inferences are magnifying the value of the product ($K > 1$).

Assume that in the first cycle iteration the trustor begins with $V = 1{,}000{,}000$ points and is able to send a remittance of 65% ($R_u = 0.65 \times 1{,}000{,}000$) of inference value to a trustee. The magnification factor perceived by the trustee is $K = 2$, thus the gain becomes 1,300,000 ($G_v = 2 \times 650{,}000$) points.

The trustee sends a portion ($q = 0.14$) of the value back by interacting with the user interface, providing a feedback label, and paying for the service. The rebate received by the trustor is 182,000 ($B_u = 0.14 \times 1{,}300{,}000$) points.

Adding the rebate to the residual value ($r_u = 0.35 \times 1{,}000{,}000$), the trustor's accumulated gain is equal to 532,000 ($A_u = 350{,}000 + 182{,}000$) points. And the trustee's gain is 1,118,000 ($N_v = 0.86 \times 1{,}300{,}000$) points.

First, the trustee's perception was that they received more value that what the trustor had to offer due to the magnification factor (win). Second, the trustor received a rebate in various formats—accruing value that was not there before (win). Third, after the aggregate across all trustees, the trustor will have accumulated more than the initial value offered (win).

In Fig. 2, we can see the shape of the curve showing the accumulated gains for both trustor and trustee for the four cycles of the experiment.

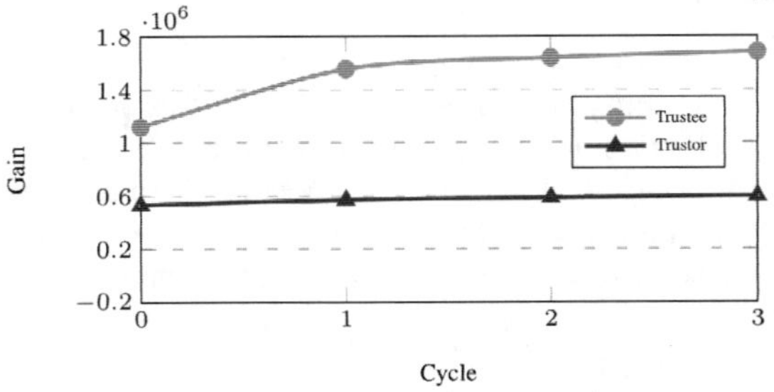

Fig. 2: Accumulated gains ($K > 1$).

B. Simulation 2: Machine Learning Inferences Are Neutral

For the second experiment, a neutral magnification factor ($K = 1$) is being simulated. The value sent by the trustor and the value received by the trustee are perceived equally.

The curve with the accumulated gains can be seen in Fig. 3. The trustee marginally sees an increase in the received value, whereas the trustor sees a small decline. This scenario could be acceptable depending on the scale of the service and number of trustees, since the trustor's final gain is the aggregate from all trustees.

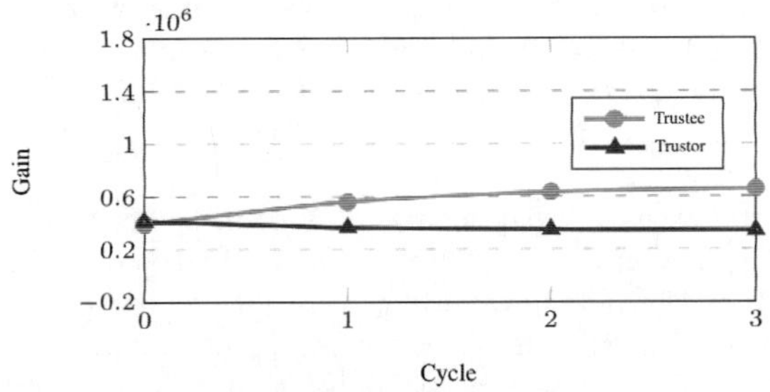

Fig. 3: Accumulated Gains ($K = 1$).

C. Simulation 3: Machine Learning Inferences Are Causing Inefficiencies

The third experiment has a curve (Fig. 4) showing a scenario where inefficiencies are being brought upon the trustee ($0 \leq K < 1$). Their gains are at best negligible, and at the same time there is a significant drop in the trustor's gains.

This situation would be plausible and acceptable only during the development phase of a product, where a trustee would have accepted to be an early adopter of the service. Otherwise, there would be no return on investment to the trustee, and a loss of value to the trustor.

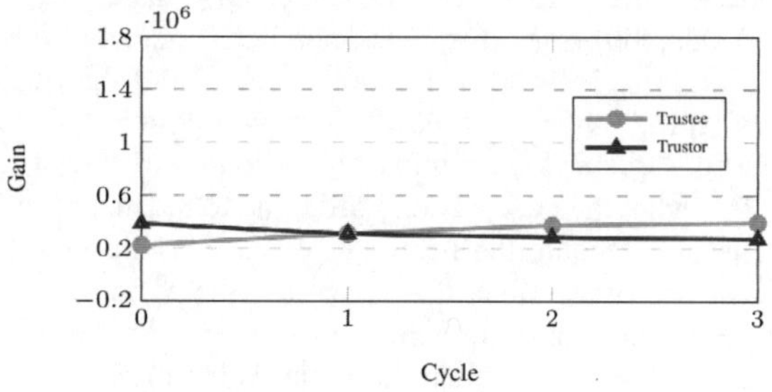

Fig. 4: Accumulated Gains ($0 \leq K < 1$).

D. Simulation 4: Machine Learning Inferences Are Rapidly Eroding Trust

The last experiment shows the worst-case scenario where machine learning inferences are eroding the trustor's trustworthiness ($K < 0$), therefore reducing the trustee's ability to be trusting. Fig. 5 show how, in this scenario, there are negative gains (loss) for trustors and trustees. They are both worse off with the service, compared to operating without it.

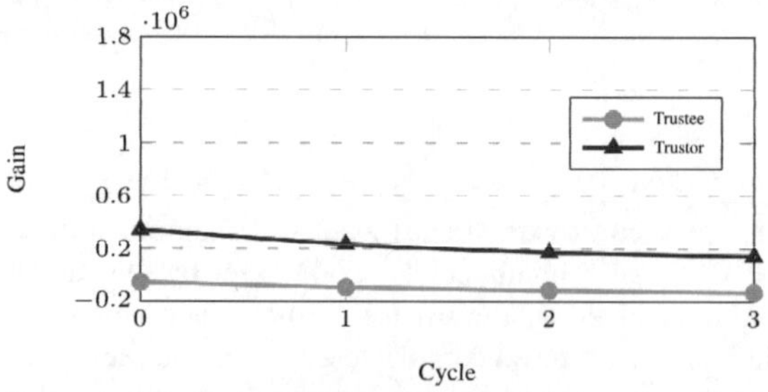

Fig. 5: Accumulated Gains ($K < 0$).

VI. Conclusion

This paper takes a step forward in contributing to the conversation to define, in a quantifiable manner, what trust in ML-based systems means. Here, we demonstrated that good machine learning inference results satisfy a valid criterion to increase a trustor's trustworthiness, allowing for trustees to be more trusting.

There exists a strong motivation for ML-based products to provide inferences only when a minimum confidence level has been cleared. It would be preferable to not produce a result than to provide a low-confidence one. When nothing is provided, a customer can still operate at their nominal level of productivity.

Plans for future research include: 1- proposing a set of criteria to define the risk associated with an inference; 2- establish a quantitative process to measure it.

References

[1] J. Berg, J. Dickhaut, and K. McCabe, "Trust, reciprocity, and social history," *Games and Economic Behavior*, vol. 10, no. 1, pp. 122–142, 1995. [Online]. Available: https://www.sciencedirect.com/science/article/pii/S0899825685710275

[2] J. von Neumann and O. Morgenstern, *Theory of Games and Economic Behavior*. Princeton University Press, 1944.

[3] D. Cirne. Simulated experiments source code. [Online]. Available: https://gist.github.com/dcirne/8c74a2d8d5adaf59f9366a5212d41f22

[4] D. Kreps, "Corporate culture and economic theory," *Perspectives on Positive Political Economy*, pp. 90–142, 1990.

[5] C. Alós-Ferrer and F. Farolfi, "Trust games and beyond," *Frontiers in Neuroscience*, vol. 13, 2019. [Online]. Available: https://www.frontiersin.org/articles/10.3389/fnins.2019.00887

Social Requirements for Designing Self-Adaptive Privacy Schemes in Cloud

The Interrelation of Social Identity with Self Disclosure Practices

Angeliki Kitsiou, Maria Sideri, Aikaterini – Georgia Mavroeidi, Katerina Vgena, Eleni Tzortzaki, Michail Pantelelis, Stavros Simou, Christos Kalloniatis
Privacy Engineering and Social Informatics Laboratory, Department of Cultural Technology and Communication
University of the Aegean
Mytilene, Greece
a.kitsiou@aegean.gr, msid@aegean.gr, kmav@aegean.gr, kvgena@aegean.gr, etzortzaki@aegean.gr, mpantel@aegean.gr, ssimou@aegean.gr, chkallon@aegean.gr

***Abstract*— This paper examines the self-presentation and self-disclosure practices of cloud services users that relate to the social group they belong to, through a quantitative survey addressed to the student population of three Universities in Greece, England, and Spain. Findings provide valuable insights regarding social identity-based users' practices and indicate important information for the design of self-adaptive privacy schemes within cloud services, setting specific social requirements based on users' social groups belonging.**

Keywords-adaptive privacy; self-disclosure practices; social requirements.

I. Introduction

Cloud services have significantly expanded in current society, transforming the way individuals and organizations store, access, and manage their data and applications. They often offer integration and interoperability capabilities, allowing different applications and systems to communicate and work together seamlessly, indicating the new notion of the Internet of Cloud [1]. This facilitates the exchange of data and information across platforms, enabling real-time collaboration, sharing, and communication among several team members regardless of their physical locations. Thus, the potential challenges and concerns associated with the expansion of cloud services are immense, such as data privacy and security, vendor lock-in and regulatory compliance [2]. Organizations and individuals should carefully evaluate their specific requirements and consider the appropriate privacy measures and service-level agreements when adopting cloud services [3]. Towards these requirements and measures, the notion of social identity has been indicated as an important factor that influences individuals' privacy preferences and concerns [4]. Social identity refers to the way individuals perceive themselves in relation to various social groups they belong to. The forming of these groups can include factors, such as nationality, ethnicity, gender, religion, profession, or interests [5]. Cloud services provide individuals with opportunities to express and project their social identities to others through profiles, content sharing, and interactions. People often join groups or follow pages related to their social identities, fostering a sense of belonging and connection. In this regard, social identity plays a key role in how individuals present themselves and manage their online image within cloud services [6]. Different social groups may have varying attitudes towards self-presentation and self-disclosure practices [7]. However, the nature of self-disclosure on cloud services raises privacy concerns, as individuals need to consider the potential risks associated with sharing personal information publicly [8]. Respectively, the variety of attitudes within cloud services concerns privacy as well, such as prioritizing the protection of personal information or embracing a more open approach. People may strategically disclose or withhold personal information in order to shape their online identity and project a desired image that aligns with their social identity and the desired/intended impression they want to create. They may share personal milestones, hobbies, achievements, opinions, or emotions, while choosing to keep other aspects of themselves and their lives private. Social identity can shape the norms and expectations around privacy within specific social groups. Group members may have shared understandings of what information is appropriate to share, the level of privacy they expect, and the consequences of privacy breaches. These group norms and the values associated with them can shape members' privacy preferences and may influence individuals' privacy management practices and decisions [9].

Privacy management, in this context, involves considering what information to disclose and how it aligns with individuals' social identity and desired impression. Users may employ privacy settings and controls to manage their self-disclosure and control who can access their shared content. Towards this, self-adaptive privacy measures and techniques have been indicated as an effective approach. Self-adaptive privacy in cloud computing refers to the ability of cloud systems to dynamically adjust privacy measures based on specific requirements and preferences of individual users or organizations. It involves tailoring privacy controls, mechanisms, and policies to meet the unique privacy needs of different users and data types [10]. In this regard, self-adaptive privacy aims at empowering users by giving them greater control over their privacy. It provides users with visibility into how their data is being handled within the cloud, offering transparency into privacy practices, and enabling informed decision-making [11]. Considering that privacy management is changing based on users' social groups, several social factors and attributes play a significant role in self-adaptive privacy approaches. These factors influence the design, implementation, and acceptance of self-adaptive privacy mechanisms and practices. Thus, as previous research indicates, these factors are usually hard to be identified or are neglected during systems' design [12]. Recent studies have focused on developing algorithmic implementations of such self-privacy adaptation methods that pay attention to users' individual attributes or context [13][14] and not on groups' norms, while other work concentrates on the user interface mechanism to adopt such adaptations in order to be protected [15].

Therefore, supporting that not only individuals' social attributes should be examined but social groups as well, this paper examines critical issues about users' social groups within cloud services related to their self-presentation and self-disclosure practices. Specifically, we aim to identify relevant determinants, based on each social group, of self-disclosure practices within the cloud. To gather the required data, a survey was conducted among the students of three Universities in Greece, England, and Spain. The findings from this study contribute to valuable insights regarding users' practices based on their belonging to a group and provide important information for the design of usable and self-adaptive privacy features within the cloud, since they promote specific privacy requirements based on users' social identity and groups, considering adaptation on a basis of group privacy management. Section II presents the research field, the methodology followed, and the implemented instrument. In Section III, the results of our survey are outlined, indicating users' self-presentation and self-disclosure practices. Section IV discusses and concludes the main findings, raising future research directions and practical implications.

II. METHODOLOGY

Supporting the arguments above suggesting that social identity pertains to how individuals shape their attitudes and behaviors within various domains of activity [5], the following foundational research question has been formulated to guide our study: RQ *"Is belonging in a social group affecting users' self-presentation and self-disclosure practices?"* To address that, the research population selected for this study included the students of three Universities in Greece, England, and Spain: University of the Aegean, University of Bournemouth, and University of Malaga, respectively. The survey was administered to undergraduate, postgraduate, and doctoral students. Due to its diverse nature in terms of geographical location and demographics, the research population holds significant potential for providing respected insights regarding users' disclosure practices within cloud-based services. It focuses on the domain of social media as the aforementioned cloud environments have been pointed out in the study as the handiest in users' everyday online practices. To ensure access to a substantial portion of the research population and facilitate the generalizability of results [16], a quantitative approach was chosen, and a structured questionnaire was developed. The researchers opted for the Hellenic Statistical Authority's categorizations when determining the values for measuring users' socio-demographics across their survey in order to ensure reliability, representativeness, and transparency. All items were compiled from previous literature and, in particular, participants were asked to identify the groups to which they belong within cloud services using a social identity taxonomy that aligns with the work of [17]. This taxonomy encompassed a range of group categories, including 15 types of groups, such as leisure groups, well-being groups, professional groups, and other user-indicated groups. In order to ensure the reliability and validity of our instrument, a comprehensive review of the literature for self-presentation and self-disclosure practices was conducted. This review allowed us to incorporate validated metrics from previous studies [18] - [21] on self-presentation and information disclosure into our instrument. These concerned 15 items, as follows: *"I share personal information, I share photos of myself, I share information about my family, I share information about my friends, I share information about my job, I share information about my hobbies, I share information about my daily activities, I share information regarding my sexuality, I share religion-related views, I share information about my political views, I state my location, I update my status, I include contact information (e.g. email, links to other profiles, personal web pages, mobile number, postal address), I have included a short cv in my profile, I tag others in the photos I share"*.

Moreover, the instrument included a set of six questions aiming at capturing participants' socio-demographic characteristics based on previous work [22]. These questions encompassed gender, age, family structure, educational level, professional experience, and monthly income. By incorporating these questions in the final part of the instrument, participants had the time required to complete it more effectively. Prior to distributing the questionnaire to the research population, a pilot study was conducted with a sample of 60 students from the three universities. The purpose of this pilot study was to test the instrument for its form, language, clarity, difficulty level, and responsiveness to respondents' interests, leading to the necessary revisions to the questionnaire items. The survey was conducted using Google Forms, which allowed for direct distribution via email. In the introductory note of the survey, the purpose, procedure, and ethical considerations were clearly explained, adhering to established research ethics and standards [23]. The collected data was then recoded and processed using IBM SPSS Statistics 28 (SPSS28).

III. RESULTS

Out of the 368 responses received, thorough checks for completeness were performed, resulting in 280 valid responses being included in the analysis. The survey involved more women than men, while a small percentage declared a different gender. Despite the distribution of ages, the majority was in the age group of 18–32. Regarding family structure, the nuclear form dominates, while it is quite interesting that some of the responders preferred not to provide an answer. Most of the participants held a Master's diploma, and 92% of the respondents have professional experience of at least 1-5 years. The majority declared a relatively low monthly income, ranging from 301 to 800€. Participants' individual attributes, presented in detail in the following Table 1, are associated with their level of social capital [24], setting the standard for a better understanding of users' self-categorization procedure in order to formulate their social identity and define their perceptions and willingness to belong to a social group.

TABLE I. RESPONDENTS' DEMOGRAPHICS

	Sample Socio-Demographics	
	Value	***Percentage%***
Gender	Male	37.5%
	Female	61.8%
	Other	0.7%
Age	18-32	58.9%
	33-47	28.6%
	>48	12.1%
Family Form	Nuclear Family	61.8%
	Large Family	7.5%
	Single-Parent Family	11.8%
	Other Form	9.3%
	Prefer not answering	9.3%
Educational Level	ICD4	36.8%
	Bachelor	23.2%
	MSc	35.7%
	PhD	3.6%
Professional Experience	1 to 5	43.6%
	6 to 10	17.5%
	11 to 15	9.6%
	16 to 20	8.9%
	21 to 25	6.4%
	>26	5.7%
Monthly Income	301–800€	40.7%
	801–1000€	16.1%
	1001–1500€	20.7%
	1501–2000€	6.1%
	2001–3000€	3.2%

The findings of our survey indicate that participants declare belonging to various social groups when adopting cloud services, namely: Companionships group (33.9%), Professional group (11.3%), Political group (3.1%), Trade union group (2.4%), Voluntary group (8.1%), Sport group (7.7%), Leisure group (11.7%), Cultural group (5.9%), Human Support group (1.5%), Scientific group (2.9%), Environmental group (2.3%), Mutual Support group (1.1%), Religious group (2%), Technological Interest group (3.1%) and Gender equality group (3.2%). Previous research has already suggested that individuals who possess multiple social identities are shaping their behaviors, respectively, within specific contexts [25]. In this regard and in order to check whether participation in a specific social group is associated with specific self-presentation and information disclosure practices, the chi-square test for two nominal dichotomous variables was used. Results are shown in Table 2, as follows.

TABLE II. SOCIAL GROUPS' DISCLOSURE PRACTICES

SELF-PRESENTATION AND INFORMATION DISCLOSURE		
Groups	***Disclosure Practices***	**Media & Services** ***Instagram, Messenger, Facebook Google services, What's up***
Companion-ship	personal information	***Messenger:*** $X^2(1)=6.844$, $p=0.009$, $\varphi_c=0.157$
	photos of myself	***Instagram:*** $X^2(1)=11.024$, $p=0.001$, $\varphi_c=0.200$ ***Messenger:*** $X^2(1)=6.517$, $p=0.011$, $\varphi_c=0.154$
	about my friends	***Messenger:*** $X^2(1)=3.957$, $p=0.047$, $\varphi_c=0.120$
	about my job	***Messenger:*** $X^2(1)=5.227$, $p=0.022$, $\varphi_c=0.138$
	about my hobbies	***Instagram:*** $X^2(1)=10.663$, $p=0.001$, $\varphi_c=0.197$ ***Messenger:*** $X^2(1)=5.632$, $p=0.018$, $\varphi_c=0.143$
	about my daily activities	***Instagram:*** $X^2(1)=10.115$, $p=0.001$, $\varphi_c=0.191$ ***Messenger:*** $X^2(1)=6.479$, $p=0.011$, $\varphi_c=0.153$
	my location	***Instagram:*** $X^2(1)=4.082$, $p=0.043$, $\varphi_c=0.122$
	I tag others in the photos I share	***Instagram:*** $X^2(1)=5.520$, $p=0.019$, $\varphi_c=0.141$
Professional	about my job	***Messenger:*** $X^2(1)=7.917$, $p=0.005$, $\varphi_c=0.169$
	religious views	***Messenger:*** $X^2(1)=5.553$, $p=0.018$, $\varphi_c=-0.142$
	a short cv in my profile	***Instagram:*** $X^2(1)=5.470$, $p=0.019$, $\varphi_c=-0.141$
	I tag others in the photos I share	***Instagram:*** $X^2(1)=5.549$, $p=.018$, $\varphi_c=-0.142$
Political	about my family	***Messenger:*** $X^2(1)=4.953$, $p=0.026$, $\varphi_c=0.134$
	about my friends	***Facebook:*** $X^2(1)=3.936$, $p=0.047$, $\varphi_c=0.119$
	about my job	***Messenger:*** $X^2(1)=6.415$, $p=0.011$, $\varphi_c=0.152$
	about my hobbies	***Facebook:*** $X^2(1)=8.561$, $p=0.003$, $\varphi_c=0.176$
	I tag others in the photos I share	***Facebook:*** $X^2(1)=7.527$, $p=0.006$, $\varphi_c=0.165$
Trade union	photos of myself	***Instagram:*** $X^2(1)=4.502$, $p=0.034$, $\varphi_c=-0.128$
	about my hobbies	***Facebook:*** $X^2(1)=6.686$, $p=0.010$, $\varphi_c=0.156$ ***Instagram:*** $X^2(1)=5.633$, $p=0.018$, $\varphi_c=-0.143$
	my location	***Instagram:*** $X^2(1)=7.107$, $p=0.008$, $\varphi_c=-0.160$

SELF-PRESENTATION AND INFORMATION DISCLOSURE		
Groups	***Disclosure Practices***	**Media & Services** ***Instagram, Messenger, Facebook Google services, What's up***
	I tag others in the photos I share	***Instagram:*** $X^2(1) = 8.209, p=0.004, \varphi_c = -0.172$
Gender equality	personal information	***Messenger:*** $X^2(1) = 4.871, p=0.027, \varphi_c = 0.133$
	about my family	***Messenger:*** $X^2(1) = 15.645, p=0.000, \varphi_c = 0.238$
	about my friends	***Messenger:*** $X^2(1) = 9.468, p=0.002, \varphi_c = 0.185$
	about my daily activities	***Messenger:*** $X^2(1) = 5.639, p=0.018, \varphi_c = 0.143$
	contact information	***Facebook:*** $X^2(1) = 5.563, p=0.018, \varphi_c = 0.142$
Religious	information about my hobbies	***Facebook:*** $X^2(1) = 5.076, p=0.024, \varphi_c = 0.136$
Voluntary	photos of myself	***Instagram:*** $X^2(1) = 4.410, p=0.036, \varphi_c = -0.126$
		What's up: $X^2(1) = 4.226, p=0.040, \varphi_c = 0.124$
	about my job	***Facebook:*** $X^2(1) = 8.503, p=0.004, \varphi_c = 0.176$
	about my hobbies	***Messenger:*** $X^2(1) = 4.735\ p=0.030, \varphi_c = 0.131$
	my daily activities	***Facebook:*** $X^2(1) = 4.720, p=0.030, \varphi_c = 0.131$
	contact information	***Google services:*** $X^2(1) = 3.878, p=0.049, \varphi_c = 0.119$
	I tag others in the photos I share	***Facebook:*** $X^2(1) = 4.268, p=0.039, \varphi_c = 0.124$
Sport	personal information	***Messenger:*** $X^2(1) = 4.467, p=0.035, \varphi_c = 0.127$
	about my friends	***Instagram:*** $X^2(1) = 4.484, p=0.034, \varphi_c = 0.127$
	about my hobbies	***Facebook:*** $X^2(1) = 5.774, p=0.016, \varphi_c = 0.145$
		Instagram: $X^2(1) = 8.501, p=0.004, \varphi_c = 0.175$
	my daily activities	***Messenger:*** $X^2(1) = 5.480, p=0.019, \varphi_c = 0.141$
	my location	***Instagram:*** $X^2(1) = 6.245, p=0.012, \varphi_c = 0.150$
	I tag others in the photos I share	***Instagram:*** $X^2(1) = 4.086, p=0.043, \varphi_c = 0.122$
Leisure	personal information	***Google services:*** $X^2(1) = 3.972, p=0.046, \varphi_c = 0.120$
	photos of myself	***Facebook:*** $X^2(1) = 4.667, p=0.031, \varphi_c = 0.130$
		Instagram: $X^2(1) = 4.730, p=0.030, \varphi_c = 0.131$
	about my hobbies	***Facebook:*** $X^2(1) = 7.015, p=0.008, \varphi_c = 0.159$
	I update my status	***Facebook:*** $X^2(1) = 4.634, p=0.031, \varphi_c = 0.130$
Cultural	about my family	***Messenger:*** $X^2(1) = 4.405, p=.0036, \varphi_c = 0.126$
	about my sexuality	***Messenger:*** $X^2(1) = 11.908, p=0.001, \varphi_c = 0.208$
	religious views	***Messenger:*** $X^2(1) = 9.344, p=0.002, \varphi_c = 0.184$
	about my political views	***Messenger:*** $X^2(1) = 8.041, p=0.005, \varphi_c = 0.171$

SELF-PRESENTATION AND INFORMATION DISCLOSURE		
Groups	***Disclosure Practices***	**Media & Services** ***Instagram, Messenger, Facebook Google services, What's up***
	my location	***Messenger:*** $X^2(1) = 8.671, p=0.003, \varphi_c = 0.177$
	contact information	***Instagram:*** $X^2(1) = 3.863, p=0.049, \varphi_c = -0.118$
		Messenger: $X^2(1) = 3.888, p=0.049, \varphi_c = 0.119$
Scientific	about my job	***Facebook:*** $X^2(1) = 9.700, p=0.002, \varphi_c = 0.187$
	about my hobbies	***Instagram:*** $X^2(1) = 4.189, p=0.041, \varphi_c = -0.123$
	about my daily activities	***Messenger:*** $X^2(1) = 4.597, p=0.032, \varphi_c = -0.129$
Environmental	personal information	***Messenger:*** $X^2(1) = 4.182, p=0.041, \varphi_c = -0.123$
Human Support	photos of myself	***Facebook:*** $X^2(1) = 7.492, p=0.007, \varphi_c = 0.164$
Technological Interest	photos of myself	***Instagram:*** $X^2(1) = 8.102, p=0.004, \varphi_c = -0.171$
	about my hobbies	***Instagram:*** $X^2(1) = 4.825, p=0.028, \varphi_c = -0.132$
	about my daily activities	***Instagram:*** $X^2(1) = 5.751, p=0.016, \varphi_c = -0.144$

Results show that there are statistically significant associations between the nominal variables of "*group participation*" and "*self-presentation and information disclosure practices*", highlighting that the group in which one chooses to participate is related to the practices that she/he chooses or avoids for self-presentation. Most of the associations were revealed for users' self-presentation and information disclosure practices on Messenger (25 associations) and Instagram (22 associations), less on Facebook (15 associations) and few (1-2) on What's Up and Google services. These results are not surprising, considering that the cumulative percent of participants using "once daily" and "several times daily" Messenger, Instagram and Facebook are, according to the results of the research, high (78.3%, 70.2% and 61.9%, respectively).

The majority of associations were positive with the exception of fifteen (15) negative revealed in the case of participating in specific types of groups (mainly trade-union, professional, technological interest, scientific, voluntary, cultural, environmental) and for specific social media, mostly Instagram and less Messenger. Although the negative associations refer to nine (9) different practices, more negative associations were revealed for practices including photos sharing ("I share photos of myself" and "I tag others in the photos I share") and for practices referring to hobbies and daily activities information sharing. This finding implies that the aforementioned practices are considered rather inappropriate by people participating in professional groups or groups that serve specific interests. Moreover, results revealed that those participating in companionship groups use more self-disclosure practices compared to others participating in other type of groups, which is explicable considering the more open goal of participation and the expected benefits from self-disclosure. Results also revealed that the self-presentation practices more used (or avoided) by people according to the type of group they belong, and the media context, were that of sharing information about hobbies (12 associations, 3 of them negative) and photos sharing of oneself (9 associations, 3 of them negative).

IV. DISCUSSION AND CONCLUSION

As the findings above indicate, social belonging in a group affects users' self-disclosure practices and, respectively, influences their privacy preferences. Self-disclosure on cloud services contributes to users' digital footprints, leaving a trace of their activities, interests, and interactions [26]. Thus, findings highlighted that users who share a similar social identity based on companionship, feel more comfortable disclosing personal information and photos within cloud services and particularly within social media. However, other users emphasizing certain aspects of their identity, mostly the professional based ones, and downplaying the others, declared to be mindful of their social identity presentation and self-disclosure on social media, considering the potential consequences and impacts on their privacy, well-being, and relationships. Evidently, previous research has shown that this digital footprint can have implications for reputation management, online perception, and potential consequences in both personal and professional contexts [27]. In this regard, the identification of social groups' self-disclosure practices on the cloud can have a significant impact on the design and implementation of self-adaptive privacy schemes, in order for users to be aware of privacy settings, critically evaluate the information shared, and maintain a balance between online and offline identities which can contribute to a more positive and authentic online presence. Considering that social groups' norms serve as guidelines for users and societies to navigate privacy boundaries and expectations, contributing to the preservation of personal autonomy, dignity, and trust [28], the identification of the practices that lead to specific group-based needs is of great importance. Since self-adaptive privacy in cloud services seeks to strike a balance between data utility and privacy protection, by tailoring privacy measures to users' needs and dynamically adapting to changing circumstances [29], users' empowerment can be enhanced when self- adaptive privacy schemes from the beginning of the design take into account groups preferences and the balance between maintaining privacy and participating in social interactions within one's social identity networks. Furthermore, incorporating the understanding of social groups' self-disclosure practices into the concept of "privacy by design" methodologies, such as the extended PriS framework for cloud computing services [30] that should be used for designing self-adaptive privacy schemes, can help ensure that privacy considerations are embedded in the development process of cloud services. Despite the limitations of our survey, concerning the weak strength of association of the nominal-by-nominal relationships *(Phi coefficient takes values between 0 and +/-1)*, our results indicate the diversity of self-disclosure practices across different social groups, providing a guide for specific social requirements that could be integrated from the initial design stages of self-adaptive privacy schemes. In this respect, the defining of the self-disclosure practices can influence the establishment of privacy defaults in cloud platforms. In Figure 1, these practices are visualized by group and cloud service, aiming to aid the self-adaptive privacy schemes designed to be aligned with the preferences of social groups by setting initial privacy defaults that reflect their common practices and expectations.

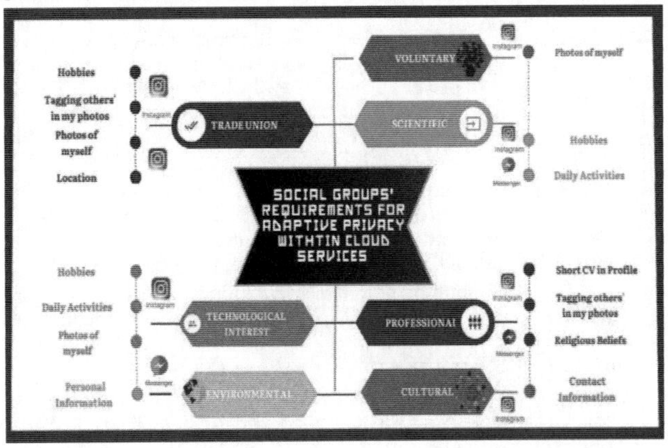

Figure 1. Social Requirements for Self-Adaptive Privacy Schemes in Cloud based on Social Groups' self disclosure practices.

Since the insights into social groups' self-disclosure practices can inform the design process, this knowledge can enable in particular the design of contextual privacy settings. These settings can dynamically adjust privacy levels based on the specific context or situation, taking into account groups' preferences in order, for example, to be more restrictive for the information of the professional groups, while more permissive for companionship or leisure groups. Finally, the provided insights into the self-disclosure practices can enhance the transparency and consent mechanisms in the self-adaptive privacy schemes. Users can be provided with clear and understandable information about how their data will be used, shared, and stored on the cloud, allowing them to make informed decisions and providing meaningful consent based on their social group norms. Therefore, users will be provided with control and agency over their information and with respect to their individual privacy preferences, reducing the risk of unintentional oversharing or undersharing.

ACKNOWLEDGMENT

H.F.R.I. Hellenic Foundation for Research & Innovation The research project was supported by the Hellenic Foundation for Research and Innovation (H.F.R.I.) under the '2nd Call for H.F.R.I. Research Projects to support Faculty Members & Researchers' (Project Number: 2550).

REFERENCES

[1] A. Cook et al., "Internet of Cloud: Security and Privacy Issues", in Cloud Computing for Optimization: Foundations, Applications, and Challenges. Studies in Big Data, B. Mishra, H. Das, S. Dehuri and A. Jagadev, Eds., Cham: Springer, pp. 271-301, 2018. doi:10.1007/978-3-319-73676-1_11.

[2] D. Peras and R. Makovec, "A conceptualization of the privacy concerns of cloud users", Information and Computer Security, vol. 30, no. 5, pp. 653-671, Mar. 2022, doi:10.1108/ICS-11-2021-0182.

[3] A. Tsouplaki, "Internet of Cloud: The Need of Raising Privacy and Security Awareness", Proc. International Conference on Research Challenges in Information Science, RCIS 2023, Springer , May 2023, pp. 542-550, doi:10.1007/978-3-031-33080-3_36.

[4] A. Kitsiou, E. Tzortzaki, C. Kalloniatis, and S. Gritzalis, "Towards an integrated socio-technical approach for designing adaptive privacy aware services in cloud computing" in Cyber Influence and Cognitive Threats, V. Benson, and J. McAlaney, Eds. Academic Press, pp. 9-32, 2020.

[5] M. Hogg, D. Abrams, and M. Brewer, "Social identity: The role of self in group processes and intergroup relations", Group Process and Intergroup Relations, vol. 20, no. 5, pp. 570–581, Jan. 2017, doi:10.1177/1368430217690909.

[6] E. E. Hollenbaugh, "Self-presentation in social media: Review and research opportunities", Review of communication research, vol. 9, pp. 80-98, Jan. 2021, doi: 10.12840/ISSN.2255-4165.027.

[7] K. Vgena, A. Kitsiou, and C. Kalloniatis, "Understanding the role of users' socio-location attributes and their privacy implications on social media". Information and Computer Security, vol. 30, no. 5, pp. 705-729, May 2022, doi:10.1108/ICS-12-2021-0211.

[8] T. Dienlin, P. K. Masur, and S. Trepte, "A longitudinal analysis of the privacy paradox". New Media and Society, vol. 25, no. 5, pp.1043-1064, June 2021, doi:10.1177/14614448211016316.

[9] A. Kitsiou, E. Tzortzaki, C. Kalloniatis, and S. Gritzalis "Identifying Privacy Related Requirements for the Design of Self-Adaptive Privacy Protections Schemes in Social Networks", Future Internet, vol. 13, no. 2, pp. 1-25, Jan. 2021, doi:10.3390/fi13020023.

[10] M. Belk, C. Fidas, E. Athanasopoulos, and A. Pitsillides, "Adaptive and Personalized Privacy and Security (APPS 2019): Workshop Chairs' Welcome and Organization". Proc. Adjunct Publication of the 27th Conference on User Modeling, Adaptation and Personalization (UMAP'19 Adjunct), ACM, June 2019, pp. 191–192, doi: 10.1145/3314183.3324963.

[11] B. P. Knijnenburg, "Privacy? I Can't Even! Making a Case for User-Tailored Privacy", IEEE Security and Privacy, vol. 15, no.4, pp. 62–67, Jan, 2017, doi:10.1109/MSP.2017.3151331.

[12] A. Kitsiou, E. Tzortzaki, C. Kalloniatis, and S. Gritzalis, "Self Adaptive Privacy in Cloud Computing Environments: Identifying the Major Socio-Technical Concepts", in Computer Security, S. K. Katsikas, F. Cuppens, N. Cuppens, C. Lambrinoudakis, Eds. Cham, Switzerland: Springer, pp. 117-132, 2020.

[13] I. Saini, S. Saad and A. Jaekel, "A context aware and traffic adaptive privacy scheme in vanets". Proc. IEEE 3rd Connected and Automated Vehicles Symposium (CAVS), IEEE, Dec.2020, pp. 1-5, doi: 10.1109/CAVS51000.2020.9334559.

[14] F. Schaub, B. Könings, and M. Weber, "Context-adaptive privacy: Leveraging context awareness to support privacy decision making", IEEE Pervasive Computing, vol. 14, no. 1, pp. 34–43, Jan - March, 2015, doi:10.1109/MPRV.2015.5.

[15] M. Namara, H. Sloan and B.P. Knijnenburg, The Effectiveness of Adaptation Methods in Improving User Engagement and Privacy Protection on Social Network Sites. [Online]. Available from: https://nru.uncst.go.ug/handle/123456789/4540 [retrieved: 10, 2023].

[16] M. Chalikias, P. Lalou, and A. Manolessou, Research Methodology and Introduction to Statistical Data Analysis via IBM SPSS STATISTICS. [Online]. Available from: https://repository.kallipos.gr/handle/11419/5075 [retrieved: 10, 2023].

[17] S. Bentley et. al., "Social Identity Mapping Online". J. of Personality and Social Psychology, vol. 118, no. 2, pp. 213-241, Feb. 2020, doi: 10.1037/pspa0000174.

[18] M. J. Hernández-Serrano, P. Renés-Arellano, R. Campos Ortuño, and B. González-Larrea, "Privacy in social networks: analysis of the Spanish teenagers' digital self-presentation risks". Revis. Lat. de Comunic. Soc., vol.79, pp. 133-154, Nov. 2021, doi: 10.4185/RLCS-2021-1528.

[19] M. Aresta, L. Pedro, C. Santos and A. Moreira, "Portraying the Self in Online Contexts: Context-Driven and User-Driven Online Identity Profiles" Contemporary Social Science, vol. 10, no.1, pp. 70–85, Jan. 2015, doi:10.1080/21582041.2014.980840.

[20] K. Vgena, A. Kitsiou, C. Kalloniatis, and S. Gritzalis, "Determining the Role of Social Identity Attributes to the Protection of Users' Privacy in Social Media", Future Internet, vol. 14, no. 9, pp. 249-267, Aug. 2022, doi:10.3390/fi14090249.

[21] Z. Jordán-Conde, B. Mennecke, and A. Townsend, "Late Adolescent Identity Definition and Intimate Disclosure on Facebook". Computers in Human Behavior, vol. 33, pp. 356–366, April 2014, doi:10.1016/j.chb.2013.07.015.

[22] A. Kitsiou, E. Tzortzaki, C. Kalloniatis, and S. Gritzalis, "Measuring Users' Socio- contextual Attributes for Self-adaptive Privacy Within Cloud-Computing Environments" in Trust, Privacy and Security in Digital Business, S. Gritzalis, E. R. Weippl, G. Kotsis, A. M. Tjoa and I. Khalil Eds. Cham, Switzerland: Springer, pp. 140-155, 2021.

[23] E. R. Babbie, The Practice of Social Research. Hamshire, UK: Cengage Learning, 2021.

[24] P. Bourdieu, "The Forms of Capital" in Handbook of Theory and Research for the Sociology of Education, J. Richardson Ed. New York: Greenwood, pp. 241-258, 1985.

[25] R. Jenkins, Social Identity. London, UK: Routledge/Taylor and Francis Group, 2008.

[26] N. Ní Bhroin et al., "The privacy paradox by proxy: Considering predictors of sharenting", Media and Communication, vol. 10, no. 1, pp. 371-383, March 2022, doi: 10.17645/mac.v10i1.4858.

[27] K. Feher, "Digital identity and the online self: Footprint strategies–An exploratory and comparative research study", Journal of information science, vol. 47, no. 2, pp. 192-205, April 2021, doi:10.1177/0165551519879.

[28] S. Gritzalis, M. Sideri, A. Kitsiou, E. Tzortzaki and C. Kalloniatis,"Sustaining Social Cohesion in Information and Knowledge Society: The Priceless Value of Privacy", in Recent Advances in Core Technologies in Informatics – Selected Papers in Honor of Professor Nikolaos Alexandris, G. Tsihrintzis and M. Virvou Eds. Vol. 14, Springer Learning and Analytics in Intelligent Systems, pp.177 - 198, 2020.

[29] A. Kitsiou et al., "Self-Adaptive Privacy in Cloud Computing: An overview under an interdisciplinary spectrum". Proc. 26th Pan-Hellenic Conference on Informatics (PCI '22), ACM, Nov. 2022, pp. 64–69, doi: 10.1145/3575879.3575968.

[30] C. Kalloniatis, "Incorporating privacy in the design of cloud-based systems: A conceptual meta-model", Information and Computer Security, vol. 25, no. 5, pp. 614–633, Nov. 2017, doi:10.1108/ICS-06-2016-0044.

Utilization of Ozone Water Generators for Preventing Infection in Home Care

Koichi Umimoto, Shinichi Iguchi, Yoshimasa Shimamoto, Katsunori Tachibana, Syunji Nagata
Department of Biomedical Science
Osaka Electro-Communication University
Osaka, Japan
e-mail: umimoto@osakac.ac.jp, hpfkp523@yahoo.co.jp, yoshi_1014shima@yahoo.co.jp, tatibana@osakac.ac.jp, narasinagatashunji@yahoo.co.jp

Yuki Nakamura
Department of Medical Engineering
Morinomiya University of Medical Sciences
Osaka, Japan
e-mail: yuki_nakamura@morinomiya-u.ac.jp

Abstract—**The prevention of opportunistic infection is important in-home care. Electrolyzation of water generates ozone water, which is strongly bactericidal. Because ozone water can be produced easily and reverts to water, it is an attractive option for hygiene management in home care. Here, we developed two devices for producing ozone water for home care and investigated the properties and bactericidal ability of the water. The first, simple device comprised a lead dioxide anode, a stainless cathode, and a diaphragm. We used the device to electrolyze 1 L of tap water and measured the ozone concentration over time. In addition, we assessed the bactericidal activity of the ozone water by performing an aerobic viable count of Escherichia coli and Staphylococcus aureus. The other device used a diamond-coated titanium plate as the anode and a stainless cathode to create ozone water from tap water flowing through an outdoor hose. The ozone concentration was measured at 0, 2, and 4 m from the hose nozzle. In the simple device, the ozone concentration was 1.1 ppm 20 minutes after starting electrolysis, but 0 ppm 70 minutes afterwards. Many colonies of E. coli and S. aureus were present in the cultures before ozone water was added, but none was detected after adding 1.1 ppm of ozone water. In the flowing water device, the ozone concentrations released at 0, 2, and 4 m were 1.6 ±0.2 ppm, 1.4±0.2 ppm and 0.6±0.3 ppm, respectively. Ozone water produced with our simple device showed strong bactericidal activity. The ozone water released within 2 m from the nozzle of the flowing water device contained more than 1.0 ppm of ozone. Thus, our devices represent an economical, environmentally friendly way to produce ozone water for use as a disinfectant in indoor and outdoor home care.**

Keywords- Home care; Ozone water; Bactericidal activity.

I. INTRODUCTION

Hygiene management for infection is required in home care, especially to prevent opportunistic infection in older adults, who have reduced resistance to infection. Generally, chemical disinfectants are used to prevent infection, however, their chemical components remain in the environment after use and contribute to global environmental pollution.

Electrolysis is a well-known technique for separating ionic substances. When water is electrolyzed with an electrolytic cell comprising two chambers separated by a diaphragm, ozone water is generated on the anode side (Figure 1). Electrolyzed ozone water is strongly bactericidal and reverts to ordinary water [1]. Economic and environmental factors make it highly suitable as a disinfectant in home care.

In this study, we developed two devices for producing ozone water for use in home care. We used the first, simple device to investigate the properties and bactericidal activity of ozone water. With the second, flowing water device, which produces ozone water for outdoor use, we studied the concentration of ozone water at different distances from the hose nozzle.

In Section 2, we present the methods of our approach. In Section 3, we give the results obtained, followed by a discussion in Section 4. Finally, we conclude our work in Section 5.

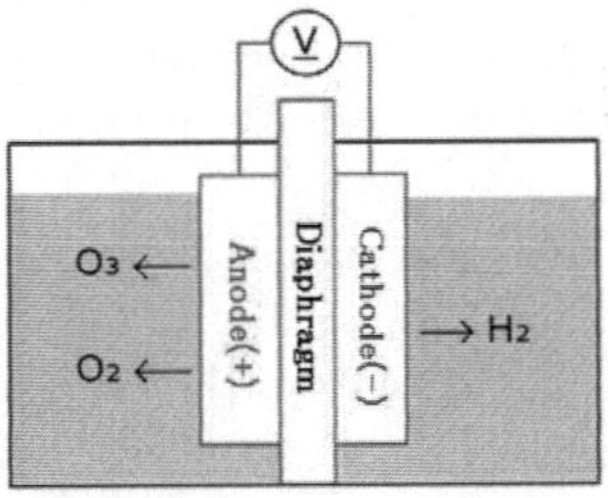

Anode side

$5H_2O \rightarrow O_2 + O_3 + 10H^+ + 10e^-$

Cathode side

$2H^+ + 2e^- \rightarrow H_2$

Figure 1. Principle of ozone water production.

II. METHODS

A. *Development of the simple device*

We developed a simple device for making ozone water. The device was a batch type, and the exterior was made of acrylic resin. The device consisted of a lead dioxide as the anode, and a stainless as the cathode, and a solid electrolyte membrane as the diaphragm. The electric power is supplied via a direct current converter (Figure 2).

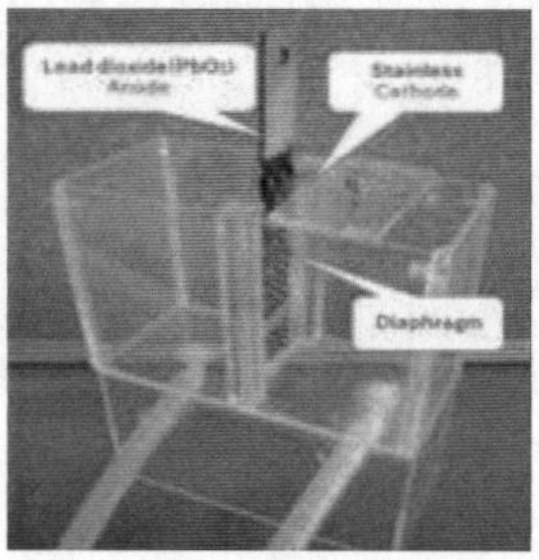

Figure 2. Prototype of batch type for producing ozone water.

B. Properties of the ozone water

We electrolyzed 1 L of tap water in the simple device by using a 20V direct current and measured the ozone concentration on the anode side. To investigate the sustainability of ozone water, we put the fresh ozone water into a beaker and measured its ozone concentration over time by 4-aminoantipirin absorption photometry.

C. Bactericidal activity

To investigate the bactericidal activity of ozone water, we prepared two strains of bacteria, *Escherichia coli* (*E. coli*) and *Staphylococcus aureus* (*S. aureus*). *E. coli* is an intestinal, gram-negative bacterium, and *S. aureus* is a gram-positive bacterium. The bactericidal activity of the ozone water was examined by cultivating the two strains of bacteria separately at 37°C for 24 hours. Then, each culture was incubated with fresh ozone water, and the solution was added to fresh petri dishes and cultivated for 48 hours. Control samples were prepared in the same way, but no ozone water was added. The bactericidal activity was assessed by counting the number of colonies of bacteria in each petri dish.

D. Development of a flowing water device

We developed a flowing water device for making ozone water, as shown in Figure 3. A diamond-coated titanium plate was used as the anode, and a stainless as the cathode. The device consisted of an electric cell with built-in electrodes and a hose, which was directly connected to an outdoor water source. The ozone water was released by pressing the hose nozzle (Figure 4).

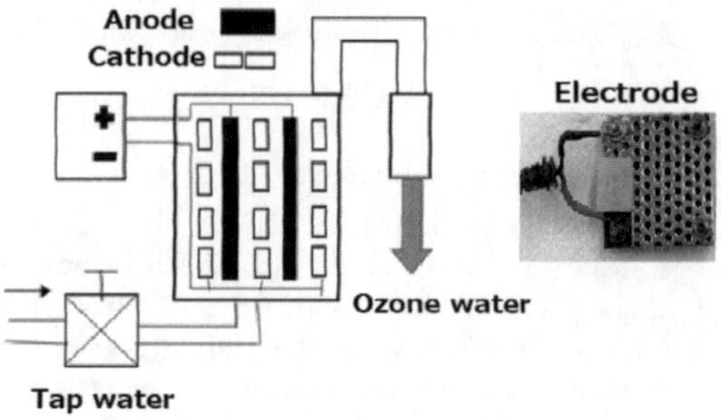

Figure 3. Principle of flowing ozone water production.

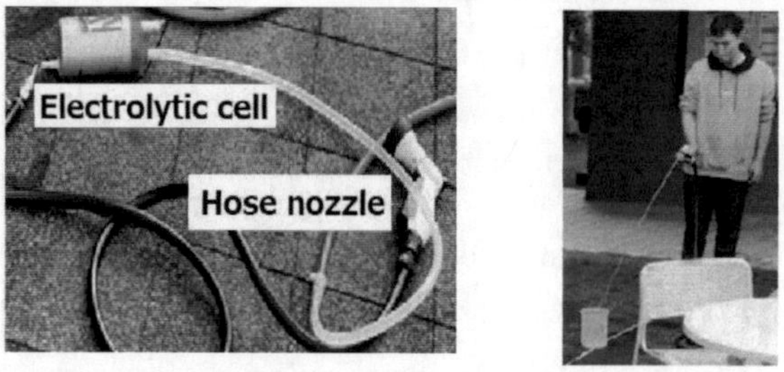

Figure 4. Prototype of the flowing water device for producing ozone water (left), and procedure for measuring the ozone concentration at various distances from the hose nozzle (right).

E. Ozone concentration in water released by the flowing water device

The leased ozone water at 0, 2, and 4 m from the hose nozzle was stored in the beaker and its ozone concentration was measured.

III. RESULTS

A. Experiments with the simple device

The ozone concentrations were 0.3 ppm at 10 minutes after the start of electrolysis and 1.1 ppm at 20 minutes, however, the concentration started to decrease immediately, and the levels were 0.3 ppm after 30 minutes and 0 ppm after 70 minutes (Figure 5).

In the control water sample, many colonies of *E. coli* (13×10^7 cfu/mL) and *S. aureus* 35×10^6 cfu/mL) were counted. However, no bacterial colonies were seen after cultivation with 1.1 ppm of ozone water (Figure 6).

B. Experiments with the flowing water device

The ozone concentration was 1.6±0.2 ppm in water at 0 m from the hose nozzle and 1.4±0.2 ppm in water at 2 m. Thus, the ozone concentration at both 0 and 2 m exceeded 1.0 ppm, i.e., the concentration that can be expected to have a sterilizing effect. However, at 4 m the concentration of ozone in the water was only 0.6±0.3 ppm (Table 1).

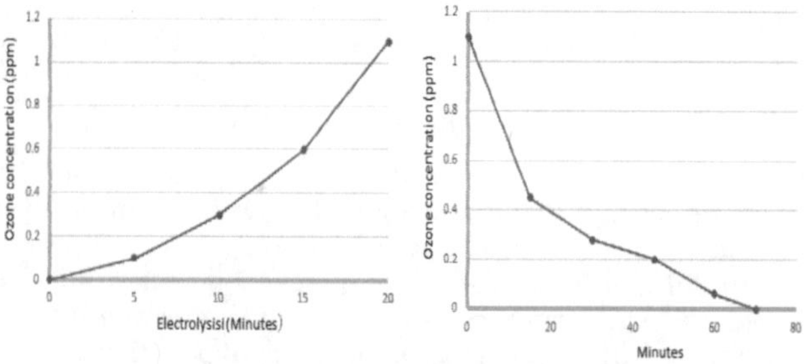

Figure 5. Changes in ozone concentration during electrolysis (left) and residual ozone concentration after ozone water generation (right).

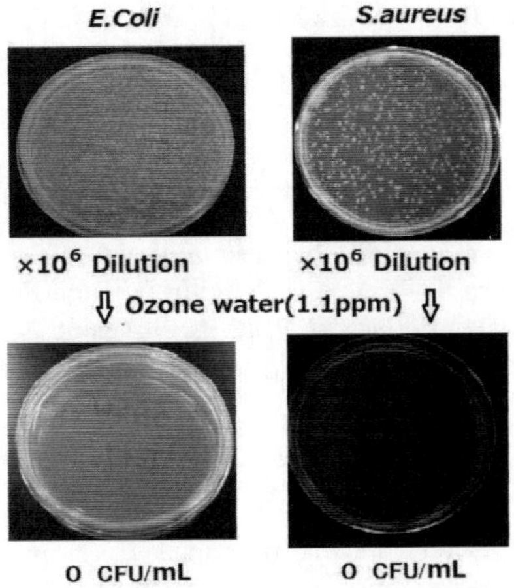

Figure 6. Bactericidal activity of ozone water.

TABLE 1. OZONE CONCENTRATION IN RELEASED WATER

Released distance of ozone water (m)	0	2	4
Ozone concentration in released water(ppm)	1.6±0.2	1.4±0.2	0.6±0.3

IV. DISCUSSION

Generally, ozone has a strong oxidative effect and is used for sterilization and deodorization in a wide range of fields, such as medicine, engineering, and agriculture. Methods for producing ozone water include electrolysis and discharge techniques. In this study, we developed a simple device to produce ozone water by electrolysis. This device is easily installed at home and required almost no maintenance; it is also cheap to use because it requires only tap water. A concentration of 1 ppm of ozone water is required for bactericidal activity, and our device produced 1.1 ppm of ozone water within 20 minutes (Figure 4) and showed strong bactericidal activity (similar to that of chemical disinfectants) against *E. coli* and *S. aureus* (Figure 5). Our experiments showed that the ozone disappeared from the water 70 minutes after the start of electrolysis (Figure 4), meaning that there was no persistence of the chemically active substance, unlike with chemical disinfectants. This lack of persistence is an advantage of ozone water and makes it suitable for disinfection in home care.

Previously, we studied the use of acidic electrolyzed water, which is produced by water electrolysis and is strongly bactericidal [2][3][4]. However, a small amount of sodium chloride is needed to produce electrolyzed water, and electrolysis generates harmful chlorine gas [5]. In contrast, ozone water can be generated from water alone and reverts to ordinary water.

In addition to hand disinfection, the prevention of infection at home requires disinfection of utensils such as tableware, cooking utensils, and sanitary appliances such as toilets. Our study shows that ozone water can be easily produced at home and used indoors to prevent infection. Our experiment with ozone water produced by a flowing water device (Table 1) showed that the released ozone water can be used as a bactericidal agent outdoors up to about 2 m from the hose nozzle. Outdoors, ozone water can be used in a wide variety of applications, e.g, the disinfection of equipment.

Our ozone water-generating devices and ozone water experiments indicate that the production of ozone water at home may be a useful approach to infection prevention in home care. Future studies should evaluate the use of ozone water in various indoor and outdoor applications and confirm its effectiveness.

V. CONCLUSION AND FUTURE WORK

We developed two devices that can be used at home to produce ozone water for infection prevention. The simple device produces 1.1 ppm of ozone water within 20 minutes of starting electrolysis, and the ozone water shows strong bactericidal activity; the ozone disappears within 70 minutes. The flowing water device maintains a bactericidal ozone concentration up to 2 m from the hose nozzle and is suitable for outdoor use. The devices are useful for producing ozone water as a disinfectant for use in home care and are beneficial from both an economic and an environmental perspective.

In the future, we will carry out the questionnaire survey using those devices in home care and summarize the points for improvement based on usage experience.

ACKNOWLEDGMENT

This research was supported in part by a Grants-in-Aid for Scientific Research from Japan Society for the Promotion of Science.

REFERENCES

[1] K. Hotta, K. Kawaguchi, K. Saito, K. Ochi, and T. Nakayama, "Antimicrobial activity of electrolyzed NaCl solution: effect on the growth of Streptomyces SPP," Actinomyatologica, vol. 8, pp. 51-56, 1994.

[2] K. Kumon, "What is functional water?" Artif. Organs, vol. 21, pp. 2-4, 1997.

[3] Y. Tatsumi, K. Umimoto, Y. Kumayama, and K. Jokei, "Effect of long-term storage on bactericidal activity of strong acidic electrolyzed water," Proceedings of IFMBE vol.14, pp. 3596-3599, 2006.

[4] K. Umimoto, H. Kawanishi, K. Kobayashi and J. Yanagida, "Development of a device to provide electrolyzed water for home care," IFMBE Proceedings vol 21, pp. 738–741, 2008.

[5] K. Umimoto, H. Kawanishi, Y. Tachibana, N. Kawai, S. Nagata and J. Yanagida, "Development of automatic controller for providing multi electrolyzed water," IFMBE Proceedings vol. 25, pp. 306-009, 2009.

Satellite Selection Algorithm to Optimize a Solution for Autonomous Driving Applications

Tiago Gonçalves
Bosch Car Multimedia
Braga, Portugal
DGAOT, Faculty of Sciences,
University of Porto
Porto, Portugal
Email:
Tiago.Goncalves4@pt.bosch.com

Gianmarco Fedeli
Bosch Car Multimedia
Braga, Portugal
Email:
Gianmarco.Fedeli@pt.bosch.com

Clara Lázaro
DGAOT, Faculty of Sciences,
University of Porto, Porto, Portugal
Interdisciplinary Centre of Marine
and Environmental Research
(CIIMAR), Matosinhos, Portugal
Email: clazaro@fc.up.pt

Hélder Silva
Algoritmi Research Centre
University of Minho
Guimarães, Portugal
Email: hdsilva@dei.uminho.pt

Telmo Vieira
DGAOT, Faculty of Sciences,
University of Porto, Porto, Portugal
Interdisciplinary Centre of Marine and Environmental
Research (CIIMAR), Matosinhos, Portugal
Email: telmo.vieira@fc.up.pt

***Abstract*— In recent years, there has been a significant exponential growth in the number of satellites from Global Navigation Satellite Systems (GNSSs). The proliferation of satellites could lead to noteworthy effects on different industries, such as aviation and autonomous driving, by substantially improving positioning accuracy and optimizing service efficiency. Nevertheless, deploying a large number of satellites comes with certain implications, such as an unavoidable increase in computational demands and higher power consumption for the receiver. A satellite selection algorithm can address these challenges by selecting a smaller subset of the total visible satellites, with comparable or even better positional accuracy. This paper introduces an algorithm for GNSS satellite selection in autonomous driving applications, which incorporates various factors including satellite elevation and signal strength. The algorithm identifies the optimal subset of satellites by applying a Sequential Updating Method (SUM) to generate multiple subsets and subsequently compare their Weighted Position Dilution of Precision (WPDOP). The subset with the lowest WPDOP is ultimately selected for use in the positioning process. The algorithm's performance is assessed in a dynamic scenario under challenging conditions, typical of autonomous driving context, and compared with other algorithms from the literature. Results show that the proposed algorithm is suitable for the target application, due to its ability to achieve higher positioning accuracy and reduce computational time compared to other methods in the literature.**

Keywords - Satellite Selection; GNSS; WPDOP; Computational Effort; Autonomous Driving.

I. INTRODUCTION

Global Navigation Satellite Systems (GNSSs) are a vital component in today's positioning and navigation landscape and stand as a key technology to society's future. A high level of maturity has been achieved with the latest generation of satellites, providing new and improved positioning signals, contributing to the achievement of accuracies that highly surpass those originally planned.

There are several error sources within a GNSS link that degrade the positioning accuracy of the system. Errors related to the atmosphere, clocks of both the satellite and receiver, the local environment, the geometry of the satellite constellations, their orbits and even intentional errors can cause discrepancies in the position of the user. To mitigate part of these effects, a multitude of correction methods have been developed, that seek to provide the best performance while offering the best price and versatility [1].

In open sky conditions, optimizing the Geometric Dilution Of Precision (GDOP) is sufficient to guarantee high accuracy solutions. When considering challenging conditions, such as a vehicle crossing an urban environment, optimizing GDOP is not enough, since different error magnitudes will affect each measurement due to multipath and Non-Line-Of-Sight (NLOS) conditions from the local environment.

With the increase in satellite number, a good satellite selection algorithm is vital to decrease the signal-processing burden of the receiver, while providing good accuracy.

A satellite selection algorithm could also benefit autonomous driving applications, contributing to achieve automation level 4, which only requires the driver to take control in very specific situations [2]. To reach automation level 5, where the vehicle is expected to operate under every condition and in every environment, GNSS could be a key component alongside other sensors, though a lot of features are still to be investigated [3]. The GNSS system can help overcome automation challenges like lane-level maneuvers, the oversight of vision systems, safety through independence, or even unlock interoperability through consistent timing and reference frames for vehicle to everything cooperation [4].

This work provides two key contributions: a satellite selection algorithm targeted for autonomous driving applications, and a performance comparison with well-known solutions from the literature using real dynamic data with a highly accurate reference ground truth. Section 2 provides background in satellite selection algorithms and Section 3 introduces the proposed solution, while Section 4 presents a performance comparison. In Section 5, a conclusion is given.

II. Background

A. Geometric Dilution of Precision

The GDOP is a metric related to the geometry of the solution, i.e., where satellites are in space, relative to the receiver. It is given by [5]:

$$GDOP = \sqrt{trace((G^T G)^{-1})} \tag{1}$$

where G is the design matrix for the position estimation solution (e.g., using a least-squares approach). For dual constellation case, the G matrix used for position and clock estimation is given by [5]:

$$G = \begin{bmatrix} e_x^{i,1} & e_y^{i,1} & e_z^{i,1} & 1 & 0 \\ \vdots & \vdots & \vdots & \vdots & \vdots \\ e_x^{i,m} & e_y^{i,m} & e_z^{i,m} & 1 & 0 \\ e_x^{j,1} & e_y^{j,1} & e_z^{j,1} & 0 & 1 \\ \vdots & \vdots & \vdots & \vdots & \vdots \\ e_x^{j,n} & e_y^{j,n} & e_z^{j,n} & 0 & 1 \end{bmatrix} \tag{2}$$

e represents the line-of-sight vector with x, y, and z components for *m* satellites of the *i-th* constellation, and *n* satellites of the *j-th* constellation. The last two columns represent the clock biases common for each measurement within constellations.

B. Optimal Method

One of the objectives of a satellite selection algorithm is to minimize the GDOP for a subset of *k* satellites from a set of *s* visible satellites. An optimal (also known as brute force) approach is to compute the GDOP value for every subset of *k* satellites from the *s* satellites available (with $k<s$).

The total number of computations of the GDOP function is given by the combinations' equation [6]:

$$C_k^s = \frac{s!}{k!\,(s-k)!} \tag{3}$$

For real-time processing, this method is only possible for a low number of satellites, due to the exponential increase in number of combinations (e.g., selecting 10 out of 15 satellites results in 3003 GDOP computations). The brute force method is considered optimal because it always produces the best possible GDOP, but at the expense of high computational cost.

Other algorithms are classified as sub-optimal or quasi-optimal, depending on how close they are to the GDOP value given by the optimal method, but with less computational effort. The Ultra-Rapid satellite selection proposed in [7] is one example, where it utilizes a constrained downdate method. This approach starts by computing the weight coefficient matrix for the all-in-view solution, and in order to avoid matrix inversions, uses the inversion lemma to find the individual contribution of each satellite. The satellite that contributes the least for the increase of GDOP is removed, and the process repeats itself until the desired subset size is achieved. A method focused on dynamic scenarios is presented in [8]. Even though being smartphone based, it is one of the few examples in literature that use dynamic data in the performance analysis, and therefore will be taken in consideration in the performance comparison.

C. Sequential Updating Method

In order to compare the highest number of satellite subsets while reducing the computation effort to a minimum, a Sequential Updating Method (SUM) is introduced in [9]. Figure 1 depicts a flowchart of the method. The process starts by choosing 4 satellites from the constellation with the most satellites to act as an initial subset. It proceeds to add each of the remaining *n*-4 satellites available to create *n*-4 subsets of size 5, with *n* being the number of visible satellites. After the creation of this group of subsets, every satellite that comes after the last satellite added in each subset is included in the subset and the subsets that had a satellite added in common will compare the trace of the inverse matrix with each other, and the one with minimal value will go to the next iteration. The process is repeated until *m* subsets with the desired size *k* remain and the one with the lowest GDOP is chosen to be used for positioning.

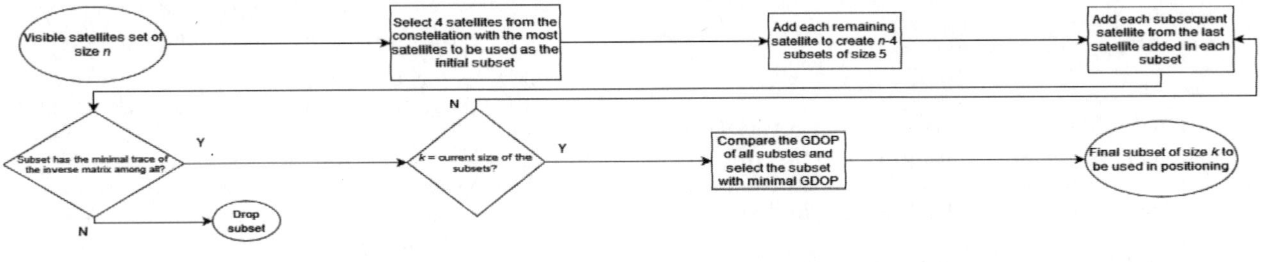

Figure 1. Process of the Sequential Updating Method.

D. Weight Function

For the purpose of creating a holistic satellite selection algorithm, a weight function is designed to provide higher weights to satellites better suited to be used in the positional solution. The proposed weight function has the form:

$$w_i = \sum_{g=1}^{F} w_g p_g \tag{4}$$

where F is the number of factors contributing to the function, w_g is the weight of factor g and p_g is the percentage assigned to the weight w_g, in order to determine the contribution to the total weight w_i. The p_g factors were determined through trial and error, iteratively refined until the optimal combination was identified, yielding the most favorable outcome.

The first two factors of the weight function are presented in [10], with those factors being the elevation and Carrier to Noise Ratio (CNR) of each satellite. The weight of the elevation factor is given as:

$$w_{el_i} = \frac{\theta_i}{\theta_{max}} \tag{5}$$

where θ_i is the elevation angle of the *i-th* satellite, θ_{max} is the maximum elevation angle among all the visible satellites at the current epoch, with all the angles being in degrees. The weight of the CNR is expressed as:

$$w_{CNR_i} = (1 + \alpha_m) \cdot \frac{CNR_i}{CNR_{max}} \tag{6}$$

with α_m being the multipath scaling factor given as [11]:

$$\alpha_m = \frac{R_{coef} - 1}{R_{coef} + 1} \tag{7}$$

where R_{coef} is the reflection coefficient and is expressed as [11]:

$$R_{coef} = \frac{10^{\frac{CNR_{max}}{20}}}{10^{\frac{CNR_i}{20}}} \tag{8}$$

For multipath free signals, the reflection coefficient is 1, while the multipath scaling factor is 0, which will not affect (6). In the case of multipath presence, the multipath scaling factor will be different than 0 and is added to '1' in (6) [12].

Another factor to complement the weight function introduced in [12] is the pseudorange variance. To calculate its value, the RTKLIB software default weighting system is used [13].

$$\sigma_i^2 = \frac{a^2}{sin^2\theta_i} \tag{9}$$

where a was determined empirically in [14] and θ_i is the elevation angle of the *i-th* satellite. Therefore, the weight of this factor is given by normalizing the pseudorange variance:

$$w_{var_i} = \frac{\max(\sigma^2) - \sigma_i^2}{\max(\sigma^2) - \min(\sigma^2)} \tag{10}$$

with the minimum and maximum values of σ^2 being calculated at each epoch.

The final factor added to this function is the CNR variation from epoch to epoch. This factor can be seen as an indicator of multipath and including its contribution in the weight function allows multipath affected measurements to have lower weight [15]. The CNR factor is expressed as:

$$\sigma_{CNR_j} = \sqrt{\frac{t-1}{t} \cdot \sigma_{CNR_{j-1}}^2 + \frac{1}{t} \cdot (CNR_i - \mu_j)^2} \tag{11}$$

$$\mu_j = \frac{t-1}{t} \cdot \mu_{j-1} + \frac{1}{t} * CNR_i \tag{12}$$

where t is the number of consecutive epochs in which the measurement was present, j represents the current epoch, σ_{CNR} and μ are the standard deviation and the mean, respectively, of the carrier to noise ratio among all satellites and CNR_i is the carrier to noise ratio of the *i-th* satellite. Hence, the weight is defined as:

$$w_{var_i} = \frac{\max(\sigma_{CNR}) - \sigma_{CNR_i}}{\max(\sigma_{CNR}) - \min(\sigma_{CNR})} \tag{13}$$

with σ_{CNR_i} being the CNR standard deviation of the *i-th* satellite, the minimum σ_{CNR} is calculated in each epoch and the maximum σ_{CNR} is a fixed value obtained by calculating the maximum σ_{CNR} of all the epochs.

III. THE PROPOSED ALGORITHM

Following the definition of the weight function, the same can be incorporated within the SUM. Before going through the SUM process, the weight of each satellite is calculated in order to create the W matrix, containing all the satellite weights. Afterwards, the weight matrix is used in the calculation of the Weighted Position Dilution of Precision (WPDOP) [16].

$$WPDOP = \sqrt{trace((G^T W G)^{-1})} \tag{14}$$

$$G = \begin{bmatrix} e_x^{i,1} & e_y^{i,1} & e_z^{i,1} \\ \vdots & \vdots & \vdots \\ e_x^{i,m} & e_y^{i,m} & e_z^{i,m} \\ e_x^{j,1} & e_y^{j,1} & e_z^{j,1} \\ \vdots & \vdots & \vdots \\ e_x^{j,n} & e_y^{j,n} & e_z^{j,n} \end{bmatrix} \tag{15}$$

$$W = \begin{bmatrix} w_1 & 0 & 0 & 0 & 0 \\ 0 & \ddots & \dots & \dots & 0 \\ 0 & \vdots & \ddots & \vdots & 0 \\ 0 & \vdots & \dots & \ddots & 0 \\ 0 & 0 & 0 & 0 & w_n \end{bmatrix} \tag{16}$$

By using the WPDOP for subsets comparisons in place of the GDOP, the positional accuracy is emphasized instead of the geometry of the satellites in the selected subset. Furthermore, the application of weights enhances the versatility and robustness since it takes in consideration multiple factors, hence making it a holistic algorithm. The proposed approach is labeled as Weighted Sequential Updating Method (WSUM) and takes the following steps:

1. Calculate the weight for each visible satellite.
2. Select the 5 satellites with the highest weight to be used as the initial subset. Making the initial subset bigger will reduce the number of iterations, therefore reducing the computational effort.
3. Go through the process of the Sequential Updating Method to find *m* subsets with *k* satellites.
4. Use the subset with minimal WPDOP for positioning.

IV. RESULTS AND ANALYSIS

GNSS data retrieved by the Vehicle Motion and Position Sensor (VMPS) designed by Bosch [17] installed in a car was used to evaluate the performance of the proposed algorithm. MATLAB was the software used to process the data and analyze results. The PC hardware is comprised of a 11th Generation Intel Core i7-11850H @ 2.50GHz, a NVIDIA RTX A3000 GPU and 32 GB of RAM. The location of the dataset collection was in Braga (Portugal) and the car goes through the urban environment of the city of Braga as well as some highway like roads. The GPS, GLONASS and Galileo constellations were considered in the experiments and Single Point Positioning (SPP) applying Kalman Filter was used to calculate the position. This dataset presents different types of conditions for the proposed algorithm to be tested, in order to verify its versatility and robustness. The optimal method, SUM, Ultra-Rapid and a smartphone-based satellite selection were also tested for comparison purposes.

The path of the car is shown in Figure 2, where the blue points coordinates were collected by the device iMar iTraceRT-MVT 600, that allows to obtain errors from the positioning system under test, to be used as a reference [19]. Throughout the experiment, there are between 0 and 23 visible satellites, as shown in Figure 3. The car went through some tunnels; therefore, no measurements were collected at some instances during the test.

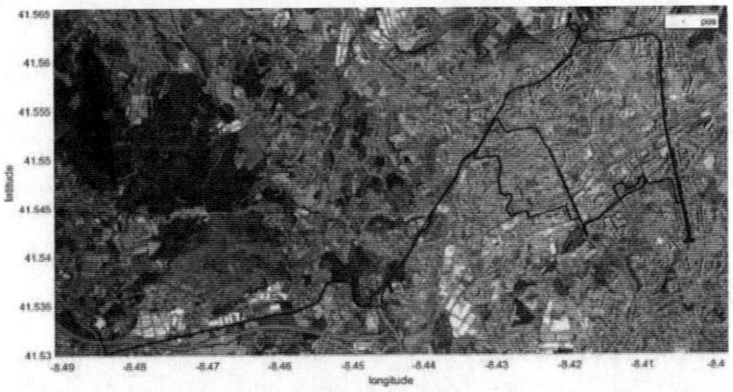

Figure 2. Path that the car went through in the city of Braga, Portugal (Satellite Image by Google Maps ©).

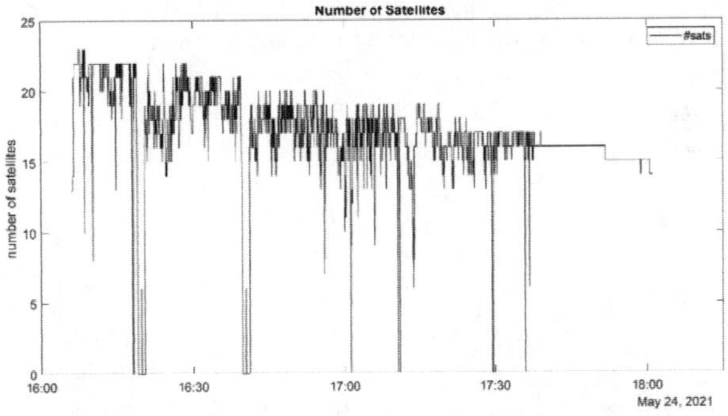

Figure 3. Number of visible satellites along the experiment.

Figures 4 and 5 show the empirical CDF of horizontal and vertical positioning errors obtained with the all-in-view (no satellite selection) solution and the four methods introduced. The WSUM exhibits an overall better horizontal error distribution compared to the other methods, while in terms of vertical error, the proposed method provides an overall better distribution until the 90th percentile.

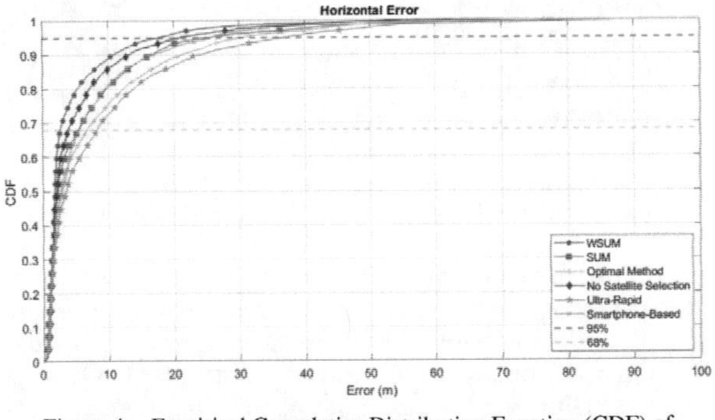

Figure 4. Empirical Cumulative Distribution Function (CDF) of horizontal positioning error for various satellite selection algorithms when selecting 9 satellites and no satellite selection.

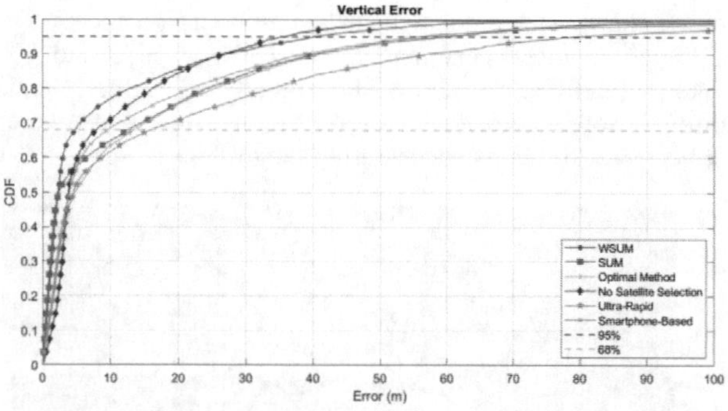

Figure 5. Empirical CDF of vertical positioning error for various satellite selection algorithms when selecting 9 satellites and no satellite selection.

Figures 6 and 7 display the distribution of the horizontal and vertical errors, respectively, where the y-axis is the percentage of trials each error range is obtained. WSUM demonstrates a higher percentage of errors between 0 and 2 meters in the horizontal category it slightly falls short of the performance exhibited by the SUM algorithm.

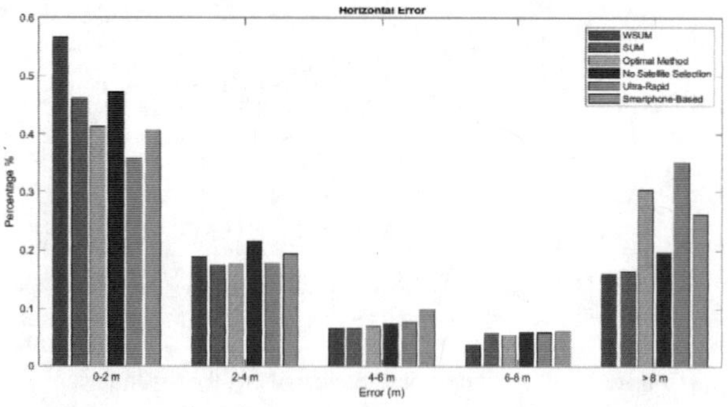

Figure 6. Percentage of trials each horizontal positional error range is obtained when selecting 9 satellites and no satellite selection.

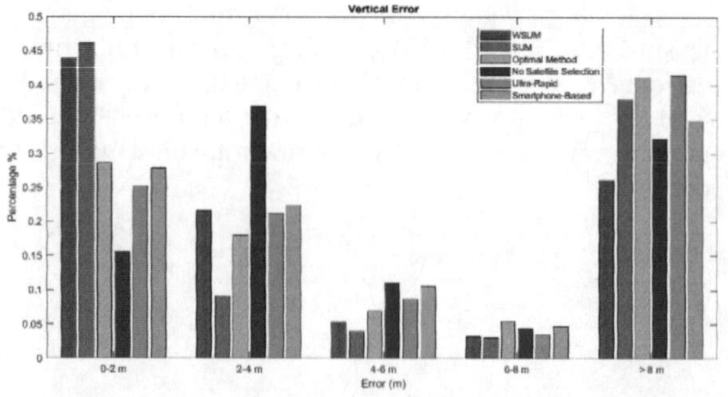

Figure 7. Percentage of trials each vertical positional error range is obtained when selecting 9 satellites and no satellite selection.

The WSUM presents 4.33 m and 8.52 m in terms of mean horizontal and vertical errors, while without satellite selection mean horizontal and vertical errors of 5.26 m and 9.52 m were obtained, respectively. The SUM, Optimal method, Ultra-Rapid and Smartphone-Based algorithms provide 6.56 m, 7.65 m, 8.93 m, and 6.25 m values of mean horizontal error, respectively, and 13.69 m, 14.30 m, 18.88 m, and 13.35 m values of mean vertical error, respectively.

Stability and computational effort are also important performance indicators of a satellite selection algorithm. Computational time is measured through the 'tic-toc' MATLAB functions and several runs were made in order to obtain the average computational time, in seconds, of each algorithm. The stability metric is measured as the ratio between number of satellites changed/removed due to algorithm decision from epoch n to epoch $n+1$ (ΔN), and number of satellites used in epoch n ($Nsat_n$):

$$Stability = \left(1 - \frac{\Delta N}{Nsat_n}\right) * 100 \qquad (17)$$

Table I shows that the increase in the size of the initial subset from 4 to 5 slightly decreases the computational time over the SUM algorithm, therefore making it faster than the original method. Stability is also displayed and while the proposed algorithm presents a lower value than SUM, it can still be labeled as highly stable.

TABLE I. STABILITY AND COMPUTATIONAL TIME OF ALL THE ALGORITHMS WHEN SELECTING 9 SATELLITES

Algorithm	Computational Time (s)	Stability
Optimal Method	**0.72261**	**94.78%**
SUM	**0.00604**	**96.63%**
Ultra-Rapid	**0.00036**	**95.51%**
Smartphone-Based	**0.00017**	**90.44%**
WSUM (Proposed)	**0.00447**	**93.55%**

When it comes to the empirical CDF of the GDOP and PDOP values, Figures 8 and 9 indicate that WSUM provides the highest values. This result is justified, given that the proposed algorithm uses the WPDOP in the comparison, thus the final chosen subset does not necessarily have the lowest values in terms of PDOP and GDOP. Furthermore, the high accuracy presented by the proposed method emphasizes the fact that a good satellite geometry does not directly translate to a good positional accuracy, and this factor by itself is not sufficient to select the best possible subset to be used in positioning.

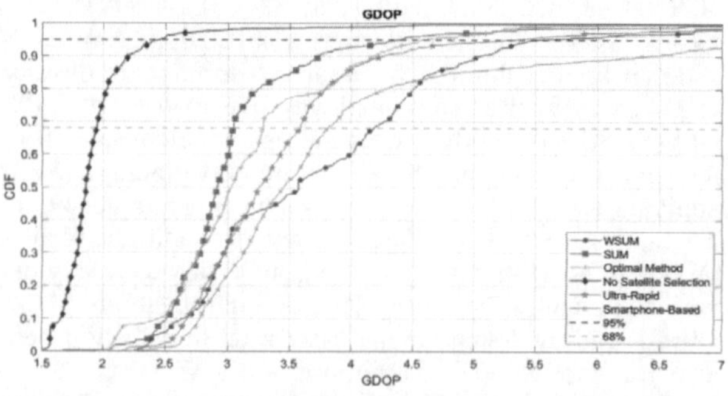

Figure 8. Empirical CDF of the GDOP for various satellite selection algorithms when selecting 9 satellites and no satellite selection.

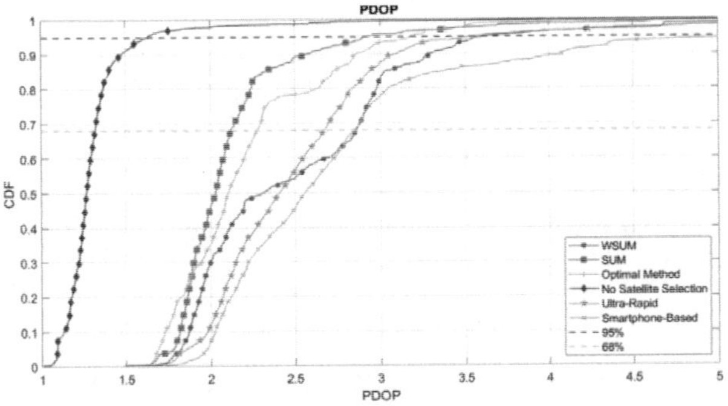

Figure 9. Empirical CDF of the PDOP for various satellite selection algorithms when selecting 9 satellites and no satellite selection.

V. CONCLUSION

In this paper, we propose a satellite selection algorithm capable of being used in dynamic scenarios in order to optimize a solution for autonomous driving. The proposed algorithm excels in providing better accuracy compared to other algorithms from the literature, as well as using all visible satellites. The computational effort was greatly minimized from the optimal method and the increase of the size of the initial subset of satellites provided a slight decrease in computational time compared to the original SUM method. The addition of the weight function did not increase the computational complexity of the proposed algorithm in any substantial way. Furthermore, it enhances the performance and versatility by making it a holistic satellite selection algorithm. Results show that the WSUM provides an improvement of 0.93 m and 1 m in terms of average horizontal and vertical error, respectively, over the use of all the visible satellites available at each epoch. Further optimizations to the proposed algorithm can be made in terms of computational effort and the implementation of Precise Point Positioning (PPP) will be made alongside the use of correction services in order to obtain higher levels of accuracy. Finally, the algorithm discussed in this paper presents a novel method that can improve positioning accuracy in challenging environments, therefore making it a promising solution to be incorporated in Highly Automated Driving vehicles.

ACKNOWLEDGMENT

This work is supported by the European Structural and Investment Funds in the FEDER component, through the Operational Competitiveness and Internationalization Programme (COMPETE 2020) [Project nº 179491; Funding Reference: SIFN-01-9999-FN-179491].

REFERENCES

[1] M. Karaim, M. Elsheikh, and A. Noureldin, GNSS Error Sources. Multifunctional Operation and Application of GPS. InTech 2018. doi: 10.5772/intechopen.75493.

[2] SAE International, "Taxonomy and definitions for terms related to on-road motor vehicle automated driving systems", 2021.

[3] ISO, "ISO/IEC TR 24027:2021 - Information technology — Artificial intelligence (AI) — Bias in AI systems and AI aided decision making", Retrieved October 11, 2023, [Online]. Available: https://www.iso.org/standard/77607.html.

[4] International Organization for Standardization, Road Vehicles – Functional Safety (ISO/DIS Standard No. 26262-6), 2018, Retrieved from https://www.iso.org/standard/68388.html

[5] E. Kaplan and C. Hegarty, Understanding GPS/GNSS: Principles and Applications, Third Edition, Artech, 2017.

[6] J. J. Spilker and B. W. Parkinson, Global Positioning System: Theory and Applications vol. 1, AAIA, 1996.

[7] C. Chi, X. Zhan, T. Wu, and X. Zhang," Ultra-Rapid Direct Satellite Selection Algorithm for Multi-GNSS", Proceedings of the International Conference on Aerospace System Science and Engineering 2019, ICASSE 2019, pp. 11–25. https://doi.org/10.1007/978-981-15-1773-0_2

[8] M. F. ElKhalea, H. M. Hendy, A. M. Kamel, I. I. Arafa, and A. Abosekeen, "Smartphone Positioning Enhancement Using Several GNSS Satellite Selection Techniques," 2022 5th International Conference on Communications, Signal Processing, and their Applications (ICCSPA), Cairo, Egypt, 2022, pp. 1-6, doi: 10.1109/ICCSPA55860.2022.10019004.

[9] A. Peng, G. Ou, and G. Li, "Fast satellite selection method for multi-constellation Global Navigation Satellite System under obstacle environments," IET Radar, Sonar & Navigation, vol. 8, no. 9, pp. 1051–1058, Dec. 2014, doi: 10.1049/iet-rsn.2013.0387.

[10] B. Wang, S. Wang, L. Miao, and S. Jun, An Improved Satellite Selection Method in Attitude Determination using Global Positioning System, Recent Patent on Space Technology, 2009.

[11] M. S. Braasch, "Multipath Effects, Global Positioning Systems: Theory and Applications", American Institute of Aeronautics and Astronautics, 1996, pp. 547-568.

[12] V. S. Srinivas, A. D. Sarma, and A. S. Reddy, "Weighted Quasi-optimal and Recursive Quasi-optimal Satellite Selection Techniques for GNSS", 2015.

[13] T. Takasu, RTKLIB: Open Source Program Package for RTK-GPS, FOSS4G 2009 Tokyo, Japan, November 2, 2009.

[14] N. Naciri and S. Bisnath, "An uncombined triple-frequency user implementation of the decoupled clock model for PPP-AR", *J Geod 95,* 2021, https://doi.org/10.1007/s00190-021-01510-y

[15] H. Tokura and N. Kubo, "Efficient Satellite Selection Method for Instantaneous RTK-GNSS in Challenging Environments," Trans Jpn Soc Aeronaut Space Sci", vol. 60, no. 4, pp. 221–229, 2017, doi: 10.2322/tjsass.60.221.

[16] E. R. Matera, A. G. Pena, C. Milner, and B. Ekambi, "Smart Exploitation of Pseudorange and Pseudorange-rate Error Characterization to Improve the PVT Solution", *32nd International Technical Meeting of the Satellite Division of The Institute of Navigation*, 2019, doi:10.33012/2019.17109

[17] Vehicle motion and position sensor, Retrieved October 11, 2023, from https://www.bosch-mobility.com/en/solutions/sensors/vehicle-motion-and-position-sensor/

[18] C. Pendão, A. G. Ferreira, A. Moreira, C. Martins, and H. Silva, "Challenges in characterization of GNSS precise positioning systems for automotive", CEUR Workshop Proceedings", 2020.

The Screen is not Flat

Luciane Maria Fadel
Graduate Program in Knowledge Engineering and Management (PPGEGC)
Federal University of Santa Catarina
Florianópolis, SC, Brazil

e-mail: luciane.fadel@ufsc.br

***Abstract*— A characteristic of the digital interface is its multidimensionality. However, its design continues to be influenced by multiple remediations, mainly from printed media, which give the interface a flat surface, suppressing its communicative and interactive potential. Interface design has dealt with this problem fragmentedly, focusing on specific elements. For the students, there remains the need to visualize the blurred screen depth. This paper outlines the multidimensionality of the interface in terms of use and aesthetics. To this end, it draws the boundaries for the aesthetics of the screen and interaction dimensions, combining 30 years of experience teaching digital design with the current literature on the topic. The results establish design dimensions that contribute to understanding the interface's imagistic potential in terms of use and aesthetics. In addition, the results highlight some of the challenges to be addressed by designers.**

Keywords-screen; interface; design; remediation; dimensions.

I. INTRODUCTION

Our society is moving towards an intensive use of screens. This use began with screens of static images such as painting and photography, which framed a moment of the imagination. From there, it migrated to screens with moving images, such as cinema, which framed a period of the imagination. When the TV occupied an essential space in our homes, its screen demanded more hours of visual contact, as it became accessible as the paintings and photographs hanging on the wall and clamored for attention as the cinema. Between one screen and another, we learned to see, accept, and apprehend its images as technology.

According to [1], technology is a complex reality involving technological knowledge and a human attitude. As an attitude, technology becomes habitual, and it is believed to make our lives easier and contribute to our comfort.

The complexity of technology also occurs in the interface design teaching, either by facing technology in its manifestation (designing) or the craft of its poetics. Poetics constitute the principles of design that best define an object or work [2]. Remediation is a central poetic of the digital interface.

Remediation is the process of representing one media into another [3]. For example, a digital calendar is expected to simulate its printed form. The months follow a table form, and the days are presented by cells. Therefore, this paper suggests that understanding the screen as flat is a consequence of the remediation process.

For [3], remediation undergoes a 4-level evolution, where the representation of a new media moves further away from the media that precedes it. Therefore, we argue that each level is reached through understanding contemporary media and recognizing its language and properties, i.e., creating its poetics.

Another poetic of digital media is its multidimensionality, rooted in the principle of numerical representation [4]. This principle enables new dimensions using the artifact through multiple aesthetic expression and interaction forms.

The poetic of multidimensionality, investigated by [5], is established by the data density that [6] defines as the intense flow of information captured and sent by the interactor+artefact. Thus, the screen mediates this data density from visible, perceived, or social dimensions. This paper focuses on the visual dimensions because it is a reasonable first step to building the base to comprehend others. In addition, teaching poetics benefits from visualizing each dimension, as the students could design each one or even play with the interconnection among dimensions to create depth.

Therefore, we argue that the screen is not flat, as its depth develops through its many dimensions. This paper draws the boundaries for the aesthetics of the screen and interaction dimensions.

The method follows qualitative research, highlighting screen dimensions from the literature and dialoguing with teaching practice. This practice enabled many observations about students' difficulties in visualizing the screen dimensions.

The remainder of this paper is organized as follows. Section 2 and Section 3 present the background review of the aesthetic and interaction dimensions. Section 4 discusses its implication on interface design. Finally, Section 5 draws a brief conclusion.

II. AESTHETIC DIMENSION

The multiple dimensions of the screen become undeniable when establishing the possibilities of the interface design aesthetic. One option is simulating three-dimensional objects, i.e., the object is created in its three dimensions. In addition, remediation, layers of information, movement, and Information Design (ID) are screen dimensions.

A. The screen interface remediation

The interface can be understood as a mediating layer between the artifact and the interactor. The user interacts with the product through the physical or digital interface. Thus, a product can be complex to manipulate, and its use requires a layer of translation of its mechanics. For example, a typewriter presents itself to the interactor through a coating, which hides its gears and leaves enough in view to be used. Therefore, [7] associates design with the interface. For the user, the interface links the user, the tool, and the action. Thus, it is likely that the more complex the object's engineering, the more critical the role of the interface as a tool facilitating use. This role becomes evident with digital interfaces, given the complexity of the artifact.

Reference [8] states that the interface is the software for the user, which means it does not matter if the algorithm is highly complex or has a layer of artificial intelligence. What the user perceives is the contact and control over the tool mediated by the interface.

Thus, digital interfaces have made this mediating layer visible (hypermediation), often because of the complexity of its use. Understanding this complexity, many designers seek to create invisible or transparent interfaces (immediacy). However, one of the main qualities of digital objects is their oscillation between hypermediation and immediacy.

This oscillation is also referred to as remediation by [3]. The authors argue that the opacity of the interface is necessary for interaction to occur, as the interactor needs to see the options to act on them (hypermediation). On the other hand, immersion happens when engaging with the content, and the interface becomes transparent (immediacy). Therefore, this oscillation is another poetic of interactive media and a dimension of the interface.

To decrease the oscillation, [9] advocates the narrativization of the interface. Lessening the oscillation can be accomplished by (1) narrativized 'look and feel' of the interface, (2) behavioral mimic and behavioral metaphors, (3) narrativized perspective, and finally, by building (4) bridges and mixed-reality interfaces.

The 'look and feel' incorporates narrative elements into the graphic representation. The aforementioned has to do with the visual identity of the artifact, as all the imagery representation should reinforce the project concept. For instance, feedback could be presented as illustrations, reinforcing the adopted narrative.

Also, interface elements can mimic behaviors or behavioral metaphors. For example, if an interface element demands an urgent response, its graphical representation can assume a hurried behavior, such as getting agitated.

Narrativized perspective, on the other hand, acts on the depth dimension of the screen. That is, the screen's graphic design makes explicit the z-axis of the spatial representation. This representation is evident in-game scenarios or environments where the interactor can move around.

Finally, data density can support the bridges and mixed-reality interfaces establishing digital and virtual connections. Augmented reality artifacts are excellent examples, as they apply new layers of dynamic data on top of the captured image of the place (Figure 1). Other bridges can be established by using interactors' information and capturing information from the environment. Locative media are examples of this dynamic.

Figure 1. Example of augmented reality artifact using Google translate App.

B. Tri-dimensional objects

Treating objects in three dimensions allows different renderings to simulate their spatiality, such as rotating the object or moving it in the screen space. So, it requires the object to be thought in true 3D, which moves away from the printed media since this support requires a 2D representation. In this case, the design domain would approach the realm of sculpture because it would encompass elements of 3D representation such as body, weight, movement, and lines of action, among others, expanding to volume treatment.

In addition to 3D representation, space simulation enables layers of movement and different forms of interaction. By treating the screen as a three-dimensional space, motion layers are created in the depth of this space, where objects can move around. For example, a disabled element can occupy a bottom layer of space and project to forward layers when enabled.

Moreover, the space can become active, posing as a design and communication element. As advocated by [10], the digital space, as a remediation of the medium, expands the possibilities of interaction as it becomes a meaningful dimension.

The screen's shape implies a reduction in the treatment of a two-dimensional space. But examples, such as the Apple Watch® bring new possibilities when the screen is designed in its three-dimensional space (Figure 2). The surface is considered spherical, which implies that the graphic elements can slide around the sphere, assuming different sizes when traversing it. They increase in the center and decrease when approaching the edges.

The treatment of the surface in 3D enables new attention arrangements, given primarily by size and position.

Figure 2. Apple Watch Interface.

C. *Information layers*

Two fronts provide an understanding of information layers: position and meaning. While the positioning layer defines different layers in different spatial positions (on any of the three axes of the screen), the meaning layer implies different degrees of importance built through Information Design using contrast, hierarchy, typography, composition, color, and image.

The positioning layer uses the spatial geometry of the screen to place the information layers. Spatial geometry implies the independence of the layers, both at the content and interaction levels.

One of the best examples of this arrangement of multiple layers on the same screen is Augmented Reality (AR) applications. AR presents a layer of dynamic information on the physical environment, whether captured by a camera or not. That is, its definition guarantees a multidimensional understanding.

AR can happen in 3 arrangements: (1) through information projected on a physical space, such as films projected on buildings; (2) using an instrument to capture the physical space and, on the same screen, insert the dynamic information; and; (3) using glasses or lenses on which the information is projected while the ocular system captures the physical space [11].

AR is distinguished from a simple projection of a video onto a screen by considering the three characteristics that [11] attributes to AR:

- It combines the real and the virtual;
- It is interactive in real-time;
- It is registered in three dimensions.

The multidimensionality of the screen is explicit, given that the interactor is the one who builds it. This co-creation allows a certain degree of control to the interactor, given the dynamism of the composite image.

In the composition of AR, one can have several layers of information organized by the distance between the object and the interactor, the screen's permanence, the interactor's importance, or any other design criterion. These criteria that are exposed by AR composition can be applied in other interface design projects. AR makes it easier to understand this multidimensional composition of information.

D. *Movement*

Movement is another screen dimension that can be understood on four approaches: moving objects, moving images, the movement of the interactor in space and navigation, or the movement of the device itself.

Given the principle of numerical representation, objects projected onto the screen can be created in true 3D, which allows the objects to be manipulated on all three axes. 3D object occupies the multidimensional space of the screen and offers many possibilities of representation. Just as the screen's surface allows it to be treated as a 3D surface, objects can also be designed with three dimensions.

The calendar, for example, which is constantly translated into digital with firm reference to its printed predecessor, i.e., two-dimensional, can be represented by a 3D object, such as a sphere. The spherical calendar allows movement to explore new possibilities of representation.

The object movement through animations, micro animations, sliding in different directions, and appearance, among others, adds dynamism to the interface elements, providing feedback to the interactor. Moving images is characteristic of media based on time, such as video, movies, or animation. These media are complex, translating narratives into different dimensions, such as time, space, or sequential images.

The interactor's movement occurs in physical space or/and on the screen, navigating among pages. As argued by [6] and [12], the former is supported by mobile technology with small screens. The device's movement brings new possibilities of embodied or haptic interaction. That is, the control of the screen can occur through actions with the device. For example, shaking the device can switch pages.

E. *Information design (ID)*

The design project also presents new dimensions because ID parallels interaction and navigation.

The layers intertwine various "designs" that increase the depth of the screen. The ID acts on the implications for the reception of the information that allows interaction and navigation. Thus, when creating a button to serve as an interaction element, the ID crafts the button to better inform about the possible action.

The Navigation Design presents the same dynamic, as it establishes a path among digital pages, while the Information Design delivers the best solutions to offer the way.

Therefore, it is considered that Navigation Design plans the possible paths; the Interaction Design proposes the mechanisms to allow the interactor to act upon the interface, while Information Design conceives these mechanisms.

III. USE AND INTERACTION DIMENSIONS

Mobility has intensified the use of digital objects. This property amplifies the concept of screen since the place of use needs to be within the covered reception area to transmit and receive data. The creation of the interface happens dynamically from the imbrication in receiving, treating, and providing the data, which is named performative cartography [12]. Thus, mobility and performative cartography become dimensions of screen use.

A. *Mobility*

Mobility, i.e., the use of digital products in different places, is supported by the technology of individual Internet access and the size of artifacts, such as smartphones and tablets, which enables their use while the interactor is on the move. Mobility has enabled data density, making space active by collecting data from interactors or delivering locative data and information. The screen has become a portal through which the information about the place is presented to the interactor. Locative media, such as games or apps, can create new dimensions of responsiveness provoked by space.

Reference [6] labeled this active space as augmented space and argued that this expansion should be seen as an idea or a cultural and aesthetic practice. This reconceptualization expands the creation possibilities, making the screen a complex space.

This complexity embraces the idea of constant monitoring, which goes unnoticed by the interactors. These two situations need to be faced as design domains. That is, monitoring is a fact, and it can be omitted or used by the digital artifact, which requires addressing it in the interface.

As a cultural practice, several objects integrate the work and leisure routine, such as ubiquitous computing, artificial intelligence, augmented reality, and wearables. Aesthetics accompanies this engineering but still disconnects from the presence of the interactor and its surroundings. In addition, these objects are still imagined alone, and thus, their ecology is not much considered. For instance, the IoT (Internet of Things) features could be integrated into the digital artifact design to improve the use of the data or functionalities.

These are some of the challenges to be thought of in the mobility dimension. These challenges are made explicit in the cultural practice of performative cartography.

B. *Performative cartography*

The double displacement of the individual in the physical environment and on the screen is known as "performative cartography" [12]. The interactor navigates the interface while the interface is formed. For example, the map in Google Maps is generated from the subject's position in space (Figure 3).

Thus, visualization and image construction co-occur in a creative process that [12] indicates is a 4D operation of a 3D space. To solve the representation dilemma, the author suggests that the 4th dimension would treat space-time instead of treating time. The argument that both time and space are revealed in use supports this suggestion. For this reason, performative cartography implies changes, differences, and a certain unpredictability of movement that forms.

Figure 3. Example of performative cartography using Google Maps.

C. *Interaction*

In addition to the device's movement, interaction with the digital object occurs in new dimensions because of interactivity. Considering that the interactors' experience with the screen occurs through actions and perceptions, that is, how they act and understand, a two-way communication process is established between the interface and the interactors. Thus, the interactivity of a narrative experience is discussed by [13] in 4 modes: cognitive, functional, explicit, and meta-interactivity. Cognitive Interactivity [13] relates to revisiting a text that conflicts with the previous understanding. Functional Interactivity deals with its physicality, usability, and Information Design. Explicit Interactivity examines the actions when using the interface, the interaction per se. And Meta-interactivity considers the involvement with the text outside the experience when the interactor talks about it.

Interaction can be interpreted through the categories pointed out by [14]. The authors list different concepts associated with interaction, such as dialogue, transmission, tool use, tool use, optimal behavior, embodiment, experience and control. Each concept conceives the relationship between product and human in a particular way. In this paper, all these concepts imply dimensions of the screen, as they establish poetics of use and meaning.

The interface establishes a conversation with the interactor through a dialog. It is expected to be a fluid conversation, either from the side of the interactors who understand how the interface works and what "response" they can send or from the side of the interface that also responds according to the interactors' emission. Therefore, it is likely that the mental model dimension of conversation is strongly considered in this design.

Interaction, as transmission, requires a design focused on the quality of the channel as it pays attention to the number of bits transmitted. In this case, the noise dimension becomes the most relevant.

For [14], interaction conceived as tool use has three implications: (1) the tool shapes how the interactor will act (focus on the task artifact); (2) the focus can be on the mediation value of the interface; (3) the focus falls on the use itself. Thus, looking at interaction as a tool requires a dimension of the extension of the body and senses, as proposed by [15].

When interaction is optimal behavior, there is a confrontation to establish the best result between performance and resources (both human and technological). Therefore, the time-space-statistical dimension [14] of the screen emerges.

Designing interaction as embodied requires situating its agents in a physical world. Reference [14] indicates that situating interaction involves intention, coupling, and context.

Conceiving interaction as experience means understanding how the interaction unfolds. It considers the qualities of the technology and not only the object's properties and turns to aesthetic, emotional, and completeness aspects. Therefore, the value dimension deepens the attribution and expectations regarding the screen. Finally, the concept of control highlights errors against an ideal, meaning the system adjusts actions following feedback.

IV. IMPLICATIONS OF THE DIMENSIONS

This paper argues that the multidimensionality of the screen is a property of digital media conceptualized in [6] principle of numerical representation. From this principle, the dimensions of the screen can be understood in the field of 1) Aesthetics, which involves the graphic qualities of the interface; 3D representation; space as a medium; layers of information; movement and the design of information, and 2) Use and Interaction, comprising at least mobility; performative cartography and interaction.

However, the new media's nature is the older media's remediation. Therefore, in order to form a new media, it is necessary to construct its poetics. Thus, determining the screen's dimensions can contribute to its definition and recognition of its language and properties. Once defined, the dimensions can be addressed in both the teaching and practice of design. Figure 4 summarizes the main findings.

A. *Teaching design*

Recognizing the multidimensionality of the screen implies responsible teaching of interface design. This responsibility lies in treating the various dimensions of the screen, starting with understanding digital technology as habitual. Therefore, this treatment suggests facing questions about the role of digital technology in everyday life, and its effect on society.

This paper proposes to address these questions focusing on the seven axes of design: composition, form, color, typography, human factors, technology, and movement. Therefore, to address the role of digital technology, design teaching could expose different contributions of the screen depending on the type of artifact in focus. For each axis, the design elements and their contribution to the role of the screen would be related. This construction promotes a critical position and develops the analytical skill of the designer. The field of Aesthetics, Use, and Interaction could elaborate on other issues raised in this paper.

The teaching of Aesthetics develops the gaze towards the interface, i.e., recognizing the interface as an active mediating field. An active media requires treating the interface as a dynamic object oscillating between opaque and transparent. In addition, the elements of the interface support and respond to the actions of the interactor, delivering information and feedback. Furthermore, teaching 3D modeling promotes the abstract reasoning of thinking about the screen space and its objects in three dimensions.

Teaching design also explores layers of information by its nature. Objects (type, form, and function), action (passive or interactive), hyperlinks in depth, design choices such as gamification and metaphors, or even behavior, such as movement, shape this nature.

The movement remains on the periphery of design projects. Thus, the urgency of teaching design to promote its integration into projects is notorious.

Teaching movement requires building the ability to deal with time and space, favoring a narrative's constitution. Teaching narrative as a poetics of design requires treating the narrativization of the interface, that is, treating the design elements as passive or active agents of the narrative. Concepts and elements of narrative will be revisited for this purpose.

Information Design is a constant in design projects, but it has been absorbed by the specialties required in digital design, such as interaction design and navigation. Teaching digital Information Design reinforces the intertwining and boundaries of these specialties.

The implications of dimensions in teaching about use and interaction lie in the recognition of mobility and performative cartography as requirements and properties of the object. Therefore, teaching can highlight such factors and discuss the axis of technology and its consequences on the artifact's use, production, and creation.

The interaction dimension implies teaching interactivity through some biases such as narrative, embodied, and agency. These biases can broaden interaction treatment and incorporate new technology methods, presenting the potential for accessibility.

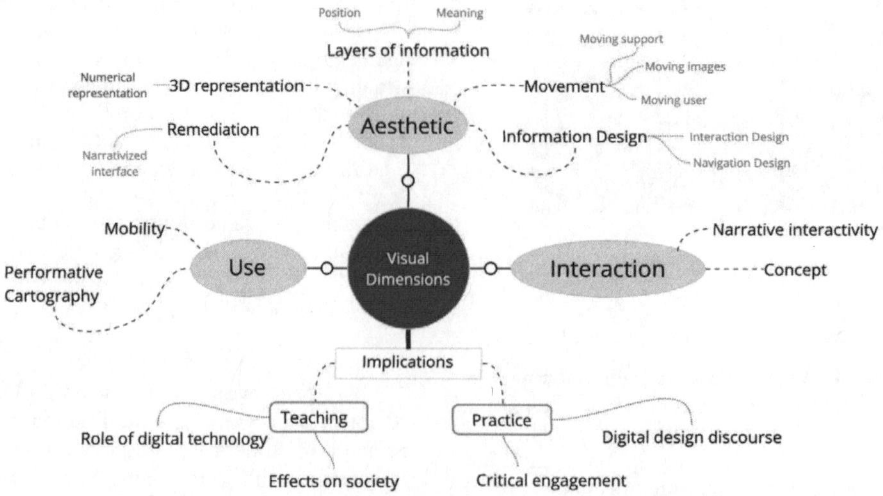

Figure 4. Visual dimensions and its implication in teaching and practice.

B. Design practice

The implications of dimensions in design practice are configured in a digital design discourse through the iterative and responsible construction and creation of artifacts that shape a cyber society. It is argued that facing the multidimensionality of the screen provokes thinking, recognizing, analyzing, and discussing interface design in its multifaceted practices.

The practice of the aesthetic dimension provides a critical engagement with the elements that contribute to the depth of the screen and its effect on reception by the interactor. It requires an active, managerial, collaborative practice that values the participation of multiple agents, human and non-human. It also requires encompassing various areas of knowledge as a source of ideas and inspiration, which can be realized in alternatives through the design method. It also allows systematizing iterative analysis processes and creating the dimensions of use and interaction.

V. CONCLUSION

The multidimensionality of the screen is a characteristic investigated by several researchers in the axes of design, such as composition, shapes, color [16], typography [17], human factors [18], technology [19], and movement [20]. The design of virtual and augmented reality artifacts has imposed the need for research on other dimensions of the artifact [21].

Establishing the boundaries of different screen dimensions inspires investigations and draws attention to the complexity of the screen. This complexity goes far beyond the reach of this paper because it involves social, emotional, psychological, historiographic, and philosophical dimensions, among others.

This paper contributes to this field of research and practice by drawing interface dimensions in terms of use and aesthetics. Our experience teaching digital design pointed to great difficulty for students in giving depth to the screen. One issue is the lack of visualization of this depth. It is hoped that multidimensional interface design supports the visualization of these dimensions.

The taxonomy of these and other dimensions presented in the literature is left as future research. In addition, future research should develop each dimension regarding design techniques to support teaching and designing a screen that explores its multidimensionality. This work is currently ongoing by this researcher.

REFERENCES

[1] A. Cupani, "Types of technology and their cultural consequences," *Revista Dialectus,* pp. 82-95, 2020.

[2] D. Bordwell, Poetics of Cinema, New York: Routledge, 2007.

[3] J. D. Bolter and R. Grusin, Remediation, MIT Press paperback edition, 2000.

[4] L. Manovich, The Language of New Media, Cambridge: MIT Press, 2001.

[5] L. M. Fadel and A. Coelho, "Augmented reality in information design," In press, 2023.

[6] L. Manovich, "The Poetics of Augmented Space," *Visual Communication,* pp. 219-240, 2006.

[7] G. Bonsiepe, Gui Bonsiepe: Interface - An Approach to Design, Jan Van Eyck Akademie, 1999.

[8] D. Norman, Design of Everyday Things: Revised and Expanded, New York: Basic Books, 2013.

[9] J. Bizzocchi, M. B. Lin and J. Tanenbaum, "Game, narrative and the design of the interface," *International Journal of Art and Technology,* vol. 4, pp. 460-479, 2011.

[10] L. M. Fadel and J. Bizzocchi, "Designing background as space medium remediation," *Estudos in Design (Online),* v. 17, 2019, pp. 5-22.

[11] R. T. Azuma, "A Survey of Augmented Reality," *In Presence: Teleoperators and Virtual Environments,* vol. 6, no. 4, 1997, pp. 355-385.

[12] N. Verhoeff, Mobile Screens The Visual Regime of Navigation, Amsterdam: Amsterdam University Press, 2012.

[13] E. Zimmerman, "Narrative, Interactivity, Play and Games," in *First Person: New Media as Story, Performance, and Game*, Cambridge, MIT Press, 2004, pp. 154-164.

[14] K. Hornbæk and A. Oulasvirta, "What is interaction?," in *CHI 2017*, pp. 5040–5052, Denver, 2017, doi.org/10.1145/3025453.3025765.

[15] M. McLuhan, "The Playboy Interview: Marshall McLuhan," *Playboy Magazine,* pp. 53-74, 1969.

[16] Z. Wang, W. Liu and M. Yang, "Data-driven multi-objective affective product design integrating three-dimensional form and color," in *Data-driven multi-objective affective product design integrating three-dimensional form and color Zeng Wang, Weidong Liu, Minglang Yang Neural Computing and Applications (NCAA)*, pp. 15835–15861, 2022.

[17] J. J. Shen, K. Jin, A. Zhang, C. Breazeal and H. W. Park, "Affective Typography: The Effect of AI-Driven Font Design on Empathetic Story Reading," in *CHI EA'23*, pp. 1–7, doi.org/10.1145/3544549.35856252023.

[18] P. J. Thomas, The social and interactional dimensions of human-computer interfaces, New York: Cambridge University Press, 1995.

[19] V. G. Motti, "Wearable Technologies: a Roadmap to the Future," in *WebMedia'20: Proceedings of the Brazilian Symposium on Multimedia and the Web*, pp. 3-4, 2020, doi.org/10.1145/3428658.3431928.

[20] R. Sun, A. V. Wallop, G. Leslie and E. Y.-L. Do, "SoniSpace: Expressive Movement Interaction to Encourage Taking Up Space with the Body," in *DIS'23 Companion Publication*, 2023, pp. 279–283, doi.org/10.1145/3563703.359.

[21] M. O. Ellenberg, M. Satkowski, W. Luo and R. Dachselt, "Spatiality and Semantics - Towards Understanding Content Placement in Mixed Reality," in *CHI EA'23,* 2023, pp. 1–8, doi.org/10.1145/3544549.3585853.

[22] J. Murray, Hamlet on the Holodeck, London: MIT Press, 1998.

Exploring the Temperature Dependent Magnetic Properties and Magnetoimpedance Effect in Fe-rich Microwires for Temperature Monitoring

Paula Corte-León
Dept. Polymers and Adv. Materials and EHU Quantum Center, Univ. Basque Country, UPV/EHU, 20018 San Sebastian, Spain
e-mail: paula.corte@ehu.eus

Valentina Zhukova, Mihail Ipatov
Dept. Polymers and Adv. Materials, Dept. Applied Physics and EHU Quantum Center,
Univ. Basque Country, UPV/EHU, 20018 San Sebastian, Spain
e-mails: valentina.zhukova@ehu.es; mihail.ipatov@ehu.es

Ivan Skorvanek, František Andrejka,
Institute of Experimental Physics, Slovak Academy of Sciences, Kosice, Slovakia
e-mail: skorvi@saske.sk; andrejka@saske.sk

Arcady Zhukov
Dept. Polym. Adv. Materials, Dept. Applied Physics and EHU Quantum Center, Univ. Basque Country, UPV/EHU, 20018 San Sebastian and Ikerbasque, Bilbao, Spain
e-mail: arkadi.joukov@ehu.es

***Abstract*—In this work, we provide new experimental results on temperature dependence of hysteresis loops and the Giant MagnetoImpedance (GMI) effect of amorphous $Fe_{75}B_9Si_{12}C_4$ microwires. We observed a remarkable improvement of GMI ratio and modification of hysteresis loops from rectangular to inclined upon heating. The observed experimental results are discussed considering relaxation of internal stresses upon heating, Hopkinson effect and modification of the thermal expansion coefficients upon heating.**

Keywords- Magnetic microwires; Magnetic softness; Giant magnetoimpedance effect; Internal stresses; Magnetic anisotropy.

I. INTRODUCTION

Amorphous magnetic materials are commonly considered among the most promising magnetic materials because of their excellent magnetic and mechanical properties [1]-[5]. Such amorphous materials can be prepared with planar (ribbons) or cylindrical (wires) shapes.

Magnetic wires can have unique magnetic properties, such as magnetic bistability [6]-[8] and/or giant magnetoimpedance, GMI, effect [9]-[11], which are suitable for development of several technological applications [12]-[15]. Therefore, research on amorphous magnetic wires has attracted substantial attention since the 70-s [6]-[15].

Recently, substantial attention has been paid to development of amorphous materials with new functionalities, such as reduced dimensions, enhanced corrosion resistance or biocompatibility [11][13]. Therefore, great attention has been paid to development of alternative fabrication methods allowing preparation of biocompatible amorphous materials with reduced dimensionality [11][13].

Accordingly, studies of glass-coated microwires with reduced diameters (between 0.5 and 100 μm), covered with thin, insulating, biocompatible and flexible glass-coating prepared by the Taylor-Ulitovsky method have attracted great attention [11] [13]. Such microwires are covered with thin, insulating, biocompatible and flexible glass-coating allowing better corrosion resistance and biocompatibility. Additionally, such microwire can present excellent magnetic softness or magnetic bistability [11] [13]. Such features of glass-coated microwires allow development of new exciting applications in various magnetic sensors, as well as in smart composites with tunable magnetic permittivity [6][11][13]-[21]. One more advantage of glass-coated microwires is their excellent mechanical properties [4] [5].

One of the most promising applications of glass-coated microwires is the external stimuli (temperature, stress, magnetic field) monitoring [22]-[25]. As was previously demonstrated [22], the dispersion of the effective permittivity, ε_{ef}, of the composites with magnetic wire inclusions depends on the metallic wires geometry, as well as on the magnetic wires impedance. The utilization of ferromagnetic wires allows tuning of this dispersion through changing the wire magnetic structure by external stimuli (magnetic field, stress or temperature) [22]-[25].

For such applications, studies of temperature dependence of the GMI effect are essentially relevant. However, there are only very few studies on temperature dependence of GMI and most studies were performed in different amorphous materials (ribbons or thick magnetic wires without glass-coating) [26]-[29].

In this paper, we provide our recent experimental results on temperature dependence of the GMI effect and hysteresis loops for Fe-rich ($Fe_{75}B_9Si_{12}C_4$) microwires.

This paper is organized as follows. In Section 2, the experimental methods, as well as the microwires characteristics analyzed in this paper are provided. Section 3 presents the experimental results dealing with temperature dependence of hysteresis loops and GMI effect. Finally, we conclude the paper in Section 4.

II. Experimental System Details

Amorphous $Fe_{75}B_9Si_{12}C_4$ glass-coated microwires (metallic nucleus diameter, d= 15.2 μm, total diameter, D= 17.2 μm) with positive magnetostriction coefficient, λ_s, ($\lambda_s \approx 38x10^{-6}$), have been prepared using the Taylor-Ulitovsky method, previously described elsewhere [16] [18].

The hysteresis loops have been measured using MicroSense EV9 Vibration Sample Magnetometer (VSM), as well as using fluxmetric methods. The latter was previously successfully employed for characterization of magnetically soft microwires at room temperature [30], while utilization of VSM magnetometry allowed to measure the hysteresis loops of 5 mm long samples from room temperature up to 300 °C, as described elsewhere [31]. The hysteresis loops were represented as the dependence of normalized magnetization, M/M_0 (where M is the magnetic moment at a given magnetic field and M_0 is the magnetic moment of the sample at the maximum magnetic field amplitude measured at room temperature) versus magnetic field, H.

Specially designed experimental set-up allows to measure sample impedance and evaluate $\Delta Z/Z$-ratio in the temperature, T, range from room up to T= 300 °C at frequencies, f, up to 110 MHz [32].

We used the GMI ratio, $\Delta Z/Z$, determined as:

$$\Delta Z/Z = [Z(H) - Z(H_{max})] / Z(H_{max}), \quad (1)$$

where Z is impedance of the wire, H and H_{max} are the applied and maximum DC magnetic fields.

III. Experimental Results and Discussion

As shown in Figure 1, a rectangular hysteresis loop is observed for as-prepared $Fe_{75}B_9Si_{12}C_4$ glass-coated microwire, as expected for Fe-rich microwire with positive λ_s [18].

A remarkable change in hysteresis loop is observed upon heating: the hysteresis loops of studied sample becomes essentially non-rectangular (see Figure 2a). The substantial effect of heating can be better appreciated from Figure 2b, where the change in the low field hysteresis loop upon heating is shown. Rectangular hysteresis loop transforms into inclined upon heating (see Figure 2b).

The observed changes in hysteresis loops upon heating are almost completely reversible: as shown in Figure 3, the

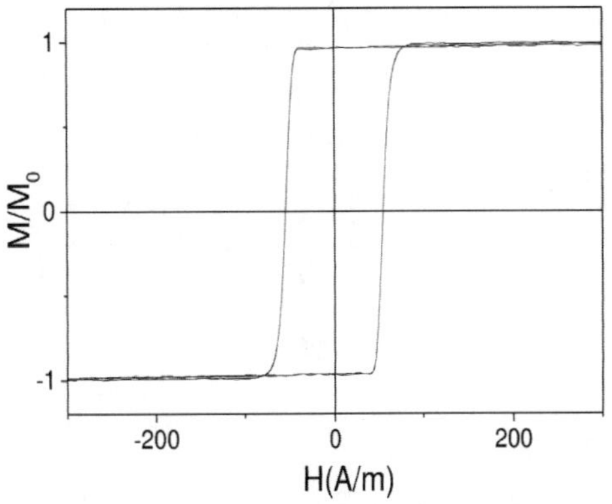

Figure 1. Hysteresis loops of as-prepared sample.

hysteresis loop measured after heating up to 300 °C and cooling back to room temperature becomes again rectangular.

The aforementioned GMI effect is successfully explained in terms of skin effect of magnetically soft conductors. The origin of the GMI effect is related to the effect of a magnetic field, H, on the penetration depth, δ, of an electrical current flowing through the magnetically soft conductor [9]-[11]. The relationship between δ and the circumferential magnetic permeability, μ_ϕ, for the case of magnetic wires is given by:

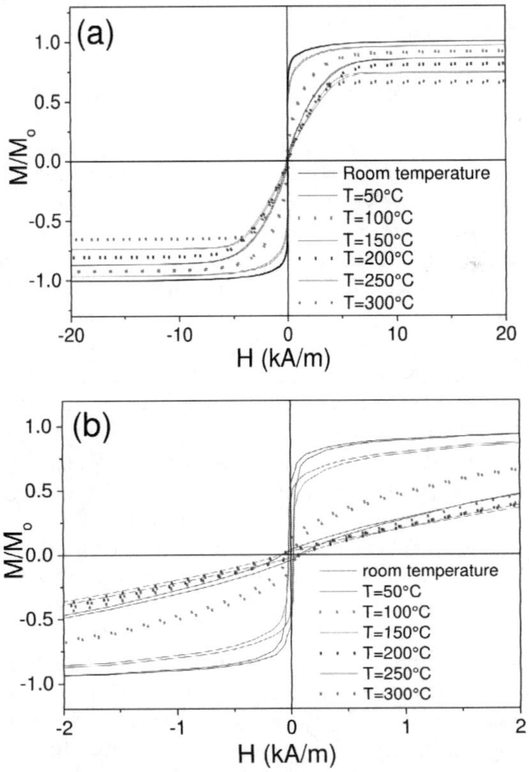

Figure 2. Hysteresis loops of studied sample, measured at different T (a). Low field hysteresis loops (b) measured at the same T.

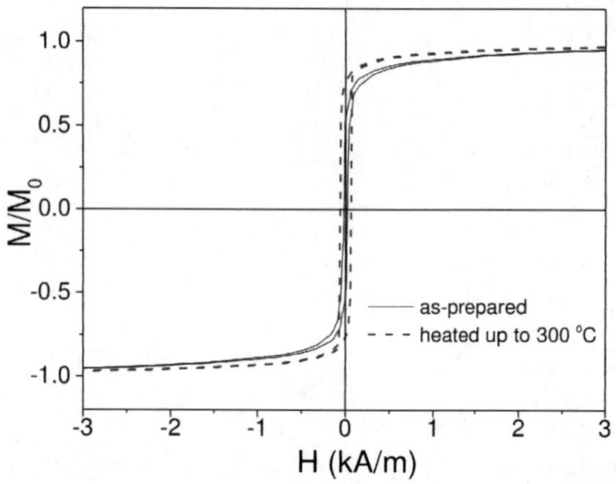

Figure 3. Hysteresis loops of studied sample, measured before and after heating up to 300 °C.

$$\delta = \sqrt{\pi \sigma \mu_\phi f} \quad (2)$$

where σ is the electrical conductivity and f the frequency of the current along the sample.

Accordingly, high $\Delta Z/Z$-ratio values are usually observed in magnetic wires with high μ_ϕ- values, typically observed in amorphous wires with low transversal magnetic anisotropy [9]-[11][23].

As reported elsewhere [11], for magnetic wires with rectangular hysteresis loops, the $\Delta Z/Z$-ratio values are usually rather low. However, the observed influence of heating on the shape of the hysteresis loops suggests a modification of the GMI effect. Figure 4 shows the results of the temperature dependence of the GMI effect of studied microwire. Indeed, evidenced from Figure 4, a remarkable increase in $\Delta Z/Z$-ratio is observed for the studied sample upon heating (see Figure 4). Temperature dependencies of maximum GMI ratio, $\Delta Z/Z_{max}$, for 50 and 100 MHz are summarized in Figure 4c.

The origin of the rectangular hysteresis loop of Fe-rich microwires is commonly attributed to the peculiar domain structure of as-prepared Fe-rich microwires consisting of axially magnetized inner single domain and outer domain shell with radial magnetization [6] [7] [33]. Axial magnetic anisotropy of as-prepared Fe-rich microwires (λ_s >0) is commonly explained considering preferentially axial character of the internal stresses arising during the fabrication process consisting of simultaneous rapid solidification of metallic nucleus surrounded by glass-coating with rather different thermal expansion coefficients [18] [34] [35]. The main origin of such stresses is the difference in thermal expansion coefficients of the glass-coating and the metallic nucleus. Accordingly, the heating effect on hysteresis loops shape must be attributed to a decrease in internal stresses upon heating.

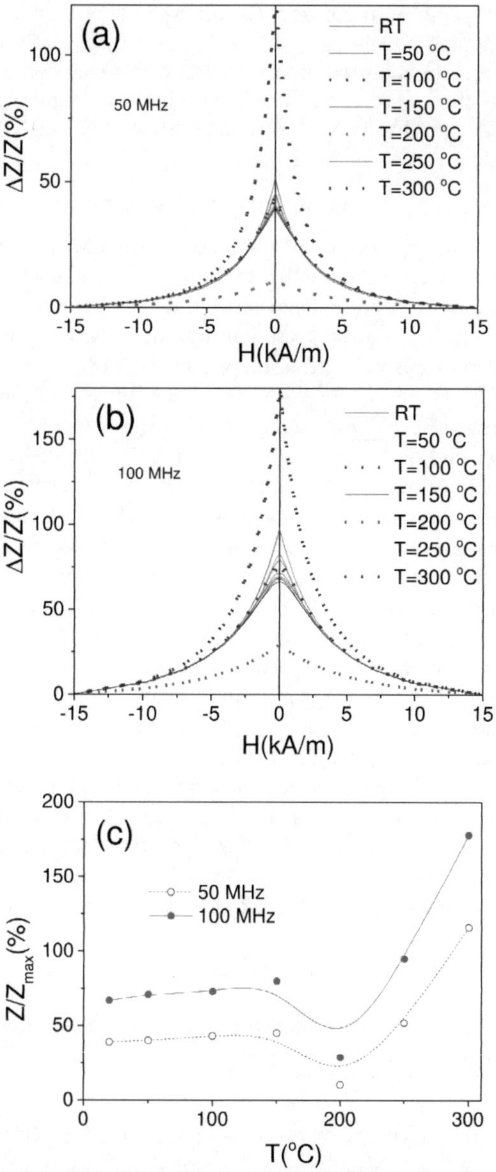

Figure 4. $\Delta Z/Z(H)$ dependencies of studied sample measured at 50 (a) and 100 MHz (b) at various temperatures and $\Delta Z/Z_{max}$ (T) dependencies evaluated for 50 and 100 MHz (c).

The transformation of the hysteresis loops from rectangular to inclined must be the main reason of remarkable GMI effect improvement.

Upon samples heating, several processes are expected: the reduction of internal stresses originated by the rapid solidification of a composite microwire with a different thermal expansion coefficient of the metal nucleus and glass coating and relaxation of internal stresses (as in any amorphous materials). Additionally, the origin of the substantial GMI effect improvement at T= 300 °C can be related to the Hopkinson effect. The Hopkinson effect is manifested as a sharp magnetic permeability maximum at temperatures slightly below the Curie temperature, T_c, [36][37]. The origin of such effect is commonly associated with a faster decrease of magnetic anisotropy constant with temperature as compared to the magnetization.

A comparison of the hysteresis loops measured at different T (see Figure 5a) shows that, indeed, higher magnetic permeability is observed at T= 300 °C, as compared to the hysteresis loops measured at T= 200 °C and 250 °C (see Figure 5 a).

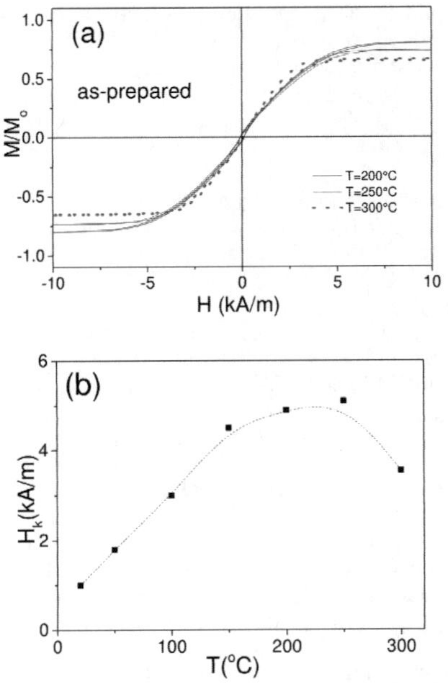

Figure 5. Change in the hysteresis of studied samples upon heating (a) and H_k(T) dependencies evaluated from hysteresis loops (c).

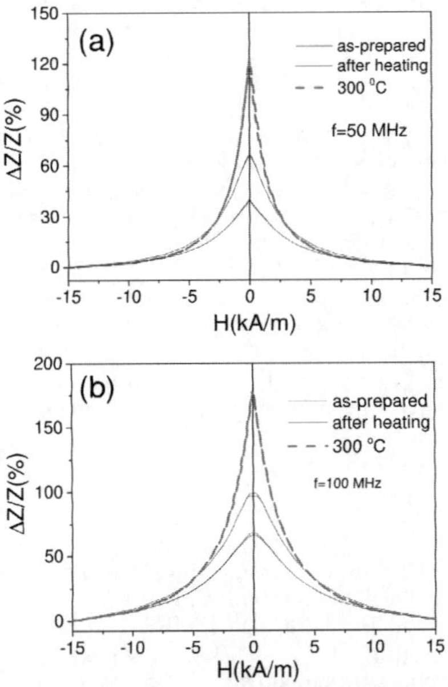

Figure 6. $\Delta Z/Z(H)$ dependencies measured at 50 MHz (a) and 100 MHz (b) at room temperature before and after heating and at T=300 °C

The evolution of average magnetic anisotropy field, H_k, upon heating is provided in Figure 5b. Such H_k –values were evaluated from the hysteresis loops, as previously described [38].

In order to separate the effect of heating from the effect of the internal stresses relaxation, the comparison of the $\Delta Z/Z(H)$ dependencies measured at room temperature before and after heating up to 300 °C is provided in Figure 6.

A comparison of the $\Delta Z/Z(H)$ dependences (see Figure 6 a,b) clearly shows some $\Delta Z/Z_{max}$ improvement after heating to 300 °C. This increase in $\Delta Z/Z_{max}$ must be related to the relaxation of internal stresses. However, the main contribution to the increase in $\Delta Z/Z_{max}$ is related to the heating itself.

The observed experimentally results on substantial temperature dependence of the GMI effect and magnetic properties of Fe-rich microwires can be useful for temperature monitoring. However, the effect of heating must be separated from the internal stresses relaxation upon heating.

IV. CONCLUSIONS

The temperature dependence of the magnetic properties and the GMI effect of amorphous FeSiBC microwires have been thoroughly analyzed using both hysteresis loops and GMI measurements. A substantial change in hysteresis loops shape and GMI effect upon heating is observed. We observed a remarkable improvement of the GMI ratio and modification of hysteresis loops from rectangular to inclined upon heating of FeSiBC microwire. The observed experimental results are discussed considering relaxation of internal stresses upon heating, Hopkinson effect and modification of the thermal expansion coefficients upon heating.

The observed significant effect of temperature on the hysteresis loop shape and the GMI effect of FeSiBC microwires coated by insulating, flexible and biocompatible glass-coating opens up the possibility of using such Fe-rich microwires for temperature sensors and for temperature monitoring in composites with magnetic microwire inclusions.

ACKNOWLEDGMENT

This work was supported by EU under "INFINITE" (HORIZON-CL5-2021-D5-01-06) project, by the Spanish MICIN under PID2022-141373NB-I00, by the Government of the Basque Country under PUE_2021_1_0009, Elkartek (MINERVA, MAGAF and ZE-KONP) projects and under the scheme of "Ayuda a Grupos Consolidados" (ref. IT1670-22). The authors are thankful for the technical and human support provided by SGIker of UPV/EHU (Medidas Magnéticas Gipuzkoa) and European funding (ERDF and ESF). The group at the Institute of Experimental Physics SAS acknowledges support from the projects VEGA 2/0148/23 and APVV-19-0369.

REFERENCES

[1] F. Fiorillo, G. Bertotti, C. Appino, and M. Pasquale, Soft Magnetic Materials (Ed. J. Webster), Wiley Encyclopedia of Electrical and Electronics Engineering, 1999, John Wiley & Sons, Inc., p. 42. doi:10.1002/047134608X.W4504.pub2.

[2] J. Durand, "Magnetic Properties of Metallic Glasses" in Topics in Applied Physics, Vol. 53, Glassy Metals II. Atomic Structure and Dynamics, Electronic Structure, Magnetic Properties, H. Beck and H.-J. Giintherodt Eds., Springer-Verlag, Berlin Heidelberg New York Tokyo, pp. 343-386, 1983.

[3] D. C. Jiles, "Recent advances and future directions in magnetic materials", Acta Mater., vol. 51, pp- 5907-5939, 2003.

[4] T. Goto, M. Nagano, and N. Wehara, "Mechanical properties of amorphous $Fe_{80}P_{16}C_3B_1$ filament produced by glass-coated melt spinning", Trans. JIM, vol. 18, pp. 759–764, 1977.

[5] V. Zhukova et al., "Correlation between magnetic and mechanical properties of devitrified glass-coated $Fe_{71.8}Cu_1Nb_{3.1}Si_{15}B_{9.1}$ microwires", J. Magn. Magn. Mater., vol. 249, pp. 79–84, 2002.

[6] M. Vázquez and D.-X. Chen, "The magnetization reversal process in amorphous wires", IEEE Trans. Magn., vol. 31, no. 2, pp. 1229-1239, 1995.

[7] K. Mohri, F.B. Humphrey, K. Kawashima, K. Kimura, and M. Muzutani, "Large Barkhausen and Matteucci effects in FeCoSiB, FeCrSiB, and FeNiSiB amorphous wires", IEEE Trans.Magn., vol. 26, no. 5, pp. 1789- 1781, 1990.

[8] A. Zhukov et al., "Frequency dependence of coercivity in rapidly quenched amorphous materials, J. Mat. Sci. Eng. A vol. 226-228, pp. 753-756, 1997.

[9] K. Mohri, T. Uchiyama, L. P. Shen, C. M. Cai, and L. V. Panina, "Amorphous wire and CMOS IC-based sensitive micro-magnetic sensors (MI sensor and SI sensor) for intelligent measurements and controls", J. Magn. Magn. Mater., vol. 249, pp. 351-356, 2001.

[10] A. Zhukov et al., Giant magnetoimpedance in rapidly quenched materials", J. Alloys Compound., vol. 814, pp. 152225, 2020.

[11] M. Knobel, M. Vazquez, and L. Kraus, Giant magnetoimpedance, Handbook Magn. Mater., vol. 15, pp. 497- 563, 2003.

[12] V. Zhukova et al., "Electronic Surveillance and Security Applications of Magnetic Microwires", Chemosensors, vol. 9, p. 100, 2021.

[13] T. Uchiyama, K. Mohri, and Sh. Nakayama, "Measurement of Spontaneous Oscillatory Magnetic Field of Guinea-Pig Smooth Muscle Preparation Using Pico-Tesla Resolution Amorphous Wire Magneto-Impedance Sensor", IEEE Trans. Magn., vol. 47, pp. 3070-3073, 2011.

[14] Y. Honkura, "Development of amorphous wire type MI sensors for automobile use", J. Magn. Magn. Mater., vol. 249, pp. 375-381, 2002.

[15] A. Zhukov et al., "Magnetoelastic sensor of level of the liquid based on magnetoelastic properties of Co-rich microwires", Sens. Actuat. A Phys., vol. 81, no. 1-3, pp.129-133, 2000.

[16] V. Zhukova et al., "Development of Magnetically Soft Amorphous Microwires for Technological Applications", Chemosensors, vol. 10, p. 26, 2022.

[17] D. Kozejova et.al., "Biomedical applications of glass-coated microwires", J. Magn. Magn. Mater., vol. 470, pp. 2-5, 2019.

[18] A. Zhukov et al., "Advanced functional magnetic microwires for technological applications", J. Phys. D: Appl. Phys., vol. 55 p. 253003, 2022, doi:10.1088/1361-6463/ac4fd7.

[19] L. Ding, S. Saez, C. Dolabdjian, L. G. C. Melo, A. Yelon, and D. Ménard, "Development of a high sensitivity Giant Magneto-Impedance magnetometer: comparison with a commercial Flux-Gate", IEEE Sensors, vol. 9 (2), pp. 159-168, 2009.

[20] D. Makhnovskiy, N Fry, and A. Zhukov, "On different tag reader architectures for bistable microwires", Sens. Actuat. A Phys., vol. 166, pp. 133-140, 2011.

[21] S. Gudoshnikov et al., "Evaluation of use of magnetically bistable microwires for magnetic labels", Phys. Stat. Sol. (a), vol. 208, no. 3, pp. 526–529, 2011.

[22] D. Makhnovskiy, A. Zhukov, V. Zhukova, and J. Gonzalez, "Tunable and self-sensing microwave composite materials incorporating ferromagnetic microwires", Advances in Science and Technology, vol. 54, pp 201-210, 2008.

[23] F. Qin and H. X. Peng, "Ferromagnetic microwires enabled multifunctional composite materials", Prog. Mater. Sci., vol. 58 (2), pp. 183-259, 2013.

[24] M. Churyukanova et al., "Non-contact method for stress monitoring based on stress dependence of magnetic properties of Fe-based microwires", J. Alloys Compd., vol. 748(5), pp. 199-205, 2018.

[25] A. Allue et al., "Smart composites with embedded magnetic microwire inclusions allowing non-contact stresses and temperature monitoring", Compos. Part A Appl., vol. 120, pp. 12-20, 2019, doi: 10.1016/j.compositesa.2019.02.014

[26] J. Nabias, A. Asfour, and J. Yonnet, "Temperature Dependence of Giant Magnetoimpedance in Amorphous Microwires for Sensor Application", IEEE Trans. Magn., vol. 53(4), p. 4001005, 2017. DOI:10.1109/TMAG.2016.2625841.

[27] J. D. Santos, R. Varga, B. Hernando, and A. Zhukov, "Enhancement of GMI effect in magnetic microwires through the relative temperature dependence of magnetization and anisotropy", J. Magn. Magn. Mater., vol. 321, pp. 3875–3877, 2009.

[28] M. Kurniawan et al., "Temperature Dependent Giant Magnetoimpedance Effect in Amorphous Soft Magnets", J. Electron. Mater., vol. 43, pp. 4576–4581, 2014.

[29] P. Corte –Leon et al., "Effect of temperature on magnetic properties and magnetoimpedance effect in Fe -rich microwires", J. Alloys Compound. vol. 946, p. 169419, 2023.

[30] L. Gonzalez-Legarreta et al., "Optimization of magnetic properties and GMI effect of Thin Co-rich Microwires for GMI Microsensors", Sensors, vol. 20, p.1558, 2020.

[31] B. Kunca et al., "Soft magnetic performance of ultra-rapidly annealed high-Bs Fe-(Co)-B nanocrystalline alloys at elevated temperatures", J. Alloys Compd., vol. 911, p. 165033, 2022, DOI: 10.1016/j.jallcom.2022.165033.

[32] F. Andrejka, "Influence of thermal treatment in external magnetic field on microstructure and magnetic properties of selected rapidly quenched alloys" (Doctoral dissertation), Technical University, Kosice, Slovakia, 2018.

[33] V. Zhukova, J. M. Blanco, A. Chizhik, M. Ipatov, and A. Zhukov, "AC-current-induced magnetization switching in amorphous microwires", Front. Phys. vol. 13, no. 2, p. 137501, 2018. https://doi.org/10.1007/s11467-017-0722-6

[34] S. A. Baranov, V. S. Larin, and A. V. Torcunov, "Technology, Preparation and Properties of the Cast Glass-Coated Magnetic Microwires", Crystals, vol. 7, p. 136, 2017.

[35] H. Chiriac and T. A. Óvári, "Amorphous glass-covered magnetic wires: preparation, properties, applications", Progr. Mater. Sci., vol. 40, no. 5, pp. 333-407, 1996.

[36] K. He, H. Xu, Z. Wang, and L. Cheng", Hopkinson effect in soft magnetic materials", J. Mater. Sci. Technol., vol. 16, pp 145-147, 2000.

[37] V. Zhukova, M. Ipatov, A. Talaat, and A. Zhukov, "Hopkinson effect in Co-rich glass-coated microwires", Phys. Status Solidi C, vol. 11, no. 5–6, pp. 1130–1132, 2014. doi:10.1002/pssc.201300715.

[38] A. Zhukov et al., "Induced Magnetic Anisotropy in Co-Mn-Si-B Amorphous Microwires", J. Appl. Phys., vol. 87, pp. 1402-1408, 2000. doi:10.1063/1.372063

SLAM-based Mapping in Truck-and-Robot System for Last-Mile Delivery Automation

Ryo Nakamura
Graduate School of Science and Engineering
Doshisha University
Kyotanabe, Japan
e-mail: ctwh0151@mail4.doshisha.ac.jp

Takeshi Kambe, Masafumi Hashimoto, Kazuhiko Takahashi
Faculty of Science and Engineering
Doshisha University
Kyotanabe, Japan
e-mail: {mhashimo, katakaha}@mail.doshisha.ac.jp

***Abstract*—This paper presents a Simultaneous Localization And Mapping (SLAM)-based mapping method for last-mile delivery automation using a scanning Light Detection And Ranging sensor (LiDAR) mounted on a quadruped robot. Distortion in scan data from the LiDAR, caused by the swinging motion of the robot, is corrected by estimating the robot's pose (three-dimensional positions and attitude angles) in a period shorter than the LiDAR scan period using an extended Kalman filter. LiDAR-scan data related to stationary objects are detected from the corrected scan data using an occupancy grid method. Local maps in small areas where robots deliver goods to customers are built using normal distributions transforms and Graph SLAM. A feature-based loop detection is also performed using surface features and point feature histograms. The local maps are corrected in the Graph SLAM framework using the scan data from LiDAR mounted on a truck stopping at robot depots. Experimental results obtained in our university campus demonstrate the effectiveness of the presented method.**

Keywords*—*LiDAR; NDT Graph SLAM; map building; loop detection; quadruped robot; delivery automation.

I. INTRODUCTION

Recently, last-mile delivery automation using wheeled and legged robots has progressed due to increased e-commerce and demand for contactless delivery during the COVID-19 pandemic [1][2]. Delivery robots are designed to move short distances at pedestrian speed. Owing to their low speed and limited range, delivery robots are usually combined with trucks to enable a fast and efficient delivery process [3][4]. As shown in Figure 1, a truck transports delivery goods with robots and releases the robots at dedicated drop-off locations (robot depots). The robots deliver goods to customers and return to the robot depots by themselves.

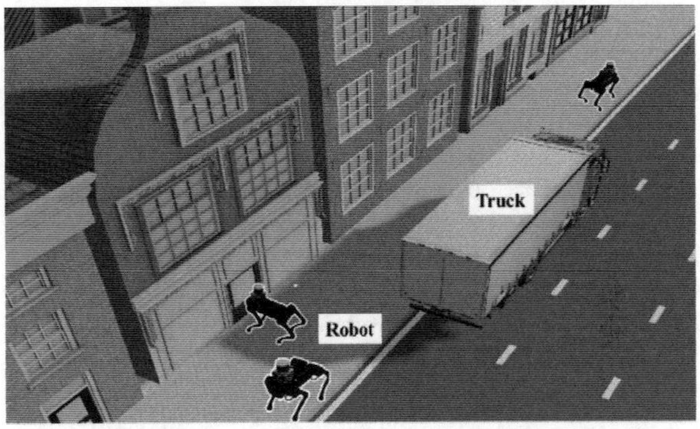

Figure 1. Image of truck-and-robot delivery system.

In such truck-and-robot delivery systems, map building (mapping) and map-matching-based self-localization using built maps are important technologies for autonomous navigation of delivery robots [5]. In the domain of mobile robotics and Intelligent Transportation Systems (ITS), many related studies using cameras and Light Detection And Ranging sensors (LiDARs) have been presented [6]–[8]. Mobile mapping systems are typically used to build High-Definition (HD) maps for autonomous driving and advanced driver assistant systems in wide road environments, such as highways and motorways. In truck-and-robot delivery systems, autonomous driving and pose estimation of trucks moving in wide road environments can be performed using HD maps. However, because HD maps building by mobile mapping systems incur high cost, Simultaneous Localization And Mapping (SLAM)-based mapping has been proposed as an efficient method for mapping narrow residential environments, in which robots deliver goods to customers.

In this paper, we focus on LiDAR SLAM-based mapping. We previously presented mapping methods using LiDAR mounted on cars, motorcycles, and driver's helmets based on Normal Distributions Transforms (NDT) SLAM [9]–[11] to build a three-dimensional (3D) point cloud map in community road environments.

To build 3D point cloud maps by robot-mounted LiDAR using scan matching based-SLAM, such as NDT SLAM and iterative closest point SLAM, the scan data captured in the LiDAR coordinate frame are mapped onto the world coordinate frame using the self-pose (position and attitude angle) of a robot. Mechanical LiDARs, where laser beams are scanned in omnidirection (rotation of 360° of the laser beams in the horizontal direction), are typically used for LiDAR-based mapping. Hence, the complete data within one scan (one rotation of the laser beams in the horizontal direction) cannot be acquired simultaneously when a robot is moving and swinging. Therefore, if such data are transformed based on the robot's pose at the same time, distortion appears in the mapping results.

To reduce the distortion in scan data, many methods for distortion correction have been presented using linear interpolation and its variants [12][13]. In our previous work, a Kalman filter-based method was presented [10][11]. Because Kalman filter-based localization is widely used in the fields of mobile robotics, distortion correction in a Kalman filter framework can be easily incorporated in the self-localization system of a robot.

Scan matching-based SLAM causes a drift (degradation of accuracy over time); to reduce the drift, Graph SLAM is typically used in conjunction with scan matching-based SLAM. In Graph SLAM, the detection of revisit places (called loops) is an important issue, and many methods for loop detection have been presented [14][15]. In our previous work, a detection method using surface features and matching distance indicators was presented [9]. However, some improvements are required to reduce missed and false detection of loops.

This paper presents a LiDAR SLAM-based mapping method for truck-and-robot delivery systems. The LiDAR SLAM-based mapping method involves integrating components that we previously proposed [9]–[11]: distortion correction of LiDAR scan data, extraction of scan data related to stationary objects from the entire corrected LiDAR scan data, and point cloud mapping based on NDT Graph SLAM. Another contribution of this paper is to improve the performance of loop detection in our previous Graph SLAM by introducing Fast Point Feature Histograms (FPFH) [16]. In addition, the mapping accuracy of robot-mounted LiDAR is improved using scan data from truck-mounted LiDAR.

The rest of this paper is organized as follows. Section II describes the experimental system. Section III explains the method of map building and correction, and Section IV presents the method of loop detection. Section V presents experimental results to verify the proposed method, followed by the conclusions in Section VI.

II. Experimental System

Figure 2 shows an overview of a quadruped robot (Unitree A1). A scanning 16-layer LiDAR (Velodyne VLP-16) and an Inertial Measurement Unit (IMU, MTi-300) are mounted on the upper part of the robot. The maximum range of the LiDAR is 70 m, the horizontal viewing angle is 360° with a resolution of 0.2°, and the vertical viewing angle is 30° with a resolution of 2°. The LiDAR provides 384 measurements (the object's 3D position and reflection intensity) every 1.33 ms (at 4.8° horizontal angle increments).

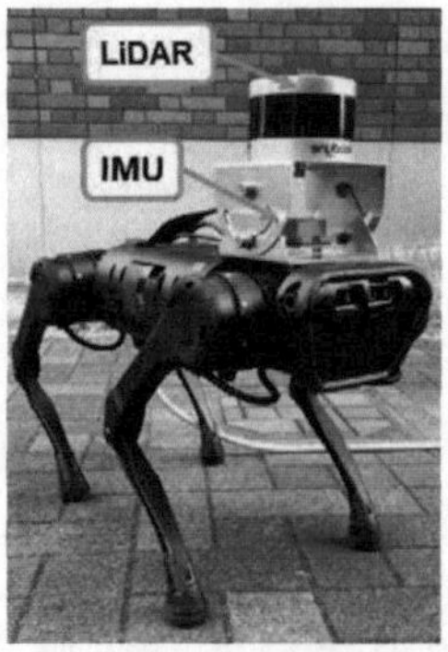

Figure 2. Overview of experimental quadruped robot.

The time that the LiDAR beam takes to complete one rotation (360°) in the horizontal direction is 100 ms, and 30,000 measurements are obtained in one rotation.

The IMU provides attitude angles (roll and pitch angles) and angular velocities (roll, pitch, and yaw velocities) every 10 ms with an attitude angle error of ±0.3° (typ.) and an angular velocity error of ±0.2 °/s (typ.).

Meanwhile, a scanning 32-layer LiDAR (Velodyne HDL-32) is used as a truck-mounted LiDAR. The maximum range of the LiDAR is 70 m, the horizontal viewing angle is 360° with a resolution of 0.16°, and the vertical viewing angle is 41.34° with a resolution of 1.33°. The time that the LiDAR beam takes to complete one rotation (360°) in the horizontal direction is 100 ms, and 70,000 measurements are obtained in one rotation.

III. Map Building and Correction

A. Local Map Building by Robot-Mounted LiDAR

The captured scan data from the robot-mounted LiDAR in a single scan are mapped onto a 3D grid map (voxel map) represented in the LiDAR coordinate frame Σ_b attached to the LiDAR. A voxel grid filter is applied to downsize the scan data. The block used for the voxel grid filter is a cube with a side length of 0.2 m.

In a world coordinate frame Σ_w, a voxel map with a voxel size of 1 m is used for NDT scan matching [17]. For the *i*-th ($i = 1, 2, \ldots n$) measurement in the scan data, the position vector in Σ_b is denoted as $\boldsymbol{p}_{bi}$ and that in Σ_w as $\boldsymbol{p}_i$. The following relation is obtained:

$$\begin{pmatrix} \boldsymbol{p}_i \\ 1 \end{pmatrix} = \boldsymbol{T}(\boldsymbol{x}) \begin{pmatrix} \boldsymbol{p}_{bi} \\ 1 \end{pmatrix} \tag{1}$$

where $\boldsymbol{x} = (x, y, z, \phi, \theta, \psi)^T$ denotes the robot's pose. $(x, y, z)^T$ and $(\phi, \theta, \psi)^T$ denote the 3D position and attitude angle (roll, pitch, and yaw angles) of the robot, respectively, in Σ_w. $\boldsymbol{T}(\boldsymbol{x})$ denotes the homogeneous transformation matrix:

The scan data obtained at the current time step t ($t = 0, 1, 2, \ldots$) are called the new input scan, and the scan data obtained in the previous time step, i.e., before $(t-1)$, are called the reference scan (local map). The robot pose at t is determined by matching the new input scan at t with the reference scan data obtained before $(t-1)$. The robot pose is used for coordinate transform using (1). The new input scan can then be mapped to Σ_w, and the local map is updated.

NDT SLAM based on NDT scan matching is performed by mapping LiDAR scan data captured in Σ_b onto Σ_w using the self-pose information of the robot. The LiDAR obtains range measurements by scanning laser beams. Thus, when a robot moves and swings, the complete scan data cannot be acquired in a single scan (LiDAR beam rotation of 360° in a horizontal plane) simultaneously. Therefore, if the entire scan data obtained within one scan are mapped onto Σ_w using robot-pose information at a single point in time, distortion arises in mapping results.

The distortion in the scan data from the LiDAR is corrected by estimating the robot's pose in a period of 1.327

ms, which is shorter than the LiDAR scan period of 100 ms. The extended Kalman filter-based algorithm [11] is applied to distortion correction based on information from NDT SLAM and an IMU.

Corrected scan data relating to road surfaces are removed using a rule-based method [11], and scan data relating to objects are mapped onto the grid map (cell size of 0.3 m in this study). Scan data relating to moving objects (called moving scan data), such as cars and pedestrians, are removed using an occupancy grid method, and those relating to stationary objects (stationary scan data) are then extracted. The stationary scan data are used for NDT SLAM-based mapping.

NDT SLAM degrades mapping accuracy over time due to accumulation errors. To reduce the error, Graph SLAM is employed. The robot poses, which are calculated by NDT SLAM every 100 ms (LiDAR scan period), are mapped onto a pose graph, as depicted in Figure 3. When revisit places (loops), where the robot has already visited places during map building, are detected using a method described in Section IV, the current robot's pose relative to its pose at the revisit node is set to the pose graph as a loop constraint (blue arrow in Figure 3). The objective function of (2) is then minimized to improve the accuracy of the map built by NDT SLAM:

$$J(\chi) = \sum_i \{(\boldsymbol{x}_{i+1} - \boldsymbol{x}_i) - \boldsymbol{\delta}_{i+1,i}\}^T \boldsymbol{\Omega}^{pose} \{(\boldsymbol{x}_{i+1} - \boldsymbol{x}_i) - \boldsymbol{\delta}_{i+1,i}\}$$

$$+ \sum_{x_A, x_B \in \text{loop}} \{(\boldsymbol{x}_B - \boldsymbol{x}_A) - \boldsymbol{\delta}_{A,B}\}^T \boldsymbol{\Omega}^{loop} \{(\boldsymbol{x}_B - \boldsymbol{x}_A) - \boldsymbol{\delta}_{A,B}\} \quad (2)$$

where the first and second terms on the right side indicate the constraints on NDT SLAM and loop, respectively. $\chi = (\boldsymbol{x}_1^T, \boldsymbol{x}_2^T, \cdots, \boldsymbol{x}_i^T, \cdots)^T$. $\boldsymbol{x}_i$ denotes the robot's pose at the i-th time step. $\boldsymbol{\delta}_{i+1,i}$ denotes the relative pose of the robot between the i-th and $(i+1)$th time steps, which is calculated from NDT SLAM. $\boldsymbol{x}_A$ and $\boldsymbol{x}_B$ denote the robot's poses at the revisit and current nodes, respectively. $\boldsymbol{\delta}_{A,B}$ denotes the relative pose of the robot at the two nodes, which is calculated from the LiDAR scan data using NDT scan matching. $\boldsymbol{\Omega}^{pose}$ and $\boldsymbol{\Omega}^{loop}$ denote the information matrices.

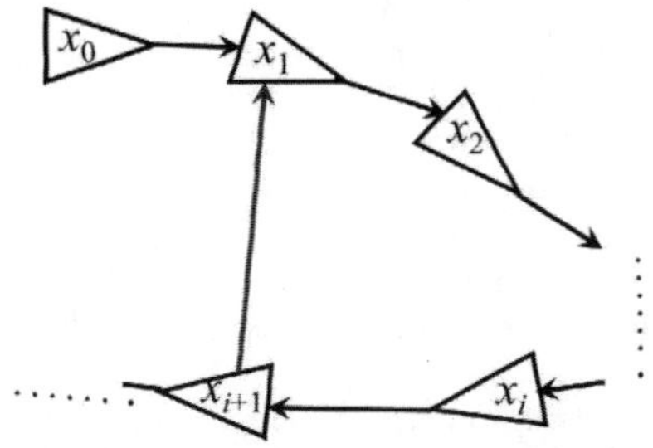

Figure 3. Pose graph for map building. The robot's poses are represented as graph nodes (black triangles), and relative poses between two neighboring nodes are represented as graph edges (black arrows).

B. Map Correction by Truck-Mounted LiDAR

When the robot returns to the robot depot, the local map built by the robot is corrected using the LiDAR scan data captured by the truck-mounted LiDAR. Such map correction is performed in Graph SLAM framework by the following steps:

Step 1: Mapping by truck-mounted LiDAR; the map is built using the truck-mounted LiDAR at the robot depot, and the truck poses, obtained by the map-matching method using an HD map, are mapped onto a pose graph, as depicted in Figure 4;

Step 2: Encounter node detection; nodes, where the robot encounters the truck are detected in the pose graph;

Step 3: Relative pose estimation; the robot's poses relative to the truck at encounter nodes are estimated from scan data captured by the truck and robot-mounted LiDARs using NDT scan matching;

Step 4: Map correction; the local map built by the robot is corrected using pose graph optimization.

The relative poses of the robot at the encounter nodes are set to the pose graph as the loop constraint (red arrow in Figure 4). The following objective function is then minimized to correct the local map:

$$J(\chi') = J(\chi)$$

$$+ \sum_{x^*, x_A \in \text{loop}} \{(\boldsymbol{x}_A - \boldsymbol{x}^*) - \boldsymbol{\delta}_A\}^T \boldsymbol{\Omega}_A^{loop} \{(\boldsymbol{x}_A - \boldsymbol{x}^*) - \boldsymbol{\delta}_A\}$$

$$+ (\boldsymbol{x}^* - \boldsymbol{\delta}^*)^T \boldsymbol{\Omega}^* (\boldsymbol{x}^* - \boldsymbol{\delta}^*) \quad (3)$$

where $\chi' = (\boldsymbol{x}^{*T}, \chi^T)^T$ and $\chi = (\boldsymbol{x}_0^T, \boldsymbol{x}_1^T, \cdots, \boldsymbol{x}_i^T, \cdots)^T$. $\boldsymbol{x}^*$ denotes the truck pose, and χ represents a set of the robot poses. $J(\chi)$ denotes the objective function of the pose graphs in (2). The second term on the right side is the constraint on the relative pose of the robot at encounter nodes $\boldsymbol{x}_A$. $\boldsymbol{\delta}_A$ denotes the robot pose relative to the truck at the encounter nodes. The third term on the right side is the constraint on the truck pose (green arrow in Figure 4). $\boldsymbol{\delta}^*$ denotes the truck pose. $\boldsymbol{\Omega}^{loop}$ and $\boldsymbol{\Omega}^*$ denote the information matrices. As the truck pose is typically obtained accurately, $\boldsymbol{\Omega}^*$ is set to a large value.

IV. Loop Detection

The method of encounter node detection during map correction (Section III. B) is similar to the method of revisit node detection (SectionIII. A). Therefore, in this section, we

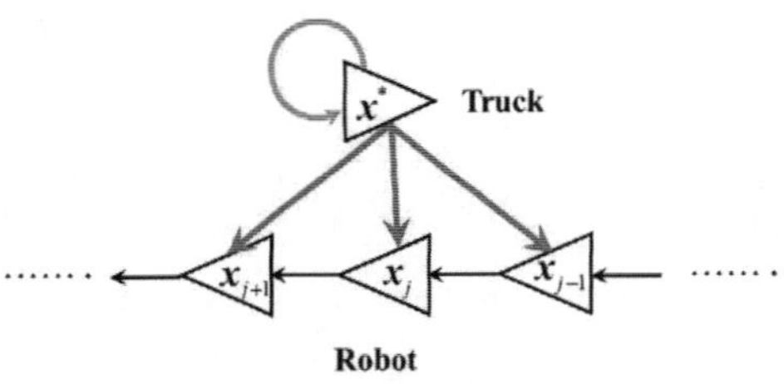

Figure 4. Pose graph for map correction.

describe the method of revisit node detection during local map building.

A. Detection of Candidate of Revisit Nodes

To detect revisit nodes, a candidate for revisit nodes is first obtained using the self-location information of the robot by NDT SLAM. If the distance of an old node from the current node is less than 10 m, the old node is recognized as a candidate for revisit nodes.

Thereafter, the Loop Probability Indicator (LPI) [18] is calculated using stationary scan data captured at the candidate for the revisit and current nodes. Each grid of the voxel map is first classified into three types: line, plane, or other voxels in Figure 5. Three eigenvalues ($\lambda_1 \geq \lambda_2 \geq \lambda_3 \geq 0$) are calculated from LiDAR scan data in voxels based on principal component analysis, and the following features are calculated:

$$q_1 = \frac{\sqrt{\lambda_1} - \sqrt{\lambda_2}}{\sqrt{\lambda_1}},\ q_2 = \frac{\sqrt{\lambda_2} - \sqrt{\lambda_3}}{\sqrt{\lambda_1}},\ q_3 = \frac{\sqrt{\lambda_3}}{\sqrt{\lambda_1}} \tag{4}$$

When the maximum values are q_1, q_2, and q_3, the voxel is determined as being of line, plane, or other types.

Based on the surface normal vector of the plane voxels, the plane voxels are further divided into nine classes: (1, 0, 0), (0, 1, 0), (0, 0, 1), $(1/\sqrt{2}, 1/\sqrt{2}, 0)$, $(1/\sqrt{2}, -1/\sqrt{2}, 0)$, $(1/\sqrt{2}, 0, 1/\sqrt{2})$, $(-1/\sqrt{2}, 0, 1/\sqrt{2})$, $(0, 1/\sqrt{2}, 1/\sqrt{2})$, and $(0, -1/\sqrt{2}, 1/\sqrt{2})$.

Two feature descriptors $\boldsymbol{U} = (u_1, u_2, \cdots, u_{11})^T$ and $\boldsymbol{V} = (v_1, v_2, \cdots, v_{11})^T$ are defined. $\boldsymbol{U}$ is calculated from LiDAR scan data captured at the candidate for revisit nodes, and $\boldsymbol{V}$ is calculated from the LiDAR scan data at the current node. u_1 and v_1 denote the numbers of line voxels in the voxel map. $u_2 - u_{10}$ and $v_2 - v_{10}$ denote the numbers of plane voxels divided into nine classes. u_{11} and v_{11} denote the numbers of other voxels.

From the feature descriptors $\boldsymbol{U}$ and $\boldsymbol{V}$, the LPI is given by

$$\mathrm{LPI} = \frac{\sum_{i=1}^{11} \{\max(u_i, v_i) - |u_i - v_i|\}}{\sum_{i=1}^{11} \max(u_i, v_i)} \tag{5}$$

A higher degree of similarity between the LiDAR scan data at both nodes leads to a larger LPI. Thus, the loop can be detected from the candidate of the revisit nodes using a large LPI value (a threshold of 80% in this study).

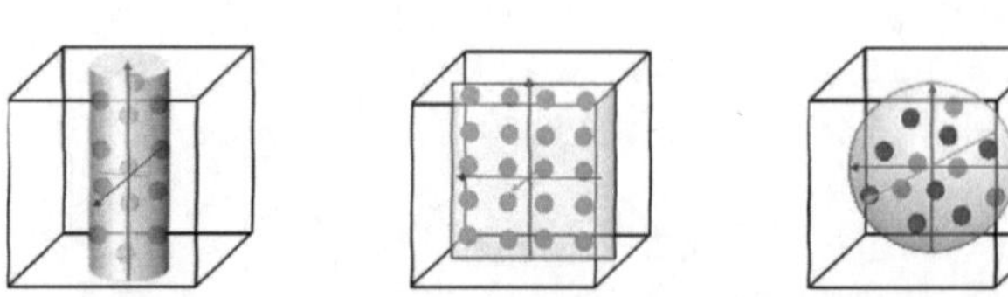

(a) Line voxel (b) Plane voxel (c) Other voxel

Figure 5. Classification of voxels.

B. Detection of Revisit Nodes and Calculation of Relative Pose

Revisit nodes are determined from the candidate for revisit nodes using a Matching Distance Indicator (MDI). From two LiDAR scan data captured at the current node and each candidate for revisit nodes, the relative pose of the robot is calculated using NDT scan matching. The MDI is then given:

$$\mathrm{MDI} = \frac{1}{N}\sum_{i=1}^{N} d_i \tag{6}$$

where N represents the number of measurements in the LiDAR scan data captured at the candidate for revisit nodes. d_i denotes the nearest neighbor distance.

A higher degree of similarity between the LiDAR scan data captured at two nodes leads to a smaller MDI. The loop can then be detected by a smaller MDI value (a threshold of 1.5 m in this study).

In NDT scan matching, if an initial value of the relative pose is given incorrectly, both the relative pose estimate and MDI become inaccurate due to local minima issues. To correctly set an initial value of the relative pose, an FPFH [16] is used.

Point features are extracted using FPFH from two LiDAR scan data captured at the current node and each candidate for revisit nodes. First, LiDAR scan data (stationary scan data) captured at the current node are mapped onto a voxel map (grid size of 0.2 m) in Σ_b and downsampled using a voxel grid filter. The centroid of the stationary scan data in the i-th voxel (i = 1, 2, ...) on the voxel map is then obtained. The centroid is called the feature point A_i. From stationary scan data captured at each candidate for revisit nodes, the feature point B_i is obtained in the same way in Σ_b.

Point feature histograms (33 dimensions in this study) are calculated based on the feature points A_i and B_i, and their feature points are matched as follows:

Step 1: The three-feature point A_i (i = 1, 2, 3) is randomly extracted from the set of feature points obtained at the current scan. Then, 100 feature points B_j (j = 1, 2, ..., 100) with similar feature histograms as those of A_i are extracted using the k-nearest neighbor method from the set of feature points obtained by each candidate for revisit nodes. We denote the triangle consisting of the three-feature point $\{A_1, A_2, A_3\}$ as A', while that consisting of any three-feature points from 100 feature points B_i as B'. The three-feature point $\{B_1, B_2, B_3\}$ is selected so that the two triangles A' and B' are congruent.

Step 2: The pose of the candidate for revisit node relative to the current node is denoted by $\delta\boldsymbol{X} = (\delta x, \delta y, \delta z, \delta\phi, \delta\theta, \delta\psi)^T$, where $\delta\boldsymbol{x} = (\delta x, \delta y, \delta z)^T$ and $\delta\boldsymbol{\theta} = (\delta\phi, \delta\theta, \delta\psi)^T$ denote the relative position and attitude angle (roll, pitch, and yaw angles), respectively.

In the matched triangles A' and B', the centroid positions of the three-feature points $\{A_1, A_2, A_3\}$ and $\{B_1, B_2, B_3\}$ are denoted by $\overline{\boldsymbol{a}}$ and $\overline{\boldsymbol{b}}$, respectively. The feature point matrices are denoted by $\delta\boldsymbol{a} = (\delta\boldsymbol{a}_1, \delta\boldsymbol{a}_2, \delta\boldsymbol{a}_3)^T$ and $\delta\boldsymbol{b} = (\delta\boldsymbol{b}_1, \delta\boldsymbol{b}_2, \delta\boldsymbol{b}_3)^T$, where $\delta\boldsymbol{a}_i \triangleq \boldsymbol{a}_i^* - \overline{\boldsymbol{a}}$ and $\delta\boldsymbol{b}_i \triangleq \boldsymbol{b}_i^* - \overline{\boldsymbol{b}}$, and $\boldsymbol{a}_i^*$ and $\boldsymbol{b}_i^*$ are the 3D positions of the feature points A_i and B_i, respectively. Based on the matrices $\boldsymbol{W}_1$ and $\boldsymbol{W}_2$, which are defined by the singular value decomposition ($\boldsymbol{H} = \boldsymbol{W}_1 \boldsymbol{\Sigma} \boldsymbol{W}_2^T$) of the matrix $\boldsymbol{H} = \delta\boldsymbol{b} \cdot \delta\boldsymbol{a}^T$, the relative position $\delta\,\boldsymbol{x}$ and the rotational matrix $\boldsymbol{R}(\delta\boldsymbol{\theta})$ related to the relative attitude angle $\delta\,\boldsymbol{\theta}$ are given by

$$\boldsymbol{R}(\delta\boldsymbol{\theta}) = \boldsymbol{W}_2 \boldsymbol{W}_1^T = \begin{pmatrix} \cos\delta\theta\cos\delta\psi & \sin\delta\phi\sin\delta\theta\cos\delta\psi - \cos\delta\phi\sin\delta\psi & \cos\delta\phi\sin\delta\theta\cos\delta\psi + \sin\delta\phi\sin\delta\psi \\ \cos\delta\theta\sin\delta\psi & \sin\delta\phi\sin\delta\theta\sin\delta\psi + \cos\delta\phi\cos\delta\psi & \cos\delta\phi\sin\delta\theta\sin\delta\psi - \sin\delta\phi\cos\delta\psi \\ -\sin\delta\theta & \sin\delta\phi\cos\delta\theta & \cos\delta\phi\cos\delta\theta \end{pmatrix} \tag{7}$$

$$\delta\boldsymbol{x} = \bar{\boldsymbol{a}} - \boldsymbol{R}(\delta\boldsymbol{\theta})\bar{\boldsymbol{b}} \tag{8}$$

Based on the relative pose, the 3D position $\boldsymbol{b}_i$ of the feature point B_i in Σ_w can be transformed to the 3D position $\boldsymbol{b}_i' = \boldsymbol{R}(\delta\boldsymbol{\theta})\boldsymbol{b}_i + \delta\boldsymbol{x}$ in Σ_b. The feature point nearest to $\boldsymbol{b}_i'$ is extracted from the set of feature points A_i (i =1, 2, ...), and the 3D position of the nearest feature point is denoted by $\tilde{\boldsymbol{a}}_i$. Then, the cost function is given by

$$J = \frac{1}{N_B}\sum_{i=1}^{N_B}(\tilde{\boldsymbol{a}}_i - \boldsymbol{b}_i')^T(\tilde{\boldsymbol{a}}_i - \boldsymbol{b}_i') \tag{9}$$

where N_B represents the number of the feature points B_i.

Step 3: Steps 1 and 2 are repeated 100 times to find the relative pose $\delta\boldsymbol{X}$ with the smallest J in (9). Then, the relative pose $\delta\boldsymbol{X}_0$ is obtained. In NDT scan matching, the relative pose $\delta\boldsymbol{X}_0$ is used as the initial value, and the iterative calculation is performed. Therefore, the accurate relative pose is calculated, and the MDI in (6) is accurately obtained.

V. FUNDAMENTAL EXPERIMENTS

Mapping experiments are conducted on our university campus, as depicted in Figure 6. A truck stops at the yellow circle in Figure 6, and the robot starts from the yellow circle, moves on the red and green paths in areas 1 and 2, and returns to the yellow circle. LiDAR and IMU data of the truck-and-robot system are recorded, and mapping is performed offline.

The distances travelled by the robot in areas 1 and 2 are 250 and 95 m. respectively, and the maximum velocity is approximately 5 km/h. Figure 7 depicts the attitude angle of the robot during movement, which is observed by the IMU.

For comparison, maps are built in the following cases:

Case 1: NDT SLAM-based local map building using robot-mounted LiDAR,

Case 2: NDT SLAM-based local map building without distortion correction of LiDAR scan data,

Case 3: NDT Graph SLAM-based local map building,

Case 4: Correction of local map using truck-mounted LiDAR.

Note that, in cases 1, 3, and 4, the distortion correction method is implemented.

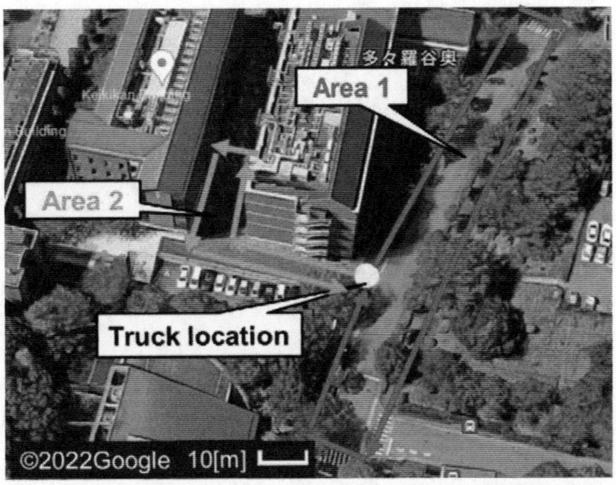

Figure 6. Experimental environment. The yellow circle indicates the truck location and start/goal position of robot. The red and green lines indicate the movement paths of robot.

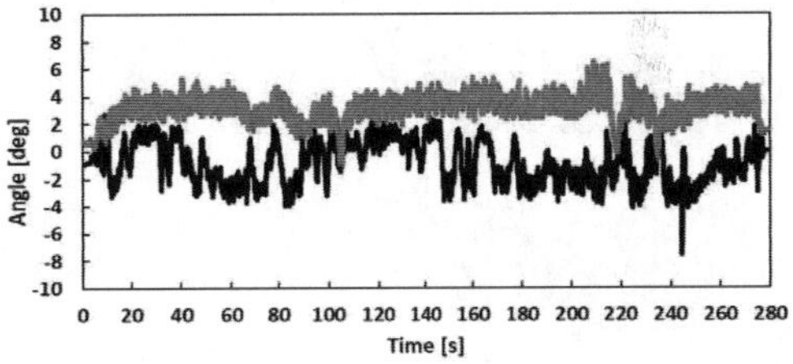

(a) Area 1

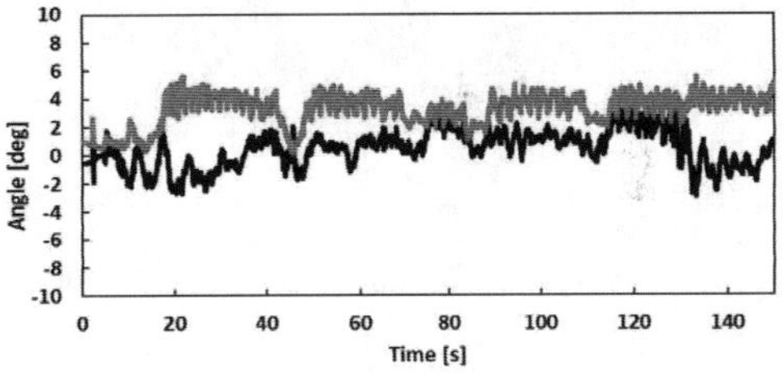

(b) Area 2

Figure 7. Roll (black) and pitch (red) angles of robot.

Figures 8 and 9 show the mapping results in areas 1 and 2 (local maps 1 and 2), respectively, using case 4. These figures show that the proposed method can build an environmental map.

In SLAM-based mapping, the mapping accuracy is equivalent to that of the self-pose estimate of the robot. Therefore, to evaluate the mapping accuracy, the error of position estimate of the robot at the goal position is measured using a GNSS/LiDAR positioning system installed on the truck.

Tables I and II show the results in areas 1 and 2, respectively, shown in Figure 6, where the robot moves twice in each area. From theses tables, we can conclude that case 3

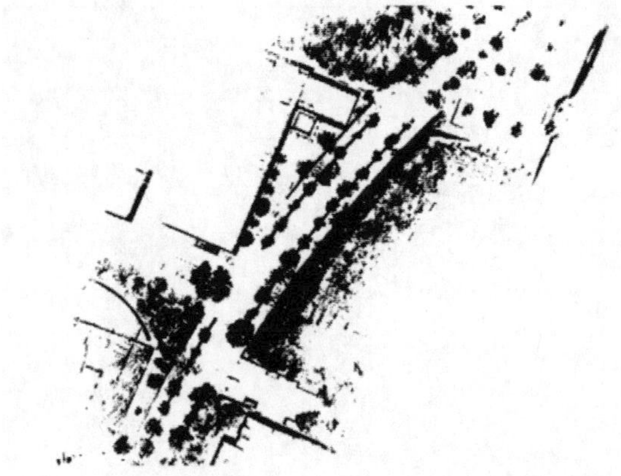

(a) Overall map (top view)

(b) Enlarged map (bird's-eye view)

Figure 8. Mapping result in area 1 (local map 1).

(a) Overall map (top view)

(b) Enlarged map (bird's-eye view)

Figure 9. Mapping result in area 2 (local map 2).

TABLE I. ERROR IN POSITION ESTIMATE OF ROBOT AT GOAL POSITION (LOCAL MAP 1).

	CASE 1	CASE 2	CASE 3	CASE 4
Run 1	3.09 m	3.63 m	0.15 m	0.13 m
Run 2	3.30 m	4.54 m	0.10 m	0.10 m

TABLE II. ERROR IN POSITION ESTIMATE OF ROBOT AT GOAL POSITION (LOCAL MAP 2).

	CASE 1	CASE 2	CASE 3	CASE 4
Run 1	0.92 m	1.17 m	0.28 m	0.10 m
Run 2	0.47 m	1.89 m	0.25 m	0.13 m

provides better results than cases 1 and 2. Furthermore, case 4 provides better results than case 3.

VI. CONCLUSION AND FUTURE WORK

This paper presented a LiDAR SLAM-based mapping method in truck-and-robot system for last-mile delivery systems. Distortion in scan data from robot-mounted LiDAR was corrected using a Kalman filter-based method. LiDAR scan data related to stationary objects were extracted from corrected scan data using an occupancy grid-based method, and local maps were built using NDT Graph SLAM.

Furthermore, a feature-based loop detection method was presented using surface features and FPFH. The local map was corrected in the Graph SLAM framework using scan data from truck-mounted LiDAR. The efficacy of the presented mapping method was demonstrated through experimental results obtained in our university campus.

We are currently performing quantitative evaluations of the proposed method in various environments. In future works, map building using small and lightweight solid-state LiDAR instead of the mechanical LiDAR used in this paper will be performed. In addition, map update and maintenance will be studied.

REFERENCES

[1] E. Shaklab et al., "Towards Autonomous and Safe Last-mile Deliveries with AI-augmented Self-driving Delivery Robots," arXiv:2305.17705, 2023.

[2] J. Hooks et al., "ALPHRED: A Multi-Modal Operations Quadruped Robot for Package Delivery Applications," IEEE Robotics and Automation Letters, vol. 5, pp. 5409-5416, 2020.

[3] V. Balaska et al., "A Viewpoint on the Challenges and Solutions for Driverless Last-Mile Delivery," Machines, vol. 10, pp. 1–15, 2022.

[4] A. Heimfarth, M. Ostermeier, and A. Hübner, "A Mixed Truck and Robot Delivery Approach for the Daily Supply of Customers," European J. Operational Research, vol. 303, pp. 401–421, 2022.

[5] L. Qingqing, J. P. Queralta, T. N. Gia, Z. Zou, and T. Westerlund, "Multi Sensor Fusion for Navigation and Mapping in Autonomous Vehicles: Accurate Localization in Urban Environments," arXiv:2013.13719, 2021.

[6] E. Yurtsever, J. Lambert, A. Carballo, and K. Takeda, "A Survey of Autonomous Driving: Common Practices and Emerging Technologies," IEEE Access, vol. 8, pp. 58443–58469, 2020.

[7] B. Huang, J. Zhao, and J. Liu, "A Survey of Simultaneous Localization and Mapping," eprint arXiv:1909.05214, 2019.

[8] S. Kuutti et al., "A Survey of the State-of-the-Art Localization Techniques and Their Potentials for Autonomous Vehicle Applications," IEEE Internet of Things Journal, vol. 5, pp. 829–846, 2018.

[9] S. Tanaka, C. Koshiro, M. Yamaji, M. Hashimoto, and K. Takahashi, "Point Cloud Mapping and Merging in GNSS-Denied and Dynamic Environments Using Only Onboard Scanning LiDAR," Int. J. Advances in Systems and Measurements, vol. 13, pp. 275–288, 2020.

[10] K. Matsuo, A. Yoshida, M. Hashimoto, and K. Takahashi, "Normal Distributions Transform-based Mapping Using Scanning LiDAR Mounted on Motorcycle," Proc. of the 5th Int. Conf. on Advances in Sensors, Actuators, Metering and Sensing, pp. 69–75, 2020.

[11] I. Yoshida, A. Yoshida, M. Hashimoto, and K. Takahashi, "Map Building Using Helmet-Mounted LiDAR for Micro-Mobility," Artificial Life and Robotics, vol. 28, pp. 471–482, 2023.

[12] S. Hong, H. Ko, and J. Kim, "VICP: Velocity Updating Iterative Closest Point Algorithm," Proc. of the IEEE Int. Conf. on Robotics and Automation, pp. 1893–1898, 2010.

[13] P. Zhou, X. Guo, X. Pei, and C. Chen, "T-LOAM: Truncated Least Squares LiDAR-only Odometry and Mapping in Real Time," IEEE Trans. on Geoscience and Remote Sensing, vol. 60, pp. 1–13, 2022.

[14] S. Arshad and G. W. Kim, "Role of Deep Learning in Loop Closure Detection for Visual and Lidar SLAM: A Survey," Sensors, vol. 21, p. 1–17, 2021.

[15] L. Huang, "Review on LiDAR-based SLAM Techniques," Proc. Int. Conf. on Signal Processing and Machine Learning, pp. 163–168, 2021.

[16] R. B. Rusu, N. Blodow, and M. Beetz, "Fast Point Feature Histograms (FPFH) for 3D Registration," Proc. of IEEE/RSJ Int. Conf. on Robotics and Automation, pp. 3212–3217, 2009.

[17] P. Biber and W. Strasser, "The Normal Distributions Transform: A New Approach to Laser Scan Matching," Proc. of IEEE/RSJ Int. Conf. on Intelligent Robots and Systems, pp. 2743–2748, 2003.

[18] F. Martín, R. Triebel, L. Moreno, and R. Siegwart, "Two Different Tools for Three-Dimensional Mapping: DE-based Scan Matching and Feature-Based Loop Detection," Robotica, vol. 32, pp. 19–41, 2017.

A Tool for Automating Sizing in Agile Development Using the COSMIC Method

Bruel Gérançon, Sylvie Trudel
Department of Computer Science
Université du Québec à Montréal (UQAM)
Montréal, Canada
e-mail: gerancon.bruel@uqam.ca, trudel.s@uqam.ca

Abstract— **Agility is one of the industry's most widely used software development approaches. It lies in the fact that an agile development project is supposed to deliver the functionalities for the product owner as soon as possible. However, automating sizing in agile development remains difficult. The software's functional size measurement methods are challenging to scale for agility. In the industry, managers and scrum masters use empirical methods to estimate the size of user stories manually. One of the pitfalls of this approach is the limited collection of data in agile projects, which makes it challenging to carry out statistical analysis to better estimate the value of appropriate efforts for the subsequent iterations of the projects. This paper presents a tool for automating sizing in agile development using the COSMIC Function Point (CFP) from User Stories written in natural language. Our tool integrates a set of techniques in Natural Language Processing (NLP), which semantically identify the triplet (subjects, predicates or verbs, objects) from items of product backlog (User Stories written in natural language) and automatically quantifies the number of verbs (data movement) which refers to the functional size. Afterward, we applied a set of rules in COSMIC to identify the types of data movement.**

Keywords - Agile; User Stories; Triplet; Natural Language Processing (NLP); Automation.

I. INTRODUCTION

The measure of the functional size of agile development projects plays an important role in software engineering. It allows project managers to establish reliable estimation and productivity models [11][18]. In other words, it is a key factor that allows for estimating the effort, the cost of developing software products, and performing an analysis of the performance of the software development team [9]. Moreover, the techniques used in agile development for writing software specification documents do not facilitate the automation of the functional size of agile development [9]. The software requirements are written in natural language and do not contain technical and specified details [10]-[12]. For this reason, it would be important to propose a new approach that facilitates measuring the functional size of agile development. How could the triplets approach help automate the functional size of agile projects?

In this article, we will review the primary technique used for writing software requirements in agile development in Section II. Section III will focus on the estimation technique in agile development. Subsequently, we will present the limitations of this technique and evaluate the possibility of automating agile developments using COSMIC. Section V will describe our proposed triplets approach for automating sizing in agile development using the COSMIC Function Point (CFP) from User Stories written in natural language and previous automation work realized with the triplets structure. Section V will introduce our new tool that automatically measures the functional size of agile development projects using the COSMIC method. Finally, we will present in Section VI the results of our research and its limitations.

II. TECHNIQUE FOR WRITING REQUIREMENTS IN AGILE

In agile development projects, the requirements are often written as structured User Stories. A User Story consists of a few lines of text describing a functionality software must offer to allow an actor or user to achieve a specific objective [4]. One of the significant advantages of this technique is that it is centered on the system user [3][4]. An often-used User Story description format is the following:

As a "user role" I want "this feature or functionality" So that I can “benefit or business value, or business reason”

III. ESTIMATION IN AGILE DEVELOPMENT PROJECTS

In this section, we present the user story points technique for estimating agile development projects, the limitations of this technique, and the sizing of User Stories with the COSMIC method.

A. User Story Points

In agile development, User Story Points (USP) are considered an estimated relative level of the effort required to complete a User Story [1][3]. Estimation is important because it allows the project manager to identify which requirements to prioritize for each iteration and whether these requirements or User Stories could be completed during the iteration [7]. Automating the measurement of the functional size of agile projects is a priority for managers and agile teams. Most agile development projects measure their requirements in user story points [2]. As part of this measure, agile teams commonly use the Fibonacci sequence to size stories (1, 2, 3, 5, 8, 13) to assign a value combining size and complexity so that this value reflects the effort to achieve the product backlog item [1][2][13][14]. The development team considers the number of User Story Points as the average size.

B. *Limitations of User Story Points*

The limitations of User Story Points for measuring agile development projects are that it is not possible to standardize their value from one project to another or from one organization to another, as this value is subjective and specific to the development team that assigned it [2][6][7]. Also, the User Story Points do not represent a measure of functional size but rather an effort estimate [1][3][8].

C. *Sizing User Stories with the COSMIC Method*

Many published works demonstrate that it is possible to manually apply a functional size measure on the items in the product backlog. For example, Trudel and Buglione [8] proposed a Guideline for sizing Agile Projects. Desharnais and al. [19] used functional size methods, such as COSMIC method, to estimate Agile User Stories. Angara et al. [6] present related work on linkages between User Stories and the COSMIC method. Furthermore, from the literature consulted, only a few tools automatically allow measuring the functional size of agile development projects (items in the product backlog) using the COSMIC method. Therefore, this paper aims to describe a tool for automating sizing in agile development projects using the COSMIC method.

IV. THE TRIPLETS APPROACH AND PREVIOUS WORK

In this section, we present the triplet approach proposed for estimating agile development projects and the previous work of automation of functional size with this approach.

A. *The Triplets Approach*

The triplets approach is a model that defines and represents the software requirements as a triplet [9][15]. Each triplet comprises a trio of concepts, such as (subject, predicate, object). The subject represents the functional user interacting with the system; a composite predicate represents the use case scenario; an atomic predicate represents the events the functional user triggers. The object represents a software component [9][10][12].

B. *Previous Works*

In our previous work, we used the triplet approach to automate functional size measurement of use cases [9]. We developed a tool for automatically generating triplets from use cases written in natural language, specifically in English or French, and calculating the functional size of the software to be measured [9]. Indeed, we decided to adapt our automation tool from requirements written as structured User Stories to measure agile development projects.

V. TOOL TO AUTOMATE AGILE PROJECT SIZING

Section II indicates that product backlog requirements are written in natural language as User Stories. We developed a tool that automatically performs the functional size measurement on the User Stories of a product backlog. Our tool integrates a set of Natural Language Processing (NLP) techniques, which semantically identifies the subjects, verbs, and objects from User Stories written in natural language. In such a perspective, we presume that a software requirement written as a User Story refers to an actor (subject) that triggers an action or a system operation (verb or data movement) on an object. Afterward, we applied several rules in COSMIC for identifying the verbs that correspond to a type of data movement (Entry, Exit, Read, Write) and quantifying the number of verbs (data movement), which refers to the functional size [9]. In the description of this User Story: "As a visitor, I want to search a product," the tool identifies "user" as the subject, "search" as the verb, and "product" as the object. In other words, the tool targets the triplet structure (subject, predicate/verb, object). In [9] and [10], we assumed that the writing of software requirements in agile, specifically in the form of User Stories, can be done with predicates of two arguments ***f (x, y)***. The predicate is expressed by a verb, which corresponds to the data movements, system operations, or methods of the object, which will be triggered following an external stimulation [9][10][15]. The "**x**" variable or subject of the action represents the user or actor, while the "**y**" variable is the object of the action. The objects represent the software classes that will be implemented. In this case, our tool automatically identifies the potential software components and methods (data movements or system operations) that will be implemented in each iteration of an agile development project. Figure 1 presents the data model built by our tool from the items in the product backlog to determine the functional size in COSMIC Function Points (CFP).

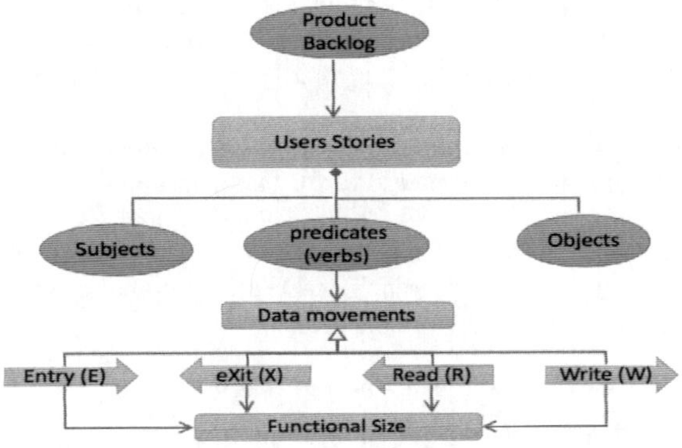

Figure 1. Data Model built by our tool.

A. *Evaluation and Validation of Results*

We tested the tool with two (2) agile development projects for which the items in the product backlog are written in the form of User Stories. First, human experts certified with the COSMIC method manually measured the functional size of the two (2) projects according to the measurement manual rules [16][17]. Second, we compared the results presented by the tool to the experts' manual measurement results, which are published and available on the COSMIC website. The research showed that our tool offers automated results consistent with the manual results, with an average accuracy of 95.97%. It was found that automated counting yields different results compared with manual counting (a difference of 4.03%). To identify the source of the discrepancies, we examined the software requirements documents (description of the User Stories) for both projects. After analysis, we identified the following main factors behind the discrepancies:

- The tool fails to determine data movements for the following Use Stories: "As a user, C-Reg requests Course Catalog to send Course Offering data"; "As a user, C-Reg requests Course Offering data (with number of students enrolled, etc.) from the Course Catalog." This is because the tool identifies the verb "requests" as a noun, not a verb. The tool fails to determine data movements for these User Stories: "As a user, C-Reg sends The Professor's selected Course offerings to the Catalog," and "C-Reg sends Professor's qualifications and department to Course Catalog to retrieve." The tool does not identify the verb "sends." This project was challenging to measure since there were a lot of unnecessary details in the description of User Stories while the User Story description format was not wholly respected. User Stories in this document are also described with passive verbs, but some User Stories are described according to the recommended standard format with active verbs. The two examples of scenarios of User Stories whose verbs are conjugated in the passive form are respectively, "Validated Course Offering IDs are sent to the Course Catalog so that it can maintain the count of Students for each Course Offering"; "Student's Schedule items are marked 'enrolled' and made persistent on C-Reg''.
- For project #2, a difference of 1 CFP was recorded between manual and automated measures for the total number of data movements (|83 CFP - 84 CFP|). The additional COSMIC Function Point (CFP) obtained by the tool occurs following a duplicate. We summarized in TABLE I the automatic size of User Stories obtained from the tool.

TABLE I. AUTOMATIC AND MANUAL SIZE OF USER STORIES

Project	**Manual Functional Sizing**	**Automatic Functional Sizing**	**Accuracy**
Case#1	109	95	93.14%
Case#2	83	84	98.80%
Total	**193**	**178**	**95.97%**

B. *The Usefulness of Functional Size Automation for Agile Development*

One of the benefits of measuring the functional size of agile development projects is that it allows project managers to establish reliable estimation and productivity models, provided the effort and time data is of good quality [11][18]. Studies and experiments have shown a strong correlation between functional size and effort and between functional size and project duration [18]. When the functional size of agile projects is known early, it would allow managers to perform an analysis of the performance of the software development team, such as development cost, productivity, and delivery rate [18]. This is admittedly a weak point of most agile methods.

It is important to mention that automated counting of agile development projects is advantageous when there are many requirements from real-life projects. Indeed, automating the measurement process of agile development is helpful because it allows measuring faster. For example, in our experiment, for a series of projects totaling 362 CFP in size, a COSMIC human expert took about 268 minutes to measure the functional size, i.e., to apply the COSMIC method and determine the functional size [10]. Other human experts would have taken around 362 minutes, a little over one minute per CFP [12]. As for the tool developed, it took approximately two (2) minutes and 3 seconds to upload the document that contains the User Stories descriptions, determine the functional size, and identify the types of data movement [10] [15]. By comparing the manual measurement effort to that of automated measurement, we found a significant difference in favor of automated measurement [10].

VI. CONCLUSION AND FUTURE WORK

This paper proposed a new tool designed to automate the functional sizing of agile development projects from the items in a product backlog. This tool can effectively identify the subjects, predicates or verbs, and objects derived from User Stories and quantifies the number of data movements, which refers to the functional size. Thus, the validation of our tool needs to cover the potential cases. In the future, extensive testing will be performed to improve the tool's efficiency. Also, we will integrate a machine learning module, which allows the tool to learn to identify the data movement for the User Stories that are not described according to the recommended standard format.

REFERENCES

[1] S. Murat, T. Hacaloglu and O. Demirors, "Effort estimation for agile software development: Comparative case studies using COSMIC functional size measurement and story points", *Proceedings of the 27th International Workshop on Software Measurement and the 12th International Conference on Software Process and Product Measurement*, pp. 41-49, 2017.

[2] T. Fehlmann and A. Gelli, "Functional Size Measurement in Agile Development: Velocity in Agile Sprints", *Proceedings of the 27th International Conference on Evaluation and Assessment in Software Engineering*, pp. 200-204, 2023.

[3] I. K. Raharjana, D. Siahaan, and C. Fatichah, "User stories and natural language processing: A systematic literature review", pp. 53811-53826, *IEEE,* 2021.

[4] K. Beck and D. West, "User Stories in Agile Development", In Scenarios, Stories, Use Cases: Through the Systems Developments Lifecycle, 2004.

[5] P. Abrahamsson, O. Salo, J. Ronkainen, and J. Warsta, "Agile software development methods: Review and analysis" *arXiv preprint arXiv:1709.08439,* 2017.

[6] J. Angara, P. Srinivas Prasad, and G. Sridevi, "Towards Benchmarking User Stories Estimation with COSMIC Function Points-A Case Example of Participant Observation" *International Journal of Electrical & Computer Engineering,* pp. 2088-870, 8, 2018.

[7] J-M. Desharnais, L. Buglione, and B. Kocatürk, "Using the COSMIC method to estimate Agile user stories", *Proceedings of the 12th International Conference on product focused software development and process improvement*, pp. 68-73, 2011.

[8] S. Trudel and L. Buglione, "Guideline for sizing Agile projects with COSMIC" *Proceedings of International Workshop on Software Measurement*, 2010.

[9] B. Gérançon, S. Trudel, R. Nkambou, and S. Robert, "Software functional sizing automation from requirements written as triplets." *International Conference on Software Engineering Advances, Barcelona, Spain, ISBN: 978-1-61208-894-5 16*, pp. 23–29, 2021.

[10] B. Gerançon, "Design and implementation of a triplet formalization technique for the automation of functional size measurement from software requirements written in natural language", Ph.D. thesis, University of Quebec at Montreal (UQAM), 2022). [Online]. Available from: https://archipel.uqam.ca/15762/1/D4212.pdf, [Retrieved: October 2023].

[11] S. Trudel, "The COSMIC ISO 19761 functional size measurement method as a software requirements improvement mechanism", Ph.D. thesis, École de Technologie Supérieure (ETS), Montreal, 2012.

[12] B. Gérançon and S. Trudel, "Improving Quality of Software Requirements by Using a Triplet Structure", *International Conference on Computational Science and Computational Intelligence (CSCI), Las Vegas, NV, USA, IEEE, Computer Society, ISBN-13: 979-8-3503-2028-2,* pp. 1884-1888, 2022.

[13] T. Hacaloglu and O. Demirors, "Measurability of functional size in Agile software projects: Multiple case studies with COSMIC FSM" *In 2019, 45th Euromicro conference on software engineering and advanced applications (SEAA),* pp. 204-211. IEEE, 2019.

[14] R.K. Mallidi and S. Manmohan, "Study on agile story point estimation techniques and challenges" *International Journal of Computer*, pp. 9-14, 2021

[15] B. Gérançon, R. Nkambou, S. Trudel and S. Robert, "A cognitive model for supporting software functional sizing automation from requirements written as triplets", *The 20th International Conference on Software Engineering Research Practice, Springer Nature, Las Vegas, USA, ISBN-13: 978-1-6654-6218-2 (IEEE),* pp. 362-373, 2022.

[16] A. Abran *et al.*, "The COSMIC Functional Size Measurement Method Version 5.0", [Online]. Available from: www.cosmic-sizing.org, [Retrieved: August 2023].

[17] M. Downing, M. Eagles, P. Hope, and Ph. James, "C-Reg Case Study v1.0.1", August 2018. [Online]. Available from: https://cosmic-sizing.org/publications/acme-car-hire-case-study-v1-0-1/, [Retrieved: August 2023].

[18] A. Abran, "Software project estimation: The fundamentals for providing high-quality information to decision-makers", John Wiley & Sons, 2015.

[19] J. Desharnais, L. Buglione, and B. Kocatürk, "Using the COSMIC method to estimate Agile user stories", *Proceedings of the 12th international conference on product focused software development and process improvement*, pp. 68-73, 2011.

Towards Hypothesis-driven Forensic Text Exploration System

Jenny Felser*, Dirk Labudde†, Michael Spranger‡
Mittweida University of Applied Sciences
09648 Mittweida, Germany
Email: *felser@hs-mittweida.de, †labudde@hs-mittweida.de, ‡spranger@hs-mittweida.de

***Abstract*—Short messages stored on mobile devices have become a crucial source of evidence in criminal investigations. However, the high volume of chat messages poses a challenge to the investigator. Topic modelling offers the potential to summarise the short messages compactly, thus effectively supporting the investigator in exploring the vast number of chat messages. This paper presents our preliminary work towards developing a forensic text exploration system based on topic modelling approaches. The two goals typically pursued by the investigator when exploring chat messages are to be supported. On the one hand, the investigator often already has a hypothesis about specific topics discussed in the chats and wants to find evidence. On the other hand, the investigator also wants to discover new topics and connections. Accordingly, in this work, we investigated unsupervised and semi-supervised approaches based on Latent Dirichlet Allocation (LDA) with the additional use of word embeddings. Overall, the evaluation of different methods using actual case data showed that the semi-supervised approach, combined with word embedding similarity, can find qualitatively better topics than unsupervised topic modelling approaches based on LDA.**

***Index Terms*—topic modelling; forensic text analysis; semi-supervised; hypothesis-driven analysis.**

I. INTRODUCTION

Nowadays, the analysis of short messages stored on mobile devices is an important part of forensic investigations. However, the high number of messages can also prove challenging for the investigator. Often, a single mobile phone stores more than 15,000 Short Message Service (SMS) and 150,000 messages from messenger services [1]. Furthermore, especially in the case of gang crime and organised crime, it is often necessary to examine the short messages of several mobile phones [1]. To assist the investigator in exploring the chat messages, the application of topic modelling is suggested. This allows to get an overview of the contents discussed in the messages and to summarise the messages as compactly as possible.

Topic modelling should best support both goals that investigators are pursuing when analysing forensic chat messages: On the one hand, investigators usually have some presumption about topics that have been discussed in the messages. Usually, at least they know the area of offence their case is about. In addition, they can obtain information about the circumstances of the offence from interrogations [2] or the case file [2]. Accordingly, one goal is to find evidence in the data for a certain hypothesis, respectively, that a topic was actually discussed in it. On the other hand, the investigators also want to discover new topics, for example about the motivation of the crime or previously unsuspected connections to certain people.

The basic aim of this paper is to investigate some methods of unsupervised topic modelling for the first scenario and semi-supervised topic modelling for the second scenario and to qualitatively evaluate and compare the results. More specifically, the unsupervised method used is weighted Latent Dirichlet Allocation (wLDA), as described by Wilson and Chew [3], while the keyword-Assisted Topic Model (keyATM) developed by Eshima et al. [4] was chosen as the semi-supervised method. In addition, an extension of keyATM is proposed based on a combination with the Cluster Words (CluWords) document representation presented by Viegas et al. [5], which additionally includes word embeddings.

The paper is organized as follows: At first, some related work is presented in Section II. Then, an overview of the data and methods is provided in Section IV. The experimental results are presented and discussed in Section V. Finally, Section VI concludes the paper.

II. RELATED WORK

To the extent of our knowledge, topic modelling has only been used by a few works in the field of forensics with the aim of compactly summarising data sets in the context of forensic investigations [6]–[9]. Furthermore, they also did not focus specifically on communication data. Instead, de Waal et al. [8] extracted topics from all textual data that need to be investigated for a case, including emails and notes in text documents, while Noel and Peterson [9] used Word documents extracted from a hard disk store as the data basis. Both works [8], [9] applied the Latent Dirichlet Allocation (LDA), as described by Blei et al. [10], as the algorithm for topic modelling. Moreover, topic modelling was used by Li et al. [7] and Busso et al. [6] to support data exploration in specific offense areas or in the analysis of concrete cases. Li et al. [7] tried to uncover various topics in conversations about corruption on Twitter using the Biterm Topic Modeling (BTM) algorithm introduced by Yan et al. [11]. Moreover, Busso et al. [6] applied the Structural Topic Model (STM), as described by Roberts et al. [12], to identify topics in a series of racist and offensive letters. Thus, in summary, unsupervised probabilistic generative models such as the LDA and its extensions were mainly applied to forensic texts. These are suitable for the second mentioned scenario regarding the analysis of forensic short messages, namely for the data exploration.

However, to the extent of our knowledge, no previous work in the forensic field has focused on the scenario where the investigator is looking for evidence of certain assumed topics in the data. The problem with unsupervised approaches is that they are not able to identify topics of interest to the investigator if they are present in the dataset only to a small extent [13], as is often the case in forensic communication data due to the prevalence of irrelevant small talk.

This problem can be addressed by incorporating the investigator's prior knowledge into the topic modelling process, for example, by using supervised approaches, e.g., [14], [15]. However, these require annotated training datasets to learn known topics. One approach to create an annotated dataset would be to collect as much case data as possible from different offence areas and label the messages with the known offence as their topic. Yet, legal questions in the respective country would first have to be clarified as to whether the merging of data from different cases is permissible. Instead, semi-supervised approaches come into consideration, which differ in the type of user input they integrate, e.g., [16]–[18]. For example, user feedback on the relevance of topics [19]–[21], information about thematic relationships between word pairs, e.g., [16], [22], [23] or user knowledge about known topics in the form of a few characteristic terms was included in topic modelling, e.g., [4], [17], [24]. The last case is most suitable for finding evidence for suspected topics. In these approaches, a distinction can be made between Targeted Topic Modelling, e.g., [17], [25], [26] and Seed-Guided Topic Modelling, e.g., [4], [24], [27].

Algorithms of Targeted Topic Modelling aimed at extracting fine-grained topics related to a specific aspect described by a single characteristic word, e.g., [17], [25], [26]. In forensic context, these approaches could be used to find different subtopics dealing exclusively with the crime under investigation, such as drug crime. The basic idea of these algorithms was to reduce the dataset to documents [17], [23], [25], word pairs [28] or words [26] that were relevant to the aspect, whereby the relevance determination was carried out with reinforcement learning [23] or based on external corpora [26], for example. However, especially when determining relevance at the document level, these approaches are accompanied by the risk that important case-relevant information can be lost if incorrectly classified as irrelevant.

In contrast, seed-guided topic modelling approaches, especially probabilistic generative models, e.g., [4], [13], [29], may be promising. Unlike other semi-supervised methods, e.g., [30], these have the advantage that they can overcome prior knowledge, if the desired topic, described by some relevant seed words, does not appear in the dataset at all, e.g., [13], [29], which is why these approaches are particularly suitable for testing hypotheses in a forensic context.

So far, however, semi-supervised probabilistic approaches have been applied and evaluated mainly on long, linguistically correct texts such as draft legislations [4] and customer reviews [31], [32]. An important contribution of this work is therefore to investigate the suitability of topic modelling for identifying case-relevant topics in forensic communication data, despite their particular challenges, such as their short length and low linguistic quality [33]. Furthermore, it is one of the first studies to include both goals, exploration and finding evidence, in topic analysis of forensic texts.

III. Data

For all experiments, WhatsApp messages from a real case about the financial support of a terrorist group, which were stored on the mobile phone of a suspected person, served as the data basis. The dataset is not publicly available, but was provided to the authors by a cooperating prosecutor for research purposes and has already been used in previous work [34]. The messages were exchanged in 146 chats between mid-December 2014 and mid-May 2019. The total of approximately 118,000 text messages in the data set were primarily in German and to a lesser extent in Turkish and Arabic. Since the focus of this work was on monolingual topic analysis, approximately 106,000 German messages were extracted by automatic language detection using Google's cld2 [35] and cld3 [36] models. Details on the vocabulary size, the number of unique tokens (besides words also punctuation marks, symbols, numbers and web links), the average frequency of words and the length of the messages can be taken from the upper section of Table I.

TABLE I
STATISTICAL DESCRIPTION OF THE DATA SET USED

Property/ Statistic	Result
vocabulary size (# unique words)	36467
# unique tokens	39039
average frequency of words	22.62
∅ message length (in words)	7.75
# conversations	15625
∅ number of messages per conversation	6.81
∅ conversation length (in words)	52.78

As can be seen from the table, the messages contained on average less than eight words including stopwords. Since the short length of the messages poses a known problem for topic modelling [37], messages that occurred in a common temporal context were aggregated into related conversations, as explained by [33], which were subsequently considered as one document. The formation of conversations was carried out with the Mobile Network Analyzer (MoNA), a forensic tool for analysing mobile communication data [1]. Information about the number of conversations, the average number of messages that made up a conversation and the length of the conversations can be found in the bottom section of Table I.

IV. Methods

In order to find suitable approaches for both scenarios of forensic data analysis, exploration and hypothesis testing, initial experiments on unsupervised and semi-supervised topic modelling were carried out. All algorithms were trained on the conversation documents described in Section III. The preprocessing as well as the training of the topic models was conducted with the statistical software R.

A. Preprocessing

Before performing topic modelling, extensive preprocessing was applied to these conversation documents, which, as shown by Churchill and Singh [38], is essential for good results in topic modelling, especially with noisy data such as forensic short messages. This included the performance of the following cleansing steps:

1) Removal of redundant whitespace
2) Removal of web links, email addresses, and mentions, as they did not contribute to the content
3) Removal of emojis, as they usually have little meaning without context in topic-word distributions
4) Removal of punctuation marks and then numbers
5) Removal of German, Turkish and English stopwords using the stopword lists provided by Diaz [39]. The removal of English and Turkish stop words was necessary despite the reduction of the data set to German messages, as it could not be excluded that Turkish idioms or anglicisms were used in messages classified as German.
6) Removal of the 100 most frequent words and the 100 words with the lowest Inverse Document Frequency (IDF)
7) Removal of all modal and auxiliary verbs as well as the most common German verbs manually selected from [40]
8) Conversion to lower case
9) Lemmatisation using the TreeTagger [41], [42], in particular to reduce the high sparsity of the communication dataset by decreasing the vocabulary size [43]
10) Tokenisation in unigrams

B. Unsupervised topic modelling

wLDA [3] was chosen as unsupervised approach. This algorithm differs from the standard LDA by integrating a term weighting scheme based on Pointwise Mutual Information (PMI) [44] into Collapsed Gibbs Sampling [45], which penalises terms that occur in many documents and are often not meaningful in topics. The term weighting scheme was used in addition to the stop word removal in order to prevent irrelevant high-frequency words, typical for colloquial texts [46], from dominating the topics. Using the cleaned conversation documents as input, the topic model was trained over 1,500 iterations, where the hyperparameters α as prior for the document-topic-distribution and β as prior for the topic-word distribution [4] were set to 0.08 and 0.01. The number of topics was set to 13 in accordance with the semi-supervised approach, which is explained in the following subsection.

C. Semi-supervised topic modelling

As a semi-supervised method, the keyATM model, as described by Eshima et al. [4], was chosen because it extends wLDA and, accordingly, unlike other seed-guided topic modelling algorithms, gives less weight to uninformative words when estimating topics. The basic idea of keyATM consists in the introduction of an additional topic-word distribution containing only seed words [4].

For each desired topic, set of seed words were created based on the so-called term tree explained by Spranger et al. [1], which describes a complex system of syntagmas, referring to case-relevant terms that occur together in a conversation. Each syntagm was considered as a set of seed words. The term tree was created semi-automatically by expanding case-relevant words provided by the prosecutor in charge of the case with further relevant words using a suggestion system of the software MoNA [1], [34]. Each syntagm respectively each set of seed words included case-relevant terms, their synonyms, spelling variants and words that are syntagmatically related to the case-relevant terms provided. As an example, a selection of terms from three out of eight seed word sets is presented in Table II. Notably, keyATM enables the specification of a seed word as a topic label before fitting the model [4]. Throughout this table and subsequent ones, English translations of terms are provided in parentheses.

TABLE II
SELECTED TOPIC LABEL AND EXAMPLES OF USED SEED WORDS FOR SEMI-SUPERVISED TOPIC DETECTION WITH KEYATM.

Topic Label	Seed Terms
Geld (money)	Euro, überweisen (transfer), Zahlung (payment)
Terror	Waffe (weapon), Anschlag (attack), Gewalt (violence)
Verein (association)	Vereinsregister (association register), rechtsfähig (judicable), Vereinsgründer (association founder)

With the created seed word sets, keyATM was trained on the cleaned conversation documents, where the hyperparameters α and β and the number of iterations were set to the same values as for the training of wLDA, as described in Section IV-B. Suplementary, specific hyperparameters for keyATM were set to the default values as suggested in the reference paper by Eshima et al. [4]. In addition to the eight seed topics, keyATM enables to find a predefined number of unseeded topics, in this case five, which mainly serve as residual topics to bundle unimportant words together [4], [24].

D. Semi-supervised topic modelling with CluWords

keyATM already aims to ensure that the seed words and their related words have a high probability in the desired topic [4]. However, this requires that the words co-occur with the seed words in documents [4], [29]. To ensure that words that are semantically very similar to the seed words are assigned high probabilities in the corresponding topic, regardless of their co-occurrence frequency, keyATM was extended with an adapted CluWords document representation, originally proposed by Viegas et al. [5]. A CluWord is defined as a set of words that have a high word embedding similarity to a term [5]. The basic idea of the approach is to insert

CluWords into the original conversation documents and then perform topic modelling on this pseudo-documents [5].

For this, word embeddings were learned first, whereby fastText [47] was chosen as the method because it can handle out-of-vocabulary words. Since the dataset of forensic short messages was considered too small to obtain meaningful word embeddings from it, instead, the unsupervised fastText skipgram-model with a window size of five and character N-Grams with a length between two and six was trained on a large external dataset to represent words as 300-dimensional word vectors. This training dataset also consisted of informal texts, namely primarily 20 million tweets provided by [48].

Subsequently, for each topic label of the seed word sets, its CluWord was created, which consisted of all words of the dataset for which the cosine similarity between their word embeddings and the word embedding of the topic label was above a threshold value of 0.45 [5]. The pseudo-documents were created by enhancing each topic label in a conversation document with its CluWord. This approach differed from the original CluWords method [5] only in the fact that the latter inserted the semantically similar words to all terms. The decision to include only the similar words to the topic labels, rather than to all the seed words, was based on the fact that the actual relevance of some seed words to the case was unclear.

The procedure for training keyATM on these pseudo-documents was analogous to Section IV-C.

V. Results

In this section, the results of the three approaches to topic modelling are presented qualitatively. The topics "Geld", "Terror" and "Verein" were selected as examples for the semi-supervised approaches. To ensure comparability, as suggested, for example by [49], among the topics of the unsupervised algorithm wLDA, those that most resembled the topics "Geld", "Terror" and "Verein" of keyATM were selected, determing the similarity with the Jensen-Shannon divergence (JSD) [50].

A. Unsupervised topic modelling

The eight words with the highest probability in the selected topics of the wLDA are shown in Table III, which also indicates the most similar seed topic in parentheses.

TABLE III
THE EIGHT MOST PROBABLE WORDS FROM THREE TOPICS OF WLDA WITH HIGH SIMILARITY TO THE SELECTED TOPICS OF KEYATM.

Topic 4 (Geld)	Topic 7 (Terror)	Topic 10 (Verein)
Euro	schlafen (sleep)	€
Geld (money)	schreiben (write)	Twitter
spielen (play)	nerven (annoy)	Stream
kaufen (buy)	Bett (bed)	first name user
holen (get)	erzählen (tell)	spenden (donate)
neu (new)	Arbeit (work)	Statement
schicken (send)	kennen (know)	first name user
PC	scheißen (shit)	zahlen (pay)

As can be seen, the fourth and seventh topics are difficult to interpret. For the fourth topic, this can be explained by the fact that topics about money and computer games seem to be mixed. Condering the seventh topic, the problem is that it generally does not contain meaningful terms, but mainly general ones. This was unexpected, as highly frequent words were removed or penalized by the adjusted Collapsed Gibbs Sampling method [4]. One possible explanation might be that the PMI weighting is unreliable for short texts, as noted by [51].

In contrast, the tenth topic could be considered relevant to the case, as it contained words such as "spenden" and "zahlen". That words like "Twitter" and the two individuals whose names appeared among the top words in the topic were related to fundraising activities and relevant to the case was evident from examining the context of these terms in the chat messages.

B. Semi-supervised topic modelling

Regarding the semi-supervised topic modelling, the eight most probable words of the three selected topics are displayed in Table IV, where the selected seed words of the respective topic are highlighted in bold and seed words of other topics are marked with an asterisk. As outlined in Table IV, the most probable words of the topic "Geld" include both seed words and intuitively associated terms like "kaufen" and "zahlen". However, these terms are quite generic, making it difficult to determine the topic's relevance to the case. Furthermore, keyATM could not identify the topic "Terror", but, instead, the topic consists of irrelevant and meaningless terms. These outcomes for both topics can be attributed to the fact that, according to Eshima et al. [4], the quality of topics is heavily dependent on the chosen seed word sets. Regarding the topic "Geld", the problem was that the seed words themselves, such as euro, were very general terms, while concerning the topic "Terror", one possible explanation for the poor results could be the low frequency of the seed words [4].

TABLE IV
THE EIGHT MOST PROBABLE WORDS OF THE THREE TOPICS "GELD", "TERROR" AND "VEREIN" USING THE ALGORITHM KEYATM.

Geld (money)	Terror	Verein (association)
Geld (money)	Bild (image)	Stream
Euro	lachen (laugh)	boy's first name
schicken (send)	kennen (know)	€*
€	stehen (stand)	Twitter
holen (get)	süß (cute)	Event
Mail	kaufen (buy)	Twitch
kaufen (buy)	Hammer (hammer)	boy's first name
Handy (mobile phone)	Son	spenden (donate)

Regarding the seed topic "Verein", the most probable words included specific terms. However, the differences with the most similar unsupervised wLDA topic were minor, as this topic already contained relevant words. Nevertheless, keyATM enhanced interpretability through automatic label assignment.

C. Semi-supervised topic modelling with CluWords

Particularly concerning the topic "Terror", the inclusion of CluWords resulted in more relevant terms appearing among the most probable words. As shown in Table V, which lists the top eight words in the three topics, the topic "Terror" included terms like "Mord" and "Durchsuchungsbefehl".

TABLE V
THE EIGHT MOST PROBABLE WORDS OF THE THREE TOPICS "GELD", "TERROR" AND "VEREIN" USING KEYATM WITH CLUWORDS.

Geld (money)	Terror	Verein (association)
Euro	Mord (murder)	€*
Geld (money)	Gesinnung (attitude)	first name user
kaufen (buy)	ermittlwn (investigate)	spenden (donate)
überweisen (transfer)	Hobbermittler (hobby investigator)	Statement
nah (close)	Verbrechen (crime)	first name user
ausgeben (spend)	Drohung (threat)	SWH
zahlen (pay)	Durchsuchungsbefehl (search warrant)	Twitter
kriegen (get)	Moschee (mosque)	Tipeee

However, further research is required to determine whether the topic "Terror" is actually related to aspects like search warrants or if its presence among the most probable words is solely due to similarity based on external word embeddings. In contrast to the topic "Terror", the most probable words of the other two topics, namely "Geld" and "Verein", strongly resembled the standard keyATM topics.

VI. CONCLUSION

Topic Modelling offers high potential for the analysis of forensic short messages, where it can be used both to find evidence for suspected topics and to explore the dataset. This paper presented our initial work on assisting the investigator with these two scenarios, for which unsupervised and semi-supervised topic modelling approaches were analysed. Overall, it was found that the unsupervised algorithm wLDA already succeeded in finding case-relevant topics. keyATM as a semi-supervised approach was able to detect a similar case-relevant topic as wLDA, but failed to find further rare topics in the messages despite the inclusion of prior knowledge. In contrast, the expansion of keyATM based on Word Embedding similarity proved to be more promising.

For this reason, there is potential in semi-supervised methods that simultaneously learn word embeddings and topics, such as the Keyword Assisted Embedded Topic Model (keyETM) proposed by Harandizadeh et al. [27]. Furthermore, a problem with semi-supervised topic modelling so far was that despite term weighting, many unimportant words appeared in the topics. To address this problem, future work intends to apply the semi-supervised Guided Topic-Noise Model (GTM) [13], which specifically addresses the high number of irrelevant words in colloquial texts. Basically, future experiments should be conducted on a comprehensive set of forensic datasets to definitely decide which approaches are particularly suited for forensic data analysis.

REFERENCES

[1] M. Spranger, J. Xi, L. Jaeckel, J. Felser, and D. Labudde, "MoNA: A forensic analysis platform for mobile communication," *Künstliche Intelligenz*, vol. 36, pp. 163–169, May 2022.

[2] H. Walder, T. Hansjakob, T. E. Gundlach, and P. Straub, *Criminalistic thinking (in German)*, 11th ed., ser. Fundamentals of criminalistics (in German). Heidelberg: Kriminalistik, 2020.

[3] A. T. Wilson and P. A. Chew, "Term weighting schemes for latent dirichlet allocation," in *Proceedings of the 2010 Annual Conference of the North American Chapter of the Association for Computational Linguistics on Human Language Technologies (NAACL-HLT)*. Los Angeles, California: Association for Computational Linguistics (ACL), Jun. 2010, pp. 465–473.

[4] S. Eshima, K. Imai, and T. Sasaki, "Keyword-Assisted Topic Models," *American Journal of Political Science*, pp. 1–21, Feb. 2023.

[5] F. Viegas *et al.*, "CluWords: Exploiting semantic word clustering representation for enhanced topic modeling," in *Proceedings of the Twelfth ACM International Conference on Web Search and Data Mining (WSDM '19)*. New York, NY, USA: ACM, Jan. 2019, pp. 753–761.

[6] L. Busso, M. Petyko, S. Atkins, and T. Grant, "Operation Heron: Latent topic changes in an abusive letter series," *Corpora*, vol. 17, no. 2, pp. 225–258, Aug. 2022.

[7] J. Li, W.-H. Chen, Q. Xu, N. Shah, and T. Mackey, "Leveraging big data to identify corruption as an SDG Goal 16 humanitarian technology," in *Proceedings of the Global Humanitarian Technology Conference (GHTC)*. Seattle, WA, USA: IEEE, Oct. 2019, pp. 1–4.

[8] A. de Waal, J. Venter, and E. Barnard, "Applying topic modeling to forensic data," in *Proceedings of Advances in Digital Forensics IV*, ser. IFIP - The International Federation for Information Processing Book Series, vol. 285. Paris, France: Springer Science+Business, Jan. 2008, pp. 115–126.

[9] G. E. Noel and G. L. Peterson, "Applicability of Latent Dirichlet Allocation to multi-disk search," *Digital Investigation*, vol. 11, no. 1, pp. 43–56, Jul. 2014.

[10] D. Blei, A. Ng, and M. Jordan, "Latent Dirichlet Allocation," *The Journal of Machine Learning Research*, vol. 14, pp. 993–1022, Mar. 2003.

[11] X. Yan, J. Guo, Y. Lan, and X. Cheng, "A biterm topic model for short texts," in *Proceedings of the 22nd International Conference on World Wide Web (WWW '13)*. Rio de Janeiro, Brazil: ACM, May 2013, pp. 1445–1456.

[12] M. E. Roberts *et al.*, "Structural topic models for open-ended survey responses," *American Journal of Political Science*, vol. 58, no. 4, pp. 1064–1082, Oct. 2014.

[13] R. Churchill, L. Singh, R. Ryan, and P. Davis-Kean, "A guided topic-noise model for short texts," in *Proceedings of the ACM Web Conference 2022 (WWW '22)*. New York, NY, USA: ACM, Apr. 2022, pp. 2870–2878.

[14] D. Ramage, D. Hall, R. Nallapati, and C. D. Manning, "Labeled LDA: A supervised topic model for credit attribution in multi-labeled corpora," in *Proceedings of the 2009 Conference on Empirical Methods in Natural Language Processing*. Singapore, Singapore: ACM, Aug. 2009, pp. 248–256.

[15] D. M. Blei and J. D. McAuliffe, "Supervised topic models," in *Proceedings of the 20th International Conference on Neural Information Processing Systems (NIPS'07)*, ser. NIPS'07. Red Hook, NY, USA: Curran Associates Inc., Dec. 2007, pp. 121–128.

[16] D. Andrzejewski, X. Zhu, and M. Craven, "Incorporating domain knowledge into topic modeling via Dirichlet Forest priors," in *Proceedings of the 26th Annual International Conference on Machine Learning (ICML '09)*. Montreal, Quebec, Canada: ACM, Jun. 2009, pp. 25–32.

[17] S. Wang, Z. Chen, G. Fei, B. Liu, and S. Emery, "Targeted Topic Modeling for focused analysis," in *Proceedings of the 22nd ACM SIGKDD International Conference on Knowledge Discovery and Data Mining*, ser. KDD '16. New York, NY, USA: ACM, Aug. 2016, pp. 1235–1244.

[18] Y. Meng *et al.*, "Discriminative Topic Mining via Category-Name Guided Text Embedding," in *Proceedings of The Web Conference 2020 (WWW'20)*. New York, NY, USA: ACM, Apr. 2020, pp. 2121–2132.

[19] H. Kim, D. Choi, B. Drake, A. Endert, and H. Park, "TopicSifter: Interactive Search Space Reduction through Targeted Topic Modeling," in *Proceedings of the IEEE Conference on Visual Analytics Science and Technology (VAST)*. Vancouver, BC, Canada: IEEE, Oct. 2019, pp. 35–45.

[20] J. Choo, C. Lee, C. Reddy, and H. Park, "UTOPIAN: User-Driven Topic Modeling Based on Interactive Nonnegative Matrix Factorization," *IEEE Transactions on Visualization and Computer Graphics*, vol. 19, no. 12, pp. 1992–2001, Dec. 2013.

[21] M. El-Assady, R. Sevastjanova, F. Sperrle, D. Keim, and C. Collins, "Progressive Learning of Topic Modeling Parameters: A Visual Analytics Framework," *IEEE Transactions on Visualization and Computer Graphics*, vol. 24, no. 1, pp. 382–391, Jan. 2018.

[22] H. Kobayashi, H. Wakaki, T. Yamasaki, and M. Suzuki, "Topic Models with Logical Constraints on Words," in *Proceedings of Workshop on Robust Unsupervised and Semisupervised Methods in Natural Language Processing*. Hissar, Bulgaria: Association for Computational Linguistics (ACL), Sep. 2011, pp. 33–40.

[23] J. Chen *et al.*, "TAM: Targeted Analysis Model with reinforcement learning on short texts," *IEEE Transactions on Neural Networks and Learning Systems*, vol. 32, no. 6, pp. 2772–2781, Jun. 2021.

[24] K. Watanabe and A. Baturo, "Seeded Sequential LDA: A semi-supervised algorithm for topic-specific analysis of sentences," *Social Science Computer Review*, pp. 1–25, May 2023.

[25] J. He, L. Li, Y. Wang, and X. Wu, "Targeted aspects oriented topic modeling for short texts," *Applied Intelligence*, vol. 50, no. 8, pp. 2384–2399, Mar. 2020.

[26] V. Rakesh *et al.*, "A Sparse Topic Model for extracting aspect-specific summaries from online reviews," in *Proceedings of the 2018 World Wide Web Conference (WWW '18)*, ser. Track: Web Search and Mining. Lyon, France: International World Wide Web Conferences Steering Committee, Apr. 2018, pp. 1573–1582.

[27] B. Harandizadeh, J. H. Priniski, and F. Morstatter, "Keyword Assisted Embedded Topic Model," in *Proceedings of the Fifteenth ACM International Conference on Web Search and Data Mining (WSDM'22)*. Virtual Event AZ USA: ACM, Feb. 2022, pp. 372–380.

[28] J. Wang, L. Chen, L. Li, and X. Wu, "BiTTM: A Core Biterms-based Topic Model for Targeted Analysis," *Applied Sciences*, vol. 11, no. 21, pp. 1–22, Oct. 2021.

[29] J. Jagarlamudi, H. Daumé III, and R. Udupa, "Incorporating lexical priors into topic models," in *Proceedings of the 13th Conference of the European Chapter of the Association for Computational Linguistics*. Avignon, France: Association for Computational Linguistics (ACL), Apr. 2012, pp. 204–213.

[30] Y. Feng, J. Feng, and Y. Rao, "Reward-Modulated Adversarial Topic Modeling," in *Proceedings of the 25th International Conference on Database Systems for Advanced Applications (DASFAA)*, ser. Lecture Notes in Computer Science (LNCS), Y. Nah *et al.*, Eds. Jeju, South Korea: Springer International Publishing, Sep. 2020, pp. 689–697.

[31] M. Tushev, F. Ebrahimi, and A. Mahmoud, "Domain-specific analysis of mobile app reviews using Keyword-Assisted Topic Models," in *Proceedings of the 44th International Conference on Software Engineering (ICSE '22)*. Pittsburgh Pennsylvania: ACM, May 2022, pp. 762–773.

[32] N. Amat-Lefort and S. J. Barnes, "Towards more convenient services: A text analytics approach to understanding service inconveniences in digital platforms," in *Proceedings of the 56th Hawaii International Conference on System Science (HICSS)*. Honolulu, Hawaii, USA: ScholarSpace, Jan. 2023, pp. 1346–1355.

[33] M. Spranger, F. Heinke, L. Appelt, M. Puder, and D. Labudde, "MoNA: Automated identification of evidence in forensic short messages," *International Journal on Advances in Security*, vol. 9, no. 1 & 2, pp. 14–24, Aug. 2016.

[34] J. Felser, J. Xi, C. Demus, D. Labudde, and M. Spranger, "Recommendation of query terms for colloquial texts in forensic text analysis," in *Proceedings of the International Workshop On Digital Forensics (IWDF)*. Hamburg, Germany: Gesellschaft für Informatik, Bonn, Sep. 2022, pp. 35–47.

[35] J. Riesa and I. Giuliani, "Compact Language Detector," Mountain View, California, United States, Aug. 2023, https://zenodo.org/records/7670098.

[36] J. Riesa, "Compact Language Detector," Mountain View, California, United States, Aug. 2023, https://github.com/CLD2Owners/cld2.

[37] I. Vayansky and S. A. P. Kumar, "A review of topic modeling methods," *Information Systems*, vol. 94, pp. 1–30, Dec. 2020.

[38] R. Churchill and L. Singh, "textPrep: A text preprocessing toolkit for Topic Modeling on Social Media Data," in *Proceedings of the 10th International Conference on Data Science, Technology and Applications (DATA 2021)*. Online Streaming: SCITEPRESS, Jan. 2021, pp. 60–70.

[39] G. Diaz, "Stopwords ISO," https://github.com/stopwords-iso/stopwords-iso, Aug. 2023.

[40] Lingolia Deutsch, "The 50 most important verbs in German (in German)," https://deutsch.lingolia.com/de/50-verben-deutsch, Oct. 2023.

[41] H. Schmid, "Probabilistic part-of-speech tagging using decision trees," in *Proceedings of International Conference on New Methods in Language Processing*. Manchester, UK: Routledge, 1994, pp. 154–164.

[42] ——, "Improvements In part-of-speech tagging with an application to German," in *Natural Language Processing Using Very Large Corpora*, ser. Text, Speech and Language Technology (TLTB), S. Armstrong *et al.*, Eds. Dordrecht, Netherlands: Kluwer Academic Publishers, 1995, no. 11, pp. 13–25.

[43] L. Hickman, S. Thapa, L. Tay, M. Cao, and P. Srinivasan, "Text preprocessing for text mining in organizational research: Review and recommendations," *Organizational Research Methods*, vol. 25, no. 1, pp. 114–146, Jan. 2022.

[44] K. W. Church and P. Hanks, "Word association norms, mutual information, and lexicography," in *Proceedings of the 27th Annual Meeting on Association for Computational Linguistics*, vol. 16. Vancouver, British Columbia, Canada: Association for Computational Linguistics (ACL), Jun. 1989, pp. 76–83.

[45] T. L. Griffiths and M. Steyvers, "Finding scientific topics," *Proceedings of the National Academy of Sciences*, vol. 101, no. 1, pp. 5228–5235, Apr. 2004.

[46] R. Churchill and L. Singh, "Percolation-based topic modeling for tweets," in *Proceedings of the 9th KDD Workshop on Issues of Sentiment Discovery and Opinion Mining (WISDOM'20)*. San Diego, USA: Association for Computing Machinery (ACM), Aug. 2020, pp. 1–8.

[47] A. Joulin, E. Grave, P. Bojanowski, and T. Mikolov, "Bag of Tricks for Efficient Text Classification," in *Proceedings of the 15th Conference of the European Chapter of the Association for Computational Linguistics*, vol. 2. Valencia, Spain: Association for Computational Linguistics, Apr. 2017, pp. 427–431.

[48] N. Kratzke, "Monthly Samples of German Tweets," Dec. 2021, https://zenodo.org/records/7670098.

[49] W. X. Zhao *et al.*, "Comparing Twitter and traditional media using Topic Models," in *Proceedings of the 33rd European Conference on IR Research (ECIR)*, ser. Lecture Notes in Computer Science (LNCS), P. Clough *et al.*, Eds. Berlin, Heidelberg: Springer Science+Business, Apr. 2011, pp. 338–349.

[50] S. M. Ali and S. D. Silvey, "A General Class of Coefficients of Divergence of One Distribution from Another," *Journal of the Royal Statistical Society*, vol. 28, no. 1, pp. 131–142, Jan. 1966.

[51] X. Li, A. Zhang, C. Li, J. Ouyang, and Y. Cai, "Exploring coherent topics by topic modeling with term weighting," *Information Processing & Management*, vol. 54, no. 6, pp. 1345–1358, Jun. 2018.

Comparison of 2D Virtual Learning Environments with Classic Video Conferencing Systems for Tertiary Education

Gerhard Hube, Kevin Pfeffel, Nicholas H. Müller
Faculty of Economics and Business Administration and
Faculty of Computer Science and Business Information Systems
Technical University of Applied Sciences Würzburg-Schweinfurt
Würzburg, Germany
e-mail: gerhard.hube@thws.de
e-mail: kevin.pfeffel@thws.de
e-mail: nicholas.mueller@thws.de

***Abstract*— This work is a follow-up to our previous study "2D Virtual Learning Environments for Tertiary Education", which was carried out in 2022. The main focus was to analyze the suitability of a 2D Virtual Learning Environment (VLE) for tertiary education using the desktop based 2D immersive environment 'gather.town'. The study was conducted with a selected course of a Master's program at the Technical University of Applied Sciences Würzburg-Schweinfurt over one semester. Accompanying the course, subjects were asked to complete the Online Learning Environment Survey (OLLES) questionnaire weekly for analysis, and additional qualitative interviews were conducted afterwards. The descriptive analysis suggests that the immersive 2D environment used is holistically suitable as a learning environment in the tertiary sector, due to high and very high values for presence, participation, collaboration and active learning. For this paper, two seminars were conducted using Virtual Learning Environments, one of them in 'gather.town' and the other in 'Zoom'. In addition to the OLLES questionnaire and the qualitative interviews, the Igroup Presence Questionnaire (IPQ) was also queried. Additionally, the exam grades were also collected as a performance measure. This made it possible to compare the different learning environments. When comparing the questionnaires, only some dimensions showed a difference between Virtual 2D Learning Environments and Classic Video Conferencing Systems. In contrast, with exam grades, subjects were found to perform better with Virtual 2D Learning Environments than with Classic Video Conferencing Systems.**

Keywords-Virtual Learning Environments; Online Teaching; Tertiary Education; 2D Environments; Desktop Virtual Reality; Zoom; gather.town.

I. INTRODUCTION

This contribution is based on the first step of the study published in 2022 in the International Journal on Advances in Systems and Measurements, vol. 15, no. 3 & 4 with the title "2D Virtual Learning Environments for Tertiary Education" [1]. As the main result of the study, the high scores of the OLLES [2] questionnaire can be mentioned. In connection with the interviews, it can be said that an Immersive 2D Environment can be used holistically as a form of teaching and has advantages over Classic Video Transmission Tools. As a practical implication, it can be deduced that the use of Virtual Learning Environments in the tertiary sector, on the one hand, can be relatively easily deployed with existing software solutions and, on the other hand, are also well received and therefore offer benefits for students.

Nevertheless, this first study was only an overview of the use of an immersive 2D environment as a learning tool within tertiary education. Group comparisons with other teaching formats were not possible. Therefore, this is the goal for this research. Here, the same teaching unit is being tested again in gather.town and at the same time another teaching unit is being tested in Zoom. Again, the OLLES questionnaire is used and additionally the Igroup Presence Questionnaire (IPQ) [3]. The IPQ is a scale for measuring the sense of presence experienced in a Virtual Environment (VE). The qualitative interviews were also be used again for data collection. In Figure 1, there is an overview of the timeline and the different learning environments and measuring instruments.

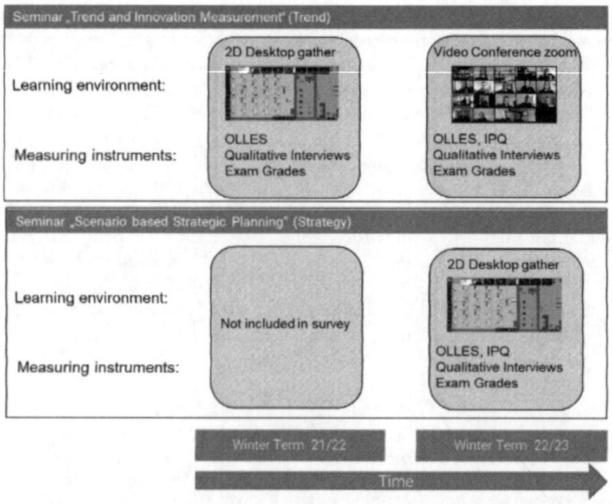

Figure 1. Overview of timeline, seminars, learning environments and measuring instruments for the study.

With the results of the different seminars and learnings environments, a comparison of the two forms of teaching can be made.

The definitions and explanations for the basic terms, as well as the overview of studies and related works about Virtual Learning Environments (VLE) and Virtual Reality (VR) in higher education were made in the study from 2022 [1].

Additional, to the literature review from our study in 2022 [1], there were several new studies published about educational online learning, especially with Learning Management Systems (LMS) like Moodle and Video Conference Systems, especially Zoom [4] - [8]. In addition, many studies about the phenomenon of "Zoom fatigue" were published [9] - [13] which underlines the need for alternative online Learning Environments like low immersive Desktop Environments. Probably because of this need, several studies appeared with gather.town as one example for this kind of Virtual Environment. Lo and Song [14] performed a review of the empirical studies in gather.town and revealed that there is still a lack in studies besides computer science courses, the examination of student's behavior and learning achievements. The authors also found out, that most of the studies had only a short duration and suggest studies with a longer duration. With this study, we evaluate Virtual Learning Environments over several semesters in the context of seminars, not in computer science, but in business administration. We also include exam grades for learning outcomes. With these conditions, we fulfill some of the requirements for further research. To summarize, so far we have looked descriptively at the suitability of 2D Virtual Learning Environments for tertiary education and now we want to test this statistically by means of a first comparison of 2D Virtual Learning Environments and Classic Video Conferencing Systems.

Following in Section 2, we explain the method used. Section 3 resumes the results, which are then discussed in detail in Section 4 with some limitations. Section 5 forms the end of the paper and contains the conclusion with the main results and future studies.

II. METHOD

In the following, we present the immersive learning environment gather.town, in which the course took place, and the measuring instruments OLLES and IPQ, which were used for the assessment. In addition, qualitative interviews were subsequently conducted with some of the subjects, which will also be presented here.

A. *Immersive 2D environment gather.town*

The software gather.town [15] was used as an immersive 2D environment. This is a web conferencing software, which allows to create a complete virtual replica of the teaching building. Within this virtual space, users can move around using avatars and interact with each other and their environment, similar to real life. If the avatars now walk around in the Virtual Environment and then meet each other at a certain distance, the camera and the microphone of the computers are automatically switched on, and the users have the opportunity to communicate. The graphical user interface is quite simple and it does not demand any special requirements to run on a variety of computers. In preparation, the entire real seminar building was recreated in the gather.town environment and the following Virtual Environment settings and software features were used:

The podium is the classic teaching situation, as shown in Figure 2. Within the gather.town environment, all students and the tutor are in one large room. The tutor stands in front at the lectern, while the students take their places at the tables. All students can see, hear and, of course, communicate with each other via camera and microphone. It is possible to share the screen to provide lecture slides or other content to all participants in the plenum area. In this way, the tutor can use lecture slides in addition to a verbal execution of the learning topic, as they would be used in a real teaching situation.

We refer to our publication in 2022 [1] for explanation of the features "Workshop", "Whiteboard", "Break Rooms" with games and yoga room, and "Interactive elements".

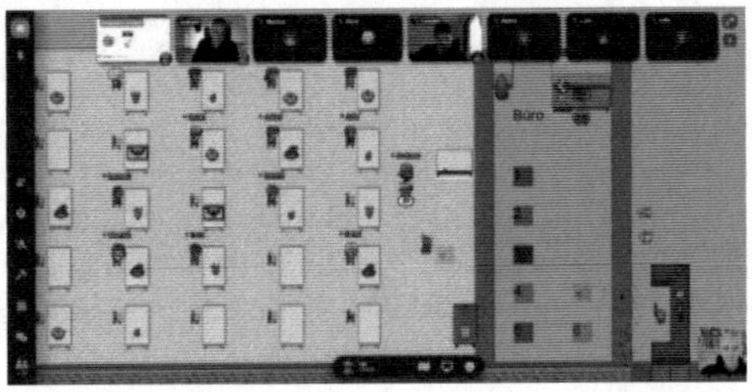

Figure 2. This is the podium. A classic teaching situation in a shared space is shown.

B. *Video conference tool Zoom*

Zoom is one of the Classic Video Conferencing Tools with quite wide spread usage for education, especially during the COVID-19 pandemic, but also after reopening universities in 2021 [4] [16]. With Zoom, it is possible for one or more people to interact through chat messages, video based visual communication, and group work [17]. Besides the communication in the whole group of participants, it is also possible to create subgroups (Break out rooms) for group work or group discussions. There is also the possibility to share the screen with other participants, to do little surveys and to use a whiteboard. The classic appearance is the monitor full of video tiles with the participants of the Zoom meeting, as shown in Figure 3.

Figure 3. Video tiles on monitor while classical Zoom video conference.

C. Measuring instrument

The OLLES questionnaire in its modified 35-item form was used as the measurement instrument [2]. The OLLES questionnaire is a web-based survey instrument for use in online learning environments in tertiary education. In this context, the OLLES questionnaire provides inferences about students' perceptions of interaction opportunities within an online environment in terms of economy and efficiency. The dimensions of the OLLES are Student Collaboration (SC), Computer Competence (CC), Active Learning (AL), Tutor Support (TS), Information Design and Appeal (IDA), Material Environment (ME), and Reflective Thinking (RT). In addition, questions about general computer use and Internet use were also recorded. All items were measured on a 5-point Likert scale [18].

The IPQ [3] was also used. The IPQ is a scale for measuring the sense of presence experienced in a Virtual Environment. Here, the sense of presence is understood as the subjective sense of being in a Virtual Environment. Also, the igroup.org project consortium states that: "the sense of presence can be separated from the ability of a technology to immerse a user. While this immersion is a variable of the technology and can be described objectively, presence is a variable of a user's experience. Therefore, we obtain measures of the sense of presence from subjective rating scales." The IPQ has three subscales and one additional general item not belonging to a subscale. The three subscales are Spatial Presence (the sense of being physically present in the VE), Involvement (measuring the attention devoted to the VE and the involvement experienced) and Experienced Realism (measuring the subjective experience of realism in the VE). There is also a general item that assesses the general "sense of being there". This item has high loadings on all three factors, with an especially strong loading on Spatial Presence. The original questionnaire was constructed in German, so we used this one, since the subjects are German native speakers. All items were measured on a 7-point Likert scale with a range from 0 to 6 [18].

For the qualitative interviews, a separate questionnaire was developed, which can be viewed in full in our previous paper [1] where the same questionnaire was used. First, an introductory question was asked in order to lead the test persons into the interview situation in a relaxed manner and to check whether they could still remember the seminar well within the Virtual Learning Environment. Building on this, at least one question was asked about each dimension of the OLLES to develop a deeper understanding of why one of the dimensions had performed well or poorly. In addition, the questions of the questionnaire still investigate whether the subjects prefer face-to-face classes, a Virtual Learning Environment such as gather.town or Classic Video Conferencing Software such as Zoom and why this is so. Finally, the questionnaire examines whether the Virtual Learning Environment gather.town was also used outside the actual seminar and, if so, for what other purposes. In addition, questions are asked about the highlights and shortcomings of the software used.

Furthermore, exam grades were collected as a form of performance measure.

D. Experimental procedure

Even before the first seminar, all test persons were familiarized with the gather.town environment resp. the Zoom environment. In particular, the basic functions were tested, so that everybody knows them and can use them independently. In addition, the OLLES questionnaire was introduced, since this was used in its original English language, but the test persons were not native English speakers.

Both seminars were held over 5 days each, with one teaching session starting in the early afternoon and lasting 5-6 school lessons each. Both seminars were held exclusively in their respective VE used. There were a total of two time measurement points, one after the first seminar and one after the last seminar. Both questionnaires were completed online directly after the seminar.

The qualitative interviews were collected a few days after the last seminar, but they were conducted within gather.town resp. Zoom. An appointment was made with a respondent within gather.town resp. Zoom, where the interview was conducted and the audio track was recorded. The audio track was then transcribed, analyzed and interpreted.

E. Sample

All data were collected at the Technical University of Applied Sciences Würzburg-Schweinfurt within the seminars "Scenario Based Strategic Planning" (from here just "Strategy") and "Trend Analysis and Innovation Measurement" (from here just "Trend") of the master study program "Integrated Innovation Management". The seminar "Strategy" was held in gather.town and the seminar "Trend" was held in Zoom, as shown in Figure 1.

For the seminar Strategy, a total of 19 subjects participated. However, only 16 subjects completed the questionnaires. This leaves n = 16 valid subjects for the final analysis. The average age of the subjects is 25.19 years, with a minimum of 22 years and a maximum of 33 years. Of the n = 16 subjects, 5 are female (31.3 %) and 11 are male (68,7 %). In addition, it must be noted that only 11 subjects could be used for the comparison of the two measurement points, since only these 11 subjects completely filled out the two questionnaires. For the remaining statistics, however, all 16 subjects can be used. In addition, for a performance comparison in the form of the scores, the scores of all 19 subjects of the seminar were used. Five randomly selected subjects were used for the qualitative interviews. Afterwards, it was checked to what extent the answers of the subjects overlapped or whether new insights could still be gained with further surveys, but a feeling of saturation set in. Therefore, n = 5 interviews were considered sufficient. Of the n = 5 subjects, 3 are female and 2 are male.

For the seminar Trend, a total of 19 subjects participated. However, only 17 subjects completed the questionnaires. This leaves n = 17 valid subjects for the final analysis. The average age of the subjects is 25.06 years, with a minimum of 22 years and a maximum of 33 years. Of the n = 17 subjects, 6 are female (35.3 %) and 11 are male (64.7 %). In addition, it must be noted that only 10 subjects could be used for the comparison of the two measurement points, since only these 10 subjects completely filled out the two questionnaires. For the remaining statistics, however, all 17 subjects can be used. For a performance comparison in the form of the scores, the scores of all 19 subjects of the seminar were used.

Four randomly selected subjects were used for the qualitative interviews. Afterwards, it was checked to what extent the answers of the subjects overlapped or whether new insights could still be gained with further surveys, but a feeling of saturation set in. Therefore, n = 4 interviews were considered sufficient. Of the n = 4 subjects, 2 are female and 2 are male.

III. Results

The results section is divided into different areas. First, there is a statistical part in which the time measurement points of the individual subjects are compared to see if there is a difference between the first time measurement point after the first seminar unit and the last time measurement point at the end of all seminar units. This is complemented by a purely descriptive part, in which the mean values of the OLLES and IPQ questionnaires are considered. Thereafter is the part in which the results of the qualitative interviews are presented. Both of these parts are again subdivided into the individual seminars. Lastly, there is a statistical part. In this part, first there are group comparisons related to the values of the OLLES and IPQ questionnaires. The data from our previous paper [1] will also be used. Finally, there is a group comparison of the exam grades as a performance measure.

A. *Results for "Strategy" using gather.town*

First, the Wilcoxon test will be used to examine whether there are differences in the OLLES test between the individual time measurement points and thus whether there was a change in the evaluation with regard to the repetition of the use of gather.town.

Two time measurement points were not available for all 16 subjects, therefore the following Wilcoxon test was only calculated with n = 11 complete subjects.

The Wilcoxon test showed that there was no difference between time measurement point 1 and time measurement point 2 regarding the OLLES questionnaire.

Next, using the Wilcoxon test will be used to examine whether there are differences in the IPQ test between the individual time measurement points and thus whether there was a change in the evaluation with regard to the repetition of the use of the gather.town environment.

There was a significant difference of the variable G (General Presence). The statistic test is $z = -2.850$ and the associated significance value is $p = .002$. Thus, the difference is significant: the central tendencies of the two time measurement points differ (Asymptotic Wilcoxon test: $z = -2.85$, $p = .002$, $n = 11$).

For the other scales, there was no significant difference between time measurement point 1 and time measurement point 2.

The next step is a descriptive analysis of the mean value variables of both time measurement points together. This also includes all measured values regardless of whether there were only one or two time measurement points for a subject.

In terms of computer use, it was found that all subjects use their computers daily or at least several times a week. In the case of Internet use, it was found that all subjects use the Internet on a daily basis.

A test for normal distribution of the OLLES dimensions revealed that the dimensions Student Collaboration (SC), Information Design and Appeal (IDA), Material Environment (ME), and Reflective Thinking (RT) are normally distributed and the dimensions Computer Competence (CC), Active Learning (AL), and Tutor Support (TS) are not normally distributed. Those descriptive values can be seen in Table 1.

A test for normal distribution for the dimensions of the IPQ revealed that the General Presence (G), Spatial Presence (SP), and Involvement (INV) variables were normally distributed, and the Experienced Realism (REAL) variable was not normally distributed. Those descriptive values can be seen in Table 2.

Next are the results of the qualitative questionnaire. A complete overview of the guideline interview can be found in our previous paper [1] and can be referred to for better understanding. Question 1 revealed that all subjects could still remember the seminar and the use of gather.town well to very well. Question 2 revealed that cooperation within gather.town was rated as sufficient to good. Walking around and interaction opportunities were rated positively. Beyond that, however, additional tools for collaborative workshops like, e.g., Miro [19] outside from the gather.town environment were more likely to be used. Nevertheless, further inquiry revealed that most subjects indicated that there was enough opportunity for successful collaboration. However, some also said that it was somewhat difficult for them to assess this, since they had only used a few functions themselves. Question 3 showed that although there were sometimes technical problems in using gather.town, as an example the browser compatibility, the use itself was always understandable and simple and therefore it did not represent a technical hurdle. Question 4 showed mixed responses. Some subjects found gather.town motivating because it has a certain gaming character and thus offers more functions and possibilities than Zoom, for example. On the other hand, however, it was also increasingly noted that concentration suffers in online seminars and a general demotivation takes place, since the exchange is missing and the classroom is generally preferred. This was also confirmed by the query. Walking around independently in gather.town is more motivating than Classic Video Conferencing Tools, but more demotivating than a seminar in a real classroom. Question 5 and the related query revealed that the tutor's contact and accessibility was good and enough opportunities were given for feedback, and further questions were answered quickly. Based on question 6, it was found that the learning materials were perceived in a very mixed way. However, the query showed that the learning environment apart from the learning materials was perceived as very interesting and appealing. Especially the "Pokémon charm" was very appealing and cute. Question 7 showed that the test persons assess their learning success minimally better

TABLE I. OLLES – STRATEGY IN GATHER.TOWN

Descriptive Analysis					
Dimension	*Mean Value*	*Standard Error of the Mean*	*Standard Deviation*	*Minimum Value*	*Maximum Value*
Student Collaboartion (SC)	3.33	0.22	0.87	1.60	4.60
Computer Competence (CC)	4.71	0.12	0.48	3.50	5.00
Active Learning (AL)	3.39	0.15	0.58	2.60	4.50
Tutor Support (TS)	3.92	0.11	0.43	3.40	5.00
Information Design and Appeal (IDA)	3.49	0.13	0.52	2.70	4.50
Material Environment (ME)	4.00	0.14	0.57	3.00	5.00
Reflective Thinking (RT)	3.13	0.23	0.57	3.00	5.00

TABLE II. IPQ – STRATEGY IN GATHER.TOWN

Descriptive Analysis					
Dimension	*Mean Value*	*Standard Error of the Mean*	*Standard Deviation*	*Minimum Value*	*Maximum Value*
General Presence (G)	1.69	0.34	1.38	0.00	4.50
Spatial Presence (SP)	2.69	0.18	0.70	1.40	3.60
Involvement (INV)	2.04	0.11	0.43	1.38	2.88
Experienced Realism (REAL)	1.78	0.11	0.45	1.25	2.75

than with Classic Video Conferencing Tools, however, they generally assess their learning success online lower than in presence, even if the test persons think that this does not necessarily have an effect on the grades, nevertheless felt on the knowledge that remains at the end. Question 8 further confirmed that subjects prefer gather.town over Classic Video Conferencing Tools like Zoom because it offers more interaction options, facilitates individual conversations, it is very easy to log in, and is generally more dynamic. However, there was also one respondent who preferred Zoom simply out of habit. Question 9 then went on to confirm that all subjects preferred face-to-face lectures. The main reasons for this are that one can interact best with each other, there is also a physical exchange with people, it is more personal and one is less distracted than at home. Question 10 showed that some subjects also used gather.town outside of the lecture for quick communication for projects, or in the work context. However, some did not continue to use it. Finally, question 11 and the two follow-up questions showed that it would be better to integrate additional tools, but gather.town was generally well received due to the diversity as well as physical activation (e.g. yoga) and provides a lot of potential for creative things. Isolated connection problems and browser incompatibility were mentioned as negative points.

B. Results for "Trend" using Zoom

First, the Wilcoxon test will be used to examine whether there are differences in the OLLES test between the individual time measurement points and thus whether there was a change in the evaluation with regard to the repetition of the use of Zoom.

Two time measurement points were not available for all 17 subjects, therefore, the following Wilcoxon test was only calculated with n = 10 complete subjects.

The Wilcoxon test showed that there was no difference between time measurement point 1 and time measurement point 2 regarding the OLLES questionnaire.

Next, using the Wilcoxon test will be used to examine whether there are differences in the IPQ test between the individual time measurement points and thus whether there was a change in the evaluation with regard to the repetition of the use of the Zoom.

The Wilcoxon test showed that there was no difference between time measurement point 1 and time measurement point 2 regarding the IPQ.

The next step is a descriptive analysis of the mean value variables of both time measurement points together. This also includes all measured values regardless of whether there were only one or two time measurement points for a subject.

In terms of computer use, it was found that all subjects use their computers daily or at least several times a week. In the case of Internet use, it was found that all subjects use the Internet on a daily basis.

A test for normal distribution of the OLLES dimensions revealed that the dimensions Student Collaboration (SC), Information Design and Appeal (IDA), Material Environment

(ME), and Reflective Thinking (RT) are normally distributed and the dimensions Computer Competence (CC), Active Learning (AL), and Tutor Support (TS) are not normally distributed. Those descriptive values can be seen in Table 3.

A test for normal distribution for the dimensions of the IPQ revealed that the General Presence (G), Spatial Presence (SP), and Involvement (INV) variables were normally distributed, and the Experienced Realism (REAL) variable was not normally distributed. Those descriptive values can be seen in Table 4.

Next are the results of the qualitative questionnaire. A complete overview of the guideline interview can be found in our previous paper [1] and can be referred to for better understanding. Question 1 revealed that all subjects could still remember the seminar and the use of Zoom well to very well. Question 2 revealed that cooperation within Zoom was rated as sufficient to good. Further inquiry revealed that most subjects indicated that there was enough opportunity for successful collaboration. However, there were problems with collaboration due to a lack of a personal level, which was especially exacerbated by cameras being turned off. Question 3 showed that there were no technical problems in using Zoom and the use itself was always understandable and simple. Question 4 revealed that the use of Zoom mostly demotivated the subjects. One respondent, however, stated that he was more motivated because of the time saved. Time saving was more often mentioned as a positive point while less involvement and more distraction at home were mentioned as negative points. One respondent therefore also felt that the sense of learning together is lost somewhere. Question 5 and the related query revealed that the tutor's contact and accessibility was good and enough opportunities were given for feedback, and further questions were answered quickly. Based on question 6, it was found that the learning materials were perceived in a very mixed way. However, the query showed that the learning environment apart from the learning materials was perceived as very neutral, sometimes even boring, but sufficient to fulfill the purpose. Question 7 showed that the test persons assess their learning success much worse than in presence. Only one respondent stated that he might have even better learning success than in presence, because this allowed him to focus exclusively on the learning content. Based on question 8, a mixed opinion emerged. Some subjects prefer Zoom because Zoom contains fewer distractions from game-like elements. Exactly the opposite, some subjects prefer gather.town because of playful elements, as these promote interpersonal relationships and group work. It was often said that the more interactive and intensive the group work, the more likely they would choose gather.town, but Zoom is perfectly adequate for normal lectures. Question 9 then went on to confirm that most subjects preferred face-to-face lectures. The main reasons for this are that it is more

TABLE III. OLLES - TREND IN ZOOM

Descriptive Analysis					
Dimension	***Mean Value***	***Standard Error of the Mean***	***Standard Deviation***	***Minimum Value***	***Maximum Value***
Student Collaboartion (SC)	3.29	0.20	0.82	1.00	4.40
Computer Competence (CC)	4.69	0.13	0.54	3.00	5.00
Active Learning (AL)	2.96	0.15	0.63	2.00	4.00
Tutor Support (TS)	3.86	0.11	0.43	3.00	4.60
Information Design and Appeal (IDA)	3.10	0.15	0.64	1.60	3.80
Material Environment (ME)	3.75	0.17	0.72	1.40	4.50
Reflective Thinking (RT)	3.18	0.23	0.96	1.20	4.90

TABLE IV. IPQ - TREND IN ZOOM

Descriptive Analysis					
Dimension	***Mean Value***	***Standard Error of the Mean***	***Standard Deviation***	***Minimum Value***	***Maximum Value***
General Presence (G)	0.82	0.32	1.31	0.00	4.00
Spatial Presence (SP)	2.45	0.19	0.78	1.20	4.00
Involvement (INV)	1.87	0.12	0.49	1.50	3.50
Experienced Realism (REAL)	1.86	0.12	0.49	1.38	3.00

personal, and they prefer the physical exchange with people before and after a lecture. They can also pay more attention when they are present, and they are less likely to be distracted. However, one respondent also prefers Zoom because of the time and cost savings in particular. Question 10 showed that some subjects also used Zoom outside of the lecture for projects, or in the work context. Others used it only during the time of the COVID-19 pandemic. Finally, question 11 and the two follow-up questions showed that Zoom is simple, runs stably and the important functions are well integrated. However, it is easier to sit back and turn off the cameras, and this means that the group loses a lot.

C. Group Comparisons

The following is a comparison of all three seminars conducted to date. These are the seminar Trend held in gather.town [1], the seminar Strategy held in gather.town and the seminar Trend held in Zoom. For an overview, see Figure 1. First, the results of the OLLES and the IPQ questionnaire are compared. Afterwards, the exam grades are compared as a performance measure.

First, the seminar Trend (gather.town) was tested with the seminar Strategy (gather.town). In total, the data of 32 subjects are compared. There are 16 from Trend (gather.town) and 16 from Strategy (gather.town). The Mann-Whitney U test showed no significance for any variable. The computer and Internet variables remained without significant difference, as did the OLLES variables. The IPQ could not be tested here, because no survey of the IPQ was conducted for the seminar Trend (gather.town).

Second, the seminar Trend (gather.town) was tested with the seminar Trend (Zoom). In total, 33 subjects are compared. There are 16 from Trend (gather.town) and 17 from Trend (Zoom). Here, the IPQ also could not be tested. The Mann-Whitney U test showed a significant difference in the Active Learning (AL) and Information Design and Appeal (IDA) variables of the OLLES.

Subjects in the gather.town learning environment perceive Active Learning ($Mdn = 3.6$) better than subjects in the Zoom learning environment ($Mdn = 3.0$), asymptotic Mann-Whitney U test: $U = 57.000$, $p = .004$. Cohen's effect size is $r = .50$, corresponding to a strong effect.

Subjects in the gather.town learning environment perceive the Information Design and Appeal ($Mdn = 3.6$) better than subjects in the Zoom learning environment ($Mdn = 3.2$), asymptotic Mann-Whitney U test: $U = 57.000$, $p = .004$. Cohen's effect size is $r = .50$, corresponding to a strong effect.

Last, the seminar Strategy (gather.town) was tested with the seminar Trend (Zoom). In total 33 subjects are compared. There are 16 from Strategy (gather.town) and 17 from Trend (Zoom). The Mann-Whitney U test showed only a significant difference in the General Presence (G) variable of the IPQ.

Subjects in the gather.town learning environment perceived General Presence ($Mdn = 1.25$) better than subjects in the Zoom learning environment ($Mdn = .00$), asymptotic Mann-Whitney U test: $U = 73.000$, $p = .019$. Cohen's effect size is $r = .41$, corresponding to a medium effect.

When comparing grades, the seminar Trend (gather.town) is compared with the seminar Trend (Zoom) first. In total 36 subjects are compared. There are 17 from Trend (gather.town) and 19 from Trend (Zoom). The Mann-Whitney U test showed a significant difference.

Subjects in the gather.town learning environment have better grades ($Mdn = 1.7$, low values represent better grades) than subjects in the Zoom learning environment ($Mdn = 1.9$), asymptotic Mann-Whitney U test: $U = 90.000$, $p = .021$. Cohen's effect size is $r = .38$, corresponding to a medium effect.

IV. Discussion

In the dimensions of computer use and Internet use, the subjects indicated that they use this on a daily basis. In addition, the gather.town environment as well as the Zoom environment and all basic functions were sufficiently explained before the start of the study. Thus, we assume that there were no poor ratings for the environments due to possible lack of technical skills.

The test whether there were differences between different time measurement points showed the following results. With the Strategy seminar and the OLLES questionnaire there was no difference in the time measurement points and with the IPQ, there was a difference in scale G (General Presence). The difference in scale G could be explained by the fact that it consists of only one question item and therefore reacts much more strongly to minimal deviations. At the seminar Trend, no significant difference was found between the two time measurement points for either the OLLES or the IPQ. Although a meta-study by Merchant et al. [20] found small effects in simulation studies in terms of number of sessions, these were measures of learning outcome and not an assessment of the immersive environment as in this study. In our previous paper [1], there were also no significant differences at several different time measurement points. Therefore, it can be assumed that it is sufficient to query the questionnaires once.

If one compares the statements of the qualitative questionnaires, it becomes clear that the same statements can be found repeatedly. Almost all subjects showed a hierarchy in their preferred choice of teaching styles. Classroom teaching is clearly preferred. This is followed by the use of 2D Virtual Environments. Classic Video Conferencing Systems are least preferred. If we take a closer look at this hierarchy, we can see that the more opportunities for interaction and the more personal a teaching style is, the more it is preferred. Subjects consistently said they preferred gather.town over Zoom because they had more human proximity and also more opportunities to interact with other students. Nevertheless, ideally, they would like face-to-face teaching. This statement seems to be even more prevalent after the COVID-19 pandemic. However, it also became clear that simple lectures could be replaced more easily by online teaching than seminars in which the focus is on working together.

The group comparisons showed that a comparison of two different seminars with different subjects in gather.town nevertheless resulted in equal evaluations of the Virtual Learning Environment regarding the OLLES questionnaire. Therefore, stable valuations can be assumed here. A comparison of the same seminar with different Virtual

Learning Environments showed that gather.town scored significantly higher on the Active Learning (AL) and Information Design and Appeal (IDA) dimensions of the OLLES questionnaire than Zoom. However, this result could not be repeated for different seminars and different Virtual Learning Environments. There was a significant difference in the G scale of the IPQ, with gather.town showing a higher general presence than Zoom. The Active Learning (AL) dimension of the OLLES specifically asks about the motivation created, as well as the feedback received through the activities or the teaching unit within the environment itself. Again, various studies already showed that motivation [21] - [25] is a crucial factor in the use of VLE's. That there was increased motivation was confirmed by the interviews. The motivation arose primarily through increased interactivity. For the test persons, it was clearly more motivating to walk through the Virtual Environment by moving the avatar and not just to sit in front of the laptop. This also led to the environment being perceived as very varied. The dimension Information Design and Appeal (IDA) of the OLLES asks in particular how creative and original presented teaching materials are and whether graphics used are helpful and visually appealing. This mainly refers to the teaching slides presented as if they were in a presentation. Since the same learning materials were used here, this difference is difficult to explain. It is possible that the actual learning environment was included in the evaluation and not just the learning materials. Perhaps this double assessment was due to the fact that, in this particular case, it was not always clear to the subjects what the individual question items referred to in this dimension. The scale G (General Presence) of the IPQ asks solely about the sense of being there. This feeling could not be created at all with Zoom and at least minimally with gather.town. However, only in one of the two tests with different seminars. Whether there is an influence of the seminar on the evaluation of a Virtual Learning Environment is difficult to say. Nevertheless, the results found could also be due to a still small sample size. Statistically, however, the difference between the two Virtual Learning Environments turned out to be smaller than the qualitative interviews suggested. In the end, only partially significant differences in the evaluation could be found and these could not be repeated.

Looking at the exam grades, a significant difference was found between the Virtual Learning Environments used. When using the gather.town environment, the subjects had better grades than using the Zoom environment. This is a medium effect. Although there was not much difference in the assessment of Virtual Learning Environments, it does seem to have an impact on performance measurement in the form of exam grades. The results also confirmed that it is only possible to compare the same seminars with each other.

V. Conclusion And Future Work

This study shows that, according to the subjects, there is a hierarchy of teaching styles. Classroom teaching is the most popular form. This is due to the direct contact with fellow students, greater motivation and the best possible opportunity for interaction in order to solve tasks in a team and learn together. This is followed by the use of a 2D Virtual Learning Environment. Here, direct contact is much more limited than in face-to-face teaching, but this can be partially replaced by the use of avatars and the resulting interaction possibilities. Thus, the test participants are also motivated to use the Virtual Learning Environment. The most unpopular are Classic Video Conference Systems. These have the least interaction possibilities and are therefore perceived as demotivating. This hierarchy, especially the preference of face-to-face personal teaching is confirmed by several other studies [26] - [29]. Also the preference for gather.town as 2D Desktop VR to Zoom as Classic Video Conferencing Tool can be explained and

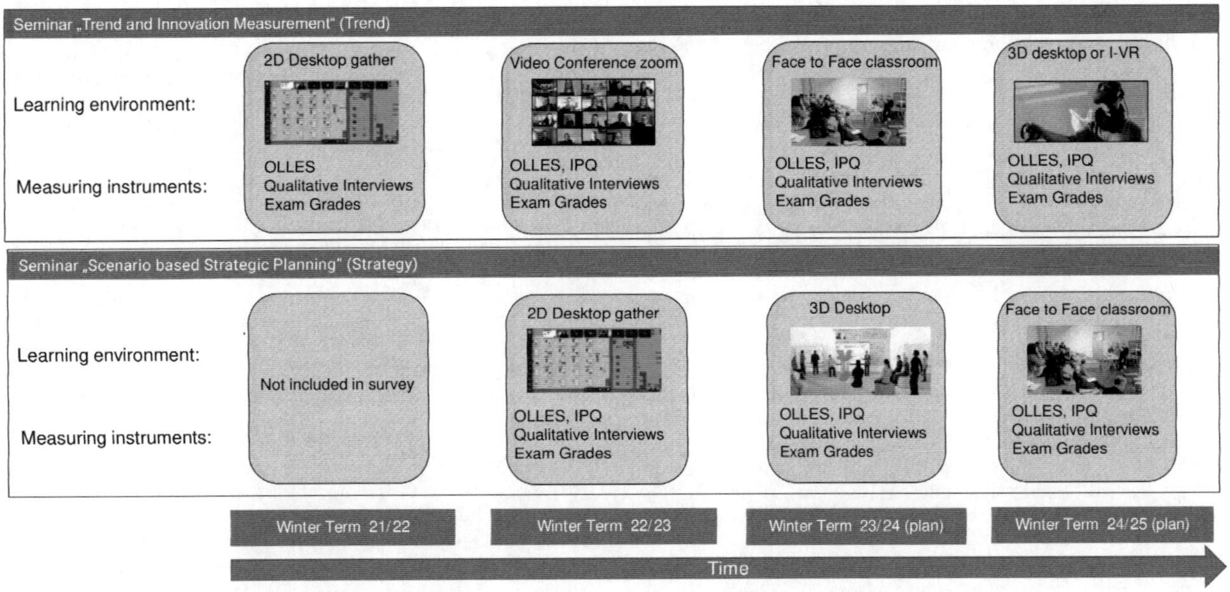

Figure 4. Overview of seminars, learning environments and measuring instruments for finished and planned studies.

confirmed by several studies [30] - [33]. It seems to be important to use VLE that are innovative, social emotional, and engage formal and informal communication, which seems to be better solved within the Virtual 2D Learning Environment gather.town.

In an evaluation of Virtual 2D Learning Environments and Classic Video Conference Systems using the OLLES and IPQ questionnaire, however, this could only be shown for some dimensions or scales. Contrary to the statements of the qualitative interviews, the quantitative evaluation of the two online teaching formats therefore seems to make no or only a very small difference. In contrast, when exam grades were measured as a performance measure, subjects were found to perform better with Virtual 2D Learning Environments than with Classic Video Conference Systems. Thus, the use of 2D Virtual Learning Environments seems to be a better choice than Classic Video Conference Systems for successful online teaching. However, it must also be noted here, that this is a field study and therefore the number of subjects is low. Future work needs to clarify whether face-to-face teaching also leads to the best performance measures. In addition, other online forms of teaching will also be tested. For this purpose, it is initially planned to hold the same seminars as in this study in the next semester once in face-to-face teaching and once in a Virtual 3D Learning Environment. An overview can be seen in Figure 4.

Since it has been found that realism plays an important factor in the evaluation of Virtual Learning Environments, this will also be used to explore which factors contribute to a higher degree of realism. For example, the change from a 2D learning environment to a 3D learning environment with 3D avatars could be an improvement. This could then be seen with a better IPQ rating. In addition, this study will be extended to the application of I-VR environments, as soon as this can be implemented with enough test persons, since sufficient equipment must be available and software must offer all necessary functions. Now, there are many indications that hybrid forms of teaching and learning will be used in the future. Above all, the type of seminar also plays a role. Roughly speaking, the more interactive the seminar, the more opportunities for interaction are required and the more the seminar should tend towards classroom teaching. It also shows that personal contact cannot be replaced and that this provides more motivation for learning. In the end, the goal should always be to provide the best possible teaching and learning experience for all involved.

REFERENCES

[1] G. Hube, K. Pfeffel, and N. H. Müller, "2D Virtual Learning Environments for Tertiary Education" International Journal on Advances in Systems and Measurements, ISSN 1942-261x, vol. 15, no. 3 & 4, pp. 81-92, 2022.

[2] J. Clayton, "Development and Validation of an Instrument for Assessing Online Learning Environments in Tertiary Education: The Online Learning Environment Survey (OLLES)," [Online]. Available from: https://espace.curtin.edu.au/handle/20.500.11937/550 2023.10.10

[3] T. Schubert, F. Friedmann, and H. Regenbrecht, "The experience of presence: Factor analytic insights," Presence, vol. 10, no. 3, pp. 266–281, 2001, doi: 10.1162/105474601300343603.

[4] G. Q. Hu, "Qualitative Analysis of Students' Online Learning Experiences after the University Reopening," Journal of Education, Humanities and Social Sciences, vol. 7, pp. 115–134, Jan. 2023, doi: 10.54097/ehss.v7i.4074.

[5] I. Assaly and U. Atamna, "Who Needs Zoom? Female Arab Students' Perceptions of Face-to-Face Learning and Learning on Zoom," Sustainability, vol. 15, no. 10, 8195, 2023.

[6] N. Kocyigit and F. Yilmaz, "Effects of Zoom Fatigues on Life Satisfaction: A Research on Teachers," [Online]. Available from: https://www.researchgate.net/publication/371970282_EFFECTS_OF_ZOOM_FATIGUE%27S_ON_LIFE_SATISFACTION_A_RESEARCH_ON_TEACHERS 2023.10.10

[7] P. Prasetyo and Z. Abidin, "Zoom Learning Media Relatioship and Interest in Learning with Learning Outcomes Civics," Akademika: Jurnal Teknologi Pendidikan, vol. 12, no. 1, pp. 153-161, 2023. doi: 10.34005/akademika.v12i01.2467

[8] L. Andrade-Arenas, W. W. Reyes Perez, and C. A. Yactayo Arias, "Moodle platform and Zoom videoconference: learning skills in the virtual modality," Indonesian Journal of Electrical Engineering and Computer Science, vol. 31, no. 1, pp. 337-349, 2023, doi: 10.11591/ijeecs.v31.i1.pp337-349.

[9] A. Carțiș, ""Zoom Fatigue" In Higher Education: Videoconferencing Impact On Students' Fatigue," Education Facing Contemporary World Issues - EDU WORLD 2022, vol. 5, pp. 1355-1364, 2023, doi: 10.15405/epes.23045.138.

[10] L. Knox, S. Berzenski, and S. Drew, "Measuring Zoom Fatigue in College Students: Development and Validation of the Meeting Fatigue Scale for Videoconferencing (MFS-V) and the Meeting Fatigue Scale for In-Person (MFS-I)," Media Psychology, Advance online publication, doi: 10.1080/15213269.2023.2204529

[11] A. Ngien and B. Hogan, "The relationship between Zoom use with the camera on and Zoom fatigue: considering self-monitoring and social interaction anxiety," Information Communication & Society, vol. 26, no. 10, pp. 2052-2070, 2023, doi: 10.1080/1369118X.2022.2065214.

[12] G. Fauville, M. Luo, A. C. M. Queiroz, A. Lee, J. N. Bailenson, and J. Hancock, "Video-conferencing usage dynamics and nonverbal mechanisms exacerbate Zoom Fatigue, particularly for women," Computers in Human Behavior Reports, vol. 10, 2023, doi: 10.1016/j.chbr.2023.100271.

[13] H. N. Shoshan and W. Wehrt, "Understanding Zoom Fatigue: A Mixed-Method Approach," Applied Psychology, vol. 71, no. 3, pp. 827-852, 2022, doi: 10.1111/apps.12360.

[14] C. K. Lo and Y. Song, "A Scoping Review of Empirical Studies in Gather.town," 11th International Conference on Information and Education Technology (ICIET), 2023, pp. 1-5, Electronic ISBN: 978-1-6654-6548-9 doi: 10.1109/ICIET56899.2023.10111430.

[15] Gather Presence, Inc. gather.town. [Online]. Available from: https://www.gather.town 2023.10.10

[16] D. Serhan, "Transitioning from face-to-face to remote learning: Students' attitudes and perceptions of using Zoom during COVID-19 pandemic," International Journal of Technology in Education and Science, vol. 4, no. 4, pp. 335-342, 2020, doi: 10.46328/ijtes.v4i4.148.

[17] Zoom Video Communications, Inc. [Online]. Available from: www. https://zoom.us 2023.10.10

[18] R. Likert, "A technique for the measurement of attitudes," Archives of Psychology, vol. 22, no. 140, pp. 5-55, 1932.

[19] Miro. [Online]. Available from: https://miro.com,f14 2023.07.11

[20] Z. Merchant, E. T. Goetz, L. Cifuentes, W. Keeney-Kennicutt, and T. J. Davis, "Effectiveness of virtual reality-based instruction on students' learning outcomes in K-12 and higher education: A meta-analysis," Computers & Education, vol. 70, no. 1, pp. 29–40, 2014, doi: 10.1016/j.compedu.2013.07.033.

[21] S. Y. Chien, G. J. Hwang, and M. S. Y. Jong, "Effects of peer assessment within the context of spherical video-based virtual reality on EFL students' English-Speaking performance and learning perceptions," Computers & Education, vol. 146, no. 3, 2019, doi: 10.1016/j.compedu.2019.103751.

[22] M. H. Kim, "Effects of Collaborative Learning in a Virtual Environment on Students' Academic Achievement and Satisfaction," Journal of Digital Convergence, vol. 19, no. 4, pp. 1–8, 2021, doi: 10.14400/JDC.2021.19.4.001.

[23] B. Yildirim, E. Sahin-Topalcengiz, G. Arikan, and S. Timur, "Using virtual reality in the classroom: Reflections of STEM teachers on the use of teaching and learning tools," Journal of Education in Science, Environment and Health, vol. 6, no. 3, pp. 231-245, 2020, doi: 10.21891/jeseh.711779.

[24] S. Mystakidis, E. Berki, J. P. Valtanen, "Deep and Meaningful E-Learning with Social virtual reality Environments in Higher Education: A Systematic Literature Review," Applied Sciences, vol. 11, no. 5, 2412, 2021, doi: 10.3390/app11052412.

[25] M. Akgün, B. Atıcı, "The Effects of Immersive virtual reality Environments on Students' Academic Achievement: A Meta-analytical and Meta-thematic Study," Participatory Educational Research, vol. 9, no. 3, pp. 111-131, 2022. doi: 10.17275/per.22.57.9.3.

[26] A. Driscoll, K. Jicha, A. N. Hunt, L. Tichavsky, and G. Thompson, "Can online courses deliver in-class results?: A comparison of student performance and satisfaction in an online versus a faceto-face introductory sociology course," Teaching Sociology, vol. 40, no. 4, pp. 312–331, 2012, doi: 10.1177/0092055X12446624.

[27] C. Stone, "Online learning in Australian higher education: Opportunities, challenges and transformations," Student Success, vol. 10, no. 2, pp. 1–11, 2019, doi: 10.5204/ssj.v10i2.1299.

[28] C. Merlin-Knoblich, P. N. Harris, and E. C. McCarty Mason, "Examining student classroom engagement in fipped and non-fipped counsellor education courses," The Professional Counselor, vol. 9, no. 2, pp. 109–125, 2019, doi: 10.15241/cmk.9.2.109.

[29] M. R. Cairns, M. Ebinger, C. Stinson, and J. Jordan, "COVID-19 and human connection: Collaborative research on loneliness and online worlds from a socially-distanced academy," Human Organization, vol. 79, no. 4, pp. 281–291, 2020, doi: 10.17730/1938-3525-79.4.281.

[30] J. Du, X. Fan, J. Xu, C. Wang, L. Sun, and F. Liu, "Predictors for students' self-efcacy in online collaborative groupwork," Educational Technology Research and Development, vol. 67, pp. 767–791, 2019, doi: 10.1007/s11423-018-9631-9.

[31] L. Caprara and C. Caprara, "Effects of virtual learning environments: A scoping review of literature," Education and Information Technologies, vol. 27, pp. 3683–3722, 2022, doi: 10.1007/s10639-021-10768-w.

[32] S. V. Mamadjanova, "Design Features of Virtual Learning Environments," European International Journal of Multidisciplinary Research and Management Studies, vol. 2, no. 6, pp. 1–5, 2022, doi: 10.55640/eijmrms-02-06-01.

[33] C. Latulipe and A. De Jaeger, "Comparing Student Experiences of Collaborative Learning in Synchronous CS1 Classes in Gather.Town vs. Zoom," SIGCSE 2022: Proceedings of the 53rd ACM Technical Symposium on Computer Science Education - vol. 1, Feb. 2022, pp. 411-417, doi: 10.1145/3478431.3499383.

Development and Application of a New Ontology in the Context of Hybrid AC/DC Grids

Alessandro Rossi
Energy Green Transition
Engineering Ingegneria Informatica
Palermo, Italy
email: alessandro.rossi@eng.it

Marzia Mammina
Energy Green Transition
Engineering Ingegneria Informatica
Palermo, Italy
email: marzia.mammina@eng.it

Jawad Kazmi
Center for Energy
AIT Austrian Institute of Technology
Vienna, Austria
email: jawad.kazmi@ait.ac.at

Zhiyu Pan
Institute for Automation of CPS
RWTH Aachen University, Aachen, Germany
email: zhiyu.pan@eonerc.rwth-aachen.de

Charles Emehel
Institute for Automation of CPS
RWTH Aachen University, Aachen, Germany
email: charles.emehel@eonerc.rwth-aachen.de

Bharath Varsh Rao
Center for Energy
AIT Austrian Institute of Technology, Vienna, Austria
email: bharath-varsh.rao@ait.ac.at

Antonello Monti
Institute for Automation of CPS
RWTH Aachen University, Aachen, Germany
email: amonti@eonerc.rwth-aachen.de

***Abstract*—The HYPERRIDE project aims to enable a unique revolution in the electrical grid infrastructure creating the conditions to really unlock a wide application of Direct Current (DC) technology in the distribution grid. By combining DC and Alternating Current (AC) technologies, HYPERRIDE will demonstrate potential solutions that are seen in AC-DC hybrid grids for Low Voltage (LV) and Medium Voltage (MV) infrastructures, as most power electronics applications use internal DC power supplies. Furthermore, HYPERRIDE provides a technology-independent specification of a FIWARE-based interoperable and secure Information and Communications Technology (ICT) platform. In this paper, after giving a quick rundown on main energy domain ontologies that share knowledge conceptualization to allow an easier systems interaction and give the system components reasoning capabilities and autonomy, the Hybrid Ac Dc Grid Ontology (HADGO) developed inside the project will be described and a real case application will be presented. The Switch Gear use case was successfully modeled and evaluated for inconsistencies using the HermiT Reasoner. Asserted and inferred facts were achieved and more use case scenarios can be updated on the HADGO ontology either through hard coding on the Protégé GUI or using the ontology learning method. A total of 301 asserted and inferred axioms were achieved using the HermiT Reasoner on the Protégé ontology development tool. The HADGO ontology is applied in the HYPERRIDE sensing and monitoring infrastructure layer. It shows the usability of HADGO ontology in a real use case scenario of a grid information system.**

Keywords-Hybrid AC/DC, Smart Grid, Ontology, ICT, Interoperability, Reasoner.

I. Introduction

The role of Distributed Energy Resources (DER) is increasing significantly in electrical power systems due to many environmental, economic, and political drivers [1]. This transition has also put the electrical distribution grid in a central role. The challenges arising from this transition are largely being addressed under Smart Grid (SG) [2] initiatives. Although there is no standard definition, in general, a SG refers to a method of incorporating intelligence into the operation of a distribution grid to increase flexibility and performance. For electrical power systems, AC distribution grids are a well-known infrastructure that has been in use for a long time. This infrastructure can be assisted by DC technologies as a possible backbone to increase, for example, Renewable Energy Sources (RES) hosting capacity; however, they must be designed on a solid basis to allow for rapid roll-out and integration. It is critical to provide and test suitable methodologies and resources to lower entry barriers for early adoption processes to maximize the implementation capability of new DC technologies. The HYPERRIDE project aims to support this transition toward the transformation in the electrical grid infrastructure by laying the groundwork for the widespread adoption of DC technology. The future distribution grid both at the Low Voltage Direct Current (LVDC) component to Medium Voltage Direct Current (MVDC) backbone is planned to be demonstrated at three pilot sites (Germany, Italy, and Switzerland) implementing relevant use cases. These pilots will provide valuable insights and help identify the gaps in knowledge and possible solutions for the various focus areas.

Interoperability among the components and sub-systems of the developed AC/DC hybrid power system solution is a key goal of the project, as having an interoperable solution has numerous benefits for all stakeholders. In general, interoperability [3] implies that information conveyed from a *sending* system to a *receiving* system can be used meaningfully by the latter, necessitating at least some interpretation and contextualization of the data. Interoperability, however, is a challenging quality attribute to achieve because, in addition to some other technical and governance challenges, it necessitates a thorough understanding of the problem, the solution, and its interrelation. Data is at the center of interoperability, necessitating its consideration in any effort to achieve a higher level of interoperability.

An ontology is a formal description of knowledge as a set of concepts within a domain and their interrelationships [4]. It provides an abstract model that can describe, in a formal language based on mathematical logic, relevant aspects (concepts, relationships, properties, facts, rules) of a phenomenon or domain of interest that is intended to be represented for some purpose. Apart from being useful for many other aspects, an ontology provides a sound basis for developing an interoperable data model that can help in the integration of SG applications. One such ontology HADGO is developed in the context of HYPERRIDE as the basis for the interoperable data models for enabling interoperability and integration of solutions in hybrid AC/DC smart grid applications.

The rest of the paper is organized as follows. Section II provides a concise review of some of the relevant ontologies and data models, Section III introduces the HADGO ontology, then in Section IV an explanation of the application of the developed ontology with some real-world use cases, is provided. Section V concludes this paper by highlighting the contribution and their effects, and also providing future research directions.

II. Background and State of the Art

The integration of software applications may entail substantial semantic difficulties when translating information from one application to another. Different terminologies may be used to describe the same domain and, when the same terminology is used, applications often associate different semantics with the terms. This hinders the exchange of information between applications. Ontologies may solve this issue by providing a way of explicitly specifying the semantics for each terminology unambiguously. The ontologies provide, indeed, a shared knowledge conceptualization that allows an easier system interaction and gives the system components reasoning capabilities and autonomy [5]. An ontology is a formal description of knowledge as a set of concepts within a domain and the relationships between them. It is an abstract model that describes, by using a formal language based on mathematical logic, relevant aspects (rules, properties, relationships, etc.) of the domain of interest to be represented for some purpose. Since terms and relations are shared by the entire community of the domain of interest, there is no ambiguity: an ontology describes specific knowledge unambiguously. Relationships between concepts enable automated reasoning on data, easy to implement in semantic graph databases that use ontologies as their semantic schema [6].

In this subsection, an overview of some open ontologies focused on various aspects of energy or power systems will be presented. Smart Appliances REFerence (SAREF) [7] is an ontology created to enable interoperability between smart devices. SAREF is based on the concept of a "device", which is a tangible object that we can easily find in households, public buildings, or offices and which can perform one or more functions. The SAREF ontology offers a list of basic functions that can be combined into a more complex function. Each function has some associated commands. A device can be found in some corresponding states that are also listed as building blocks. A device that wants its functions to be discoverable, registerable, and remotely controllable by other devices in the network offers a service. The service specifies the device that is offering it and its functions. A device is also characterized by an energy/power profile that can be used to optimize the energy efficiency in a home or office that is part of the building. SAREF is expressed in Web Ontology Language Description Logic (OWL-DL) and contains 124 classes, 56 object properties, and 28 datatype properties [8].

SAREF for Energy (SAREF4ENER) is Web OWL-DL ontology that is one of the many (SAREF4INMA [9]; a SAREF extension for the industry and manufacturing domain, building devices and topology [10], etc.) extensions of SAREF with new classes and properties, focusing on demand response scenarios, where customers can offer flexibility to the smart grid to manage their smart devices using a Customer Energy Manager. SAREF4ENER has been created in collaboration with Energy@Home and EEBus, which are major Italy- and Germany-based industry associations, to enable the interconnection of their different data models [11].

SmArt eneRGy dOmain oNtology (SARGON) [12] is an extension of the SAREF ontology to cross-cut domain-specific information that represents the smart energy domain. SARGON ontology is powered by smart energy standards and Internet of Things (IoT) initiatives, and real use cases. It involves classes, properties, and instances explicitly created to cover the building and electrical grid automation domain. This study exhibits the development of SARGON and demonstrates it through a web application to cross-cut domain-specific information that represents the smart energy domain and is powered by smart energy standards and IoT initiatives, as well as real use cases. SARGON involves classes, properties, and instances explicitly created to cover the building and electrical grid automation domain. The SARGON ontology network consists of several interconnected domain ontologies related to the smart grid and building automation:

- Person, Company, Building, and Address ontologies contain data for describing the nature of a person, company, building, and address, besides spaces and geometrical data such as area, place, floors, etc.;
- Device inherits all classes of SAREF ontology and extends it according to energy equipment which includes industrial equipment, energy generators, and system resources, such as Phasor Measurement Units, Proportional-Integral-Derivative controllers, converters, etc.;
- Services provides ontologies for services in the smart grid and building automation like controlling, monitoring, and protection;

- Common Information Model (CIM) and International Electrotechnical Commission (IEC) 61850 present terms and relations in the power grids. It identifies the list of classes and variant instances that can be used for monitoring and controlling smart grids according to the standards.

The ontologies of the SARGON network have been harmonized to enable data portability for different applications in smart energy systems including building automation and power grid monitoring and controlling. Those ontologies are intended to be used together with FIWARE Next Generation Service Interface Linked Data (NGSI-LD), a standard defined by European Telecommunications Standards Institute (ETSI) Industry Specification Group for cross-cutting Context Information Management [13].

OntoMG [14] is an ontology-based information model for microgrids that aims to solve interoperability issues (syntactic and semantic) encountered between microgrid components. It is compliant with the CIM and the IEC 61850 standards. OntoMG integrates six packages, each related to a specific aspect involved in the achievement of the microgrid objectives:

- The identification aspect (Id) consists of associating a unique identity for each stakeholder enabling an easier component recognition and implicit information extraction
- The operation aspect (Op) aims at optimizing the network operations
- The mobility aspect (Mob) captures component displacements during their lifetime
- The economical aspect (Eco) aims at minimizing total costs while considering the components' participation in the Energy Market
- The ecological aspect (Ecolo) is related to the component participation in/on the environment
- Multi-roles aspect is related to the component roles during his operation in the system.

Semantic ontologies have been proposed by several research projects and initiatives to represent data related to the energy domain used by different Energy Management Systems deployed in different smart grid scenarios, such as smart homes, urban environments (e.g., buildings, districts, cities, etc.), organizations, microgrids or Virtual Power Plants and Demand Response management. Ontology for Energy Management Applications (OEMA) [15] is an attempt to unify existing heterogeneous ontologies that represent different energy-related data. The OEMA ontology network is made up of eight interconnected domains and each ontology represents one or various energy domains: Infrastructure Ontology, Energy and Equipment, Geographical, External factors, Person and Organisation Ontology, Energy Savings, Smart Grid Stakeholders, Person and organization, Units of Measurement. These ontologies are connected by a core Ontology Network.

III. HYPERRIDE AC/DC GRID ONTOLOGY

The HADGO is developed to help in defining, modeling, and analyzing a hybrid AC/DC power grid that can then be used in different use cases in the context of the H2020 HYPERRIDE project and beyond. Some of these use cases that were considered during the formulation of the ontology include but are not limited to power-flow calculation, cascading effects calculation, critical components identification, etc. However, the demonstration of such applications is beyond the scope of this document.

An overview of the HADGO is presented in Figure 1. The figure is very detailed and shows not only the entity classes and their relationships but also highlights the object properties that are used for such relationships, as well as the entity class that is the domain and range of these properties. The ontology contains around 50 asserted entity classes. From these entity classes, Figure 2 highlights (half) the classes at the top two layers.

Additionally, the ontology contains around 186 axioms with 116 logical axioms with several object and data properties. Adopting the naming conversion usually used in ontology authoring, a prefix of `hadgo` is used with all the members of the HADGO ontology making the name following the format `hadgo:<member>`.

Developing data models in a diverse and uncoordinated manner typically results in textitdata stovepipes issues, which can lead to a total/partial failure in attaining interoperability and impede the ontology's reusability potential while also making integration difficult. When developed appropriately, ontologies can help in achieving consistency in the usage of terms and meaning leading towards achieving a common understanding and further avoiding frequent adoptions [16].

Ontological realism [17], is being advocated as one of the best practices [16] [18] for ontology development. It refers to developing an ontology to be more like a reality model than a data model to maximize its utility and stability. In this development method, the resulting ontologies serve as representations of the entities to which the data pertains rather than the data itself.

Furthermore, in the formulation of ontology, the principle of *single inheritance* is used. According to this concept, in ontology, each entity class must be a subclass of precisely one other entity class, and anything belonging to a parent term also belongs to all child terms at lower levels. This means that each asserted taxonomy has a single root node and that each ontology has one or more asserted taxonomies as suitable components.

Keeping this background in mind, the HADGO is being developed using ontological realism as well as the single inheritance rules. The knowledge is derived from some experimental and benchmark hybrid AC/DC grid models in conjunction with expert judgments, and opinions from the involved experts.

A. Entity Classes

An introduction to top-level entity classes, as highlighted in Figure 2, is provided in this section. The classes include `hadgo:PowerGrid`, `hadgo:Component`, `hadgo:ComponentType`, `hadgo:FunctionType`,

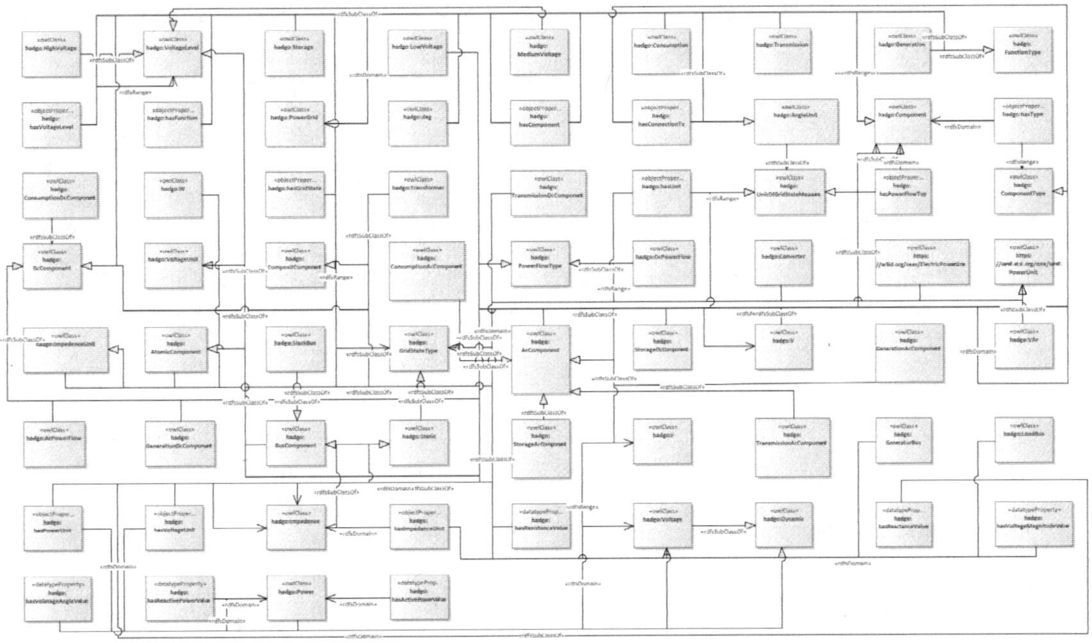

Figure 1. A partial view of the ontology with some entity classes, data, object properties, and relationships.

hadgo:GridStateType, hadgo:PowerFlowType and hadgo:VoltageLevel. All of these entity classes are sub-classes of owl:Thing entity class, which is the default way of defining classes using the Web Ontology Language (OWL).

1) PowerGrid class: The hadgo:PowerGrid is the umbrella entity class that can represent an AC, DC, or hybrid grid. It is also one of the top-level classes and a direct sub-class of owl:Thing. The usage, relationships, object, and data properties for the hadgo:PowerGrid are summarized with the diagram shown in Figure 1. It has relations with most of the other high-level entity classes as the power grid is modeled using this class as the base. It can then include several hadgo:Component (and its specialized sub-classes like hadgo:AcComponent or hadgo:DcComponent). Many functional and inverse object properties help in adding more semantics to the relationship.

2) Component class: The hadgo:Component is one of the major entity classes in the HADGO. The hadgo:Component has two sub-classes for modeling an AC component hadgo:AcComponent and a DC component hadgo:DcComponent. Both AC and DC components are then divided into four sub-classes that distinguish them based on the type of function (hadgo:FunctionType) they are performing in the model. The asserted function types, that a component can have are defined to be either hadgo:Generation, hadgo:Storage, hadgo:Conumption, or hadgo:Transmission.

Figure 1 again can be referred to for showing the usage of the hadgo:Component entity class. Each component instance can have multiple object properties and relationships. One such relationship is with the hadgo:ComponentType entity class which helps in specifying the type of the specific instance of a component. A component can be either an hadgo:AtomicComponent or an hadgo:ComponentComponent meaning that it consists of more than one components. The hadgo:ComponentComponent are specialized be of two kinds hadgo:Transformer and hadgo:Converter.

Furthermore, each hadgo:Component instance can have object properties that assign some hadgo:GridStateType. These hadgo:GridStateType can be either hadgo:Dynamic or hadgo:Static and represents hadgo:Voltage, hadgo:Power and hadgo:Impedance.

Each component instance must have a relationship with hadgo:VoltageLevel which defines, as the name suggests, the voltage level on which the component is operating. The asserted values as the range of object property are hadgo:HighVoltage, hadgo:MediumVoltage, and hadgo:LowVoltage.

3) ComponentType entity class: The hadgo:ComponentType entity class is defined to assert the types an hadgo:Component can have. The two specializations for this entity class are further defined as being hadgo:AtomicComponent and hadgo:ComponentComponent. The former covers the component instances that are atomic and usually have a single function. In contrast, the latter covers the component instances that can be composed of more than one component. The hadgo:ComponentComponent are further specialized with two sub-classes hadgo:Converter which represents

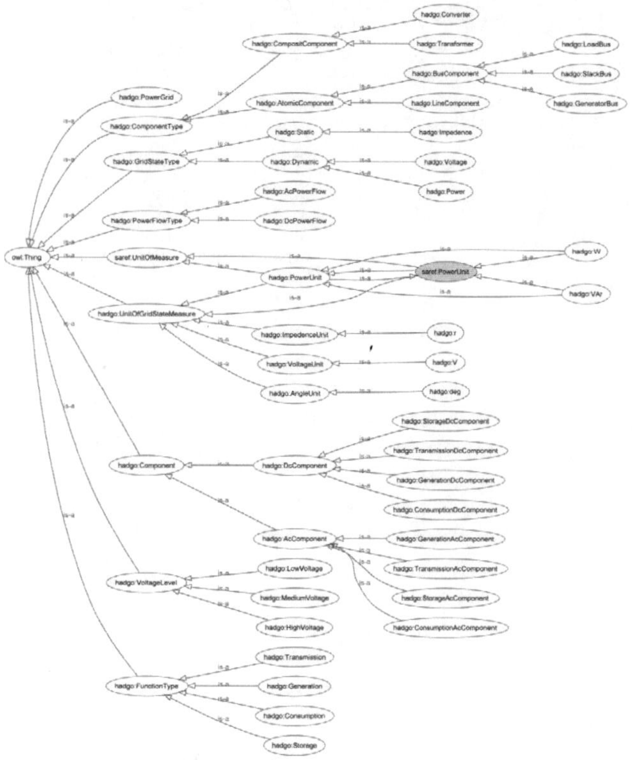

Figure 2. Hierarchy of major asserted entity classes in HADGO.

an AC/DC converter as well as `hadgo:Transfomer`.

Similarly, `hadgo:AtomicComponent` is specalized with two sub-classes that are `hadgo:BusComponent` and `hadgo:LineComponent`, which are self-explanatory. However, `hadgo:BusComponent` is further classified into three specialized sub-classes that are `hadgo:GeneratorBus`, `hadgo:LoadBus` and `hadgo:SlackBus`.

4) FunctionType class: The `hadgo:FunctionType` entity class defines the different types of function that a `hadgo:Component` can assume. The relationships and constraints are imposed using some object properties defining `hadgo:Component` as the domain and `hadgo:FunctionType` as the range. There are four specializations defined as the sub-classes that are `hadgo:Transmission`, `hadgo:Storage`, `hadgo:Generation`, `hadgo:Consumption`.

5) GridStateType class: The entity class `hadgo:GridStateType` represents the measurable grid states that an instance of a component can have. There are two sub-classes defined as `hadgo:Static` and `hadgo:Dynamic`. The two sub-classes for the `hadgo:Dynamic` are `hadgo:Voltage` and `hadgo:Power` while `hadgo:Static` only has one that is `hadgo:Impedence`.

6) PowerFlowType class: The entity class `hadgo:PowerFlowType` represents the power flows that an instance of a component in the grid can have. Changing this value affects the way this instance can be connected to other instances of the components and the type of object properties it can have. There are two specializations, `hadgo:AcPowerFlow` and `hadgo:DcPowerFlow` representing AC and DC power flow respectively.

7) VoltageLevel class: The entity class `hadgo:VoltageLevel` represents the voltage level an instance of the `hadgo:Component` can have and it defines the voltage level on which the component is operating. The three asserted sub-classes are `hadgo:HighVoltage`, `hadgo:MediumVoltage`, and `hadgo:LowVoltage`.

8) UnitOfGridStateMeasure class: The entity class `hadgo:UnitOfGridStateMeasure` represents the units that are used for measuring `hadgo:GridStatType` that a `hadgo:Component` instance can have. This entity class has children and grandchildren that define first the phenomenon and then define the respective unit.

IV. REAL CASE SCENARIO

The switchgear as a data instance was modeled on the HADGO ontology and validated with the HermiT Reasoner. The validated switchgear instance was provisioned on Entirety docker container on the HYPERRIDE ICT platform.

A. HADGO Switchgear Instance Modeling and Validation

The switchgear use case as an application ontology was modeled on the HADGO reference ontology in Section III above using the Protégé ontology modeling tool. The Switchgear concept was modeled as a class, and its object and data property were modeled for all its data instances.

The Hermit Reasoner was selected as the Logic evaluation solver for the switch gear data instance for the HADGO ontology and some inconsistencies during the use case modeling were observed and resolved based on the explanation results from the log output. All the instance assertions for both data and object properties were modeled and synchronized and can be used as anchor terms during ontology matching or ontology alignment which can be learned statistically or modeled and updated with Protégé.

The data instance as well as the assertions and properties defined and inferred for the Switchgear use case will also serve as a ground truth and data lineage for all future switchgear-based data analytics in the hybrid AC/DC Domain. Figure 3 below shows the modeled switch gear use case as an asserted hierarchy.

TABLE I
SUMMARY OF HADGO ASSERTED AND INFERRED FACTS ACHIEVED USING HERMIT REASONER

S.#	Fact Type	Count
1	Total Axioms achieved	301
2	Classes	63
3	Object Property	18
4	Data Property	12
5	Individual	1

The HermiT Reasoner, which is based on the Tableau Algorithm, carries out OWL Logic computation on the modeled HADGO reference ontology with the Switch Gear use case. From the decidability and satisfiability Logic computation by the HermiT Reasoner on the modeled HADGO ontology, Table I summarizes the asserted and inferred Facts validated on ontology.

These results validate the HADGO ontology as a Reference Ontology for any Hybrid AC/DC or DC grid. The Owl file in Turtle format is shown in the Appendix and can be run by anyone for verification and extension.

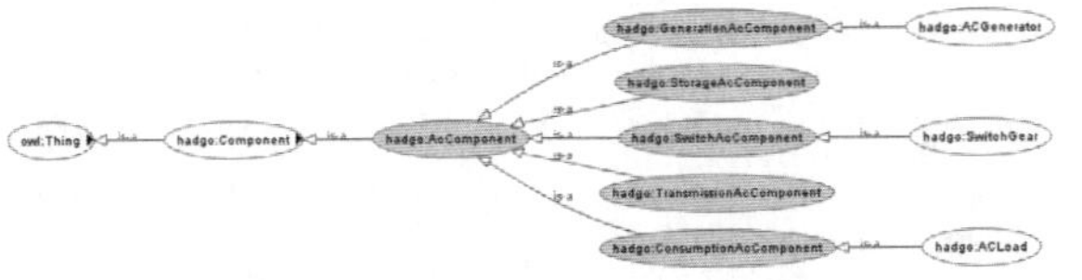

Figure 3. Hadgo Switch Gear Use Case Ontology Hierarchy.

From the HADGO base ontology, the inferred axioms data were exported and the metric was compared between the base ontology including the asserted and inferred axioms, and that of only the inferred axioms. The combined chart is shown in Figure 4 Therefore we have a total of 301 axioms in the base ontology out of which 117 are inferred axioms and 184 are asserted axioms.

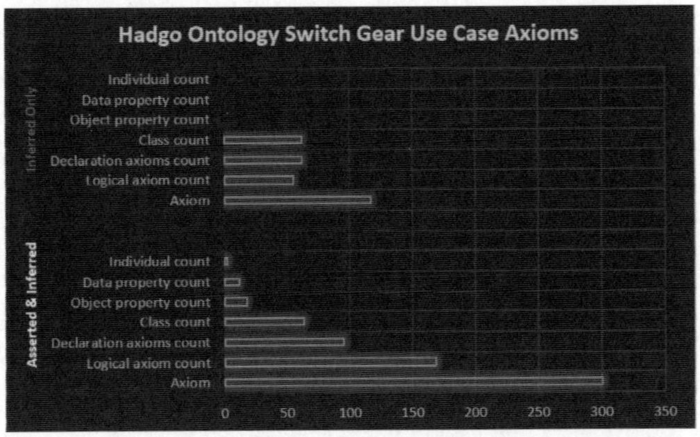

Figure 4. HADGO Ontology Switch Gear Use Case Axioms.

The achieved inference from the Switchgear use case modeling update on HADGO confirms that the logical restrictions, class constructors, class disjoint, and pairwise disjoint on multiple classes and the partitions carried out on during the HADGO ontology development were effective. It was found during the experiment that the more axioms were asserted from the domain knowledge of the AC/DC grid, the more inferred axioms were obtained.

B. HADGO Switchgear Entity Provisioning and application

The developed HADGO ontology is used in the HYPERRIDE sensing and monitoring infrastructure layer, as part of the work done for the definition of a reference ICT Platform in the AC/DC grid context [19]. The first step is to collect the sensor data through the MQTT Broker. The IoT Agent is connected with the MQTT Broker and ORION Context Broker. The Entirety [20] creates the entity of the device. The HADGO ontology is integrated into the Entirety to harmonize the data according to [21]. The data are saved in the MongoDB and the QuantunLeap subscribes to the context broker and forwards the data to the CrateDB. Finally, the data are monitored in the Grafana.

TABLE II
LIST OF COMPONENTS USED FOR TESTING THE REAL CASE SCENARIO

S.#	Component Type	Component Name
1	Main contactors	Schaltbau CT1230/08 + CT1130/08
2	Current sensors	LEM LF 1010-S current transducer
3	Voltage sensors	LEM DVM 3000 voltage transducer
4	Controller	WAGO 750 Series Modbus Bus-coupler

To test the sensing and monitoring layer, the platform is implemented on the German pilot side. The switch gear data is collected and monitored with the developed platform. The switch gear is a self-build type. The important components used are described in Table II.

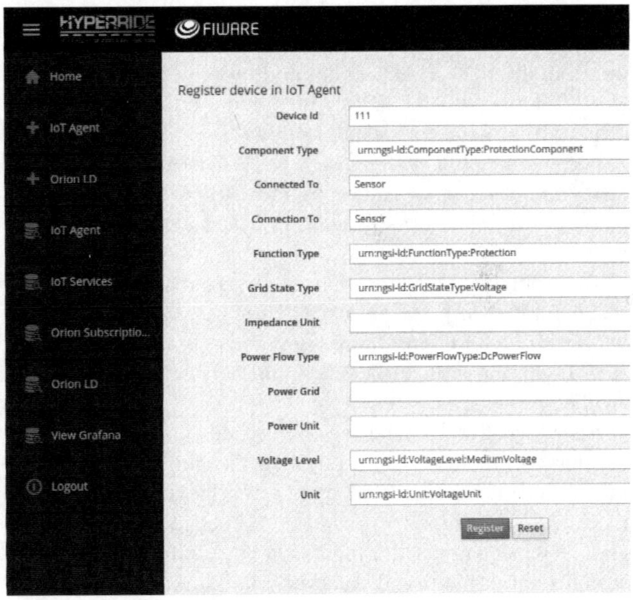

Figure 5. Register Device in IoT Agent.

The development is based on the following steps. First, the IoT agent for switch gear is created in Entirety based on the HADGO ontology. The process is shown as follows in Figure 5. The parameters of the table are defined in the data model in the code as NGSIv2, NGSI-LD, and JSON formats. The Quantum Leaps part is to read the formats of NGSIv2, NGSI-LD, and JSON. Also, the Orion Context Broker has a role here for the Format checking. The data is now uploaded to the CrateDB. Then, the data are illustrated with Grafana in Figure 6.

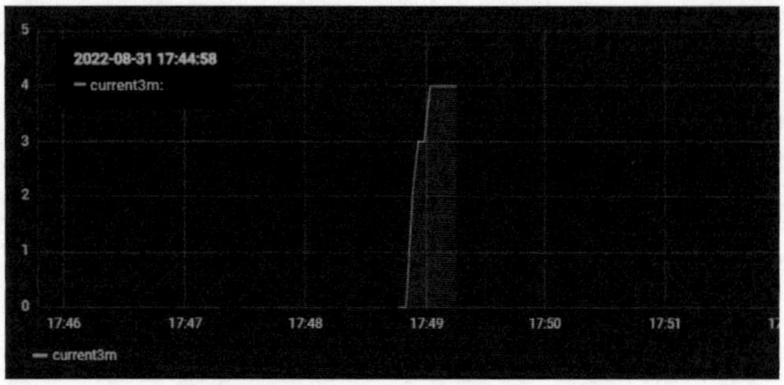

Figure 6. Monitoring the switch gear data.

V. CONCLUSION

The HADGO ontology is a proposed core reference ontology for the AC/DC and DC smart grid. The UML information modeling for the software applications implementation was carried out with Enterprise Architect while the ontology modeling was implemented with Protege. New AC/DC and DC grid entities with their subclasses and superclasses were developed and described for the new grid concepts. For the relationships, object properties and data properties were developed and described. For the individual, a use case of Switch Gear was described and object and data assertion were defined. The HADGO ontology was validated using the HermiT Reasoner and 301 asserted and inferred axioms were achieved in this experimental study.

For future work, more unary predicates and binary predicates axioms can be added as individuals to the HADGO ontology to increase its ground truth and axioms knowledge base.

To enable more application of the HADGO ontology at scale, future work on ontology learning can be carried out on the HADGO reference ontology using unstructured, semi-structured, and structured data from the pilot sites of hybrid AC/DC power grid.

Also, statistical methods can be carried out on the HADGO ontology for more AC/DC entity classification and relationship prediction on the modeled ontology. This helps to achieve more inferred axioms to increase the scope of data models and knowledge graphs for more data integration in information systems applications and databases.

ACKNOWLEDGMENT

The research leading to these results has received funding from the European Union H2020 Framework Programme (H2020/2014-2020) under Grant Agreement No 957788.

REFERENCES

[1] M. Fan, H. Liang, Z. Zhang, A. Su, and W. Chen, "Cost-benefit analysis of integration der into distribution network," in *CIRED 2012 Workshop: Integration of Renewables into the Distribution Grid*, 2012, pp. 1–4.

[2] "IEEE Smart Grid Vision for Computing: 2030 and Beyond Reference Model," *IEEE*, pp. 1–18, 2016.

[3] R. Jochem and T. Knothe, "Interoperability requirements derived from interoperability dimensions," in *Enterprise Interoperability II*, R. J. Gonçalves, J. P. Müller, K. Mertins, and M. Zelm, Eds. London: Springer, 2007, pp. 39–50.

[4] N. Guarino, D. Oberle, and S. Staab, *What Is an Ontology?* Berlin, Heidelberg: Springer Berlin Heidelberg, 2009, pp. 1–17. [Online]. Available: https://doi.org/10.1007/978-3-540-92673-3_0

[5] M. Ciocoiu, D. Nau, and M. Grüninger, "Ontologies for integrating engineering applications," *J. Comput. Inf. Sci. Eng.*, vol. 1, pp. 12–22, 03 2001.

[6] L. D. Lauretis, S. Costantini, and I. Letteri, "An ontology to improve the first aid service quality," in *2019 IEEE International Conference on Systems, Man and Cybernetics (SMC)*, 2019, pp. 1479–1483.

[7] J. S. S. Melo, T. A. Neves, and L. E. dos Santos, "Saref: Sistema de apresentação remota por reconhecimento facial," *CNJ*, vol. 6, pp. 77–92, 2022.

[8] L. Daniele, F. den Hartog, and J. Roes, "Created in close interaction with the industry: The smart appliances reference (saref) ontology," in *International Workshop Formal Ontologies Meet Industries*. Springer, 08 2015, pp. 100–112.

[9] M. de Roode, A. Fernández-Izquierdo, L. Daniele, M. Poveda-Villalón, and R. García-Castro, "Saref4inma: A saref extension for the industry and manufacturing domain," *Semantic Web Journal*, vol. 11, pp. 911–926, 2020.

[10] M. Poveda-Villalón and R. García-Castro, "Extending the SAREF ontology for building devices and topology," in *Proceedings of the 6th Linked Data in Architecture and Construction Workshop, London, United Kingdom, June 19-21, 2018*, ser. CEUR Workshop Proceedings, M. Poveda-Villalón, P. Pauwels, and A. Roxin, Eds., vol. 2159. CEUR-WS.org, 2018, pp. 16–23. [Online]. Available: https://ceur-ws.org/Vol-2159/02paper.pdf

[11] ETSI, "SAREF4ENER: an extension of SAREF for the energy domain created in collaboration with Energy@Home and EEBus associations," https://saref.etsi.org/saref4ener/v1.1.2/, 2020, [Online; accessed 2023-09-29].

[12] M. Haghgoo, I. Sychev, A. Monti, and F. Fitzek, "Sargon – smart energy domain ontology," *Smart Cities*, 12 2020.

[13] "ETSI GS CIM 009 V1.2.2 (2020-02); Context Information Management (CIM); NGSI-LD API," *ETSI Group Specification*, 2020.

[14] K. Salameh, R. Chbeir, H. Camblong, G. Tekli, and I. Vechiu, "A generic ontology-based information model for better management of microgrids," in *Artificial Intelligence Applications and Innovations*, R. Chbeir, Y. Manolopoulos, I. Maglogiannis, and R. Alhajj, Eds. Cham: Springer International Publishing, 2015, pp. 451–466.

[15] J. Ariza, F. Larrinaga, and E. Curry, "A unified semantic ontology for energy management applications," in *2nd International Workshop on Ontology Modularity, Contextuality, and Evolution (WOMoCoE 2017) - WSP/WOMoCoE@ISWC - Vienna*, 10 2017.

[16] R. Rudnicki, B. Smith, T. Malyuta, and W. Mandrick, "White Paper: Best Practices of Ontology Development," https://www.nist.gov/system/files/documents/2021/10/14/nist-ai-rfi-cubrc_inc_002.pdf, Oct 25 2016, [Online; accessed 2023-04-24].

[17] B. Smith and W. Ceusters, "Ontological realism: A methodology for coordinated evolution of scientific ontologies," *Appl Ontol.*, vol. 5(3-4), pp. 139–188, 2010.

[18] Y. Alfaifi, "Ontology development methodology: A systematic review and case study," in *2022 2nd International Conference on Computing and Information Technology (ICCIT)*, 2022, pp. 446–450.

[19] M. Mammina, A. Rossi, D. Arnone, G. Zizzo, S. Moradi, and P. Smith, "Predictions in Resilient Hybrid AC/DC Grids Leveraged by an Interoperable and Secure ICT Platform," in *2022 IEEE International Conference on Environment and Electrical Engineering and 2022 IEEE Industrial and Commercial Power Systems Europe (EEEIC / ICPS Europe)*, 2022, pp. 1–6.

[20] M. Haghgoo, I. Sychev, A. Monti, and F. H. Fitzek, "Entirety—semanntic provisioning and governing iot devices in smart energy domain," *SoftwareX*, vol. 18, p. 101081, 2022.

[21] Z. Pan, G. Pan, and A. Monti, "Semantic-similarity-based schema matching for management of building energy data," *Energies*, vol. 15, no. 23, p. 8894, 2022.

An Autonomic Approach to Security Incident Response and Prevention in Cloud Computing

Glenn Russell, Roy Sterritt
School of Computing
Ulster University
Belfast Campus,
Northern Ireland
email: russell-g6@ulster.ac.uk |
r.sterritt@ulster.ac.uk

***Abstract*—An autonomic approach for responding to security incidents is proposed, which aims to replace traditionally people intensive, reactive, and technically complex methods for responding to security incidents. In addition, the approach provides the ability for systems to evolve in response to the nature of the attacks, building an immunity iteratively based on real environmental conditions. The solution works alongside existing systems and controls, addressing failures to resolve the complexities of security engineering in heterogenous systems spanning endpoints, traditional data centres, private cloud, and public cloud.**

***Keywords*—autonomic computing; security; infosec; incident response; cloud computing; control.**

I. INTRODUCTION

Cloud computing is a paradigm for providing information technology infrastructure and services to users who do not want to own and operate their own physical equipment and want to be able to deploy and scale their applications at will. There are many benefits to this, which have led to ever increasing adoption of cloud computing services, at the expense of more traditional data centres. It was predicted that 2022 [1] would see spending on public cloud services of $482.155 billion, an increase of 21.7% over 2021, and an increase of 53.6% over 2020. There is no sign of this increase in spending abating. IBM [2] lists the benefits as:

- **Flexibility** allows services to be accessed and scaled to fit ever changing demands, from anywhere on the Internet.
- **Efficiency** means that users do not need to spend money on physical equipment, much of which may be redundant, while being able to bring applications to market quicker.
- **Strategic value** is derived from having access to the latest technology as it becomes available, from new processors to the latest machine learning platforms.

Private cloud is where a company or entity make use of their own networking and compute to provide services to users via the use of virtualisation technologies, such as OpenStack [3]. This allows services to be provisioned using an Application Programming Interface (API), then torn down again via the same API when the services are no longer needed. Like private cloud, *public cloud* aims to provide flexible and scalable resources to users, but this service is provided by a third-party, such as Amazon, in the form of Amazon Web Services (AWS) or Google in the form of Google Cloud Platform (GCP).

Services provided by cloud match those available in traditional data centres, but are categorised into several distinct areas. *Infrastructure as a Service (IaaS)* provides basic computing infrastructure in the form of virtual machines, networking, and storage. This is a core element of all clouds, both public and private, and has arguably [4] become increasingly commoditised. AWS have the Elastic Compute Cloud (EC2) service for virtual machines, while GCP has Google Compute Engine (GCE) providing the same service, as just two examples. *Platform as a Service (PaaS)* is an abstraction which prevents the user from needing to manage compute directly, and instead provides a framework for building and deploying applications. As part of this, advanced features, such as identity, access management and security are usually provided. Examples of this are Google App Engine, Heroku and Vertex AI [5]. *Software as a Service (SaaS)* removes practically all responsibility from the user of managing and running an application (other than managing user access), and instead provides direct business value. Examples of this are Salesforce, public GitHub, and Google Docs [6]. Finally, *Container as a Service (CaaS)* refers to a service which orchestrates many different sub-components running in containers into a fully managed distributed application. While the term is agnostic of any given implementation of the technology, this usually refers to Kubernetes [7], a platform developed by Google to manage massive applications. Each of the major public clouds offer managed Kubernetes services; GCP provides Google Kubernetes Engine (GKE), Azure provides Azure Kubernetes Service (AKS), and AWS provides Elastic Kubernetes Service (EKS). Out of the various service offerings offered in cloud, CaaS is the closest to offering autonomic capabilities. Casalicchio argues [8] that container orchestration does not include any autonomic features because of a reliance on hypervisors and simplistic heuristics for actions like scaling, but this misses two key points. The hypervisor is not the autonomic management agent in a CaaS, it is the master node [9] along with the *Kube-Controller-Manager*, and secondly that the process of scaling pods and nodes is already autonomic in the case of managed offerings, such as GKE.

Underlining this shift in how Information Technology (IT) services are deployed and managed are the kind of workloads being run on clouds. They are no longer the reserve of small, rapidly innovating start-ups, but are used by over 90% of the largest companies in the world [10]. Large financial institutions like CapitalOne closed the last of their data centres in 2020, relying entirely on Amazon Web Services to run their entire I.T. estate [11]. However, with this seismic shift in how services are run, so have these new services been exposed to new kinds of threats. While a threat is often thought of as a malicious actor, whether that be a script kiddie or hacker collective, the most significant cause of breaches is human error. In fact, IBM found [12] that human error is the root cause in 95% of cases. The combination of simple to deploy services with complex and difficult to fully understand API configurations means that even before services are deployed, vulnerabilities are already built into a service. With the ease with which new Tools, Techniques, and Procedures (TTPs) are brought to bear by attackers on the Internet, security practitioners are facing multiple threats from internal and external vectors. This has led to both a shortage of trained cyber professionals [13] and burnout among existing people [14]. Clearly, the burden on cyber professionals is increasing, with 2021 seeing a 1885% increase in ransomware attacks alone [15].

Security in IT systems (often referred to simply as *Cyber*) is a central concern in how people conduct their lives, how nations and governments run their countries and manage their societies. The digitisation of society, while providing an unprecedented level of access to information and communication, has introduced an equal and opposite issue in exposing our society to threats that transcend both physical, national, and geographical boundaries.

Hagen et al. [16] refer to the challenges of physical distance, borders and time diminishing. However, the impact of this is that society has become much more susceptible to various kinds of malignant activity from threat actors that ranges from causing reputational damage in the form of web site defacement, hacktivism from organisations like Anonymous [17], or even attack from nation states. Cryptographer and security expert Bruce Schneier predicted [18] the rise of rapid automated attacks, perpetrated from a distance, and the subsequent proliferation of these techniques would require only a single skilled threat actor, while the ability to communicate at will over long distances in secret would mean that a technique could simply be copied by others. The prevalence and effectiveness of cyber-attacks by nation states has resulted in a move to defensive postures that will possibly include what is euphemistically called a kinetic response – a cyber-attack could soon lead to a physical military response [19]. Given the state of current computing paradigms and the associated financial and societal risks, methods must be developed which can remove the burden of securing of those paradigms as much as possible from the human.

In Section 2, security in cloud computing is examined, focusing on defense in depth. Section 3 focuses on Autonomic Cloud Computing for security. Section 4 goes into more detail on applying these autonomic principles for security. Section 5 proposes an Autonomic Incident Response System, and finally the paper concludes with Section 6.

II. SECURITY IN CLOUD COMPUTING

Regardless of the computing paradigm being deployed, effective security programmes adopt some fundamental principles, which can be utilised regardless of the computing paradigm. The principle of these approaches is *defense in depth* (Figure 1), which calls for a series of defensive mechanisms which are layered to protect valuable data and information. Having multiple layers of security ensures that there are redundant controls in place if a specific control is compromised [20]. However, these layers are typically not environment aware. An example here is a firewall that is used to block non-authorised network traffic, which protects a virtual machine, which runs anti-virus software, which is detecting malware. Neither security control is aware of the other, or shares information about their environment. This is a major shortcoming and prevents contextual knowledge from being shared to protect other assets if a machine is infected with malware. Ideally, the anti-virus agent would let the firewall know that a piece of malware would try to attack other assets (this process is referred to as *traversal*) by passing metadata, which notes a particular traffic of network traffic using five-tuple [21] data along with a file hash as part of a message payload. The firewall could then react to the attack in real-time. At the same time, the malware metadata could be used by another component, such as a malware sandbox where it could be detonated to provide further data to further enhance defensive measures, or even to maintain a chain of custody for forensic analysis of a breach. This process is part of what is referred to as *incident response*, which is a procedure for dealing with a security incident.

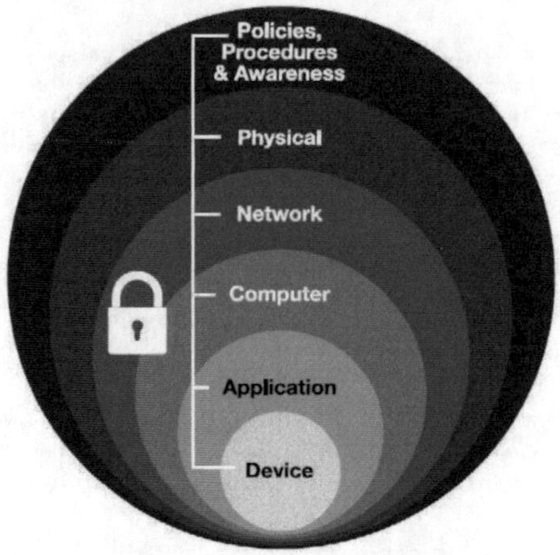

Figure 1. Defense in depth.

The scenario described is already understood by security practitioners (though this is a simpler use case), but there are two issues which make this process very resource intensive and increasingly unmanageable:

- The incident response process is manual, meaning it is very resource intensive and requires specific expertise.
- There are many of these incidents per day, and too few people to respond. This has led to the prevalence of a condition called *alert fatigue*, which is the scenario where security teams have too many alerts to be able to work effectively [22].

The security industry has attempted to resolve these core issues by introducing new kinds of tools and automation to make the job of the security team easier. There are several classes of tools to achieve this. An ad-hoc nomenclature exists which describes the types of security data that are used in cloud and security platforms. An *Indicator of Compromise* (IoC) is a digital artifact, such as a file, hash or configuration that is a sign of an attack. These can be shared among systems so that they can all be protected by detecting an attack. Organisations called *Information Sharing and Analysis Centers (ISACs)* exist for industry verticals where trusted partners can share these using threat sharing platforms, e.g., the *Financial Services ISAC (FS-ISAC)*. A *vulnerability* is a package or system misconfiguration that is susceptible to attack, and lastly an *exploit* is a piece of software or technique that can be used to take advantage of a vulnerability. *Security Information and Event Management (SIEM)* platforms perform two main functions. Firstly, they collect log and event information from networks and devices and store the data so that it can be searched. Logs could take the form of access logs, network traffic information, web requests or DNS requests. All this log data enables the second purpose of these platforms, which is to look for anomalies in the logs that may be indicative of a breach or attempted attack, both in real-time and as part of a forensic analysis of a breach. For example, if a log message indicates a particular IP address is performing thousands of requests a second, it may be indicative of a DDoS attack. Rules are written which describe these conditions, and when these conditions are detected, alerts are raised which are handled by a human operator. It does so in real-time, but as the volumes of logs have increased exponentially, these platforms are having trouble scaling to meet demand. *Threat intelligence* seeks to augment a SIEM by providing information about malicious sources, which can be then used in real-time to filter alerts, reducing the cognitive load on the security practitioner. Practically, if a SIEM has a known list of IP addresses that it knows are a source of malicious traffic, then it can prioritise alerts on those rather than attempting to filter and analyse all sources.

Integrating SIEM, threat intelligence and other tools, such as Endpoint Detection and Response (EDR) tools together and providing procedures for responding to threats are *Security Orchestration, Automation and Response (SOAR)* platforms Repetitive processes can be handled automatically, and a SOAR platform could be used to respond to a malware attack as described, or to automatically shut down a virtual machine if it is found to be infected with a critical vulnerability. Like a SIEM, these rules or playbooks must be manually written for the platform to be effective. With so many different tools and techniques, there is a significant challenge in simply being able to integrate them. The single common standard for sharing vulnerability information for many years has been the *Common Vulnerabilities and Exposures (CVE)* standard [23], which is how software vulnerabilities, such as Heartbleed [24] are communicated for consumption by human and machine alike. It describes details, such as whether the vulnerability can be exploited over a network or without authentication to the host system. In recent years, several other standards have emerged under the stewardship of Oasis in the form of the *Structured Threat Information eXpression (STIX)* standard, and complementary *Trusted Automated eXchange of Indicator Information (TAXII)* standard. These formats are XML-based and are used to describe all manner of threats, such as malware or network-based attacks, independent of any single vendor or implementation, and indicators of compromise using the embedded CyBOX standard. The *Security Content Automation Protocol (SCAP)* is a standard proposed by NIST [25] that allows for automated vulnerability management and is in use by many major security solutions. *Common Vulnerability Scoring System (CVSS)* is an important standard because it attempts to add a dynamic weight to a vulnerability through its *environmental* score. If a vulnerability is exposed directly to the Internet, then the weight is increased to reflect the higher risk of exploitation, or if mitigated by a network control, it is greatly reduced for the opposite effect. Other standards exist expressing similar data, but in summary, there are many standards that support integration of various security tools and processes.

The integration of various log sources, security platforms and controls together are an ideal outcome, which in theory should produce an effective immune system that can detect and respond to threats more effectively. The reality is far from the truth. The result of efforts by security vendors to solve these many problems has resulted in an explosion in complexity of security tools which require all new skills to be able to operate and interpret. In fact, deploying new security tools may not improve security at all, but have the opposite effect due to a decreasing ability to detect an attack [26]. Even in the case where a tool adopts an open standard, such as SCAP, if other tools in the environment do not at least support it also, then the ability to integrate is greatly reduced.

III. AUTONOMIC CLOUD COMPUTING AND SECURITY

While autonomic computing is a well-defined domain, it does not hold exclusivity over the main features of an autonomic system, and cloud computing platforms exhibit several features which classify aspects as autonomic. Indeed, Cloud Computing was Autonomic Computing's major impact success during its 2nd decade [27]. These principles are refined into just four, so-called *self-CHOP*.

- Self-*Configuration*
- Self-*Healing*
- Self-*Optimisation*
- Self-*Protection*

Self-configuration is supported by both IaaS and PaaS services to build distributed applications. Etchevers et al. [28] outline various methods to achieve this. Virtualisation and corresponding formats are a focus of the paper which concludes that the formalisms and mechanisms offered by industry are basic, non-exhaustive and non-extensible. A key point from the paper is that vendors are moving towards common APIs, such as OVF to describe applications. However, the paper does not explore the practice of *configuration management*, which addresses the shortcomings identified by providing the ability to autonomously configure multiple applications and multiple fine-grained applications. Popular tools in this space are *Puppet*, *Chef*, *Ansible* and *Terraform*. Each of these tools possess a management component or master which configures new and existing components, such as new servers coming online via an agent or surrogate agent process. Both the master and agents are akin to an *autonomic manager*, which exchange information on the desired state of an environment and the actual state. *Configuration drift* (Figure 2) is where the configuration of a service differs from the expected configuration, and it is this that the master attempts to correct for each service. It does so iteratively through a process called *eventual consistency*, in which the master issues commands over a secure channel to make corrections, and the services (in fact, an autonomic manager) respond with a snapshot of their current state. This continues until there is no configuration drift. This mechanism results in what is a *self-healing* process that can operate with any aspect of the cloud that can be managed programmatically. Configuration management tools can integrate with any aspect of a cloud environment, including security controls. This results in a *declarative* capability to define the desired state of an environment. While this implies a static system, these tools also allow rules to be added which dictate how a system should behave under load or when failures occur, which gives the environment the ability to define *fault tolerance* declaratively and have the managers enact it. Cloud is also *self-optimising* because it can scale many aspects of the environment according to pre-defined conditions and rules. This ability to pre-programme the addition and removal of services from the environment results in *apoptotic* services. Servers may be started (using the autonomic processes available from configuration management tools) based on some collection of metrics, such as requests per second to an application or increased CPU usage. Then when loads fall back under some threshold (which could be static or learned over time) servers are shut down again. The ability to shutdown services in response to some environmental event is a key part of an autonomic security capability. For example, if a server is compromised, it should be quarantined, snapshotted for forensics, then shutdown before it can be used by an attacker to traverse the network. What is lacking in cloud is the integration and proliferation of these events in a way which is standardised and in real-time. The environmental event could come from a SIEM platform or threat intelligence platform using STIX.

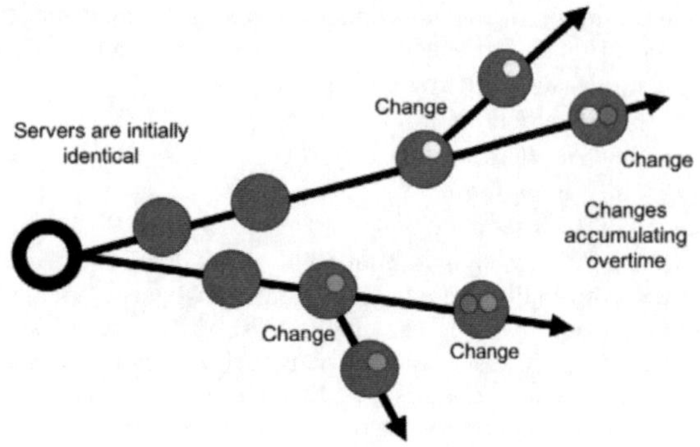

Figure 2. Configuration drift.

The ability to declare what a cloud environment should look like and have configuration management processes configure and heal services gives us the ability to build *self-protecting* systems. However, this is where the current state of cloud largely fails to embrace autonomic principles. To self-protect, a component must be aware of internal and external threats, and this complexity is why securing any IT system, not just cloud is becoming exponentially more difficult. Consider the following incident example:

- Configuration manager defines a network and application which runs on port 443.
- The application uses version 10.1 of a web server.
- A new server starts up and it's agent communicates with the master to retrieve it's configuration and install the application running on port 443.
- The new server reports back to the configuration manager which compares declared versus actual state, sees they are the same, so no further action is taken.
- Thirty minutes later, the new server checks again with the master to compare declared state. They are the same, so no changes are required.
- A new zero day exploit on the web server being used is found. There is no patch available yet, but metadata is available.
- An application is running for which there is no defence yet.

There are several possible mitigations for this. The use of a SOAR platform may be able to automatically shut this service down or create a firewall rule that blocks traffic to this port. The issue is that the SOAR does not know about the zero day to be able to take an action in the first place. A threat intelligence feed could provide this information automatically, but there will always be a lag between a zero day being found and exploited and the time it is detected and mitigated. Even the associated CVE may not contain enough metadata to be assist an autonomous security platform, and there is often a lag of days or weeks before information is available in the National Vulnerability Database (NVD), examined in detail by Ruohonen [29]. In addition, in real-world scenarios, services are simply not shut down and security controls automatically configured without oversight, due to the risk of business outages or even inadvertently introducing even more vulnerabilities into a system. Security platforms, such as IBM QRadar Risk Manager [30] disabled features which allowed the automatic configuration of security controls for these reasons. Even in an environment where a mature configuration management strategy is in place, security tools are in place and well-tuned, incidents cannot be responded to in real-time.

IV. APPLYING AUTONOMIC PRINCIPLES TO SECURITY

Clearly, there are significant efforts to bring the power of automation to bear on the dual problem of ever-increasing complexity, and ever more scarce resources when it comes to dealing with it. Cloud has nascent support for an autonomous approach to security in the form of configuration management tools APIs (though unique to each cloud implementation). Defence in depth strategies call for multiple independent components working together to provide layered security, and while individual controls are effective at addressing specific kinds of controls, such as protecting a web application or defending a network, they are not *context-aware* because they do not understand the environment in which they are operating. (This means that if a vulnerability is present, it is not clear how critical it is. It could be hidden behind many other controls or exposed directly to the Internet). This is a key requirement of eight conditions that IBM define [31] as features of an autonomic system, which are:

- The system is aware of the resources it can access and why it is connected to other systems.
- It can automatically configure itself based on its environment.
- It must be able to optimise itself for efficiency.
- It must be resilient in the face of problems through self-healing or avoiding issues.
- It must protect itself against attacks.
- It must adapt to its environment by establishing connections with adjacent systems.
- It should rely on open standards.
- It can predict demand for its resources and adapt in a manner transparent to other systems.

Research in autonomic security is relatively non-existent but is gaining momentum in industry. Google have labelled their own initiatives as the "10x SOC", referring to a *security operations center* which can be considered the central nervous system in an enterprise. The focus of this effort is to address the issues set out by this paper, in terms of throughput achieved over current methods [32]. As is predictable for a vendor publication, prominence is given to specific products, but nevertheless, it identifies the following building blocks of an autonomic SOC:

Products, including Chronicle, Looker and BigQuery, which mirror the functionality of a SIEM in providing analysis of logs and events.

Integrations to EDR, SOAR, etc.

Blueprints, including network forensics and telemetry.

Content, which includes rules, logs and security detection playbooks.

Despite originating from a deeply technical company like Google, their full paper [33] does not propose an autonomic solution, and falls short of any kind of technical insight into an approach, but it does serve to underline the finding of this paper so far, and that is the components are available to build an autonomous system. What is lacking is cohesion in the form of an *autonomic communications channel* and standardised message formats. This paper has identified several open message formats that can be used to communicate security information between all kinds of components.

Thus, reviewing the eight attributes of an autonomic system and combining it with what has been identified so far in terms of cloud and security technology, we can map the eight autonomic principles as defined by IBM to an autonomic security solution for cloud environments.

- It can be *aware* of systems that it is connected to via the use of configuration management declared state.
- It can *configure* itself and other components via configuration management agents.
- It can *optimise* itself through metrics gathered from the environment via manager components and data generated by the cloud platform to block threats not previously seen.
- It can *self-heal* by turning off infected or compromised hosts using SOAR or restarting services that unexpectedly crash or fail.
- It can *protect* itself by declaring known state, and fixing configuration issues if configuration drift is detected.
- It can *partially adapt* to its environment by using the declared state to understand adjacent systems and use environment information to modify its own behaviour.
- Many *open standards* exist which allow components to communicate, such as STIX, TAXII, SCAP and ATT&CK.
- It can *predict* demand and future events by using environment information and threat intelligence data.

To achieve an autonomic solution, cloud and security technology must operate as a single immune system, rather than as vestigial appendages to one another.

V. AN AUTONOMIC INCIDENT RESPONSE SYSTEM

This paper has summarised the many challenges facing security practitioners as they secure and defend their platforms against both internal and external actors. It has also researched the current state of cloud as a means for managing complex distributed applications. In doing so, a complex and heterogenous landscape of point solutions and loose integrations has been identified which increases complexity rather than reduces it. Proposing a solution which introduces yet another security tool to actively manage will not resolve the issues in a meaningful way. Therefore, the following must be true of any solution:

- The solution must augment existing tools and platforms. i.e., the solution should utilise existing security services or agents as their managed component.
- The solution should adopt autonomic principles in a manner which does not increase the cognitive load on security practitioners. It will do this by automating incident response and cutting the human out of the loop.
- The solution must adopt open standards to enable messages and knowledge to be shared among components of the solution.

An autonomic solution requires that the following components be present in the solution:

- An **autonomic element** which is a combination of a managed component and an autonomic manager
- The **managed component** which in this case could be any kind of security apparatus that we would to managed autonomically, e.g., a firewall or user access list.
- The **autonomic manager**, which operates the managed component based on feedback, such as messages received from the environment.
- Communication between the autonomic elements will be achieved with an **autonomic communications channel**. As part of this, messages will be formatted according to open standards, such as STIX, CyBOX and SCAP.

The **environment** should be considered as the full extent of a cloud deployment which hosts infrastructure that provides some value, of any combination of services. In the case of a website, this could be virtual machines, databases, message queues and an in-memory cache, for example. A defence in-depth strategy (Figure 3) calls for multiple layers of security. The solution proposes that each logical layer of such a strategy is secured by an autonomic element as described.

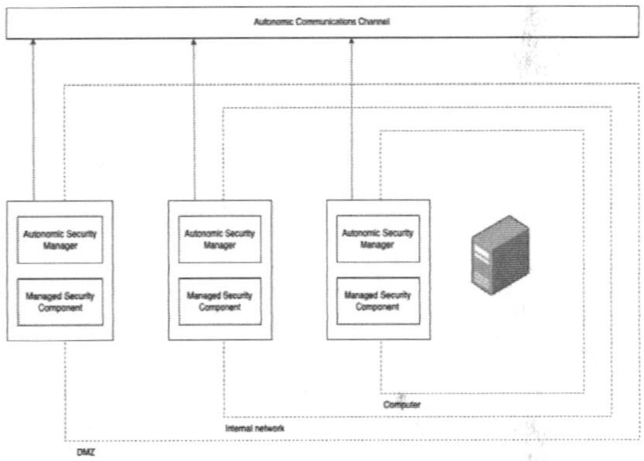

Figure 3. Autonomic defence in depth.

Autonomic elements must consume and emit the following kinds of messages:

- **Indicator of compromise** data will be passed between autonomic elements using the OpenIOC standard. This is our *reflex signal*, to which the system is expected to respond, which should result in a mitigation. Examples of this message may be an IoC for a piece of malware identified by an EDR solution (the managed component) and published to the autonomic communications channel by an attached autonomic manager.
- **Vulnerabilities** will be expressed using the CVE format and associated *Common Platform Enumeration (CPE)* format which allows specific operating system, package, and version information to be expressed. An example message would specify that OpenSSL version 1.1.3 on Linux has a critical vulnerability.
- **Mitigations** required for managed components will be passed using the *SCAP* standard, which contains machine readable data expressing how the

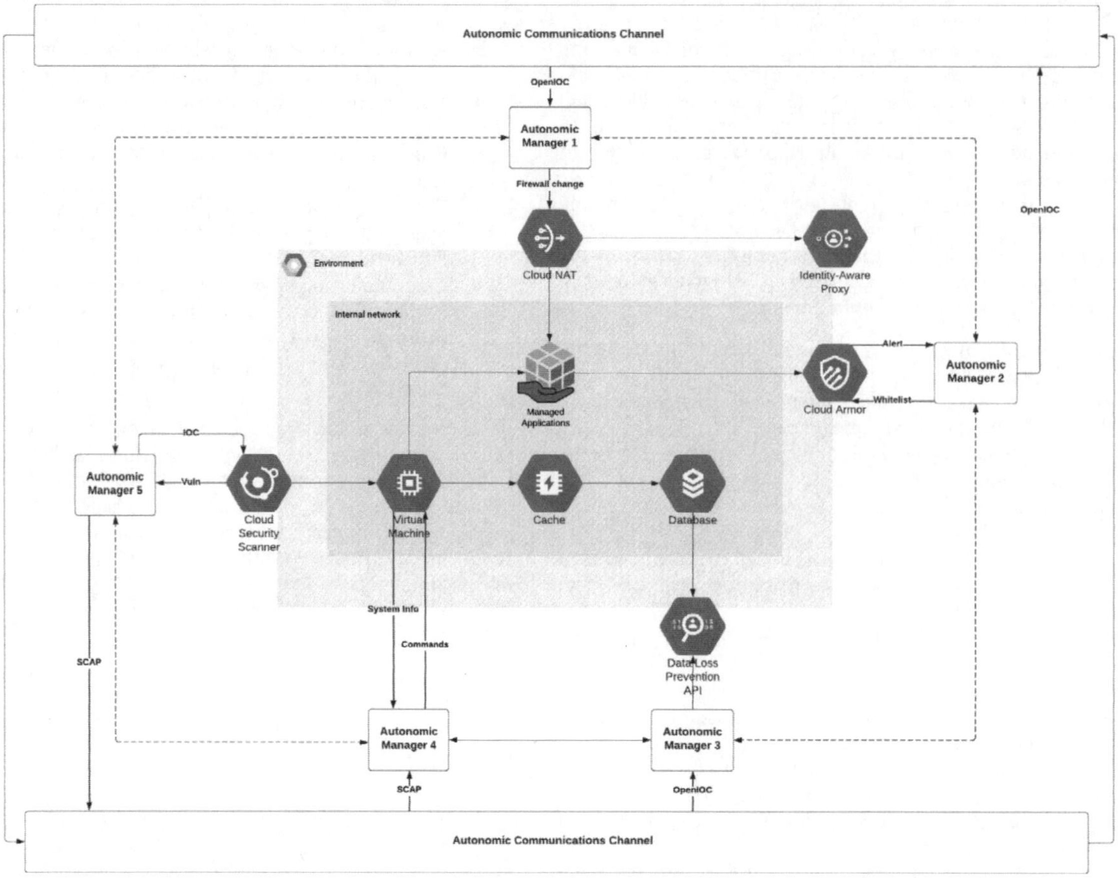

Figure 4. Autonomous secure cloud environment.

environment state should be modified to remediate a vulnerability, possibly an apoptotic response to the reflex signal. An example SCAP message would specify that a certain Windows 11 Pro service should be disabled.

A scalable and fault tolerant message bus, such as Kafka or RabbitMQ will constitute the **autonomic communications channel** which each autonomic manager will both subscribe and publish to. These message queues are built to ensure that messages are always delivered and can scale up to many millions of messages per second, so important security events are guaranteed to be delivered. Each managed component is an existing security control or cloud service. The autonomic manager integrates with it via existing APIs and acts as a gateway between control specific messages and the standardised formats the solution is relying on. While each autonomic element receives every reflex signal being triggered, it is up to each specific element to decide how to react to it, and if it also needs to transmit a reflex signal in turn. By combining both cloud services and security controls into a single autonomous system, an immune system is created which removes the need for a human in the loop because existing security tools integrate poorly with the environment they are protecting.

To understand how the solution would work, consider Figure 4. AM5, which manages a vulnerability scanner, detects a vulnerability on a VM and emits an SCAP message with remedial details. AM4 receives the message and issues a system command which updates the environment state with the remedial action and the change is made as configuration drift has occurred between the desired state and actual state. AM1, AM2 and AM3 receives the message but does not perform any action.

In another scenario, AM3 detects that data is being sent to an unauthorised IP outside of the environment. It emits an OpenIOC message. AM1 receives the message and instantly enacts a change to the environment to block this network traffic. In addition, AM2 receives the message and queries the Cloud Armor Web Application Firewall (WAF) for all traffic sent from the offending external IP address and emits an OpenIOC message. Upon receiving the message AM5 conducts a vulnerability scan of the web applications being hosted that interacted with the external IP, based on the messages from AM2.

At no point in these interactions is a human necessary to perform any action. This fact is the advantage of an autonomic security solution, as the workload on security practitioners is greatly reduced.

VI. CONCLUSIONS

So far, the security industry has failed to take advantage of the many features covered by this paper, and only increased the complexity of systems overall, failing to take advantage of autonomic principles in favour of artificial complexity.

Taking a devil's advocate position, a serious ethical issue with the solution is the consumption of data which has historically been heavily biased against network traffic originating in certain regions, and weight that traffic is much more negatively based on this fact alone. In this solution, this will manifest itself in the number of IoCs being flagged as originating in regions, such as Russia or China. The root cause of this is the bias in threat intelligence which is either directly or indirectly consumed by security tools and cloud platforms. This will directly lead to users from those areas being treated differently than others based on an explicit bias. However, the move to purely autonomous security platforms can greatly reduce this issue by removing very real cognitive bias introduced by human operators. Of course, the irony of the tendency to instantly associate any activity from Russian and Chinese sources is that although both these countries are undeniably involved in cyber warfare as nation states [34], in the case of Russia at least they have not launched a mass surveillance and illegal wiretapping campaign to match the scope of that perpetrated by GCHQ and the NSA in the form of the PRISM programme [35]. So, in this case, a very real bias results in blind spots as teams may not consider 'friendly' nation states as potential sources of attack. This is underlined by the simple fact that attempting to search for material associated with nation state threat actors will yield results that are almost exclusively non-western countries. Finally, to underline the effect of cognitive bias, consider the conflict between Russia and Ukraine and its impact on the security practitioner. Given the clear distinction in the roles of aggressor and victim as portrayed in western media, this could result in a human unconsciously giving more weight to a Russian IoC than a Ukrainian IoC. The ability for an autonomous system to operate purely on observations and data effectively negates this very real shortcoming in 'human-in-the-loop' security platforms. Lastly, it is worth noting (at least as of 2013) that Russia was only fourth in the rankings for sources of cyber-attacks, while the US was second [36]. Autonomicity provides the opportunity to remove bias from the system along with its stated aim of intelligent self-management.

ACKNOWLEDGEMENTS

The first author managed development of IBM QRadar Risk Manager [30] product for IBM. Product names may be a registered trademarked by their respective owners, all rights reserved. This paper was produced as part of COM760 Autonomic Computing & Robotics on Ulster University's MSc in Artificial Intelligence.

REFERENCES

[1] Gartner, "Gartner Says Four Trends Are Shaping the Future of Public Cloud," Gartner, 2 August 2021. [Online]. Available: https://www.gartner.com/en/newsroom/press-releases/2021-08-02-gartner-says-four-trends-are-shaping-the-future-of-public-cloud. [Accessed 10, 2023].

[2] IBM, "Benefits of Cloud Computing," 10 October 2018. [Online]. Available: https://www.ibm.com/uk-en/cloud/learn/benefits-of-cloud-computing. [Accessed 05, 2022].

[3] OpenStack, "The Most Widely Deployed Open Source Cloud Software in the World," OpenStack, 1 March 2022. [Online]. Available: https://www.openstack.org/. [Accessed 10, 2023].

[4] A. McLean, "Has IaaS commoditisation triumphed?," 2014. [Online]. Available: https://www.comparethecloud.net/editor-recommends/has-iaas-commoditisation-triumphed-over-iaas-differentiation/. [Accessed 10, 2023].

[5] Google, "Overview of Generative AI on Vertex AI," 11 2023. [Online]. Available: https://cloud.google.com/vertex-ai/docs/generative-ai/learn/overview. [Accessed 11, 2023].

[6] S. Dawson, "What Is SaaS? (With 23 Successful SaaS Examples)," 11 2022. [Online]. Available: https://dawsonsimon.com/saas-examples. [Accessed 11, 2023].

[7] CNCF, "Production-Grade Container Orchestration," CNCF, 1 March 2022. [Online]. Available: https://kubernetes.io/. [Accessed 10, 2023].

[8] E. Casalicchio, "Autonomic Orchestration of Containers: Problem Definition and Research Challenges," in *VALUETOOLS'16: Proceedings of the 10th EAI International Conference on Performance Evaluation Methodologies and Tools on 10th EAI International Conference on Performance Evaluation Methodologies and Tools*, 2016.

[9] R. Mohamed, "Kubernetes Cluster vs Master Node," Suse, 16 April 2019. [Online]. Available: https://www.suse.com/c/kubernetes-cluster-vs-master-node/#:~:text=What%20is%20Master%20Node%20in,the%20frontend%20to%20the%20cluster.. [Accessed 10, 2023].

[10] T. Luxner, "Cloud computing trends and statistics: Flexera 2023 State of the Cloud Report," Flexera, 5 April 2023. [Online]. Available: https://www.flexera.com/blog/cloud/cloud-computing-trends-flexera-2023-state-of-the-cloud-report/. [Accessed 10, 2023].

[11] S. Fregoni, "Capital One closes all data centers, relies on AWS on-demand infrastructure," Silicon Angle, 1 December 2020. [Online]. Available: https://siliconangle.com/2020/12/01/capital-one-closes-all-data-centers-to-rely-on-aws-on-demand-infrastructure-reinvent/. [Accessed 10, 2023].

[12] M. Ahola, "The Role of Human Error in Successful Cyber Security Breaches," usesecure, April 2019. [Online]. Available: https://blog.usecure.io/the-role-of-human-error-in-successful-cyber-security-breaches#:~:text=According%20to%20a%20study%20by,have%20taken%20place%20at%20all!. [Accessed 10, 2023].

[13] J. Legg, "Confronting The Shortage Of Cybersecurity Professionals," Forbes, 21 October 2021. [Online]. Available: https://www.forbes.com/sites/forbesbusinesscouncil/2021/10/21/confronting-the-shortage-of-cybersecurity-professionals/?sh=d27c8f178b9b. [Accessed 10, 2023].

[14] J. Coker, "Stress and Burnout Affecting Majority of Cybersecurity Professionals," Info security group, 2021 September 2021. [Online]. Available: https://www.infosecurity-magazine.com/news/stress-burnout-cybersecurity/. [Accessed 10, 2023].

[15] A. Taylor, "There's a huge surge in hackers holding data for ransom, and experts want everyone to take these steps," Fortune, 22 February 2022. [Online]. Available: https://fortune.com/2022/02/17/ransomware-attacks-surge-2021-report/#:~:text=Governments%20worldwide%20saw%20a%201%2C885,SonicWall%2C%20an%20internet%20cybersecurity%20company. [Accessed 10, 2022].

[16] D. J. Hagen and D. O. Lysne, "Protecting the Digitized Society—the Challenge of Balancing Surveillance and Privacy.," JSTOR, 2016. [Online]. Available: https://www.jstor.org/stable/26267300?seq=1#metadata_info_tab_contents. [Accessed 10, 2023].

[17] V. Karagiannopoulos, "A decade since 'the year of the hacktivist', online protests look set to return," 29 June 2021. [Online]. Available: https://theconversation.com/a-decade-since-the-year-of-the-hacktivist-online-protests-look-set-to-return-163329. [Accessed 10, 2023].

[18] B. Schneier, Secrets and Lies: Digital Security in a Networked World, with New Information about Post-9/11 Security, 2nd edition, Indianapolis: Wiley Publishing, 2004.

[19] K. Townsend, "UK Warns That Aggressive Cyberattack Could Trigger Kinetic Response," 15 May 2018. [Online]. Available: https://www.securityweek.com/uk-warns-aggressive-cyberattack-could-trigger-kinetic-response. [Accessed 10, 2023].

[20] Forcepoint, "What is Defense in Depth?," Forcepoint, 2022. [Online]. Available: https://www.forcepoint.com/cyber-edu/defense-depth. [Accessed 10, 2023].

[21] M. Rouse, "What Does 5-Tuple Mean?," 21st May 2014. [Online]. Available: https://www.techopedia.com/definition/28190/5-tuple#:~:text=Explains%205%2DTuple-,What%20Does%205%2DTuple%20Mean%3F,and%20the%20protocol%20in%20use.. [Accessed 10, 2023].

[22] D. Raywood, "Alert Fatigue and Overload an Issue for Majority of Security Analysts," 9th July 2020. [Online]. Available: https://www.infosecurity-magazine.com/news/alert-fatigue-overload-issue/. [Accessed 10, 2023].

[23] Mitre, "CVE® Program Mission," 2022. [Online]. Available: https://www.cve.org/. [Accessed 10, 2023].

[24] Mitre, "Heartbleed CVE," 2014. [Online]. Available: https://cve.mitre.org/cgi-bin/cvename.cgi?name=cve-2014-0160. [Accessed 10, 2023].

[25] NIST, "Security Content Automation Protocol," 2022. [Online]. Available: https://csrc.nist.gov/projects/security-content-automation-protocol. [Accessed 10, 2023].

[26] Ponemon institute, "The 2020 Cyber Resilient Organization Study by the Ponemon Institute," IBM, 2022. [Online]. Available: https://www.ibm.com/account/reg/us-en/signup?formid=urx-45839. [Accessed 10, 2023].

[27] R. Sterritt, "Keynote: 20 Years of Autonomic Computing," in *17th International Conference on Autonomic and Autonomous Systems (ICAS)*, Online (Covid-19), 2021.

[28] X. Etchevers, T. Coupaye, F. Boyer and N. De Palma, "Self-configuration of distributed applications in the cloud," July 2011. [Online]. Available: https://www.computer.org/csdl/proceedings-article/cloud/2011/4460a668/12OmNznCl2S. [Accessed 10, 2023].

[29] J. Ruohonen, "A look at the time delays in CVSS vulnerability scoring," 2 December 2017. [Online]. Available: https://www.sciencedirect.com/science/article/pii/S2210832717302995#b0080. [Accessed 1, 2023].

[30] IBM, "IBM QRadar Risk Manager," 24 January 2022. [Online]. Available: https://www.ibm.com/docs/en/qsip/7.3.2?topic=manager-qradar-risk. [Accessed 05, 2022].

[31] IBM, "An architectural blueprint for autonomic computing," June 2005. [Online]. Available: https://www-03.ibm.com/autonomic/pdfs/AC%20Blueprint%20White%20Paper%20V7.pdf.

[32] I. Ghanizada and A. Chuvakin, "Modernizing SOC ... Introducing Autonomic Security Operations," 21 July 2021. [Online]. Available: https://cloud.google.com/blog/products/identity-security/modernizing-soc-introducing-autonomic-security-operations. [Accessed 10, 2023].

[33] I. Ghanizada and A. Chuvakin, "Autonomic Security Operations," 2 July 2021. [Online]. Available: https://services.google.com/fh/files/misc/googlecloud_autonomicsecurityoperations_soc10x.pdf. [Accessed 10, 2023].

[34] Mandiant, "Advanced Persistent Threat Groups," [Online]. Available: https://www.mandiant.com/resources/apt-groups. [Accessed 10, 2023].

[35] The Guardian, "UK gathering secret intelligence via covert NSA operation," 7th June 2013. [Online]. Available: https://www.theguardian.com/technology/2013/jun/07/ uk-gathering-secret-intelligence-nsa-prism. [Accessed 05, 2022].

[36] N. Knell, "Top 10 Countries Where Cyber Attacks Originate," 23 April 2013. [Online]. Available: https://www.govtech.com/security/hacking-top-ten.html. [Accessed 10, 2023].

AC/DC: Autonomic Computing to Maintain Drone Fleet Continuity

Fiachra Merwick, Roy Sterritt
Ulster University
Belfast, Northern Ireland
email: fiachra.merwick@gmail.com
| r.sterritt@ulster.ac.uk

Abstract— **This paper aims to review the current state of the art of autonomic computing as it relates to the management of a fleet of drones being used for surveillance. Drones, for the purposes of this paper, refer to unmanned aerial vehicles that incorporate sensors for autonomous detection and surveillance. As economies of scale and improvements in the technology continue to materialize, fleets of drones become a viable commercial option to perform surveillance. In order to ensure self-management of these complete systems, an architecture is proposed to ensure the self-Configuring, Healing, Optimizing and Protection (self-CHOP) properties of the system are realized. The theoretical implementation of this autonomic computing solution is then discussed with respect to both its advantages and ethical implications.**

Keywords—Autonomic Computing; UAV; swarm; self-management.

I. Introduction

Autonomic Computing is a term originally derived and proposed by IBM in 2001, which describes the area of self-governing systems [1]. It has been compared with some biological functions of the human body which are essentially self-managed, not requiring conscious thought, such as the nervous system which self regulates the body [2]. As the predicted increase in complexity of computer systems would far outweigh the number of operators required to maintain them at that time, it was imperative to develop a discipline of computing whereby the systems would manage themselves to a certain degree, often occurring in the background unbeknownst to both the user and the operator [3]. This initial concept gave rise to the idea of the CHOP properties, which defines self-managing systems as being self–configuring, self-healing, self-optimising and self-protecting [4]. The self in this instance refers to the information system [5].

Recent improvements in drone technology, or more specifically Unmanned Aerial Vehicles (UAVs), which incorporate autonomous flight capabilities, have led to the ability to deploy UAVs in commercial settings for surveillance purposes [6]. There are still many hurdles to overcome with respect to ` the technology, however, incorporating a fleet of UAVs will become increasingly commercially viable as the technology scales and the scope of work/area of surveillance increases [7].

One distinction that is important to make is the difference between the terms autonomous and autonomic. Although IBM initially described Autonomic computing as self-governing [1], a more recent distinction between autonomy and autonomicity is that autonomy is self-governing and autonomicity is self-managing. Self-governing relates to the "delegation of responsibility to the system to meet the defined goals of the system (automation of responsibility including some decision making for the success of tasks), whereas autonomicity is system self-management (automation of responsibility including some decision making for the successful operation of the system)" [8].

Surveillance systems using UAV technology have the advantage of being adaptive with respect to automation for both flight controls, altering coverage and improving flight efficiency, as well as the object or risk detection models used to power the sensing portion of the system. This is particularly important where surveillance is used as a deterrent to criminal activity or threats, as individuals that pose the threat may adapt to the safeguards put in place, thus there is more scope to keep up with any potential changes in the behaviour of those that pose the threat.

The main objectives of this paper are to:

- Identify the current state of the art in UAV surveillance technology.
- Outline requirements of an autonomic system as it relates to a surveillance system comprising of multiple UAV's.
- Propose an autonomic solution to ensure appropriate self-management as fleets of UAV's begin to scale.
- Consider both the suitability and ethical implications of this proposal.

The format of the remainder of this paper is organised in the following manner: Section 2 details previous work carried out relating to the development and use of autonomic computing, focussing on its use in multi agent systems. Section 3 introduces an architecture that could be implemented to ensure self-management of the system. Section 4 discusses the results and provides a conclusion to the study.

II. Related Work

A. *Autonomic Computing*

A self-managing or autonomic system is summarised in [9] by four general properties, which include both objectives and attributes. The objectives of the system are to be self-configuring, self-healing, self-optimising and self-protecting. The attributes help to define the implementation of the system in order to achieve the objectives and can be categorised as self-aware, self-situated, self-monitoring and self-adjusting [10]. This is represented as a quality tree presented in Figure 1 and accurately captures the elements of autonomic computing [10].

Figure 1. Autonomic Computing Tree [10].

a) Self-Configuring

This can be described as the system's ability to "automatically install, configure or integrate new software components" [10] or more simply, the ability to "readjust itself automatically" [9].

b) Self-Healing

This is the ability of the system to recover from a fault, including identifying the fault and repairing it where possible.

c) Self-Optimisation

This is the system's ability to improve its performance against its ideal performance, which is known by the system, by measuring its current performance and implementing policies that attempt to improve it.

d) Self-Protecting

The system will have awareness of potential threats and will defend itself from these threats, whether they be accidental or malicious in nature.

The autonomic element, shown in Figure 2, is a control loop that manages the self-monitoring of a system, which was coined as MAPE by IBM. This refers to the functions of Monitoring, Analyzing, Planning and Executing [11]. The autonomic managers also communicate with each other using a reflex signal, which ensures the robustness of the system.

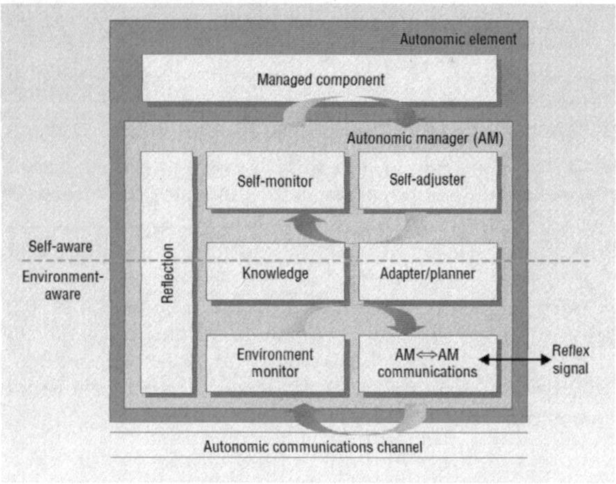

Figure 2. Control loops in an autonomic element [11].

B. Heartbeat Monitoring

The reflex signal, introduced in the previous paragraph, is a crucial element in the design of autonomic systems and heartbeat monitoring can enable achieving this. It is noted in [4] that there is a facility designed within Grid computing to detect and report on whether processes are still alive. The idea behind heartbeat monitoring is that a process or agent within a system continuously broadcasts a signal to indicate its health.

The important aspect of heartbeat monitoring is that it reduces the amount of data sent by an agent or process, by just transmitting a simple signal. It is only in the absence of receiving this signal that the reflex signal then performs more complex tasks and more detailed information can be sent [11].

Ultimately, this can then be used to ensure the self-CHOP objectives can be met by the system.

C. UAVs

The concept of a large fleet of UAV's operating autonomously and self-managing using autonomic computing methods with a surveillance objective as topic for investigation was inspired by research carried out for NASA on the use of swarms for future missions, where a swarm describes a "large number of simple entities that have local interactions (including interactions with the environment)" [12].

The limitations in the use of induvial UAVs are highlighted in [13], noting the limited battery life and field of view and suggests a swarm of UAVs working in collaboration with each other as a sustainable solution. It is quite evident from recent studies that the main stakeholders when it comes to swarm technology for surveillance are world militaries [14], [15], [16]. This raises some ethical concerns with respect to the development and improvement of the technology.

In a review of communication architectures for swarms of UAV's by [17], autonomic computing, as per the goals, objectives and attributes outlined in Figure 1, is not referred to specifically, and is not encompassed by the architectures; however, many aspects of autonomic computing are considered.

A more robust autonomic computing approach to communication between multiple agents is taken by [18], where computer vision is the primary method of communication using optical character recognition.

The following section attempts to improve on the swarm communication architecture by implementing an autonomic computing approach, inspired by [18], with due consideration to each aspect of the system goals.

III. AC/DC Architecture

A comprehensive review of UAV swarm communication architectures is provided in [17]. The "Single-Group Swarm Ad hoc Network" architecture is used as the baseline architecture in this proposal and will be enhanced using lessons learned from [18]. A schematic of the infrastructure is shown in Figure 3, where U-T-U stands for UAV-to-UAV communication and U-T-I stands for UAV to base infrastructure communication.

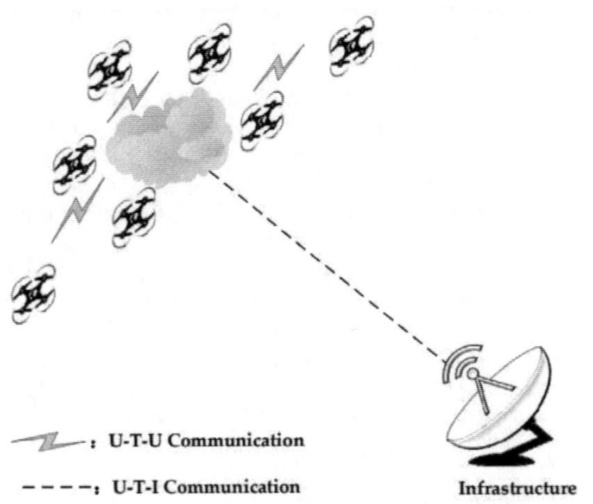

Figure 3. Single-Group Swarm Ad hoc Network architecture [17].

In a "single-group swarm Ad hoc network", there is no dependence on the base station infrastructure providing communication to all UAVs, therefore eliminating a single point of failure in the system. At any given instant, the closest UAV to the base station infrastructure, known as the "gateway UAV" sends and receives information at high power, with only low power transmission being required to transmit and receive information between the remaining UAVs.

Although "UAVs in the swarm can share situation information in real time to optimize collaborative control and improve efficiency" [17], loss of the gateway UAV may constitute a single point of failure if the loss is not managed appropriately, and this is where an autonomic solution fits in perfectly to maintain the continuous deployment of the swarm without human intervention. This is due to the fact that the gateway UAV contains additional transceivers to allow it to communicate at high power to the base station infrastructure.

An enhancement is proposed for this infrastructure by including heartbeat monitoring, similar to that described in [11] [18]. Autonomic elements, as per Figure 2, will be incorporated in each individual UAV of the swarm, as well as the base station infrastructure.

The concept is that each UAV in the swarm will be emitting an "*I am alive*" signal. This will be received by both surrounding UAVs using the U-T-U communication and by the base station infrastructure using the U-T-I communication, for the UAV sending the high-power transmission. If this signal is not received at any instance, then an algorithm, as specified in Figure 4, will be executed.

```
Swarm autonomously performing surveillance of environment
if "I am Alive" signal not received then
    Determine last known GPS position
    Closest UAV to the GPS position self identifies
    Closest UAV moves to within imaging range of the gps position
    Closest UAV runs computer vision algorithm for detection of obstacles and UAVs
        If unexpected objects found by computer vision then
            Relay signal to reconfigure the route planner for the swarm
        Elsif threat is identified by computer vision then
            Relay signal to reconfigure the route planner for the swarm
            Report threat findings to base station operator
            Endif
        If lost UAV found by computer vision then
            Send communication of updated GPS location and video for recovery team
        Endif
    If signal received by base station then
        Dispatch new Gateway UAV to replace lost UAV
        Establish new connection between the gateway UAV and the swarm and base station
    Else
        Dispatch generic UAV to replace the lost UAV
    Endif
Endif
```

Figure 4. Proposed algorithm for reflex signal, inspired by [18].

The successful implementation of this algorithm will rely on the swarm of UAVs and the base station operating as autonomic managers and it aims to:

1) Dispatch a new UAV: This will ensure self-healing of the system is achieved, specifically addressing the issue of gateway UAV loss and re-establishing the connection between the swarm and the base station infrastructure.

2) Send the closest UAV by GPS position: This is carrreid out to monitor the location of the lost UAV and identify any obstacles or threats and the location of the lost UAV. This ensures the system achieves the self-protection objective, if threats or new obstacls do exist.

3) If applicable, update the routing plan for the swarm: Based on the findings from point 2, this aspect will help achieve the self-configuration and self-optimisation of the autonomic system by ensuring repetition of the UAV loss will not occur due to spacial or external threats.

4) If applicable, send information on lost UAV: Also, based on the findings from point 2, this aspect will help achieve self-healing to a degree, although the underlying motivation for the execution of this procedure is for an operator to use this data for physical retrieval and inspection of the site of the loss.

IV. CONCLUSION & FUTURE WORK

The proposed autonomic solution is an enhancement to the current state of the art of UAV swarm communication technology, as informed by the reviewed literature. The main advantage of incorporating an autonomous computing element to the swarm architecture is ensuring self-configuration and self-healing of the system, particularly in the case where the gateway UAV is lost.

The heartbeat reflex signal methodology is a good fit for the autonomic elements of this architecture, as it is imperative for UAVs to consume as little power as possible and a simple signal achieves that requirement. The result of the implementation, which achieves the self-CHOP objectives, will be UAV swarms operating without operator intervention, for the most part, though it is noted that the physical nature of robotic swarms will always require some physical involvement.

Although this enhancement will improve upon swarm route optimisation and threat avoidance, a real ethical concern is raised, as military usage of these swarms is inevitable. It is difficult to state, prior to implementation, if this could be used purely defensively, or offensively also. However, it is clear from both the research carried out and the reasons behind implementation of the autonomic elements of the system, such as healing due to loss of UAVs and optimisation after identification of threats to the system, that military use is the use case that would ultimately benefit the most.

Autonomic computing and its implementation in systems is not as widely known or publicised as autonomous implementations, however it is clear from the research carried out for this paper and the potential implication of the implementation of the proposal in this paper, that without autonomic computing, the autonomous algorithms may be rendered useless.

ACKNOWLEDGEMENTS

This paper was produced as part of COM760 Autonomic Computing & Robotics for Ulster University's MSc. in Artificial Intelligence.

REFERENCES

[1] P. Horn, "Autonomic Computing: IBM's Perspective on the State of Information Technology," *IBM,* October 2001.

[2] S. Dobson, R. Sterritt, P. Nixon and M. Hinchey, "Fulfilling the vision of Autonomic Computing," in *Computer*, 2010, pp. 35-41.

[3] C. Franke, W. Theilmann, Y. Zhang and R. Sterritt, "Towards the Autonomic Business Grid," *Fourth IEEE International Workshop on Engineering of Autonomic and Autonomous Systems,* pp. 107-112, 2007.

[4] R. Sterritt and S. Chung, "Personal Autonomic Computing Self-Healing Tool," *Proceedings of the 11th IEEE International Conference and Workshop on the Engineering of Computer-Based Systems,* pp. 513-520, 2004.

[5] T. Wong, M. Wagner and C. Treude, "Self-Adaptive Systems: A Systematic Literature Review Across Categories and Domains," *Information and Software Technology,* vol. 148, 2022.

[6] K. Kanistras, G. Martins, M. J. Rutherford and K. P. Valavanis, "A survey of unmanned aerial vehicles (UAVs) for traffic monitoring," *2013 International Conference on Unmanned Aircraft Systems (ICUAS),* pp. 221-234, 2013.

[7] Y. Zhou, B. Rao and W. Wang, "UAV Swarm Intelligence: Recent Advances and Future Trends," *IEEE Access,* vol. 8, pp. 183856-183878, 2020.

[8] W. Truszkowski, L. Hallock, C. Rouff, J. Karlin, J. Rash, M. G. Hinchey and R. Sterritt, Autonomous and Autonomic Systems: With Applications to NASA Intelligent Spacecraft Operations and Exploration Systems, London: Springer, 2009.

[9] R. Sterritt, G. Wilkie, G. Brady, C. Saunders and M. Doran, "Autonomic Robotics for Future Space Missions," *European Space Agency,* 2015.

[10] R. Sterritt and D. Bustard, "Autonomic Computing - a means of achieving dependability?," *10th IEEE International Conference and Workshop on the Engineering of Computer-Based Systems,* pp. 247-251, 2003.

[11] M. G. Hinchey and R. Sterritt, "Self-Managing Software," *Computer,* vol. 39, pp. 107-109, 2006.

[12] M. G. Hinchey, J. L. Rash, W. F. Trusz, C. A. Rouff and R. Sterritt, "Autonomous and Autonomic Swarms," in *Software Engineering Research and Practice (SERP)*, 2005.

[13] M. G. Cimino, M. Lega, M. Monaco and G. Vaglini, "Adaptive Exploration of a UAVs Swarm for Distributed Targets Detection and Tracking," in *Proceedings of the 8th International Conference on Pattern Recognition Applications and Methods*, 2019.

[14] Z. Xiaoning, "Analysis of military application of UAV swarm technology," *2020 3rd International Conference on Unmanned Systems (ICUS),* pp. 1200-1204, 2020.

[15] M. Campion, P. Ranganathan and S. Faruque, "UAV swarm communication and control architectures: a review," *Journal of Unmanned Vehicle Systems,* pp. 93-106, 2018.

[16] Y. Wang, P. Bai, X. Liang, W. Wang, J. Zhang and Q. Fu, "Reconnaissance Mission Conducted by UAV Swarms Based on Distributed PSO Path Planning Algorithms," *IEEE Access,* vol. 7, pp. 105086-105099, 2019.

[17] X. Chen, J. Tang and S. Lao, "Review of Unmanned Aerial Vehicle Swarm Communication Architectures and Routing Protocols," *Applied Sciences,* vol. 10, p. 3661, 2020.

[18] C. Saunders, R. Sterritt and G. Wilkie, "Computer Vision Techniques for Autonomic Collaboration between Mobile Robots," *The Seventh International Conference on Adaptive and Self-Adaptive Systems and Applications,* pp. 51-57, 2015.

Autonomic Computing in the Cloud: An Overview of Past, Present and Future Trends

Alistair McLean, Roy Sterritt
School of Computing, Ulster University
Belfast, Northern Ireland
Email: Mclean-a13@ulster.ac.uk | r.sterritt@ulster.ac.uk

Abstract - **The use of cloud computing has grown at an exceptional rate, with offerings from major cloud providers removing the requirement for organisations to acquire and maintain their own infrastructure. However, the complexity of computer-based systems deployed to the cloud means that efficient and effective management of resources is difficult for humans to achieve. The application of autonomic computing to this environment has solved the problem of complexity and management by creating systems that can self-manage through self- and environmental awareness. This work aims to investigate how the application of autonomic computing has advanced the field of cloud computing with an overview of historical developments, current state-of-the-art solutions, and expected future trends. Investigation shows that optimisation of cloud services with respect to operational costs, energy consumption, Service Level Agreements (SLAs), and Quality of Service (QoS) has, and remains to be, an active area of research. With the protection of data and services in the cloud being a priority for users, we discuss advancements in the application of security-aware components for autonomic cloud computing. Ethical implications of cloud computing are discussed, principally the energy consumption of data centres, highlighting the growing research in the field of energy efficient computation and resource management. The contribution of this paper is Systematization of Knowledge (SoK).**

Keywords – Cloud Computing; Autonomic Computing; Autonomous Systems; Service Oriented Architecture.

I. INTRODUCTION

Cloud computing has dramatically changed the way businesses approach creating, deploying, maintaining, scaling, and financing their information technology services. Small to Medium-sized Enterprises (SMEs) can benefit from accessing vast computational resource without the unaffordable upfront costs of provisioning and maintaining their own hardware or data centres [1][2]. Additionally, the diverse offerings from cloud computing providers today appeals to a range of consumers, from SMEs to large multinational corporations. The adoption rate of cloud technologies over the last few decades has been high and it is expected that organisations will continue to embrace cloud computing, with adoption of public cloud services accelerating [3][4].

Simultaneously, organisations have been working on improving the dependability of their systems. In an increasingly technological world, the reliance on computing systems is more important than ever. The criticality of computing systems is such that unplanned application downtime and critical IT failures can have massive business impact – potentially costing large organisations hundreds of thousands of dollars per hour [5]. Autonomic computing is an area that emerged to help address the challenge of creating reliable, fault tolerant, self-managing systems. The principles of autonomic computing are now commonplace, having already been incorporated into many computing systems. Work in the area has proposed that *all* computer-based systems should indeed be autonomic [6].

The aim of this paper is to detail how the principles of Autonomic Computing have been applied throughout the emergence of Cloud Computing. This section continues with "what is Cloud Computing?" and "what is Autonomic Computing?", followed by a history of the areas in Section 2. Section 3 then looks at the current state of the art, and Section 4 describe potential future trends before the paper concludes.

A. *What is Cloud Computing?*

Cloud computing is a method of utilising remote computing resource and capacity provided by means of an Internet service [7]. It has become customary in the field of cloud computing to describe cloud service models with the "as a Service" (aaS) phrase – prepended by the technology on offer [8]. Although there have been many takes on this "as a Service" approach – the major cloud service providers have generally adopted a three-tier approach, each tier representing a distinct level of resource abstraction and control. They include:

1. Software as a Service (SaaS)
2. Platform as a Service (PaaS)
3. Infrastructure as a Service (IaaS)

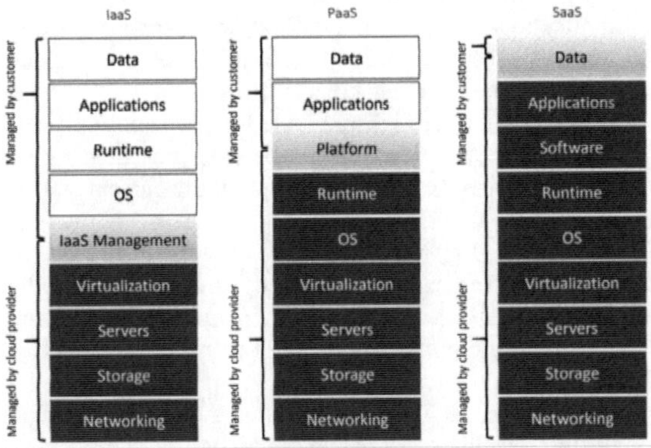

Figure 1. Representation of resource abstraction and level of control for the three main service models [9].

Figure 1 shows an example of how the level of control between the cloud provider and the customer varies between service models.

B. *What is Autonomic Computing?*

Inspired by the autonomic nervous system where bodily functions are unconsciously regulated, autonomic computing is a design model that aims to create computer-based systems that, through self- and environmental awareness, act to self-Configure, self-Heal, self-Optimise, and self-Protect (self-CHOP) [6][10].

An established method for achieving self- and environmental awareness in computing systems is by use of autonomic managers [11]. An autonomic manager cycles through a four-step control loop entailing Monitoring, Analysing, Planning, and Executing (MAPE) managed elements in a system, while consulting Knowledge (MAPE-K). Sensors collect information from the autonomic element and from its environment, with effectors able to complete executable tasks to accomplish system adaptation [12]. Figure 2 shows the high-level design of an autonomic manager.

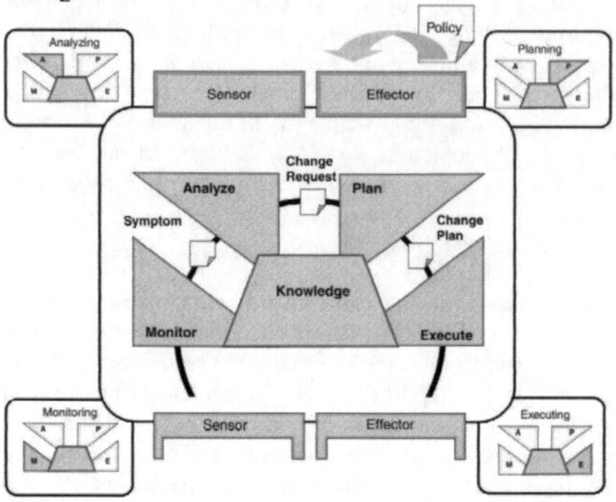

Figure 2. Autonomic manager utilising a MAPE-K control loop [11].

The *monitoring* stage collects information from the managed resource and prepares this data for analysis. Information collected may include data, such as performance metrics, capacity utilisation, response times, and health status of other managed elements in the environment. Communication between autonomic managers, including reporting of their health status, can facilitate self-healing and self-protecting mechanisms [13][14].

The *analysis* stage is responsible for determining if self-adjustment is necessary based on the data presented by the monitoring process. Comparison between the current state of the system and the ideal state of the system, dictated by policy, supports decision making at this stage of the control loop. Predictive forecasting techniques can also be utilised to determine the likelihood of self-adjustment in the future, allowing for pre-emptive change in the system to facilitate self-CHOP behaviour.

The *planning* stage naturally follows the analysis stage. If analysis determines that change is necessary, the plan acts on the change request to structure the workflow.

Execution puts the change workflow into action to update the state of the system through effector interfaces with managed resources.

Knowledge extends the standard MAPE control loop, allowing data to be shared between each of the four stages and between multiple autonomic managers in a system. Knowledge in an autonomic system may include information, such as decision-making governance policies, symptom diagnostics, and solutions.

II. HISTORY OF THE AREA

The emergence of cloud computing has provided many benefits to users including increased flexibility and scalability of resources, reduced time to market for applications, and financial savings on infrastructure cost and maintenance. However, the growth of this field has increased the complexity of computer-based systems making it harder for humans to manage, further emphasising the importance of autonomic computing to create self-managing systems [15][16].

A. *Runtime Management*

Large-scale distributed applications deployed to the cloud are adaptive and evolve throughout the lifetime of their execution. Early research identified the benefit of non-static techniques, which continually assess the demands and priorities of systems at runtime. One such proposed architecture was the Autonomic Runtime Manager (ARM), which used MAPE techniques to self-optimise the system. Experiments using wildfire simulation showed that the use of dynamic ARM optimisation improved performance by up to 45% compared with static techniques [17].

B. *Service Level Agreements*

Autonomic computing as a concept showed great promise for the management of infrastructure, however some outstanding issues meant that application within a cloud environment was not a simple task. Notably, existing frameworks did not account for virtualisation layers, and conflicts could arise between SLA and other targets, such as energy efficiency. This led to research proposals, such as extending the traditional MAPE-K loop to include an Adaption phase to balance virtualisation in the cloud. The adaptation phase of the suggested A-MAPE-K loop could establish SLA contracts, tailor monitoring processes, or handle attribute inconsistencies prior to application deployment [18]. The result being that cloud providers and consumers could create SLAs on demand, with self-management of infrastructure considering multiple goals simultaneously. Other work included flexible and reliable management of SLAs, with improved monitoring to prevent SLA violations [19].

C. *Scaling Optimisation*

The ability for cloud consumers to scale up their resources when required, and decommission or scale down when demand is reduced, has been one the greatest benefits of cloud computing. This elastic quality reduces the need for vast resource redundancy in preparation for peak demand – the infrastructure can simply scale up its capacity during peak times. This has the benefit of reducing the running costs for cloud providers, with cloud consumers only paying for the resources that are needed to maintain QoS. However, the processes involved with scaling resources up and down take time and have associated costs and therefore research has aimed to optimise this autonomic process. One such paper utilises machine learning techniques to classify Virtual Machines (VM) in a system during the analysis stage of the MAPE-K loop [20]. The VMs are labelled with a status of "Normal", "Underutilized", or "Overutilized" at each layer of the system based on their workload.

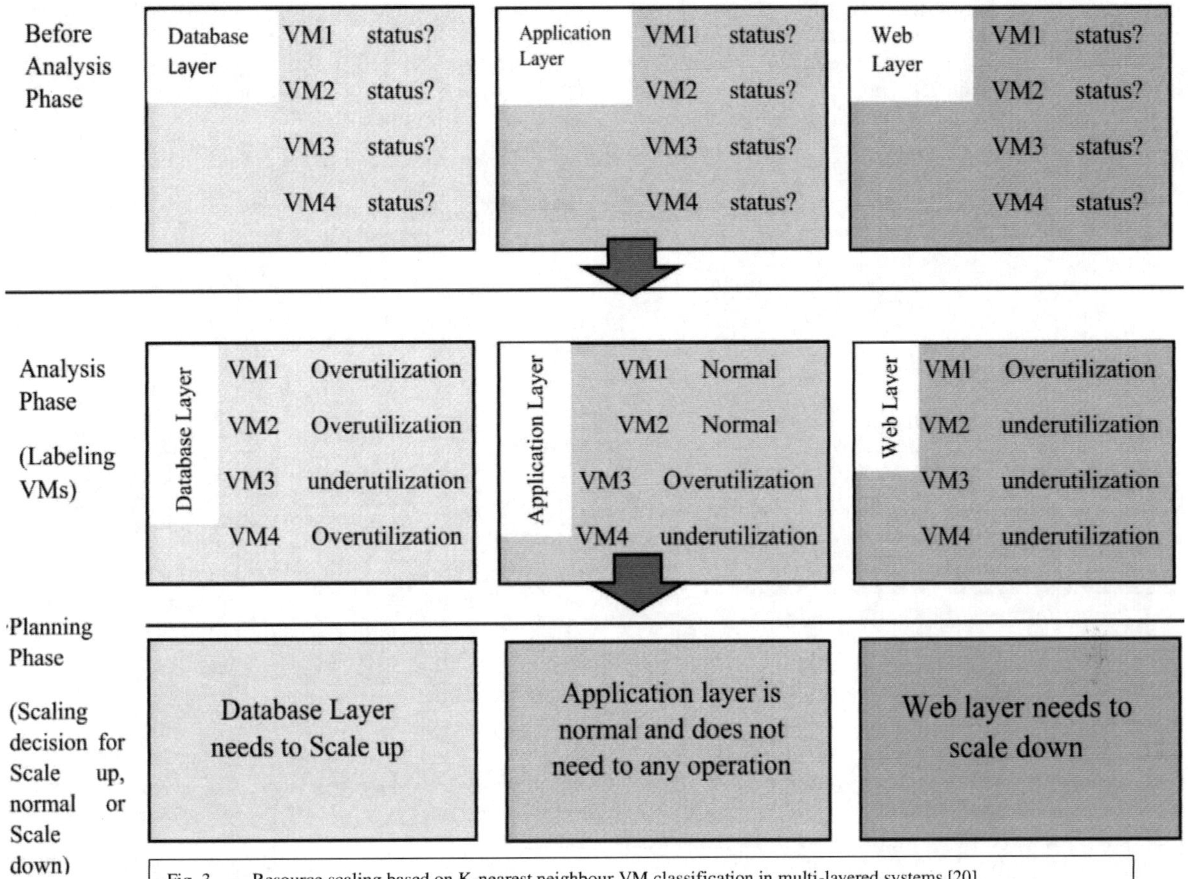

Fig. 3. Resource scaling based on K-nearest neighbour VM classification in multi-layered systems [20].

Figure 3 shows how labelling the VMs can inform the autoscaling decision process at each layer. Experimental results of simulations using this method discovered benefits including improved VM utilisation, shorter response times for customer requests, and lower operating costs for the cloud consumer.

III. CURRENT STATE OF THE ART

Work in the field of autonomic cloud solutions is well established [43]. Indeed, Cloud Computing was Autonomic Computing's major impact success during its 2nd decade [43].

Figure 4 shows a proposed taxonomy of the field, based on literature review, showing existing solutions categorised as either feature or parameter based [21]. The taxonomy is further divided into autonomic management, performance management, security-aware, and QoS-aware solutions.

A. *Autonomic Management*

Service, workload, and resource management are all types of autonomic management methodologies actively studied in research.

Service management concerns the ability to effectively manage the autonomic processes to abide by SLA and QoS agreements between cloud consumers and cloud providers. The efficiency of this process has been actively studied, with research revealing innovative solutions to improve on the existing methods. One such solution used a game theory approach to manage capacity of IaaS services [22]. Using simulations and real deployments to Amazon EC2, they report efficiency improvements of up to 70% when compared with other state of the art solutions. Other research has shown how an unsupervised machine learning approach can improve the performance of autonomic cloud managers, reporting reduction of SLA violations by up to 62% [23].

Workload management is important for adapting to the heterogenous demand throughout the system lifecycle. The trade-off between the benefit of auto-scaling and the cost of addition resources on the cloud has been an area of interest in industry and an active research topic. In the context of cloud web applications, one paper proposed an autonomic approach to optimise profits through consideration of revenue and costs models alongside performance objectives [24]. Although the scalability of the cloud is one of its greatest selling points, this research highlights the need to assess the business requirements to ascertain if the revenue generated by the additional resources will justify the costs of those additional resources. Their autonomic solution, implemented in a hybrid cloud setting, showed considerable profit improvement compared with other baseline methodologies.

Resource management is concerned with the availability and optimisation of resources at system runtime. It is important that resources are highly available to meet QoS demands, and that they are adequately utilised for greater cost benefit to the cloud consumer. An autonomic approach to resource provisioning has been presented, which uses Bayesian learning techniques and time series prediction models for scaling decisions in fog computing environments [25]. Simulation results of this novel approach shows benefits, such as decreased operating costs, decreased delays, and higher resource utilisation. Another approach that uses Reinforced Learning (RL) combined with autonomic computing benefitted from cost reductions of up to 50% whilst increasing resource utilisation by up to 12% [26].

B. *Security-Awareness*

The increased interest in cloud computing has necessitated consideration of how to protect systems deployed on such infrastructure. In the spirit of autonomic computing, self-protection is a key requirement of any system. Predominantly, self-protection of cloud resources and cloud data have been of significance in research.

It is important that sensitive data used in the cloud is protected in storage and during transmission to and from the cloud. There have been encouraging proposals to improve existing systems in this area [27]. Furthermore, existing security techniques have been evolving to better protect resources on the cloud. One of the latest proposals in this area, a system called SECURE [28], has shown promising improvements over other techniques, emphasising better QoS during security attacks.

C. *QoS-Awareness*

It is obvious that computing systems that can achieve higher QoS ratings will deliver greater benefit to organisations. The ability for autonomic systems to have QoS-awareness [29] is therefore another area of interest in research. An example of this research is a proposed "Agriculture as a Service" [30] using a QoS-aware autonomic information system. The system gathers information from Internet of Things (IoT) devices and, through analysis of QoS objectives with the use of fuzzy logic, makes appropriate decisions that are autonomically implemented. Simulations have shown resource management benefits of the system including lower execution costs, lower latency, and shorter execution times when compared with existing systems in the area.

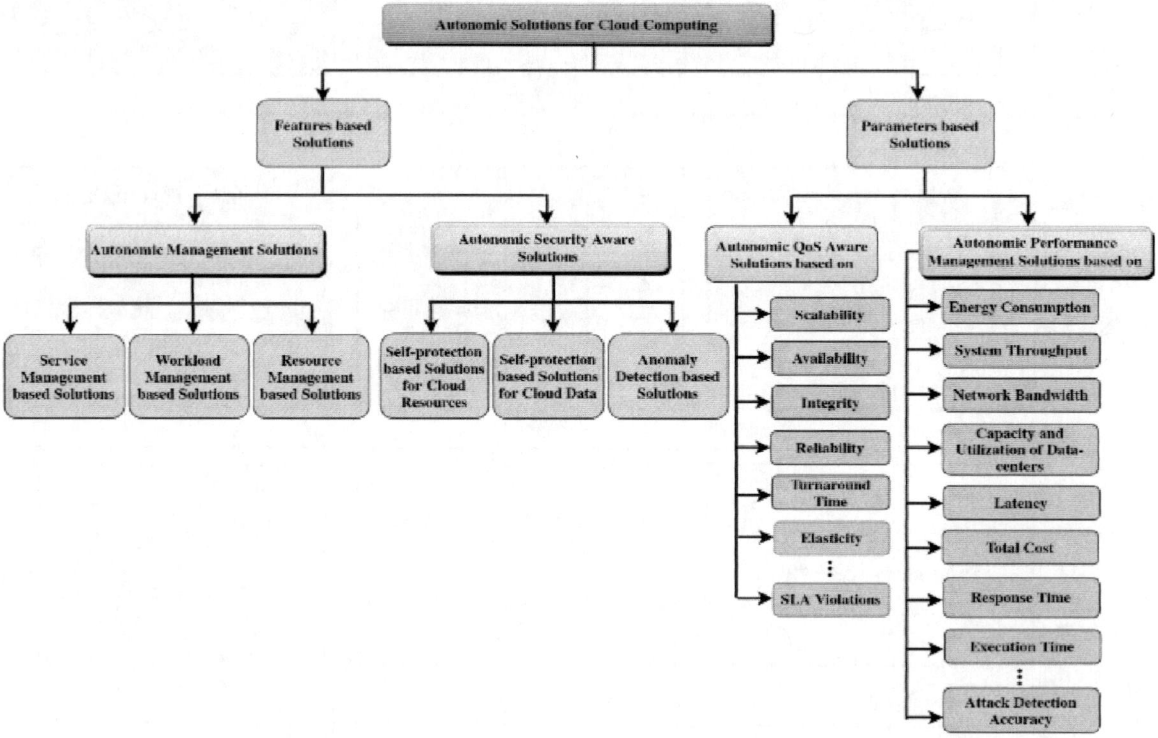

Figure 4. Overview showing the taxonomy of existing autonomic cloud solutions based on review of literature [21].

D. *Performance Management*

The amount of computing power necessary to facilitate the scale of cloud computing today creates an ethical conundrum. The greater demand for processing capacity is causing energy consumption of cloud technologies to continuously grow. As mentioned, the adoption of cloud computing is likely to continue accelerating therefore it has become important to investigate other methods of addressing energy consumption in the cloud. This is where performance management plays a role, aiming to improve performance efficiency of cloud systems (getting better performance for the same energy usage). A proposed system called DREAM [31] tackles the issue of high energy consumption in mobile cloud systems. Their system specifically addresses high energy consumption related to cloud CPU and network usage by smartphones. Through optimisation techniques they were able to show energy reductions of up to 35% compared with other methods with similar performance.

IV. POTENTIAL FUTURE TRENDS

We have already seen many examples of successful implementation of autonomic cloud solutions and improvements. However, some areas will benefit from continued research and innovation.

A. *Cloud Privacy and Security*

Relinquishing control of system and user data to the cloud provider will be a concern for many cloud consumers, therefore, work in the field of security-aware solutions will continue [32]. It has been speculated that the emergent field of "confidential computing" is the future of the cloud [33]. Confidential computing gives cloud consumers full control over their sensitive workloads. It explicitly details the computing components that they must trust, whilst providing strong protection from other components, and preventing attacks from other cloud users. Although still in its initial stages, it is expected that the field will grow rapidly to become as popular as some of the most prevalent privacy mechanisms of today.

B. *IoT Ecosystems*

Although seemingly two independent fields, the IoT and cloud computing are closely linked. IoT "generally refers to scenarios where network connectivity and computing capability extends to objects, sensors and everyday items not normally considered computers, allowing these devices to generate, exchange and consume data with minimal human intervention" [34]. Quite often, it is cloud computing services that are facilitating IoT devices, but as the number of connected devices increases, cloud technologies are struggling to sustain real-time demand [35]. It is expected that research will continue to investigate autonomic processes to handle the complexity and demands of IoT systems [36]-[39].

C. *Energy Consumption and Sustainability*

As mentioned, the enormous demand for computational processing and data storage on the cloud means that energy efficiency is a high priority topic. Data centres consume huge amounts of energy with high utilisation of resources, large operating costs, and substantial carbon footprints. In addition to using cleaner energy sources to power data centres, it is paramount that progress continues in the field of computational energy efficiency. We have already described some of the successes in this endeavour, but it is expected that research and development into energy-efficient computation will continue to improve as energy consumption of the cloud grows [40]-[42].

V. CONCLUSIONS

Autonomic computing has been a key facilitator in the advancement of cloud computing. With the scale and complexity of cloud computing systems growing, autonomic computing has helped deal with the difficulty of managing these systems. Autonomic computing has shown great advantages, including improved dependability of systems, through the ability to self-configure, self-heal, self-optimise, and self-protect.

Historically, we have seen the challenges and successes of applying autonomic principles to a cloud infrastructure. The ability to manage autonomic elements at runtime in a heterogenous environment was achieved with innovations on the topic of ARM. SLA violations drove advancements in autonomic techniques to create a tailored approach for cloud applications, for example the proposal of an A-MAPE-K control loop within autonomic managers. Furthermore, identifying that the process of resource scaling could be optimised with respect to time and cost saw the introduction of other technologies, such as those used in machine learning, to support decision making.

Evaluation of the current state of the art highlighted new innovative solutions alongside considerable improvements to existing autonomic techniques in the cloud. Autonomic management solutions have been able to drastically reduce SLA violation occurrence rates, increase resource utilisation, and reduce operational costs of resources resulting in increased profit. Development of self-protecting security-aware solutions has expanded on existing security techniques whilst improving the QoS of systems under attack. QoS-aware systems have shown resource management benefits including lower costs, improved latency, and shorter execution times. Performance management research is extremely important for both cloud providers and cloud users, with the aim being to improve energy efficiency of computation. Innovation in this field has shown promise with proposed solutions achieving considerable energy reductions whilst maintaining performance.

The current state of the art in autonomic cloud computing is promising. Further work in the area will likely see optimisations with respect to self-CHOP and MAPE mechanisms in cloud-based computing systems. As the digital age continues, with more and more data generated every day, the importance for cloud providers to handle data in an efficient and secure manner will increase. It is expected that optimisation of cloud security will continue to be an active research topic in the future. Additionally, in the interest of sustainable ethical practices and Corporate Social Responsibility (CSR), cloud providers are becoming increasingly pressured to address the scale of their operational energy consumption. With the vast energy demands of data centres used to provide cloud computing services continually growing, it is expected that research into energy efficient computation will long continue.

ACKNOWLEDGEMENT

This paper was produced as part of COM760 Autonomic Computing & Robotics for Ulster University's MSc. in Artificial Intelligence.

REFERENCES

[1] P. Modisane and O. Jokonya, "Evaluating the benefits of Cloud Computing in Small, Medium and Micro-sized Enterprises (SMMEs)", *Procedia Computer Science*, vol. 181, pp. 784-792, 2021.

[2] A. Khayer, M. Talukder, Y. Bao, and M. Hossain, "Cloud computing adoption and its impact on SMEs' performance for cloud supported operations: A dual-stage analytical approach", *Technology in Society*, 60, p.101225, 2020.

[3] A. Adamuthe and G. Thampi, "Technology forecasting: A case study of computational technologies", Technological *Forecasting and Social Change*, 143, pp. 181-189, 2019.

[4] Flexera, "*2023 State of the Cloud Report*" [online] Available at: https://info.flexera.com/CM-REPORT-State-of-the-

Cloud?lead_source=Website%20Visitor&id=Blog, 2023, [Accessed Oct. 2023].

[5] S. Elliot, "DevOps and the cost of downtime: Fortune 1000 best practice metrics quantified", *International Data Corporation (IDC)*, 2014.

[6] R. Sterritt and M. Hinchey, "Why Computer-Based Systems Should Be Autonomic", *12th IEEE International Conference and Workshops on the Engineering of Computer-Based Systems (ECBS'05), pp. 406-412,* 2005. doi: 10.1109/ECBS.2005.75.

[7] V. Arutyunov, "Cloud computing: Its history of development, modern state, and future considerations", *Scientific and Technical Information Processing*, vol. 39 issue 3, pp. 173-178, 2012.

[8] Y. Duan, G. Fu, N. Zhou, X. Sun, N. Narendra, and B. Hu, "Everything as a Service (XaaS) on the Cloud: Origins, Current and Future Trends", *IEEE 8th International Conference on Cloud Computing*, pp. 621-628, 2015.

[9] J. Surbiryala and C. Rong, "Cloud Computing: History and Overview", *IEEE Cloud Summit, pp. 1-7,* 2019.

[10] R. Sterritt, "Towards Autonomic Computing: Effective Event Management", *Proceedings of 27th Annual IEEE/NASA Software Engineering Workshop (SEW)*, IEEE Computer Society, pp. 40-47, 2002.

[11] IBM, "An Architectural Blueprint for Autonomic computing", IBM White Paper 3rd Ed., 2005.

[12] R. Kazhamiakin, S. Benbernou, L. Baresi, P. Plebani, M. Uhlig, and O. Barais, "Adaptation of Service-Based Systems", *Service Research Challenges and Solutions for the Future Internet*, pp.117-156, 2010.

[13] R. Sterritt and D. Bantz, "PAC-MEN: Personal Autonomic Computing Monitoring Environment", *Proceedings 15th International Workshop on Database and Expert Systems Applications, 2004.*

[14] R. Sterritt and S. Chung, "Personal Autonomic Computing Self-Healing Tool", *Proceedings of the 11th IEEE International Conference and Workshop on the Engineering of Computer-Based Systems, 2004.*

[15] J. Kephart, "Research challenges of autonomic computing", *Proceedings of the 27th International Conference on Software Engineering, 2005. ICSE 2005.*

[16] R. Sterritt and M. Hinchey, "Autonomicity An Antidote for Complexity?", *IEEE Computational Systems Bioinformatics Conference - Workshops (CSBW'05),* 2005.

[17] J. Yang, H. Chen, S. Hariri, and M. Parashar, "Autonomic runtime manager for adaptive distributed applications", *Proceedings 14th IEEE International Symposium on High Performance Distributed Computing (HPDC-14), 2005.*, 69-78, 2005.

[18] M. Maurer, I. Breskovic, V. Emeakaroha, and I. Brandic, "Revealing the MAPE loop for the autonomic management of Cloud infrastructures", *IEEE Symposium on Computers and Communications (ISCC),* 2011.

[19] V. C. Emeakaroha, R. N. Calheiros, M. A. Netto, I. Brandić, and C. A. Rose, "DeSVi: An Architecture for Detecting SLA Violations in Cloud Computing Infrastructures", Available at: https://www.semanticscholar.org/paper/DeSVi-%3A-An-Architecture-for-Detecting-SLA-in-Cloud-Emeakaroha-Calheiros/d4c8a4c9d6fa921e20e479714e1a14d92b948ad9, 2010, [Accessed Oct. 2023].

[20] A. Mazidi, M. Golsorkhtabaramiri, and M. Tabari, "Autonomic resource provisioning for multilayer cloud applications with K-nearest neighbor resource scaling and priority-based resource allocation", *Software: Practice and Experience*, 50(8), pp. 1600-1625, 2020.

[21] N. Agrawal, "Autonomic cloud computing-based management and security solutions: State-of-the-art, challenges, and opportunities", *Transactions on Emerging Telecommunications Technologies*, 32(12), 2021.

[22] D. Ardagna, B. Panicucci, and M. Passacantando, "Generalized Nash Equilibria for the Service Provisioning Problem in Cloud Systems", *IEEE Transactions on Services Computing*, 6(4), pp. 429-442, 2013.

[23] R. Uriarte, F. Tiezzi, and S. Tsaftaris, "Supporting Autonomic Management of Clouds: Service Clustering with Random Forest", *IEEE Transactions on Network and Service Management*, 13(3), pp.595-607, 2016.

[24] N. Beigi-Mohammadi, M. Shtern, and M. Litoiu, "Adaptive Load Management of Web Applications on Software Defined Infrastructure", *IEEE Transactions on Network and Service Management*, 17(1), pp. 488-502, 2020.

[25] M. Etemadi, M. Ghobaei-Arani, and A. Shahidinejad, "Resource provisioning for IoT services in the fog computing environment: An autonomic approach", Computer *Communications*, 161, pp. 109-131, 2020.

[26] M. Ghobaei-Arani, S. Jabbehdari, and M. Pourmina, "An autonomic resource provisioning approach for service-based cloud applications: A hybrid approach", *Future Generation Computer Systems*, 78, pp. 191-210, 2018.

[27] A. Sarhan and S. Carr, "A Highly-Secure Self-Protection Data Scheme in Clouds Using Active Data Bundles and Agent-Based Secure Multi-party Computation", *IEEE 4th International Conference on Cyber Security and Cloud Computing (CSCloud)*, pp. 228-236, 2017.

[28] S. Gill and R. Buyya, "SECURE: Self-Protection Approach in Cloud Resource Management", *IEEE Cloud Computing*, 5(1), pp. 60-72, 2018.

[29] S. Singh, I. Chana, and M. Singh, "The Journey of QoS-Aware Autonomic Cloud Computing", *IT Professional*, 19(2), pp. 42-49, 2017.

[30] S. Singh, I Chana, and R. Buyya, "Agri-Info: Cloud Based Autonomic System for Delivering Agriculture as a Service", *Internet of Things*, 9, 100131, 2020.

[31] J. Kwak, Y. Kim, J. Lee, and S. Chong, "DREAM: Dynamic Resource and Task Allocation for Energy Minimization in Mobile Cloud Systems", *IEEE Journal on Selected Areas in Communications*, 33(12), pp. 2510-2523, 2015.

[32] S. Gill and A. Shaghaghi, "Security-Aware Autonomic Allocation of Cloud Resources", *Journal of Organizational and End User Computing*, 32(3), pp. 15-22, 2020.

[33] M. Russinovich et al., "Toward confidential cloud computing", *Communications of the ACM*, 64(6), pp. 54-61, 2021.

[34] K. Rose, S. Eldridge, and L. Chapin, "The internet of things: An overview", *The Internet Society (ISOC),* pp. 1–50.

[35] S. Gill, S. Tuli, M. Xu, I. Singh, K. Singh, D. Lindsay, S. Tuli, D. Smirnova, M. Singh, U. Jain, H. Pervaiz, B. Sehgal, S. Kaila, S. Misra, M. Aslanpour, H. Mehta, V. Stankovski, and P. Garraghan, "Transformative effects of IoT, Blockchain and Artificial Intelligence on cloud computing: Evolution, vision, trends and open challenges", *Internet of Things*, 8, 100118, 2019.

[36] A. Zyane, M. Bahiri, and A. Ghammaz, "IoTScal-H: Hybrid monitoring solution based on cloud computing for autonomic middleware-level scalability management within IoT systems and different SLA traffic requirements", *International Journal of Communication Systems*, 33(14), 2020.

[37] A. Lam, O. Haugen, and J. Delsing, "Dynamical Orchestration and Configuration Services in Industrial IoT Systems: An Autonomic Approach", *IEEE Open Journal of the Industrial Electronics Society*, 3, pp. 128-145, 2022.

[38] S. Rahman and G. Jackson, "Autonomic Methods for Mitigating Threats to the Internet of Things (IoT)", *International Conference on Computational Science and Computational Intelligence (CSCI),* pp. 1302-1307, doi: 10.1109/CSCI.2017.227, 2017.

[39] E. Mezghani, S. Berlemont, and M. Douet, "Autonomic Coordination of IoT Device Management Platforms", *IEEE 29th International Conference on Enabling Technologies: Infrastructure for Collaborative Enterprises (WETICE),* 2020.

[40] T. Tekreeti, T. Cao, X. Peng, T. Bhattacharya, J. Mao, X. Qin, and W. Ku, "Towards Energy-Efficient and Real-Time Cloud Computing", *IEEE International Conference on Networking, Architecture and Storage (NAS),* 2021.

[41] S. Simaiya, V. Gautam, U. Lilhore, A. Garg, P. Ghosh, N. Trivedi, and A. Anand, "EEPSA: Energy Efficiency Priority Scheduling Algorithm for Cloud Computing", *2nd International Conference on Smart Electronics and Communication (ICOSEC),* 2021.

[42] M. Xu, A. Toosi, and R. Buyya, "A Self-Adaptive Approach for Managing Applications and Harnessing Renewable Energy for Sustainable Cloud Computing", *IEEE Transactions on Sustainable Computing*, 6(4), pp. 544-558, 2021.

[43] T. Lorimer and R. Sterritt, "Autonomic Management of Cloud Neighborhoods through Pulse Monitoring," 2012 IEEE Fifth International Conference on Utility and Cloud Computing, Chicago, IL, USA, 2012, pp. 295-302, doi: 10.1109/UCC.2012.60

[44] R. Sterritt, "Keynote: 20 Years of Autonomic Computing," in International Conference on Autonomic and Autonomous Systems (ICAS), Online (Covid-19), 2021.

Autonomic Computing for Autonomous Vehicles

Alastair Martin and Roy Sterritt
School of Computing, Ulster University
Belfast, Northern Ireland
eMail: Martin-A68@ulster.ac.uk | r.sterritt@ulster.ac.uk

***Abstract*—Autonomous Vehicles (AVs) offer huge potential benefits to society in terms of safety, business opportunities and improved transport experiences. But AVs are very complex, and although prototypes have been successfully tested on public roads, major challenges remain before the technology can be rolled out to the mass market. This Systematization of Knowledge (SoK) paper looks at how the techniques and solutions developed in Autonomic Computing (AC) could be applied to AVs to help overcome some of these challenges. It gives some specific examples and concludes that while more research and development is needed, it is already clear that AC will need to be a central component of AV technology.**

Keywords—Autonomous Vehicle; Autonomic Computing.

I. Introduction

Autonomous Vehicles (AVs) offer huge potential benefits in areas, such as:

- *Safety*. The World Health Organisation estimates there are about 1.25 million fatal traffic accidents per year, and the US Department of Transport estimates 93% of accidents are caused by driver error [21]. AVs have the potential to significantly reduce these figures.
- *Business opportunities*. AVs have the potential to improve efficiency, and free up driver time for other tasks.
- *Improved consumer centric experience*. AVs will facilitate easier access to personal transport for disabled or young people, autonomous parking and improve traffic conditions.

AVs have been in development for several decades, and further development will be needed before they will be ready for the mass market. Section II of this paper looks at the history of AV technology. Section III gives an overview of Autonomic Computing. Section IV outlines the challenges still facing AVs and Section V looks at how the principles of AC could be applied to AVs to help overcome the challenges and achieve the benefits outlined above.

II. History of Autonomous Vehicles

An AV, sometimes referred to as a "self-driving car", is a vehicle that can operate without input from a human driver. Early concepts proposed embedding guidance systems in roads. But, by the 1980s, car manufacturers and research universities had switched their attention to vehicles that were self-navigating, and this has been the main focus of attention since then.

The AV industry was given a big boost when the Defence Advanced Research Projects Agency (DARPA) in the United States organised a series of prize competitions for AVs from 2004 – 2007 called Grand Challenges. By 2007, the event was called the DARPA Urban Challenge, and teams had to design an AV that could navigate through an urban environment, while obeying traffic laws and avoiding obstacles.

The potential of AV technology for public use was starting to become clear, and numerous partnerships were formed between universities and industry to push it forward. Perhaps the most famous example is Stanford University's Sebastian Thrun, a member of the team that won the DARPA Grand Challenge in 2005 [1][22]. He went on to co-found Google's Self-Driving Car project in 2009. This is often seen as the start of the commercial phase of AV development.

By 2016, the Society of Automotive Engineers (SAE International) had defined a 6-level scale of automation, known as SAE J3016 [8].

- *Level 0 – No automation*. The driver is responsible for being aware of the environment, and for all driving tasks on a continuous basis. Some warning and emergency assist systems do fall into this category, e.g., park distance control, and anti-lock brakes.
- *Level 1 – Driver assistance*. Some tasks involving speed and steering are executed by the car, e.g., Adaptive Cruise Control (ACC) and Lane Keeping Assist (LKA). But the driver is responsible for all other aspects of driving.
- *Level 2 – Partial Automation*. The driver can "take their hands of the wheel" for some operations, e.g., Advanced automatic parking and Traffic Jam Assist. But the driver must still activate and deactivate the systems, and must monitor the environment at all times and be prepared to take full control at any point.
- *Level 3 – Conditional Automation*. The AV can manage all aspects of driving and safety in some circumstances, e.g., "Highway Chauffeur". The driver does not need to constantly monitor the driving tasks, but does need to be able to take over control at short notice if conditions require it.
- *Level 4 – High Automation*. Similar to Level 3, but does not need the human driver to provide a fall back because the AV can slow or safely stop if necessary.
- *Level 5 – Full Automation*. The AV is capable of performing all driving tasks in all conditions. A human driver does not need to be present.

Cars at level 1 are now widely available. Cars with level 2 capabilities are also on sale, although some functionality may be disabled, depending on local regulations – it can be switched on via "over the air update". Vehicles with higher levels of autonomous behaviour are still in development. The latest Gartner hype cycle for Connected Vehicles and Smart Mobility (Figure 1) shows many of the key enabling technologies are in the trough of disillusionment. The SAE [7] is upbeat about this, suggesting it means that "the hard work of commercializing many significant technologies is underway. Over the next five years or so, many technologies on this Hype Cycle will become productive parts of the automotive and smart-mobility ecosystem."

III. Overview of Autonomic Computing

Computer systems are becoming increasingly complex, and also becoming increasingly important to people and businesses. This leads to the twin problems of increased costs of managing and maintaining the systems, and the increased cost implications of faults and failures. To address these twin challenges, the concept of Autonomic Computing was proposed, where "autonomicity implies self-managing" [2].

The goals of AC are to reduce the costs of managing and maintaining complex systems and reducing the likelihood and impact of faults and issues.

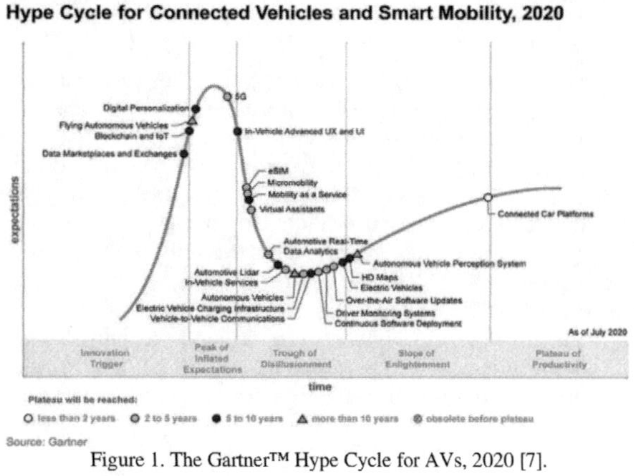

Figure 1. The Gartner™ Hype Cycle for AVs, 2020 [7].

"Self-managing" is often split into four autonomic system objectives [3]:

- *Self-Configuration* – the system re-adjusts itself to support a change in circumstances or new objectives.
- *Self-Healing* – the system can recover automatically when a fault occurs, or proactively avoid health problems.
- *Self-Optimisation* – the system can measure current performance, adjust to improve and react to policy changes.
- *Self-Protection* – the system can defend itself against accidental or malicious attacks, is aware of threats and can defend itself against them.

To achieve these objectives, an AC system needs to be self-aware, aware of its environment, and have the ability to monitor and adjust. An AC system, and in particular the policies that drive monitoring and adjustment, can be designed and built, or can learn and adapt using AI.

IBM did some of the initial work on AC. In 2003, they proposed the idea of an autonomic element, consisting of a managed element and an autonomic manager [4], see Figure 2. The autonomic element runs a continuous control loop that *Monitors* the managed element via sensors and *Analyses*, *Plans* and *Executes* updates based on *Knowledge* about the element. This is known as MAPE-K.

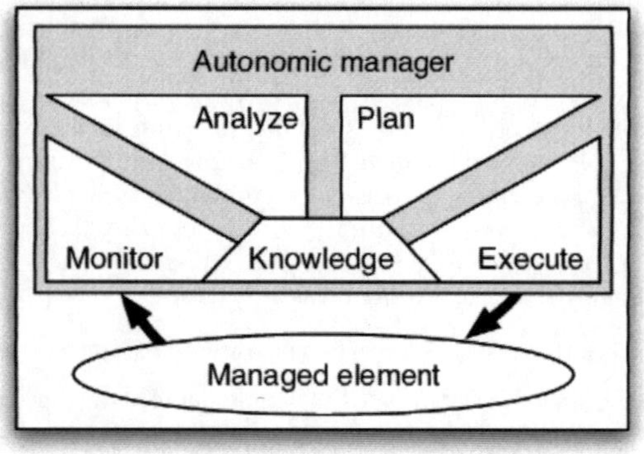

Figure 2. MAPE-K control loop [4].

There have been many impressive advancements in AC since the initial proposals in the early 2000s, but the breadth of the original vision, and the ever increasing complexity of computer systems, means there is still much to do [5]. There is a balanced review on some of the early successes of AC versus the hype in [6]. This "hype-cycle" (a term coined by Gartner) is common to many areas of technology (including AVs – see Figure 1 – as well as AC).

IV. CURRENT STATE OF AV TECHNOLOGY

An Autonomous Vehicle architecture is made up of three functional blocks [21]:

- *Data Acquisition*. This can be through sensors like RADAR, LIDAR and camera, and via communication with other cars or the internet.
- *Data processing*. This takes in the data and uses it for situational and environmental awareness. It then merges that with navigation and path planning logic to determine the next actions to take.
- *Actuation*. Carry out the actions to ensure a safe and smooth journey.

There are two basic architectural approaches [23]:

- *Centralised System Architecture*, where the sensors and data inputs feed into a single computation unit, which in turn drives the actuators.
- *Distributed System Architecture*, where functional subcomponents of the overall system are implemented in separate local units, and are connected using a shared communications bus.

The centralised approach is relatively simple in theory, with all logic collocated and no communications delays to manage. But an overall AV solution is very complex, and a centralised approach is difficult to build and test incrementally. There is also a single point of failure (the central computation unit) and it is difficult and expensive to design and build a backup.

In contrast, the components in a distributed system can be designed and tested separately, and can be removed, replaced or upgraded independently. The system can also be made more robust to point failures, and redundancy can be built in more easily and at lower cost.

In spite of rapid progress, and broad consensus on the best architecture, numerous challenges still need to be overcome before AVs will be ready for commercial roll out. These include:

- *Software reliability*. A recent Which? report [9] found that electric car manufacturer Tesla – a major AV innovator – was the least reliable car brand in the UK in 2021. And most of the faults reported were "software problems" and not problems with the electric motors or batteries. This suggests that major improvements in the design, implementation and operation of vehicle software systems will be needed before more complex, safety critical AV solutions can be launched.
- *Interpretable and Verifiably Safe solutions*. AVs must be safe and efficient. Rule based systems, designed manually by humans, are explainable and testable, but tend to behave overly cautiously. On the other hand, solutions based on machine learning often give better results but are hard to explain and do not offer any formal safety guarantees.
- *Reliability of Communications*. AVs require fast and reliable communications, and will place large and unique demands on the emerging 5G network.

- *Legal and regulatory issues.* Some countries and states allow limited testing of AVs on the public road, but the wider legal and regulatory framework for public use of AVs still needs to be sorted out. In particular, insurance and legal liability in the case of accidents remain difficult areas.
- *Data Privacy.* AVs collect huge amounts of data about their own vehicle and other road users, and this can lead to complex ethical issues. Two examples highlighted in [11] are:
  - If an AV detects another car that is owned by a driver that the insurance company knows has had multiple accidents, should the AV take an alternative route to avoid the risky car?
  - If an AV detects another car performing a dangerous or illegal manoeuvre, should it report it to the police? Or to their insurance company?

  These issues need more debate, and potentially some sort of industry wide ethical framework, to resolve.
- *Public perception.* AVs are already much safer than human controlled cars in terms of accidents per million kilometres driven. But there have been some high profile incidents that have dented public confidence in computer based solutions. These include one in 2016, when a Tesla in automatic mode crashed into a truck killing the driver, and one in 2018, when an Uber autonomous car hit and killed a pedestrian [13].

V. The Future – Applying AC principles to AVs

Autonomous Vehicles overlap with several big technology trends, including Artificial Intelligence (AI), Internet of Things (IoT), mobile communications (5G), security and personal data. And looking at the issues outlined in the previous section, it is apparent that the principles of Autonomic Computing would also be crucial to making AV technology a success.

A recent Institution of Engineering and Technology (IET) comment article [10] highlighted the importance of "Start Early and Think Big" when it comes to getting the benefits of automation. We need to spot the systemic issues early and address them before the implementation approach becomes irreversible. To ensure the right strategy, we first need to understand any commercial constraints, such as cost, attitude to risk and regulatory restrictions. We then draw out the high-level technical requirements and constraints, and feed those into the core solution.

The similarities between AV technology and AC are striking. At the core of both is the need to collect data on their environment, interpret that data and then plan and take appropriate action. Both have evolved towards a distributed architecture, and to using Artificial Intelligence (AI) to improve the analyzing and planning stages of the process. And both have worked to balance the potential of machine learning against the need for explainable and verifiable solutions. It therefore makes sense that AC should be at the core of AV design, and that AVs should look to AC for ideas and inspiration.

The following subsections outline some future AV trends and possible areas where AC principles could add value.

A. *Internet of Things (IoT)*

Autonomic Computing was originally proposed for relatively static systems like computer networks in an office, or the nodes in a telecommunications network. More recently researchers have looked at how to apply AC techniques to the more dynamic architecture of the IoT [14]. An AV can be thought of as a complex object in the IoT, and some of the principles being considered for IoT in general will also apply to AVs.

In the original context of AC, the managed resources were typically clusters of machines in a grid, application servers, routers, and so on. An IoT environment is made up of a far wider range of heterogeneous devices, which may often be mobile. And the number of devices and their arrangement can be highly dynamic. This is particularly true of AVs, where the AV can be talking to a wide, and rapidly changing, variety of AVs and roadside devices as it drives along. Similarly, the autonomic managers in the original AC context were often software components in a relatively centralized solution, whereas in an IoT environment the autonomic managers are more likely to be distributed across many different types of devices.

This leads to new challenges, including:

- How to implement and manage device to device communication.
- Additional self.* objectives, like self-adaptation and self-organization, are more important in a dynamic IoT context.
- Decision making is more likely to be de-centralized.
- Security and device identification.
- Failure recovery and adaptation strategies will be different, because IoT environments are often remote with fewer options for remote human intervention.

AVs should study and adopt AC techniques developed for IoT.

B. *5G Mobile Communications*

AVs are a classic example of the IoT goal that envisages the interconnection of objects that have historically been offline. The term Vehicle to Everything (V2x) has been coined to cover this interconnectivity, including Vehicle to Vehicle (V2V), Vehicle to roadside infrastructure (V2I) and Vehicle to the internet, including links to backend systems like car manufacturers and insurance companies (V2N).

All this communication requires bandwidth and flexibility and is increasingly being enabled using 5G networks. A study [12] of one million connected cars, found that "connected cars have distinct sets of characteristics, including those similar to regular smart phones (e.g. overall diurnal pattern), those similar to IoT devices (e.g. mostly short network sessions), but also some that belong to neither type (e.g. high mobility)".

AVs will place new demands on 5G networks, which in turn will place new demands on the autonomic management of those networks. Research is already underway on how to use "Machine Learning for Autonomic Network Management in a Connected Cars Scenario" [15] to address these new challenges. One critical factor for AVs is performance. Network degradations could impact safety, so the 5G autonomic management systems needs to detect this in advance and take action, for example by being aware of rush hour traffic patterns, or more irregular hot spots caused by road works or accidents and adjusting 5G capacity in anticipation.

C. *Safety Critical Engineering and MAPQE-K*

There is a view that Autonomic Computing is not an entirely new concept, but is related to existing concepts like dependability, and builds on existing engineering principles like fault tolerance and safety critical systems standards and design [19].

Safety and dependability are critical considerations in the aircraft industry, and the increasing complexity of aircraft suggests that the self.* properties of AC could be desirable in avionics software platforms. But the rigid aircraft certification processes, and the current requirements for static and pre-determined behaviour, are at odds with the flexible, adaptive nature of AC.

One paper [20] proposes a novel architecture that modifies the typical AC MAPE-K approach by adding in a "*Qualifier*" step – creating MAP-*Q*E-K. Safety critical aircraft systems are based on Design Assurance Levels (DAL). The proposal is that the M, A and P steps could be low-level DAL, but the new *Qualifier* step along with *Execute* would be high level DAL and would act as a robust gatekeeper for any changes being carried out on the managed element. By isolating the complex MAP stages in a low DAL partition, with only the simpler Q and E steps requiring high DAL, it is hoped that an acceptable solution could be reached. The updated architecture is outlined in Figure 3.

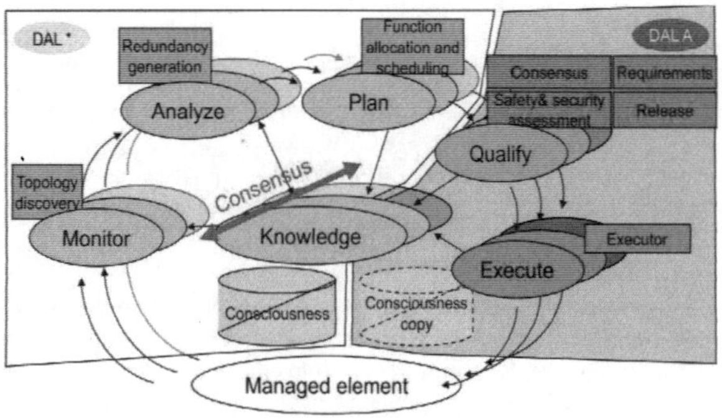

Figure 3. MAP-QE-K with DALs (from [20]).

A similar approach could be considered for AVs, to help balance the often-competing demands of verifiable and explainable solutions and acceptable levels of performance.

D. *Reinforcement Learning*

AVs must be safe and efficient. Manually designed rule-based systems are explainable and verifiable but need to act conservatively to ensure safety. On the other hand, Machine Learning (ML) based solutions often give better results but are hard to explain and do not offer any formal safety guarantees.

One paper [16] looked at a novel form of Reinforcement Learning (a type of ML) that can generate safe and efficient policies, while also being easy to interpret and open to formal proofs of safety. The paper focuses on the specific scenario of an AV over-taking other vehicles, but the "Verifiable Software Reinforcement Learning" approach proposed could be adapted to other challenges in AV, including how to use AC principles in an AV context.

E. *Other areas*

There are numerous other areas where AC techniques (both new and adapted from other domains) could be applied to AVs. Here are three examples.

- *Security* is a big concern for AVs, including cyber security, denial of service attacks (DOS), and protection of personal information. There has been some work done in this area, for example the "COSCA framework for CONseptualising Secure Cars" [25], but more work is needed. AVs could potentially adopt AC techniques like ALice (Autonomic License Signal) for positively identifying actors.
- *Fix Over the Air (FOTA).* This is already possible in some modern cars (e.g. Tesla), to both fix problems, and to enable new (potentially paid for) features. AVs are likely to require much more interaction with the manufacturer and other businesses and authorities, for example to update the vision system to recognise new road signs, and to update the AC MAPE-K control loop with new strategies.
- *Swarm intelligence and AC* have been studied in the context of space exploration [17]. Some of the concepts could be applied to AVs [18], including ideas around cooperation (e.g. to improve traffic flow) and sharing of information (e.g. about slippery road surfaces). Other proposals (e.g. self-destructing a faulty satellite) might not be so appropriate in an AV context.

VI. CONCLUSION AND DISCUSSION

Autonomous Vehicle technology is hugely complex and ambitious, but there are big potential rewards in terms of safety, business opportunities and better customer experiences.

There is a lot of overlap between AVs and other big technical areas, particularly Artificial Intelligence (AI), Internet of Things (IoT) and Fifth Generation Mobile Networks (5G). To this list we should add Autonomous & Autonomic Computing (Figure 4).

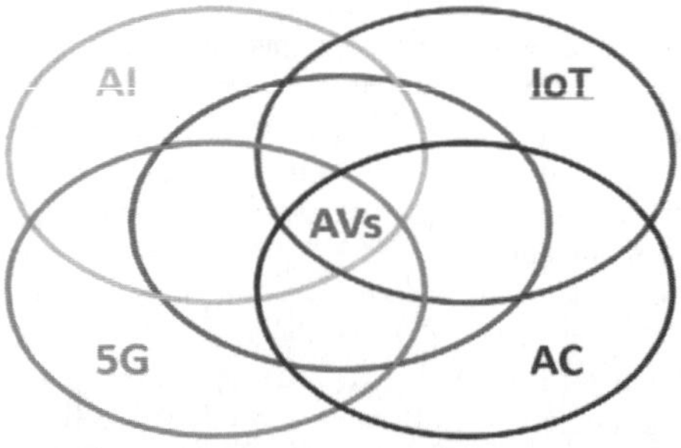

Figure 4. the complex interactions and overlaps between five technical areas.

This paper has outlined the current state of AVs and some of the challenges that still need to be overcome before AVs are ready for "prime time". These include technical, ethical and legal challenges. The paper has also highlighted the similarities and overlaps between AV technology and AC, and has identified several areas where AC techniques and practices could help address AV challenges (and in some cases there has already been progress). Many more examples exist, and more research and development are needed, but it is clear that AC principles will need to be a central part of AV technology if it is to be a success.

ACKNOWLEDGEMENTS

This paper was produced as part of COM760 Autonomic Computing & Robotics for Ulster University's MSc in Artificial Intelligence.

REFERENCES

[1] G. Seetharaman, A. Lakhotia, and E. P. Blasch, "Unmanned vehicles come of age: The DARPA grand challenge," in Computer, vol. 39, no. 12, pp. 26-29, Dec. 2006, https://doi.org/10.1109/MC.2006.447

[2] R. Sterritt and M. G. Hinchey, "Why Computer-Based Systems Should be Autonomic", In Proc. 12th Annual IEEE International Conference and Workshop on the Engineering of Computer Based Systems (ECBS 2005) - Greenbelt, MD, USA, pp. 406-412, Apr. 2005. https://doi.org/10.1109/ECBS.2005.75

[3] M. G. Hinchey and R. Sterritt, "Self-managing software", IEEE Computer, vol. 39, no. 2, pp.107-109, 2006. https://doi.org/10.1109/MC.2006.69

[4] J. O. Kephart and D. M. Chess, "The vision of autonomic computing", IEEE Computer, vol. 36, no.1, pp. 41–50, 2003.

[5] S. Dobson, R. Sterritt, P. Nixon, and M. Hinchey, "Fulfilling the Vision of Autonomic Computing", IEEE Computer, 43(1), pp. 35-41, 2010, https://doi.org/10.1109/MC.2010.14.

[6] R. Sterritt and M. G. Hinchey, "Birds of a Feather Session: Autonomic Computing: Panacea or Poppycock?", IEEE Workshop on the Engineering of Autonomic Systems (EASe 2005) at 12th Annual IEEE International Conference and Workshop on the Engineering of Computer Based Systems (ECBS 2005) - Greenbelt, MD, USA, Apr 2005, pp. 335-341, doi:10.1109/ECBS.2005.22

[7] B. Visnic, "2020 Gartner Hype Cycle for Connected Vehicles and Smart Mobility", Society Automotive Engineers International, (sae.org), 2020. [retrieved Oct. 2023].

[8] SAE, "J3016C: Taxonomy and Definitions for Terms Related to Driving Automation Systems for On-Road Motor Vehicles", Society Automotive Engineers International (sae.org), 2021. [retrieved Oct. 2023].

[9] J. Loughran, "Electric vehicle reliability survey paints bad picture for Tesla owners", E&T Magazine (theiet.org), Engineering & Technology, 3 March 2022.

[10] M. Cheah, "Want to benefit from automation? Start early, and think big", E&T Magazine (theiet.org), Engineering & Technology, 10 March 2022.

[11] R. Zallone, "Artificial Intelligence vs Autonomous Cars vs General Data Protection Regulation", 2020 AEIT International Conference of Electrical and Electronic Technologies for Automotive (AEIT AUTOMOTIVE), 2020. Doi:10.23919/AEITAUTOMOTIVE50086.2020.9307410.

[12] C. E. Andrade et al., "Connected cars in cellular network: a measurement study", In Proceedings of the 2017 Internet Measurement Conference (IMC '17). Association for Computing Machinery, New York, NY, USA, pp235–241, 2017. Doi:10.1145/3131365.3131403

[13] D. Wakabayashi, "Uber's Self-Driving Cars Were Struggling before Arizona Crash." The New York Times, 23 Mar. 2018, www.nytimes.com/2018/03/23/technology/uber-self-driving-cars-arizona.html [retrieved Oct. 2023]

[14] M. Tahir, Q. Mamoon Ashraf, and M. Dabbagh, "Towards Enabling Autonomic Computing in IoT Ecosystem," 2019 IEEE Intl Conf on Dependable, Autonomic and Secure Computing, Intl Conf on Pervasive Intelligence and Computing, Intl Conf on Cloud and Big Data Computing, Intl Conf on Cyber Science and Technology Congress (DASC/PiCom/CBDCom/CyberSciTech), 2019, pp. 646-651, doi:10.1109/DASC/PiCom/CBDCom/CyberSciTech.2019.00122

[15] G. Velez, M. Quartulli, A. Martin, O. Otaegui, and H. Assem, "Machine Learning for Autonomic Network Management in a Connected Cars Scenario", Communication Technologies for Vehicles. Nets4Cars/Nets4Trains/Nets4Aircraft 2016. LNCS, vol. 9669. Springer, doi:10.1007/978-3-319-38921-9_12.

[16] L. M. Schmidt, G. Kontes, A. Plinge, and C. Mutschler, "Can You Trust Your Autonomous Car? Interpretable and Verifiably Safe Reinforcement Learning," 2021 IEEE Intelligent Vehicles Symposium (IV), 2021, pp. 171-178. doi:10.1109/IV48863.2021.9575328.

[17] R. Sterritt, "Apoptotic computing: Programmed death by default for computer-based systems", IEEE Computer, Vol. 44, No.1, pp. 59-65, Jan. 2011, doi: 10.1109/MC.2011.5.

[18] Y. Anand and R. Ajithkumar, "Autonomous Car With Swarm Intelligence", 2019 2nd International Conference on Intelligent Computing, Instrumentation and Control Technologies (ICICICT), 2019, pp. 1659-1662, doi: 10.1109/ICICICT46008.2019.8993301.

[19] R. Sterritt and M. Hinchey, "Autonomicity - an antidote for complexity?", 2005 IEEE Computational Systems Bioinformatics Conference - Workshops (CSBW'05), 2005, pp. 283-291, doi: 10.1109/CSBW.2005.28.

[20] B. Annighoefer, J. Reinhart, M. Brunner, and B. Schulz, "The Concept of an Autonomic Avionics Platform and the Resulting Software Engineering Challenges", 2021 International Symposium on Software Engineering for Adaptive and Self-Managing Systems (SEAMS), 2021, pp. 179-185, doi:10.1109/SEAMS51251.2021.00031.

[21] R. Hussain and S. Zeadally, "Autonomous Cars: Research Results, Issues, and Future Challenges", IEEE Communications Surveys & Tutorials, 21(2), pp. 1275-1313, 2019, doi:10.1109/COMST.2018.2869360.

[22] M. Buehler, K. Iagnemma, and S. Singh, eds. "The 2005 DARPA grand challenge: the great robot race", vol. 36. Springer, 2007.

[23] K. Jo, J. Kim, D. Kim, C. Jang, and M. Sunwoo, "Development of Autonomous Car—Part I: Distributed System Architecture and Development Process," IEEE Transactions on Industrial Electronics, 61(12), pp. 7131-7140, Dec. 2014, doi:10.1109/TIE.2014.2321342.

Development of Free Space Microwave Sensing of Carbon Fiber Composites with Ferromagnetic Microwire Inclusions

Valentina Zhukova, Mihail Ipatov, Paula Corte-León, Alvaro Gonzalez, Alfonso García- Gómez
Dept. Polym. Advanced Materials, Dept. Applied Physics and EHU Quantum Center, Univ. Basque Country, UPV/EHU, 20018 San Sebastian, Spain
e-mails: valentina.zhukova@ehu.es; mihail.ipatov@ehu.es; paula.corte@ehu.eus; alvaro.gonzalezv@ehu.eus; alfonso.garciag@ehu.eus

Francisco Javier Vallejo, Peio Olaskoaga
Ideko Technology Centre, Elgoibar, Spain
e-mails: fjvallejo@ideko.es; polaskoaga@ideko.es

Johan Malm, Christer Johansson
RISE Research Institutes of Sweden, Digital Systems, Göteborg, Sweden
emails: johan.malm@ri.se; christer.johansson@ri.se

Rafael Garcia-Etxabe
GAIKER Technology Centre, Basque Research and Technology Alliance (BRTA), Spain
e-mail: etxabe@gaiker.es

Arcady Zhukov
Dept. Polym. Advanced Materials, Dept. Appl. Physics and EHU Quantum Center, Univ. Basque Country, UPV/EHU, 20018 San Sebastian and Ikerbasque, Bilbao, Spain
e-mail: arkadi.joukov@ehu.es

***Abstract*—In this work, we provide new experimental results on studies of composites with glass-coated ferromagnetic microwires aligned with the requirements of carbon composites. This work focuses on the free space microwave measurements of composites made from carbon fibers and ferromagnetic microwires inclusion focusing on the electromagnetic properties. We prepared and measured hysteresis loops and the magnetoimpedance effect of several microwires and selected Co-rich microwires with better magnetic softness and higher magnetoimpedance effect. We observed that, by using a low frequency modulating magnetic field allows us to distinguish the microwave signals originated by ferromagnetic microwires inclusions from that generated by the carbon fibers. The location of carbon fibers near magnetic microwires has a critical effect on the response signals (parameters S amplitude) obtained from such composites.**

Keywords-magnetic microwires; magnetic softness; carbon fiber composite; magnetoimpedance effect.

I. INTRODUCTION

Amorphous soft magnetic materials, prepared by rapid melt quenching, can present excellent magnetic softness together with superior mechanical properties [1]-[5]. Thus, abrupt deterioration of the magnetic softness and mechanical properties (such as tensile yield) upon the devitrification of amorphous precursor is previously reported [4]. Additionally, the fabrication process of amorphous materials involving rapid melt quenching is fast and inexpensive [1]-[5]. Accordingly, amorphous soft magnetic materials are useful for numerous industrial applications (mostly for design of magnetic devices and magnetoelastic sensors) [8]-[12].

The development of novel applications of amorphous materials requires new functionalities, i.e., reduced dimensions, enhanced corrosion resistance or biocompatibility of the sensing material [11][13]. Therefore, great attention has been paid to development of alternative fabrication methods allowing preparation of amorphous materials at micro-nano scale involving melt quenching [11][13].

Glass-coated microwires prepared by the Taylor-Ulitovsky technique fit most of the requirements: such magnetic microwires have micro-nanometric diameters (between 0.5 and 100 μm), covered with thin, insulating, biocompatible and flexible glass-coating and can present excellent magnetic softness or magnetic bistability [5] [11] [13]. Such features of glass-coated microwires allow development of exciting new applications in various magnetic sensors, as well as in smart composites with tunable magnetic permittivity [6][11][13]-[20]. One more advantage of glass-coated microwires is their excellent mechanical properties [4] [5].

Recently, the stress dependence of hysteresis loops and Giant Magnetoimpedance, GMI, effect have been proposed for the mechanical stresses monitoring in Fiber Reinforced Composites (FRC) containing microwires inclusions or using magnetoelastic sensors based on stress dependence of various magnetic properties [10] [20] [21].

One of the common problems in composite materials is monitoring of stresses and temperature. Usually, composite stress monitoring is performed by different sensors, like the pressure transducers and dielectric sensors [21]. However, these employed sensors are not wireless [21]. One of the proposed solutions for non-destructive FRC monitoring is by using of piezoelectric fibers with diameters of 10 to 100 μm [22]. However, this solution requires electrodes to supply an electrical field, occupying a significant amount of space.

Among the promising solutions, addressing the problem of non-destructive FRC monitoring is a new sensing method involving free space microwave spectroscopy using inclusions of ferromagnetic microwire presenting the high frequency impedance quite sensitive to applied stress and magnetic field [21]. The aforementioned glass-coated microwires with metallic nucleus diameters of 0.2 - 100 μm can present excellent mechanical and corrosive properties (if produced with an amorphous structure), and hence perfectly suitable for the requirements of this technique, making it suitable for remote stresses and temperature monitoring in FRCs [18]-[21].

For the proposed application involving the non-destructive FRC monitoring glass-coated microwires must present good magnetic softness and high magnetoimpedance, MI, effect [18] [21]. Magnetic softness of amorphous microwires is substantially affected by the chemical composition of metallic nucleus: better magnetic softness and higher MI effect are reported for Co-rich microwires with vanishing magnetostriction [1] [5].

Accordingly, in this paper, we present our latest results on studies of magnetic properties of glass-coated Co-rich microwires and on our attempts to wirelessly health monitoring of composites containing both carbon fibers and ferromagnetic glass-coated microwires.

This paper is organized as follows. In Section 2, the experimental methods as well as the microwires characteristics analyzed in this paper are provided. Section 3 deals with experimental results dealing with free space microwave measurements of composites containing both carbon fibers and ferromagnetic glass-coated microwires. Finally, we conclude the paper in Section 4.

II. EXPERIMENTAL SYSTEM DETAILS

Generally, we prepared and analyzed two different types of magnetic amorphous microwires: i) amorphous microwires with high positive magnetostriction coefficients, λ_s, (Fe-rich) and ii) amorphous microwires with vanishing λ_s (Co-Fe-based microwires). We studied microwires with metallic nucleus diameters, *d*, ranging from 22 up to 38 μm and a total diameter, D, up to 45 μm, prepared using the modified Taylor-Ulitovsky method described elsewhere [11] [17]. The Taylor-Ulitovsky method allows the preparation of metallic microwires (with typical diameters of the order of 0.1 to 100 μm) covered with an insulating glass coating [11] [17].

Magnetic hysteresis loops of studied microwires have been measured using the fluxmetric method, previously described in detail elsewhere [16]. The hysteresis loops were represented as the dependence of normalized magnetization, M/M_0 (where M is the magnetic moment at a given magnetic field and M_0 is the magnetic moment of the sample at the maximum magnetic field amplitude almost at magnetic saturation) versus magnetic field, H. Such format of hysteresis loops allows better comparison of microwires with different chemical composition and diameters. The homogeneous axial magnetic field was produced by a long solenoid (about 1 cm in diameter and 12 cm in length). All the measurements were performed at low magnetic field frequencies (100 Hz).

The sample impedance, Z, in extended frequency range has been evaluated using the micro-strip sample holder from the reflection coefficient, S_{11}, obtained using Vector Network Analyzer (VNA), as previously described [23]. Such micro-strip holder with sample has been placed inside a long solenoid generating a homogeneous magnetic field, H. The GMI ratio, $\Delta Z/Z$, is obtained from $Z(H)$ dependence as:

$$\Delta Z/Z = [Z(H) - Z(H_{max})]/Z(H_{max}), \quad (1)$$

where H and H_{max} are given and maximum applied fields respectively.

The composites containing both carbon fibers and ferromagnetic glass-coated microwires were manufactured in the INFINITE project (Horizon Europe) at IDEKO's facilities (see Figure 1).

Figure 1. Image of the carbon fiber composite with magnetic microwire inclusions (the vertical lighter fibres) with 5 mm spacing.

The amorphous structure of all the microwires has been

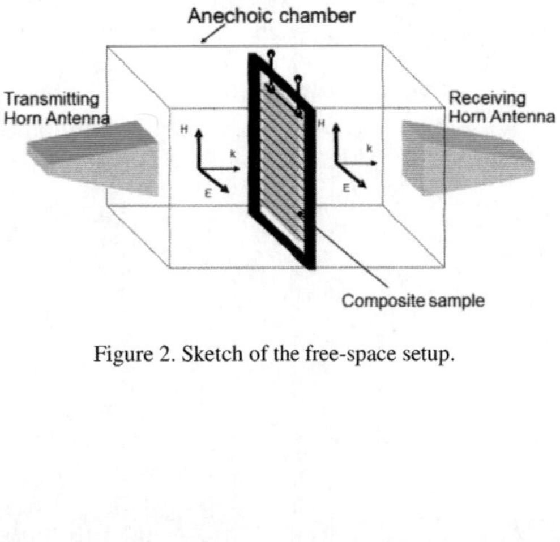

Figure 2. Sketch of the free-space setup.

proved by the X-ray Diffraction (XRD) method. Typically, the crystallization of amorphous microwires was observed at Tann ≥ 500 °C [16].

For wireless measurements we used the free space measurement setup (see Figure 2) consisting of two broadband horn antennas (1-17 GHz) fixed to the anechoic chamber and a vector network analyzer, previously employed for the characterization of the composites with magnetic wire inclusions [18,21]. Such setup allows to characterize the composite of 20 x 20 cm^2.

III. EXPERIMENTAL RESULTS AND DISCUSSION

Previous studies have demonstrated that the magnetostriction coefficient, λs, is primary affected by the composition of the microwires. Vanishing λs –value ($\lambda s \approx 10^{-7}$) is predicted in $(Co_{1-x}Fe_x)_{1-y}(Si\text{-}B\text{-}C)_y$ amorphous alloys at $0.05 \leq x \leq 0.1$ and $0.15 \leq y \leq 0.30$ [17] [24]. Therefore, we prepared $Co_{64.6}Fe_5B_{16}Si_{11}Cr_{3.4}$ glass-coated microwires with metallic nucleus diameter, *d*, of 22 and 38 μm, which previously showed high MI effect [17].

For comparison, we also prepared and measured magnetic properties of Fe-rich microwires ($Fe_{77.5}B_{15}Si_{7.5}$) with d=23 μm, D=37 μm and high and positive λs ($\lambda s \approx 40 \times 10^{-6}$).

The hysteresis loops of studied microwires are provided in Figure 3. As observed from Figure 3, both Co-rich microwires show good magnetic softness: a coercivity, H_c, about 16-20 A/m and a magnetic anisotropy field, H_k, about 150 A/ m. In contrast, a rectangular hysteresis loops and $H_c \approx 100$ A/m are observed for $Fe_{77.5}B_{15}Si_{7.5}$ glass-coated microwires (d=23 μm, D=37 μm) (see Figure 3c).

Figure 3 shows the results on GMI effect of these microwires. As evidenced from Figure 4, both Co-rich microwires present high MI effect (maximum $\Delta Z/Z$ up to 220 % at 100 MHz, see Figures 4 a,b). However, for $Fe_{77.5}B_{15}Si_{7.5}$ microwire the observed MI effect is rather low: up to 2% at the same frequency (100 MHz) (see Figure 4c). Consequently, Co-rich microwires with better MI effect have been selected for the composite preparation.

As reported elsewhere [25] [26], magnetic properties and MI effect of amorphous ferromagnetic microwires are substantially affected by applied stress and by heating. Therefore, the main advantage of utilizing of magnetic microwires inclusions in carbon fiber composites is the possibility for stress and/or temperature monitoring. Very few previous publications have reported attempts to prepare such composites, while Fe-rich microwire inclusions were used and the carbon fiber content was rather low [27].

The expected problem with composites containing conductive carbon fibers is that they can substantially interfere with the microwave signal from the magnetic microwire inclusions [27]. Therefore, we propose to apply a low frequency modulating magnetic field to distinguish the microwave signals from magnetic microwires from that originated by conductive carbon fibers, since only the magnetic microwires responds to the modulating field.

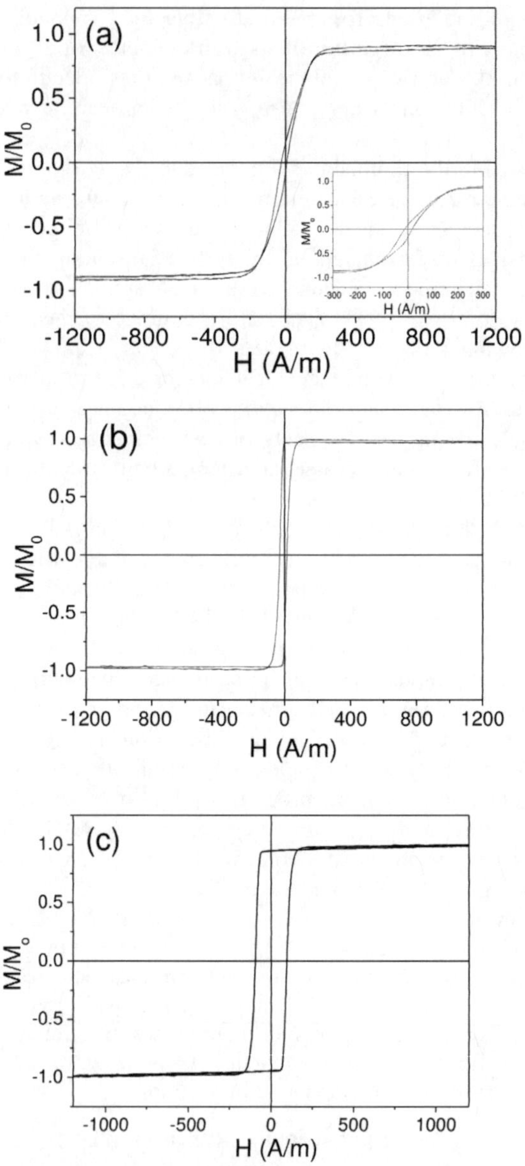

Figure 3. Hysteresis loops of $Co_{64.6}Fe_{5.0}B_{16.0}Si_{11.0}Cr_{3.4}$ microwires (a,b) with d≈22 μm, D≈24μm and d=38 μm, D=43.5 μm respectively and $Fe_{77.5}B_{15}Si_{7.5}$ microwires with d=23 μm, D=37 μm (c).

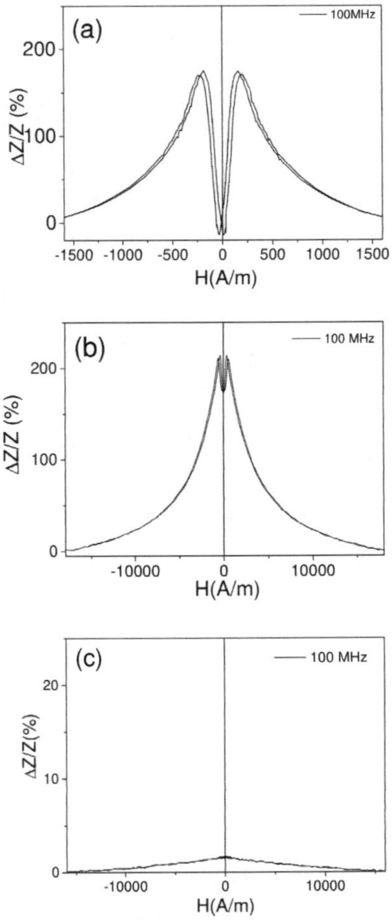

Figure 4. *ΔZ/Z(H)* dependencies measured in $Co_{64.6}Fe_{5.0}B_{16.0}Si_{11.0}Cr_{3.4}$ microwires with d≈22 μm (a), d=38 μm (b) and in $Fe_{77.5}B_{15}Si_{7.5}$ microwires (c).

In Figure. 5a, the microwave signals are shown (S parameters) measured at 2 GHz. As observed, the signals measured under these conditions are comparable to the noise level. In order to separate the microwave signal from ferromagnetic microwires, we used an external low frequency modulated magnetic field. As shown in Figure 5b, application of such modulated magnetic field (80 Hz) allows a sensitive and stable extraction of the response signal (R and T coefficients) from the ferromagnetic microwires inclusions.

However, the position of carbon fibers in vicinity of magnetic microwires critically affect the signals (S parameters) obtained from such composites.

In Figure 6 are provided the examples of the influence of thin insulating plastic layer (30 μm thick) between the ordered microwires and carbon fiber composite on S_{11} parameters

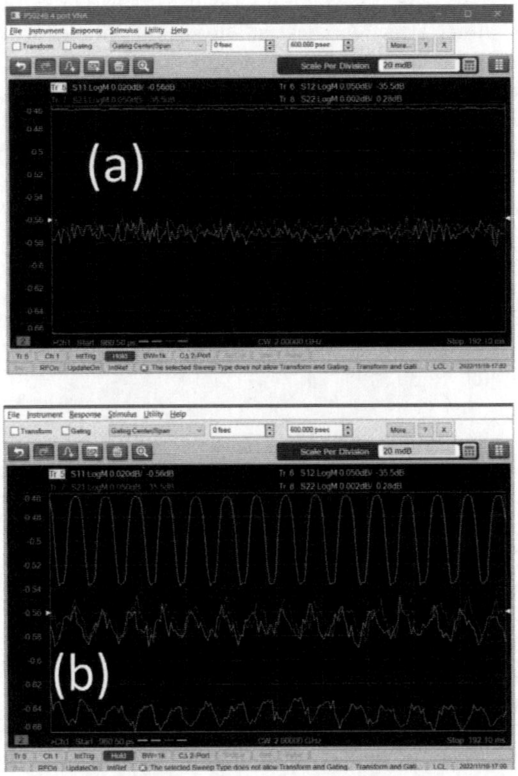

Figure 5. Microwave signals from the composites measured at 2 GHz (a) and the same signal with an external low frequency modulated magnetic field (80 Hz) (b). Line colors: yellow-S_{11}; green-S_{22}, blue and magenta: S_{12} and S_{21} respectively.

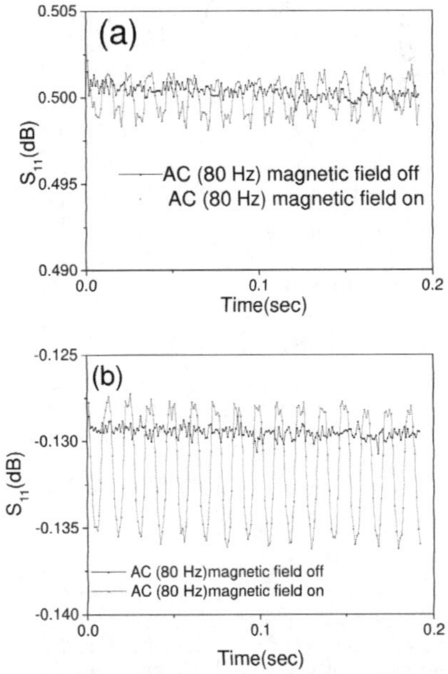

Figure 6. Effect of insulating plastic layer between the microwires and Carbon fibre composite on S_{11} parameter. Measurements with plastic layer (a) and without plastic layer (b).

As observed, the presence of even such thin insulating layer allows affecting substantially the amplitude of the S_{11} parameter signal originated by magnetic microwires.

The aforementioned examples provide the routes for development of the composites made from the carbon fibers and magnetically soft amorphous glass-coated microwires inclusions.

The key results are that use of a low frequency modulating magnetic field allows to distinguish the microwave signals originated by ferromagnetic microwires inclusions from that generated by the carbon fibers. However, the position of carbon fibers in vicinity of magnetic microwires critically affect the signals obtained from such composites.

IV. CONCLUSIONS

We have explored the feasibility of developing composites containing carbon fibers and glass-coated magnetic microwires inclusions using the free space microwave spectroscopy aligned with the requirements of carbon composites. For the preparation of such composites, we selected Co-rich microwires with better magnetic softness and higher magnetoimpedance effect. We experimentally demonstrated that the application of low frequency magnetic field allows to distinguish the microwave signals originated by ferromagnetic microwires inclusions from the signal generated by the carbon fibers. However, the location of carbon fibers near magnetic microwires has a critical effect on the signals (parameter S) obtained from such composites.

ACKNOWLEDGMENT

This work was supported by EU under "INFINITE" (HORIZON-CL5-2021-D5-01-06) project, by the Spanish the Spanish MICIN under PID2022-141373NB-I00, by the Government of the Basque Country under PUE_2021_1_0009, Elkartek (MINERVA, MAGAF and ZE-KONP) projects and under the scheme of "Ayuda a Grupos Consolidados"(ref. IT1670-22),The authors thank for technical and human support provided by SGIker of UPV/EHU (Medidas Magnéticas Gipuzkoa) and European funding (ERDF and ESF).

REFERENCES

[1] P. Corte-Leon et al., "Magnetic Microwires with Unique Combination of Magnetic Properties Suitable for Various Magnetic Sensor Applications", Sensors, vol. 20, p. 7203, 2020.

[2] J. Durand, "Magnetic Properties of Metallic Glasses" in Topics in Applied Physics, vol. 53, Glassy Metals II. Atomic Structure and Dynamics, Electronic Structure, Magnetic Properties, Editors: H. Beck and H.-J. Giintherodt, Springer-Verlag, Berlin Heidelberg New York Tokyo, pp. 343-386, 1983

[3] T. Goto, M. Nagano, and N. Wehara, "Mechanical properties of amorphous $Fe_{80}P_{16}C_3B_1$ filament produced by glass-coated melt spinning", Trans. JIM, vol. 18, pp. 759–764, 1977.

[4] V. Zhukova et al., "Correlation between magnetic and mechanical properties of devitrified glass-coated $Fe_{71.8}Cu_1Nb_{3.1}Si_{15}B_{9.1}$ microwires", J. Magn. Magn. Mater., vol. 249, pp. 79–84, 2002.

[5] A. Zhukov et al., "Giant magnetoimpedance in rapidly quenched materials", J. Alloys Compound., vol. 814, pp. 152225, 2020.

[6] V. Zhukova et al., "Electronic Surveillance and Security Applications of Magnetic Microwires", Chemosensors, vol. 9, p.100, 2021.

[7] K. Mohri, T. Uchiyama, L. P. Shen, C. M. Cai, and L. V. Panina, "Amorphous wire and CMOS IC-based sensitive micro-magnetic sensors (MI sensor and SI sensor) for intelligent measurements and controls", J. Magn. Magn. Mater., vol. 249, pp. 351-356, 2001.

[8] T. Uchiyama, K. Mohri, and Sh. Nakayama, "Measurement of Spontaneous Oscillatory Magnetic Field of Guinea-Pig Smooth Muscle Preparation Using Pico-Tesla Resolution Amorphous Wire Magneto-Impedance Sensor", IEEE Trans. Magn., vol. 47, pp. 3070-3073, 2011.

[9] Y. Honkura, "Development of amorphous wire type MI sensors for automobile use", J. Magn. Magn. Mater., vol. 249, pp. 375-381, 2002.

[10] A. Zhukov et al., "Magnetoelastic sensor of level of the liquid based on magnetoelastic properties of Co-rich microwires", Sens. Actuat. A Phys., vol. 81, no. 1-3, pp.129-133, 2000.

[11] V. Zhukova et al., "Development of Magnetically Soft Amorphous Microwires for Technological Applications", Chemosensors, vol. 10, p. 26, 2022

[12] L. Ding, S. Saez, C. Dolabdjian, L. G. C. Melo, A. Yelon, and D. Ménard, "Development of a high sensitivity Giant Magneto-Impedance magnetometer: comparison with a commercial Flux-Gate", IEEE Sensors, vol. 9, no.2, pp. 159-168, 2009.

[13] D. Kozejova et al., "Biomedical applications of glass-coated microwires", J. Magn. Magn. Mater., vol. 470, pp. 2-5, 2019.

[14] D. Makhnovskiy, N Fry, and A. Zhukov, "On different tag reader architectures for bistable microwires", Sens. Actuat. A Phys., vol. 166, pp. 133-140, 2011.

[15] S. Gudoshnikov et al., "Evaluation of use of magnetically bistable microwires for magnetic labels", Phys. Stat. Sol. (a), vol. 208, no. 3, pp. 526–529, 2011.

[16] L. Gonzalez-Legarreta et al., "Optimization of magnetic properties and GMI effect of Thin Co-rich Microwires for GMI Microsensors", Sensors, vol. 20, p.1558, 2020.

[17] A. Zhukov et al., "Advanced functional magnetic microwires for technological applications", J. Phys. D: Appl. Phys., vol. 55, p. 253003, 2022.

[18] D. Makhnovskiy, A. Zhukov, V. Zhukova, and J. Gonzalez, "Tunable and self-sensing microwave composite materials incorporating ferromagnetic microwires", Advances in Science and Technology, vol. 54, pp 201-210, 2008.

[19] F. Qin and H.X. Peng, "Ferromagnetic microwires enabled multifunctional composite materials", Prog. Mater. Sci., vol. 58, no. 2, pp.183-259, 2013.

[20] M. Churyukanova et al., Non-contact method for stress monitoring based on stress dependence of magnetic properties of Fe-based microwires", J. Alloys Compd., 748, no.5, pp. 199-205, 2018.

[21] A. Allue et al., "Smart composites with embedded magnetic microwire inclusions allowing non-contact stresses and temperature monitoring", Compos.Part A Appl., vol. 120, pp. 12-20, 2019, doi: 10.1016/j.compositesa.2019.02.014

[22] L. J. Nelson, "Smart piezoelectric Fibre composites", Mat. Sci. and Tech., vol. 18, pp.1245-1256, 2002.

[23] A. Zhukov, M. Ipatov, P. Corte-Leon, J. M. Blanco, L. González-Legarreta, and V. Zhukova, "Routes for

Optimization of Giant Magnetoimpedance Effect in Magnetic Microwires", IEEE Instrumentation & Measurement Magazine, vol. 23, no. 1, pp. 56-63, 2020 DOI: 10.1109/MIM.2020.8979525

[24] M. Churyukanova et al., "Magnetostriction investigation of soft magnetic microwires", Phys. Stat. Sol. A, vol. 213, no. 2, pp. 363-367, 2016.

[25] P. Corte-Leon et al., "Stress dependence of the magnetic properties of glass-coated amorphous microwires" J. Alloys Compound, vol. 789, pp. 201-208, 2019, doi: 10.1016/j.jallcom.2019.03.044

[26] P. Corte -Leon et al., "Effect of temperature on magnetic properties and magnetoimpedance effect in Fe -rich microwires", J. Alloys Compound. vol. 946, 169419, 2023, doi: https://doi.org/10.1016/j.jallcom.2023.169419

[27] Y. Luo et al., "Left-handed metacomposites containing carbon fibers and ferromagnetic microwires", AIP Advances vol. 7, 056110, 2017.

Electric Network Frequency Optical Sensing Devices

Christos Moysiadis, Georgios Karantaidis, Constantine Kotropoulos
Department of Informatics, Aristotle University of Thessaloniki
Thessaloniki, 54124, Greece
Email: {mousiadi, gkarantai, costas}@csd.auth.gr

***Abstract*—Electric Network Frequency (ENF) acts as a fingerprint in multimedia forensics applications. In indoor environments, ENF variations affect the intensity of light sources connected to power mains. Accordingly, the light intensity variations captured by sensing devices can be exploited to estimate the ENF. A first optical sensing device based on a photodiode is developed for capturing ENF variations in indoor lighting environments. In addition, a device that captures the ENF directly from power mains is implemented. This device serves as a ground truth ENF collector. Video recordings captured by a camera are also employed to estimate the ENF. The camera serves as a second optical sensor. The factors affecting the ENF estimation are thoroughly studied. The maximum correlation coefficient between the ENF estimated by the two optical sensors and that estimated directly from power mains is used to measure the estimation accuracy. The paper's major contribution is in the disclosure of extensive experimental evidence on ENF estimation in scenes ranging from static ones capturing a white wall to non-static ones, including human activity.**

Keywords*—Electric Network Frequency (ENF), optical sensor based on a photodiode, CMOS-based GoPro Hero8 camera, ENF estimation in video.

I. INTRODUCTION

The widespread and ever-increasing use of social media and the vast amount of video recordings shared online have exposed individuals to perpetrators seeking illicit profits. A plethora of tools can alter and manipulate digital content, as well as metadata information. Through editing, the content and the time the recording was captured can be altered for fraudulent purposes.

The Electric Network Frequency (ENF) signal is employed as an authentication signature in a wide range of multimedia applications, starting from audio [1] and proceeding to video, e.g., [2]–[5]. The ENF is embedded in digital content captured by microphones, devices plugged into power mains, or near power sources. It fluctuates around its fundamental frequency at 50 Hz in Europe and 60 Hz in the U.S. due to the instantaneous differences between the consumed and the produced electric load in the power grid. The ENF can also be found in the higher harmonics of the fundamental frequency [6]. A lot of effort has been paid to develop ENF estimation algorithms [7]–[15], tested mainly for audio forensics applications.

The application domain of ENF-related authentication research has been shifted to images and video. It has been found that ENF can be embedded in video recordings through the intensity variations of different light sources. A systematic study of ENF estimation in digital video recordings captured by various optical sensors was presented in [16]. An algorithm for detecting the presence of ENF was proposed in [3]. Simple Linear Iterative Clustering (SLIC) was employed to derive superpixels. It was attested that the algorithm could operate in short clips regardless of the camera sensor type. Extension of [3] was presented in [5], allowing to handle both static and non-static video recordings. An analytical model for video recordings captured by a rolling shutter mechanism was proposed in [17]. A novel method of ENF estimation in video employing a rolling shutter mechanism was developed in [18]. There, parametric and non-parametric spectral estimation approaches were combined to estimate accurately the ENF. The rolling shutter mechanism was modeled in [19], resorting to multirate signal processing theory.

In this paper, two optical devices are developed to measure the ENF signal in indoor environments illuminated by two different light sources. The intensity emanating from light sources fluctuates due to the ENF variations in the power grid. Taking advantage of this fact, the first optical sensor based on a photodiode measures the light intensity fluctuations. To evaluate the accuracy of the ENF signal captured by the photodiode-based sensor, a ground truth ENF is essential. For this reason, a device that records the ENF signal directly from power mains is also implemented. Luminance variations were also recorded in an indoor environment employing a common Complementary Metal-Oxide-Semiconductor (CMOS)-based GoPro Hero8 camera, which was set to record at 30 fps at a resolution of 1080p with the anti-flicker effect turned off to resemble the operation of a surveillance camera. The camera serves as a second optical sensor. Comparing the ENF extracted from the photodiode against that estimated by the GoPro camera, useful conclusions are drawn regarding their effectiveness. The experiments involved various setups, such as varying video duration and distance between the optical sensor and the white wall background and introducing moving objects or human activity. The Maximum Correlation Coefficient (MCC) between the ENF estimated by either optical sensor and that estimated from power mains was employed as a metric to assess the ENF estimation accuracy.

The paper's major contribution is in the disclosure of extensive experimental evidence, which demonstrates that under certain conditions, the photodiode sensing device delivers a reliable reference (i.e., ground truth) ENF signal, extending the work in [16]. This could benefit practitioners and find use in real-life applications where it is quite difficult to acquire ground truth ENF through a Frequency Disturbance Recorder (FDR). Several spectral analysis methods were employed for ENF estimation, such as the Short-Term Fourier Transform (STFT), the Blackman-Tukey (BT) spectral estimate, the Estimation of Signal Parameters with Rotational Invariant Techniques (ESPRIT) [20], as well as the spectrum combining approach [11].

The remainder of the paper is as follows. Section II briefly describes ENF fundamentals. Section III details the design and implementation of sensing devices. Section IV discusses ENF estimation. Section V concludes the paper and suggests future research topics.

II. ENF Fundamentals

The ENF is embedded in video recordings captured by optical sensors in indoor environments illuminated by fluorescent lamps, halogen lamps, or incandescent bulbs. In particular, light intensity fluctuates at twice the fundamental frequency of ENF, i.e., 100 Hz in Europe and 120 Hz in the U.S.

The low sampling rate of optical sensors results in severe aliasing and, consequently, hinders ENF estimation. To determine the aliased frequencies and estimate the ENF signal in video recordings, one should apply the sampling theorem [21]. The aliased frequency f_A emanated from halogen/incandescent illumination is given as $f_A = |\hat{f}_N - \gamma\, f_s| \leq \frac{f_s}{2}$, where f_s denotes the sampling frequency of the camera, $\hat{f}_N$ is the frequency of light source illumination, and γ stands for an integer factor [22].

The STFT is employed for ENF estimation following the procedure in [5]. That is, for a window $w(t)$ L samples long centered around lG, where G is the hop size in samples, the Discrete-Time Fourier transform of the lth segment of $x(t)$ is computed [23]:

$$X_l(\omega) = \sum_{t=-\infty}^{\infty} x(t)\, w(t-lG)\, \exp\left(-j\omega t\right). \tag{1}$$

The BT spectral estimate is a refined periodogram [20]:

$$\hat{\phi}_{BT}(\omega) = \sum_{\zeta=-(M-1)}^{M-1} w(\zeta)\, \hat{r}(\zeta)\, e^{-j\omega\,\zeta} \tag{2}$$

where $\hat{r}(\zeta) = \frac{1}{N}\sum_{t=\zeta+1}^{N} x(t)x(t-\zeta)$, $-(M-1) \leq \zeta \leq M-1$, is the standard biased estimate of $r(\zeta)$ and $w(\zeta)$ is an lag-window of even symmetry.

The spectrum combining approach delivers an accurate power spectrum based on a weighted summation of multiple spectral bands from around the signal harmonics [11]. Each band's local Signal-to-Noise Ratio (SNR) is employed to calculate the corresponding weights. The weighted summation is given by:

$$S(\omega) = \sum_{z=1}^{Z_a} w_z\, \phi_{BT}(z\,\omega) \tag{3}$$

where $\phi_{BT}(z\,\omega)$ is the zth harmonic scaled power spectrum, w_z weighs the harmonic spectral bands around each harmonic taking into consideration the local SNR, and $Z_a = 7$ denotes the number of harmonics considered.

ESPRIT was also used to estimate the ENF signal. The size of the sample covariance matrix was set to 10×10, and the line spectrum model was set to 3. Due to lack of space, the interested reader is referred to [5] [20].

III. Devices Design and Implementation

To collect light intensity fluctuations using a photodiode, following the paradigm in [16], a first circuit was designed based on the photodiode BPW21. This photodiode was chosen due to its excellent light and spectral sensitivity in the visible range. A common and robust way to amplify the photocurrent generated by a photodiode is to utilize two operational amplifiers with a positive and a negative feedback loop to stabilize its behavior and produce a linear correlation between the light intensity and the current generated [24]. The operational amplifiers OP07D were used as current-to-voltage converters to capture the fluctuations and pass them to the laptop sound card. The voltage from the power mains was dropped to 18 Volts Alternating Current (AC) using a center-tapped transformer. Also, a full bridge rectifier and a voltage regulator pair (LM7805/7905) were used to convert the AC voltage to Direct Current (DC) to power the operational amplifiers. The next step was to wire appropriately the two amplification stages of the operational amplifiers. A combination of positive and negative feedback occurred in the first stage to amplify and clean the initial signal collected from the photodiode. In contrast, the signal was further amplified in the second stage by incorporating another negative feedback stage.

Fig. 1. Circuit photograph.

A second circuit was implemented to extract the ENF from the power mains. A transformer lowered the power mains AC voltage from 220 Volts to 18 Volts. A voltage divider further decreased the voltage to about 3 Volts peak-to-peak in accordance with the laptop sound card voltage tolerance [25]. The next stage included a high pass filter to eliminate the DC component with a cutoff frequency of 32 Hz. Finally, an anti-aliasing filter stage was deployed to control the cutoff frequency set at the Nyquist frequency. More specifically, since we wanted to sample the signal at 1 KHz, we set the value of $R4$ to 33 KΩ to filter the signal at around 500 Hz. The ENF extracted from power mains served as reference ENF. In practice, the reference ENF is recorded by an FDR, which provides accurate measurements up to $\pm 5 \cdot 10^{-4}$ Hz [9].

To record simultaneously the ENF mains signal and the light intensity signal at a proper voltage level, we employed a 3.5 mm stereo jack cable to feed the ENF mains signal to the left channel of the sound card and the light intensity signal from the photodiode to the right channel of the sound card. The developed devices are depicted in Figure 1. On the left, the transformer of the circuit is depicted. The breadboard containing the circuit to extract the ground truth ENF from the power mains is shown on the top. The photodiode circuit, the full bridge rectifier, and the voltage regulation stages can be seen at the bottom. On the right, the 3.5 mm audio jack is depicted.

The diagram of the devices is shown in Figure 2. On the left, a 230/18V center-tapped transformer is shown. The top comprises a voltage divider and two filtering stages for acquiring the power mains voltage. The central part of the diagram depicts a full bridge rectifier followed by a voltage regulator pair to convert the AC signal to +5/-5V DC rails, which are fed into the operational amplifiers. The photodiode and its two-stage amplification circuit can be seen on the right. A MATLAB script [26] was written to capture both signals.

IV. Device Experimental Evaluation

Two sets of experiments were conducted to evaluate the performance of the designed devices.

In the first set of experiments, a GoPro Hero 8 camera was employed to record a white wall inside a living room. Three different factors were taken into consideration: (i) two different light sources, namely, a halogen lamp and an incandescent bulb; (ii) different distances between the camera and the wall; and (iii) various video recording durations. In the second set of experiments, the same camera was used to collect video recordings under realistic conditions. Video recordings, ground truth ENF, and code can be found at [27].

A. *First set of experiments*

To assess the impact of the light source on the accuracy of ENF estimation, camera recordings of a white wall illuminated by either a halogen lamp or an incandescent bulb were collected. Unless otherwise stated, the ENF estimation from video recordings was carried out using the SLIC-based approach [3] [5] and employing the STFT. Comparisons were made against the ENF estimated from the power mains using STFT. The camera was mounted at different distances from the white wall background, namely 0.5 m, 1 m, 1.5 m, 2 m, 2.5 m, 3 m, and 3.5 m. The varying distances are found to affect the ENF estimation, as can be seen in Table I. When a halogen lamp illuminated the scene, the top measured MCC was 0.9778 at a 1 m distance between the camera and the white wall. When an incandescent bulb illuminated the scene, the top measured MCC was 0.9738 at the same distance.

Apart from the type of light source and the distance between the camera and the white wall, the duration of video recordings may vary. Since video duration is not known apriori, it is very important to challenge our ability to find a match in such circumstances. For that reason, we conducted another experiment that considered all three factors. A halogen lamp and an incandescent bulb were employed, while the camera

TABLE I. MCC Between the ENF Estimated from Video and Power Mains for Varying Distances

Distance (m)	**Halogen**	**Incandescent**
0.5	0.8271	0.9232
1	**0.9778**	**0.9738**
1.5	0.9058	0.8235
2	0.9746	0.9394
2.5	0.9210	0.9512
3	0.8266	0.7510
3.5	0.7646	0.8525

was mounted at three different distances from the white wall background, i.e., 1 m, 2.5 m, and 3.5 m. Although the initial total duration of the recording was 8 min, we estimated the ENF for video durations $g = 1, 2, \ldots, 8$ min, as depicted in Figure 3. When the camera was mounted at a distance of 1 m, setups including either a halogen lamp or an incandescent bulb yielded high MCC values even for a short video duration of 1 min. Table II summarizes the MCC measurements. The top MCC for each light source is shown in boldface. Underlined MCC indicates the second and third best MCC for each pair of light sources and distance.

TABLE II. MCC Between the ENF Estimated from Video and Power Mains for Varying Video Durations

Duration (min)	**1**	**2**	**3**	**4**	**5**	**6**	**7**	**8**
1 m Halogen	**0.9936**	0.9699	0.9790	0.9818	0.9838	0.9845	0.9828	0.9778
2.5 m Halogen	0.8793	0.7613	0.8545	0.8958	0.9211	0.9032	0.9077	0.9211
3.5 m Halogen	0.9555	0.7668	0.7958	0.7867	0.7708	0.7720	0.7691	0.9211
1 m Incandescent	**0.9905**	0.9422	0.9299	0.9180	0.9162	0.9333	0.9611	0.9211
2.5 m Incandescent	0.9902	0.9530	0.9334	0.9382	0.9393	0.9455	0.9487	0.9512
3.5 m Incandescent	0.9612	0.8704	0.8489	0.7901	0.7754	0.8393	0.8277	0.8525

To further assess the developed devices' performance and attest that the designed photodiode-based device delivers an accurate ground truth ENF, we used the same set of recordings against either the ENF extracted from power mains or the photodiode. Spectrum combining was used to estimate the ground truth ENF. The ENF estimation from video recordings was carried out by employing the BT spectral estimate. For varying distances between the camera and the white wall, as well as for both light sources, the same trend in MCC was observed in Table III.

TABLE III. MCC Between the ENF Estimated from a Video Recording and Either the Power Mains or the Photodiode-device Output

Distance (m)	**0.5**	**1**	**1.5**	**2**	**2.5**	**3**	**3.5**
Mains (Halogen)	0.9888	0.9989	0.9904	0.9928	0.9968	0.9932	0.9344
Photodiode (Halogen)	0.9	0.9998	0.999	0.9996	0.9998	0.9995	0.9445
Mains (Incandescent)	0.9938	0.9983	0.8892	0.9949	0.9977	0.99	0.9944
Photodiode (Incandescent)	0.9999	0.9998	0.8905	0.9998	0.9999	0.9997	0.9991

The ENF estimated at the output of the photodiode-based device was compared to the ENF measured at power mains. Spectrum combining was used in both cases. The ENF was also extracted from the recording captured by the camera, which was placed 2 m far away from the white wall for both illumination sources and various video durations using SLIC and STFT. The top MCC value of 0.9964 was observed between the ENF extracted from a 2-minute video when an incandescent bulb illuminated the scene and that measured from power mains. Regarding the photodiode-based device,

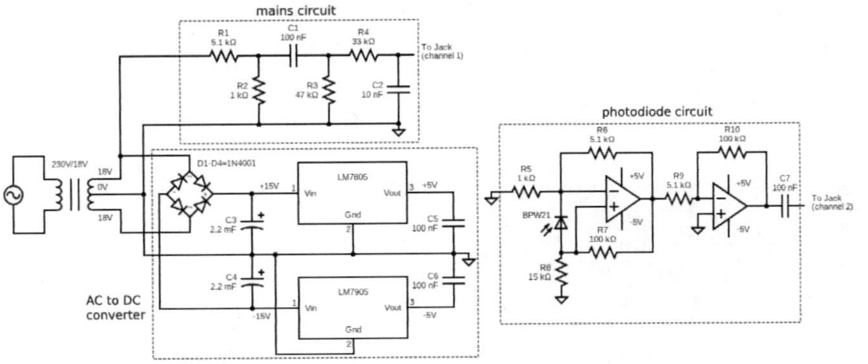

Fig. 2. Detailed circuit diagram of the developed devices.

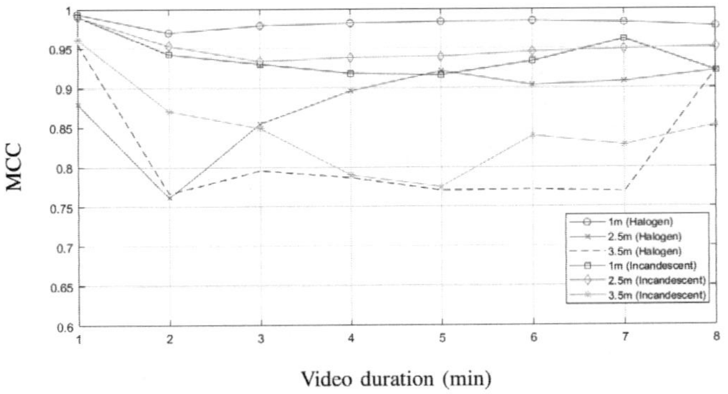

Fig. 3. MCC between the ENF estimated from a camera recording and the ENF measured at power mains for varying video duration and distance.

the top MCC value of 0.9982 was observed between the ENF extracted from an 8-minute recording when an incandescent bulb illuminated the scene and that measured from power mains. The MCC is plotted for various recording durations of the video and the photodiode signals in Figure 4.

The MCC measurements are listed in Table IV. Top MCCs are shown in boldface for each optical sensor.

TABLE IV. EFFECT OF VARIOUS DURATIONS AND TWO DIFFERENT LIGHT SOURCES IN MCC

Duration (min)	**1**	**2**	**3**	**4**	**5**	**6**	**7**	**8**
Camera (Halogen)	0.9652	0.9951	0.9950	0.9948	0.9935	0.9941	0.9934	0.9928
Camera (Incandescent)	0.9808	**0.9964**	0.9877	0.9905	0.9897	0.9941	0.9939	0.9950
Photodiode (Halogen)	0.9935	0.9945	0.9956	0.9953	0.9954	0.9951	0.9944	0.9941
Photodiode (Incandescent)	0.9843	0.9904	0.9881	0.9873	0.9943	0.9949	0.9955	**0.9982**

Furthermore, it is demonstrated that the ENF measured at the output of the photodiode-based device can be employed as a ground truth ENF. The MCC measurements between the ENF estimated from the photodiode-based device and the power mains using spectrum combining are reported. Seven recordings of 8-minute duration each were captured. When a halogen lamp was employed, the top measured MCC was 0.9988, while the top MCC was 0.9989 for the incandescent bulb. For all recordings, the MCC exceeded 0.99 regardless of the light source illuminating the scene, as seen in Table V.

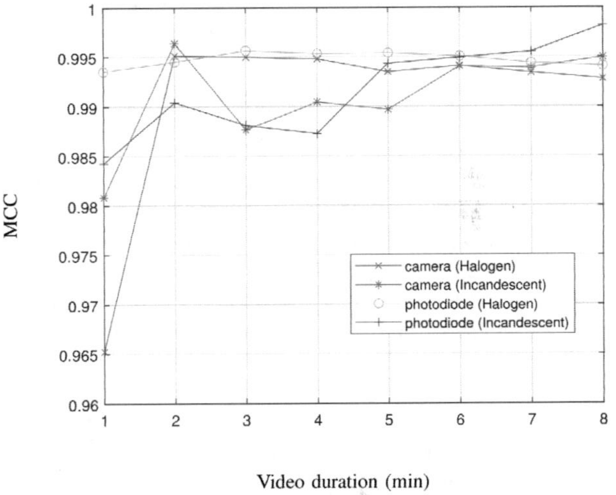

Fig. 4. MCC between the ENF estimated from both optical sensors' recordings and power mains.

TABLE V. MCC BETWEEN THE ENF EXTRACTED AT THE OUTPUT OF THE PHOTODIODE DEVICE AND THE POWER MAINS

# Recording	**Halogen**	**Incandescent**
1	0.9906	0.9946
2	**0.9988**	**0.9989**
3	0.9904	0.9975
4	0.9941	0.9982
5	0.996	0.9979
6	0.9934	0.9918
7	0.9935	0.9935

B. Second set of experiments

A challenging set of experiments was conducted to test the ability to timestamp non-static video recordings whose snapshots are shown in Figure 5. Top left: Non-static video of a scene with various textures and reflection coefficients illuminated by a halogen lamp, where a moving jacket is introduced to the scene referred to as video (a). Top right: A dimly lit hallway illuminated by a halogen bulb displaying human activity of varying obstruction referred to as video (b). Bottom left: A video of a person moving in and out of a very complex scene illuminated by a halogen lamp in medium lighting condition referred to as video (c). Bottom-right: The same scene as in the bottom-left when the lighting conditions are dimmer due to a low-power incandescent bulb, referred to as video (d). Each recording had a duration of 10 minutes.

Fig. 5. Snapshots from 4 non-static videos.

The ENF estimation from video recordings was carried out by applying the SLIC-based approach [3] [5], bandpass filtering around the aliased light flickering captured by the camera for various filter orders as was set in each experiment, and ESPRIT unless otherwise stated. Using spectrum combining, comparisons were made against the ENF estimated from either the power mains or the photodiode. The objective is to find the best parameters yielding a satisfactory MCC compared with the ground truth from both the mains power and the photodiode.

For video (a), the experiment took place in a well-lit environment with many textures. A jacket moved in front of the camera throughout the video, not causing sudden changes in the overall light intensity. A high MCC of 0.997 was measured using SLIC, bandpass filtering with pass-band [9.9, 10.1] Hz of order ν = 111, and STFT for segment duration of 21s.

Video (b) involves a person moving in and out of the frame in a dim environment. Despite the fact that more than half of the scene consists of dark objects with low reflection coefficients, an adequate MCC of 0.8133 and 0.8131 was obtained, respectively, when the ENF estimated from the video was compared against the ENF extracted from power mains or that captured by the photodiode-based sensing device. Figure 6 depicts the MCC between the ENF estimated from the video and the ground truths captured by mains or photodiode for varying durations. The pass-band used in the experiment was [9.99, 10.19] Hz. It is shown that the best results are acquired for a segment duration of 133 s when a bandpass filter order of ν=51 was employed. When the ground ENF was captured by the photodiode, the highest MCC value was observed for a segment duration of 109 s.

The final two experiments involving videos (c) and (d) are the most challenging, containing a great number of objects, different surfaces, and shadows. In the former, the scene was illuminated by a halogen lamp. Applying SLIC and a bandpass filter of order ν=211 before ESPRIT was used for

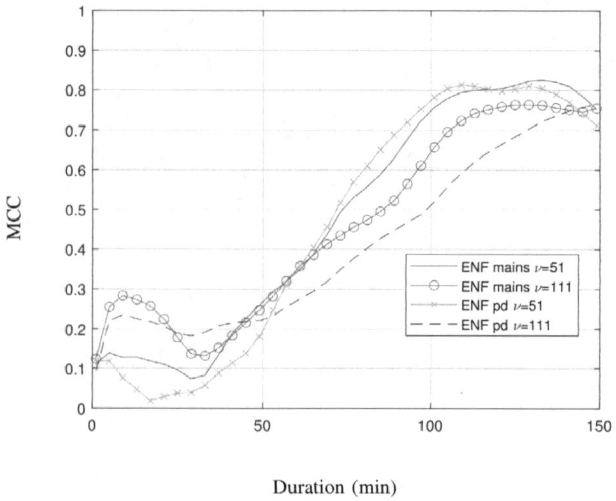

Fig. 6. MCC between the ENF estimated from video (b) and either ground truth (mains or photodiode).

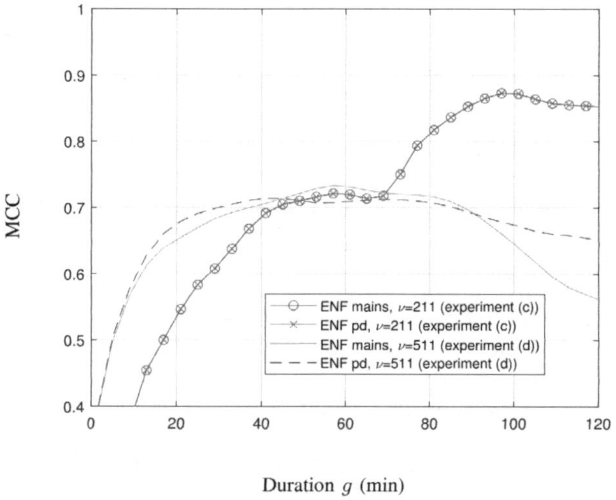

Fig. 7. MCC of the ENF estimated from the videos (c) and (d) against the ground truths (mains and photodiode).

ENF estimation, an MCC of 0.8736 was obtained for both ground truths. In the latter, we expected to acquire a lower MCC due to the lower overall light intensity fluctuation in proportion to the obstruction the moving person causes to the scene. The procedure is as above, with the difference that a bandpass filter of an order of ν=511 was used. An MCC of 0.7336 was obtained when the ENF extracted from the video was compared to the ENF from power mains, while an MCC of 0.7143 was measured when compared to the ENF from the photodiode. Figure 7 depicts the MCC obtained in both cases as a function of the segment duration. It is seen that the MCC between the ENF estimated from the video and either ground truth ENF follows the same trend for video (c). In contrast, the MCC is slightly higher when the comparison is made against the ENF from the power mains than the ENF from the photodiode. The pass-band in experiments (c) and (d) was [9.99, 10.19] Hz and [10.04, 10.14] Hz, respectively.

V. Conclusions

An optical sensor based on a photodiode has been developed to capture light intensity variations and enable ENF extraction in real-life scenarios. Multiple experiments have been conducted when a camera is used as a second optical sensor to record static and non-static videos. Experiments have attested that the ENF estimated from the photodiode device using the spectrum combining approach can be employed as a reference signal for either a halogen or an incandescent bulb. The MCC between the ENF estimated from a camera recording and the ENF estimated from either the power mains or the photodiode-device output follows the same trend, confirming that the photodiode-device can provide a reliable reference ENF signal.

It has been demonstrated that collecting a valid ground truth is possible without needing a device plugged into power mains. This fact allows battery-powered devices to be used as a means to extract ENF. Future research would address ENF estimation in indoor environments where LED bulbs illuminate a scene. LED lighting is now more than ever commercially available, replacing older lighting technology such as incandescent bulbs at an increased rate. Therefore, it is urgent to challenge the ability to timestamp video recordings in such environments.

Acknowledgements

G. Karantaidis' research work was supported by the Hellenic Foundation for Research and Innovation (HFRI) under the HFRI PhD Fellowship grant (Fellowship Number: 820). C. Kotropoulos' research was funded by the Hellenic Foundation for Research and Innovation (HFRI) (Faculty Support Code: 388).

References

[1] C. Grigoras, "Digital audio recording analysis: The electric network frequency (ENF) criterion," *Int. J. of Speech Language & the Law*, vol. 12, no. 1, pp. 63–76, 2005.

[2] A. Hajj-Ahmad, A. Berkovich, and M. Wu, "Exploiting power signatures for camera forensics," *IEEE Signal Process. Letters*, vol. 23, no. 5, pp. 713–717, 2016.

[3] S. Vatansever, A. E. Dirik, and N. Memon, "Detecting the presence of ENF signal in digital videos: A superpixel-based approach," *IEEE Signal Process. Letters*, vol. 24, no. 10, pp. 1463–1467, 2017.

[4] D. Nagothu, Y. Chen, E. Blasch, A. Aved, and S. Zhu, "Detecting malicious false frame injection attacks on surveillance systems at the edge using electrical network frequency signals," *Sensors*, vol. 19, no. 11, p. 2424, 2019.

[5] G. Karantaidis and C. Kotropoulos, "An automated approach for electric network frequency estimation in static and non-static digital video recordings," *Journal of Imaging*, vol. 7, no. 10, 2021.

[6] C. Grigoras, "Applications of ENF criterion in forensic audio, video, computer and telecommunication analysis," *Forensic Sci. Int.*, vol. 167, no. 2-3, pp. 136–145, 2007.

[7] D. P. Nicolalde and J. A. Apolinario, "Evaluating digital audio authenticity with spectral distances and ENF phase change," in *Proc. IEEE Int. Conf. Acoustics, Speech and Signal Process.*, 2009, pp. 1417–1420.

[8] M. Huijbregtse and Z. Geradts, "Using the ENF criterion for determining the time of recording of short digital audio recordings," in *Proc. Int. Work. Computational Forensics*, The Hague, The Netherlands, 2009, pp. 116–124.

[9] O. Ojowu, J. Karlsson, J. Li, and Y. Liu, "ENF extraction from digital recordings using adaptive techniques and frequency tracking," *IEEE Trans. Inf. Forensics and Security*, vol. 7, no. 4, pp. 1330–1338, 2012.

[10] D. Bykhovsky and A. Cohen, "Electrical network frequency (ENF) maximum-likelihood estimation via a multitone harmonic model," *IEEE Trans. Inf. Forensics and Security*, vol. 8, no. 5, pp. 774–753, 2013.

[11] A. Hajj-Ahmad, R. Garg, and M. Wu, "Spectrum combining for ENF signal estimation," *IEEE Signal Process. Letters*, vol. 20, no. 9, pp. 885–888, 2013.

[12] G. Hua, Y. Zhang, J. Goh, and V. L. L. Thing, "Audio authentication by exploring the absolute-error-map of ENF signals," *IEEE Trans. Inf. Forensics and Security*, vol. 11, no. 5, pp. 1003–1016, 2016.

[13] A. Skodras, A. Triantafyllopoulos, I. Krilis, and A. Foliadis, "A Hilbert-based approach to the ENF extraction problem," *IEICE Proc. Series*, vol. 24, no. A3-3, 2016.

[14] A. Hajj-Ahmad, C. Wong, S. Gambino, Q. Zhu, M. Yu, and M. Wu, "Factors affecting ENF capture in audio," *IEEE Trans. Inf. Forensics and Security*, vol. 14, no. 2, pp. 277–288, 2019.

[15] G. Karantaidis and C. Kotropoulos, "Blackman–Tukey spectral estimation and electric network frequency matching from power mains and speech recordings," *IET Signal Process.*, vol. 15, no. 6, pp. 396–409, 2021.

[16] R. Garg, A. L. Varna, A. Hajj-Ahmad, and M. Wu, ""seeing" ENF: Power-signature-based timestamp for digital multimedia via optical sensing and signal processing," *IEEE Trans. Inf. Forensics and Security*, vol. 8, no. 9, pp. 1417–1432, 2013.

[17] S. Vatansever, A. E. Dirik, and N. Memon, "Analysis of rolling shutter effect on ENF-based video forensics," *IEEE Trans. Inf. Forensics and Security*, vol. 14, no. 9, pp. 2262–2275, 2019.

[18] P. Ferrara, I. Sanchez, G. Draper-Gil, H. Junklewitz, and L. Beslay, "A MUSIC spectrum combining approach for ENF-based video timestamping," in *2021 IEEE Int. Work. Biometrics and Forensics*. IEEE, 2021, pp. 1–6.

[19] H. Su, A. Hajj-Ahmad, R. Garg, and M. Wu, "Exploiting rolling shutter for ENF signal extraction from video," in *Proc. IEEE Int. Conf. Image Process.*, 2014, pp. 5367–5371.

[20] P. Stoica and R. L. Moses, *Spectral Analysis of Signals*. Pearson Prentice Hall Upper Saddle River, NJ, 2005.

[21] A. V. Oppenheim and R. W. Schafer, *Discrete-Time Signal Processing*, 3rd ed. Upper Saddle River, NJ, USA: Prentice Hall Press, 2009.

[22] A. Hajj-Ahmad, S. Baudry, B. Chupeau, and G. Doërr, "Flicker forensics for pirate device identification," in *Proc. 3rd ACM Work. Inf. Hiding and Multimedia Security*, 2015, pp. 75–84.

[23] J. B. Allen and L. R. Rabiner, "A unified approach to short-time Fourier analysis and synthesis," *Proc. of the IEEE*, vol. 65, no. 11, pp. 1558–1564, 1977.

[24] W. Hernandez, "Input-output transfer function analysis of a photometer circuit based on an operational amplifier," *Sensors*, vol. 8, no. 1, pp. 35–50, 2008.

[25] A. Triantafyllopoulos *et al.*, "Exploring power signatures for location forensics of media recordings," IEEE Signal Processing Cup 2016, Tech. Rep., 2016.

[26] C. Moysiadis, "ENF Sensing Device," accessed on October 10, 2023. [Online]. Available: https://github.com/chrismoi/ENF-Sensing-Device

[27] C. Moysiadis, G. Karantaidis, and C. Kotropoulos, "Video, Ground truth, and code," accessed on October 10, 2023. [Online]. Available: https://github.com/chrismoi/Electric-Network-Frequency-Optical-Sensing-Devices

Physical Demonstrator of Medical Imaging Unit: Threat Analysis and Protection Strategies in Cybersecurity

Marina Galiano Botella
CSIRT-CV
Valencia, Spain
csirtcv@gva.es

Abstract- **Cyberattacks on healthcare systems are increasing. For this reason, there is a need to investigate and protect the operation of the technologies involved in healthcare facilities. One of the technologies with the greatest impact on healthcare has been diagnostic imaging. To cover this need for protection, a physical demonstrator of a Medical Imaging Unit has been developed, using the specific technologies of this system. In addition, abuse cases are specifically developed for this system. The purpose of this demonstrator is to help in the training on the operation and use of the technologies of a Medical Imaging Unit, to raise awareness among professionals and organizations, to determine the scope that an attack on the system could have and to generate measures to reduce or mitigate the impact.**

Keywords- health, cybersecurity, radiology, medical imaging.

I. INTRODUCTION

The use of Information Communications Technologies (ICTs) has become essential to meet the challenges faced by the healthcare system. In this sense, the use of some ICT tools such as electronic prescriptions or the Electronic Health Record has meant a great advance in the efficiency and effectiveness of the use of healthcare resources. Another technology that has led to a revolution due to its digitalization is diagnostic imaging.

In recent years, diagnostic imaging has advanced exponentially, becoming the focus of attention of engineers and scientists in order to improve medical imaging [1].

Healthcare systems are increasingly under attack by cybercriminals [2], [3]. Areas of hospitals that use these technologies can sometimes find themselves unprotected due to their rapid advancement and the increasing connectivity of devices to the Internet.

As shown in Fig. 1, during 2022, the healthcare sector was one of the most targeted. There are several reasons why the healthcare sector is targeted by cyberattackers. The first is that the information handled is highly sensitive and therefore offers great value to attackers. The second is the need to require the immediacy of the operation of the entire structure. A hospital cannot stop, since it has patients who need treatment, and whose lives depend on the uninterrupted operation of the hospital facilities. It is for this reason that many hospital systems are subject to computer attacks, such as ransomware (which involves encrypting and rendering computer systems unusable unless a ransom is paid). In such cases, hospital systems are forced to comply with ransom demands in order to continue operating.

A cyberattack on a hospital can have repercussions on the different systems and the usual operations of the facility. The attack can block the systems, making it impossible to access patients' medical records and forcing professionals to make medical reports manually. On the other hand, there are many consequences when the computer system is blocked, such as the cancellation of medical appointments, delays in surgical operations and the loss of electronic documents used by the hospital system such as procedures, among others.

Patient medical records are highly valuable on the dark web due to their comprehensive and sensitive information. This data, including personal, medical, and financial details, is used for identity theft, financial fraud, extortion, and healthcare scams. These records are targeted for their potential in both criminal activities and unauthorized research or commercial use.

In order to understand the scope of cyberattacks on healthcare environments, the objective is to develop a physical demonstrator of a medical environment. The medical environment will seek to represent a typical radiology or medical imaging unit of a hospital. This environment will realistically represent the delivery of medical images from a hospital. In addition, the mock-up of the environment will be

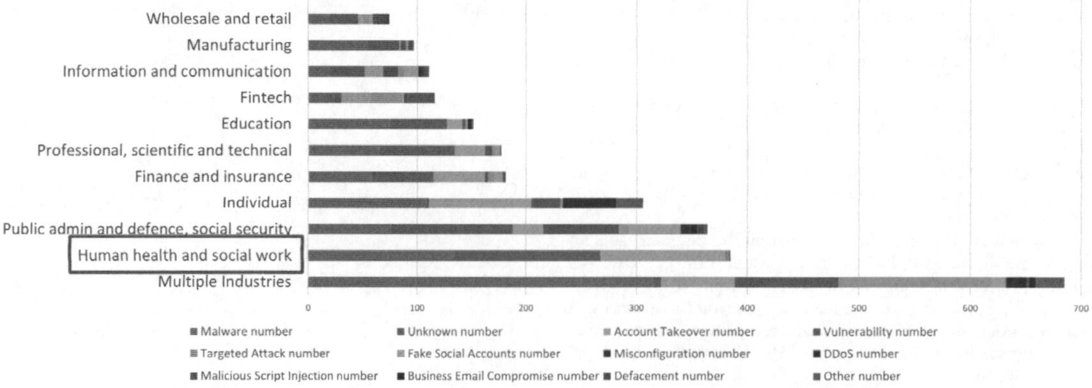

Fig. 1. Attacks by targets breakdowns in 2022 per sector. Data retrieved from [9].

done in such a way that it is as visual as possible when representing different abuse cases or attacks to the medical environment.

The simulation environment aims to investigate and analyze in depth the systems and threats that involve the hospital sector in the area of medical imaging, raise awareness among people and organizations involved in the health sector and test the different systems of the network of the Medical Imaging Unit, being able to determine the scope of the attacks and generate measures to reduce or mitigate the impact. For this purpose, during the project, several abuse cases will be developed, cyberattacks to the environment and its systems, to know the scope of these and use them in future awareness sessions.

The rest of the paper is structured as follows. In Section II, we present the devices that integrate the demonstrator, the defined architecture, and the cases of abuse to be developed. In Section III the results of the cases of abuse developed and launched are presented. Finally, we conclude our work in Section IV highlighting the most relevant aspects of the work performed.

II. MATERIALS AND METHODS

The Medical Imaging Unit environment developed represents 6 medical imaging rooms with 5 different techniques: 2 X-ray rooms, 1 Computerized Tomography (CT), 1 Magnetic Resonance Imaging (MRI), 1 mammography and 1 ultrasound. These imaging techniques are all simulated using PCs with Ubuntu 18.02 OS installed, except for the ultrasound scanner, for which the actual device is physically used, Chison ECO2.

The environment has been designed so that training and demonstrations can be carried out as visually as possible. For this reason, screens have been used to display the images that each modality would be taking in each room, in a simulated way. On the other hand, the modalities of each room have been 3D printed, as well as other decorative objects.

The environment uses the Digital Imaging and Communications in Medicine (DICOM) [4] standard for transmission, storage, retrieval, printing, processing and visualization of medical images and their information. It is used both as a storage format and as a transmission protocol for medical images.

The open source software used for the DICOM server is ORTHANC [5]. This software is used as the Picture Archiving and Communication System (PACS) of the environment. In addition, a PC with OS Windows 10 is used to perform consultations within the network, simulating that of a doctor's or radiologist's health practice. The architecture is shown in Fig. 2.

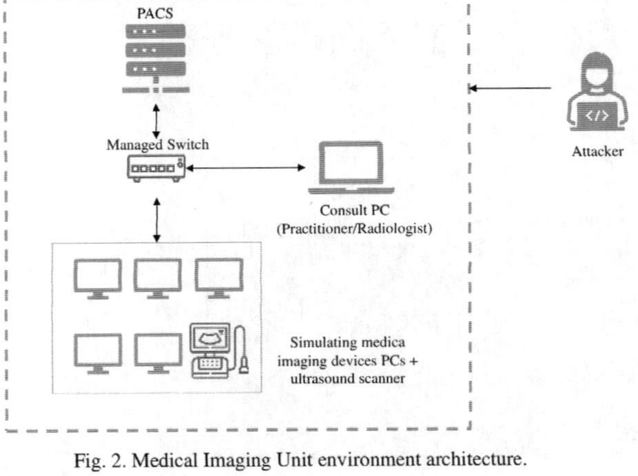

Fig. 2. Medical Imaging Unit environment architecture.

ORTHANC has been configured so that the consultation PC can access the PACS web server and upload and download images, delete patients and other default permissions.

In order to develop abuse cases in the Medical Imaging Unit physical demonstrator, the use of DICOM within the environment has been understood. The use of C-ECHO, C-STORE, C-MOVE, C-FIND and C-RETRIEVE has been studied in depth [6]. A specific configuration was performed in the environment when performing the abuse cases. The server configuration allowed C-ECHO, C-FIND and C-STORE from all devices within the network, while C-MOVE and C-RETRIEVE were only allowed for the specific asset simulating the radiography consultation equipment.

The abuse cases are developed in Python 3 using mostly the *pydicom* library for working with images in DICOM format [7]. The abuse cases should be launched from the radiologist's consulting PC, simulating that one of the radiologists' PCs has been compromised. However, depending on the network topology, these abuse cases could be launched from any network access point.

The proposed abuse cases are:

A. *Convert an image to DICOM*

The objective of the attack is to convert jpeg or png files into DICOM files so that a medical image can be replaced by the desired image and uploaded to PACS. There are multiple programs and libraries that can convert an image from a specific format to DICOM. In this case, the *Python-GDCM* library has been used [8].

B. *Steganography in DICOM*

The goal of the attack is to embed a message in a DICOM file in a hidden way so that it can be used as a means of communication between cyber attackers. For steganography of messages in a DICOM image, we focus on its metadata. DICOM has its own function which is to create private blocks to store patient information that has not been matched to any of the base fields of the DICOM metadata. Therefore, several private blocks are created, and the text is encrypted using Base64. The size of the image is not a limiting factor as these images are usually around 5MB in size.

C. *Modify metadata*

The objective of the attack is to acquire the image from the PACS, modify the metadata and replace it in the PACS. In this case, the original metadata is changed to that of another patient, potentially creating confusion for clinicians reviewing the patient, modality or clinician who performed the assessment.

D. *DICOM image modification*

The objective of the attack is to obtain a medical image from the PACS and modify the DICOM image by varying the pixels in such a way that it cannot be readable. In this way, we can darken the image or create areas with more brightness that may look like pathologies. We can also modify the image with another image, leaving the original metadata but completely modifying the image.

E. *Exfiltration of information*

The aim of the attack is to extract the medical images available in PACS in order to modify them and delete the original ones. In this way, the saved images of patients would not correspond to the original ones. In addition, these images are connected to patient data, and private health data can be obtained.

F. *Export metadata*

The aim of the attack is to obtain confidential patient information. To do this, all this data is stored in a local file.

The abuse cases are compiled into a single script that can be launched automatically, making it unnecessary for the attacker's technical knowledge to compromise hospital patient data.

III. RESULTS

The medical environment has been built taking into account that it must be a mobile unit, compact and easy to move without losing sight of the functionality of the environment, represented in a single module and with the capacity to integrate new modules. The visualization of the environment is shown in Fig. 3.

Therefore, the training and execution of attacks in the environment are more visual. In addition, when investigating the operation of the DICOM standard, tests can be performed without having to consider that the system shutdown may be critical or that the safety of any patient dependent on the operation of the devices may be involved.

The results obtained with the developed abuse cases are shown and discussed below.

A. *Convert an image to DICOM*

The image conversion is successful, but the DICOM file gets a unique identifier (UID) related to JPEG. When uploading the file to the DICOM server, the configuration of the server must be taken into account, since if it is not in promiscuous mode or does not accept these UIDs or image types, the upload may be rejected. Another alternative proposed is to modify the UID of the image created, pretending that it has been obtained from one of the modalities of the Medical Imaging Unit. This case of abuse is the beginning of most of the more developed cases, being essential in some occasions.

B. *Steganography in DICOM*

The private blocks have been created correctly and the Base64 encrypted message has been successfully included. The image has hardly suffered any variation in the image size as estimated, and in addition, the encrypted message is well camouflaged as there are several fields with numbers in the metadata that doctors do not usually check. On the other hand, more robust encryption could be used for future iterations or other steganography methods could be sought where the patient's image is involved instead of the metadata itself. These types of communications have been used by advanced persistent threat (APT) groups in social networks or other environments. They are not currently known to be used in healthcare settings, but it is a starting point to consider monitoring.

C. *Modify metadata*

Patient data can be changed for images previously downloaded from PACS. This may have an impact on the study not being found in common searches if the main search fields such as patient name or patient ID number have been modified.

D. *DICOM image modification*

Image modification using pixels can cause initial chaos for the radiologists who have to treat that image or for the physician who receives it this way post image processing. However, it could be easily reversible for a skilled technician. On the other hand, medical images could be exchanged between patients, leading to misdiagnosis by medical staff. However, the rise of AI also makes it increasingly difficult to distinguish real medical images from those generated by an algorithm. An example of substitution in the Medical Imaging Unit is shown in Fig. 4. This is one of the cases of abuse with the greatest impact both because of its visual nature and because it could lead to a real diagnosis, since the patient could be diagnosed with a pathology that he/she does not suffer from or even not be diagnosed with one that he/she does suffer from, putting his/her life at risk.

E. *Exfiltration of information*

This case of abuse is only possible if the compromised machine requesting it has permission to obtain such images, as is the case with a radiology station. However, proper network segmentation, or monitoring of strange or abundant requests, can help prevent this type of attack in a hospital environment. Cyberattackers sometimes get this information from patients along with their medical images in order to sell them on the

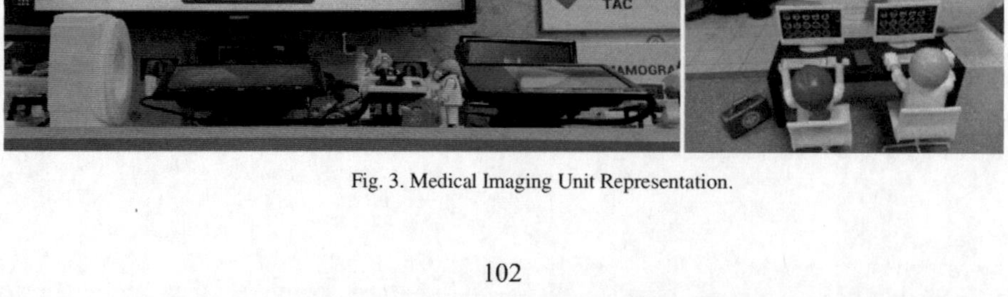

Fig. 3. Medical Imaging Unit Representation.

dark web. Proper segmentation, permissions management and monitoring of the DICOM standard could help prevent and detect this type of attack.

F. Export metadata

In the Medical Imaging Unit, this case could be executed from any point in the network since the only thing obtained was the patient data and not the image itself. An expert attacker could obtain them despite being a complex protocol. Segmentation and configuration of permissions on each device is essential to prevent this type of attack. In addition, monitoring the requests helps to detect them.

In many cases, the measures that are implemented or advised in hospital environments for the prevention and detection of these attacks are usually technical. Some of these countermeasures are:

- Use strong passwords.
- Encrypt DICOM communications.
- Perform periodic audits on medical network.
- Monitor DICOM requests and accesses through web interface.
- Network segmentation.
- Implement security measures as firewalls.

However, not all of them must be of this technical nature. It is crucial for cyberattack prevention to involve all staff and raise their awareness of cybersecurity. These countermeasures are based on awareness and training in cybersecurity, and of course, targeting this education to the healthcare sector. Raising awareness of the hospital's internal processes and the repercussions that misuse of systems can bring is indispensable. It is also very important to create security procedures to help implement these cybersecurity practices.

The development and construction of the Medical Imaging Unit, in addition to the creation of the abuse cases, helps to conduct more visual training sessions that reinforce this message.

The creation of the abuse cases has helped to gain a deeper understanding of the risks that can exist in a hospital, so that once they are known, they can be mitigated.

IV. CONCLUSIONS

The developed Medical Imaging Unit environment helps the different teams involved in cybersecurity to improve their knowledge of healthcare environments, as well as to test in a real simulated environment using the developed abuse cases. Attack teams can identify vulnerabilities and exploit them without risk of causing harm to either facilities or patients, while defense teams can monitor such actions. The execution of the abuse cases assists in the threat analysis of an attacker compromising an in-network system in a hospital with access to medical images of a hospital's patients. Finally, these abuse cases can be used in conferences, lectures, and trainings for cybersecurity awareness in healthcare environments, as well as to teach new professionals how to defend and attack such facilities for ethical purposes.

REFERENCES

[1] M. Desco and J. J. Vaquero, 'Más de un siglo de imagen médica' [in English: Over a century of medical imaging], Arbor, vol. CLXXVII, no. 698, pp. 337–364, Feb. 2004, doi: 10.3989/arbor.2004.i698.611.

[2] 'Ciberataque al hospital Clínic de Barcelona | Hospital Clínic Barcelona' [in English: Cyberattack to Barcelona's Hospital Clinic], Clínic Barcelona. https://www.clinicbarcelona.org/prensa/ultima-hora/ciberataque-al-hospital-clinic-de-barcelona (accessed Mar. 23, 2023).

[3] E. Press, 'Lockbit se disculpa por el ataque de ransomware a un hospital infantil y ofrece la herramienta para liberar los sistemas' [in English: Lockbit apologises for ransomware attack on children's hospital, offers tool to free systems], Jan. 03, 2023. https://www.europapress.es/portaltic/ciberseguridad/noticia-lockbit-disculpa-ataque-ransomware-hospital-infantil-ofrece-herramienta-liberar-sistemas-20230103122550.html (accessed Mar. 23, 2023).

[4] 'DICOM'. https://www.dicomstandard.org/ (accessed Feb. 28, 2022).

[5] 'Orthanc - DICOM Server'. https://www.orthanc-server.com/ (accessed Mar. 23, 2023).

[6] '9.3 Protocol', https://dicom.nema.org/dicom/2013/output/chtml /part07/sect_9.3.html, (accessed Mar. 23, 2023).

[7] 'Pydicom |', https://pydicom.github.io/ (accessed Sep. 01, 2023).

[8] 'python-gdcm: Grassroots DICOM runtime libraries', 2023, [MacOS, Microsoft: Windows, POSIX, Unix]. Available: https://github.com/tfmoraes/python-gdcm/ (accessed Sep. 01, 2023).

[9] '2022 Cyber Attacks Statistics – HACKMAGEDDON', [Online]. Available: https://www.hackmageddon.com/2023/01/24/2022-cyber-attacks-statistics/ (accessed Nov. 06, 2023).

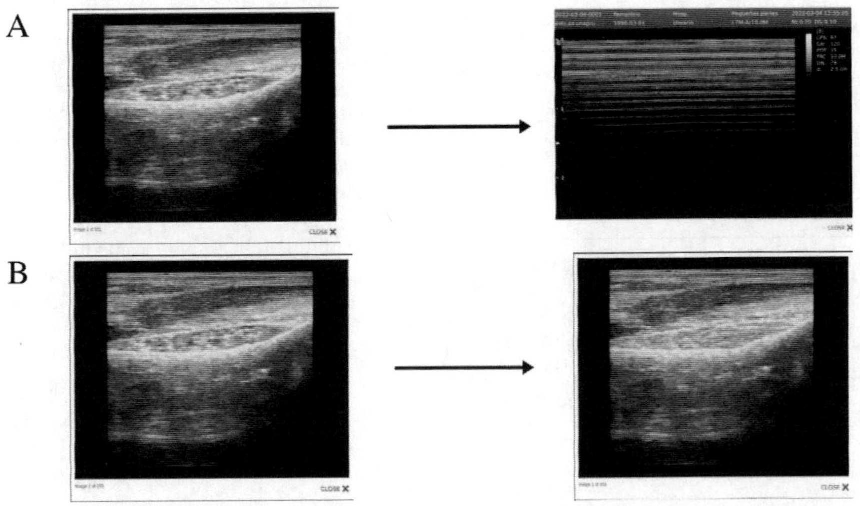

Fig. 4. Modification of a medical image. A. Image changed. B. Image modified by AI.

Towards a Secure City: The Contribution of the Smart City Physical Demonstrator in Threat Assessment

Marina Galiano Botella
CSIRT-CV
Valencia, Spain
e-mail: csirtcv@gva.es

Eduardo Ortega Serrano
S2 Grupo
Valencia, Spain
e-mail: csirtcv@gva.es

Elvira Lara Maudos
S2 Grupo
Valencia, Spain
e-mail: csirtcv@gva.es

Abstract- **Smart Cities are susceptible to cyberattacks due to the large amount of data being collected and shared in real time across networks and connected systems. Cyberattacks on Smart Cities can have serious consequences, such as unauthorized access to sensitive information, sabotage of critical infrastructure, and disruption of essential services. Prior studies have developed testbeds in the context of Smart Cities, but these have not been primarily focused on cybersecurity. Furthermore, existing research on cybersecurity within Smart Cities often comprises literature reviews rather than practical experimentation in a test environment. In this paper, we propose a Smart City physical demonstrator. It aims to investigate and analyze in depth these systems to know the scope of the different attacks and generate measures to mitigate the risks and impact. In addition, the demonstrator seeks to raise awareness of Smart City users and organizations involved in its development. The physical demonstrator of a Smart City serves as an invaluable resource for cybersecurity teams, empowering them to enhance their understanding of Smart City environments.**

Keywords- Smart City; cybersecurity; traffic; waste; electrical vehicles.

I. INTRODUCTION

Smart Cities are born with the aim of reducing the consumption of resources and improving the efficiency of the management of services, as well as improving the quality of life of citizens, reducing pollution and making cities safer and more livable. On the other hand, the revolution brought about by the Internet of Things (IoT) has made feasible the precise and instantaneous measurement of many variables that affect the environment of cities, making it possible for the first time to make decisions based on instantaneous, highly accurate data.

The rapid transition to smart cities has led to the rapid adoption of the devices being used without regard to cybersecurity. This is reflected in some cyberattacks on smart cities that leave the city without the software necessary for city management, resulting in loss of police records or other court documents [1]. For these reasons, it is evident the need to have a thorough understanding of the implicit risks of this digital transformation and to be prepared to respond effectively to the possible risk scenarios to which a Smart City may be subjected. In short, a correct transition towards a Smart City model must be accompanied by a correct securitization specialized in cybersecurity.

Among the systems that can be found in Smart Cities, traffic management, waste management and electric vehicle charging systems, are of particular interest. These systems are the ones that have been selected to make a physical demonstrator of a Smart City, based on the city of Valencia, Spain. The components used in the environment can be found in real Smart City locations, as well as with the same configurations.

A. Traffic management

Traffic management is represented by the use of a camera. Cameras play an important role in traffic management in modern cities. They enable traffic operators to monitor and control vehicle flow, detect traffic violations and generally improve road safety. Cameras can be used to monitor traffic lights and crosswalks, detect vehicles in bus lanes or exclusive lanes, as well as to detect traffic violations, such as speeding, red light violations or using a cell phone while driving. In addition, cameras can be used to collect traffic data, which helps to plan and improve city infrastructure [2].

B. Waste management

Waste management in the demonstrator is represented by an urban waste sensor installed inside a container. These sensors are an important tool for improving waste collection efficiency, as they allow city operators to monitor container filling and plan waste collection more effectively. Sensors can also help reduce collection costs, as operators can collect containers only when they are full, rather than on a defined schedule. In addition, some of these sensors can be used to measure air quality, providing valuable data for urban planning and environmental management [3][4].

C. Electric vehicle charging systems management

In this case, electric vehicle charging is represented by an outdoor charging station. Electric vehicle chargers are essential in Smart Cities because they enable the transition towards a more sustainable and cleaner mobility. These chargers are important for urban planning, as they enable energy demand management and optimization of power grid usage [5]-[7].

The objectives of the demonstrator are to investigate and analyze in depth the systems and threats to which Smart Cities are exposed, raise awareness among people and organizations using the systems, and perform tests on these systems to know the scope of the different attacks and thus be able to generate measures to reduce or eliminate the impact.

Within the paper's structure, in Section 2, the related work concerning testbeds, digital twins and cybersecurity in Smart Cities will be presented. In Section 3, the testbed setup and the proposed cybersecurity investigation methods for Smart Cities will be outlined. In Section 4, the outcomes and consequences of the conducted attacks will be presented. In Section 5, conclusions are summarized, project challenges are discussed, and future work is highlighted.

II. STATE OF ART

Significant technological advancements in replicating environments have occurred, as we have witnessed a noticeable shift from traditional testbeds to what we now refer to as digital twins [8]. These digital twins are highly detailed digital representations of physical products and even entire environments, playing a pivotal role in various applications, including Smart Cities [9]-[12]. While there are numerous testbeds specializing in Smart Cities [13]-[15], it is less common to find initiatives that integrate these testbeds with digital twins. Additionally, these approaches often overlook the aspect of cybersecurity.

However, it is important to note that, on occasion, potential applications in the field of cybersecurity that these digital twin models offer are mentioned [11]. Cybersecurity stands as a critical element in Smart Cities, and the capability to simulate and analyze cyber threats in virtual environments can be essential for protecting critical infrastructure and intelligent systems within the city.

Conversely, the continuous increase in cyberattacks directed at the Smart Cities sector has spurred the creation of studies that analyze trends and types of attacks that have occurred or could potentially occur within these smart cities [16]-[19]. Some of them apply new technologies such as Deep Learning or other kinds of Artificial Intelligence (AI) [20][21]. Nevertheless, it is relevant to mention that most of these studies tend to consist of literature reviews or compilations of existing data, rather than conducting actual attacks in a controlled testing environment. For this reason, the project focuses on creating a hybrid testbed that combines real systems with typical elements of a digital twin. The goal of this testbed is to represent a Smart City and be useful for conducting cybersecurity tests on a small and large scale, allowing us to observe the impacts of cyberattacks. It also serves as a means of raising awareness about these environments.

III. MATERIALS AND METHODS

The Smart City demonstrator mainly represents three management systems: traffic, waste and electric vehicle chargers. For each of these systems, a traffic camera, a waste sensor and an electric vehicle outdoor charging station have been used as main elements, respectively. In addition, there are several PCs for the management of the devices. It should be noted that the connection of all devices is wired directly to the managed switch except for the waste management sensor, which communicates with a router to provide Internet connection and to communicate with a real pre-production platform.

The environment has been designed with the aim of making the training and demonstrations as visual as possible. For this purpose, there are different visualization screens where the consequences of an attack on one of these systems can be shown. To play the role of an external attacker, there is a laptop from which some of the malicious behaviors can be simulated in order to affect the infrastructure of a Smart City.

When monitoring the environment, a port mirror is used on the switch to study attacks from a defensive perspective.

Figure 1 shows the pre-construction design of the Smart City. The laboratory consists of five assemblable parts (racks).

- Main rack: The electrical cabinet containing the switchgear, network electronics and device control elements is located in this rack. In addition, there is a display at the top for the management of the devices in the environment.
- Rack 1: Contains the electric vehicle charging station.
- Rack 2: The waste management system has been installed, which includes a trash container and the sensor installed inside it.
- Rack 3: It contains the traffic camera system. The camera is installed in the upper part and the display screen in the lower part.
- Rack 4: Contains two screens showing the city's pre-production platform and viewing environment.

The abuse cases will be developed in Python 3, compiled into a single script that can be launched automatically, making it unnecessary for the attacker to have technical knowledge to compromise the different components of the Smart City. For attacks on the charger and camera, the attacker's PC will be connected via an ethernet cable, while attacks on the debris sensor will be done wirelessly.

The abuse cases proposed for development are described below:

A. *Ransomware attack on the charging infrastructure*

The goal of the attack is to power down the charger's sockets. In this way, the attacker would disable the charger and ask for a ransom to restore the charger to its normal state. During the attack, it will be shown that an attempt is made to enable the charger, but it automatically reverts to the disabled state.

B. *Man in the Middle (MitM) in the charging system*

The purpose of the attack is to show the customer that their vehicle is charging when it is not. Thus, the blue light indicating "charging" status will illuminate but the charging socket will actually be powered down.

C. *Obtaining camera credentials*

The purpose here is to obtain the camera's credentials via web cookie or via brute force by performing an attack on its sending protocol Real-Time Streaming Protocol (RTSP).

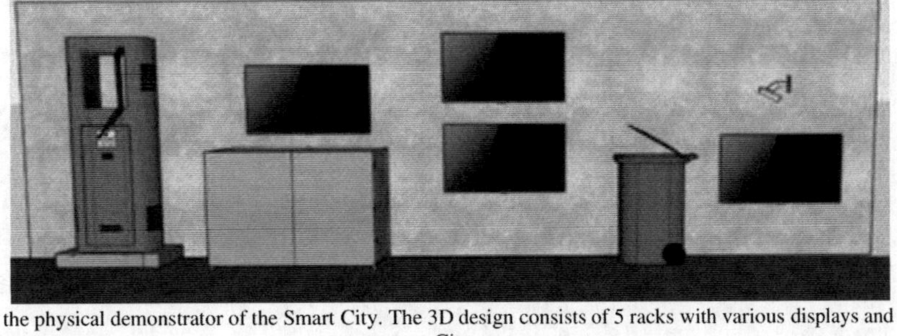

Figure 1. 3D design of the physical demonstrator of the Smart City. The 3D design consists of 5 racks with various displays and real systems of a Smart City.

D. *Attack on the camera access token*

By means of the user's access token, different configuration elements such as zoom, brightness or intensity can be changed so that the image displayed does not correspond to the real image.

E. *Obtaining credentials from the waste management sensor*

This represents a method of extracting authentication credentials through tools against the Message Queuing Telemetry Transport (MQTT) protocol.

F. *MitM between the waste management sensor and the management platform*

Tampering in the middle of the communications between the sensor and the sensor management web page to steal information or enter modified information.

IV. RESULTS

The Smart City demonstrator consists of several modules. Figure 2 shows the visualization of the Smart City racks. The image illustrates the structure of racks 2 and 4 in the Smart City prototype with the displays and the waste management sensor. Also, it shows the racks 1 and 3 where the charger of the electric vehicle charging management system and the camera of the traffic management system are located, respectively.

The abuse cases are currently under development. However, an analysis of the implications of each of the attacks in case of success has been carried out.

A. *Ransomware attack on the charging infrastructure*

Removing the availability of charging devices can create a significant logistical problem in the city. If the problem extends to several systems and for an extended period of time, it could create a sense of discomfort and dissatisfaction in the population by not being able to use the electric vehicle charging services of their city, undermining the mobility capacity of its inhabitants.

B. *MitM in the charging system*

The spoofing of a charge may cause complaints from the population to increase and saturate certain citizen services or even if this extends to several devices, the technical staff will not be able to cover the repair of all of them.

C. *Obtaining camera credentials*

Obtaining the credentials of traffic cameras may involve having access to modify the credentials and restrict workers' access to them or even power down the cameras. This would force technicians to go in person camera by camera to reset them.

D. *Attack on the camera access token*

Altering camera visual settings means that traffic control center workers cannot do their job properly or the camera cannot analyze the data correctly. If one of the cameras records videos and uses AI algorithms to count vehicles but the zoom has been changed, this data would include errors.

E. *Obtaining credentials from the waste management sensor*

Obtaining passwords via MQTT would be an initial step in order to be able to modify data emitted by the sensor. These consequences are explained in the following abuse case.

F. *MitM between the waste management sensor and the management platform*

The data that can be manipulated is whether the trash container is full or not, forcing a vehicle to travel to the site, when it is not necessary, wasting resources. On the other hand, the trash container could be full, and no vehicle could appear, causing the neighbors' discomfort and the proliferation of pests.

In the future, luminaires will be incorporated into one of the racks. In addition, the different abuse cases for each of the systems will be implemented, while in parallel we will analyze how to detect these attacks defensively, while analyzing the repercussions of each of the abuse cases.

Finally, these abuse cases can be used in new research on industrial cybersecurity, conferences, lectures and trainings for cybersecurity awareness in Smart Cities environments, as well as, to train new professionals in attack and defense of such facilities for ethical purposes.

V. CONCLUSIONS

The Smart City physical demonstrator represents a valuable tool for cybersecurity teams, allowing them to improve their knowledge of these Smart City environments, test in a real simulated environment, and conduct research. Thanks to this technology, attack teams can identify vulnerabilities and exploit them without the risk of causing damage to either facilities or users, giving them the opportunity to gain hands-on experience in a controlled environment.

On the other hand, defense teams can monitor the actions carried out by attack teams, which allows them to learn about

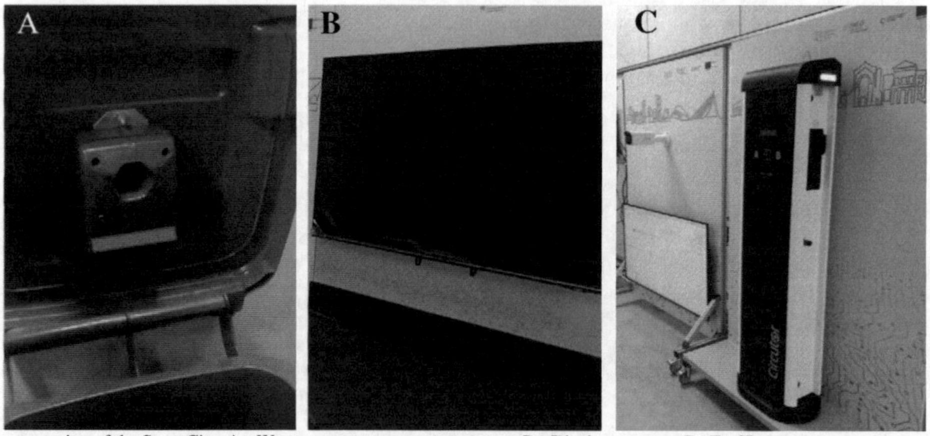

Figure 2. Representation of the SmartCity. A - Waste management system sensor. B - Display screens. C - Traffic management camera and electric vehicle charger.

existing vulnerabilities in the system and improve their protection strategies. In addition, the detected abuse cases can be used in conferences, lectures and trainings to raise community awareness about the importance of cybersecurity in Smart Cities.

In short, the Smart City physical demonstrator is presented as a fundamental tool for teaching and training new professionals in the field of Smart Cities cybersecurity. This technology allows users to learn how to defend and attack such facilities for ethical purposes, thus contributing to the construction of a safer and more secure environment.

Smart City systems are characterized by their large-scale complexity, making it impractical to acquire numerous physical devices for conducting real-scale testbeds. As a result, virtualization of these systems becomes a crucial avenue for experimentation. Furthermore, the rapid proliferation of new devices in the Smart City landscape necessitates ongoing vigilance to identify and integrate these devices into testbeds effectively.

In addition, achieving highly realistic configurations for these testbeds is a primary objective, as it allows for more accurate experimentation. However, achieving absolute fidelity to real-world configurations can prove challenging, given that each organization or municipal body may possess specific and unique configurations that deviate from the initial design parameters. This divergence can necessitate adjustments in testbed setups to accommodate these variations.

Furthermore, in addition to the incorporation of luminaires, there is a need to conduct a comprehensive analysis of the systems currently deployed within Smart Cities that hold the potential for integration into the testbed environment. This necessitates an examination of emerging attack vectors and the development of use cases for training and awareness in the field of cybersecurity.

Expanding the testbed environment is achievable through the integration of a 3D model representing a Smart City. This model facilitates the scalability of attacks across multiple devices, enabling a comprehensive evaluation of attack pathways and their real-world impact on an urban setting. Additionally, the introduction of new technologies, particularly those involving AI, holds promise for enhancing anomaly detection and countering attacks. This may also involve deploying AI-driven surveillance systems, which, it is important to note, can be vulnerable to manipulation by potential attackers, adding an additional layer of complexity to the research.

REFERENCES

[1] "SAMSAM Ransomware Suspected in Atlanta Cyberattack - Noticias de seguridad - Trend Micro ES". https://www.trendmicro.com/vinfo/es/security/news/cybercrime-and-digital-threats/samsam-ransomware-suspected-in-atlanta-cyberattack (accessed Sep. 01, 2023).

[2] A. M. de Souza, C. A. Brennand, R. S. Yokoyama, E. A. Donato, E. R. Madeira, and L. A. Villas, "Traffic management systems: A classification, review, challenges, and future perspectives", *International Journal of Distributed Sensor Networks*, vol. 13, no. 4, p. 1550147716683612, Apr. 2017, doi: 10.1177/1550147716683612.

[3] B. Esmaeilian, B. Wang, K. Lewis, F. Duarte, C. Ratti and S. Behdad, "The future of waste management in smart and sustainable cities: A review and concept paper", *Waste Management*, vol. 81, pp. 177–195, Nov. 2018, doi: 10.1016/j.wasman.2018.09.047.

[4] A. Hussain *et al.*, "Waste Management and Prediction of Air Pollutants Using IoT and Machine Learning Approach", *Energies*, vol. 13, no. 15, Art. no. 15, Jan. 2020, doi: 10.3390/en13153930.

[5] M. S. Mastoi *et al.*, "An in-depth analysis of electric vehicle charging station infrastructure, policy implications, and future trends", *Energy Reports*, vol. 8, pp. 11504–11529, Nov. 2022, doi: 10.1016/j.egyr.2022.09.011.

[6] A. Khaksari, G. Tsaousoglou, P. Makris, K. Steriotis, N. Efthymiopoulos, and E. Varvarigos, "Sizing of electric vehicle charging stations with smart charging capabilities and quality of service requirements", *Sustainable Cities and Society*, vol. 70, p. 102872, Jul. 2021, doi: 10.1016/j.scs.2021.102872.

[7] B. P. Rimal, C. Kong, B. Poudel, Y. Wang, and P. Shahi, "Smart Electric Vehicle Charging in the Era of Internet of Vehicles, Emerging Trends, and Open Issues", *Energies*, vol. 15, no. 5, Art. no. 5, Jan. 2022, doi: 10.3390/en15051908.

[8] R. Vrabič, J. A. Erkoyuncu, P. Butala, and R. Roy, "Digital twins: Understanding the added value of integrated models for through-life engineering services", Procedia Manufacturing, vol. 16, pp. 139–146, 2018, doi: 10.1016/j.promfg.2018.10.167.

[9] L. Deren, Y. Wenbo, and S. Zhenfeng, "Smart city based on digital twins", Comput.Urban Sci., vol. 1, no. 1, p. 4, Dec. 2021, doi: 10.1007/s43762-021-00005-y

[10] G. White, A. Zink, L. Codecá, and S. Clarke, "A digital twin smart city for citizen feedback", Cities, vol. 110, p. 103064, Mar. 2021, doi: 10.1016/j.cities.2020.103064.

[11] M. Jafari, A. Kavousi-Fard, T. Chen, and M. Karimi, "A Review on Digital Twin Technology in Smart Grid, Transportation System and Smart City: Challenges and Future", IEEE Access, vol. 11, pp. 17471–17484, 2023, doi: 10.1109/ACCESS.2023.3241588.

[12] H. Xia, Z. Liu, M. Efremochkina, X. Liu, and C. Lin, "Study on city digital twin technologies for sustainable smart city design: A review and bibliometric analysis of geographic information system and building information modeling integration", Sustainable Cities and Society, vol. 84, p. 104009, Sep. 2022, doi: 10.1016/j.scs.2022.104009.

[13] M. Zaman, N. Puryear, N. Zohrabi, and S. Abdelwahed, "Development of the OpenCyberCity Testbed: Smart City Research Innovation and Opportunities", in Proceedings of the ACM/IEEE 14th International Conference on Cyber-Physical Systems (with CPS-IoT Week 2023), San Antonio TX USA: ACM, May 2023, pp. 233–234. doi: 10.1145/3576841.3589612.

[14] R. Sell, R.-M. Soe, R. Wang, and A. Rassõlkin, "Autonomous Vehicle Shuttle in Smart City Testbed", in Intelligent System Solutions for Auto Mobility and Beyond, C. Zachäus and G. Meyer, Eds., in Lecture Notes in Mobility. , Cham: Springer International Publishing, 2021, pp. 143–157. doi: 10.1007/978-3-030-65871-7_11.

[15] L. Sanchez *et al.*, "SmartSantander: IoT experimentation over a smart city testbed", Computer Networks, vol. 61, pp. 217–238, Mar. 2014, doi: 10.1016/j.bjp.2013.12.020.

[16] V. Garcia-Font, C. Garrigues, and H. Rifà-Pous, "Attack Classification Schema for Smart City WSNs", Sensors, vol. 17, no. 4, p. 771, Apr. 2017, doi: 10.3390/s17040771

[17] A. A. Elsaeidy, A. Jamalipour, and K. S. Munasinghe, "A Hybrid Deep Learning Approach for Replay and DDoS Attack Detection in a Smart City", IEEE Access, vol. 9, pp. 154864–154875, 2021, doi: 10.1109/ACCESS.2021.3128701.

[18] M. Alamer and M. A. Almaiah, "Cybersecurity in Smart City: A Systematic Mapping Study", in 2021 International Conference on Information Technology (ICIT), Amman, Jordan: IEEE, Jul. 2021, pp. 719–724. doi: 10.1109/ICIT52682.2021.9491123.

[19] M. Kalinin, V. Krundyshev, and P. Zegzhda, "Cybersecurity Risk Assessment in Smart City Infrastructures", Machines, vol. 9, no. 4, p. 78, Apr. 2021, doi: 10.3390/machines9040078.

[20] C. Ma, "Smart city and cyber-security; technologies used, leading challenges and future recommendations", Energy Reports, vol. 7, pp. 7999–8012, Nov. 2021, doi: 10.1016/j.egyr.2021.08.124.

[21] Md. M. Rashid *et al.*, "Adversarial training for deep learning-based cyberattack detection in IoT-based smart city applications", Computers & Security, vol. 120, p. 102783, Sep. 2022, doi: 10.1016/j.cose.2022.102783.

Hybrid Networking Platform for Minority Groups in Accessing Labour Market

Understanding the Role of Online and Offline Social Capital Interplay in Resource Accessibility

Cecilia Olivieri
X23 Science in Society
Treviglio, Italy
e-mail: cecilia.oliveri@x-23.org

Agathe Semlali
X23 Science in Society
Treviglio, Italy
e-mail: agathe.semlali@x-23.org

Davide Carminati
X23 Science in Society
Treviglio, Italy
e-mail: davide.carminati@x-23.org

Lorenzo Maggio Laquidara
X23 Science in Society
Treviglio, Italy
e-mail: lorenzo.maggio@x-23.org

Abstract—**Social interactions and resource accessibility have long been central elements in social research. Social capital, an idea pioneered by Pierre Bourdieu, is an extremely effective concept for reading and interpreting social interactions. The rise of communication technologies and online social networks has further shaped human interactions and created new avenues for social ties. Although the analysis of offline and online networks separately is supported by an extensive bibliography, the interplay between the two still needs further development. The study addresses the gap in understanding the relationship in mutual influence between online and offline networks, particularly within migrant communities and minority groups. Focusing on a case study platform, connecting young Afrodescendant women and orienting them to their professional career, this research explores how the hybrid nature of the platform (promoting both virtual and in person networks) impacts the interplay between online and offline social capital of the platform's members and their ability to access resources. To achieve these goals, mixed-methods Social Network Approach (SNA) and a one-year longitudinal approach are employed. By uncovering the complexities of online and offline social capital dynamics, especially within marginalized groups, the study offers insights for effective platform-networking-building and highlights resource accessibility potential for similar platforms development.**

Keywords-online networks; migrations; discourse network analysis; participatory research; gender.

I. INTRODUCTION

Understanding human social interactions and resource accessibility has long been a focal point in social research. In fact, investigating their functioning can offer an insightful vehicle to better understand research and policy issues such as migration, employment, social inclusion, and community development, just to name a few. Social capital was first conceptualized by seminal social scientist Pierre Bourdieu in his 1986 study on exclusion dynamics in French high society [3]. Social capital represents the aggregate of the actual potential resources that are linked to the possession of a durable network or, in other words, to membership in a group [15]. Social capital is a multifaceted construct, reflecting the multifaceted nature of human relationships. One's own social capital consists of ties of various kinds (i.e., weak/strong, frequent/sporadic, direct/indirect) and nodes (that is, individuals, groups, institutions, or other entities). Each of them influences an individual's social standing and resource accessibility in relation to their social surroundings.

The above-mentioned theories have been strongly applied to the field of migration [10] and minority groups studies [1] since they provide a deep understanding of the dynamics by which these groups constitute, maintain, and exploit their network for resource accessibility [19]. In this context, networks represent a meaningful resource, as they provide a means through which individuals belonging to multiple marginalized or disadvantaged groups can access a diverse range of support, knowledge, and opportunities. However, a detailed investigation of these ties, their nature, origins, and constitution can reveal the particular kind of resources that flow among them. The complexity of such ties and networks and how they are established and maintained has become more complex over time [10].

The rise of new communication technologies and online social networks has added a new dimension to this understanding. The spread of Information and Communication Technology (ICTs) and social media has transformed interpersonal connections and communications and affected the ways in which people create and maintain social ties [12]. Online networks, made possible by digital platforms, occupy an increasingly relevant role in shaping modern social interactions, especially in the COVID-19 pandemic's aftermath. Indeed, this change has imposed the need to complexify the view and analysis of all social fields, including migration and minority studies.

Despite the relevance and permeability of such new human connection forms, the relationship between the online and offline dimensions needs further investigation [11]. Indeed, it is crucial for forthcoming research to delve into the specific domains where online and offline networks converge, not only enhancing the comprehension of network outcomes, but also elucidating the underlying mechanisms through which ties influence outcomes in both contexts [16].

In this research, relying on an online platform fostering Afrodescendant networks case study, we intend to delve more into the interplay between the online and offline social capital by filling the above-mentioned gap. Through the analysis of this case study, we will explore (i) the role of this hybrid nature platform (active both virtually and offline, through in person activities) in promoting online and offline social capital at individual and community level, and (ii) how these different forms of social capital interplay and influence one another. The first objective will be reached by deepening the factors enabling such connections and the effectiveness in accessing resources, while the second one by delving into the mutual networking dynamics. The ultimate scope of the research is to provide a tridimensional and in depth understanding of the networking phenomena related to the hybrid nature of the platform. From this baseline, we intend to implement and strengthen the impact in networking-building and resources-access of the platform, by extracting meaningful insights from online and offline networks interactions. The rest of the paper is structured as follows. In Section II, we present the case study the research is investigating. Finally, we conclude our work in Section III, to present our research methodologies.

II. THE CASE STUDY

This study intends to reach our research objectives by addressing a critical real-world issue that intersects with minority groups' online and offline social capital dimensions - and their mutual interplay - and access to economic opportunities. Afrodescendant women, in most countries, are disproportionately prone to unstable and precarious jobs [18]. Gender-based inequality often intercepts ethnic-based discriminations, resulting in fewer economic prospects for Afrodescendant women. These inequalities arise from a combination of factors, including overrepresentation in informal employment [7] and limited educational opportunities [1]. In this panorama, the online and offline network dimensions generate a form of social capital, thus representing a decisive factor for access or exclusion from the labor market group [5]. In particular, migrant organizations, active both online and offline, are mostly considered important means of support for ethnic minorities [14]. In addition to specific services, these organizations have indeed a major role in increasing the social engagement and in reducing the social exclusion of their users, so in strengthening their social capital [4].

We intend to consider the case study of an online platform, mainly active in the Ile-de-France area, orienting young Afrodescendant women to their professional career, as a means of understanding online and offline network interplay and resource access promotion. This community was created with the scope of connecting young graduates, employees and expert Afrodescendant women and creating an inclusive space for sharing experiences, knowledge and support. It is a hybrid platform with both a virtual dimension - mainly oriented towards offering webinars, training activities and digital networking - and an in-presence dimension that complements the networking experience with proximity and human involvement through activities and workshops.

The hybrid character of this platform on the one hand and the target group participating in it on the other, will make it possible to investigate the relationship between the two network dimensions in a privileged field of investigation for access to resources such as that of minority groups. The reference to this case study will be functional to the extraction of actionable insights that can substantively enhance the efficacy of networking-building and resource access within similar contexts.

III. EMPLOYED METHODOLOGY AND CONCLUSION

Qualitative and language-based approaches represent a promising attempt to provide narratives informed by migrants' voices and experiences. These approaches allow the researcher to get a progressively accurate knowledge of the community structure [8] [10] and multifocality [13]. This combines with ideas of community members shaping, mapping and evaluating their network and the resources linked to its belonging.

For us to achieve these goals, our methodology will rely on mixed-methods Social Network Approach, or SNA [4]. Our data collection strategy will consist of in-depth, semi-structured interviews, on a sample of ten subjects. Semi-structured interviews make it possible to explore processes and human experiences participation and resources access within the studied network [2]. On the other hand, quantitative SNA techniques [6] will be used, in order to map the existing formal connections and their characteristics. Network member features, their degree of activity within the network, and their virtual connections will be mapped and analyzed. Such a protocol will produce quantitatively built network maps, which will represent network tie directionality and strength [6]. The quantitative and qualitative data collected will be jointly analysed [17]. In conclusion, a longitudinal approach [9] will allow us to study how the interplay between the two online and offline spheres evolves over one year. The same data collection and elaboration processes will be indeed conducted twice along the study, with ten to twelve months of distance between the first and second interview.

REFERENCES

[1] F. Anthias, "Transnational mobilities, migration research and intersectionality" in Nordic Journal of Migration Research, 2(2), pp. 102-110, 2012.

[2] E. Babbie and J.D. Edgerton, "Fundamentals of social research", Cengage, Canada, 2023.

[3] P. Bourdieu, "The Forms of Capital. Handbook of Theory and Research for the Sociology of Capital", J. G. Richardson. New York, Greenwood Press, pp. 241-58, 1986.

[4] A. D'Angelo, "Migrant organisations: embodied community capital?" In Migrant capital: Networks, identities and strategies. London: Palgrave Macmillan UK, pp. 83-101, 2015.

[5] R. Dekker, G. Engbersen and M. Faber, "The use of online media in migration networks" in Population, Space and Place, 22(6), pp. 539-551, 2016.

[6] G. Edwards, "Mixed-method approaches to social network analysis", 2010.

[7] E. Kofman and P. Raghuram, "Gender and global labour migrations: Incorporating skilled workers" in Antipode, 38(2), pp. 282-303, 2006.

[8] C. Noy, "Sampling knowledge: The hermeneutics of snowball sampling in qualitative research" in International Journal of social research methodology, 11(4), pp. 327-344, 2008.

[9] J. P. Ryan et al., "A coastal ocean extreme bloom incubator" in Geophysical Research Letters, 35(12), 2008.

[10] L. Ryan, U. Erel, and A. D'Angelo, "Introduction understanding 'migrant capital'" in Migrant capital: Networks, identities and strategies. London: Palgrave Macmillan UK, pp. 3-17, 2015.

[11] L. Ryan, "Telling network stories: researching migrants' changing social relations in places over time. Global Networks, 21(3), pp. 567-584, 2021.

[12] J. Sajuria, J. vanHeerde-Hudson, D. Hudson, N. Dasandi and Y. Theocharis, "Tweeting alone? An analysis of bridging and bonding social capital in online networks" in American Politics Research, 43(4), pp. 708-738, 2015.

[13] G. Solano, V. Schutjens and J. Rath, "Multifocality and opportunity structure: towards a mixed embeddedness model for transnational migrant entrepreneurship" in Comparative Migration Studies, 10(1), pp. 1-24, 2022.

[14] R. Zetter and M. Pearl, "The minority within the minority: Refugee community-based organisations in the UK and the impact of restrictionism on asylum-seekers" in Journal of Ethnic and Migration Studies 26, pp. 675–697, 2020. doi:10.1080/71368050

[15] C. Kent, A. Rechavi and S. Rafaeli, "The Relationship Between Offline Social Capital and Online Learning Interactions" in International Journal of Communication, 13, pp. 1186–1211, 2019.

[16] J. Bisbee and J. M. Larson, "Testing Social Science Network Theories with Online Network Data: An Evaluation of External Validity" in American Political Science Review, 111(3), pp. 502–521, 2017.

[17] A. Bryman, Social Research Methods. 4th., 2012.

[18] UN Office of the High Commissioner for Human Rights (OHCHR), "Women and girls of African descent: Human rights achievements and challenges (2018)", 2020.

[19] E. Sommer and M. Gamper, "Beyond structural determinism advantages and challenges of qualitative social network analysis for studying social capital of migrants" in Global Networks, 21(3), pp. 608-625, 2021.

Verification Tasks through Deep Learning in a Semantic Information Extraction System

Angel Luis Garrido
University of Zaragoza
Universitat Politecnica de Valencia
Zaragoza, Spain
Email: garrido@unizar.es

Norman U. Bellorín
InSynergy Consulting S.A.
Madrid, Spain
Email: nbellorin@isyc.com

Alvaro Peiró
InSynergy Consulting S.A.
Madrid, Spain
Email: apeiro@isyc.com

Eduardo Mena
I3A, University of Zaragoza
Zaragoza, Spain
Email: emena@unizar.es

***Abstract*—Nowadays, the use of applications that validate identity documents is already widespread. The problem is when, for multiple reasons, the image sent to these systems is impossible to process, either due to lack of definition, because the image is incomplete, or simply because it is not the correct document, among other reasons. To bypass this type of errors, a prior image verification process is proposed, which avoids the superfluous use of resources for an unattainable validation. For this, we have designed a working methodology that combines several Artificial Intelligence techniques: computer vision, deep learning, and semantics tools. The proposal has been implemented and evaluated in a real environment with promising results.**

Keywords-Computer vision; Knowledge-Based Systems; Deep Learning.

I. Introduction

In any company, document management is a necessary task for developing business functions, but it requires much time and dedication. The reason is not because of its difficulty, but because of the need to be methodical and exhaustive, which may become impractical if working with many documents. To solve this situation, companies use Document Management Systems (DMS) to store, share, track, and manage files or documents. Among other functions, the DMS software can usually handle document digitization processes for verification tasks. For instance, users attach the images of identity cards captured by a camera, and their validation is typically done using external commercial tools. After the analysis, the validation software returns the information embedded in the image. The identity document may include the identifier, name, surname, and validity date. All this data allows identity verification by comparing it with the user's data stored in the system. An analysis carried out during six months with 359,885 identity documents for validating resulted in 24% of invalid documents that could not be processed by a validation software. The study was in collaboration with InSynergy Consulting [1], a significant company in Spain devoted to developing specific software for managing documents.

The contribution of this work is, given the high number of errors, to propose a verification methodology to identify the type of identity document attached to an image and validate its visual quality. This will avoid generating validation requests that will be erroneous, either due to the poor quality of the image or because the typology of the document was mistaken. Our proposed methodology combines several techniques: computer vision, deep learning, and ontologies. Although many works can be found in the literature that addresses this issue [2] [3] [4], as far as we know, none of them approach it from this point of view, and they do not use the support of semantic technologies to improve the results.

We have applied our proposal in a real environment in collaboration with InSynergy. In this context, we have performed a set of preliminary tests with an actual document dataset, and we have integrated it with the Analysis and Semantic Interpretation (AIS) system [5] [6]. This information extraction system uses the ICIX architecture [7], showing the feasibility and the benefits of our approach. The rest of this paper is organized as follows. Section II describes the methodology used. Section III depicts the experiments, and finally, Section IV addresses the conclusions and future work.

II. Methodology

In this section, we will explain the main steps (see Fig. 1) of the proposed methodology:

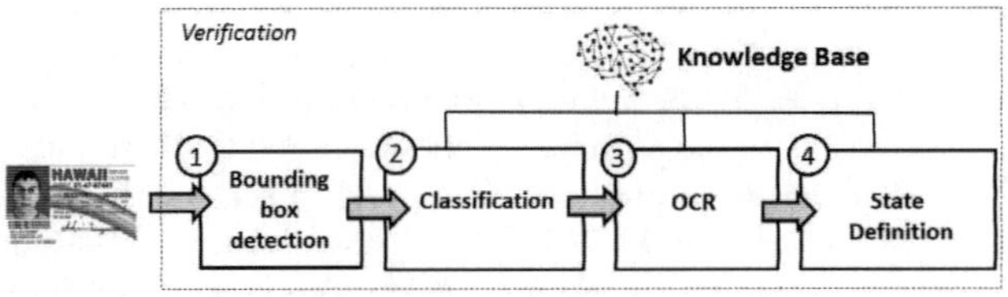

Figure 1. Overview of the proposed methodology.

1) *Bounding box detection.* In this step, the image of the identity document will be analyzed to extract only the area in which the document is located to reduce background noise and to help the system improve the classification of the document. The objective is to identify the edges from sudden changes in brightness, or limits defined through changes in reflectance or illumination in the image. To do this, an adaptation of the Canny [8] algorithm was made and it was empirically validated. This approach simplifies the image so that only the

outline of the objects is drawn. Since all edge detection results are easily affected by noise in the image, it is essential to filter out the noise to avoid incorrect detection.

2) *Classification.* An image classification algorithm based on deep learning techniques is responsible for classifying the typology of the attached identity document in the images uploaded by end users. A multiclass classification model has been developed. This model, which allows cataloguing the identity documents, differentiates the typology, the front and back, as well as the nationality of the document. The information to assist this process is obtained from a knowledge base of the AIS system, described in [5], which stores this data.
3) *Optical Character Recognition (OCR).* The visual quality of the attached image will be determined when the fields of an identity document are read, and its quality will be verified. If most of these labels are read (name, surname, date of birth, gender, etc.), the visual quality of the document is considered acceptable. This process is assisted by an OCR tool and the knowledge base of AIS, which also stores the typology of the fields in each of the different identity documents.
4) *State definition.* The results of previous tasks are analyzed, and an outcome (satisfactory/failed) is determined. This step is also supported by the knowledge base, which includes a set of rules that allow you to decide if the document is suitable to be sent to the validation stage.

III. Experiments

Experiments have been executed under Linux using *Google Colaboratory (Colab)*, computer vision libraries such as *OpenCV 4.6.0*, and the Google Colab environment. On the other hand, *TensorFlow* and *Keras* libraries have been employed to develop and train neural networks. For the experiments, we used a dataset with 1,120 images of identity documents (front and back), passports, and an error class. This dataset can not be public due to data protection laws.

The results of the training are shown in Fig. 2. Then, cross-validation was performed on the entire data set, which placed the success rate at 98.77%. The final validation confusion matrix is shown in Fig. 3. It is observed how the multilayer model improves the results of the single-layer model. Finally, after implementing the entire system with its various stages, the validation error rate (errors and false positives) decreased from the initial 24% to 2%.

IV. Conclusions and Future Work

The contribution of this work is to propose a new resolution scheme for the problem of verifying the quality of identity documents, within the context of an information extraction system. In this way, we drastically improve the success rate of the validation process by avoiding carrying it out if the image quality is inadequate. To achieve this, we propose a methodology that combines computer vision techniques,

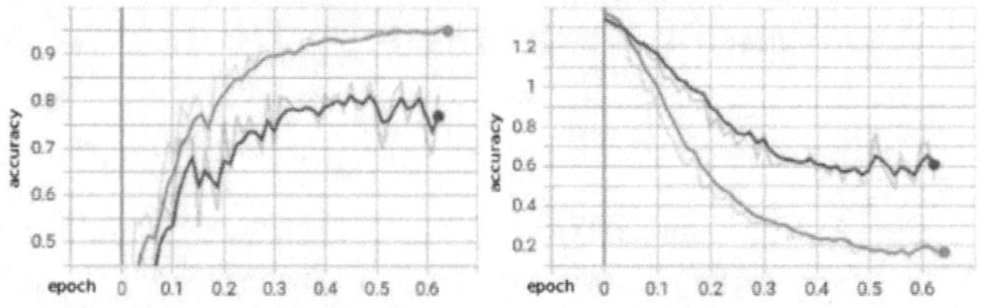

Figure 2. Training results, accuracy and loss, respectively. The top line is the multilayer model, and the bottom line is the single-layer model.

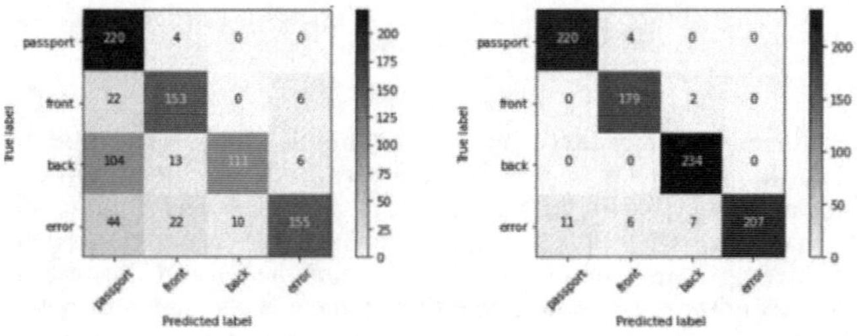

Figure 3. Confusion matrix using the single-layer or multilayer model, respectively.

classification through deep learning, and OCR checks, using an internal knowledge base to orchestrate all the steps. As future work, we are planning to use transfer learning techniques, to retrain models without losing previous training work, or without having to load the entire data set into memory.

Acknowledgment

This research work has been supported by the OTRI Project ICIX9 2019/0628-21 at the University of Zaragoza, by the Spanish project PID2020-113903RB-I00 (AEI/FEDER, UE), and by DGA/FEDER. The authors want to acknowledge Dr. Carlos Bobed for his valuable collaboration.

References

[1] http://isyc.com/, [last access Nov. 2023].

[2] M. K. Gupta, R. Shah, J. Rathod, and A. Kumar, "Smartidocr: Automatic detection and recognition of identity card number using deep networks," in *IEEE Sixth International Conference on Image Information Processing (ICIIP)*, vol. 6, 2021, pp. 267–272.

[3] L. Zhao, C. Chen, and J. Huang, "Deep learning-based forgery attack on document images," *IEEE Transactions on Image Processing*, vol. 30, pp. 7964–7979, 2021.

[4] D. P. Van Hoai, H.-T. Duong, and V. T. Hoang, "Text recognition for vietnamese identity card based on deep features network," *International Journal on Document Analysis and Recognition (IJDAR)*, vol. 24, pp. 123–131, 2021.

[5] M. G. Buey, A. L. Garrido, C. Bobed, and S. Ilarri, "The AIS project: Boosting information extraction from legal documents by using ontologies." in *ICAART (2)*, 2016, pp. 438–445.

[6] M. G. Buey, C. Roman, A. L. Garrido, C. Bobed, and E. Mena, "Automatic legal document analysis: Improving the results of information extraction processes using an ontology," *Intelligent Methods and Big Data in Industrial Applications*, pp. 333–351, 2019.

[7] A. L. Garrido, A. Peiro, C. Bobed, E. Mena, and C. Morte, "ICIX: A semantic information extraction architecture," in *Proceedings of the 25th International Database Engineering & Applications Symposium*, 2021, pp. 75–83.

[8] E. A. Sekehravani, E. Babulak, and M. Masoodi, "Implementing canny edge detection algorithm for noisy image," *Bulletin of Electrical Engineering and Informatics*, vol. 9, no. 4, pp. 1404–1410, 2020.

Model-supported Software Creation: Towards Holistic Model-driven Software Engineering

Hans-Werner Sehring
Department of Computer Science
Nordakademie
Elmshorn, Germany
e-mail: hans-werner.sehring@nordakademie.de

***Abstract*—Software typically is developed based on descriptions of a relevant section of the real world, the problem as well as its solution. Methodologies and tools have evolved to create and manage such descriptions, and to finally implement software as specified. Model-Driven Software Engineering (MDSE) is one approach of model management. A series of models that build upon each other by means of model transformation is used to describe a software solution in increasing detail. While MDSE gained a fair amount of attention, it is not equally successful in all application domains. We claim that one reason for this is that MDSE is well-suited for formal domains and computation-centric solutions. But it is not equally suited for software development processes with a high degree of creativity involved, like, for example, solutions with a focus on human-machine interaction or content-centric applications. One reason is the fact that properties of such software are designed by experts of certain domains who use specific notations and tools. In this paper, we discuss an approach for the creation of software that requires models that are either defined in specific notations used by experts or that do not allow formalized model transformations. The approach relies on artifacts created using a heterogeneous set of languages. These artifacts are described by formal models that add semantics and that relate the informal artifacts. For such an approach, we coin the term "model-supported software creation" in this paper.**

Keywords*—*model-driven software engineering; model-driven architecture; software engineering; software architecture

I. Introduction

Software is, in most of the cases, used to represent and solve real-world problems. In order to be able to do so, a relevant section of the real world needs to be captured, and the problem as well as its solution need to be described in sufficient detail. This includes defined requirements, test cases, conceptual models, domain models, etc.

Methodologies and tools have evolved that capture problems and solutions, model the real world with respect to the problem at hand, and finally allow implementing software as specified.

The various description artifacts involved in software engineering processes call for means to manage these descriptions. In particular, they have to be related to each other to reach goals like, for example, those of coherence and traceability.

Classical software engineering has a typical sequence of an analysis phase, resulting in requirements, design phases, resulting in solution designs, and implementation phases, resulting in working software. In agile approaches, these phases may be very condensed. The artifacts (descriptions, models, code, etc.) created in each phase build upon each other. Still, they are formally unrelated. Those artifacts contributing to a phase consider the artifacts from previous phases, though.

Model-Driven Software Engineering (*MDSE*) or *Model-Driven Software Development* (*MDSD*) is one approach to a more formal management of artifacts. A series of models that build upon each other is used to describe a software solution in increasing detail. Typically, the models are refined or transformed up to the point where actual running software can be generated out of the most precise model.

While MDSE gained a fair amount of attention, it is not equally successful in all application domains. We claim that one reason is that MDSE is well-suited for formal domains and computation-centric solutions. But is is not equally suited for software development processes with a high degree of creativity involved. For example, while it is feasible to model technical domains, for example, involving mathematics and physics, it is less common to formally model solutions with a focus on creative and subjective aspects. Human-machine interaction (online shops, for example) or content-centric applications (personalized marketing websites, for example) are examples found in typical customer-facing commerce systems.

For models that experts require in specific notations, and for ones that do not allow formalized model transformations, a different approach is discussed in this paper. It relies on models created using a heterogeneous set of languages that are described by formal models that add semantics and that relate the informal artifacts.

We introduce the name *Model-Supported Software Creation* (*MSSC*) in this paper to emphasize the fact that (formal) models are supporting a creative process, but are not the central resource of the process, and to describe the wider range of activities involved.

Section II of this paper revisits some approaches to MDSE. Shortcomings of simple MDSE applications are examined in Section III. Requirements to a holistic MSSC approach are listed in Section IV. Section V presents the *Minimalistic Meta Modeling Language* (*M³L*) and how it is applied to holistic MSSC. We conclude the paper in Section VI.

II. Model-driven Software Engineering

Various approaches to software generation from models are discussed. In this section, we briefly revisit some of these.

A. Model-driven Architecture

The *Model-Driven Architecture* (*MDA*) [1] of the Object Management Group (OMG) is an early and well received proposal for an MDSE approach. It assumes models to be created on (originally) three levels of abstraction. A *Computation-Independent Model* (*CIM*; this term is not used in current specifications) describes the software to be developed from the perspective of the subject domain, as domain concepts or requirements. It typically is an informal description, for example, done in natural language. A first formal model is a *Platform-Independent Model* (*PIM*), formulated in the MDA's *Meta Object Facility* (*MOF*). It is transformed into a *Platform-Specific Model* (*PSM*) that in turn is used to generate a working implementation.

B. Software Generation

Software generation has gained particular attention since this step in an MDSE process can well be formalized.

a) Metaprogramming: Programs that generate programs are an obvious means to software generation. The development of such generators tends to be costly, but results may be targeted optimally to the application at hand.

b) Templates: Code with repeating structures can be formulated as templates with parameters for the variations of that uniform code. For *Concept-Oriented Content Management* [2], for example, code for CRUD operations is generated. This code does not differ in functionality, but in the data types used for domain entities.

c) Generative AI: The currently emerging generative AI approaches based on large languages models provide another means to generate code from descriptions. Based on a library of samples, they allow interactively generating code from less formal descriptions, in particular natural language expressions.

C. Domain-specific Languages

Languages can be associated with metamodels [3]. This means that a model of a software application can be expressed by a language for a subject domain. Such a language is called a *Domain-Specific Language* (*DSL*).

The software generation process is simplified to defining an application using a DSL, allowing to define the application in terms of the subject domain. There is a trade-off regarding the degree of abstraction: The more domain knowledge is put into the DSL, the simpler it is to define an application. But a more specialized DSL also means that the range of application that can be defined becomes more limited.

D. Generic Software

The aim of MDSD and MSSC is custom software that is tailored to solve one specific problem. Generic software, on the other hand, encapsulates some domain knowledge that is applicable in a set of scenarios.

The concrete application is defined by setting parameters of the generic software. The application areas of generic software are defined by the degree to which domain knowledge was generalized and parameterized.

There are varying degrees of parameterization. This relates to so-called low code and no code approaches. These are also based on a generalized software that maps a section of the real world, and they allow software to be customized within the limits of the chosen section.

III. MDSE in Practice

MDSE approaches are not equally successful in all application domains [4]. We see two main obstacles to applying MDSE in some areas: heterogeneous modeling artifacts and the stages of a software development that are covered.

A. Heterogeneous Modeling Artifacts

MDSE typically is based on a modeling framework that supports all stages of a software development process. This requires that model artifacts on every stage can be expressed in a language that is supported by that framework. In many cases, it is even required that all models involved are formulated within the same metamodel.

Some application domains call for specific kinds of artifacts that rely on certain established notations and cannot be forced into a form given by a central metamodel. For such application domains, the properties of software are designed by experts of certain fields who use specific notations and tools. One example of such an application domain is digital communication like marketing and sales communication over a website.

In the retail sector, for example, we note that customers interact with retail companies at different touch points, interact on changing communication channels, use different payment methods, are subject to different legal and tax systems, etc. In such scenarios, a series of experts needs to gather (a part of) the domain knowledge on one modeling stage in order to communicate it to experts of the next stage (domain expert to requirements engineers, these in turn to architects as well as test engineers, architects to developers, and so on).

User experience designers and user interfaces designers, for example, work with artifacts like personas, customer journeys, wireframes, style guides, click dummies, prototypes, etc. Such artifacts support creative processes. They are adequate means to communicate with business experts, and they are used by programmers to build usable software.

A pure MDSE approach of generating such artifacts from models is not adequate for the work of experts and their clients. It might be hindering the creative process.

B. Coverage of all Project Stages

Modeling starts at the point where there is consensus about the kind of software to be developed. In fact, projects start at an earlier stage at which a (business) need arises. In a commercial setting, this may be, for example, increased revenue, a certain number of new customers, or customer satisfaction. A solution approach is not given. At this stage, it is not even decided that new or improved software will be part of the solution.

The same holds for project stages after software generation, namely roll-out, operations, and support.

TABLE I. STAGES OF SOFTWARE CREATION

Creation stage	Model entities on the stage
(Business) Goals	KPIs OKRs
Subject domain model	Information architecture Interaction design Wireframes Processes, data flows
Requirements	Solution hypothesis Functional ~ Non-function ~ Customer journeys Touch points
Solution architecture	Interfaces High-level architecture Functional mapping
Software architecture(s)	Components communication between those components interfaces to the environment constraints of the resulting software system requirements met by the architecture rationale behind architecture decisions
Code	Metaprogramming Software generators Domain-specific languages
Systems architecture	Infrastructure definition Automated deployments
Operations	Service level agreement Monitoring

IV. HOLISTIC MODEL-DRIVEN SOFTWARE CREATION

In Section III, we pointed out two shortcomings with basic MDSE approaches: Firstly, they do not consider early project stages that precede software development. Secondly, they are not suited to utilize heterogeneous models that are formulated in different languages, are not all equally formal, etc.

As noted in the introduction section, we use the term MSSC to describe a holistic approach to software creation that in contrast captures all aspects of a project, not only the software development phases, and that can cope with heterogeneous and informal modeling artifacts.

In the following, we point out the modeling stages we consider relevant for software creation processes, and we outline typical model transformations of model-based development processes.

A. Modeling Stages

Table I gives an overview over typical stages of software creation and some examples of artifacts they deal with.

a) Business Goals: A project starts with the identification of a problem to be solved. In many cases, the problem does not lie within the computing domain. Accordingly, the desired solution is typically formulated by means of (business) goals that shall be reached (see Section III-B).

Goals have to be measurable in order to judge the success of a project. *Key Performance Indicators* (*KPIs*) or *Objectives and Key Results* (*OKRs*) are often used to define target values that can be measured. The values that are measured often lie in the business domain and have to be determined by controlling means on the business level. The success of a software solution that helps reaching the goal is then proven implicitly.

Since formal goals are set up as a first abstraction of the business goals to be reached, they are subjective and depend on a stakeholder who defines them. Approaches like i* [5] aim to model this subjectivity.

b) Subject Domain Model: The later stages of software design require a certain understanding of the problem domain, for example, typical concepts of the area the software is to be applied in. The requirements relate to the domain concepts.

Modeling means abstracting from the domain that is represented. Therefore, domain concepts cover a section of the subject domain that is relevant for the solution.

In the MDA approach, the CIM may include the stage of domain modeling.

c) Requirements: Requirements characterize the properties of a software solution. This means that this stage only is entered if it is decided that software helps reaching the defined goals. It also means that a first software solution hypothesis has been recognized and is being detailed through requirements.

There is a wide range of requirements: functional requirements and the diverse kinds of non-functional requirements. Additionally, constraints that limit the solution space belong to this stage.

Other entities of this modeling stage depend on the problem at hand. For example, conceptions of interactive applications for digital communication typically begin by identifying personas as role models of target groups, determine the customer journeys as the sequence of interactions users have at different touch points, before finally deriving artifacts like the information architecture. To design user interfaces, artifacts like wireframes, style guides, and click dummies are used to help defining subject domain concepts and requirements.

There are various tools to help managing functional requirements. Deductive databases can help validating and completing requirements [6].

d) Solution Architecture: Solution architecture is the set of high-level definitions that relate subject domain concepts to technical solutions.

As a high-level architecture, it does not prescribe an actual implementation in full detail. It may contain the choice for certain implementation technologies and products, though, in particular if they are crucial to meeting some requirements or to conform to the constraints.

Based on the chosen components, a solution architecture defines the interfaces required to implement the processes and data flows identified as requirements. For example, in a digital communication like an e-commerce website, the information demand at every touch point is derived from the customer journeys, and data flows are designed accordingly.

e) Software Architecture: The detailed design of the software to be developed is part of the software architecture. It details definitions from the solution architecture up to the point where they are concrete enough to guide the coding stage.

Shaw and Garlan [7] point out that there are different approaches to the different perspectives on software. In a structural approach, the software architecture is composed of components, communication between the components, product configurations, references to the requirements and constraints from the requirements stage, boundaries within which the software is designed to work as specified, the rationale of design decisions, and design alternatives that were considered.

Many other architecture definitions contain similar modeling entities. *Architectural Description Languages* (*ADLs*) allow capturing these aspects.

Shaw and Garlan point out that besides structural models, there are also framework models, dynamic models, and process models. The latter, for example, focus on the dynamic aspects of the software.

f) Code: When architecture models are precise enough, code can be generated out of them using one of the approaches from Section II-B.

In practice, coding is a manual task in most cases. The architecture definition serves as a guideline to programming, documentation, and quality assurance. Detailed design decisions are added in the coding stage.

g) Systems Architecture: The systems architecture describes how software is deployed and set up. It defines computing and communication infrastructure.

Deployment diagrams describe how software is packaged and distributed on the infrastructure. Infrastructure and network diagrams illustrate the technical setup.

Typically, infrastructure is virtualized and created automatically from scripts in the *Infrastructure as Code* approaches. This allows continuous deployments of many software components, for example, in contemporary composable architectures.

h) Operations: Part of the requirements are typically formulated towards operations. *Service-Level Agreements* (*SLAs*) define measurable goals to systems operation. Fulfillment of these goals is controlled by means of monitoring and timely maintenance in the case of incidents. To this end, monitoring and logging concepts connect development and operations.

B. Model Refinement and Transformations

An MDSE process relies on a series of models where models are created from existing models by means of *model transformation*. A model on one stage is created based on the input of models of earlier stages or by refining models from the same stage. There are three typical kinds of model transformations.

Figure 1a shows the basic structure of model transformations on one stage and between stages. Figures 1b to 1g show examples of typical model transformations between different stages.

a) Model Combination: Domains often rely on base domains. For example, business tasks rely on mathematics. Accordingly, models are defined by integrating (existing) models of the base domains. This way, models are reused.

b) Model Refinement: Within one stage, models are refined to more concrete models of the same stage. This way, the work in each stage starts with first, coarse-grained models, that are then transformed into more concrete models. Different refinements of one model may cover different perspectives on the (software) solution. The process of refining involves

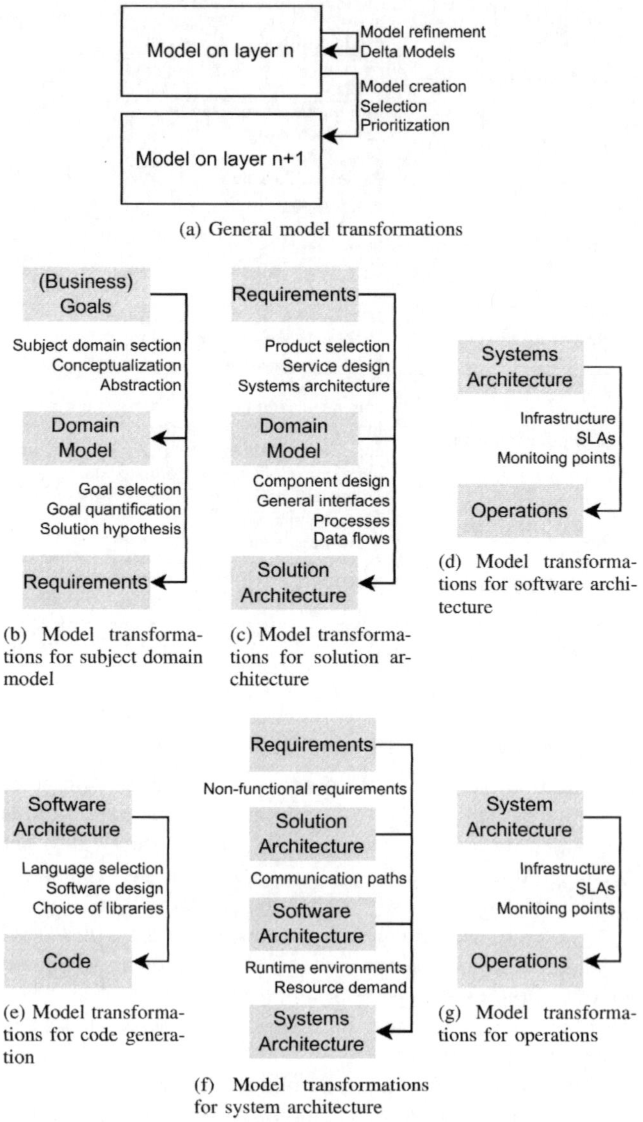

(a) General model transformations

(b) Model transformations for subject domain model

(c) Model transformations for solution architecture

(d) Model transformations for software architecture

(e) Model transformations for code generation

(f) Model transformations for system architecture

(g) Model transformations for operations

Figure 1. Different kinds of model transformations.

decision making. Decisions can be documented by explicitly stating delta models that explicitly represent the refinements.

c) Model Creation from Existing Models: When processing from one stage to another, initial models are required for the subsequent stage that is entered. These models shall be related to the most concrete models of the preceding stage. In some cases, models can be transformed when proceeding to a subsequent stage. In this case, the transformation establishes the relationship. If new models have to be created, the model elements should be explicitly linked to the elements from models on which they are based. For example, Shaw [7] demands that a software architecture description refers to requirements.

V. An MSSC Approach with the M³L

An MSSC approach includes the creation and utilization of diverse artifacts. Each of them serves a specific purpose, and each is maintained by experts using established tools. Though the artifacts from different stages of a software creation process are related, they typically cannot be expressed using the same language. They differ, for example, in the level of detail, the degree to which they follow a formalism, and the syntactic representation targeted at different audiences.

When, in contrast to MDSE, no single modeling language can be used for a universal model, an overarching modeling framework is required for model coherence [8]. Such a framework cannot host the artifacts themselves. It shall, however, put the artifacts in context and relate them to each other.

Relationships between artifacts clarify their contribution to the software creation process. They explicate the provenance of models, they put models in context, and they are the basis for traceability and, therefore, the ability to cope with change.

In this paper, we propose using the *Minimalistic Modeling Language*, *M³L* (pronounced "mel") [9], as the modeling framework required for MSSC.

A. A Brief Introduction to the M³L

The M³L is a meta modeling language. As such, it can be employed for models for different kinds of applications.

In this section, we give a brief overview over the syntax of the language. Sample applications in the subsequent sections will demonstrate its use.

A statement **A** defines or references a *concept* named *A*. The M³L does not distinguish definitions from references. If **A** does not exist, it is defined.

Concepts can be *refined* with "is a": `A is a C`. Using the clause "is the" defines a concept to be the only specialization of its base concept.

Concepts can be put in *context*. A statement `A { B }` defines *B* in the context of *A*. *B* is said to be the *content* of *A*. References are valid in the context they are defined in and in all subcontexts. This means, that statements `A { B }` and **C** make *B* and *C* visible in the context of *A*, but *B* is not part of the content of *C* or of the topmost context.

Concepts can be defined differently in different contexts. For example, the statements `A { B is a C }` and **B** define *B* as a specialization of *C* in the context of *A*, but without base concept in the topmost context.

A concept in a nested context is referenced as `B from A`.

Semantic rules can be defined on concepts, denoted by "|=". A semantic rule references another concept that is delivered when a concept with a semantic rule is referenced. Like for any other reference, a non-existing concept is created on demand.

Context, specializations, and semantic rules are employed for *concept evaluation*. A concept evaluates to the result of its syntactic rule, if defined, or to its *narrowing*. A concept *B* is a narrowing of a concept *A* iff

- *A* evaluates to *B* through specializations or semantic rules, and
- the whole content of *A* narrows down to content of *B*.

To evaluate a concept, syntactic rules and narrowing are applied repeatedly.

With this evaluation, for example, a conditional statement can be defined as (given *Statement*, *Boolean*, *True*, and *False*):

```
IfThenElse is a Statement {
  Condition is a Boolean
  ThenStmt is a Statement
  ElseStmt is a Statement }
IfTrue is an IfThenElse {
  True is the Condition } |= ThenStmt
IfFalse is an IfThenElse {
  False is the Condition } |= ElseStmt
```

Concepts can be marshalled/unmarshalled as text by *syntactic* rules, denoted by "|-". A syntactic rule names a sequence of concepts whose representations are concatenated. A concept without a syntactic rule is represented by its name. Syntactic rules are used to represent a concept as a string as well as to create a concept from a string.

For example, rules for language-dependent code generation:

```
Java{IfThenElse |- "if" "(" Condition ")"
                    ThenStmt FalseStmt  .}
```

B. Dimensions of Model Relationships

The three model relationships named in Section IV-B can be expressed with the M³L. This way, models are put in context. The following examples outline basic modeling approaches for the three relationships.

a) Combining models: For example, on the layer of domain models, a model

```
ProductDescriptions is a DomainModel {
  ProductData
  PaymentMethods from Commerce
  PackagingInformation from Logistics }
```

combines parts of product details that come from different specialized models (assuming that concepts for models *Commerce* and *Logistics* are given).

Likewise, on the layer of solution architecture, a model

```
OurInfoSys is a PlatformIndependentModel {
  AppServer from SWComponents
  DBMS from SWComponents
  DataSchema from DBModeling
  WebServer from SWComponents
  WebPage from WebDesign }
```

combines technical components from different technical descriptions.

b) Refining models: One model can be created as a refinement of another. Concepts in the content of the refined model are inherited and can be refined further.

An example from the solution architecture layer is:

```
OurInfoSysConcept is an OurInfoSys {
  RDBMS from SWComponents is the DBMS
  ProductDataSchema
    is an RDBSchema from DBModeling,
       the DataSchema
  WebServer from SWComponents
    is a ServletEngine from Java }
```

In this example, two aspects of the conceptual model are refined: From a technical perspective, the *DBMS* is more concretely specified to be a relational DBMS (*RDBMS*), and the *WebServer* to be implemented as a Java Servlet engine (*ServletEngine*). Regarding the domain model, it is defined that the data schema is defined to store products (*Product-DataSchema*).

c) Creating models in subsequent stage: A model can be explicitly created as a transformation of another model using a semantic rule. In the example of the information system:

```
OurInfoSysConcept |= OurInfoSysDataLayer {
 RDBMS
 ProductDataSchema {
  ProductsTable is a Table from DBModeling
 } }
```

RDMBS from the source model *OurInfoSysConcept* is re-introduced in the transformed model. The database schema *ProductDataSchema* is additionally redefined by naming one table. *WebServer* from *OurInfoSysConcept* is not considered in the transformed model, since it only models the data layer of the information system.

C. Software Creation with the M³L

The models in MDSE ultimately reach the stage of generating code. The M³L allows creating code using syntactical rules that can be added to models with sufficient concreteness.

Using the example from above, part of the information system based on a relational database can be defined to create a relational schema by SQL statements as follows:

```
OurInfoSysDBIm is an OurInfoSysDataLayer {
 ProductDataSchema {
  ProductsTable |- "PRODUCTS("Columns")" .
 } |- "CREATE TABLE " ProductsTable . }
```

By defining the syntactical rules in the context of an implementation model, different code generation schemes can be defined for one software model.

VI. Summary and Outlook

This section sums up this paper and outlines future work.

A. Summary

In this paper, we revisit MDSE approaches and conclude that they are successful in certain application areas, while they are not established in many other areas. In particular, in digital communication, for example, in the construction of commerce or marketing websites or mobiles apps, they are not used in practice. One reason for this is a mismatch between established means of conceptual work and formal models.

Under the name of Model-Supported Software Creation (MSSC) we study requirements to models for such kind of applications. As early results, MDSE approaches cover the stages of software creation well, but they do not cover early inception phases. We claim that models used in MSSC need to be able to cope with less formalism and preciseness as required by typical MDSE approaches. Instead, they must deal with heterogeneity and subjectivity.

We outline model creation with the M³L as a step towards MSSC. It allows providing descriptive models of the artifacts used in practical approaches and relating them as to drive holistic software creation processes.

B. Outlook

We are at the beginning of our investigations towards MSSC. Consequently, there are numerous questions to be answered in the future. We highlight two of them.

There are numerous approaches to generate code from models, and code written in a formal language can be managed in a structured way. The syntactic rules of the M³L, for example, allow this. To include artifacts from other stages into the modeling process (like requirements or design documents), abstractions are needed to reference, include, or generate parts of artifacts the same way it is possible for code.

Testing is typically not found in model-based processes. Though there may be no need to test generated software, a kind of testing is required, nevertheless. This may include model checking on each stage of the process and analysis of models that are the result of model transformations.

In MSSC processes, success should ultimately be judged based on the degree to which business goals have been reached. To this end, they must be formalized, and effects of the running software need to be measured.

Acknowledgment

Numerous discussions on topics of modeling and software engineering led with colleagues, partners, and clients are highly appreciated. The author thanks the Nordakademie University of Applied Sciences for funding the publication of this work.

References

[1] Object Management Group. *Model Driven Architecture (MDA)*, MDA Guide rev. 2.0, OMG Document ormsc/2014-06-01, [Online] Available from: https://www.omg.org/cgi-bin/doc?ormsc/14-06-01. 2023.9.5.

[2] H.-W. Sehring, S. Bossung, and J. W. Schmidt, "Content is Capricious: A Case for Dynamic System Generation," Proc. 10th East European Conference (ADBIS 2006), Springer, 2006, pp. 430-445.

[3] T. Kühne, "Matters of (Meta-) Modeling," Software & Systems Modeling, vol. 5, pp. 369-385, Dec. 2006.

[4] J. Cabot, R. Clarisó, M. Brambilla, and S. Gérard, S., "Cognifying Model-Driven Software Engineering," Proc. Software Technologies: Applications and Foundations (STAF 2017), Springer, 2018, pp. 154-160.

[5] E. S. K. Yu and J. Mylopoulos, "From E-R to "A-R" – Modelling strategic actor relationships for business process reengineering," Proc. 13th Int. Conf. on the Entity-Relationship Approach (ER'94), Springer, 1994, pp. 548-565.

[6] H. W. Nissen, M. A. Jeusfeld, M. Jarke, G. V. Zemanek, and H. Huber, "Managing multiple requirements perspectives with metamodels," in IEEE Software, vol. 13, no. 2, pp. 37-48, March 1996.

[7] M. Shaw and D. Garlan, "Formulations and Formalisms in Software Architecture," Computer Science Today: Recent Trends and Developments, Lecture Notes in Computer Science, vol. 1000, pp. 307-323, 1995.

[8] S. Bossung, H.-W. Sehring, M. Skusa, and J. W. Schmidt, "Conceptual Content Management for Software Engineering Processes," Proc. Advances in Databases and Information Systems, 9th East European Conference (ADBIS 2005), Springer, 2005, pp. 309-323.

[9] H.-W. Sehring, "On Integrated Models for Coherent Content Management and Document Dissemination," Proc. 13th International Conference on Creative Content Technologies (CONTENT 2021), 2021, pp. 6-11.

Improvement of Fatty Acids Composition of a Microalga Isolated from the Moroccan Seawater for Biodiesel Production

Salima Ouled Hajja
Geosciences, Water and Environment Laboratory (L-G2E) Faculty of Sciences
Mohammed V University (UM5) in Rabat
Rabat, Morocco
Email: fatiallalatserine@gmail.com

Miloudia Slaoui, Houria El Bakraoui
Energy, Materials and Sustainable Development (EMDD) Laboratory, Higher School of Technology-SALE, CERN2D
Mohammed V University (UM5) in Rabat
Rabat, Morocco
Emails: smslaoui2@gmail.com, houriya1234@gmail.com

***Abstract*— The cellular biochemical composition of the isolated microalga Chlorella sp. was investigated in both favorable and nitrogen-depleted circumstances, with a particular focus on lipid classes and fatty acid distribution. When algal cells were grown in nitrogen-starvation media, the lipid and carbohydrate content increased, but the protein content decreased. Under control conditions, glycolipids were the most abundant lipid component at about 58.2% of total lipids, however under nitrogen stress conditions, neutral lipids became more prevalent at 74.8% of total lipids. The level of TAGs in nitrogen stressed cells was more than four times greater than in control cells. Oleic acid was the most prevalent fatty acid (47.2%) in the neutral lipids fraction. Under nitrogen stress, lipid quality analysis revealed that this alga has the potential to be used as a biodiesel feedstock.**

Keywords- Chlorella sp; biodiesel; stress conditions; Nitrogen; Phosphorus; bioenergy.

I. INTRODUCTION

Overuse of fossil fuels has resulted in an energy crisis and environmental issues [1]. Considering this, sustainable bioenergy, particularly biodiesel, has received a lot of attention in recent years. Biodiesel is a compound composed of fatty Acid Methyl Esters (FAME), created normally by the transesterification of vegetable oils or animal fats [1]. Microalgae are now seen as a viable feedstock for biodiesel production due to many benefits, including high photosynthetic efficiency, quick growth rate, and high lipid content [2]. In contrast to terrestrial energy crops, these organisms exhibit a significant lipid yield per unit of marginal land, possess the capability to harness sunlight and other nutrients to recycle carbon from fossil sources, and contribute positively to the environment [3]. The widespread commercial production of Microalgae biodiesel faces limitations due to various techno- logical and economic constraints [4]. Therefore, it is crucial to enhance both the yield of microalgal biomass and lipid production to maintain competitiveness and economic viability [5]. Various factors, including culture conditions like nitrogen and phosphorus stress, cultivation methods, temperature, light intensity, light/dark cycles, salinity, and pH, wastewater type can influence these parameters [6] – [8].

Chlorella has long been used commercially to make bioactive chemicals, animal feed, and nutrition for humans. Due to their high lipid output and environmental adaptability, reports of the potential of chlorella for the manufacture of biodiesel has increased in recent years [9]. There have been claims that several species of Chlorella might boost the lipid accumulation under conditions of nutritional restriction or famine. Given the preceding knowledge, it is critical to explore the buildup of lipids in microalgae growing under stress condition. In addition, total lipids are a useful tool for identifying oleaginous species and their fatty acid profiles offer a more targeted indication of the kind of substrate that is best for producing biodiesel.

In light of this, the purpose of this research is to assess the effects of nitrogen stress on biomass production, lipid accumulation, and fatty acid composition of an isolated microalga, Chlorella sp., cultured in f/2 medium.

II. METHODS

The strain Chlorella sp. investigated in this study was isolated from saltwater near Sidi Moussa beach in Morocco. Before being transferred to 100 mL beakers, the seawater samples were collected and filtered. Microalgae were identified using an optical microscope (Nikon ECLIPSE E200). Serial dilution was utilized to generate a pure culture. By inserting a loop of sample culture from the highest dilution tubes on the agar growth medium, a sterile loop was employed to form parallel streaks on the agar growth media. The petri dishes were covered with parafilm and incubated at 25°C. After 30 day of incubation, f/2 medium has been employed in the maintenance of the culture of this species in 100 mL Erlenmeyer flask.

The cellular biochemical composition of the isolated microalga Chlorella sp. was investigated in both favorable and nitrogen-depleted circumstances, with a particular focus on lipid classes and fatty acid distribution after six days of cultivation. Carbohydrate concentration was determined by the phenol-sulfuric acid method. Total lipid extraction from dry biomass was carried out using the Bligh and Dyer technique. 100 milligrams of dry cells are maintained in 3.5 mL of a chloroform/methanol/water (2/1/0.5 v/v/v) mixture. The mixture was centrifuged for 15 minutes at 4000 rpm after vertexing, and the organic phase was extracted and deposited in a tube that has been previously dried and weighed.

The lipid content was determined by using the following equation:

$$\text{Lipid content (\%)} = ML/MA*100$$

where ML (g) is the mass of the extracted lipids (corresponding to the difference in mass of the empty tubes and containing the dry lipids) and MA (g) is the mass of dry algal biomass. 500 μL of chloroform was used to resuspend the extracted lipids. 100 μL of this mixture was combined with 800 μL of 10% Boron trifluoride-methanol solution in a screw tube, and the combination was then heated to 100 ◦C in a water bath for 15 minutes. 750 μL of the solvent (100 μL of heptadecane in 10 mL of hexane) and 1.5 mL of water were added after cooling, and the mixture was vortexed for 2 minutes. The upper phase was retrieved with a Pasteur pipette, and 10 μL of it was injected into an Agilent gas chromatography (6850) system to characterize the methyl esters.

III. RESULTS AND DISCUSSION

Results indicate that, when algal cells were grown in nitrogen-starvation media, the lipid and carbohydrate content increased but the protein content decreased. Under control conditions, glycolipids were the most abundant lipid component about 58.2% of total lipids, however under nitrogen stress conditions, neutral lipids became more prevalent 74.8% of total lipids. The level of TAGs in nitrogen stressed cells was more than four times greater than in control cells. Oleic acid was the most prevalent fatty acid (47.2%) in the neutral lipids fraction. Similar trends have been documented in the cells of Chlorella vulgaris [10].

IV. CONCLUSION AND FUTURE WORK

The primary components of microalgal biomass consist of protein, carbohydrate, and lipid. Our findings demonstrated that when subjected to nitrogen deprivation, there was an elevation in carbohydrate and lipid content, accompanied by a reduction in protein content. Hence, environmental stress conditions play a crucial role in enhancing lipid quality for biodiesel production. Although nitrogen starvation can significantly increase the content of neutral lipids in microalgae, its main drawback is the limited biomass production.

Therefore, in the future work, it will be essential to further optimize the culture conditions for the isolated microalgae *Chlorella sp.* to achieve the desired quantity and quality of lipids for biodiesel production such as providing high light levels, limiting other nutrients.

REFERENCES

[1] J. Liu, J. Huang, Z. Sun, Y. Zhong, Y. Jiang and F. Chen, "Differential lipid and fatty acid profiles of photoautotrophic and heterotrophic Chlorella zofingiensis: assessment of algal oils for biodiesel production," Bioresource Technology, vol. 102, pp. 106–110, 2011.

[2] Q. Hu, M. Sommerfeld, E. Jarvis, M. Ghirardi, M. Posewitz, M. Seibert, and A. Darzins, "Microalgal triacylglycerols as feedstocks for biofuel production: perspectives and advances," The Plant. J, vol. 54, pp. 621–639, 2008.

[3] H. Li, "Environment-Enhancing Process for Algal Wastewater Treatment, Heavy Metal Control and Hydrothermal Biofuel Production: A Critical review", Bioresource Technology, vol. 298, pp. 122 421, 2020.

[4] F. Chu, "Enhancing Lipid Production in Microalgae Chlorella PY-ZU1 with Phosphorus Excess and Nitrogen Starvation under 15% CO2 in a Continuous Two-Step Cultivation Process," Chemical Engineering Journal, vol. 375, pp. 121912, 2019.

[5] K. R. Renjith, G. John, S. Muraleedharan Nair and N. Chandramohanakumar, "Biodiesel Prospective of Five Diatom Strains Using Growth Parameters and Fatty Acid Profiles", Biofuels. 8, no.1, pp. 81-89, 2017.

[6] M. A. Yaakob, R. M. S. R Mohamed, A. Al-Gheethi, R. Gokare, and R. R. Ambati, "Influence of Nitrogen and Phosphorus on Microalgal Growth, Biomass, Lipid, and Fatty Acid Production: An Overview", Biomolecule, vol. 10, pp. 393, 2021.

[7] H. El. Bakraoui, M. Slaoui, D. Hmouni, and F. El aamri, "Impact of color of light and nitrogen concentration on Pavlova sp. biomass, cells size and biochemical composition," Biofuels, 2022.

[8] H. EL Bakraoui, M. Slaoui, J. Mabrouki, D. Hmouni and C. Laroche "Recent Trends on Domestic, Agricultural and Industrial Wastewaters Treatment Using Microalgae Biorefinery System," Applied Sciences, vol. 13, no.1, pp. 68, 2022.

[9] X. P. Zhou, L. Xia, H. M. Ge, D. L. Zhang, and C. X. Hu, "Feasibility of biodiesel production by microalgae Chlorella sp. (FACHB-1748) under outdoor conditions," Bioresource. Technology, vol. 138, pp. 131-135, 2013.

[10] S. H. Ho, S. W. Huang, C. Y. Chen, T. Hasunuma, A. Kondo, C. Chang, and J. S, "Characterization and optimization of carbohydrate production from an indigenous microalga Chlorella vulgaris FSP-E" Bioresource. Technology, vol. 135, pp.157-165, 2013.

Sensorization and Optimization of Industrial Graphic Arts Machinery Using Artificial Intelligence Techniques

Angel Luis Garrido
University of Zaragoza
Henneo Media
Zaragoza, Spain
Email: garrido@unizar.es

Jonathan Rodríguez
Technical Office Manager
Henneo Print
Zaragoza, Spain
Email: jonathan.rodriguez@henneoprint.com

Mariano Sánchez
Maintenance Head
Henneo Print
Zaragoza, Spain
Email: msanchez@henneoprint.com

José Manuel Antón
Production Manager
Henneo Print
Zaragoza, Spain
Email: jmanton@henneoprint.com

Roberto Castán
Development Department
Hiberus Tech.
Zaragoza, Spain
Email: rcastan@hiberus.com

Susana Sangiao
Development Department
Hiberus Tech.
Zaragoza, Spain
Email: ssangiao@hiberus.com

Carlos Bobed
IIS Department
I3A, University of Zaragoza
Zaragoza, Spain
Email: cbobed@unizar.es

Eduardo Mena
IIS Department
I3A, University of Zaragoza
Zaragoza, Spain
Email: emena@unizar.es

***Abstract*—Today, manufacturing companies have technologies that allow them to monitor the different processes carried out in their facilities. These technologies, based on Real-Time Operating Systems and Internet of Things paradigms, are mature, and their application is widespread in different sectors. The problems come when factories own old machinery and legacy systems, and when the processes are poorly automated, which is a typical scenario in the graphic arts industry. To solve this situation, we propose a comprehensive management framework that obtains real-time information through Sensing systems and Artificial Intelligence technologies. The advantages obtained are the unification of information, the simplification of obtaining information by different departments, the automation of processes, and the support in planning tasks. We are currently testing our proposal in a real environment with promising results.**

Keywords-Sensors; Knowledge-Based Systems; Internet of Things; Machine Learning.

I. INTRODUCTION

Nowadays, manufacturing companies have technology that allows them to monitor the processes performed in their facilities. These technologies, based on Real-Time Operating Systems (RTOS) and Internet of Things (IoT) paradigms, are in a mature state, and their use is already being normalised by factories from diverse sectors [1]. The problems come when a series of circumstances occur, such as those listed below:

- Factories with old machinery.
- Machines and information systems without connection among them in the same manufacturing tasks.
- Presence of manual and little automated processes.

In those cases, when it is necessary to modernise the production systems, there is no choice but to carry out retrofitting work [2], which involves the replacement of existing parts or the incorporation of new ones to improve the characteristics of the machine or device. Ontologies and knowledge bases are often found in the literature as common resources for integrating legacy industrial systems with current systems [3] [4]. Still, as far as we know, there are no application studies in the graphic arts sector.

Precisely, if we focus on the graphic arts sector, in the specific scenario of printing publications with large rotary machines, the three situations mentioned above usually come together [5]. The life cycles of the machinery are very long, so it is easy to find rotary presses that are 20 years old or more, in perfect operation, logically dragging with them old computer systems that are complex to interconnect with current systems. The disadvantage is that the electronic and computer systems are based on legacy systems, and when they were manufactured, the RTOS and IoT paradigms were barely developed. Furthermore, many of the processes in these factories are still semi-automated, or even manual.

To work in this environment, we propose a comprehensive management framework that obtains information in real-time from both the old machinery and the legacy systems, through sensorization techniques and Artificial Intelligence (AI) technologies such as semantics management tools and machine learning. We are currently testing our proposal in collaboration with Henneo Print [6], a significant company in Spain devoted to printing all kinds of publications. The rest of this paper is organized as follows. Section II describes the graphic arts working context. Section III depicts the proposed architecture, and finally, Section IV addresses the conclusions and future work.

II. Graphic Arts context

There are two types of technologies when printing publications with large rotary presses: the so-called "coldset" (with cold ink) and the so-called "heatset" (hot ink, because a press-dryer intervenes in the process). The coldset technology is used to print newspapers, and heatset is used to print leaflets, books, and magazines, products that require a higher quality.

In the coldset stage, job planning is relatively simple, since publications generally have a fixed periodicity (daily, weekly, monthly, etc.) and very stable delivery windows. But, in the heatset stage, planning is fully variable as it is specified by customers. So, any delay entails a critical modification of the factory's global planning. It is a much more dynamic and unstable work environment, and many factors come into play, so decision-making becomes complicated, and tools are necessary to assist managers in their daily work, both in terms of machine maintenance and production planning.

Therefore, today's challenge in this sector is to computerise heatset processes at printing plants by incorporating RTOS and IoT technologies on old machinery and systems. In other words, we need suitable information to assist complex tasks such as planning tasks or maintenance reporting.

III. Architecture

In Fig. 1, we can see the different elements of the proposed architecture and the relations among them:

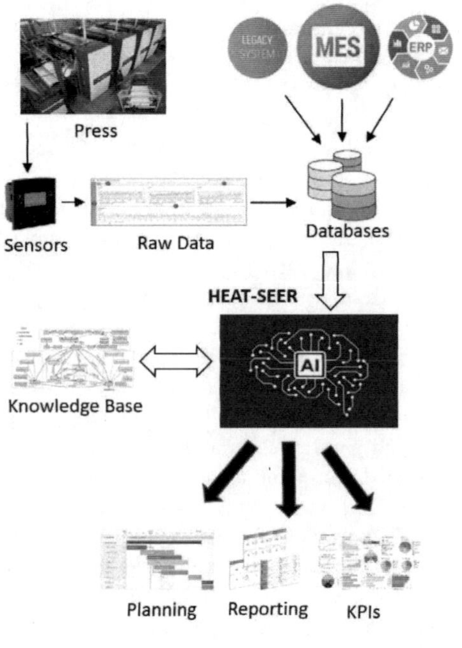

Figure 1. Overview of the proposed architecture.

Through retrofitting techniques and incorporating specific sensors, raw information is obtained from different aspects of the press: speed, temperature, electrical consumption, etc. At the same time, the most relevant information from the other systems existing in the factory has been considered: the Manufacturing Enterprise System (MES), the Enterprise Resource Planning (ERP), and specific systems, which, in most cases, are legacy systems. All the data stored on those systems are collected from their respective databases by *"Heat-Seer"*, an AI system, which, guided by the historical information and business rules contained in a specific knowledge base, is capable of performing the following tasks:

1) To assist the technical office in its planning tasks, simulating different production scenarios. It uses business rules and information obtained through machine learning from historical production data.
2) To automate data collection tasks and reporting for the production and maintenance departments.
3) To show *Key Performance Indicators* (KPI), the critical quantifiable indicators of progress toward an intended result. In this case, business results.

After passing the sensorization and information collection phase, the architecture implementation and testing work is underway, along with the development of the AI tool.

IV. Conclusions and Future Work

The contribution of this work is to propose a methodology for the problem of optimizing production tasks such as reporting, planning or maintenance when using legacy systems and machinery in the graphic arts sector. The advantages obtained will be the unification of information that allows data exploitation by different departments, the automation of processes, and the creation of new tools that will enable, for example, the planning and simulation of varying manufacturing scenarios. In future work, we have planned to integrate the knowledge base with a conversational system that allows operators to resolve doubts regarding work procedures using natural language.

Acknowledgment

This work is being supported by the Heat-Seer Project (no. 22021/C005/00148375) - Action co-funded by Red.es and the European Union through the European Regional Development Fund (ERDF), by the Spanish project PID2020-113903RB-I00 (AEI/FEDER, UE), and by DGA/FEDER.

References

[1] Y. Jiang, S. Yin, J. Dong, and O. Kaynak, "A review on soft sensors for monitoring, control, and optimization of industrial processes," *IEEE Sensors Journal*, vol. 21, no. 11, pp. 12 868–12 881, 2020.

[2] A. Alqoud, D. Schaefer, and J. Milisavljevic-Syed, "Industry 4.0: a systematic review of legacy manufacturing system digital retrofitting," *Manufacturing Review*, vol. 9, p. 32, 2022.

[3] G. Bitsch, P. Senjic, and J. Askin, "Integration of legacy systems to cyber-physical production systems using semantic adapters," *Procedia CIRP*, vol. 118, pp. 259–263, 2023.

[4] B. A. Mozzaquatro, R. Melo, C. Agostinho, and R. Jardim-Goncalves, "An ontology-based security framework for decision-making in industrial systems," in *2016 4th International Conference on Model-Driven Engineering and Software Development (MODELSWARD)*. IEEE, 2016, pp. 779–788.

[5] S. Baray, S. Hameed, and A. Badii, "Analysing the factors responsible for effectiveness of implementation and integration of enterprise resource planning systems in the printing industry," *Journal of enterprise information management*, vol. 21, no. 2, pp. 139–161, 2008.

[6] https:\\henneoprint.com, [last access Nov. 2023].

Cod Catch Forecasting through Machine Learning Algorithms at the Haul Level

Huamin Ren
School of Economics, Innovation and Technology
Kristiania University College
Oslo, Norway
email: huamin.ren@kristiania.no

Yajie Liu
Faculty of Bioscience, Fisheries and Economic
UiT The Arctic University of Norway
Tromsø, Norway
email: yajie.liu@uit.no

Keshav Prasad Paudel
Faculty of Bioscience, Fisheries and Economic
UiT The Arctic University of Norway
Tromsø, Norway
email: keshav.p.paudel@uit.no

***Abstract*—This paper leverages historical fishing data in conjunction with machine learning algorithms to uncover fishing patterns and more precisely forecast fishing catches. The introduction of Machine Learning techniques into the fishing industry holds significant promise for enhancing operational performance. Such methodologies can promote great efficiency and enhance the decision-making processes, optimizing factors such as fishing effort, location, and catch rates. Preliminary results illustrate the efficacy of three distinct machine learning algorithms: Linear Regression, RANdom SAmple Consensus (RANSAC), and Light Gradient Boosting Machine (LightGBM). Throughout our experimentation, it became evident that the modeling performance is profoundly influenced by the sampling strategy. This influence likely stems from inherent noise in the data, which degrades overall performance. Our findings offer insights into the effective employment of machine learning algorithms for data selection and modeling.**

***Index Terms*—Machine learning, big data, fishing catch, forecast.**

I. Introduction

Machine Learning (ML) has emerged as a valuable tool for processing and analyzing big data [1]. Moreover, it proves to be an effective and efficient approach in tackling the key methodological issues and challenges encountered in modeling and analyzing various datasets in resource management. The integration of big data and Machine Learning can help to improve fisheries management, optimize resource allocation, enhance productivity and profitability, and overall sustainability. The machine learning can help fishers optimize their fishing efforts by analyzing historical catch data along with environmental factors such as ocean temperature, salinity, etc.

Norway has one of the world richest fishing grounds, making Norway the largest fishing country in Europe. Fishery has been an important contributor to the Norwegian Economy after the petroleum industry. Fish catches are affected by a multitude of factors including fishing effort, location, types of fishing vessels, socio-economic conditions and environmental variables. Climate is changing and the effects of climate change have been observed, including higher temperature, shrinking glaciers, altered precipitation patterns, frequent extreme weather, sea level rise and more acidic oceans. These changes are happening faster in the pole areas than the rest of the world. This climate changes have shifted the productivity of marine fisheries resources and habitats. Combing extensive data and ML algorithms to explore fishing patterns and forecast fish catches is a crucial aspect of aquatic research because of its relevance to establishing effective fishery management and resource allocation systems. In particular, it empowers fishers to make better decisions by optimizing their fishing strategies, thereby maximizing fishing productivity and profitability while reducing operational costs in a dynamic environment [2].

Research on fishery catch forecasting has considered both long-term catch forecasting on a scale of months or years and short-term forecasting on a scale of days. The fishery industry has reported challenges, particularly in short-term catch data, when faced with limitations of available data. Due to work cycles or actual work conditions, fishery practitioners responsible for catch data often do not have complete and detailed records, leading to a lack of real data and inaccuracies [3]. In a fisheries management context, a more detailed information on the catch composition including type of the fish at the actual haul may allow for better adaptations of management measures. In other words, at the scale of the individual fishing operation (with each haul or each trip considered), a better information on the type and catch distributions of target species may be learnt [6] [7], which not only helps spatial avoidance but could also increase the profit of fishing. Therefore, We investigate each catching behavior from the haul and attempt to study the fish catch in the long-term. We propose machine learning approaches into modelling the fish catch w.r.t. fishing location, vessel and gear type, the time of catch and other external factors.

The main objective of the paper is to use ML to explore fishing patterns and forecast fish catches. Particularly, we investigate the application of ML methods for enhancing fish catch forecasting. The structure of the paper is as follows. Section II provides an overview of the most recent developments in the field, highlighting the growing importance of ML techniques in addressing fish catch forecasting challenges. In Section III, we introduce our proposed ML methods and compare them with existing approaches, and then we demonstrate their performance in Section IV. In Section V, we summarize our findings and outline the future directions of our research.

II. RALATED WORK

While Machine Learning (ML) and Artificial Intelligence (AI) have seen widespred application in various fields, their use in natural resource management, especially in fisheries, remains relative limited. Studies such as that of Zhang et al. [3] applied ML algorithms and ensemble learning model to predict the location of albacore tuna fishing in the South Pacific, revealing that the ensemble learning model achieves higher accuracy estimates than machine learning models. Similarly, L. F. Rahman et al. [15] developed an ML approach to predict marine capture fisheries and aquaculture production in Malaysia based on past production data and climate variables, highlighting the better performance of ensemble ML model compared to the single ML model. Compared to advancements seen in machine learning application in other fields such as computer vision and healthcare systems, the progress in employing machine learning algorithms for predicting fish catches remains relatively nascent. Nonetheless, nmerous emerging research avenues in fisheries show promise. Notable attempts, like those in [8] [9] and [10], endeavor to automatically predict fish catches using past catches and meteorological information. Anothe study, [11] emphasized that prediction errors should be evaluated in a manner that goes beyond mere consideration of absolute error, regardless of the predicted value. To illustrate this, it is important to recognize that an error of 100 kg in a predicted fish catch of 5000 kg should not be treated equivalently to the same error occurring in a prediction of 500 kg. This perspective does not align with fishers' practical understanding As a result, it is suggested that evaluation metrics should be tailored to optimize prediction errors in a way that aligns with the fishers' intuition and real-world experience.

Research exploring the impact of climate change on fish catch remains limited, but has seen recent advances. For instance, O. S. Kjesbu et al. [4] examined the effect of climate change on the migration patters of North Pacific spiny dogfish, employing a ML approach. additionally, Wikstrom [14] evaluated supervised ML algorithms to predict recreational fishing success and found that random forest algorithm proved the most effective in the experiments and a combination of variables contributes optimal predictions.

III. METHOD

A. Problem Formulation

Given data $D = (x_1, y_1), (x_2, y_2)...(x_i, y_i), ...(x_M, y_M,$ where M is the number of the collected data. Each x_i is the n-dimensional vector, which represents the relative attributes per haul per catch, for example, start position width, start position length, sea depth start (meters), duration - (minutes), stop position width, stop position length, sea depth stop (meters), draw distance (meters), species, round weight, etc. There are 43 attributes in our studies data after some cleaning. From the data set, we estimated the model parameter vector θ appropriately expressed as:

$$y = f(x; \theta) \tag{1}$$

Our objective is to establish the estimation of Y, represented as $\hat{Y}$, by modelling of X, so that it satisfies:

$$min\|\hat{y}_i - y_i\|_2, \text{ where } \hat{y}_i = f(x_i; \theta) \tag{2}$$

B. Proposed Pipeline

We have applied three machine learning methods to implement the modelling f in Eq. 2 and compared their performance on cod catch forecasting.

1) Linear Regression

   Linear Regression learns a model by minimizing the objective function in Eq. 2:

$$f(x; \theta) = \theta_i x_i + b \tag{3}$$

   Equivalently, the objective is to minimize the loss in the equation below.

$$(\theta^*, b^*) = argmin_{\theta,b} \sum_{i=1}^{M} (y_i - \theta x_i - b)^2 \tag{4}$$

2) RANSAC

   RANSAC algorithm normally performs the following steps [12].

   Step1 Selection of samples randomly from D and have a sample set S.

   Step2 Model estimation by using S.

   Step3 Counting the number of data with estimation error within parameter ϵ.

   Step4 Terminate the algorithm when the number of data satisfying Step3 exceeds a threshold, and model is built using those data. Otherwise, iterate the procedure from Step1.

3) LightGBM

   LightGBM is based on Gradient Boosting Decision Tree (GBDT) [13], which is a widely-used machine learning algorithm, due to its efficiency, accuracy, and interpretability. However, GBDT is facing challenges, especially in the tradeoff between accuracy and efficiency, due to the reason that conventional implementations of GBDT need to scan all the data instances to estimate the information gain of all the possible split points. Therefore, their computational complexities will be proportional to both the number of features and the number of instances. To address such limitation, LightGBM was proposed by applying two new techniques called Gradient-based One-Side Sampling (GOSS) and Exclusive Feature Bundling (EFB), see more details in [5].

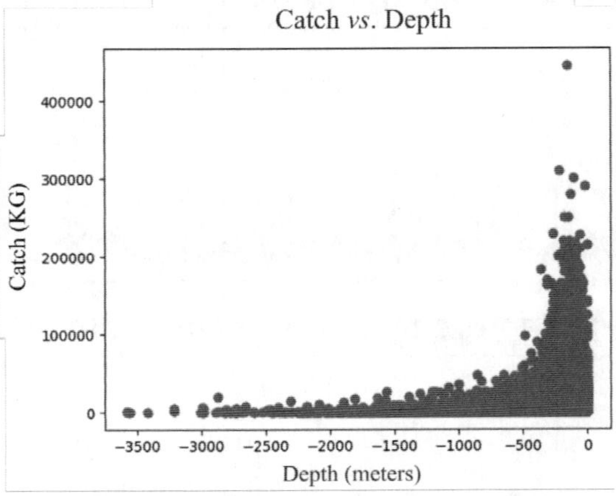

Fig. 1: Catch by depth.

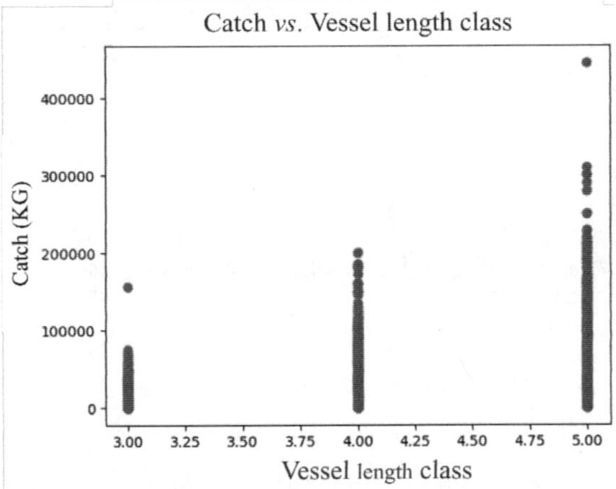

Fig. 2: Catch by vessel length class.

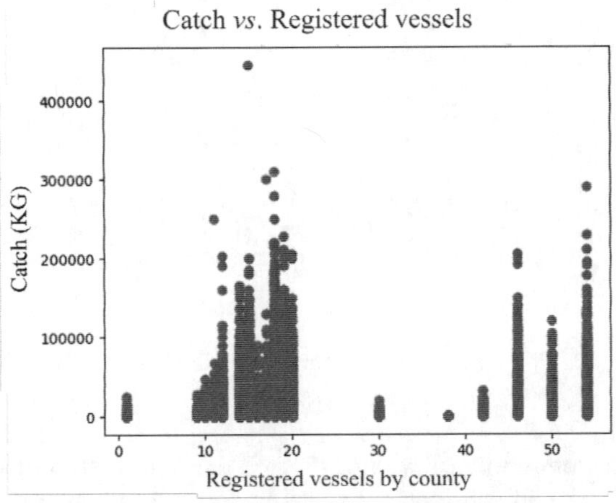

Fig. 3: Catch with registered vessels by county.

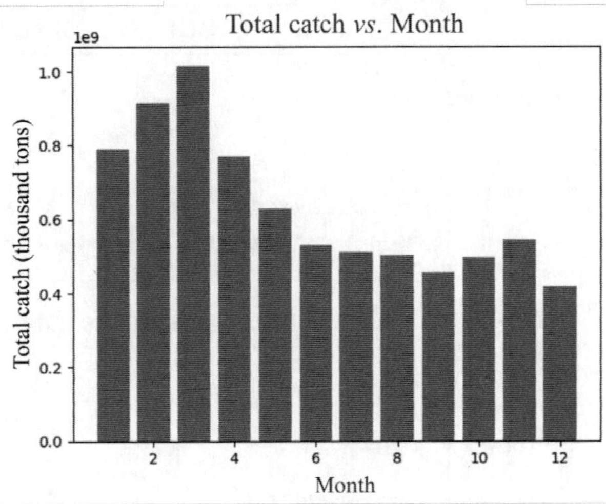

Fig. 4: Catch by the harvesting month.

IV. Experimental Results

A. Dataset Description

We used cod fishery as a case study to test the modeling and prediction. The historical fishing data were extracted from the Vessel Monitoring System (VMS) from the Norwegian Fisheries Directorate, ranging from 2000 - 2022. The dataset compromises haul time, draw distance, fishing location (width, length, depth), catch weight, and vessel characteristics (e.g., length, tonnage, engine power, etc.). We visualized, explored, and analyzed spatial relationships in ArcGIS Pro [16] to identify and remove records with unreliable position (i.e., vessel positions and/or fishing activities on land). The einvironmental variables included two oceanographic variables: Sea Surface Temperature (SST) and sea surface CHlorophyll a concentration (CHLa), three bathymetric and/or topographic variables: depth, slope and terrain ruggedness (rugosity), and two distance related variables: distance to coast and distance to nearest port were used in this study. SST and CHLa were derived from Moderate Resolution Imaging Spectroradiometer (MODIS) satellite measurements. The level 3 (4 km resolution) monthly average SST data for both Aqua and Terra satellites from the NASA Ocean Color [17] were downloaded. Observations from the four temperature images for each month (both Terra and Aqua, day – 10:30, 13:30, respectively – and night – 22:30, 01:30 respectively) were combined to calculate the monthly mean SST. Similarly, MODIS/Aqua monthly level 3 data of chlorophyll concentration were obtained from the NASA [17], Goddard Earth Science [18], and Distributed Active Archive Center [19]. The General Bathymetric Chart of the Oceans (GEBCO) gridded bathymetric data were sued. Slope was calculated from the depth data (GBECO 2023 grid). Rugosity, a measure of terrain complexity or the seabed roughness, was derived using the Benthic Terrain Modeler (BTM version 3.0). It is woth noting that seabed roughness is strongly correlated to biodiversity in marine environments.

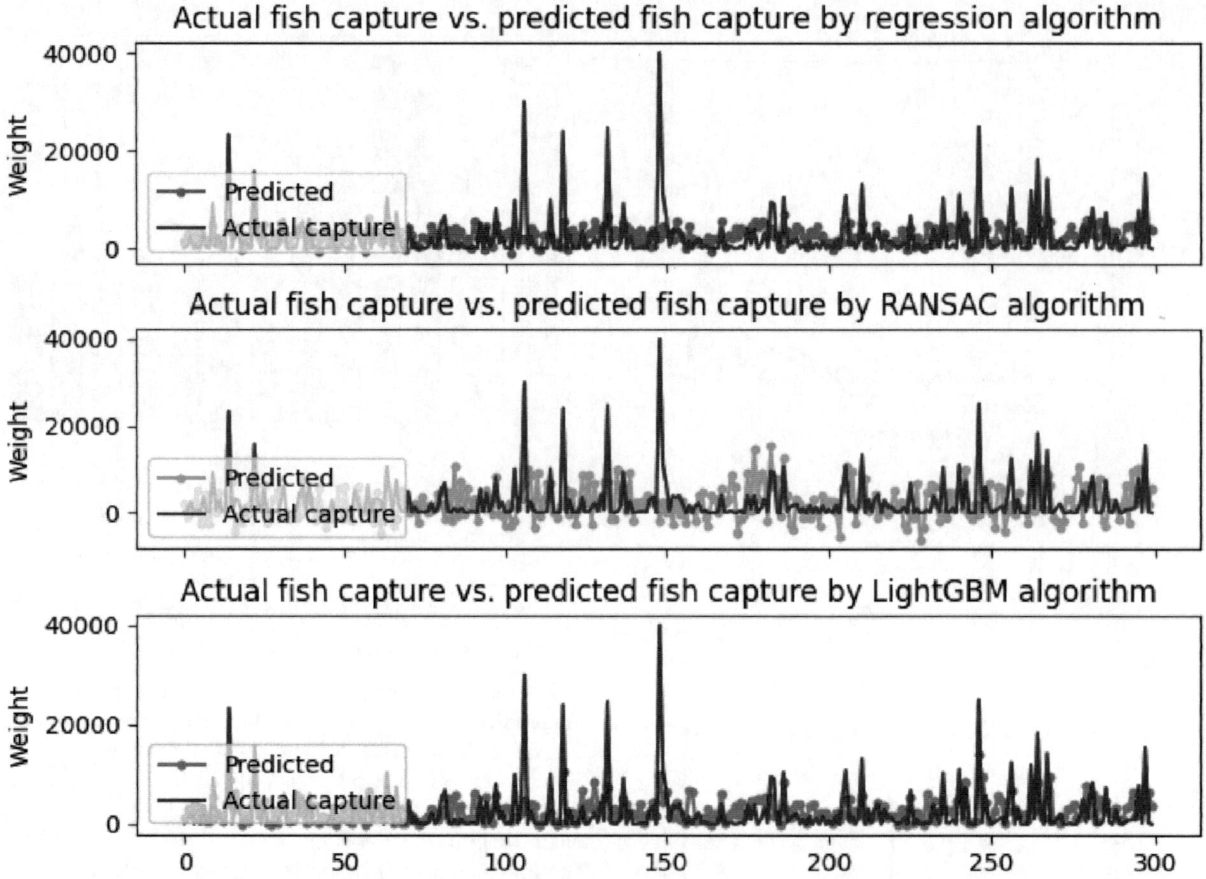

Fig. 5: Predictions of Fish catches with Regression/RANSAC/LightGBM algorithm.

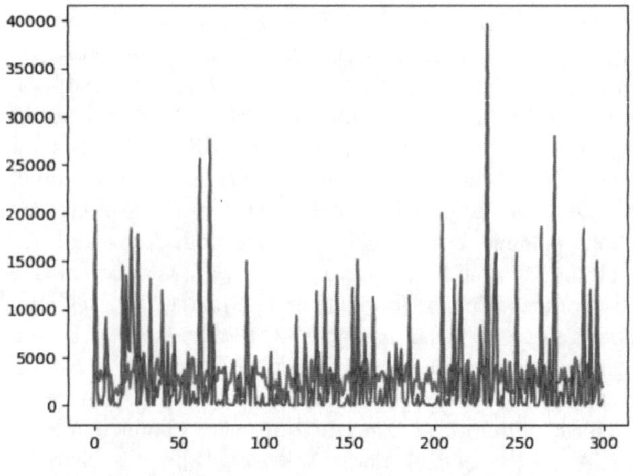

Fig. 6: Fish catch performance with Linear Regression.

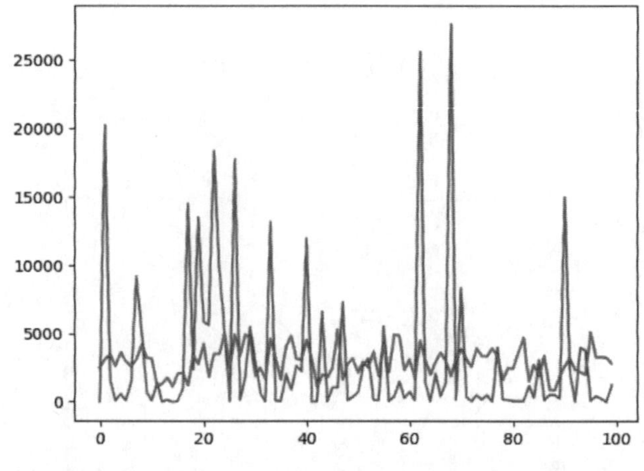

Fig. 7: Fish catch performance with RANSAC algorithm.

B. Data visualization

We conducted an in-depth analysis of the data to determine the correlation between catch weight (kg) and various influencing factors. Initially, we investigated the relationship between locations and fish capture rates. The correlation between catch and depth is illustrated in Fig. 1, and the relationship between catch and vessel length class can be observed in Fig. 2. Further insights related to catch and registered vessels by county are presented in Fig. 3. Then, the monthly total catch is depicted in Fig. 4 (calculated by total weight in thousand tons). The fish catch shows a strong correlation with factors, such as the county where the vessel is registered, the traveling distance, and the fishing month.

C. Performance of machine learning algorithms without parameter tuning

To visualize the forecasting of fish catch based on different modeling approaches, refer to the accompanying figures. Fig. 6 illustrates the performance of a linear regression model, while Fig. 7 depicts the performance using the RANSAC algorithm. A comparative assessment of both figures clearly indicates that RANSAC generally demonstrates superior performance over linear regression. The x-axis represents sampled data points. Additionally, it should be noted that the initial 100 data points in Fig. 6 correspond exactly to the first 100 data points in Fig. 7. These outcomes may be due to considerable noise in the training data, which adversely impacts the forecasting accuracy. Employing RANSAC allows for a more selective use of data for training, potentially mitigating this issue.

The comparative analysis in Fig. 5 shows that LightGBM outperforms the other two models. Due to misreporting data per trip, or per vessel often contains noise, which can substantially degrade model performance. LightGBM's data sampling strategy results in improved forecasting accuracy and performance. In gradient boosting, data points with larger gradients (errors) are crucial for calculating information gain. The Gradient-based One-Side Sampling (GOSS) technique in LightGBM retains these critical data points and conducts random sampling on the remaining data.

V. Conclusion and Future Work

We have applied three machine learning methods on historical fishing data in this paper to tackle a fish catch forecasting problem. Specifically, we conducted preliminary analyses to showcase the effectiveness of linear regression, RANSAC, and LightGBM, comparing their performances in fish catch predictions. Our current method still exhibits limitations in terms of model performance, particularly when dealing with data that contains a significant amount of noise. Throughout our experiments, it became evident that the influence of the sampling strategy should not be underestimated. Therefore, a more robust fish catch forecasting model that integrates advanced data sampling techniques will be one of our future research directions.

As our research evolves, several promising directions have captured our attention. A notable focus is the transformation of haul-level data into time series formats, targeting more vessel-focused or trajectory-driven models. Furthermore, we will delve into the influence of psychological factors and introduce a novel metric for assessing the accuracy of fish catch forecasting. This is especially crucial since existing error-based metrics may not fully integrate external variables and the perspectives of the fishermen.

References

[1] L. Wang and C. A. Alexander. "Machine learning in big data", International Journal of Mathematical, Engineering and Management Sciences, 1(2), pp.52, 2016.

[2] K. Sakaguchi and N. Yamashita, "Method to forecast the catches of Japanese common squid Todarodes pacificus in the Sea of Okhotsk off Hokkaido," Bull. Japanese Soc. Fisheries Oceanogr., vol. 79, no. 2, pp. 43–45, 2015.

[3] Y. Zhang, M. Yamamoto, G. Suzuki and H. Shioya, "Collaborative Forecasting and Analysis of Fish Catch in Hokkaido From Multiple Scales by Using Neural Network and ARIMA Model," IEEE Access, vol. 10, pp. 7823-7833, 2022. doi: 10.1109/ACCESS.2022.3141767.

[4] O. S. Kjesbu et al., "Highly mixed impacts of near-future climate change on stock productivity proxies in the North East Atlantic. Fish and Fisheries", pp. 1–15. 2021. https://doi.org/10.1111/faf.12635

[5] G. Ke et al., "LightGBM: A highly efficient gradient boosting decision tree", Proc. Adv. Neural Inf. Process. Syst., vol. 30, pp. 3146–3154, 2017.

[6] M. Robert et al., "Spatial distribution of discards in mixed fisheries: species trade-offs, potential spatial avoidance and national contrasts", Reviews in Fish Biology and Fisheries, Vol. 29, pp. 917–934, 2019.

[7] S. Kristian, B. Plet-Hansen and C. U. François, "The value of commercial fish size distribution recorded at haul by haul compared to trip by trip", ICES Journal of Marine Science, vol. 77, Issue 7-8, pp. 2729–2740, December 2020. https://doi.org/10.1093/icesjms/fsaa141

[8] T. Komatsu, I. Aoki, I. Mitani, and T. Ishii, "Prediction of the catch of Japanese sardine larvae in Sagami Bay using a neural network," Fisheries Science, vol. 60, no. 4, pp. 385-391, Dec. 1994.

[9] J. R. Leathwick, J. Elith, M. P. Francis, T. Hastie, and P. Taylor, "Variation in demersal fish species richness in the oceans surrounding New Zealand: an Analysis using boosted regression trees," Marine Ecology Progress Series, vol. 321, pp. 267-281, Sept. 2006.

[10] Y. Kokaki, N. Tawara, T. Kobayashi, K. Hashimoto, and T. Ogawa, "Sequential fish catch forecasting using Bayesian state space models", Proc. ICPR2018, pp. 776-781, Aug. 2018.

[11] Y. Kokaki, T. Kobayashi and T. Ogawa, "Psychological measure on fish catches and its application to optimization criterion for machine-learning-based predictors", OCEANS 2019 - Marseille, Marseille, France, pp. 1-5, 2019. doi: 10.1109/OCEANSE.2019.8867405.

[12] T. Watanabe, "Initial Performance Improvement for Fuzzy RANSAC Algorithm Based on Weighted Estimation Model", International Conference on Image Processing and Robotics (ICIP), Negombo, Sri Lanka, pp. 1-6, 2020. doi: 10.1109/ICIP48927.2020.9367332.

[13] J. H Friedman. "Greedy function approximation: a gradient boosting machine", Annals of statistics, pp 1189–1232, 2001.

[14] J. Wikström. "Evaluating supervised machine learning algorithms to predict recreational fishing success : A multiple species, multiple algorithms approach", 2015. https://api.semanticscholar.org/CorpusID:109388862.

[15] L. F. Rahman et al., "Developing an Ensembled Machine Learning Prediction Model for Marine Fish and Aquaculture Production", Sustainability , 13 (16), 9124, 2021. https://doi.org/10.3390/su13169124.

[16] Environmental Systems Research Institute (ESRI). ESRI Spatial Analyst. Retrieved from https://www.esri.com/en-us/arcgis/products/arcgis-spatial-analyst/ArcGIS. [Last accessed Oct. 2023]

[17] NASA Ocean Biology Processing Group. Sea-viewing Wide Field-of-view Sensor (SeaWiFS) Level-3 Ocean Color Data. Retrieved from https://oceancolor.gsfc.nasa.gov/l3/, [Last accessed Oct. 2023]

[18] Goddard Earth Science (GES)- Distributed Active Archive Center (DAAC). Retrieved from https://daac.gsfc.nasa.gov/, [Last accessed Oct. 2023]

[19] Distributed Active Archive Center (DAAC). Retrieved from https://www.earthdata.nasa.gov/eosdis/daacs, [Last accessed Oct. 2023]

[20] FAO Major Fishing Areas. Retrieved from https://www.fao.org/fishery/en/area/27/en, [Last accessed Oct. 2023]

Non-deterministic Operation Profiles Based on Multi-Layer Interest Landscapes for Autonomous Robotic Teams

Florian Segor, Igor Tchouchenkov, Aleksej Buller, Matthias Kollmann
IAS - Department of Interoperability and Assistance Systems
Fraunhofer IOSB
Karlsruhe, Germany
e-mail: {florian.segor, igor.tchouchenkov, aleksej.buller, matthias.kollmann}@iosb.fraunhofer.de

***Abstract*—Distributed deployment of cooperating unmanned vehicles is increasingly becoming a key element for expanding the range of operations in many domains. The Management by Objective Demonstrators is used to investigate procedures and potential solutions for a holistic approach to generate cooperating vehicle teams based on global planning paired with local reactive autonomy of individual vehicles. The implemented procedures deducing local autonomy from global planning are presented. Based on this, the use of operation profiles for aerial reconnaissance, which are intended to enable cooperative team behavior with respect to the global mission, are analyzed. The operation profiles are compared to traditional methods and their advantages and disadvantages are highlighted.**

Keywords-swarming; mission planning; reactive autonomy; reconaissance.

I. INTRODUCTION

Available autonomy within modern robotic systems is constantly increasing, opening up new fields of application and possible scenarios for corresponding systems. Autonomous Systems (AS) will be more and more considered critical for various types of missions in the future. As much as these increasing demands may drive AS development, many acute issues remain to be solved addressing individual solutions and specific operation requirements.

Our vision is to evoke an intelligent, effective and efficient cooperating behavior by creating autonomous responsiveness of individual robots to the individual situation while considering the overall mission objective, the actions of assigned team members, as well as the environment and its potential dynamic change. The concept of local responsiveness based on global planning is providing this autonomous decision-making capability to individual vehicles organized in a team. In the work presented here, the basic approach to achieve this system autonomy as a part of the flexible control chain of the Management by Objective Demonstrator [1] is described. The performance of this solution is discussed in the context of a specific application scenario - the coordinated deployment of multiple AS operating in a team to fulfill aerial reconnaissance.

The Management by Objective Demonstrator (MOD) is designed as a multi-layered flexible stacked architecture, integrating a modular, adjustable control chain of planning, monitoring, and evaluation algorithm. This is used to prepare and schedule collective actions at the global team level with respect to the mission objective, allocate resources, and provide the (physical or simulated) asset a framework for coordinated actions following the task-oriented Operation Profiles (OP) herein discussed. In this holistic approach, the OPs are used to create local behavior of the AS (also referred to as Reactive Artificial Intelligence (RAI)). These profiles provide the single team members the capability to autonomously decide and operate in their dedicated environment, while the global planning process assures that the mission target is fully contained by the cooperative assets.

In comparison with traditional planning and operating alternatives for aerial reconnaissance, the advantages and disadvantages of the proposed non-deterministic movement profiles for autonomous operation are discussed and the possible applications are analyzed.

The paper is structured as follows: After a brief overview of the state of the art in Section II, the concept of the Management by Objective Demonstrator is described in Section III. The structure of the multi-layer interest landscapes as well as their concrete application are considered in Section IV, and the simulated results are discussed in Section V. The paper is closed with a final discussion in Section VI.

II. STATE OF THE ART

Research and development in the environment of the parallel application of several, possibly heterogeneous sensor carriers, are a fast-growing field in different research areas [2]-[4].

Tan et al. [5] address the problem of navigating multiple individual vehicles in a swarm with respect to an anticipated environmental model. In order to navigate the vehicles, an Artificial Potential Field (APF) is generated that maps the obstacles and destinations of each vehicle as a mathematical function of attraction and repulsion. Each vehicle uses this information to find its way through obstacles to its destinations. This is a widely used approach (e.g., see [6][7] or [8]) that leads to good results if the environmental model is sufficiently precise in correctly representing the goals of the individual Unmanned Surface Vehicle (USV) or team members and real-world objects. As a promising approach, we have investigated APF solutions, but our findings indicated that, whilst providing inherent advantages regarding the determination of speed and course, pure APF introduces some significant shortcomings related to the movement decisions of an AS in complex situations (e.g., singularities).

Alfeo et al. [9] propose to encode the waste management infrastructure into a map by using artificial pheromones and organize the waste disposal process by mimicking the biological models of stigmergy-based foraging. While the described approach is extremely relevant for the self-organization of a swarm, it bases it movement decisions on the fixed and reduced possibilities provided by the underlaying model of the existing streets. While this is perfectly sufficient for the waste disposal in urban area, it is not sufficient to organize a team of AS in a less-structured area, e.g., an open field.

In [10], the authors describe a multi vehicle approach using an artificial pheromone approach, that seems to be promising. Based on the different objectives of a task, diffusing and bleeding (fading out and fading in) pheromones are used to guide the assets to scan the positions with increased uncertainty of a designated target cell for potential threatening persons or vehicles. In contrast, the solution presented here operates on geographical coordinates and not with an artificial division of the real world into cells. Additionally, we calculate with a significantly larger movement variance (currently 360 possibilities in two dimensions). Other aspects such as task assignment, which is also discussed in [11], are components of the higher Artificial Intelligence (AI) in the MbO Demonstrator that are not considered in detail in this paper.

The proposed OPs for aerial reconnaissance are considering two basic approaches: the linear OP and the non-deterministic OP. The search patterns used in the linear approach are basically discussed in [12] and [13]. In [14], two basic search patterns, a linear approach as well as a tube approach are also studied in different embodiments for cooperative use. It is interesting to note here that the vehicles reconnoiter the identical area in parallel and no local separation by assigning sub-areas is proposed. However, the coordination effort seems to be significantly higher in this case, since the planned trajectories are in close proximity to each other. Correspondingly, a higher effort must be expended to enable secure operation. The same applies to the tube approach. Similarly, Choi et al. are creating a path following a spiral pattern [15]. While this circular approach can be well performed by the afterwards described interest landscape, it follows a clear and predictive behavior and is, therefore, not further investigated in this context. Fricke et al. are also proposing a distributed deterministic spiral search algorithm mainly as benchmark for non-deterministic solutions [16]. While this approach seems to show good results, it suffers from the fact that the search needs to be started in the center of the search area, which is a very specific situation not suitable for a generic solution.

III. MANAGEMENT BY OBJECTIVE DEMONSTRATOR CONCEPT

Autonomous Systems operating in a team to cooperatively solve a common problem is challenging from a technical perspective as well as from an organizational one. A multitude of solutions, technologies and strategies that solve specific aspects of autonomous UxV operation do exist. But it certainly requires a holistic approach considering the challenges to enable the efficient, effective and flexible operational use of such a Systems of Systems (SOS) in a real-world application. We addressed this problem by introducing the Management by Objective (MbO) concept [1]. MbO is not primarily focusing on the autonomy of the system, but on the question how a single operator can be meaningfully involved in the team's actions [17] [18]. Direct monitoring of individual vehicles is inefficient, as it usually exceeds the capacity of the operator, especially in high workload situations spread over a varying number of independent vehicles (see, e.g.: [19] [20]). Therefore, the MbO approach is not focusing on vehicle control, but on tuning the results or mission products (see Figure 1). The interaction between the operator and the assets take place via the adaption of the global mission tasks or finetuning of the mission product requirements.

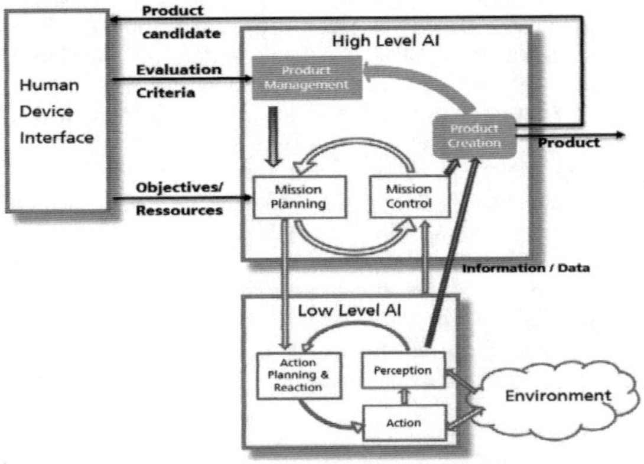

Figure 1. Management by Objective control cycles for AS as used in the MOD.

The concept can be decomposed into three main aspects: Mission Management, Product Creation and Asset Autonomy (see also Figure 1). The Mission Management, as part of the high-level AI, is fully responsible for planning and control of the cooperative actions. It is monitoring and analyzing the progress of the mission with respect to the defined parameters and objectives and is providing and manipulating the data basis of the low-level AI (reactive AI as part of the Asset Autonomy) for controlling the physical asset. The Product Creation within the high-level AI is responsible for processing collected data and provides aggregated products to the operator for evaluation. At the same time, the extracted information from the products is used as feedback to the Mission Management. The operator intervenes in the mission by adjusting the planning specifications based on the information retrieved.

Three different configurations of the MOD have been evaluated in different physical system configurations. Within the full centralized configuration, the high-level AI is a unique centralized instance accompanied by a number of also centralized Low Level AI Instances that only transfer control commands via dedicated wireless links to the interlinked assets. In the second configuration, the low-level AI is hosted on board the asset assuming the physical assets provide appropriate capacities. The third tested configuration is the full distributed approach, where the higher and the lower AI are hosted within the assets and each asset is capable of creating mission data for itself as well as for all team members.

Converting a task into a cooperative mission, based on given OPs, is a central component of the high-level AI. It is important to understand how the cooperative mission plan is translated into information measurable by the asset, in order to act autonomously. To solve this the MOD is using OPs as described in Section IV to transform the abstract mission specification into measurable representations, that can be interpreted by any low-level AI.

To create these representations, we propose to use a Multi-Layer Artificial Interest Landscape (ML-AIL) (similar to [21] [22]). The single layers of the ML-AIL are representing a specific object context or dimension, separating different types of information instead of a single merged source. Hence, we separate targets, obstacles, team members, etc. into the individual layers of the interest field and treat them according to their associated sensing algorithms. The output of the corresponding stack of sensing algorithms is fused into a control decision (see Figure 2). This approach increases the computational workload linearly to the used number of layers, but also allows to create differentiated decisions regarding the divergent mappings of the surroundings of the AS. The behavior can be optimally tuned, considering cooperative mobile objects (team members), static and mobile obstacles, mission targets (static and dynamic), as well as the physical characteristics of the asset.

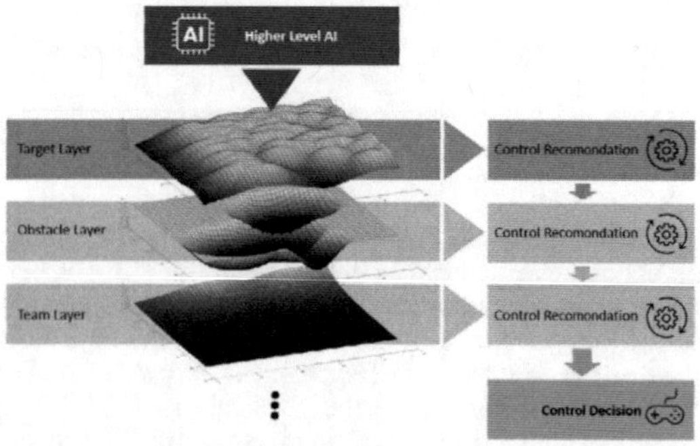

Figure 2. Multi-Layer Artificial Force Field Concept.

The current MoB is operating on three different AIL layers with the capability to add additional layers as needed:

The Target Layer is mimicking the biology inspired foraging process (e.g., see [8][9][23]). At the initial stage of a task-to-mission conversion the higher AI creates a collection of target features with appropriate parameterization, based on the mission requirements and the mission-specific chosen behavior patterns for the team and the team members. In the case of the herein discussed systematic area reconnaissance mission, the result is a set of uniformly distributed features with similar interaction behavior; in case of a non-deterministic approach the resulting features are randomly distributed with deviating interaction behavior. Defined sub-goals, a priori knowledge, mission requirements or the specified treatment of certain known objects or regions (e.g., bridges, buildings or streets that should be monitored more intensively) can be translated into accordingly adapted features, that represent the significantly higher interest in these regions. The AS is able to recognize the increased importance of these objects when analyzing the Target Layer of the ML-AIL and transfer this sensing results into corresponding target-based action recommendations. The basic behavior is not changed, but the specified areas receive increased attention. Scanning the areas is prioritized and happens on a more frequent basis (see also Section IV).

The Obstacle Layer represents the known environmental information and is translated into an AIL by the higher AI algorithms when composing the mission. Based on a real-world model, objects relevant for the mission area are extracted, translated into features of negative interest (leading to an avoiding behavior) and stored in the AIL. Objects that are detected during the mission, for example prior unknown obstacles, are dynamically integrated into this AIL and synchronized between the team members.

The Cooperative Layer is closely related to the obstacle layer and is used to store cooperative obstacles and team relevant information, as well as their history. The individual AS constructs an individual image of the current state of the team using the status information received from the other team members, e.g., to inject marker based stigmergy comparable to the concepts using an artificial pheromone trail. At the same time, it can also be used to correlate specific mission data. For example, a target may be specifically assigned to an AS, but if this target is covered and processed by another AS, the team layer information can be used to indirectly manipulate the target layer of the original assigned AS.

The individual layers use a geographic coordinate system and are described by a collection of data points called features. Each feature has inherent information, about the interaction between the layers, as well as between the layer and the AS, to be performed at layer update, based on the current situation.

As representatives of real-world objects, like obstacles or team members and virtual action or interest points, the content in the individual layers of the AIL are composed of pheromone-like interest features with an inherent information set. This contains the type (e.g., obstacle, target, POI, no-go, track, etc.), position and spatial extent, as well as the behavior during interaction with any AS.

Based on the type of the features the significance of the measured value is determined, e.g., the boundaries of a feature of type "no-go" should not be violated while the boundaries of a feature of type "obstacle" must not be violated.

Decision of the AS is based on the sensing of these features. We distinguish between an attracting and repelling influence leading to avoiding or a searching behavior. In combination with the effect on the perception (the strength of the measurement taking the distance between AS and the feature), these values are used for the sensing within the single layers. Further important parameters used to modify the interaction are the dynamic degradability (the impact on the strength of the feature under influence of an AS, e.g., if mimicking the foraging process the maximum measurable strength of a visited feature is decreased), the recovery procedure (if an who fast a once depleted feature can recover and to what maximum strength), the range of perceptibility (the distance in which the AS is still capable to sense the Feature) or the affiliation (a feature to AS mapping, providing the possibility to assign specific features to specific assets).

For the translation of the AIL into movements of the AS, we use a temporal projection of the current geographical position P to potential future positions P'_j based on the current speed $\vec{v}$ of the AS (see Figure 3). Depending on the precision necessary to operate the physical asset in the given environment the granularity of P'_j can be adapted. The MOD currently calculates with a scheme consisting of 360 anticipated future geographical positions, one position per full degree ($j = 360$). For each P'_j a State S_j is calculated based on the measured influence ($\vec{F_r}$ and $\vec{F_a}$) of a subset $M_{sub} = \{T_{sub}, W_{sub}, C_{sub}\}$ of the surrounding objects in the associated AIL Layer (Target T, World W, Cooperative C) filtered by the sliding window only considering relevant objects in range of the original position P.

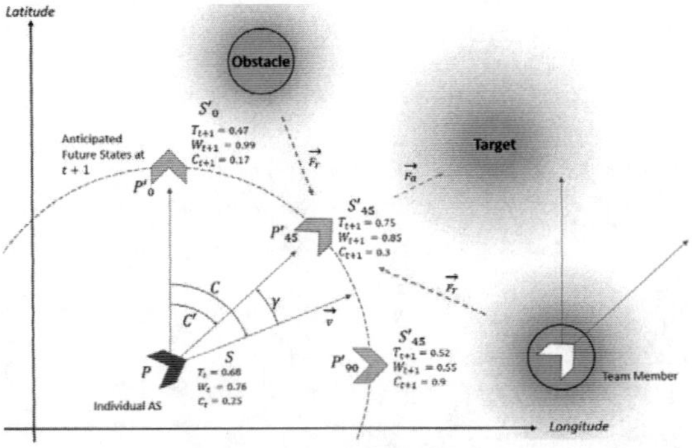

Figure 3. Sensing and decision making based on the ML-AIL for local reactive autonomy.

As impact calculation of each feature upon S_j different approaches have been implemented and evaluated (1) and (2).

$$\frac{F}{{d_f}^2 + \sigma} \quad (1)$$

F is the current maximum value of the feature to be measured, d_f corresponds to the distance and σ is the slope coefficient that describes the fuzziness or expansion of the feature. A higher σ increases the distance and strength of the measurement of the feature.

Alternatively, the harmonic oscillation approach was tested, where a full computation of the P'_j values is not necessary. Based on the observation that each feature-specific value in S_j given by (1) behaves computably for all other P'_j based on a shifted harmonic oscillation function (2), regarding the given maximum measurement of the corresponding feature.

$$u * \sin(\omega j + \varphi) \quad (2)$$

Here $u = \frac{F}{2}$ translates the function to oscillate between the maximum measurable F, ω identifies the constant angular velocity and $\varphi = -\frac{\pi}{2} - S_a$ is the phase shift, where S_a corresponds to j of the maximum measurement identical with the vector indicating the direction of the feature.

Single feature measurements are not summed up, so that strong features superimpose weaker one's or the ones that are further away. If, nevertheless, features are measurable above the baseline of the dominant feature, the harmonic oscillations are sequence wise composed. In both approaches, the output of T_{sub}, W_{sub} and C_{sub} is fused afterwards and the result is an anticipated best future state used by the low-level AI to identify the current intension C', as well as the angle offset γ. Based on this intension, the asset specific short-range navigation path is identified and translated into control commands.

IV. Creating Team Based Multi-Layer AIL for Reconnaissance Missions

The distributed multi-layer AIL approach for mission conversion in a coordinated team allows to create a specific mission environment for each AS. A central question is how to design the main target layer of the AIL via the translation of the mission aspects into corresponding features and how these features should be parameterized, so that the AS can fulfill its task in the mission context.

In this context, several scenarios were investigated and evaluated for suitability with different feature distributions. Where possible, traditional methods were used as benchmarks. The results are compared in Section V.

A. Area Reconnaissance

A basic task, in which a team approach is valuable to increase efficiency, is reconnaissance for mapping and clearance of large areas with a parallel and coordinated deployment of several reconnaissance vehicles. This scenario requires, that the entire area defined in the mission (target area) must be inspected completely.

In traditional approaches, a pre-planned trajectory for a single (or multiple) vehicle(s) is created to ensure complete coverage (see Figure 4).

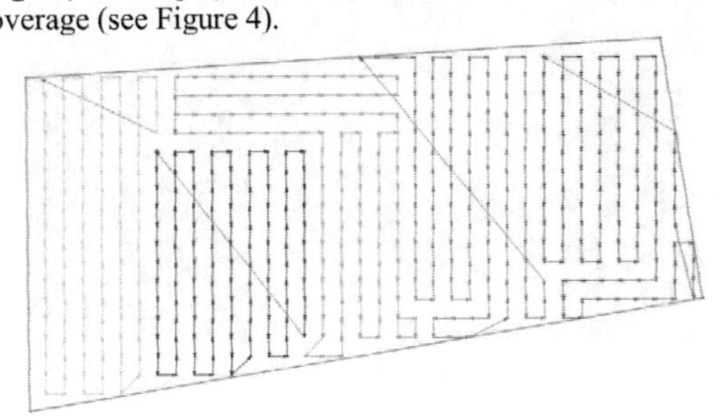

Figure 4. Pre-calculated Flightpath for five AS.

When using the ML-AIL in the MbO Demonstrator, preplanning is not intended. The AS acts autonomously and makes decisions based on the interpretation of the individual ML-AIL.

Following the classical reconnaissance approach, we use a linear feature distribution oriented horizontally (see Figure 5), vertically or along the main orientation of the target area. The special arrangement of the paths is defined by the resolution of the desired footprint, taking a potential overlap into account.

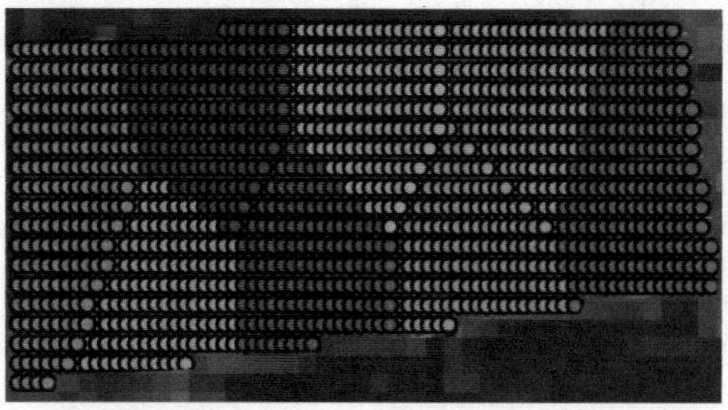

Figure 5. Linear Feature Distribution for 8 AS.

In order to allow evenly spaced tracks with a minimum of course adjustments, the features are compacted in the direction of the main axis. Without condensing the features in the ML-AFF in the direction of the main axis, the AS do not recognize the axis of operation when they are converted into local control commands. Accordingly, the decisions would lead to movements with significantly less focus, which creates disadvantages in terms of endurance and mission time.

B. *Area Reconnaissance based on Chaotic Profiles*

Regardless of the generation of the reconnaissance patterns, linear behaviors suffer from some drawbacks. In non-cooperative scenarios, when the searched object does not intent to be localized, or the objects to be searched are placed unfavorably with respect to the individual areas to be searched, a linear behavior may be disadvantageous. Chances to avoid detection are significantly higher when the movement pattern of the searchers are predictable since it is easy to anticipate which areas will be checked next.

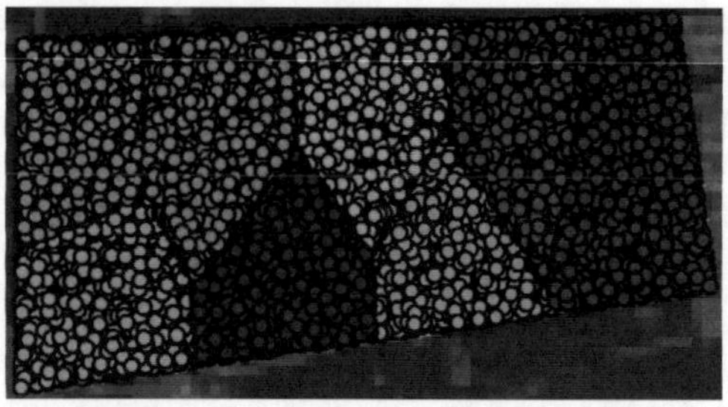

Figure 6. Chaotic Feature Distribution for 8 AS.

At the same time, large, contiguous areas remain unobserved for a long period. For this form of reconnaissance and surveillance missions, we introduced a chaotic, non-deterministic operational profile. For this purpose, the features for the operation area are not ordered linearly, but placed randomly and more densely (see Figure 6). At the same time, the features are generated with divergent properties in terms of their temporal existence and life cycle, resulting in a high fluctuation in the target layer of the ML-AIL. This fluctuation allows the AS to move unpredictably and individually in the operation area, regardless of the prior made movement decisions. In a short-term aspect this behavior leads to a more well-distributed coverage of the area, as the targets are not sequentially organized (all parts of the mission region are potentially visited next) and the feature distribution can attract the AS to search in a non-deterministic manor. However, this unpredictable behavior is bought by the drawback that a complete monitoring of the whole area, where all regions are reliable searched, is not guaranteed.

C. *Object Search based on Chaotic Profiles*

In contrast to the complete static area reconnaissance, where ideally every location is scanned only once by the sensor of the AS, the search for target objects in an area does not need to fulfill these requirements. In this case the mission target is to localize the searched objects as fast as possible. In case of static searched objects, the preconditions are close to the ones for the area reconnaissance. If targets are considered mobile, the complete coverage of the area cannot guarantee a detection rate of 100%, since a searched object may well pass undetected from a region not yet visited into a region already finally processed (active evasion) during the search phase.

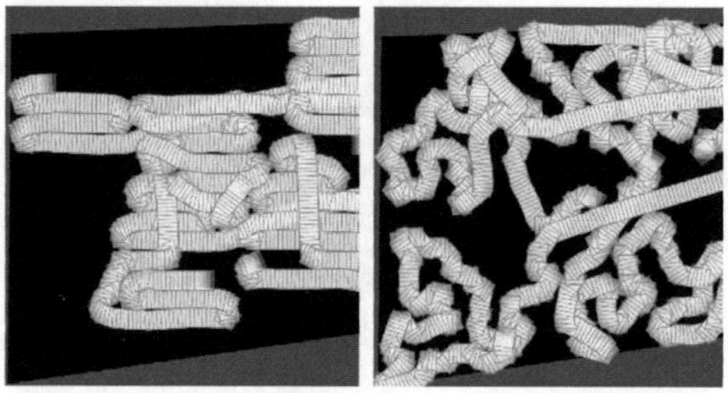

Figure 7. Left: linear reconnaissance of eight AS after 15 Minutes, right: chaotic reconnaissance of eight AS after 15 Minutes.

In this case, the proposed chaotic non-deterministic OP (see Figure 7, right side) provides some advantages over the deterministic one (see Figure 7, left side): First, the non-deterministic behavior of the AS does not allow the searched object to predict the operations of the searchers and, thus, makes it significantly more difficult to evade detection. Secondly, a scanned area is not excluded from further operations, so that even if the detection is successfully avoided, hiding in already scanned areas is not permanently promising.

D. *Area Reconnaissance with Mission Focus*

To fully exploit the strengths of a non-linear, chaotic search approach, mission planning should consider a priori information and co-translate it into feature data for the ML-AIL. In this scenario we assume that the entire mission area, as marked in the yellow rectangle (see Figure 9), is of importance. The probability that the searched objects are located on or close by the red marked areas (building, road, or forest edge) is assumed to be significantly higher than in the rest of the area.

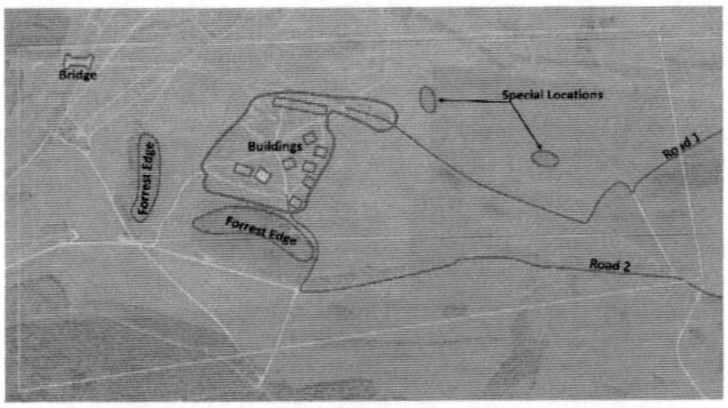

Figure 8. Mission area with high priority regions.

To have these areas searched preferably, mission planning must mark them as prioritized targets. The entire mission area is flooded with random distributed target features of variable expression, as in the basic chaotic approach. At the same time, features are placed in said regions that have a higher attraction and thus, will be preferably investigated. The chaotic, non-deterministic mission profile is preserved, while prioritizing appropriate objects and regions.

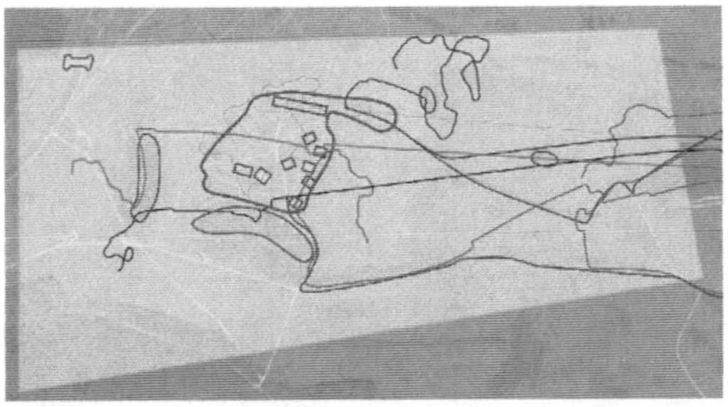

Figure 9. Chaotic Reconnaissance with high priority regions (eight AS after 15 Minutes).

Figure 9 shows that the cooperating AS are scanning the area according to the chaotic behavior profile. However, especially at the beginning of the mission, a variance can be recognized with respect to the regions marked with increased importance. The individual assets operate in their subareas with a primary focus on the prioritized regions.

V. RESULTS

To analyze efficiency and effectiveness of the proposed chaotic OPs in comparison with traditional approaches, a series of simulations were conducted and analyzed.

The simulation is conducted in a fixed mission area with a total size of 2.03 square kilometer, defined as the main target area (see also Figure 9). In order to increase the measurability and to simplify the evaluation procedure, a reduced sensor footprint is assumed, corresponding to a ground resolution of 60x60 meters. The position angles of the sensor carrier are not considered and thus, have no effect on the simulated footprint, except for direction changes. The footprint is steadily aligned in nadir. The team consists of homogeneous virtual AS, moving at a maximum speed of approximately 20 km/h and reaching a maximum rotation rate to the vehicle's rotation axis of 28 deg/s. Tests were performed with several simulated vehicles, while the main test series was limited to missions with 5 and 8 vehicles. To complement the measurements of the Reconnaissance Factor (RF) (percentage of overall scanned area), objects were randomly placed in the target area to be found in mission. A hidden object is considered found if it is inside the simulated sensor footprint. The mission duration is defined by the timespan necessary for the assets to conclude the preplanned linear operation path, but is extended to follow the development over time for the other OPs.

All four described methods were tested and compared:

1. Linear search with deterministic pre-planned paths.
2. Autonomous linear search with quasi deterministic search behavior
3. Aerial reconnaissance with non-deterministic motion profiles
4. Multi Target search with non-deterministic motion profiles and prioritized areas.

The analysis shows, that linear methods achieve satisfactory results in terms of the Reconnaissance Factor (RF) (see Figures 11-14). The meander-shaped motion profiles allow a continuous scanning of the entire area, where only few areas are left out. As outcome, the linear methods achieve a stable RF of more than 90% to the end of the mission with the selected movement pattern. This is valid for teams of five vehicles as well as for eight assets and can be qualified increased close to 100% using a higher overlap and full utilization of the area with a small extension in mission duration. Compared to the preplanned linear approach, the procedure degrades slightly when operating autonomously. This can be explained by the absent pre-mission optimization and the associated potential lengthened route traveled in case of a non-optimized area entry as well as transversal movements via already scanned areas, especially at the end of the mission in case of remaining isolated sub-areas.

Both, the chaotic and the multi-target chaotic procedures, can perform comparable, especially at the beginning of the mission. Significant performance losses manifests during the second half of the mission. This can be expected, since by design, the chaotic profiles do not exclude areas that have already been scanned from further processing. Thus, these areas are potentially scanned several times, while the trajectories are not aligned for minimal footprint overlap. In consequence, the profiles cannot compete with the linear optimized ones. The RF ranges from 60% to 80% at the end of the mission, depending on the mission type but reaches up to 90% in the simulation context with the appropriate time addition.

It can be observed, that increasing the number of assets in linear procedures, allows a continuous increase in performance, which in turn results in a reduction of the mission duration. However, it is most interesting to note that the chaotic procedures seem to benefit more from increasing the number of team members. In particular, the degradation of performance in the second half of the mission is significantly reduced by the use of eight assets compared to the mission with five assets, resulting in a final RF of more than 80% (compare Figure 10 and Figure 11).

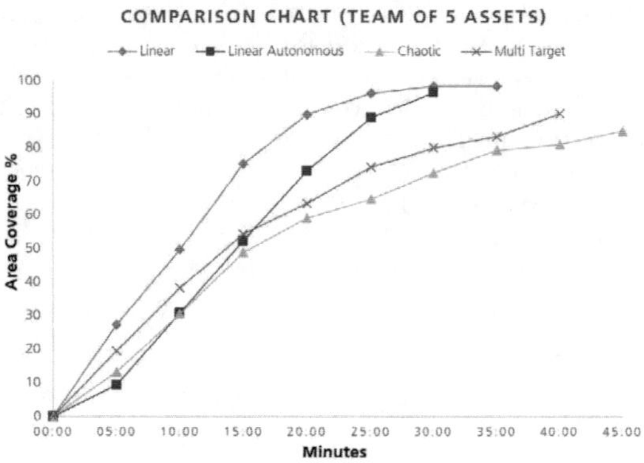

Figure 10. Comparison of mission performance for five AS.

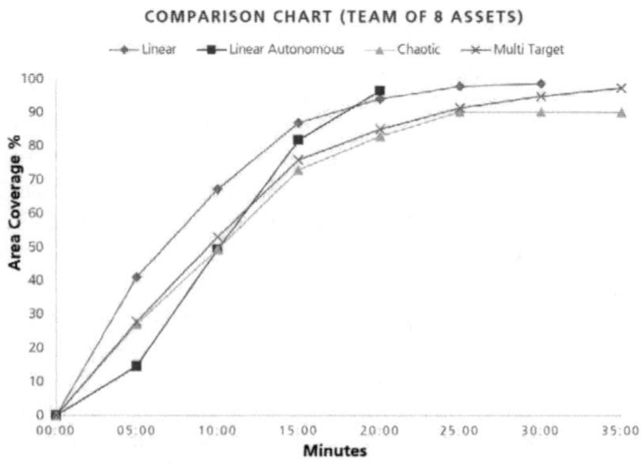

Figure 11. Comparison of mission performance for eight AS.

Analyzing the performance of the profiles regarding the detection of local static objects, the linear methods show merits to a limited extent. Especially at the beginning of the mission, the chaotic methods are at least on par or demonstrate significantly better results. During the second half of the mission, linear methods can catch up and compensate the weak start, while all methods tend to stagnate to the mission end (see Figure 12 and Figure 13).

The initial difficulties of the linear methods can be explained by the applied search patterns. Whether logically planned or linearly autonomously searched, the AS always start at a corner or edge of a region and work their way forward in a clearly structured manner. If targets are not present at the edges of the area the linear approach may take longer to achieve success. The chaotic procedures cover the area more evenly / widely distributed and thus, can show faster results in the first halve. In particular, the multi target method has an advantage over the purely random or linear methods, as the regions with an expected higher density of targets are prioritized.

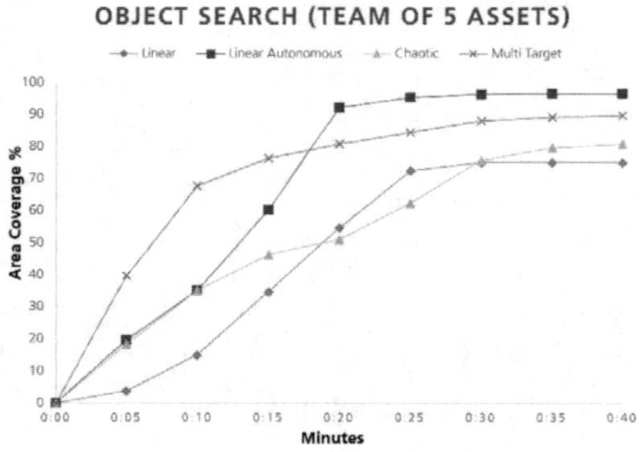

Figure 12. Comparison of object detection for five AS.

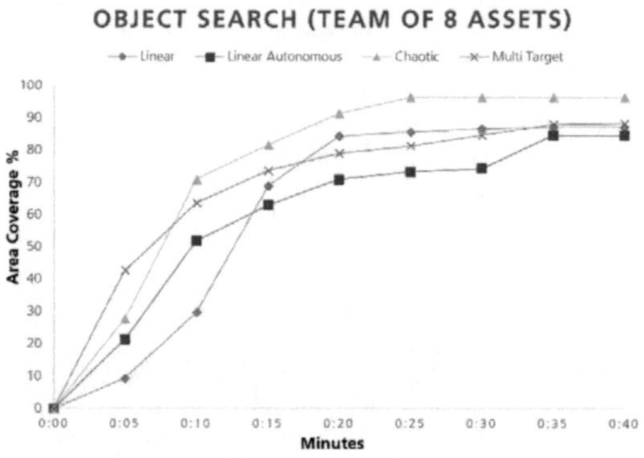

Figure 13. Comparison of Object Detection for Eight AS.

In the second half of the mission, this advantage is partially lost, which can also be explained by the multiple searched areas and the non-footprint-optimized path. As a result, significantly less area is observed (see also Figure 12 and Figure 13), which makes it more difficult for the search method to find the last targets.

VI. CONCLUSION AND FUTURE WORK

In this paper, we have presented and investigated several methods for team-based area reconnaissance. We have described how these methods are implemented in our MbO demonstrator to allow a team of vehicles (simulated or real) to cooperatively work on a joint mission.

Encoding a Multi-Layered AIL via varying feature deployment in the lower AI layer of the MbO demonstrator, based on the planning data provided by the higher AI control cycles, have been described and how the ML-AIL is used to generate action recommendations and consolidated decisions to control the physical vehicle. Since the translation of a mission objective into feature distribution is the essential step to enable efficient and effective mission delivery by multiple vehicles, we simulated procedures for cooperative area reconnaissance and search for hidden objects in teams of vehicles in the MbO demonstrator. This showed that, as expected, the proposed chaotic procedures perform less optimal in terms of RF compared to preplanned linear or autonomous linear procedures. At the same time, however, they offer advantages in terms of hidden object search, whilst the benefits of apparently chaotic movement profiles with regard to the unpredictability of the movement is not measurable in this context. Nevertheless, we expect a significantly improved search performance, especially in the case of non-cooperative evasive targets. As result the advantages of non-deterministic methods prevail the disadvantages in comparison to linear methods in applications that require an unpredictable behavior.

At the same time, the experiments have shown potential for future improvement of the non-deterministic methods. Especially, if the higher AI is qualified via advanced planning algorithms to provide an improved feature distribution and parameterization in the context of mission objectives and environmental data, we expect a performance increase that further reduces the deviation to the linear profiles. Increased cross-correlation of layers of the ML-AFF in the lower AI cycle, especially to account for sensor footprint and team behavior are additional promising candidates for further development and performance enhancement.

REFERENCES

[1] F. Segor, I. Tchouchenkov, A. Buller, M. Kollmann, and W. Müller, "Controlling swarm complexity: a management by objective approach," Open Architecture/Open Business Model Net-Centric Systems and Defense Transformation, vol. 11015, pp. 211-220, 2019.

[2] M. Schranz, M. Umlauft, M. Sende and W. Elmenreich, "Swarm Robotic Behaviors and Current Applications," Front. Robot. AI vol. 7, pp. 36, 2020, doi: 10.3389/frobt.2020.00036.2020.

[3] J. Barca and Y. Sekercioglu, "Swarm robotics reviewed," Robotica, vol. 31, pp. 345-359, 2013, doi:10.1017/S026357471200032X.

[4] R. Arnold, K. Carey, B. Abruzzo and C. Korpela, "What is A Robot Swarm: A Definition for Swarming Robotics," 2019 IEEE 10th Annual Ubiquitous Computing, Electronics & Mobile Communication Conference (UEMCON), New York, NY, USA, 2019, pp. 0074-0081, doi: 10.1109/UEMCON47517.2019.8993024.

[5] G. Tan, J. Zhuang, J. Zou, L. Wan and Z. Sun, "Artificial potential field-based swarm finding of the unmanned surface vehicles in the dynamic ocean environment," International Journal of Advanced Robotic Systems, vol. 17, no. 3, 2020.

[6] F. Bounini, D. Gingras, H. Pollart, and D. Gruyer, "Modified artificial potential field method for online path planning applications," 2017 IEEE Intelligent Vehicles Symposium IV, pp. 180-185, 2017, doi:10.1109/IVS.2017.7995717.

[7] H. Lyu and Y. Yin, "COLREGS-Constrained Real-time Path Planning for Autonomous Ships Using Modified Artificial Potential Fields," The Journal of Navigation, 72, pp. 588-608, 2018, doi:10.1017/S0373463318000796.

[8] P. Lin, W. Y. Choi, J. H. Yang, and C. C. Chung, "Waypoint Tracking for Collision Avoidance Using Artificial Potential Field, " Proceedings of the 39th Chinese Control Conference, pp. 5455-5460, 2020.

[9] A. L. Alfeo et al., "Urban Swarms: A new approach for autonomous waste management," 2019 International Conference on Robotics and Automation (ICRA), pp. 4233-4240, 2019, doi: 10.1109/ICRA.2019.8794020.

[10] J. A. Sauter and K. Bixler, "Design of unmanned swarm tactics for an urban mission," Proc. SPIE 11021, Unmanned Systems Technology XXI, vol. 110210, pp. 124-139, May 2019, doi: 10.1117/12.2518116.

[11] W. Liu, X. Zheng, and Z. Deng, „Dynamic collision avoidance for cooperative fixed-wing UAV swarm based on normalized artificial potential field optimization," J. Cent. South Univ. 28, 3159–3172, 2021, https://doi.org/10.1007/s11771-021-4840-5.

[12] F. Segor, A. Bürkle, M. Kollmann, and R. Schönbein, "Instantaneous Autonomous Aerial Reconnaissance for Civil Applications - A UAV based approach to support security and rescue forces," 6th International Conference on Systems ICONS, pp. 72-76, 2011.

[13] E. Santamaria, F. Segor, and I. Tchouchenkov, "Rapid aerial mapping with multiple heterogeneous unmanned vehicles," ISCRAM, vol. 6, pp. 592–596, 2013.

[14] R. R. Hashemi, L. Jin, G. T. Anderson, E. Wilson and M. R. Clark, "A comparison of search patterns for cooperative robots operating in remote environment," Proceedings International Conference on Information Technology: Coding and Computing, Las Vegas, NV, USA, 2001, pp. 668-672, doi: 10.1109/ITCC.2001.918874.

[15] Y.-H. Choi, T.-K. Lee, S.-H. Baek, and S.-Y. Oh, "Online complete coverage path planning for mobile robots based on linked spiral paths using constrained inverse distance transform," IEEE/RSJ International Conference on Intelligent Robots and Systems, 2009. IROS 2009, pp. 5788 -5793.

[16] G. M. Fricke, J. P. Hecker, A. D. Griego, L. T. Tran and M. E. Moses, "A distributed deterministic spiral search algorithm for swarms," 2016 IEEE/RSJ International Conference on Intelligent Robots and Systems (IROS), Daejeon, Korea (S), 2016, pp. 4430-4436, doi: 10.1109/IROS.2016.7759652.

[17] M. L. Cummings, S. Bruni, S. Mercier and P. J. Mitchell, "Automation Architecture for Single Operator, Multiple UAV Command and Control," Technical Report, Massachusetts Institute of Technology: Cambridge, MA, USA, 2007.

[18] L-F. Bluhm, C. Lassen, L. Keiser, and J. Hasbach, "Swarm View: Situation Awareness of Swarms in Battle Management Systems," STO-MP-SCI-341, 2021.

[19] M. L. Cummings and P. J. Mitchell, "Predicting Controller Capacity in Supervisory Control of Multiple UAVs," in IEEE Transactions on Systems, Man, and Cybernetics - Part A: Systems and Humans, vol. 38, no. 2, pp. 451-460, March 2008, doi: 10.1109/TSMCA.2007.914757.

[20] B. Mekdeci, and M. L. Cummings, "Modeling Multiple Human Operators in the Supervisory Control of Heterogeneous Unmanned Vehicles," A. f. Machinery, Proceedings of the 9th Workshop on Performance Metrics for Intelligent Systems, (S. 1-8). Gaithersburg, Maryland, 2009, doi:10.1145/1865909.1865911.

[21] C. R. Tinoco and G. M. B. Oliveira, "Heterogeneous Teams of Robots using a Coordinating Model for Surveillance Task based on Cellular Automata and Repulsive Pheromone," 2019 IEEE Congress on Evolutionary Computation (CEC), 2019, pp. 747-754, doi: 10.1109/CEC.2019.8790266.

[22] J. T. Ebert, M. Gauci, and R. Nagpal, "Multi-Feature Collective Decision Making in Robot Swarms," In Proceedings of the 17th International Conference on Autonomous Agents and MultiAgent Systems (AAMAS '18). International Foundation for Autonomous Agents and Multiagent Systems, Richland, SC, 1711–1719, 2018.

[23] G. Wang et al., "Emergent Field-Driven Robot Swarm States," Phys Rev Lett. 2021 vol. 126, no. 10, pp. 108002.

Applying Multimodal Data to Meta Learning for Time-Series Analysis in CPS

Philipp Ruf, Christoph Reich
Institute for Data Science, Cloud Computing and Security *(IDACUS)*
Hochschule Furtwangen University (HFU)
Furtwangen, Germany
email:{Philipp.Ruf, Christoph.Reich}@hs-furtwangen.de

Djaffar Ould-Abdeslam
IRIMAS
Université de Haute-Alsace (UHA)
Mulhouse, France
email: djaffar.ould-abdeslam@uha.fr

***Abstract*—Up until now, it has been shown that big parts of the so called Industry 4.0 are impacted by Machine Learning (ML) in some way or another. In many shopfloor situations, there are different sensors involved and all data is eventually structured, accumulated and prepared for application in various ML-based scenarios, e.g., predictive maintenance of a machine, quality monitoring of manufactured workpieces or handling domain-specific aspect of the respective fabricator or product. As the physical environment of Cyber Physical System (CPS) can change rapidly, the overall Data Acquisition (DAQ) process and ML training is impacted, too. This work focuses on datasets which consist of small amounts of tabular information and how to utilize them in image-based Neural Networks (NN) with respect to meta learning and multimodal transformations. Therefore, the conceptual utilization of an DAQ system in industrial environments is discussed regarding a variety of techniques for preprocessing and generating visual material from multimodal data. The outcome of such operations is a new dataset which is then applied in model training. Therefore, the presented approach is three-fold. In first analysing the concept of predicting the similarity of structured and numerical data in different datasets, indicators of the feasibility when applying the methodology in related but more sophisticated learning scenarios can be gained. Although ongoing time-series data is differing from simple multi-class data in terms of a chronologically dimension, basic classification concepts are applied to it and evaluated. In order to extend the similarity prediction with a temporal component, the discussed methods are extended by multimodal transformations and an subsequent utilization in Siamese Neural Networks (SNN). By discussing the concept of applying visual representations of structured time-series data in a meta-learning context, known trends and historic information can be utilized for generating real-world test-samples and predicting their validity on inference.**

Keywords*—*Data Acquisition; Time-Series Analysis; Multimodal Data; Meta Learning; Cyber Physical Systems.

I. INTRODUCTION

In recent years, the application of Machine Learning (ML) techniques has increased in many parts of the manufacturing domain. Since industrial-grade Internet of Things (IoT) setups, which are also known as Cyber-physical System (CPS), are fusing more and more with ML-based solutions, the term Artificial Intelligence of Things (AIoT) [1] has also been introduced as descriptive expression. The complexity of such a system is increasing with the utilization of additional sensors which are distributed in the environment or placed inside the manufacturing machines. Therefore, concepts regarding a fully integrated and distributed ML-based Continuous Integration/ Continuous Delivery (CI/CD) pipelines [2] can enhance the overall project structure and management. There are many different quality properties when it comes to CPS-based data [3], [4], especially when it is applied in an subsequent ML model training or inference phase.

In reality, there are situations in which only a few data points are available for the utilization in the training a model. Current proposals which tackle such restrictions are summarized as Few-Shot Learning (FSL) [5], where one differs between transfer learning and a variety of meta-learning techniques, e.g., metric-, optimization- and model-based approaches. Metric learning is commonly assessing the similarity or dissimilarity of two samples, based on a calculation which corresponds to their respective distances [6]. Thereby, the distances between mismatches is maximized while the length of an edge to a positive element, e.g., a matching sample, is minimized, enabling analysis through clusters. One metric-based FSL technique makes use of so called Siamese Neural Network (SNN)s, which utilizes a pair of identical neural networks which are sharing the same weights for processing the respective element of a sample pair, eventually determine their distances. This enables real-world applications, as for example calculating the similarity of hand-written signatures or the structure of human faces [7], where only a few data points of each class are used during model training. Although there are some established strategies for producing effective Convolutional Neural Network (CNN)-based ML models from only a few structured data points, the majority of published work targets image-based implementations. When there are multiple modalities of a specific happening, the transformation and fusion of multimodal data [8], e.g., generating another representation of a modality or combining them, is often part of the solution. Such approaches are usually of generative nature, based on a pre-defined grammar or is utilizing dictionaries for translating between unimodal signal structures. When transforming and fusing structured modalities within a unstructured modality as in a visual representation, established image-based frameworks can be utilized anyhow. Another aspect of this work is the transformation of different datasets samples into visual data, e.g., creating image representations of the *Iris* [9] dataset, the *"Mill Data Set"* [10] as well as of the *Sunspots* [11] dataset.

In addition to applying such new and synthetically generated datasets for training a model in SNN manner, additional experiments are considering ML approaches regarding the original, numeric data. In visualizing and comparing results of the respective approaches across the three varying datasets, selected aspects of utilizing meta-learning approaches for classifying multimodal time-series data are discussed.

A brief overview of requirements in the AIoT domain, as well as procedures regarding multimodal data transformation and applicable meta-learning methods is given in Section II. By discussing the overall methodology and utilized datasets in Section III, a deeper contextual understanding of the experiments, which are carried out and discussed in Section IV, can be gained. The work on hand is concluded in Section V.

II. Related Work

In the last years, the potential of end-user IoT hardware has evolved significantly, even allowing for small-scale CPS setups. In [12], the ML-focused Data Acquisition (DAQ) system dAta collectoR sysTem witH distribUted sensoRs (ARTHUR) was proposed, suggesting Raspberry-Pi hardware as worker nodes in combination with a distributed edge-cloud environment. In [13], a comprehensive overview of the AIoT domain is given, clarifying enabling technologies and architectural elements of distributed and ML-dependent operations. By considering Artificial Intelligence (AI) tools for utilization in the IoT domain, a overview of potential use-cases and open challenges is discussed. Although the ARTHUR system is applicable in the work on hand, no holistic view of comprehensive hardware considerations or use-case specifics is given.

In [8], the different approaches in the domain of multimodal ML are extensively discussed. When having multiple modalities of a specific event or happening, as for example acoustic emission, vibration data, temperature and a visual observations, there are situations in which a *multimodal fusion* can be appropriate. In using such an approach, there is an increased robustness of predictions due to handling missing values by design, as well as exposing complementary information which may be missed when processing unimodal samples by themselves. Although multimodal transformations are used on various datasets throughout the work on hand, the focus is on applying the resulting representation with respect to a time-series classification. Obviously, the feature-dimension, e.g., modalities, of available samples is also impacting the choice of an target representation. In [14], a simple two-dimensional plot of numeric values was applied to a CNN for further classification. Naturally, this transformation must be well-defined, which is why multiple preprocessing steps like cropping, rotating or framing had to be carried out. The approach of generating visual material differs from the proposal on hand, although a well-defined target transformation is necessary for stable predictions. The augmentation of image data was discussed in [15], where a variety of visual manipulation techniques were described with respect to their utilization in deep learning approaches. Although approaches like kernel filters, random erasing or color space transmissions could be part of the multimodal transformation or simply be utilized for increasing the available test- and training data, no additional augmentation was implemented in the work on hand. In [16], a solution to a temporal Common Representation Learning (CRL) problem regarding image and time-series data was introduced. The main idea is that the additional result of an image classification is enhancing the time-series classification task based on a triplet loss calculation, while the actual inference of the model is exclusively concerned with time-series data. In both synthetic, e.g., time-series sinus value with noise and Gramian Angular Summation Field (GASF) image representation, and real-world handwriting recognition datasets, the cross-modal triplet selection enhanced the inference even though only the main-modality was present. In [17], numeric data was used for generating image filters which were applied to a base-image in order to classify tabular data. Therein, a specifically formed matrix was converted into a convolutional kernel which was applied in the CNN, significantly altering the base-image in a recognizable and class-dependent manner.

In general, deep metric learning consists of informative input samples, structure of the network model, as well as a metric loss function [6]. In the context of chosing a metric loss function, there are various approaches for finding relations between samples [18] and relations between the respective sample's features. Usually approaches are based on distance metrics [6], which are implemented in order to assess sample distances in a triplet, e.g., an anchor element and a positive, as well as a negative element. The aim is to learn a metric which represents negative element further away from the anchor, than the positive element. In his studies regarding the likeness of different human races, Mahalanobis proposed a measure procedure in 1930, where the *Mahalanobis Distance* was applied for the purpose of craniometry, e.g., determining the proportions of the human skull. Since then, his method was increasingly applied and extended in a variety of domains [19], ranging from archaeology to medical diagnosis and remote sensing while solving a multitude of problems like classification, numerical taxonomy or statistical pattern recognition. In [18], the Sparse Compositional Metric Learning (SCML) approach was introduced, where the focus was on learning the Mahalanobis distances which are parameterized by a positive semidefinite square matrix. The metrics are learned as a sparse combination of rank-one basis elements, enabling local, global and multitask metric learning.

In [20], a approach for learning to determine the identity of a masked person was proposed, where a triplet loss function is applied for learning meta-features by considering positive and negative examples within a SNN while using only a few image samples during the training. In [21], a unsupervised meta learning method was proposed in the context of multivariate time-series, e.g., data that contains multiple time-dependent features. A time- and memory efficient system was proposed for learning the universal embeddings in time-series datasets, using an encoder which employs dilated causal convolutions, as well as triplets where elements can be of varying length. Although there is the commonality of triplet creation in time-series data, the approach on hand focuses on the classification of potential future samples. In [22], a framework for image-based feature extraction regarding visual time-series data was proposed with respect to plant phenotyping, e.g., observations of biologic material over time. Therein, a novel transfer learning approach of finding feature representations from image time-series data was proposed. In applying an pretrained *ImageNet* architecture as basic feature extractor, triplet based learning is applied for reducing dimensionality. A siamese-like architecture was proposed, where a series of five temporal subsequent images are processed by five SNN, each consisting of a feature extractor and a ranking module. In [23], two ML approaches, e.g., using a CNN, as well as an SNN, were presented for analyzing supernova phenomenon time-series data with respect to the classification of spectral light-curves, e.g., deciding if the combination of green, red near-infrared and infrared is a type 'I.a supernovae' or not. The CNN approach is initially processing a matrix with four rows, each of which is representing a ongoing color time-series, transforming it into a one-dimensional representation and subsequently analyzing and classifying the sample combination. In the SNN approach, an additional anchor element, which is a subset of the actual anchor's time-series data, is applied in order to tackle the sparsity of available data. Although the work on hand is utilizing SNN technology for classification, the primal focus is on using multimodal transformations in a temporal context.

III. Environment and Methodology of the Experiments

The generic and distributed DAQ system ARTHUR [12] can be applied for rapid prototyping of productive CPS environments with respect to streaming data, it's analysis and utilizing AI operations, while relying on low-cost end-user IoT hardware and open source technologies. The DAQ showcases are demonstrated using a *Redis* streaming system for transmitting data originating from different sensors, which are mounted on Raspberry Pi embedded devices, towards a cloud infrastrucure. Every shopfloor, e.g., a collection of spatial close worker nodes, is managed by a coordinating node and occurring data can be preprocessed, e.g., cleansed, taken into consideration for aggregation or even be utilized in other quality assuring procedures like applying ML models for predicting live insights into manufacturing processes. In Figure 1, the context of applying deep integrated systems like ARTHUR is depicted in a high-level manner with respect to the overall methodology of the approach on hand. Every worker node is equipped with a so called Digital Twin (DT), which is the intermediate between the phsyical and digital world, e.g., a set of logic for actuating the physical as well as the digital environment according to sensed information. By implementing the multimodal transformation of information which was gathered regarding one or multiple shopfloors, devices or sensors, in a cloud environment, virtual resources

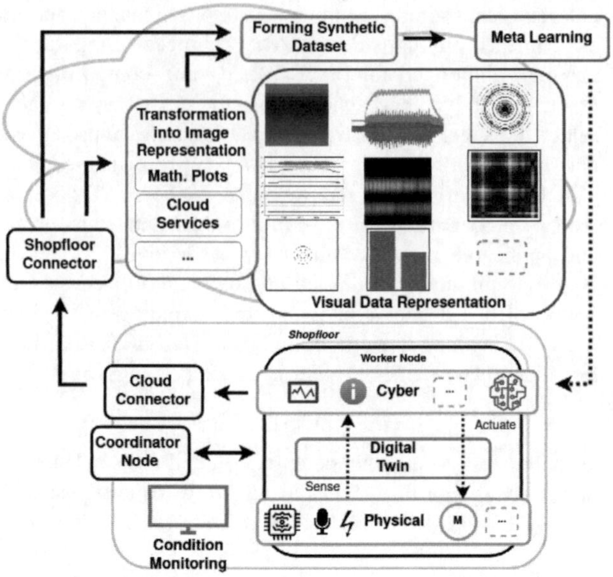

Figure 1. A High-level depiction of the overall pipeline of transforming structured shopfloor data into visual material and its utilization within cloud-based machine learning environments.

can be utilized. With subsequently processing the generated dataset in multiple meta learning approaches, a way of training models for a multitude of situations is given. In deploying the resulting model at a respective worker or coordination node, added value can be created for multiple use-cases, as for example predictive maintenance, the quality of a respective work piece, an assessment of a manufacturing machines tools, and many others.

A. Utilized Datasets

In the following, three relative simple but fundamentally differing and well-known datasets are described with respect to their utilization for meta-learning in Section IV. While choosing them, a restriction was that each of them should differ in the primarily domain of application or utilization, e.g., data for classification of samples, for finding trends and for classification in the context of time-series data.

1) Iris: The *Iris* [9] dataset consists of 150 samples of three different flower species, differing in petal and sepal length and width. Specifics of how the respective species are distinguishing themselves from each others can be obtained from Figure 2-a, which contains all available values. In this balanced dataset, no kind of preprocessing other than translating the respective species labels into a numerical representation has been done for the experiments. Although there are many possibilities of applying the Iris dataset, there is no relation to an additional dimension for expressing variations in time.

2) NASA Milling: The well known *NASA Ames & UC Berkeley "Mill Data Set"* [10] contains multimodal data of a milling machine's runs under various operating conditions and is content of several works. In [24], a summary of best

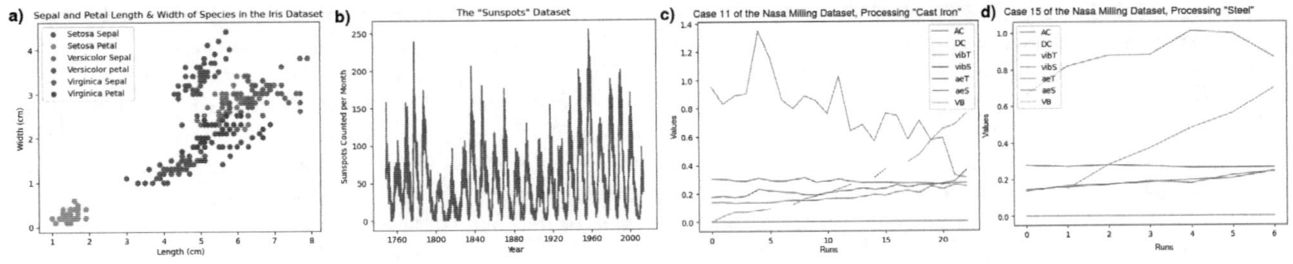

Figure 2. Depiction of datasets which were utilized in the experiments: a) Values in the Iris dataset; b) Plot of the Sunspots dataset; c) & d) Measured tool-wear values (VB) across two cases in the NASA Milling dataset, expressing the mean values of processing two different materials throughout multiple runs.

practices for applying ML in Computer Numeric Control (CNC) machining was given, while considering the dataset from [10]. Therein, each of the recorded runs was visually inspected with the aim of selecting an approximate region of *stable cutting* and additionally extract *sub-cuts* using a sliding-window of 1024 data points, which were labeled according to [25]. In [26], the concept of autoencoders is demonstrated for predicting the tool wear over time using self-supervised ML techniques and anomaly detection with respect to the Milling [10] dataset. The dataset contains data of 167 distinct recordings of occurred vibration, acoustic emission and consumed current of an spindle's individual cuts on different working material types. There are 16 cases, varying in amount of cuts from six to 23, where different parameters are applied, e.g., material type, feed rate of the cutting tool and the depth of an cut. For each of the 167 cuts, 9000 sampling points were collected at 250Hz and persisted within an structured MATLAB array. After each of the recordings, a manual assessment, e.g., an numeric representation *VB*, was carried out with respect to the tool's flank wear, manually measuring the tool's unwanted contact with already finished parts of an workpiece using an microscope. According to [25], the flank wear status can be interpreted as healthy when $VB < .2mm$, worn or degraded when $.2mm < VB < .7mm$ and failed when $VB > .7mm$ is exceeded. Given that definition of an appropriate working condition, the obvious approach is a three-class classification problem. When applying this interpretation to the whole dataset, a representation of the VB's distribution can be further taken into consideration regarding the most appropriate ML strategy. On one hand, a ML model which utilizes a binary classification with respect to a VB threshold of $.2mm$ is presumably directly applicable. On the other hand, a more granular view of the tool wear could be applied in business models where non-premium customers are satisfied with products which were manufactured with a certain degree of tolerance.

In Figure 2-c, the median values across the 11th case in the dataset are plotted. For the sake of visibility, the power consumption, e.g., information regarding AC and DC during the runs, was set to zero as it would conceal graphs of the vibration and acoustic emission. Therein, it is clearly visible that the VB value is increasing over the 23 runs of case 11 when processing cast iron. In comparison with the processing of a steel-based workpiece, a different course of sensed information is recognizable, as shown in Figure 2-d.

There was a certain kind of preprocessing necessary for further utilization in the experiments. First, the milling data [10] was extracted from the matlab structure and visually inspected. Although the majority of runs are free from sensing errors, some obviously inaccurate recordings can be determined by considering the plotted information. Those specific runs had been manually excluded from the experiment. By associating all available runs to the respective measured tool wear status, e.g., healthy, degraded or failed, three classes can be distinguished. Since there are samples for which no such value has been measured, a median value is calculated between the surrounding runs where the flank wear was determined.

3) Sunspots: The *Sunspots* [11] dataset consists of monthly observations regarding the number of counted sunspots, e.g., activities at the surface of the sun. Although there is only one target value, e.g., the number counted within a respective month as depicted in Figure 2-b, there are many observations ranging from January 1749 until September 2013, resulting in 3177 ongoing time-depended data points. Although there are well-proven and established preprocessing techniques for time-series data like normalizing values, solely the original data was considered in the experiments.

B. Visual Representation of Structured Data

Although the data available in CPS environments is usually structured, e.g., numerical values, a transformation of these modalities into visual material is almost always possible. When effectively applying a CNN as feature extractor regarding visual material, the focus is primarily on textures, e.g., a distinction between intact grass and burned grass will be more successful than learning to predict the number of grass stalks within a picture. In Figure 1, examples of data transformation are contained and some of them are exemplary discussed in the following, although there are virtually no boundaries to creativity.

1) *Feature-wise Color Pixels*: Each numeric feature of a sample can be represented by a RGB color representation, e.g, three features may be normalized to values from zero to 255. On the other hand, each feature may

be represented by a gray-scale pixel. When consistently concatenate such pixel representations, time-series can be expressed, which is also true for all following transformations.

2) *Geometric Shapes*: There is a multitude of two-dimensional shapes which can be applied as feature representation, e.g., cubes, circles or triangles, where a second dimension may be expressed by the color, stroke-width or filling of the shape with a color map. Dependent on amount of features per sample pentagons, heptagons and higher-dimensional shapes can be build or multiple basic shapes may be projected on top of each other.
3) *Visual Data Analysis Approaches*: Dependent on the dataset, different approaches like pie charts, bars, lines or cycle plots can be applied as representation of multivariate data. When for example generating a polygon radar plot, the feature's value is corresponding to a vertex within the plot, preserving their relative magnitude.
4) *Time-Series Plots*: When there is a temporal component to a dataset, the values can simply be represented by a line- or scatter plot, where multiple modalities are specifically colored or styled. Dependent on the respective problem, a grid, axis, labels and legends can be either an obstacle or support when analyzed by the CNN.
5) *Gramian Angular Fields*: This method effectively interprets a time-series as an polar coordinate system, which is then transformed into an Gramian Angular Field representation. As there are many textures within the resulting image, it is assumed to be an appropriate transformation for utilization within an CNN.

C. Utilizing Triplets with Time Series Data

In the following, a brief overview of the applied distance learning and sampling strategies is given.

a) Learning with SCML: As the SCML methodology is by now a established approach, it will be utilized in experiments where only numerical data is considered. This well-performing meta-learning technique will be used for creating (baseline) models, which will be assessed and compared to performances of subsequent experiments.

b) Learning with Siamese Neural Networks: One assumption of the work in hand is, that when the amount of existing image representations is way to low for traditional ML approaches, it may be sufficient for SNN-based approaches anyhow. Commonly, SNN architectures are created with respect to the comparison of two visual inputs. Throughout the three datasets, the capability of processing visual representations of numeric data in SNNs is investigated.

c) Triplet Sampling for Time-Series Data: Although there are many real-world applications of predicting the similarity of two data points, no standard exists regarding the crafting of triplets with respect to time-series data. Another aspect to consider is that the problem formulation is moved from predicting a class affiliation by the relation of anchor, positive and negative elements, towards an assessment of their respective appropriateness. When considering classification with respect to a regression problem, an *approximate regression* may be conducted by classification, e.g., a situation in which well-defined classes are utilized as a representation of an associated value. The choice of such a strategy may also be impacted by a multitude of aspects, as one might for example differentiate if possible data values are recurrent, exponential, linear or seemingly random. For example, there can be a static or dynamic 'sliding window', where triplet elements are positive when the window has proceeded the anchor within a certain threshold, negative respectively when the threshold was exceeded, e.g., learning to predict if a specific time-frame is associated with a preceding one. Another strategy may be a distinction and classification by splits for days, weeks, months or certain events. One might also copy the positive sample as the negative but overwriting a specific part with random or conditional values. A completely different approach was proposed in [21], where samples can be of different length and the positive element is a random subset of the anchor time-series, while the negative element is outside the anchor time frame, another modality respectively when multivariate time-series data is available. In [22], six triplets are defined for a pre-defined "time course", where direclty neighboring elements, e.g., t+1, are treated as positives and non-neighboring elements as negative element. Specifics of the further applied approach for utilizing time-series data in distance learning by forming triplets is depicted in Figure 3. The values involved in this example are depicted as circle representation and associated with eight consecutive events, e.g., *t0 - t7* of the Sunspots [11] dataset, e.g., sample nr. 1000 to 1007 which are observations between April and November of 1832. Throughout this example, it is recognizable that the *Frame Length* is constant over all triplet elements and amounts to four. In order to form a positive triplet element, the initial frame which is expressed by the anchor element, e.g., *t0 - t3*, is shifted by the amount of *Positive Offset* to the succeeding position, e.g., *t1 - t4*. A negative or non-conforming element is formed by selecting elements within a time-window of length *Negative Length*, which is positioned *Negative Offset* elements in the future regarding when the positive element has ended, and overwriting the end of the positive time-frame with it.

IV. Experiment Description

In the following experiments, the datasets which were described in Section III-A are applied to different meta-learning approaches. In addition to processing the raw data for learning a metric with SCML, synthetic datasets are formed by generating different data representations and train on them in an SNN. The experiments aim at investigating different possibilities of multimodal data transformations with respect to meta learning in an temporal context.

A. Learning Classification Metrics

Although the Iris [9] dataset has no temporal component, it was applied during experiments as additional indicator of the respective methodologies appropriateness. When forming triplets with elements of the three classes and implement a

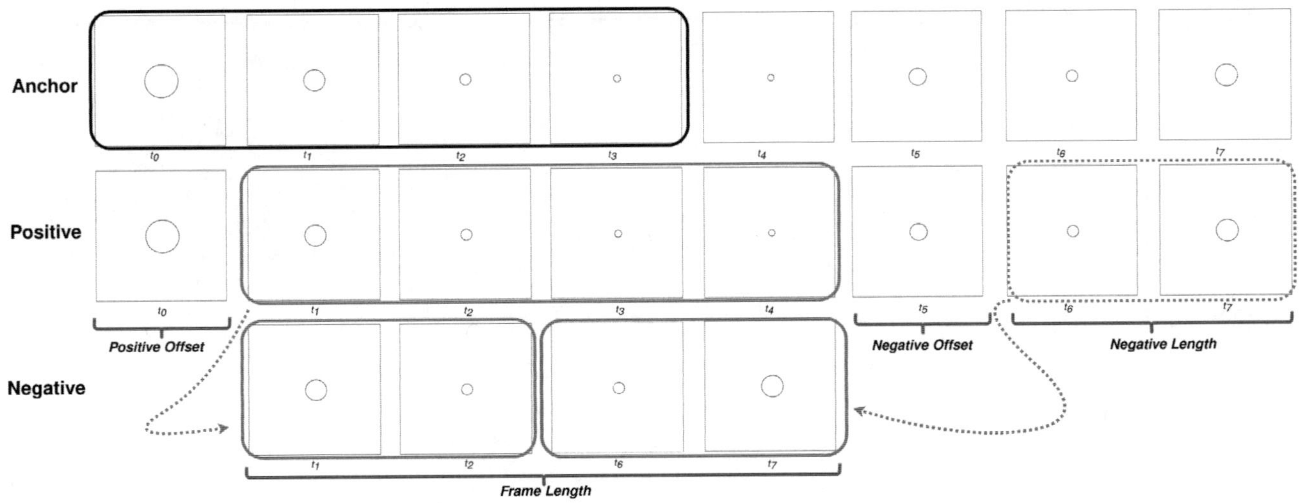

Figure 3. An example of the configurable parameters when forming triplets in ongoing unimodal time-series data, using circle representations.

random selection of the negative class, the performance of a SCML models is exceeding 90% accuracy with even a very smal amount of triplets, as depicted in Figure 4-a. The SCML algorithm was additionally applied to a simplified version of the NASA milling time-series dataset. Based on the flank wear status metric as defined in [25], three classes were considered, creating conditions similar to the Iris dataset. For synthetically decreasing the available information in training, solely the the minimum, maximum and median of values associated with a single run, e.g., power consumption, acoustic emission and vibration values of the complete time-series, were considered, alongside the processed material. The results are depicted in Figure 4-b and are supporting the assumption that measuring of distances between data points which represent different states can be applied in such time-series prediction scenarios, too.

B. Classification in Time-Series Forecasting

As there is no classification in the Sunspots [11] time-series dataset, triplets have been generated by a configurable function, as already described in Section III-C. The impact of all applicable parameters was investigated in multiple benchmarks, where the SCML model training indicated that different offset sizes have not a huge impact within this dataset. Therefore, the subsequent experiments results are depicted in Figure 4-c, where different total- and negative frame lengths were tested and results suggest that the negative frame length is the most impacting parameter. This was confirmed during experiments where the *Positive Offset* parameter was set to the value of *Negative Length*, where comparable results were achieved.

C. Classifying Image Representations in CNN

In order to assess the capabilities of SNN regarding a visual representation of structured data, multimodal transformations were carried out, beginning with the *Iris* [9] dataset. Beginnig with the official tensorflow tutorial examples on CNNs and making minor adjustments in the dense layer and loss function, a grayscaled *Filled Pie* representation was passing the 90% threshold within six epochs. The aim of the actual, subsequent, experiment was to reach this encouraging result using the same transformations in an SNN.

D. Classification of Time-Series in SNN

With having promising results from the previous experiments which were based on structured data, the following image-based approaches were conducted. The SNN architecture begins with implementing a batch normalization of the inputs, followed by a two-dimensional convolutional layer with a stride of 2x2, 16 filters and 'tanh' activation function. Afterwards, a two-dimensional average pooling layer with a pool-size of 2x2 is applied. This combination of convolutions and average pooling resumes to 32, 64, 128 and finally 256 filters, before it is flattened, normalized and applied to a dense layer with 'l2' kernel regularizer, 'tanh' activation function and ten units. This SNN structure is effective utilized as feature extractor of the information present in the image representations and trained with categorical crossentropy, RMSProp optimization with a learning rate of 0.001 and an euclidean distance function. In training multiple models with different amounts of triplets, viable results are emerging, as depicted in Figure 4-d.

1) Milling: For demonstrating the utilization of tabular data in image-based ML methods, the numeric values of the mill dataset [10] were transformed into various visual representations, divided into test- and train sets and subsequently fed to an SNN in order to train a model for categorizing the flank wear of an work piece. A simple RGB plot transformation was applied regarding the various runs modalities, e.g., acoustic emission, power consumption and vibration. The results of training on different amounts of triplets in this three-class

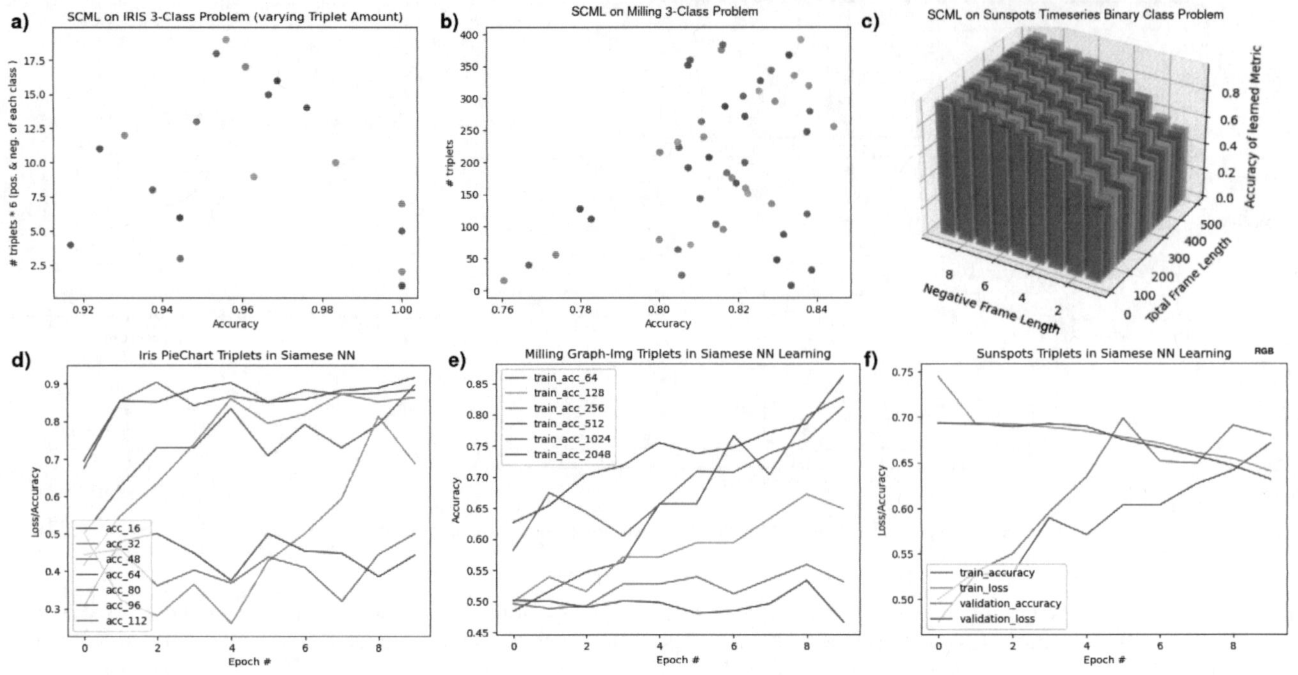

Figure 4. Results of the Experiments: **a)** *SCML* on different amounts of triplets for classifying samples in the Iris dataset; **b)** *SCML* on minimum, maximum and median values in the NASA Milling dataset; **c)** Impact of the 'Negative Length' parameter training on different amounts of triplets with positive and negative offset of 1; **d)** *SNN* training on grayscale *Pie-Chart* transformation in the Iris dataset; **e)** Training a *SNN* with different amounts of triplets in the NASA Milling dataset consisting of the particular signals *RGB plots*; **f)** Training a *SNN* with all possible Sunspots sample triplets with Frame-Length of 23, offsets of 1 and Negative-Frame-Length of 4, transformed as *Gramian Angular Field* RGB image.

classification problem are depicted in Figure 4-e. Therein, an accuracy similar to when utilizing SCML is recognizable.

2) Sunspots: Since there is only one value in samples of this time-series data, it cannot be put into relation with another modality. Therefore, the *Gramian angular field* transformation was applied to the Sunspots [11] dataset. Since the total frame length parameter of a triplet element is apparently not a impacting factor, a window-length of 23 was chosen. In setting the offsets both to one and configuring the negative frame length to four, results similar to when training a SCML model on numeric data were expected. In Figure 4-f, the results of this experiment are shown.

E. Discussion of the Obtained Results

All in all, the experiments with SCML achieved good accuracy results, even on a small amount of training triplets. Although the chosen transformations have a heavy impact on the feature extraction of SNN approaches, the results indicate a comparative accuracy. In comparing different learning approaches or variations in their configuration, the significance of model candidates can be determined. There are also situations, where depending on the problem on hand and the amount of available data, such examinations require the concurrent long-term utilization of multiple ML models on production data.

1) Structured Data: The experiments with the Iris [9] and Milling [10] dataset have shown, that a classification based on the numeric values is realizable using an approach of distance-based SCML. In Figures 4 a) and d), it can be found that the random selection of triplets is causing doubtable results, e.g., accuracy scores of 1.0, where triplets are heavily biased. As there is a decent score for SCML computations right away, the SNN approach begins to perform on $triplets \geq 80$ and stabilizes after four epochs. When considering Figures 4 b) and e), an related aspect is the flank wear assessment, which is causing an unbalanced dataset interpretation as there are naturally less samples for runs with a failed tool than for degraded or healthy ones. Another point is that the image representation in e) contains more information in terms of signals when compared to the SCML experiment from b), but is missing the type of processed material.

2) Similarity in Time-Series Classification: When considering Figures 4 c) and f), the experimentation with the Sunspots [11] dataset suggests that with a growing *negative frame lenght* parameter, accuracy is non-stop increasing. The chosen total and negative frame length of 23 and for is scoring approximately 75% accuracy with SCML approach as contrasted with nearly 70% after eight epochs of training on the SNN, while the loss is steadily decreasing. Although the used dataset may allow for an arbitrary elevation of this parameter, the respective use case data must allow for generating 'realistic' negative samples, as well as different strategies of selecting samples for the actual inference of the model. When increasing the positive offset, the assumptions about future values, which are usually not available in a productive environment, must be formalized. Therefore, historic data may be analyzed for finding trends, outliers or other significant observations, which can be combined with, or appended to, current values. When there is only a small amount of possibilities or there are unlimited resources, the model can be inferred with a multitude of samples which consist partly of random values and determining the most likely synthetic element.

V. Conclusion and Future Work

In this work, an overview of the utilization of multimodal data in meta-learning strategies was given with respect to time-series analysis in the context of CPS operations. Therefore, different approaches of distance-learning were investigated and applied in experiments using SCML and SNN. In implementing a novel approach of compiling temporal triplets, a classification of future time-series data seems possible. Although the results are capable of improvement, it was shown that strategies for predicting specific situations in CPS environments are possible for even small datasets using meta-learning approaches.

As this paper is concerned with basic experimentation, a better suited SNN architecture may be found and applied to additional datasets, using a broader variety of multimodal transformations and preprocessing approaches. In addition, problem-specific significance tests could be implemented for determining the feasibility of model candidates. There are many promising applications of DT technology, as for example the management and representation of concurrent modules in a ML pipeline or model-specific preprocessing operations on inference. The utilized datasets could in general be extended with augmented [15] versions, e.g., adding samples which initially were copies of the originals but are subject to random noise, blurring, colorizing, rotating and other image manipulation techniques. Such a methodology could then be assessed with respect to increasing the samples of poorly-represented classes and impacts on prediction accuracy. Regarding the Milling [10] dataset, a more ganular flank-wear classification, as for example in .2mm steps, could contribute to more stable predictions. Another factor cold be to additionally fuse the information of the applied material with the respective signal plots, increasing the specifics of samples and potentially the model's accuracy, too. When forming a series of temporal subsequent same-class samples, effects of the structured time-series data could also be represented as video stream and further be interpreted by ML methods for classifying short visual sequences, challenging aspects like the compilation of triplets, real-time inference or multimodal fusion.

Acknowledgement

This work as outcome of the project DQ-Meister*in with the project number P2021-01-013 has received funding from the Carl Zeiss Stiftung.

References

[1] E. Raj, D. Buffoni, M. Westerlund, and K. Ahola, "Edge mlops: An automation framework for aiot applications," in *2021 IEEE International Conference on Cloud Engineering (IC2E)*. IEEE, 2021, pp. 191–200.

[2] P. Ruf, M. Madan, C. Reich, and D. Ould-Abdeslam, "Demystifying mlops and presenting a recipe for the selection of open-source tools," *Applied Sciences, MDPI*, vol. 11, no. 19, p. 8861, 2021.

[3] N. Zubair, A. Niranjan, K. Hebbar, and Y. Simmhan, "Characterizing iot data and its quality for use," 06 2019.

[4] V. Jane *et al.*, "Survey on iot data preprocessing," *Turkish Journal of Computer and Mathematics Education (TURCOMAT)*, vol. 12, no. 9, pp. 238–244, 2021.

[5] A. Parnami and M. Lee, "Learning from few examples: A summary of approaches to few-shot learning," *arXiv preprint arXiv:2203.04291*, 2022.

[6] M. Kaya and H. Ş. Bilge, "Deep metric learning: A survey," *Symmetry*, vol. 11, no. 9, p. 1066, 2019.

[7] X. Chen and K. He, "Exploring simple siamese representation learning," *CoRR*, vol. abs/2011.10566, 2020. [Online]. Available: https://arxiv.org/abs/2011.10566

[8] T. Baltrušaitis, C. Ahuja, and L.-P. Morency, "Multimodal machine learning: A survey and taxonomy," *IEEE transactions on pattern analysis and machine intelligence*, vol. 41, no. 2, pp. 423–443, 2018.

[9] R. A. Fisher, "Iris," UCI Machine Learning Repository, 1988, DOI: https://doi.org/10.24432/C56C76.

[10] A. Agogino and K. Goebel, "Best lab, uc berkeley. "milling data set ", nasa prognostics data repository," 2007, nASA Ames Research Center, Moffett Field, CA.

[11] J. Rogel-Salazar, "Sunspots - Monthly Activity since 1749," http://doi.org/10.6084/m9.figshare.6728255.v1, 2018.

[12] N. Schneider, P. Ruf, M. Lermer, and C. Reich, "Arthur: Machine learning data acquisition system with distributed data sensors," in *Proceedings of the 13th International Conference on Cloud Computing and Services Science - Volume 1: CLOSER*, INSTICC. SciTePress, 2023, pp. 155–163.

[13] B. Chander, S. Pal, D. De, and R. Buyya, "Artificial intelligence-based internet of things for industry 5.0," in *Artificial Intelligence-based Internet of Things Systems*. Springer, 2022, pp. 3–45.

[14] A. Sharma, E. Vans, D. Shigemizu, K. Boroevich, and T. Tsunoda, "Deepinsight: A methodology to transform a non-image data to an image for convolution neural network architecture," *Scientific Reports*, vol. 9, 08 2019.

[15] C. Shorten and T. M. Khoshgoftaar, "A survey on image data augmentation for deep learning," *Journal of big data*, vol. 6, no. 1, pp. 1–48, 2019.

[16] F. Ott, D. Rugamer, L. Heublein, B. Bischl, and C. Mutschler, "Cross-modal common representation learning with triplet loss functions," 2022, oSF Preprints.

[17] L. Buturović and D. Miljković, "A novel method for classification of tabular data using convolutional neural networks," *bioRxiv*, 05 2020.

[18] Y. Shi, A. Bellet, and F. Sha, "Sparse compositional metric learning," in *Proceedings of the AAAI Conference on Artificial Intelligence*, vol. 28, no. 1, 2014.

[19] G. J. McLachlan, "Mahalanobis distance," *Resonance*, vol. 4, no. 6, pp. 20–26, 1999.

[20] F. Boutros, N. Damer, F. Kirchbuchner, and A. Kuijper, "Self-restrained triplet loss for accurate masked face recognition," *arXiv preprint arXiv:2103.01716*, 2021.

[21] J.-Y. Franceschi, A. Dieuleveut, and M. Jaggi, "Unsupervised scalable representation learning for multivariate time series," *Advances in neural information processing systems*, vol. 32, 2019.

[22] P. A. Marin Zapata, S. Roth, D. Schmutzler, T. Wolf, E. Manesso, and D.-A. Clevert, "Self-supervised feature extraction from image time series in plant phenotyping using triplet networks," *Bioinformatics*, vol. 37, no. 6, pp. 861–867, 2021.

[23] A. Brunel, J. Pasquet, J. Pasquet, N. Rodriguez, F. Comby, D. Fouchez, and M. Chaumont, "A CNN adapted to time series for the classification of supernovae," *arXiv preprint arXiv:1901.00461*, 2019.

[24] T. von Hahn and C. K. Mechefske, "Machine learning in cnc machining: Best practices," *Machines*, vol. 10, no. 12, p. 1233, 2022.

[25] Y. Cheng, H. Zhu, K. Hu, J. Wu, X. Shao, and Y. Wang, "Multisensory data-driven health degradation monitoring of machining tools by generalized multiclass support vector machine," *IEEE Access*, vol. 7, pp. 47 102–47 113, 2019.

[26] T. V. Hahn and C. K. Mechefske, "Self-supervised learning for tool wear monitoring with a disentangled-variational-autoencoder," *International Journal of Hydromechatronics*, vol. 4, no. 1, pp. 69–98, 2021.

A Multivocal Review on Derivation Games

Diego Castro, Claudia Werner
Programa de Engenharia de Sistemas e Computação - COPPE
Universidade Federal do Rio de Janeiro
Rio de Janeiro, Brazil
email: {diegocbcastro, werner}@cos.ufrj.br

***Abstract*—Games have emerged as a prominent form of entertainment, hence establishing the gaming business as a highly lucrative sector. Nevertheless, the process of developing a game can be extremely complex, involving a multitude of activities, components, and team members, making some games take a long time to be produced. The game community has already engaged in the creation of its own games. This practice is commonly referred to as modding. The application of mods in game development can provide several benefits, including enhanced longevity of games, reduced production expenses, and accelerated creation of diverse games within reduced timelines. Nevertheless, the existing mod development process predominantly lacks a structured framework. Hence, the objective of this study is to conduct a comprehensive evaluation that clarifies the main attributes, benefits, difficulties, and methodologies employed in the creation of mods.**

***Index Terms*—Game, Mods, Derivation, Structured review, Multivocal review.**

I. INTRODUCTION

By conducting a brief search, it is feasible to identify numerous games available for purchase, as well as several websites that offer modifications for these games. A modification, also referred to as a "mod," involves one or several alterations or adjustments made to a game, which could be related to its mechanics, dynamics, or any other basic element. The classification of it may differ contingent upon the degree of modification: these categorizations involve terms such as patches, tweaks, add-ons, and other designations [1–3]. This method of modifying games can result in a variety of advantages for the company that created the original titles. Among the primary advantages there are: an increase in the number of users, the number of sales, and the longevity of the game [4].

With this is mind, the paper presents a review of the use of mods in development of games. The method used in this research was Multivocal review that is a more complete examination of the literature that aims to elicit as much information as possible about a specific subject; hence, it incorporates data from both white (academic papers, books, etc.) and gray (blogs, websites, videos, etc.) sources. This strategy is typically utilized when there is substantial community support for the study subject and it is necessary to verify practical knowledge on a particular subject [5].

The subsequent sections of this paper are outlined as follows: Section 2 provides a concise overview of the research procedure used in this study. Section 3 includes a comprehensive analysis of the data encountered during the search process. Finally, Section 4 offers a concluding summary of the paper.

II. RESEARCH PROTOCOL

As mentioned, this research conducted two literature reviews applying distinct search strategies (one for each review): a Mapping Literature Review (MLR) and a Multivocal Review (RM). The first study's objective was to collect data from white literature (academic papers), while the second served as a supplement by collecting data from gray literature (websites, blogs, etc.) [5].

In the initial phase of the investigation, three search databases were utilized, following the recommendation of B. Kitchenham et al. [6]. The search string was executed on the main search engines: Scopus, ScienceDirect, IEEEXplore.

In order to facilitate the execution of this study, a fundamental search string was formulated based on the PICOC framework, which covers the following components: Population, Intervention, Comparison, Outcome, and Context [6]. Combining domain-specific keywords with the logical operator "OR" and fields with the logical operator "AND" produced the search string. This string was utilized for the duration of the search. To validate the search string, two control papers (Modding as part of game culture [3], Serious mods: A case for modding in serious games pedagogy [7]) were used to generate and execute the string in the Scopus database, the first database to which the string was applied. This validation technique seeks to ensure the quality of the search string by returning only relevant articles and author knowledge.

According to some scholars, snowball processes can mitigate the lack of other search engines and supplement the strategy by conducting search through the references and citations of the papers. In order to minimize the loss of some papers and broaden the scope of the search, the forward and backward (one-level) snowballing procedure was employed to verify the references and citations of papers for relevance [8]. The procedures, inclusion and exclusion criteria, quality criteria and research questions will be described below.

The research execution procedure consisted of the following steps:

1) Execute the search string. For searches in gray literature, it was searched for each search string up to page 10 of

google. The search strings were formed by combining the keywords of population and intervention;
2) Apply the inclusion / exclusion criteria based on the title;
3) Apply the inclusion / exclusion criteria based on the abstract;
4) Apply the inclusion / exclusion criteria based on the full text;
5) Apply the quality criteria; Apply snowballing backward;
6) Apply snowballing forward. For searches in gray literature, the snowballing was performed on site references, on links contained within the site.

The inclusion criteria, exclusion criteria, quality criteria, and research questions used in the study were:

Inclusion Criteria:

- Viability Study: The document must be in the context of Mods;
- The document must be in the context of Games and Software Reuse;
- The document must provide data to answer at least one of the research questions;
- The paper must be written in English.

Exclusion Criteria:

- Conference call;
- Studies that can not be fully accessed;
- tudies that are not in the area of Computer Science or Engineering.

Quality Criteria:

The quality criteria employed are derived from Lincoln and Guba, with the objective to evaluate the author's credibility, the transferability of ideas to the new paper, the reliability of the information, and the confirmability of the information [9].

- Is the publishing organization reputable?
- Has the author published another work in the area?
- Does the author have expertise in the area?
- Is the article clear?
- Are the references documented?
- Does this enrich the research?

Research Questions:

- **Q1:** What modifiers are used to create games from other games?
- **Q2:** What characteristics are needed to derive a game?
- **Q3:** What are the advantages and difficulties of creating games from others?
- **Q4:** What tools strategy or frameworks support these changes?

III. Results Analysis

The first phase provided a total of 923 papers. This number was reduced to 14 after the inclusion and exclusion criteria were applied to the publications. From these studies, the snowballing process was carried out, and a total of 245 more papers were evaluated. After this approach, 9 papers were included, totaling 23 papers read and assessed.

Based on the findings of the initial phase, it was determined that the gaming community is quite active in terms of development, enhancements, and modifications. Consequently, a new phase was introduced to the study. In addition to the investigation, a search for gray literature was conducted.

TABLE I
SEARCH STRING OF MUTATOR AND GAMES.

TITLE-ABS-KEY ((*game*) AND (mutator OR variant OR mods OR modification OR conversion OR add-on OR tweak OR modding) AND (tools OR approach* OR method* OR ideas OR framework* OR mechanics OR interpretation*) AND (creation OR production OR development OR elaboration OR generation OR practice)) AND (LIMIT-TO (SUBJAREA, "COMP") OR LIMIT-TO (SUBJAREA , "ENGI"))

The gray literature search encompassed up to page 10 of Google for each of the search keywords, resulting in 700 links that required validation. The inclusion and exclusion criteria were implemented after visiting each link, resulting in the selection of 21 links for the quality criteria step. Ten links were selected and approved based on the following criteria. The snowball effect was achieved by utilizing backlinks (website reference connections). As a consequence, the entire procedure was restarted for the authorized connections, and 335 additional links were validated. Lastly, fourteen additional documents were added in the search the snowballing process. Table I shows the search string used in the search. The appendix demonstrates the papers and links that were analyzed in this review.

Q1: What modifiers are used to create games from other games?

Increased accessibility to personal computers and the expansion of the Internet, which is disseminating an increasing quantity of content, are closely related to the rise of the mod trend [10]. The community and academy are increasingly generating game adaptations, which help game developers in a variety of ways, such as recruiting new players, prolonging the life of a game, providing new perspectives for the game, and fixing bugs. In general, modifications are referred to as mods and can be viewed as alterations to the original game [1]. In general, a mod is an original game that has had one or N alterations or modifications made to its mechanics, dynamics, rules, or some of its components [11].

Mods are as diverse as the games themselves. They vary in size and complexity and can make minor adjustments to the original game or completely alter its visual design [12]. Modding is the process and technique of modifying or adapting video games. It is frequently a "Do It Yourself" (DIY) strategy that teaches social and technical skills affiliated with innovation by reusing the concept of an existing game. Numerous aspects of the game, including the user interface, game items, bug fixes, characters, and regulations, are modifiable [4]. By altering the rules of a game, for instance, players are able to construct a unique gaming experience [13].

Developing mods is possible by applying mutators to a game. A mutator is a modification to an existing game; for instance, applying mutator M to game G results in the creation of a new game named G [M] [14]. Depending on the number of mutators utilized, a game may be classified in a variety of ways. There are numerous adaptations and modifications, each serving a distinct purpose [1, 4]. Each of them will be described in more detail in the following [1-3][8][16-27].

Interface customization: The interfaces are designed to emphasize the visual component of the game in order to enhance the experience. This customization entails making changes to the visual element, such as remodeling the accessories, skin, shader, or animation of a character or a game map, altering the game's colors, or altering the information displayed on the screen;

Partial Conversions: Add a new map, a new character, and a new item; increase the game's pace; add small mechanisms, bots, and rules. It is still possible to classify partial modifiers according to the modifications they execute. **(1) Mutators/tweaks:** Modify or add restricted features that have no effect on the game's functionality or mechanics. They may include modifying the game's theme song, increasing the game's speed, or modifying some graphic elements and minor rules. **(2) Add-ons:** They serve as supplementary elements within the game, performing minor adjustments such as modifying the theme's music, accelerating the game, or adjusting minor graphical components and rules. **(3) Mod: Mods:** They are the intersection of the previous two, as they retain the capacity to change rules and configurations.

Total Conversions: Certain changes are so drastic that they result in the creation of new games. A well-known conversion is the CounterStrike mod, which was based on Half-Life. In general, the number of modifiers used differentiates a partial conversion from a complete conversion. When a significant number of modifiers are applied to the point where something new is generated, a complete conversion occurs.

Others: Machinima: It could be seen as the outcome of changes that influence the visual replay of game usage sessions. In this type of modification, games are used for other purposes, such as telling a story, making a movie, or replicating a gaming experience. **Patch:** They frequently concentrate on addressing unresolved problems and creating technical enhancements. This modification is known as an unofficial or fan patch when it is created by a community.

Q2: What characteristics are needed to derive a game?

A game is a type of software development in which designers, developers, and software engineers work together to create an experience for players to live through the game [15]. Once the game is out, the contributors devote their time to updating and adding content to the main game. Modifications may include new game models, textures, music, and mechanisms, as well as complete remakes [15].

There are two primary methodologies for mod development. The first scenario occurs when there is a need for expansion in a particular game by introducing new elements, while the second scenario occurs while seeking games that offer similar characteristics to those wanted in the game under development [16]. Both need the same characteristics.

A game is made up of components that work together to generate the final output. The required qualities for their construction can be determined by defining games. Games are activities that occur in an abstract environment where decisions, actions, and rules are developed with the objective of accomplishing a leisure activity in the form of entertainment or amusement [17]. On this premise, the following aspects must be decided prior to the construction of any game: rules, actions, behaviors, objective, game loop, difficulty, and rewards [16, 18].

Each of the characteristics necessary for the interpretation and evolution of a game will be exemplified below. These features were divided into four broad categories that capture the attributes of the games at a higher level of abstraction. It should be noted that game mechanics were previously divided into actions and behaviors [17-19][23][24][29][32].

[Avatar]

Operation rules: Rules about the player. E.g.: the player can only carry one weapon at a time [4][14][18][28][33-35]; **Transition rules/states**: Understanding the character's state transitions. E.g.: the player can only shoot if he/she has a weapon in his/her hand [16, 19–23]; **Actions**: Commands that can be executed by the character. E.g.: shooting and walking [4, 19, 20, 22–24].

[Game world]

Levels: The game's stages. Strongly influenced by the gameplay that can change from one stage to the next [16, 19–23, 25]; **Rules of objects**: Rules of the objects contained in the world. E.g.: when an object must be locked or unlocked [4, 16, 20, 23, 24, 26]; **Behavioral rules**: Rules of behavior that the world can exhibit. Eg .: if the player collects a specific item it can start to rain [15, 16, 23–25, 27]; **Temporal states**: It works like a state machine; depending on the world's state, it can only go to a specific one [4, 16, 23, 25, 27]; **Mission**: What you want to achieve/complete [4, 15, 16, 19, 20, 23, 25]; **Obstacles**: What you must overcome in the game, its difficulties [7, 15, 20, 22, 23, 25, 27].

[Game play]

Winning and losing conditions: Conditions to win or lose the game [7, 12, 16, 20, 23, 27]; **Strategic dilemmas**: Strategies that can be used in the game. E.g.: combo attacks [7, 12, 16, 20, 23, 27]; **Chains of actions**: Chain of actions that can be combined. Eg .: player action with a map action [16, 20, 22, 27].

[General features]

Rules: Encapsulates the logic inside the system [4, 13, 16, 20, 21, 23, 24, 28]; **Score**: The points obtained by the player throughout the game [16, 20–23, 27]; **Behaviors**: Commands that are executed by the system [4, 16, 20, 21, 23, 27]; **Goal**: What you want to achieve/complete [4, 16, 19, 20, 23, 25]; **Challenge**: What must be accomplished to achieve the goal [4, 7, 16, 20, 21, 23]; **Rewards**: reaching the goal [4, 16, 20, 23, 24, 28]; **Game loop**: Flow of engagement of the game. It is the execution of the game where the player seeks a goal by executing a challenge and being rewarded with something [4, 20–22, 27]; **Interface**: The visual of the game, the game's sprites, and graphics [7, 19, 21, 23–25, 28]; **Entities**: Objects and elements instantiated within the game [12, 21, 23, 24, 27].

Q3: What are the advantages and difficulties of creating games from others?

Generalizing mod developers' intentions is difficult. There are several elements that contribute to a user producing a mod. Attempting new things, resolving bugs, creating new characters, increasing the difficulty of the game, gaining advantages in the game, extending the game's life cycle, the software was originally designed for a significantly different environment and may require improvement, the official developer is unable to deal with the problems, and so on are among the most significant ones [4, 29].

Modifiers, like games, are complex and time-consuming to create. The time it takes to create a mod varies greatly. The construction process might vary in duration, ranging from a few days to a somewhat longer period, while offering the advantage of using reusable components. As previously mentioned, creating a game can be incredibly time consuming and can take years. However, the time necessary to release a mod is far shorter [4]. Mods allow the community to add to the original game. Depending on the nature of the mod, it may only require one or several releases. For example, a mod that improves the texture of a game may only require one version.

The potential to increase the longevity of games is another advantage that can be ascribed to the employment of modifiers. Every game has an effective life cycle. Modifiers, on the other hand, can extend the life of the game by adding additional instructions, characters, levels, and other factors, giving players more areas to explore [4, 20, 30]. Using the same logic, modifications may help boost sales, income, and profits for original games, as many people purchase the original game in order to play the mod [4, 11, 29].

Another significant advantage of modifications is their ability to draw new players to the game, so extending its longevity. For example, Dota 2 was a Warcraft mod that reached 450,000 daily players five years after its debut and 16 years after the original game's release. As a result, the game's player base and longevity grow [4, 31].

Despite all of the benefits stated so far, there are still issues and hurdles to be aware of when building mods. The first and most serious issue is the initial investment required to create a mod, which is required to comprehend the source code, reverse engineer it, and extract its functionality [21, 32]. Following this line of thought, various investigations have already been conducted with the product line. However, this strategy necessitates an initial expenditure to understand the project's first characteristics [21, 32].

Q4: What tools or frameworks support these changes?

A variety of frameworks and tools make it easier to construct customizations. However, cloning and do-it-yourself have been the most popular methods of mod development thus far. The modder chooses the base game to be modified, confirms the properties he or she wishes to change, and then creates the new game [32]. This less complex approach, known as opportunistic reuse or ad hoc reuse, consists of cloning, copying, and stretching. Opportunistic reuse gives immediate benefits and achieves the intended result. However, project quality is not a priority; extensive reworking results in unanticipated behavior and an unstable software structure [23].

Typically, technologies that allow access to an unencrypted internal representation of the game software are used to modify games. While it may appear that game makers want to dissuade players from customizing their games, this is not the case. In order to increase sales and market share, video game developers are increasingly providing software tools for personalizing their products [29]. Software Development Kits (SDKs) for games/domains provided by game development studios to users represent a current business method for engaging users and assisting in product creation outside the company [1, 15, 33]. In addition to SDKs, which are the most popular manner of accessing the game's source code, various other platforms enable access to and allow alterations to the game's source code. The Creation Kit, GECK, Construction Set, MODKit, REDKit, Modbuddy, and D'jinni are among the most important ones [4].

Another possibility for the development of modifiers is through free software games, in which the end user has complete access to the game's source code and may modify it as desired [1]. However, this strategy is used by small businesses or anonymous developers.

Finally, there are companies that help and support the development of adjustments with the purpose of decreasing difficulties, enhancing game quality and consistency, and developing new ideas. This strategy seeks to improve the game sold by leveraging the suggestions of consumers. The Unreal engine was designed to provide users access to all of its technological components. This allowed it to conduct a number of tournaments known as Unreal Tournaments, in which the developer could express his or her creativity while producing mods [4, 12]. Other firms allow alteration construction as well, although without direct access to the components. Blizzard Entertainment's World of Warcraft, for example, provides a User Interface (UI) modification tool that allows add-ons to modify the user interface panel, resulting in a better gameplay experience.

IV. Conclusion

Game companies are growing in size, earning billions of dollars per year, releasing a significant number of titles each year, and attracting fans of all ages and genres. However, as previously mentioned, designing a game may be a time-consuming process that can take years to finish. The gaming community, on the other hand, is expanding on a daily basis. With such a vast user base, some members may be concerned or disgruntled about having to wait so long for a game to be launched.

In light of this consideration, the current paper presents a multivocal study of papers that involve information associated with the development of modifications (mods). The primary objective was to find the essential characteristics required for mod creation, as well as to explore the associated challenges and advantages. Additionally, the study aims to identify the most commonly employed techniques in this process.

Through the review, it is possible to conclude that the mod process is widely utilized in the gaming community, with numerous benefits and few disadvantages, but numerous challenges. The current strategy to mod development lacks a standardized protocol, as it is being conducted in an ad-hoc manner. Therefore, the primary objective of this research paper is to categorize the fundamental attributes, techniques, and resources employed in mod development.

In subsequent research efforts, it is anticipated that the insights gleaned from this comprehensive analysis will serve as a foundation for the development of an innovative mod creation methodology.

REFERENCES

[1] W. Scacchi, "Modding as a basis for developing game systems," *Proceedings of the 1st international workshop on Games and software engineering*, pp. 5–8, 2011.

[2] ——, "Modding as an open source approach to extending computer game systems," *Proceedings of IFIP International Conference on Open Source Systems*, pp. 62–74, 2011.

[3] A. Unger, "Modding as part of game culture," *Computer Games and New Media Cultures*, pp. 509–523, 2012.

[4] D. Lee, D. Lin, C.-P. Bezemer, and A. E. Hassan, "Building the perfect game–an empirical study of game modifications," *Empirical Software Engineering*, pp. 1–34, 2020.

[5] V. Garousi, M. Felderer, and M. V. Mäntylä, "Guidelines for including grey literature and conducting multivocal literature reviews in software engineering," *Information and Software Technology*, vol. 106, pp. 101–121, 2019.

[6] M. Petticrew and H. Roberts, *Systematic reviews in the social sciences: A practical guide*. John Wiley & Sons, 2008.

[7] V. McArthur and R. J. Teather, "Serious mods: A case for modding in serious games pedagogy," *Proceedings of IEEE Games Entertainment Media Conference (GEM)*, pp. 1–4, 2015.

[8] R. C. Motta, K. M. de Oliveira, and G. H. Travassos, "Characterizing interoperability in context-aware software systems," *Proceedings of VI Brazilian Symposium on Computing Systems Engineering (SBESC)*, pp. 203–208, 2016.

[9] Y. Lincoln and E. Guba, "Naturalistic inquiry. encyclopedia of research design. 2455 teller road, thousand oaks california 91320 united states," 2016.

[10] O. Sotamaa, "On modder labour, commodification of play, and mod competitions," *First Monday*, vol. 12, no. 9, 2007.

[11] W. Scacchi, "Computer game mods, modders, modding, and the mod scene," *First Monday*, 2010.

[12] D. B. Nieborg, "Am i mod or not?—an analysis of first person shooter modification culture," in *Creative Gamers Seminar—Exploring Participatory Culture in Gaming, University of Tampere, Finland (14–15 January)*, 2005.

[13] G. Cheung and J. Huang, "Remix and play: lessons from rule variants in texas hold'em and halo 2," in *Proceedings of the ACM 2012 conference on Computer Supported Cooperative Work*, 2012, pp. 559–568.

[14] B. T. Claude Chaunier, Torben Mogensen, "Mutators," http://www.di.fc.ul.pt/~jpn/cv/mutators.htm, online; accessed 04 March 2021.

[15] L. Poretski and O. Arazy, "Placing value on community co-creations: A study of a video game'modding'community," in *Proceedings of the 2017 ACM Conference on Computer Supported Cooperative Work and Social Computing*, 2017, pp. 480–491.

[16] D. Abbott, "Modding tabletop games for education," *Proceedings of International Conference on Games and Learning Alliance*, pp. 318–329, 2018.

[17] G. Xexéo, A. Carmo, A. Acioli, B. Taucei, C. DIpolitto, E. Mangeli, J. Kritz, L. Costa, and R. Monclar, "What are games?" *LUDES. Rio de Janeiro*, vol. 1, pp. 1–30, 2013. (In Portuguese).

[18] J. Ehrmann, C. Lewis, and P. Lewis, "Homo ludens revisited," *Yale French Studies*, no. 41, pp. 31–57, 1968.

[19] R. Al-Washmi, J. Bana, I. Knight, E. Benson, O. A. A. Kerr, P. Blanchfield, and G. Hopkins, "Design of a math learning game using a minecraft mod," in *European conference on games based learning*, vol. 1. Academic Conferences International Limited, 2014, p. 10.

[20] K. Bilińska, A. Dewalska-Opitek, and M. Hofman-Kohlmeyer, "To mod or not to mod—an empirical study on game modding as customer value co-creation," *Sustainability*, vol. 12, no. 21, p. 9014, 2020.

[21] W. D. Mendonça, W. K. Assunção, and L. Linsbauer, "Multi-objective optimization for reverse engineering of apo-games feature models," in *Proceedings of the 22nd International Systems and Software Product LineConference, vol. 1*, 2018, pp. 279–283.

[22] S. Zuppiroli, P. Ciancarini, and M. Gabbrielli, "A role-playing game for a software engineering lab: Developing a product line," in *2012 IEEE 25th Conference on Software Engineering Education and Training*. IEEE, 2012, pp. 13–22.

[23] C. Lima, W. K. Assunção, J. Martinez, W. Mendonça, I. C. Machado, and C. F. Chavez, "Product line architecture recovery with outlier filtering in software families: the apo-games case study," *Journal of the Brazilian Computer Society*, vol. 25, no. 1, pp. 1–17, 2019.

[24] R. Damaševičius and D. Ašeriškis, "Visual and computational modelling of minority games," *TEM J*, vol. 6, no. 1, pp. 108–116, 2017.

[25] M. F. Shiratuddin and W. Thabet, "Utilizing a 3d game engine to develop a virtual design review system," 2011.

[26] J. Åkesson, S. Nilsson, J. Krüger, and T. Berger, "Migrating the android apo-games into an annotation-based software product line," in *Proceedings of the 23rd International Systems and Software Product LineConference, vol. A*, 2019, pp. 103–107.

[27] G. A. Cignoni, "Reporting about the mod software process," in *European Workshop on Software Process Technology*. Springer, 2001, pp. 242–245.

[28] S. George, É. Lavoué, and B. Monterrat, "An environment to support collaborative learning by modding," in *European Conference on Technology Enhanced Learning*. Springer, 2013, pp. 111–124.

[29] S. Agarwal and P. Seetharaman, "Understanding game modding through phases of mod development." *Proceedings of ICEIS*, pp. 114–121, 2015.

[30] O. Sotamaa, "When the game is not enough: Motivations and practices among computer game modding culture," *Games and Culture*, vol. 5, no. 3, pp. 239–255, 2010.

[31] H. Postigo, "Of mods and modders: Chasing down the value of fan-based digital game modifications," *Games and Culture*, vol. 2, no. 4, pp. 300–313, 2007.

[32] J. Krüger, W. Fenske, T. Thüm, D. Aporius, G. Saake, and T. Leich, "Apo-games: a case study for reverse engineering variability from cloned java variants," in *Proceedings of the 22nd International Systems and Software Product LineConference, vol. 1*, 2018, pp. 251–256.

[33] M. M. Hofman-Kohlmeyer, "Players as content creators. the benefits of game modding according to polish users," *International*

Scientific Journal News, vol. 2, pp. 8–26, 2019.
[34] J. Debbiche, O. Lignell, J. Krüger, and T. Berger, "Migrating java-based apo-games into a composition-based software product line," in *Proceedings of the 23rd International Systems and Software Product LineConference, vol. A*, 2019, pp. 98–102.
[35] T. Dey, J. L. Massengill, and A. Mockus, "Analysis of popularity of game mods: A case study," in *Proceedings of the 2016 Annual Symposium on Computer-Human Interaction in Play Companion Extended Abstracts*, 2016, pp. 133–139.
[36] T. Tengtrirat and N. Prompoon, "Applying exception handling patterns for user interface customization in software games modification," in *Proceedings of the International MultiConference of Engineers and Computer Scientists*, vol. 1, 2013.
[37] R. F. Patterson, "Mod (video gaming)," https://civilization.fandom.com/wiki/Mod_(video_gaming), online; accessed 05 March 2021.
[38] C. Weeke, "Appropriation & motivation in game modification," *Erasmus University Thesis Repository*, 2020.
[39] R. Ramadan, "Does game modding require programming?" https://www.quora.com/Does-game-modding-require-programming, online; accessed 09 March 2021.
[40] N. Poor, "Computer game modders' motivations and sense of community: A mixed-methods approach," *New media & society*, vol. 16, no. 8, pp. 1249–1267, 2014.
[41] E. Champion, *Game mods: design, theory and criticism*, Lulu.com, 2013.

APPENDIX

A. First Stage

(1:) Building the Perfect Game – An Empirical Study of Game Modifications [4]; (2:) To mod or not to mod—an empirical study on game modding as customer value co-creation [20]; (3:) Modding tabletop games for education [16]; (4:) Migrating Java-based apo-games into a composition-based software product line [34]; (5:) Product line architecture recovery with outlier filtering in software families: the Apo-Games case study [23]; (6:) Apo-games-a case study for reverse engineering variability from cloned Java variants [32]; (7:) Multi-objective optimization for reverse engineering of apo-games feature models [21]; (8:) Visual and computational modelling of minority games [24]; (9:) Placing value on community co-creations: A study of a video game 'modding' community [15]; (10:) Analysis of popularity of game mods: A case study [35]; (11:) Serious mods: A case for modding in serious games pedagogy [7]; (12:) Design of a math learning game using a Minecraft mod [19]; (13:) Applying exception handling patterns for user interface customization in software games modification [36]; (14:) An environment to support collaborative learning by modding [28]; (13:) Reporting about the Mod software process [22]; (15:) A Role-Playing Game for a Software Engineering Lab: Developing a Product Line [22]; (16:) Remix and play: Lessons from rul ts in texas hold'em and halo 2 [13]; (17:) Modding as part of game culture [3]; (18:) Utilizing a 3D game engine to develop a virtual design review system [25]; (19:) Modding as an open source approach to extending computer game systems [2]; (20:) When the game is not enough: Motivations and practices among computer game modding culture [30]; (21:) Modding as a basis for developing game systems [1]; (23:) Of mods and modders: Chasing down the value of fan-based digital game modifications [31]; (23:) Am I Mod or Not? - an Analysis of First Person Shooter Modification Culture [12].

B. Second Stage

(1:) Mod (video gaming) [37]; (2:) Appropriation & Motivation in Game Modification [38]; (3:) Players as Content Creators the Benefits of Game Modding According to Polish Users. [33]; (4:) Understanding Game Modding through Phases of Mod Development [29]; (5:) Does game modding require programming? [39]; (6:) Computer game modders' motivations and sense of community: A mixed-methods approach [40]; (7:) Game Mods: Design, Theory and Criticism [41]; (8:) Computer game mods, modders, modding, and the mod scene [11]; (9:) On modder labour, commodification of play, and mod competitions [39]; (10:) Am I Mod or Not? - An analysis of First Person Shooter modification culture [12].

Exploring Product Line Concepts in Game Building

Diego Castro, Claudia Werner
Programa de Engenharia de Sistemas e Computação - COPPE
Universidade Federal do Rio de Janeiro
Rio de Janeiro, Brazil
email: {diegocbcastro, werner}@cos.ufrj.br

***Abstract*—The gaming industry is one of the most influential in the world and attracts a wide variety of audiences. However, game development can be a time-consuming effort. Therefore, it is necessary to reduce this development time. Software Reuse Techniques have demonstrated their capacity to reduce game development time and costs. One of the main approaches used in reuse is Software Product Line (SPL), which has been successfully adopted by different companies for the purpose of generating software on a large scale. In light of this, the purpose of this paper is to provide an overview of what it would be like to use SPL for support in game development.**

***Index Terms*—Game, Mods, Derivation, Variations, Software Reuse.**

I. Introduction

Games have emerged as a highly prevalent mode of entertainment, attracting fans of diverse preferences and generating substantial revenue in a period of several years [1]. The game development process, despite its huge fan community, has demonstrated an exhaustive and non-systematized process, resulting in prolonged release timelines for certain games [2].

The practice of Software Reuse has been widely employed in the industry as a means to mitigate development time and costs. Various ways have been adopted, ranging from opportunistic reuse to the implementation of a Software Product Line (SPL) procedure [3]. SPL is the focus of this work.

Given the aforementioned discussion, the objective of this study is to present a preliminary concept of utilizing SPL for game building, with the aim of mitigating the time and costs resources required in the existing procedure.

The rest of the paper is structured as follows. In Section 2, a brief contextualization of the problem related to the concept introduced in this study is provided. In Section 3, the suggestion for solving the situation at topic is presented, while Session 4 provides the final conclusions of this study.

II. Contextualization

As previously mentioned, the gaming industry has experienced significant growth in recent years, accumulating a substantial and dedicated community. Considering the fact that the process of game production remains expensive, characterized by substantial costs and lengthy development periods, certain enthusiasts exhibit impatience towards the release of the games, encouraging them in the creation of their own versions of those games. The phenomenon of game creation by the community is commonly referred to as modding. It can be conceptualized as a manifestation of players' artistic freedom in remaking and reinterpreting the original game, comparable to the opportunistic reuse process [4]. In this context, the original game serves as a structure upon which a new game is constructed.

The main goal of the SPL method is to create new products by using the "variation points" present in an SPL of the original product [3]. For instance, consider a software X with Y characteristics. These characteristics can be altered, eliminated, or expanded by introducing new features. Consequently, this process results in the creation of new products with Y+1 characteristics, imagining that we were adding a new feature to the software.

However, the process of building mods, like the process of building games, has some issues, with a focus on:

- The lack of specific tools for mods;
- The fact that building a mod can be time-consuming despite being faster than building a game;
- Making the source code available to be modified.

Specifically, the latter issue has already been addressed by major companies, who have made Software Development Kits (SDKs) accessible to users for modifying the original games [5, 6]. This enables users to make alterations to characters, maps, and incorporate minor modifications. Nevertheless, the availability of such services is limited to certain companies, and it should be noted that the scope of modifications that can be made is restricted, limited to certain mechanics and aesthetics of the game.

III. EngageSPL

This study proposes the creation of a platform that incorporates SPL concepts in order to address the issues identified in the development of mods and games, as previously examined. The primary objective of the platform is to facilitate the effective development of several versions of a game by streamlining the process and minimizing complications. This helps with large-scale game development.

The primary concept underlying the platform involves organizing the game's characteristics into a hierarchical structure, called feature tree. This arrangement simplifies the process of selecting, modifying, adding, or removing these aspects. The platform was designated as ENgine for GAme GEneration through Software Product Line (EngageSPL).

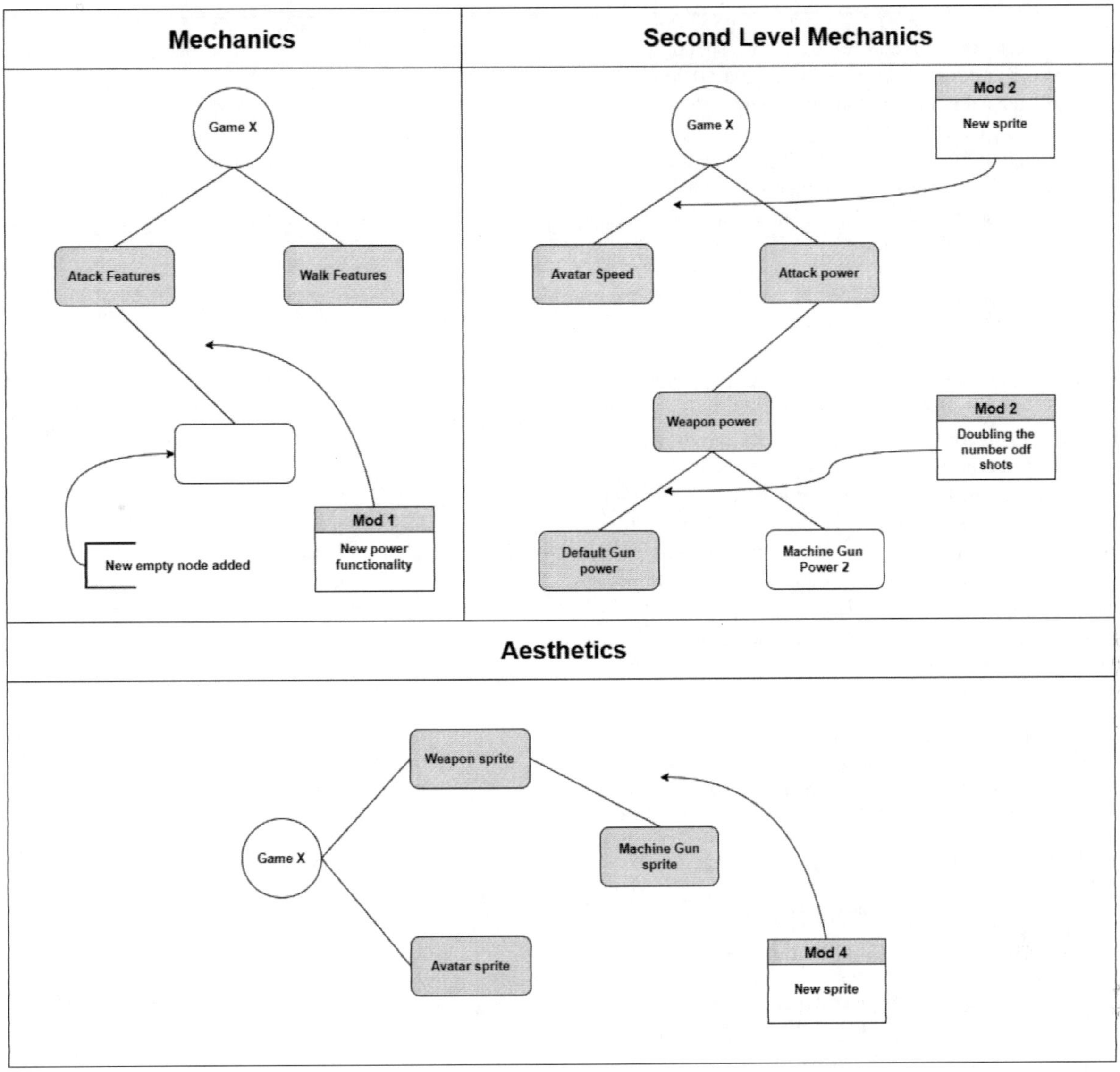

Figure 1. SPL of EngageSPL.

The primary objective of EngageSPL is to offer a comprehensive range of tools that facilitate the expansion of gaming. The platform is designed to enable the creation of a game with the ability to subsequently generate multiple video games with distinct characteristics by leveraging variation points within the functionality tree. Initially, it was thought that the platform could have 3 feature trees based on elements of tTtrad [7] framework, each of which will be highlighted below.

The elemental tTtrad is a widely recognized paradigm within the game industry. The properties of games are categorized into four distinct groups [8], however, in this work only 2 will be highlighted (Mechanics and Aesthetics).

- **Mechanics**: can be interpreted as the rules and activities that may occur during the course of the game.
- **Second level mechanics**: while the tTtrad elements do not include the second level mechanics, this study will incorporate them to elucidate the mechanics that arise from the combination of primary mechanics. The incorporation of this element will be implemented to augment the level of dynamism inside the proposed adjustments for the advancement of the games.
- **Aesthetics**: Can be defined as the graphical part of the game.

Consequently, there will be three trees: one for the mechanisms of the first level, one for the second, and a third tree for selecting the game's aesthetics. Initially, the technology and story elements of the tTtrad were eliminated from the work. The first is due to the ease of building for multiple platforms using current engines, and the second is due to the difficulty of implementing the game context to dynamically generate the narrative.

Figure 1 depicts the three trees that correspond to each component of the previously specified elementary tTtrad. This figure demonstrates the integration of a new mechanic into the hierarchical structure of the tree, with the alteration of some mechanisms at the second level. Ultimately, there exists the potential to visually represent the alteration of an aesthetic entity. Hence, the user has the ability to choose desired characteristics and determine the manner in which modifications are implemented to the existing features inside the game through the utilization of this tree structure.

IV. Conclusion

The gaming industry is seeing substantial growth, with gaming businesses expanding in scale and generating billions of dollars in annual revenue. These companies are consistently publishing a considerable number of titles across many genres, drawing a diverse range of fans. Nevertheless, as commented before, the process of game development can be a time-consuming endeavor that may span several years until its finalization. In contrast, the gaming community is experiencing continuous growth on a daily basis. Given the extensive user base, certain individuals within the community may express concerns or dissatisfaction regarding the prolonged waiting period for the commencement of a game.

References

[1] S. Pashkov, "Video game industry market analysis: Approaches that resulted in industry success and high demand," *Vaasan Ammattikorkeakoulu University of Applied Sciences - VAMK*, p. 40, 2021.

[2] K. Bilińska, A. Dewalska-Opitek, and M. Hofman-Kohlmeyer, "To mod or not to mod—an empirical study on game modding as customer value co-creation," *Sustainability*, vol. 12, no. 21, p. 9014, 2020.

[3] C. W. Krueger, "Software reuse," *ACM Computing Surveys (CSUR)*, vol. 24, no. 2, pp. 131–183, 1992.

[4] D. Abbott, "Modding tabletop games for education," *Proceedings of International Conference on Games and Learning Alliance*, pp. 318–329, 2018.

[5] S. Agarwal and P. Seetharaman, "Understanding game modding through phases of mod development." *Proceedings of ICEIS*, pp. 114–121, 2015.

[6] W. Scacchi, "Modding as an open source approach to extending computer game systems," *Proceedings of IFIP International Conference on Open Source Systems*, pp. 62–74, 2011.

[7] M. de Lemos Uliano and M. L. de Faria, "Benchmark analysis of board games with a narrative focus based on jesse schell's elementary tetrad," *Revista Poliedro*, vol. 4, no. 4, pp. 092–114, 2020. (In Portuguese).

[8] J. Schell, *The Art of Game Design: A book of lenses*. CRC press, 2008.

Application of Three-Phase Methodology for Retrofit 4.0 in Legacy Industrial Plants

Andrei Tchepurnoy Machado, Renan Yamaguti, Raphael Montali Assumpção, Omar Carvalho Branquinho, Paulo Cardieri
School of Electrical and Computer Engineering, University of Campinas, Brazil
a263837@dac.unicamp.br, renan.o.yamaguti@gmail.com, r075126@dac.unicamp.br, omar.branquinho@gmail.com, cardieri@unicamp.br

Abstract—**This work presents the non-invasive Retrofit 4.0 in a metal-mechanical industry employing the Three-phase Methodology (TpM) for Industrial Internet of Things (IIoT). Retrofitting 4.0 involves integrating legacy industrial machinery into a real-time monitoring environment using a data network, aligning with Industry 4.0 principles. The primary objective of this endeavor is to monitor production performance and anticipate plant enhancements through real-time monitoring of machine operation cycles and Receiver Signal Strength Indicator (RSSI) variations. These variations are tied to the movement of sector operators' quantities. Due to the absence of an online monitoring system, certain production processes suffer from information gaps and reliance on manual production data entry. Using the TpM, a Proof of Concept (PoC) was conducted with two motivations: monitoring machine operating cycles through current sensors and evaluating personnel movement through RSSI. For the PoC implementation, a wireless sensor network was designed for data transmission, without the need to alter the manufacturing processes, ensuring non-invasive monitoring. The results for the operating cycle and operator movement were effective, integrating this industry and its legacy into the IIoT context, enabling a non-invasive Retrofit 4.0 in conjunction with a guiding methodology.**

Keywords- TpM Three-phase Methodology (TpM), Proof of Concept (PoC), Industrial Internet of Things (IIoT), Wireless Sensor Network (WSN), Key Performance Indicator (KPI), Receiver Signal Strength Indicator (RSSI), Computer Numeric Control (CNC).

I. INTRODUCTION

This paper addresses the challenge faced by legacy industries in Brazil and other countries, which cannot fully adopt Industry 4.0 due to the cost and complexity of replacing existing systems with IIoT solutions. In Brazil, there are extensive legacy industrial complexes that are gradually transitioning to Industry 4.0 [13], with a significant need for modernization without replacing the existing infrastructure. Many of these plants are highly efficient and effectively deliver the desired final products or services, but with some hidden production performance data mismatches sometimes, enforcing the needs of an evasive approach in many cases to attend the correct 4.0 transition. Despite meeting their demands, these industries have an underlying need to integrate into IIoT for advantages such as productivity and efficiency. The article proposes the adaptation of the TpM [1] [2] for a non-invasive Retrofit 4.0, aiming to develop an IIoT solution through a Proof of Concept in a metal-mechanical sector company.

The approach focuses on operational improvements without altering any manufacturing processes, highlighting the relevance of IIoT for industrial efficiency. The article presents a structured framework, including conceptual review, proposal, description of the proof of concept, execution steps, results analysis and conclusion, the objective is to emphasize the importance of IIoT in enhancing financial outcomes in modern industries. The case study involves establishing a connection between a legacy sector of an industrial plant and a 4.0 industrial environment.

This connection aims to address two Key Performance Indicators (KPIs): monitoring machine cycles through specific current draw motor values and observing RSSI variations caused by personnel movement that affect signal propagation.

This paper is structured as follows. In Section II, we explain the Three-phase Methodology and the industrial scenario. In Section III, we detail our proposal for methodology chain application in Retrofit 4.0 through PoC. Section IV describes the PoC with TpM chaining and motivations. In Section V, we present the results analysis. We conclude our work in Section VI.

A. Related work

The Industry 4.0 revolution is in full swing, and many traditional industrial facilities are on the path to transformation through Retrofit 4.0. Below are some significant research examples focusing on the modernization of legacy industrial plants.

Article [9] describes the transition from a traditional production line to Industry 4.0 using logical connectors, which function as management interfaces. This retrofit, combining both hardware and software, is invasive and might not be suitable for all industries.

Article [4] highlights the use of energy sensors to monitor KPI´s in traditional CNC machines. This data is wirelessly transmitted and can be monitored in real-time through a mobile app.

Article [10] focuses on monitoring drilling machines, capturing data such as rotation speed and drilling depth. The data is converted into packets and transmitted to an edge device on a wireless sensor network.

II. THE THREE-PHASE METHODOLOGY AND THE INDUSTRIAL SCENARIO CONSIDERED

In this section, we review some concepts related to our proposal. We begin by reviewing TpM as a methodology for

IoT solutions [1] [6]. We adapt this approach to the specific monitoring needs of the industry targeted in the proof of concept. Next, we examine the industry's structure as defined by [5], encompassing the levels of enterprise and factory. This analysis served as a basis for applying TpM to the non-invasive Retrofit 4.0, facilitating the industry's transition to IIoT.

A. *Three-phase Methodology – TpM*

The Three-phase Methodology was created for the development of IoT solutions. However, it is not designed for IIoT and is a generic proposal not directly suitable for Retrofit 4.0. The methodology segments the analysis into three phases:

Phase 1 - Business Consideration: It establishes the fundamentals for a viable IoT solution, detailing the business and identifying needs. A 6-level reference model [8] is adopted, differentiating between streaming and static data [3].

Phase 2 - Requirements Gathering: In this phase, the focus is on collecting requirements for an IoT solution aligned with the business needs. A "top-down" approach is adopted, considering display, abstraction, storage, edge, connectivity, and data acquisition.

Phase 3 - Implementation: In this phase, the IoT solution is implemented, adopting the appropriate technologies to meet the requirements defined in Phase 2. Aspects related to variable analysis, connectivity, edge elements, storage, and the creation of a platform for data display and analysis are addressed.

B. *Industry Structure*

This work proposes an approach that combines a methodology for developing IoT solutions with the industrial structure outlined by [5]. The industrial structure is divided into Enterprise Level, responsible for strategic management, and Factory Level, where production processes and quality control take place, shown in Figure 1.

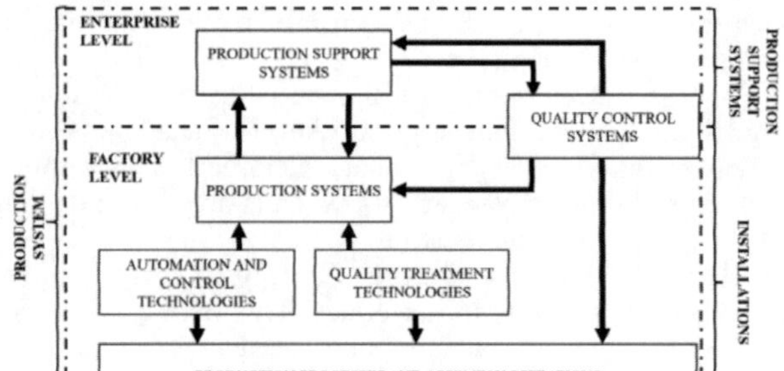

Figure 1. Division of the Production system [5].

The IoT solution aims to drive the efficiency and growth of the company, benefiting it with increased revenues through internal investment, encompassing manufacturing processes and impacting the entire organization.

III. PROPOSAL

This paper proposes a PoC for the application of the TPM to enable an IoT solution through Retrofit 4.0 in industrial environments. The focus is to demonstrate how this approach can enhance revenues at the enterprise level. The combination of the TPM with IoT within the context of Retrofit 4.0 aims to optimize manufacturing operations, improve efficiency, and drive growth in business revenues, the TpM phases are incorporated, and the scalability of this methodology allows for the organized inclusion of new projects. The segmentation of project phases creates a connection with the divisions of the production system defined by [5]. This exemplifies the collaborative utilization of the TPM in deploying Retrofit 4.0 to drive business expansion through IoT.

The segmentation of project phases using the TPM establishes a connection between Figure 1 and the divisions of the production system according to [5], as illustrated in Figure 2.

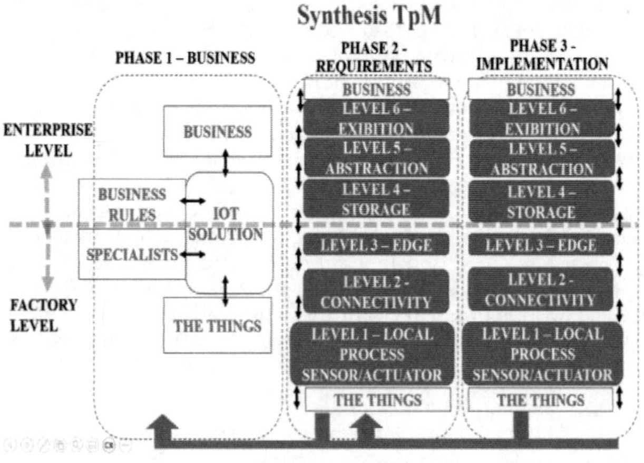

Figure 2. Incorporating TpM project phases into company areas [1].

The proposal for Retrofit 4.0 in the industry combines the concepts of the production system [5], the IoT reference model [3], and the TpM.

In Figure 2, Phase 1 is associated with the enterprise level, along with part of Phases 2 and 3 up to storage at the enterprise level. The remaining portions of Phases 1, 2, and 3 are connected to the factory level, encompassing assets, experts, edge elements, connectivity, sensors, and actuators.

Phase 1 establishes the foundation for Phases 2 and 3 of Retrofit 4.0. The process begins with a business assessment at the enterprise level to determine the feasibility of the IIoT solution, assured by a methodology. Furthermore, the proposal motivates the company to develop scalable IoT solutions over time. With the adoption of Retrofit 4.0, IIoT solutions are created in an organized manner, avoiding isolated approaches within the factory. This guides the industry in effectively crafting IIoT solutions aligned with its overarching goals.

IV. Proof of Concept

A. *Description of the TpM phases for the PoC*

1) PHASE 1 BUSINESS

A survey carried out in the company identified a lack of real-time automatic monitoring in the production line, with the chamfer-grinding department as the focal point. Currently, the control is manual, involving data input into terminals and storage on a server. This leads to gaps in records and a lack of information about events preceding performance drops.

a) Motivation

The initial motivations are twofold:

1- To monitor the performance of a machine within the sector.

2- To conduct real-time monitoring of operator's movement within the same sector [7].

Motivation 1: To monitor the current values of an AC motor in a machine, focusing on KPIs such as "machine in cycle" and "machine stopped."

Motivation 2: To implement a wireless sensor network to measure operator's movement through radio signal variations within the sector during different shifts.

The study proposes the establishment of a wireless sensor network with multiple strategically positioned links across the factory floor. The objective is to monitor variations in movement through RSSI and install a current sensor on a machine number 6 Rectifier Device (RD) model that is the chamfer griding machine located in the specified sector, to monitor the electric current of the specific motor shown in Figure 4 (drag rectification engine) during operations or inactivity.

The PoC entailed a detailed study of machine locations, considering distances and the feasibility of wiring. A wireless sensor network was chosen due to the impracticality of wiring in the environment. The necessary RSSI variations also proved crucial in monitoring operator movement during different shifts: four operators from 7:00 AM to 5:30 PM, two from 5:30 PM to 9:30 PM, and four again from 9:30 PM to 6:20 AM.

Motivation 1 – Monitoring machine cycles

The current measurement was conducted using a 10A current sensor on the specific AC motor of the RD6 machine, connected to the analog ports of the ATMEGA controller in the radio device. Figure 3 illustrates the RD6 machine and the rectified piece.

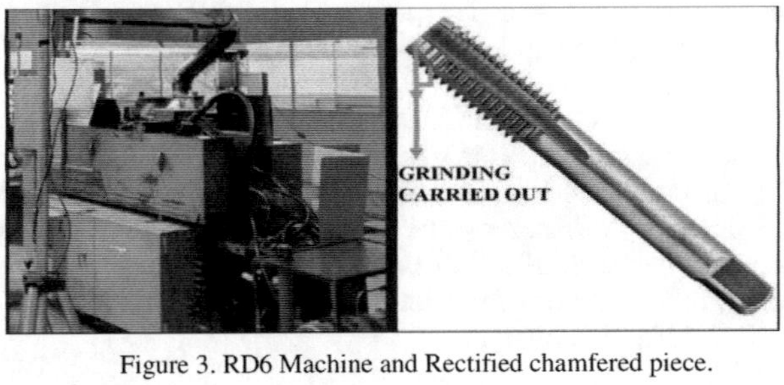

Figure 3. RD6 Machine and Rectified chamfered piece.

The radio device's firmware was configured to detect current values and transmit them in packets through the wireless sensor network [12] [14] [15].

Figure 4 illustrates the process of current measurement and the connection to the WSN up to the "Sensor Base" [11] (an edge element in Layer 3 of the TpM). This base receives machine data and forwards it to a computer in the factory office (Layers 4, 5, and 6 in the TpM) using a physical USB connection via an RJ45 CAT5 Ethernet cable, as depicted in Figure 5 from Motivation 2. Other devices within the WSN serve as sensor nodes, retransmitting the signal.

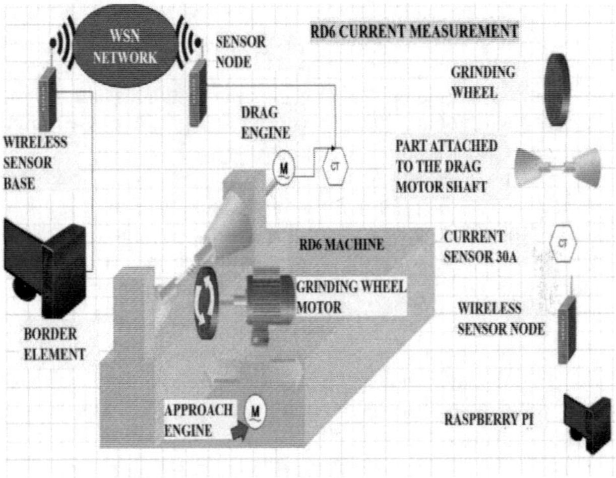

Figure 4. RD6 Current Measurement.

From Figure 4, it is noteworthy noting that the RD6 machine comprises three distinct AC motors. The first motor controls the platform's movement, the second one maintains continuous rotation of a grinding wheel, and the third one, known as the 'drag motor,' is activated by the operator after inserting the piece to be rectified.

The measurement of current in the drag motor is critical in determining whether the machine is operational or stopped. During operation, the drag motor consumes between 1 and 1.5 A for approximately 30 seconds when used for grinding a piece. After this interval, the motor no longer consumes current (0 A).

Motivation 2 – RSSI measurement to detect Operator's movement In The Area.

A wireless sensor network was used to monitor the operators' movement in the chamfer grinding sector by analyzing variations in movement through RSSI. Figure 5 provides a detailed view of the network and showcases the "things" of the associated IoT solution.

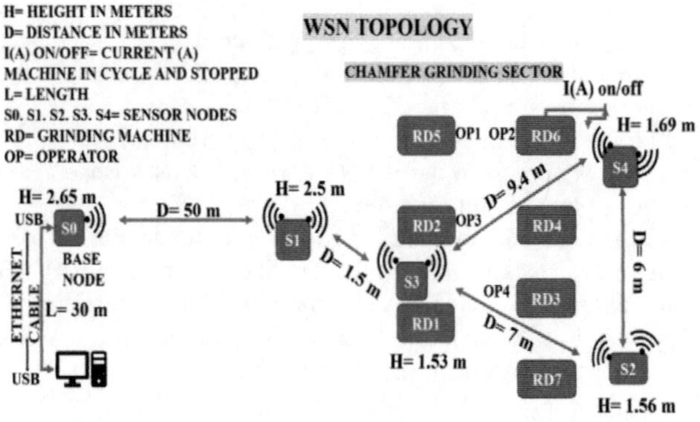

Figure 5. WSN topology.

The topology of a WSN defines the distances and heights of the sensor nodes, illustrating the propagation environment from the base station to the sensor nodes.

Before continuing with the PoC, it is necessary to collect all necessary information regarding production environments of the specified sector including routines, machines work type and specific rules. Meetings with designated specialists and understanding of business rules aligned with the things can define the bases of the PoC deployment.

b) Business Rules

The current scenario involves understanding production performance and management, emphasizing the lack of real-time monitoring in production. There is a need to supervise both machines and operators, and it is crucial for the IIoT solution to be non-intrusive to avoid disrupting production.

c) Specialist

The designated company expert engineers of the production plant explained the operation of the machines and their components. A study identified relevant parameters and a suitable sector for prototyping. The parameters to be collected and the best approach for the IIoT solution were defined.

d) Things

Details about the location, machinery, and processes were provided. The chamfer grinding sector, being the oldest in the company, was chosen for the Proof of Concept. After being approved at the enterprise level, the PoC was implemented in the factory through connected devices.

2) *PHASE 2: REQUIREMENTS*

a) Level 6 Exibition

Methods were established to quantify and display data for the enterprise level, including RD6 machine operation cycles, idle times, and personnel movement with 4 and 2 operators during different shifts.

b) Level 5 Abstraction

During two-and-a-half-hour measurements intervals in each shift, algorithms analyzed the collected digital data and presented it graphically.

c) Level 4 Storage

For the execution of the PoC, which took place after processing, the files stored the raw data from machine cycles and operator activity.

d) Level 3 Edge Element

Edge component responsible for collecting raw data during the testing period.

e) Level 2 Connectivity

Data transmission takes place through a wireless sensor network due to the absence of wiring in the environment. RSSI variation is crucial for monitoring operators across different shifts. The shifts are as follows: 4 operators from 7:00 AM to 5:30 PM, 2 operators from 5:30 PM to 9:30 PM, and 4 operators from 9:30 PM to 6:20 AM.

f) Level 1 Local Node / Sensing

The key parameters to be measured are the current of the motor in the machine during movement or idle states, and the variations in RSSI to monitor the number of operators in the sector.

3) *PHASE 3 IMPLEMENTATION*

During implementation, a framework is utilized, aligned with the technology, to define the elements according to the reference model [8].

a) Level 1 Local Node

In WSN, a node on the RD6 machine includes a current sensor and an S4 sensor for data transmission. The current is measured by a sensor capable of up to 10 A, connected to the RD6's drag AC motor and the ATMEGA controller of the radio device.

The firmware of the radio device has been adjusted to transmit the current values over the wireless network. Figure 4 illustrates the process up to the sensor base. This base receives and forwards the data to a computer in the factory office through USB connections and an RJ45 CAT5 Ethernet cable.

b) Level 2 Connectivity

The radio sensor devices, internally developed by the WISSTEK/Unicamp lab, operate at 915 MHz with 2-FSK modulation and 125 kHz channels. They feature an RF module with an integrated microcontroller, transceiver, and RF amplifier, achieving a transmission power of up to 500mW (27 dBm).

The devices were configured to operate on channel 4 (915-928 MHz) with a power of 5 dBm (31mW). RSSI and current measurements were collected during shifts with 4 and 2 operators, totaling approximately 2 and a half hours measurement per shift. The data, including RSSI and current, is sent to the base node and processed on the computer.

The RSSI measurements are recorded and graphically analyzed in LOG_TXT files, with received power values from the sensor nodes (in dBm) in the LOG_RSSI_TXT file. Routes configured with multiple hops generate noticeable RSSI variation based on the movement of operators in the sector. Figure 6 illustrates the WSN topology with the specification of hops for each route.

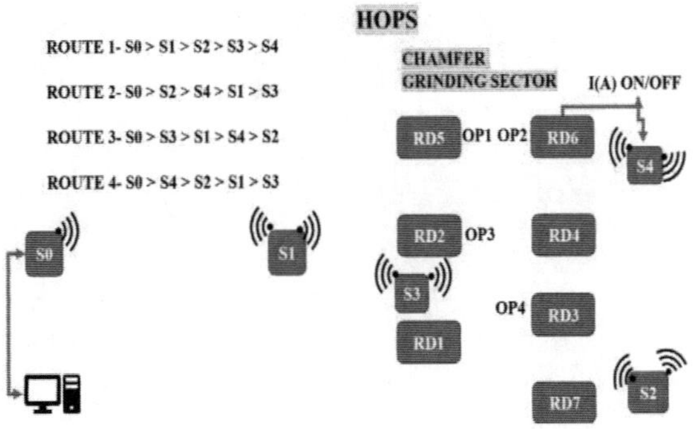

Figure 6. Hops.

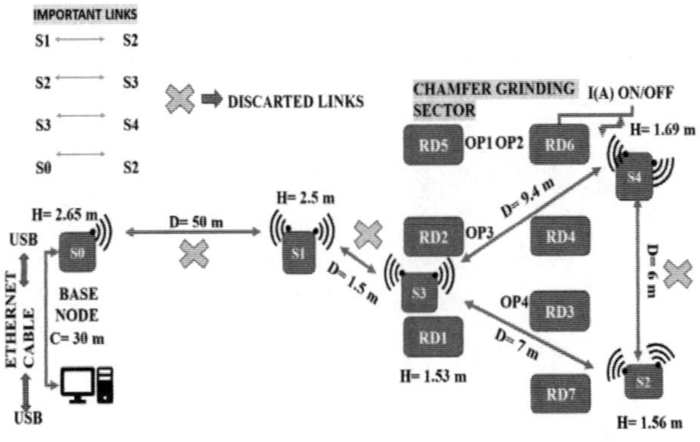

Figure 7. Important Links.

c) Level 3 Edge

A Raspberry Pi computer was installed and connected to the base node to store and display the data. Current values were collected, converted into packets, and subsequently processed at the edge element. At this element, thresholds were configured to differentiate between the machine's operating cycle (ON) and the stopped state (OFF) based on the current values. Current measurements stay within the established thresholds, corresponding to the machine's operating cycle, with values ranging from 1.0 A to 1.6 A.

d) Level 4 Storage

On the Raspberry Pi, the data is stored in CSV-compatible formats for later conversion in Excel.

e) Level 5 Abstraction

The raw data collected by the edge element was processed through algorithms and analyzed in Excel.

f) Level 6 Exibition

Illustrates the collected data with graphics and statistics analysis.

V. RESULT ANALYSIS

A. RSSI

For the analysis of RSSI variation results, we considered only the links that were physically installed, traversing the production sector. These links are more susceptible to RSSI variations due to operator movement.

Based on the measurement logs, we could observe the correlation between the line-of-sight location of the link and the RSSI variations, resulting in a more realistic scenario. Figure 7 shows the relevant links for analysis, selected from the result records, excluding irrelevant links.

Figure 8 shows the RSSI measurement over time in two distinct scenarios: when 4 and 2 operators were close to the machines.

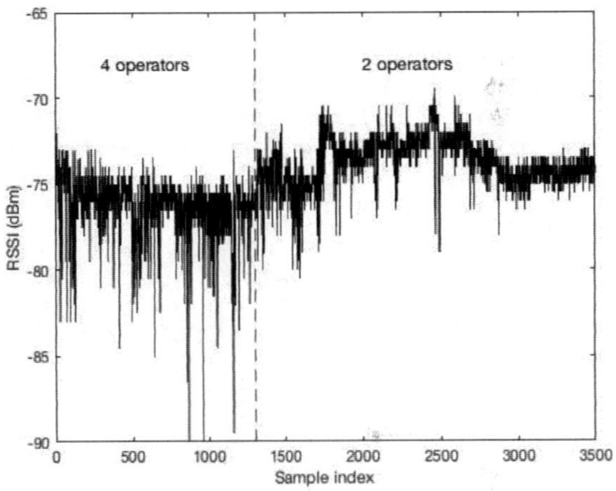

Figure 8. RSSI Variations.

It is clear, from this figure, that the level of RSSI variation is affected by the number of nearby operators.

To quantify the level of RSSI variation, we calculated the standard deviation of the RSSI measurements over a window of $L = 100$ measurements, using equation (1)

$$V(k) = \sqrt{\frac{1}{L-1}\sum_{i=k}^{i=k-L+1}[T(i) - \mu(k)]^2} \quad (1)$$

where L is the window length and T(i) are the RSSI measurements. The quantity $\mu(k)$ is the mean RSSI calculated as the equation (2)

$$\mu(k) = \sum_{i=k}^{i=k-L+1}\frac{T(i)}{L} \quad (2)$$

Figure 9 displays the standard deviation with 4 and 2 operators.

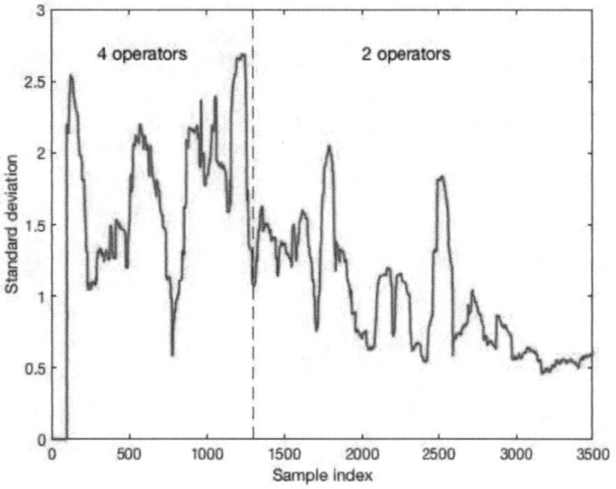

Figure 9. Std deviation.

This figure clearly shows that the standard deviation tends to be higher when there are more operators close to the machine, indication that RSSI measurements can be used to monitor operator's movement.

B. RD6 Machine Current Measurement

A pie chart illustrates the active and inactive time ratio and ON and OFF cycles in Figure 10. Figure 11 displays the measurement of motor current during operation and at rest in a zoom view.

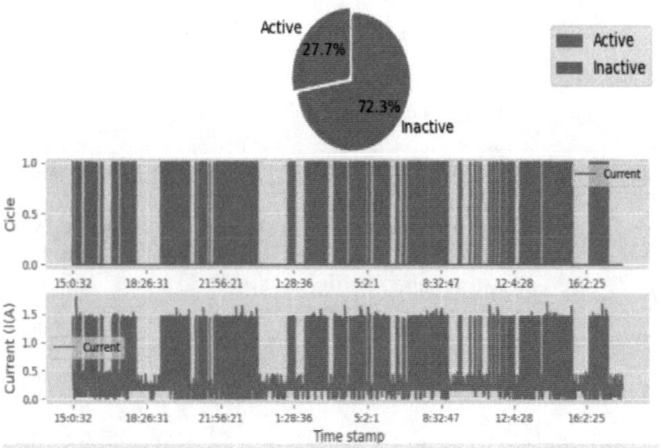

Figure 10 - Cycle ON OFF.

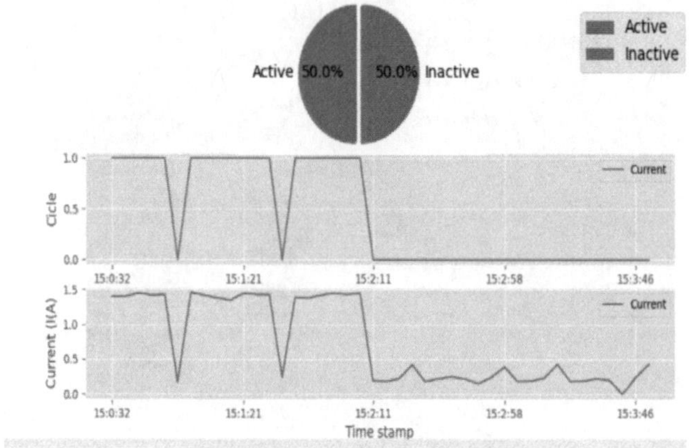

Figure 11. ON OFF ZOOM.

VI. CONCLUSION

Retrofit 4.0 followed the principles of the production system and the reference model, adopting TpM at every stage. The method played a pivotal role in shaping the IIoT solution, from understanding the business to implementing the proof of concept. The PoC met the expectations of the enterprise sector, demonstrating the effectiveness of the solution at the factory level.

The results of the PoC described the industrial environment, serving as a baseline for comparing variations in production performance and identifying gaps. The RSSI measurements revealed sector movement more clearly in the curve with four operators compared to that with two. RSSI variations can be used to interpret different patterns of human movement.

The monitoring of the RD6 machine's motor current demonstrated effectiveness in tracking the "ON" and "OFF" states. This allows real-time recording of production performance, indicating rework, production adjustments, and technical improvements. Both RSSI and current have proven to be powerful tools for productive management within the context of Industry 4.0.

The TpM application for Retrofit 4.0 through PoC proved effective contributing to a non-invasive transition process for legacy industrial plant and shown various possibilities of KPI´s management, like control machine work cycle and personal behavior in our study case, narrowing control gap which is reflected on production performance data.

ACKNOWLEDGEMENTS

This study was financed in part by the Coordenação de Aperfeiçoamento de Pessoal de Nível Superior - Brasil (CAPES) - Finance Code 001, and by Conselho Nacional de Desenvolvimento Científico e Tecnológico - Brazil, Grant 313213/2021-6.

REFERENCES

[1] L. C. B. Ferreira, O. Branquinho, P. Chaves, P. Cardieri, F. Fruett, and M. Yacoub, "A PBL-Based Methodology for IoT Teaching," in IEEE Communications Magazine, vol. 57, no. 11, pp. 20-26, November 2019, doi: 10.1109/MCOM.001.1900242.

[2] L. C. B. Ferreira, P. Chaves, R. Assumpção, O. C. Branquinho, F. Fruett, and P. Cardieri, "The Three-phase Methodology for IoT Project Development", Internet of Things, vol. 20, 2022, ISSN 2542-6605, https://doi.org/10.1016/j.iot.2022.100624. https://www.sciencedirect.com/science/article/pii/S2542660522001056.

[3] J. Green, CTO of Cisco's Data and Analytics Business Group, "IoT Reference Model", IoT World Forum, October 2014, Chicago USA, pp. 1-12, https://dl.icdst.org/pdfs/files4/0f1d1327c5195d1922175dd77878b9fb.pdf

[4] F. Lima, A. A. Massote and R. F. Maia, "IoT Energy Retrofit 4.0 and the Connection of Legacy Machines Inside the Industry 4.0 Concept," IECON 2019 - 45th Annual Conference of the IEEE Industrial Electronics Society, Lisbon, Portugal, 2019, pp. 5499-5504, doi: 10.1109/IECON.2019.8927799.

[5] M. Groover, "Automation, production systems, and computer-integrated manufacturing". ISBN 978-85-4301-501-9. Groover, Mikell, In Portuguese, Pearson Prentice Hall, 2011.

[6] D. Chew, The Wireless Internet of Things: A Guide to the Lower Layers, Wiley-IEEE, 2018.

[7] H. Wang, F. Zhang, and W. Zhang, "Human Detection through RSSI Processing with Packet Dropout in Wireless Sensor Network", Journal of Sensors, 2020, pp. 1-9, 2020, https://doi.org/10.1155/2020/4758103.

[8] A. L. Boni Deo, Master´s Thesis, "Proposal for an open-source reference model for IoT – focus on SMEs.", in Portuguese, Pontifical Catholic University of Campinas, 2018, Brazil.

[9] J. Palmeira, G. Coelho, A. Carvalho, P. Carvalhal and P. Cardoso, "Migrating legacy production lines into an Industry 4.0 ecosystem," 2022 IEEE 20th International Conference on Industrial Informatics (INDIN), Perth, Australia, 2022, pp. 429-434, doi: 10.1109/INDIN51773.2022.9976084.

[10] S. Kolla, D. Lourenço, A. Kumar, and P. Plapper, "Retrofitting of legacy machines in the context of Industrial Internet of Things (IIoT)" Procedia Computer Science, pp. 62-70, 2022, 10.1016/j.procs.2022.01.205.

[11] P. Chaves, R. Assumpção, L. Ferreira, P. Cardieri, O. Branquinho, and F. Fruett, "A remote emulation environment for the teaching of low - power wireless communications", Computer Applications in Engineering Education, 2021, 29. 10.1002/cae.22397.

[12] C. Bell, "Beginning Sensor Networks with Arduino and Raspberry Pi", doi: 10.1007/978-1-4302-5825-4, © Press 2013.

[13] S. L. Stevan, M. O. Leme, and M. M. D. Santos, "Industry 4.0: Fundamentals, Perspectives, and Applications", São Paulo Brazil, Érica publisher, 2018.

[14] E. Gaura, L. Girod, J. Brusey, M. Allen and G. Challen, "Wireless Sensor Networks: Deployments and Design Frameworks". Springer publisher, Eds. 2010, https://doi.org/10.1007/978-1-4419-5834-1.

[15] H. A. P. Zanetti and C. L. V. Oliveira, "Projects with Python and Arduino: How to Develop Practical Projects in Electronics, Automation, and IoT" in Portuguese Edition, Erica publisher, 2020.

BCI-based Game Control to Boost Focus and Attention in Students

Komalpreet Kaur
Department of Computer Science
Salem State University
Salem, MA, USA
kkaur@salemstate.edu

Manish Wadhwa
Department of Computer Science
Salem State University
Salem, MA, USA
mwadhwa@salemstate.edu

***Abstract*—This study presents a non-invasive Electroencephalogram (EEG) based Brain-Computer Interface (BCI) system to control games developed for the purpose of increasing focus and attention in students. For the study, data was collected from 6 subjects. Each subject played a focus game designed to evaluate their attention and focus before being trained through a P300-based speller. In order to evaluate the effect of training, subjects were asked to play the focus game again. The EEG data collected from the subjects during the P300-based Speller game training phase was analyzed to see the attentivity of the subjects. As per the classification accuracies obtained for all the subjects, the subjects were attentive and focused during the training phase. This training phase resulted in an improvement in their focus game performance metrics. P300-based BCI system can be effectively used to enhance focus and attention in students.**

***Index Terms*—BCI; EEG; ERP, P300-based Speller.**

I. INTRODUCTION

The phenomenon of diminished focus and attention among college students has garnered increasing attention in recent years due to its multifaceted implications on academic performance and overall well-being. This issue is closely linked to the pervasive use of digital technologies, particularly smart phones and laptops, which provide constant access to a multitude of distractions, including social media, instant messaging, and online entertainment. Research suggests that this constant connectivity and exposure to digital stimuli can lead to reduced cognitive control, making it increasingly challenging for college students to sustain their attention on academic tasks such as lectures, reading assignments, and studying. Furthermore, the demands of the college environment, including high-stress levels, irregular sleep patterns, and over commitment to extracurricular activities exacerbate this problem. Understanding the underlying factors contributing to the lack of focus and attention is pivotal for designing effective interventions and support systems aimed at enhancing the learning experience and academic outcomes for college students.

The main purpose of the study is to use a non-invasive Electroencephalogram (EEG) based BCI system to control games that are designed to improve focus and attention. Brain-Computer Interface (BCI) is a technology that enables communication between the human brain and a computer based external device [4] [5]. There are several ways in which a BCI can be implemented. BCI based training sessions have been used to enhance children's engagement in reading [9]. P300-based Speller is the most commonly used BCI system that is based on oddball paradigm [6]. P300-based Speller has been used to treat attention-deficit/hyperactive disorder in children [7]. For this study, P300-based Speller Game was utilized as a training tool to help enhance the cognitive abilities of students. The P300 response is a prominent positive deflection in the EEG signal, appearing approximately 300 ms after the presentation of the attended stimulus as shown in Figure 1. P300 deflection is widely considered to be an important indicator of attention and focus. In Figure 1, the target ERP (Event Related Potential) shown in blue shows a positive peak between 200 and 300 millisecond.

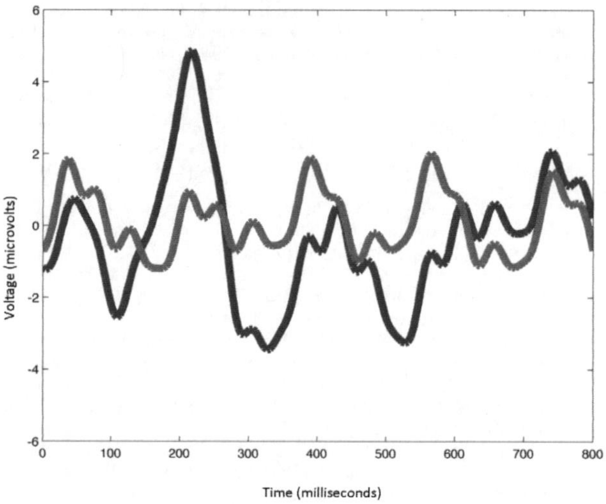

Fig. 1. Average P300 Response for Subject C. The blue waveform represents the Target ERP while the red corresponds to the Non-target ERP.

There are studies that have used BCI-based systems to improve the focus and attention in subjects. Authors in [1] [2] proposed an online EEG based neurofeedback game for enhancing attention and memory. In both the studies, subjects were asked to memorize a set of numbers in a matrix and later correctly fill the matrix. The focus of the study was mainly on memory of the subjects. The authors in [3] used a P300-based BCI Interface for improving attention. The game used in the study was challenging enough for the subjects to be attentive all the time.

The primary goal of this study is to explore the effect of P300-based Speller Game with and without feedback on enhancing the focus and attention of the subjects. The study is proposing a very simple, but monotonous game for the subjects to test their attention and focus.

The rest of the paper is organized as follows. Section II presents the materials and methodology used for this study. The section provides information about the subjects who participated in the study for data collection and the procedure used to collect the data. In Section III, preliminary results obtained from the EEG and the focus game data are presented. Section IV concludes the paper with the discussion of the current study and presents the future plan of action.

II. Materials and Methods

A. *Subject Information*

Since human subjects are a part of this study, the study was approved by the university's Institutional Review Board (IRB). After the approval, a number of emails were sent to all the students of the computer science department seeking volunteers for the study. Seven subjects from the department gave their formal consent to be a part of this study. To keep the study as unbiased as possible, the emails were not sent directly by the project investigators but by the department administrative assistant. One of the subjects, out of these seven, reported as being neurodivergent and thus was not considered for further study. This is to remove any biases. Only six subjects were thus considered for this study.

B. *Procedure*

The procedure used for the study is shown in Figure 2. All the three tasks were completed in a single session and it took around an hour for the subjects to finish all the tasks. During all the tasks, subjects sat in a comfortable chair approximately 75 cm from the monitor. EEG was collected using g.Nautlius Multipurpose 16-channel EEG cap. The headset has 16 electrodes (FP1, FP2, F3, FZ, T7, C3, CZ, C4, T8, P3, PZ, P4, PO7, PO8, and OZ) to record the data. All the electrodes were reference to the right ear and amplified, bandpass filtered from 0.5 - 500 Hz, and digitized at 1200 Hz.

- Pre-training Focus Game - A Focus Game was designed for the purpose of this study. The purpose of the Focus Game was for the subjects to play a game that was very monotonous and at the same time required attention and focus. In the Focus Game, subjects were asked to click on a moving target on the screen. The target could appear anywhere on the screen and at a variable rate. Figure 3 shows the Focus Game layout. The subjects had to click on a randomly appearing black box on a gray background on the screen. This box would disappear in a matter of 100 milliseconds so the subjects had to move their cursors quickly and click on the box before it disappeared and appeared somewhere else. The Focus Game lasted for five minutes and the moving target appeared 50 times in total.
- Training: P300-based Speller Game - As a part of the training phase, after completing the Focus Game task, subjects were asked to train via P300-based Speller Game. Each session of the P300-based Speller Game consisted of 4 experimental runs. Each run was composed of a 5 letter word. This set of characters that was consistent for all the subjects was from a 6×6 matrix displayed on the monitor, as shown in Figure 4. The rows and columns of the matrix were intensified for 100 ms with 25 ms between the intensifications [8]. There was a gap of 2 seconds between each run. A sequence of 12 row/column intensifications constituted one character epoch.

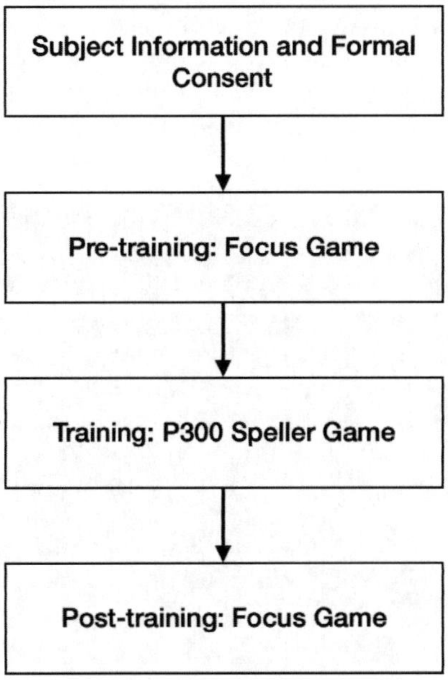

Fig. 2. Procedure used for this study.

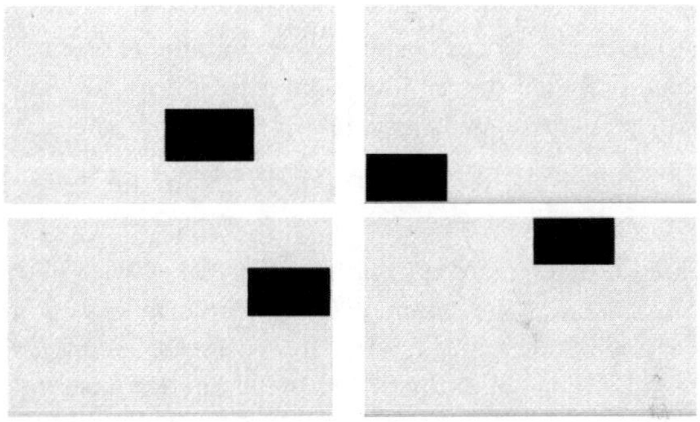

Fig. 3. Focus Game.

Words were presented on the top left corner of the monitor, and the character currently specified for selection was listed in parentheses at the end of the letter string. To better understand, for example, in Figure 4, D is the first letter of the word DICE. P300 response is generated for letter D when the fourth column and the first row of the matrix flashes.

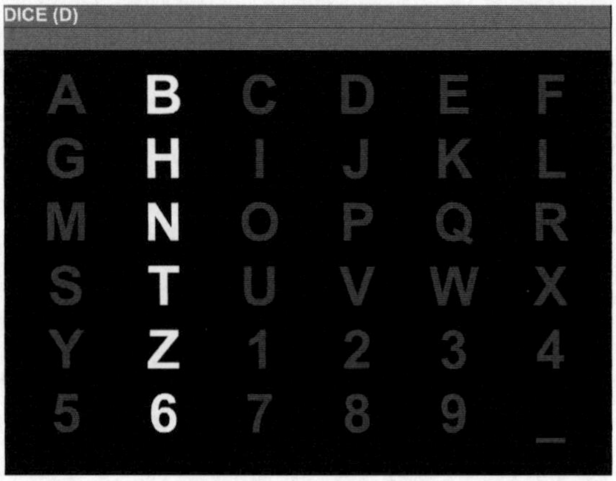

Fig. 4. The 6×6 matrix used in this study. A row or column intensifies for 100 ms every 175 ms. The letter in the parentheses at the top of the window is the current target letter "D". For this target, a P300 should be elicited when the fourth column or first row is intensified [8].

- Post-training Focus Game - After the training using P300-based Speller Game, subjects were asked to play the Focus Game again to see the impact of training.

III. Preliminary Results

A. EEG Analysis

The EEG data recorded during the training was analyzed to identify the P300 brain activity response and used to train a machine-learning model. To access the quality of the recorded EEG signal, offline P300-based Speller accuracy was computed. For each subject, an optimal classifier based on Random Forest (RF) was trained. For each channel of the data, 800 ms of the data segments were extracted following each flash for analysis. A feature vector corresponding to each stimuli was created by concatenating the extracted data segments by channel. All data were lowpass filtered to 20 Hz and decimated to 240 Hz, to smooth the data while retaining sufficient samples for classification model. A Random Forest classifier was trained using these features. In order to compute the classification accuracies, 80% of the data was used for training and the remaining 20% was used for testing. Table I reports the classification accuracies obtained for all the subjects.

TABLE I
Training and Testing Classification accuracies for six subjects.

Subject	Training Accuracy (%)	Testing Accuracy(%)
A	99.9	99.7
B	99.5	99.4
C	99.6	99.6
D	99.6	99.8
E	99.4	99.4
F	99.8	99.9

The classification accuracies achieved for all the subjects are exceptionally high. This shows that the subjects were attentive and focused during the training phase.

B. Focus Game Score

To see the impact of P300-based Speller training, subjects played the Focus Game again. To determine whether the P300-based Speller Game contributed to enhanced motivation and focus of the subjects, the scores of the Focus Game were compared. Table II presents the improvement obtained in the Focus Game scores for all the subjects.

TABLE II
Improvement in Focus Score for six subjects.

Subject	Improvement in Score (%)
A	20
B	2
C	2
D	10
E	4
F	7

In order to confirm if the improvement in the scores was statistically significant, the p-value was computed. The p-value of 0.03049 was obtained, which is much lower than 0.05, thus indicating the results obtained are statistically significant.

IV. Conclusion and Future Work

As can be seen from the results, training of the subjects via P300-based Speller Game helps improve their focus and attention. For all the subjects, there was an improvement in the Focus Game score after the training phase. The authors plan to consider three future directions, as follows.

- In this study, subjects were not given any feedback while they were training via the P300-based Speller Game. It is being anticipated that giving subjects neurofeedback while they are training, will have a very strong positive impact on the overall performance. The authors plan to implement neurofeedback as a part of the future work.
- The EEG data recorded during the focus game was not analyzed and thus is another potential candidate for the future work. With the analysis of this data, we may be able to find out what changes in the brain activity lead to such improvements.
- The EEG data recorded in this study does not specifically consider which brain areas were activated during EEG recordings. In our future work, we plan to record the brain areas that get activated during the focus activities. Let us say if only a few channels are being activated then instead of using all the 16 channels as done in this study, we only need to use those channels. This will reduce the setup time of data recording using EEG cap. Lesser data will make analysis quicker and comparatively easier and will allow for data collection from more subjects.

This study has the potential to make significant contribution to the field of education and technology by providing insights on how the P300-based Speller Game can be effectively used to enhance students' focus and attention. The results of this study could lead to the development of new educational tools and methods that utilize BCI technology to improve student engagement and performance in the classroom. Ultimately, our goal is to make learning a more interactive and effective experience for students.

REFERENCES

[1] K. P. Thomas, A. P. Vinod, and C. Guan, "Design of an online EEG based neurofeedback game for enhancing attention and memory." 2013 35th Annual International Conference of the IEEE Engineering in Medicine and Biology Society (EMBC), Osaka, Japan, pp. 433-436, 2013.

[2] J. R. Wang and S. Hsieh, "Neurofeedback training improves attention and working memory performance." Clinical Neurophysiology, vol. 124, issue 12, pp. 2406-2420, 2013.

[3] A. Mahnaz, I. H. Robertson, and T. E. Ward, "A P300-based brain-computer interface for improving attention." Frontiers in human neuroscience vol. 12, 2019.

[4] G. Schalk and E. C. Leuthardt, "Brain-computer interfaces using electrocorticographic signals." IEEE Reviews in Biomedical Engineering, vol. 4, pp 140-154, 2011.

[5] J. R. Wolpaw and E. W. Wolpaw, "Brain-computer interfaces: principles and practice." Oxford University Press, 2012.

[6] E. W. Sellers, D. J. Krusienski, D. J. McFarland, T. M. Vaughan, and J. R. Wolpaw, "A P300 event-related potential brain–computer interface (BCI): the effects of matrix size and inter stimulus interval on performance." Biological psychology, vol. 73, no. 3, pp. 242–252, Elsevier publishers, 2006.

[7] D. A. Rohani, H. B. D. Sorensen and S. Puthusserypady, "Brain-computer interface using P300 and virtual reality: A gaming approach for treating ADHD." 2014 36th Annual International Conference of the IEEE Engineering in Medicine and Biology Society, Chicago, IL, USA, 2014.

[8] L.A. Farwell and E. Donchin, "Talking off the top of your head: toward a mental prosthesis utilizing event-related brain potentials." Electroencephalography and Clinical Neurophysiology, Volume 70, Issue 6, pp 510-523, 1988.

[9] J. Huang et al., "FOCUS: enhancing children's engagement in reading by using contextual BCI training sessions." In Proceedings of the SIGCHI Conference on Human Factors in Computing Systems, Association for Computing Machinery, New York, NY, USA, pp 1905-1908, 2014.

Commute Tracking Mentor Tool for Automobile to Decrease Car Accidents

Mario Ervin, Kanwalinderjit Kaur
Department of Computer Science
California State University, Bakersfield
Bakersfield, California, USA
{mervin2, kgagnej}@csub.edu

***Abstract*— In 2020, nearly 39,000 lives were lost to motor vehicle accidents, and 2.3 million people were injured. In addition, over 5 million not-fatal crashes occurred. New and emerging technology is being introduced and included in automobiles. Vehicles have been equipped with new features and gadgets to assist drivers with commuting. However, regardless of these features, driver error directly causes many accidents. Artificial Intelligence (AI) is used for this research to study and analyze driving patterns. This solution differs from others because the focus is on improving driving behaviors rather than providing the driver with tools that will only assist when the driver is making errors. This proposed solution is implemented and tested on smartphones using the data collected from a mobile app called Phyphox. The goal is to determine and detect irregular driving patterns from the driver to assess and improve their driving skills.**

Keywords—ride, automobiles, acceleration rate, driver-vehicle interaction, machine learning.

I. INTRODUCTION

In 2020, the U.S. The Department of Transportation (DoT) reported 5,215,071 police-reported crashes. Among those crashes, 35,766 were fatal and took the lives of nearly 39,000 loved ones. The report provided by the U.S. DoT does show a decrease in overall car accidents compared to the previous year. However, speed-related crashes increased by 17%, and alcohol-impaired driving crashes up by 14% compared to the previous years' numbers.[6]. There are very few solutions to decreasing these numbers and improving driving scores. Liberty Mutual insurance company has an app, RightTrack, that evaluates its members driving habits. In addition, State Farm also has an app, Drive Safe & Save that is similar to RightTrack. Liberty Mutual's app tracks the user's Acceleration, Braking, Location, Phone Motion, Speed, and more. However, it will evaluate only for 90 days and give a score to determine the pricing of their car insurance. State Farm provides a discount that is adjusted at every new policy renewal. The app limits itself because of the duration its members use it for. Liberty Mutual could provide weekly scores and monthly pricing based on their monthly score. This would encourage drivers to drive safer and adjust their driving skills to be safer and save money. RightTrack uses the user's mobile device to track all data because most smartphones have various sensors to measure the metrics mentioned earlier.

This paper provides a solution to address speeding, distracted drivers, and other factors that result in traffic accidents. The Commute Tracking Mentor (CTM) tool studies drivers' patterns and suggests improving their driving. In addition, the tool is tasked with understanding driving habits and behaviors. The paper aims to demonstrate the use of CTM in analyzing data and determining maneuvers made by the driver. Along with this demonstration, the goal is to improve driving skills and make drivers more aware of recurring errors that could lead to accidents.

The rest of the paper is organized as follows. Section II discusses related work on traffic accidents. Section III discusses the problem that is trying to be addressed and the motivation for the research. Section IV explains the approach and preparation for the data collection. Section V reviews the tool's results and analysis, and Section VI concludes the paper.

II. LITERATURE REVIEW

Reducing traffic accidents will determine how drivers are held accountable. Car companies have added various features that assist the driver. For example, Auto Emergency Braking, or Smart Brake system, is designed to assist the driver in braking by detecting when the car is approaching another vehicle or object at a high acceleration rate. Car features that help the driver by alerting them will not reduce accidents. Priyanka et al. [7] focus on drivers by focusing on unintended acceleration and drowsiness by the driver. Their attention is channeled to solutions that react to users' driving actions, not driving behaviors. The authors in [7] suggest using ultrasonic sensors that use sound waves to determine the distance to an object. This proposition is similar to most intelligent braking systems in newer vehicles. In addition, they propose using a heartbeat sensor that will be attached to the driver's seatbelt. The driver's heartbeat is monitored, and when spiked or presents abnormal rhythms paired with the ultrasonic sensors will cause the car to decelerate and brake. The second solution is to detect if the driver is sleeping or beginning to fall asleep using the input obtained by a webcam using image processing tools [7]. This paper gives an example of technology being researched and created to react to driver behavior rather than improve driver behavior. Although these are excellent additions to a vehicle that will prevent various traffic accidents, they only give drivers the false belief that their hiccups and errors will be stopped due to car features. They do not encourage drivers to drive better, but rather give comfort to making mistakes.

Automobiles of the future could have customizable Driver-Vehicle Interaction (DVI) engines with an interaction system to learn driving propensity and behaviors, as Choi et al. [4] suggested. A successive and repetitive cycle to customize and personalize real-time driving environments will be developed utilizing Machine Learning (ML) [4]. This will allow DVI engines to adjust and adapt to their driver and tailor certain features to them. The learning process is solely to create a better DVI engine for the driver rather than provide feedback to drivers. A great addition is sending the driver an assessment of their performance.

The explainability offered to drivers can inspire the development of training methods and evaluation metrics that guarantee trustworthiness and consistency [2]. In addition, evaluation metrics can be organized and tuned to fit the overall goal of this research. Using the same evaluation metrics for diverse design objectives can be problematic when selecting measurement methods [2]. For CTM, evaluation metrics made preemptively were adjusted and followed an interactive design process. This process and focus ensure that the tool is constantly evolving and improving to ensure feedback given to drivers allows them to identify accurately what driving behaviors can be improved.

Ali et al. [1] use evaluation metrics to evaluate their predictive model's performance. Accuracy is one of their metrics and represents the percentage of correctly classified

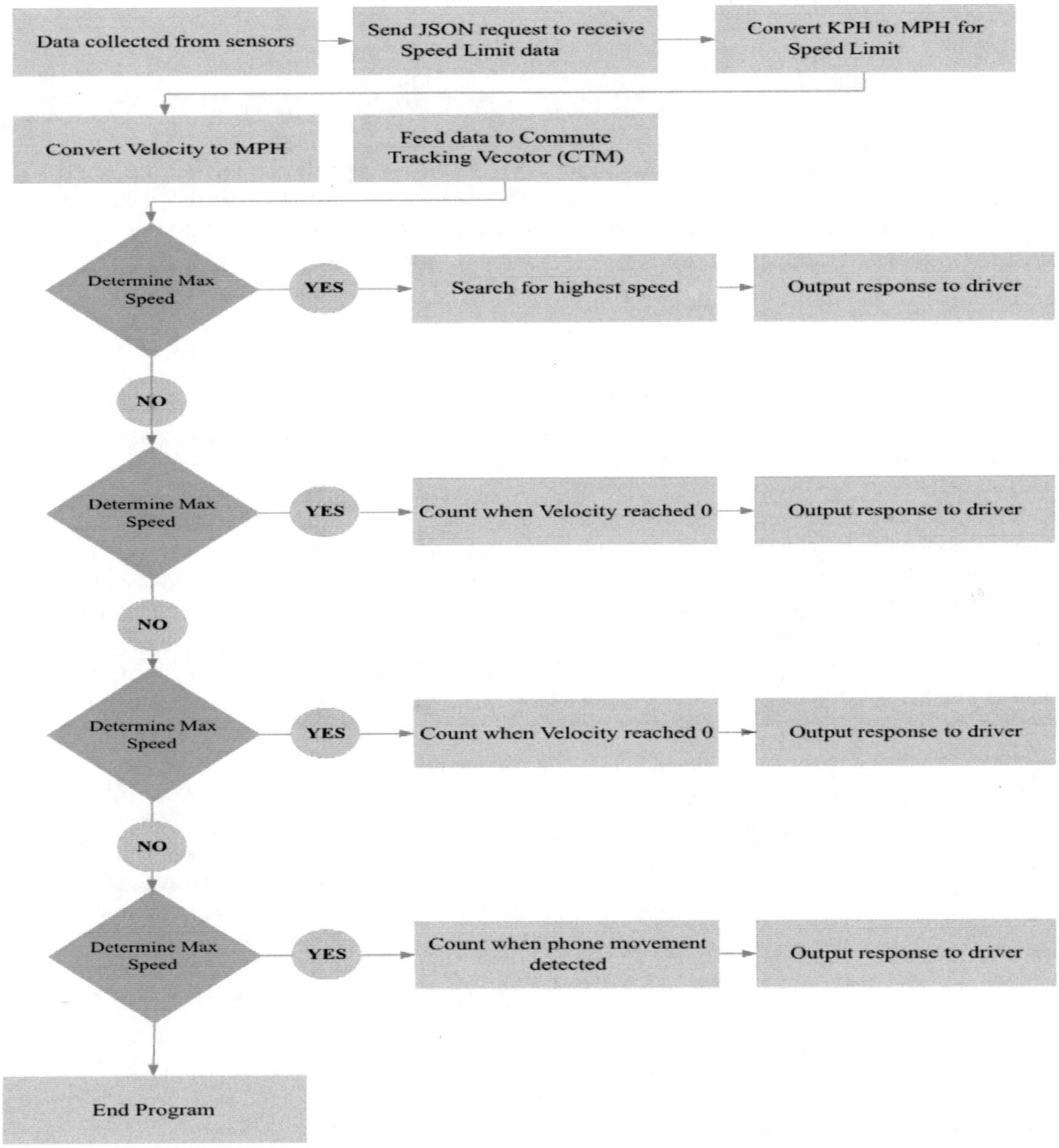

Figure 1. Flow chart demonstrating the data collection and analyzation process of CTM.

subjects in the test dataset. Another metric is sensitivity, which conveys information about correctly classified patients' percentages. Metrics have been organized for CTM to identify when the driver has stopped their vehicle abruptly or identify their maximum speed. Identifying and analyzing this data throughout their car ride summarizes their actions. In addition, this metric can be tuned to identify poor and good drivers among the datasets.

Unlike previous work, in this paper, the pairing of CTM and mobile phone data is the ambitious factor in addressing drivers' behavior using data collected from their driving patterns. AI will be used as a decision support/augmentation tool rather than as the automation of decision-making [3]. A significant difference in this paper's work is that the environment is not simulated and is recorded in real drivers' performances. Various hardware and software algorithms are being developed; however, they are being tested in simulated environments instead of real driving ones [5]. This is mainly due to the danger of testing and analyzing specific scenarios such as drowsiness and drunk driving. Lastly, CTM focuses on learning drivers' behaviors and providing feedback.

III. PROBLEM STATEMENT AND MOTIVATION

The focus of this paper is to study driving patterns from the driver and detect different drivers' behaviors while they drive. Behaviors can include when the driver is speeding or stops abruptly. The focus of this paper will help address car accidents. If car accidents can be reduced, fewer people will lose their lives each year, and even more will not be injured. This paper proposes a solution that will lead to safer roads for automobiles. Each year, car accidents have a significant effect on countless individuals and their families. Lives are lost, and families are scarred and endure unbearable suffering. The motivation lies in being able to prevent these tragedies. In addition, the motivation is grounded in the belief that through research and practical solutions, car accidents can become less common, lives can be saved, and families can remain intact.

IV. METHODOLOGY/APPROACH

Data collection involves observing automobile trips from Point A to Point B. Data was collected using a mobile app called Phyphox. This app allows users to use tools such as a Gyroscope and Accelerometer in our phone to track the phones movement and its surroundings. Phyphox can gather data without inconveniencing the driver. Data collection was gathered, handled, and utilized with various resources. All experiments used an iPhone 13 Pro Max, the Phyphox app, and an automobile. After experiments, drivers can store the data locally on their phones or export it to another storage type (Google Drive, Dropbox, etc.). The flow diagram in Figure 1 presents a step-by-step process of collecting and processing the data. Data is collected from the sensors and saved locally onto the mobile device.

The Location sensor is then accessed to obtain the Longitude and Latitude. Those coordinates are sent using a JavaScript Object Notation (JSON) request to a Google Application Programming Interface (API). The API it is sent to is the Road API. The API sends back the speed limits of the roads the drivers drove on. This speed limit data is used further when analyzing the driver's commute. The following process is the removal of any unused sensor data from data sheets. Decluttering unnecessary data allows CTM to process and analyze data more efficiently. In the following process, math calculations convert data into Miles Per Hour (MPH). The speed limit data is received in Kilometers Per Hour (KPH); therefore, using Eq. (1), the data is converted into miles per hour:

$$MPH = kph \div 1.60934 \qquad (1)$$

The Velocity data is received from the Location sensor. Velocity is needed to track the drivers' speed throughout their commute. It is measured in meters per second (m/s); therefore, the data needed to be converted to MPH. Eq. (2) was used in the conversion process:

$$MPH = velocity \div 0.44704 \qquad (2)$$

The data is pushed to CTM to begin analysis and provide feedback. CTM can determine the maximum speed reached, total stops, and whether the driver exceeded or remained under the limit. CTM has demands and uses a standard prompt response. However, CTM will add additional comments for the driver.

For this research, the following sensors were selected for the simple experiment: Gyroscope, Longitude, Latitude, Direction, and Velocity. Once set up, the driver must choose their simple experiment in the home screen and push start in the top right corner of the screen. An experiment would begin before leaving Point A and stop when the destination, Point B, was reached.

The Location sensor has seven parameters being collected. Displayed in Figure 2 are two of the four parameters collected from the Location sensor. The four parameters focused on in this paper are Longitude, Latitude, Velocity, and Direction. These parameters enable us to determine the max speed, speed limits, total stops, and directional changes. This is possible because the Location sensor uses the raw data from the phone's Global Positioning System (GPS).

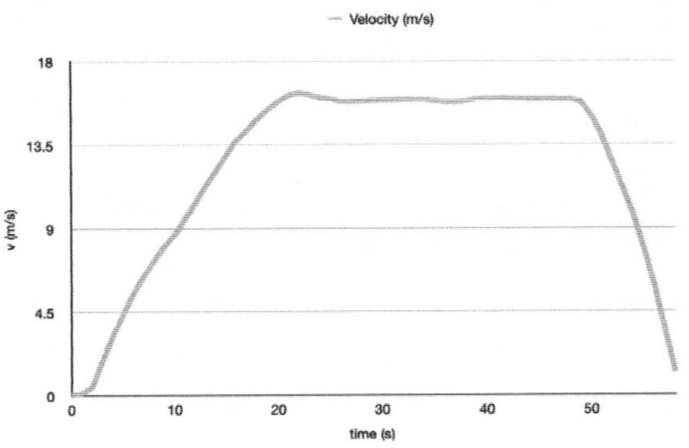

(a)

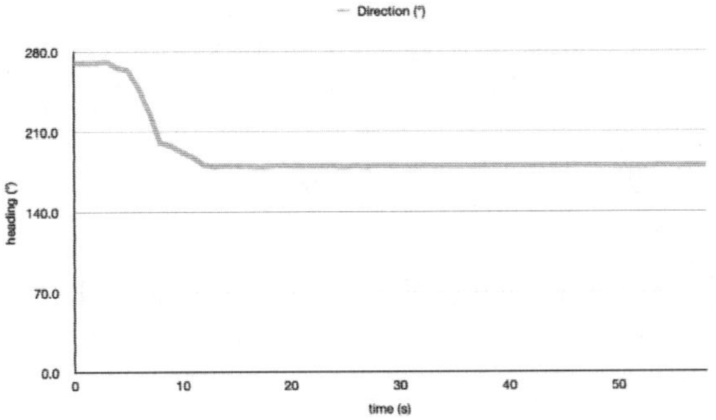

(b)

Figure 2. Velocity (a) and Direction (b) graphs of a 60-second car ride.

The Velocity graph (a) provides the most accurate vehicle speed data. In the graph, the velocity steadily increases, reaching its maximum velocity at 20 seconds. Toward the end of the journey, the vehicle has a relatively quick decrease in velocity. In Direction graph (b), the vehicle makes a turn early in the ride. This appears only to last a few seconds, eventually leveling into a linear road for the duration of the ride.

The second pair of parameters used from Location is Latitude and Longitude. The coordinates assist the CTM in identifying the minimum speed limit on roads the drivers travel on. The coordinates are sent using JSON. The coordinates arrive at a Google API called Roads API. Roads API accepts Hypertext Transfer Protocol Secure (HTTPS) requests with latitude/longitude coordinates. It uses the points to identify road segments and can return speed limits found. Once this data is received from Roads API, the speed limits are sent to CTM. CTM can see when the driver is below or above the speed limit, allowing the driver to be flagged for going above the speed limit.

These sensors provide the data and knowledge for CTM to accurately analyze their drivers' commutes. Precise points in the driver's commute make it possible to focus on improving their performance and behaviors in particular areas. Data collection, sanitization, and CTM flow are reliable and effective. CTM is given a CSV file where it can begin to analyze and provide the best and most applicable feedback to the driver.

V. RESULTS AND ANALYSIS

CTM's analysis and understanding of drivers' behavior are remarkable. The goal was to determine four data metrics: Exceeded Speed Limit Count, Max Speed, Total Stops, and Total Abrupt Stops. In Table I, five test samples are presented. This data comes from one specific driver who took similar routes when recording their data and driving. The data collected by the sensors is recorded every second the experiment is running. The average seconds for these experiments were a little under 560 seconds, about 9 minutes. In the first column, the driver's speed is investigated. The max speed reached is consistent, remaining between 57 and 64 MPH. The max speed was determined because of the Location sensor mentioned earlier. The Velocity parameter allows to determine the speed.

The following two columns analyzed when the driver was at rest. In the Total Stops, the data is consistent. As mentioned, the driver took an identical route from Point A to Point B; therefore, shouldn't the Total Stops be identical? The answer is no. The driver was unlucky in Test Sample 1, stopping ten times. This could be due to getting a red light or stopping abruptly because of other factors on the road. However, the driver was highly unlucky in Test Sample 5. They stopped a total of 40 times. In reality, this sample is a demonstration of inconsistencies that were found within the CTM analysis. It is important to note and understand that AI is not perfect, but it can be trained to be nearly perfect. This requires more data to train models and provide better and more accurate results.

Total Abrupt Stops were analyzed by analyzing the deceleration of the vehicle the Total Abrupt Stops were able to be determined. If the vehicle's speed decreased by less than 6.7 MPH in one second, it would be considered an abrupt stop. In the following equations, a is the vehicle's deceleration in m/s^2. Eq. (3) demonstrates the math needed to decide:

$$athreshold = \frac{6.7\,MPH}{1s} \times 0.44704\,\frac{m}{s^2} \quad (3)$$

Once the threshold as given in the above equation is calculated, the MPH that occurred is compared with the following second. If the threshold exceeds the following MPH, then CTM will flag that as an abrupt stop. Eq. (4) demonstrates a visual of how CTM is pairing the thresholds and MPH. In Eq. (4), the current speed is compared to the previous speed multiplied by the threshold.

$$MPH\,(i + 1) < MPH(i) \times athreshold \quad (4)$$

Abrupt stops can occur for various reasons. To name a few: distracted driving (driver is on their phone, looking at something, not in front of the vehicle, stop light changes), other drivers abruptly stopping for unknown reasons, or something occurring in the road that forces the driver to stop. Abrupt stops can be avoided by safely following other drivers to react to their stops, keeping eyes on the road at all times, examining the surroundings of the path ahead, and lastly, abiding by the speed limit given for that specific road.

TABLE I. TEST SAMPLE ANALYSIS AND PERFORMANCE

Test Sample	Max Speed	Total Stops	Total Abrupt Stops	Above Speed Limit	Phone Movement
1	64	10	5	271	8
2	57	8	3	301	7
3	60	7	4	246	5
4	57	8	4	279	12
5	58	40	2	232	7

The next column investigates when the driver exceeded the speed limit. The average the driver exceeded the speed limit in seconds was 266 throughout the five samples. They are not very safe drivers. CTM can provide feedback to the driver and notify them where they were speeding. This is an important aspect of CTM because it can interact with the driver and make recommendations. A recommendation could suggest the driver depart to their desired location sooner, so they are not rushing to their destination.

Finally, while the program was running, the drivers could not navigate through their mobile devices without ending the data collection process. CTM was tasked with analyzing drivers operating their mobile devices, but there would be minimal movement between the driver and their device. The final column reports the number of seconds the driver's phone moved. CTM flags when the device is moved. The phone movement mainly occurred when drivers had their devices in their hands, began to run a simple experiment or end one, and then placed their phones down.

Displayed in Figure 3 are three graphs from the gyroscope sensor. In graphs (a) and (b), there are no movements detected in their respective directions; however, in graph (c), there was a movement made in the direction Z. This was an intentional movement made to test CTM on being able to detect this movement. CTM was able to confirm movement for 4 seconds successfully.

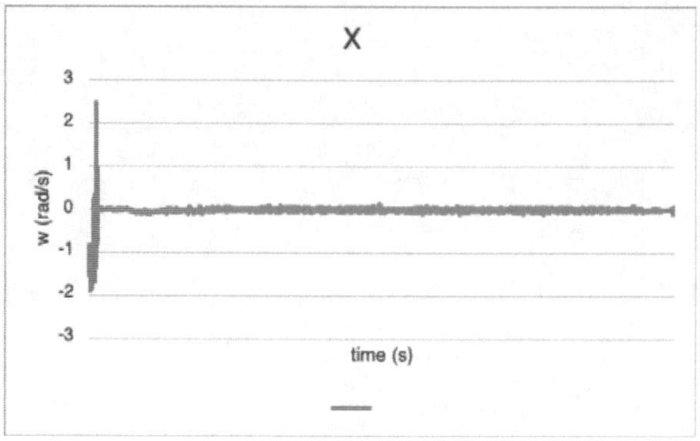

(a)

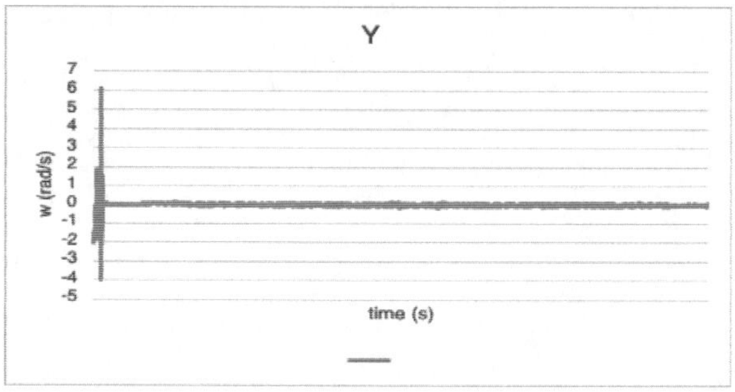

(b)

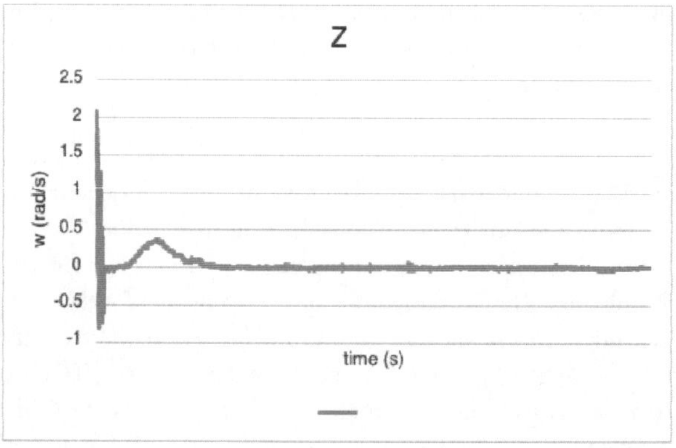

(c)

Figure 3. The X (a), Y (b), and Z(c) Gyroscope graphs of a 60-second car ride.

This overview of mobile device's sensors and data gathering, and analysis demonstrates the capabilities of providing a detailed response for the user's commute. The significance of these results is the opportunity to improve driving patterns and behaviors in aspiration to decrease automobile accidents. In addition, it focuses on the correction of the driver and not the automobile. Mobile devices are in the hands of billions of people and go wherever their user goes; therefore, the accessibility to this tool is obtainable. CTM could be integrated with automobiles; however, this will be another price tag car companies will attach to their vehicles, thus deterring people from this technology and making it accessible. The accessibility, efficiency, and consumable format that this app offers will allow a wide range of applicants to contribute to safer roads.

VI. CONCLUSION AND FUTURE WORK

This research paper has presented a comprehensive solution to address road safety and traffic accidents through AI-driven driving behavior analysis. Automobile accidents primarily occur due to driver errors. This knowledge emphasizes the urgency of finding innovative and practical solutions to improve drivers' skills and behaviors. Car companies cannot continue to focus solely on the equipment and features that will react or assist drivers but focus on improving the drivers' driving capabilities. The solution provided in this paper is utilizing mobile devices to track driving patterns and drivers' maneuvers. Liberty Mutual's RightTrack app and its counterparts have demonstrated that with an incentive involved, driving behaviors can be improved using solely a mobile device. Leaders that can provide incentives are universities, car insurance companies, and government institutions. Solving this problem will require a collective effort and innovative ideas that will lead to better solutions. While some metrics require refinement, the paper's approach significantly promotes responsible driving and expresses its efforts to reduce automobile accidents.

For future work, the goal would be to bundle the device's sensors, data analysis, and a user interface that allows a descriptive and straightforward overview of results into a mobile app. This will allow for a more simplistic data process and a more straightforward data-gathering method. Furthermore, this will allow us to track and analyze when the driver is operating their mobile device. Device movement can be tracked using a Gyroscope, and the operation of the mobile device can be tracked through a mobile app—the possibility to see when they are navigating through their device while the vehicle is moving is obtainable.

Secondly, similarly to how authors in [4] focus on adaptive cockpits and DVI engines, CTM can adapt over time to understand the drivers and how to improve their behaviors. Drivers could have a specific CTM trained solely on their data, allowing the CTM to make concrete suggestions that will be more applicable to their driver.

Lastly, bringing CTM to a larger pool of test subjects will bring exponential growth to the improvement of this tool. Reaching out to large organizations like universities or car companies will open the door to providing better incentives to use the app and perform well. For example, students at university receive scholarship money for good driving behavior, or car companies can offer a specific program to reward their drivers for good behavior. In addition, and most importantly, CTM will be brought to more people, further improving driving behaviors and decreasing traffic accidents. CTM has been proven to study and determine driving behaviors and patterns. It will be an excellent tool and solution to decreasing traffic accidents.

REFERENCES

[1] L. Ali, "An automated diagnostic system for heart disease prediction based on $\chi 2$ statistical model and optimally configured Deep Neural Network", *IEEE Access*, vol. 7, pp. 34938–34945. doi.org/10.1109/access.2019.2904800

[2] S. Ali et al., "Explainable artificial intelligence (XAI): What we know and what is left to attain trustworthy artificial intelligence", *Information Fusion*, vol. 99 doi.org/10.1016/j.inffus.2023.101805

[3] Y. Duan, J. S. Edwards, and Y. K. Dwivedi, "Artificial Intelligence for decision making in the era of big data – evolution, challenges, and research agenda", *International Journal of Information Management*, *48*, pp. 63–71, 2019. doi.org/10.1016/j.ijinfomgt.2019.01.021

[4] J. -K. Choi, K. Kim, D. Kim, H. Choi, and B. Jang, "Driver-adaptive vehicle interaction system for the advanced digital cockpit," 2018 20th International Conference on Advanced Communication Technology (ICACT), Chuncheon, Korea (South), 2018, pp. 307-310, doi: 10.23919/ICACT.2018.8323736.

[5] H. B. Kang, "Various Approaches for Driver and Driving Behavior Monitoring: A Review," 2013 IEEE International Conference on Computer Vision Workshops, Sydney, NSW, Australia, 2013, pp. 616-623, doi: 10.1109/ICCVW.2013.85.

[6] "NHTSA Releases 2020 Traffic Crash Data", *U.S. Department of Transportation*, www.transportation.gov/briefing-room/nhtsa-releases-2020-traffic-crash-data, 2020.

[7] S. Priyanka, G. Hemalatha and C. Saranya, "Sudden unintended acceleration avoidance and drowsiness detector for automobile accidents prevention," 2017 Third International Conference on Science Technology Engineering & Management (ICONSTEM), Chennai, India, 2017, pp. 964-967, doi: 10.1109/ICONSTEM.2017.8261346.

Direct Democracy System Architecture for Sustainable Community Participation

Aderonke Thompson, Nikolaos Papakonstantinou, Dharmendra Sharma

Safe and Connected Society
VTT Technical Research Centre of Finland
Espoo, Finland
e-mails: ext-aderonke.thompson@vtt.fi, Nikolaos.papakonstantinou@vtt.fi, Dharmendra.Sharma@vtt.fi

Abstract— **Active community participation without being tagged as hate speech contribution has been an established desirable element for citizens towards achieving a sustainable democratic process in communities across the world. Significant contributions to bridge this gap have been proposed by means of web technology adoption. Unarguably, in the context of free communication, anonymity is sought for serious contributions. Thus, in this paper, we examine four state-of the-art democracy platforms based on open-source technologies vis-à-vis their system architecture and features. It is observed that, while some of these platforms provide active democratic citizens participation, by e-voting, none of them adopts anonymity and full decentralization technology open-source platform in the discussion forum, which is a pivot for the waned participants' trust with the conventional centralized system that is inherently prone to single-point of failure problems; this is also prone to the vulnerabilities of data at rest, in transit and storage. Consequently, we propose a full decentralized system, based on blockchain technology that is capable of being integrated with the state-of-the-art system to ensure trust, tamper-resistance, sybil-resistance, accountability, reliability, transparency, and security, using a tokenization with the exclusive consideration of gas optimization technique to lower the cost each citizen will incur using the system.**

Keywords-architecture; anonymity; sybil-resistance; decentralization; blockchain.

I. INTRODUCTION

Governance, an outcome of citizens' choice, is evolving in organizations and communities around the world with a consensus that a good governance is quintessential for inclusion and diversity of citizens. It is a decision-making process among available options to select who governs. Of all governance types, democratic governance is the most embraced and sought after since every citizen has a platform to exercise their franchise during the electioneering process. Conversely, as laudable as the democratic governance is, the process is plagued with insincerity and mostly lacks credibility, in addition to a high cost; authors in [27] emphasize adequate fairness and transparency as a wit towards realizing a sustainable and smart governance that integrates citizens' livelihood improvement.

The following problems have been identified to be a major concern in traditional and existing electronic voting protocol:

i. the anonymity of ballot and privacy.
ii. single point of failure.
iii. inefficient authentication mechanism.
iv. votes are not universally verifiable.

Elections form the basis of governance in a democratic setting, which is the current and most acceptable type of governance that enables citizens' participation. It is a political process that requires citizens vote according to their opinion. This is done from small communities to various organizations, states, and the country at large. The process requires a high degree of trustworthiness since it is geared towards selection of capable officers that citizens deem fit for a particular position of leadership. In recent years, traditional voting systems such as paper-based voting have been heavily used, which requires voters to cast votes in appointed polling stations; the process should be transparent, secure, and reliable to ensure credibility. Since improvement is always sought, it is no doubt that advancement in Science and Technology (S&T) has impacted this increasingly evolving sphere. This advancement is principally the result of the efforts to have a secure, provable, transparent system with robust voter authentication and identification. Thus, since it is the most acceptable form of governance by citizens, advancement is incessantly sought on the overall voting system's resilience and efficiency.

E-voting is a method that digitizes voting and promises to resolve the issues and challenges related to manual voting elections on a software platform using an electronic device. Yet, the inadequacy of the e-voting systems is largely due to design flaws of centralization such as codebase, database, monitoring tools of the required infrastructure. This implies a single point of failure in secure design principles model in OWASP Software Assurance Maturity Model (SAMM) [28]. The overall impact that is beyond voters' control is that, as soon as ballot is marked and a vote is cast, the entire trust of the process lies upon the organization to ensure that there is no fraud [1]-[3]. Therefore, voters' trustworthiness become an illusion due to the non-availability of independently provable tools as anticipated by voters; that is, the degree of components compliance in relation to security characteristics as shown with its specified functionality [4], The highlighted points either hypothetically diminish voters' participation, or imposes reservations on election outcome.

Nakamoto [13] introduced blockchain technology with the development of the first cryptocurrency called Bitcoin. Blockchain stores blocks that contain a set of data such that every next block is linked to the previous one in the form of a linked list and a cryptographically secure way so that it becomes impossible to change anything in the previous blocks without rendering the blockchain invalid. It is a decentralized distributed system of nodes that works in a coordinated way with the help of a consensus protocol. It is pertinent to note that blockchain technology is not sufficient to eliminate some of the susceptible vulnerabilities of e-voting such as device compromise, voter coercion, identity verification, user error as well as network attacks [16][29].

This paper explores the use of blockchain and tokenization to facilitate secure e-voting applications with the ability to assure voter anonymity, sybil-resistance, voter's eligibility, vote integrity, and end-to-end verification. This proposed system leverages fundamental blockchain features such as a self-cryptographic validation structure through hashes and public availability of distributed ledger of records that is accessible to everyone. Blockchain technology plays a key role in the domain of electronic voting due to the inherent nature of preserving anonymity, as well as maintaining a decentralized and publicly distributed ledger of transactions across all the nodes. This paper presents a detailed design of the proposed e-voting protocol, which can achieve an end-to-end verifiable, sybil-resistant and secure election process. The rest of this paper is structured as follows. Section II presents a review of the state-of-the-art architecture with related works. Section III describes the proposed system. Section IV highlights the challenges of the existing system. Section V conclusion wraps up the article with acknowledgement.

II. LITERATURE REVIEW

All the state-of-the-art platforms considered are active web applications serving many communities across the globe - DemocracyOS, Consul Democracy Decidim and D-Cent. The core and common characteristic of these platforms leverage the benefit of open-source software for cost-effectiveness, flexible and agile development processes, robust community-driven support, and easy license management. In addition, these applications hinge on the high degree of open-source community on responsiveness to information security continuous integration and deployment to fix emerging bugs.

A. *State-of-the-art*

DemocracyOS focuses on solving the increasing challenge of unsatisfactory expression of democratic issues through inadequate binary choices and decreasing reductionist proxies; the continuous clashing proxy representation with individual's interest, consequential crisis arisen from these issues cut across the world. Then, government insistence of citizens' exclusion from such conversations should be addressed since decisions made affect all the citizens. Because technology has a strong democratizing potential in citizens horizon; harnessing the collective wise, pluralistic views ensure choosing from pre-set options to actively designing the options dynamically.

Hence, DemocracyOS is developed to achieve construction, institutional-building, and productive participatory discussion, rather than agitation, protest and citizens taking to the streets, by making information accessible to citizens. DemocracyOS pioneered creating a link between two types of formal code, otherwise known as digital software (the net) and the legal contractual system currently operating in most governmental processes. The design is for parliaments and other institutions saddled with collective decision task; being a mix among direct and representative democracy targeting the act of voting and voting on their representative selection modality alongside these beneficiaries - Argentina netizens, non-governmental organizations as regulators, developers, and hacktivists globally for law markup language towards legislative sources data standardization [5].

CONSUL as a non-profit organization reinforces the quality, neutrality, and credibility of global citizen participation in democratic process integration with independence, transparency rule of law and inclusion. Municipalities of Madrid, Buenos, Porto Alegre New York among other institutions across 35 countries actively deploy and interact with the platform. CONSUL is designed for citizens to voice their concerns and participate through proposal development, votes for new laws, debates, crowd laws, participatory budgets, and consultations. Proposal and debates are citizen-centric considering environments are utilities that make life easy. CONSUL was a response to the 2011 15M Spanish indignados for "real democracy" demand sequel to some prevalent issues such as financial and housing crises, lack of job prospects for youth, corruption as well as lack of political legitimacy of democratic institutions [6]. The platform provides democratic processes and institution improvement by fostering a new way of citizens engagement coupled with active participation, accountability and transparency of public issues affecting the citizens. The impact of the project has continued to rise across the city of Madrid and across the world as some organizations have adopted the platform for various democratic discussions and voting processes.

Decidim contributes the societal democratization processes through the construction of technology, methodologies, practices, standards actions, narratives, and values in a collaborative and reflective way. Adoption of the platform cuts across cities and organizations worldwide such as city council, an association, NGO, a university, trade union and neighbourhood association [7].

D-Cent, an acronym for Decentralized Citizens ENgagement Technologies, an EU-funded project from October 2013 to May 2016. D-Cent is a next generation open- source, distributed, and privacy-aware tools for direct democracy and economic empowerment. D-Cent is a multidisciplinary testbed platform for emerging social movements, new models for citizen control of personal and social data in addition to privacy and security by design. D-Cent is characterized with real-time notifications about issues of concerns; policies and proposals collaborations; collective municipal budgeting and give freecoin incentives to citizens [8]. Table 1 gives the summary of the four state-of-the-art.

TABLE 1. STATE-OF-THE-ART PLATFORMS

Sate-of-the-art	Decidim.org	DemocracyOS	Consul Democracy	D-Cent
Purpose	It ensures participatory democracy, that is, a platform for common citizens to participate in the decision/policy by submitting proposal and this proposal can be voted for/against.	It ensures participatory democracy with Global rule of Law in 140 Countries	It ensures participatory democracy	It enables prompt information to the citizens with real-time notifications about issues of concern an open-source platform.
Source Management	Barcelona, Spain	Argentina	City of Madrid	EU
Benefits	It can be integrated with any system that requires collective, participatory decision/policy making.	It allows debate current legislation for robust public debate.	It can be integrated with any system that requires collective, participatory decision/policy making	It supports collection of various open-source tools to enable participatory governance. Some tools are blockchain based
Features	Strategic planning, participatory processes, assemblies, initiatives and citizen consultations, participatory budgeting, networked communication, accountability, equity and transparency, levels of abstraction (process and activities are separate, social contract, community	User-friendly, Collaboration between citizens and government, simple, bill tracking, Standard repository for global public documents, accountability, and civic watchdog capabilities	Customisable, secure, on-going support, proposals, participatory budgeting, debates Collaborative, legislation, incentive	Open authentication and distributed identity management, Citizen's control and data ownership, Open source and open standards, Blockchain trust Propose and draft, Decide and vote Incentivized usage
Technologies	Ruby on Rails, Vue.JS, Postgres, SQL,	GitHub is not available	Ruby on Rails, Postgres, SQL, Docker Elasticsearch	Ruby, Docker
Platform	Web	Web	Web	Web
Web Technology	Partial decentralization Web 2.0 decentralised approach to decision making,	Web 2.0	Web 2.0	Web 2.0

B. *State-of-the-art Architecture*

The four states-of-the-art architecture reveals the functional focus and target in a unique way that suites the stakeholders which are the citizens. Decidim and D-Cent system architecture are available from their detailed system documentation - Figures 1 and 2 respectively, it is assumed that the core architecture is tailored with the general e-voting model system-specific requirements:

i. Multi-user: a few voters can vote simultaneously.
ii. System Security: The overall system security is paramount to protect identity theft and system manipulation by outsiders or third parties.
iii. Accessibility: voters can access the system from any location using secure Internet and/or mobile devices through a web browser.
iv. Availability: the system must have high availability during an election campaign.

C. *Related Works*

This section elucidates existing studies stressing their motivations, objectives, methodologies, contributions to knowledge, and limitations.

[15] presents "Blockchain technology-based e-voting system". The authors stated that elections become a pertinent occurrence during democratic process, however, distrust has been the bane of electioneering process from global perspective. Some giant economies still suffer from these concerns: flawed legal system, fraudulent characterized voting system, electronic vote machine hacking, election manipulation, and booth capturing square measure are the key challenges facing the electoral system. The authors preferred the e-voting solution to the highlighted challenges. The drawback of this research is that it does not satisfy some electronic voting requirements such as anonymous vote-cast.

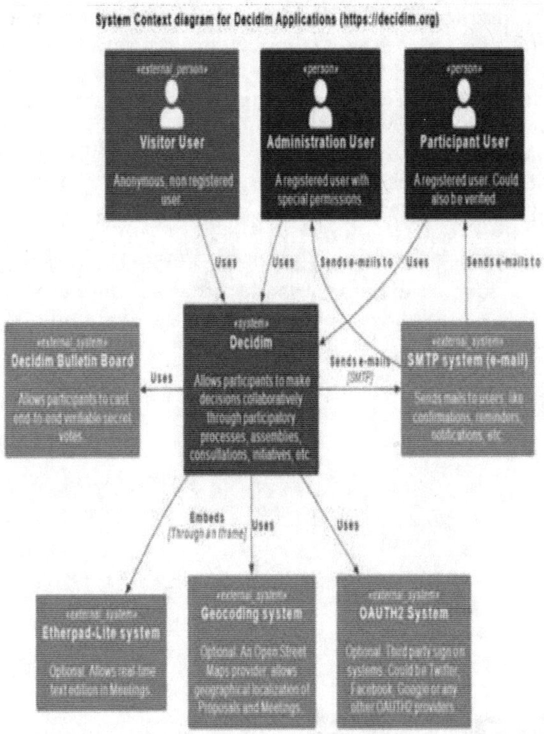

Figure 1. System Architecture for Decidim Application [26]

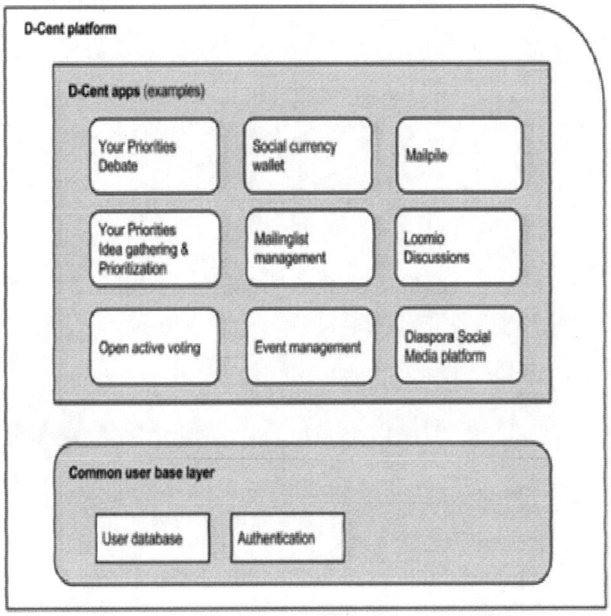

Figure 2. System Architecture for D-Cent Application [27].

[16] presents "An E-Voting Protocol with Decentralization and Voter Privacy". The focus of the study is to adopt a blockchain-based e-voting protocol that meets electronic voting requirements. Additionally, editing feature is integrated to allow voters change of mind in case it occurs within a given period. Decentralization, network peers for voters' control, and a degree of centralization is required to achieve the set objectives. Other highlights are pros and cons of blockchain adoption empirically in development/deployment and usage contexts with complex applications prospects. The drawback of this research is that there is a Central Authority (CA), as centralization point of the protocol with trustworthiness assumption. However, a malicious act from the CA brings distrust that might result to arbitrarily manipulation of cast votes for unaccredited voters; this is non-conformity to e-voting requirement.

[17] presents a "Blockchain-based e-voting approach in P2P Network". The study adopted Distributed Ledger Technology (DLT) to circumvent vote forging options plus non-repudiation and users' one-time login. Integrating the techniques with the DLT and secure e-voting user authentication in the p2p network is proposed such that trust is enhanced via vote forgery circumvention. This research was proposed because of the internet and information technologies advancement, organizations are moving from on-premise to cloud-based platforms. The drawback of this research is that a secure device is required to cast votes. Although, authors stated that the system is secure, but the system is vulnerable and susceptible to malware attacks from hackers to cast or alter vote. A major strength of the system is voter access to vote only once with no editing feature in the case of unintended errors during the voting process.

In [18], the authors explore the difficulties and uses of electronic voting procedures in elections, emphasizing the vulnerability to fraud and the demand for safe and reliable vote information. The paper advocates using blockchain technology to build a decentralized system that can validate voting data and guard against manipulation to address these problems. The decentralization of blockchain makes data backup and tracking simpler, hence maintaining the validity of the voting data. Electronic voting can use blockchain technology to increase the results' authenticity and safeguard the vote data integrity.

In [19], the authors aimed at establishing trust in the E-voting system. They examined issues with current electronic voting systems, such as fraud, a lack of transparency, and security threats like intimidation and bribery. The paper suggests a fair and transparent electronic voting system built on blockchain technology to address these problems. Therefore, their system employs a time-release encryption technique to ensure voting process fairness and a receiver-denial encryption scheme to ensure coercion resistance.

III. PROPOSED SYSTEM

Technology paradigm has continued to impact governance mechanisms and processes that culminate into a sustainable society; this study seeks to bridge the gap by adopting tokenization and blockchain technology. Electronic-voting requirements are in two parts, viz, generic, and system-specific. The generic requirements applying to general e-voting scheme, as presented by [20] and [21], include:

i. Privacy: Anyone cannot know for whom the voter voted. The ballot is hidden from outside observers.

ii. Individual verifiability: The ability of a voter to verify that the ballot has been counted.
iii. Eligibility: Only the legal voters can enroll in the voting event.
iv. Accuracy/Integrity: Every vote should be counted correctly.
iv. Fairness: Nothing can influence the result of voting. If the system leaks the voting result or the authority adds a voter during the voting, the event can be defined as unfair.
v. Uniqueness: Every voter can only vote once. The voter will have no permission to vote more if he votes.
vi. Robustness: Anyone.

A. *Integrated System Approah*

Information and data are critical to technical assessment and decision-making in a software system development lifecycle; therefore, ensuring system architecture aligns with system requirements is fundamental to achieving stakeholders concerns towards a set of consistent views and models. The state-of-the-art architectures align with the integrated system design approach [22] from the three concerned perspectives - stakeholder, system, and trades; stakeholders being the citizens, trades being the objectives and capabilities of the platforms; while system is the technology specifications deployed including security-driven constraints. In DDemo, emphasis is on system self-protection against sybil attacks, and secure system management. A rider to the integrated system approach is the state-of-the-art is compliance with the OWASP Software Assurance Maturity Model (SAMM) of people, process, and technology, it is an effective approach to system design [23].

B. *System Architecture*

System architecture is the fundamental concepts or properties of a system in its environment embodied in its elements, relationships, and in the principles of its design and evolution [24][25].

Stakeholders' perspective for free speech can be handled with the system architecture in Figures 3 and 4 to integrate full decentralization into the state-of-the art.

C. *Proposed System Overview*

The proposed-voting protocol implements decentralized data storage using blockchain technology to make the election procedure more decentralized, transparent, and secure. There are two (2) prominent group-oriented digital signatures that support both user-authentication and anonymity which are: Group signature and Ring signature. The signatures are modern cryptographic primitives, and they provide privacy preserved authentication feature. This type of signature preserves users' privacy by granting users the ability to get verified while also hiding their identities in a group. Signatures can be generated by a user who belongs to a group by representing a group. The signer can employ other users public key without their consent to hide his identity i.e., a user adds himself into any set of his choice and produces a signature. The e-voting protocol uses the ring signatures for privacy enhancement and multi signatures to create consensus between groups, the system integrates strong identity with tokenization. and it is linked to other verified identities to improve the system authentication which is important to voting eligibility requirement and overall system security. The proposed system consists of three phases; each phase contributes to the demonstration of the system's effectiveness to achieve an end-to-end verifiable e-voting scheme that satisfies all voting requirements.

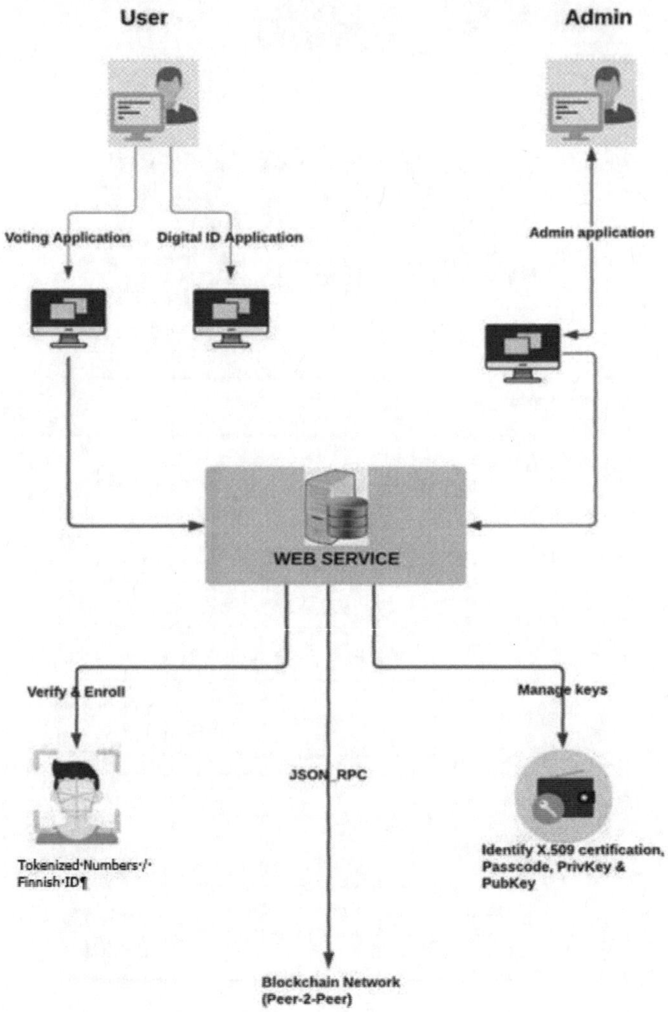

Figure 3. Proposed System Architecture.

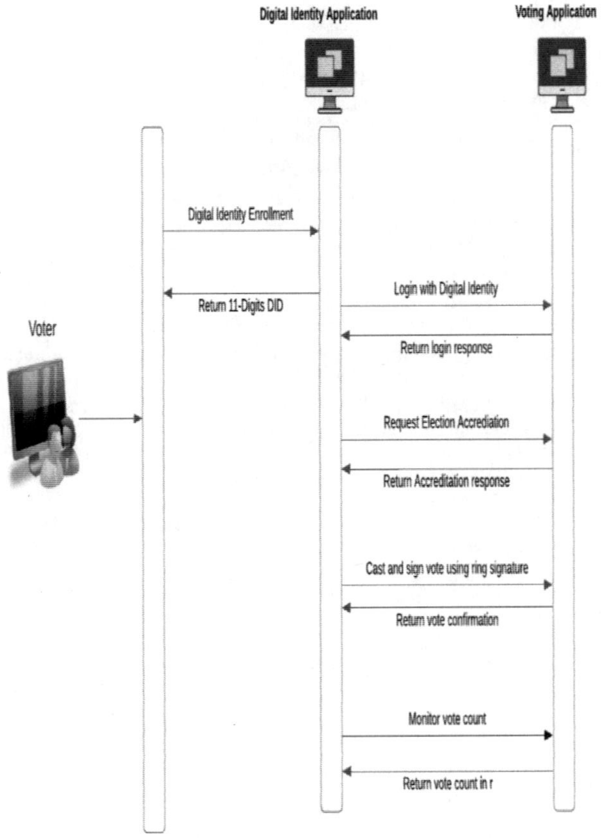

Figure 4. Proposed protocol voting phase and identity enrollment.

IV. CHALLENGES OF THE EXISTING SYSTEM

Hackers can compromise the integrity of the e-voting which is seen as a major disadvantage in the voting system. This could be done either physically or remotely where a malicious attacker changes millions of the vote data undetected. In the e-voting system, fraud is easier to perform. Identification of the voters would have to occur using participants' unique credentials such as his social security number, drive license. Perpetrators can acquire these pieces of information, logging themselves in the system and casting a vote for someone else. If someone gets a large amount of such unique identifiers with a data breach, they would be able to cast thousands of fraudulent votes. The manufacturers of these e-voting machines can be bias, causing influences in votes. Private companies who develop and distribute these e-voting systems would lock away their source code. Some companies that get hired by the government to implement these e-voting systems can act unbiased in inaccurately collecting and reporting votes. These acts do not guarantee a fair and unbiased election.

V. CONCLUSION

This paper presents the architecture of state-of-the-art platform for direct democracy participation and proposed a more secure platform with sybil resistant feature in addition to anonymity of participants using blockchain technology that meets the fundamental e-voting properties that provide full decentralization and places as much control of the process in the hands of the voters and the public. This is ongoing research; in which the system's application development is ongoing using solidity and react programming languages with gas optimization integration to ensure a lightweight feature and reduce cost for community participants. Thereafter, performance evaluation will be conducted using standard metrics.

ACKNOWLEDGMENT

The research is sponsored by the European Research Consortium for Informatics and Mathematics (ERCIM) and the host Institution – VTT Technical Research Institute of Finland.

REFERENCES

[1] D. Z. Tharindu, and K. B. N. Lakmali, Blockchain based e-voting system. International Journal of Soft Computing and Artificial Intelligence, vol. 7, Issue.1, May-2019. http://www.iraj.in/journal/journal_file/journal_pdf/4-570-15641401811-7.pdf.

[2] S. A.-B. Salman, S. Al-Janabi, & A. M. Sagheer, A Review on E-Voting Based on Blockchain Models. Iraqi Journal of Science, pp. 1362–1375, 2022. https://doi.org/10.24996/ijs.2022.63.3.38

[3] https://wentzwu.com/2021/08/02/systems-engineering-confidence-trust-and-assurance/ Accessed April 3, 2023.

[4] International Organization for Standardization/International Electrotechnical Commission/Institute of Electrical and Electronics Engineers 2011 ISO/IEC/IEEE 42010 – Systems and Software Engineering – Architecture description. https://www.iso.org/standard/50508.html

[5] https://worldjusticeproject.org/our-work/programs/democracyos, Accessed April 6, 2023.

[6] https://oecd-opsi.org/innovations/consul-project/, Accessed April 6, 2023.

[7] https://decidim.org/, Accessed April 6, 2023.

[8] https://dcentproject.eu/about-us/, Accessed April 6, 2023.

[9] H. Yi, Securing e-voting based on blockchain in P2P network. EURASIP Journal on Wireless Communications and Networking, 2019 (1). https://doi.org/10.1186/s13638-019-1473-6

[10] C. Angsuchotmetee and P. Setthawong, BlockVOTE : An Architecture of a Blockchain-based Electronic Voting System. ECTI Transactions on Computer and Information Technology (ECTI-CIT), 14(2), 174-189, 2020. https://doi.org/10.37936/ecti-cit.2020142.227455.

[11] M. Bernard, The 5 Big Problems With Blockchain Everyone Should Be Aware Of, retrieved from https://www.bernardmarr.com/default.asp?contentID=1354

[12] Y. Wu, An E-voting System based on Blockchain and Ring Signature [Master's thesis, University of Birmingham]. Dgalindo, 2017, https://www.dgalindo.es/mscprojects/yifan.pdf.

[13] S. Nakamoto, "Bitcoin: a peer-to-peer electronic cash system", Bitcoin, https://bitcoin.org/bitcoin.pdf, 2019.

[14] L. Dan, Could Estonia Be the Model for Secure Online Voting?. GovTech, https://www.govtech.com/blogs/lohrmann-on-cybersecurity/could-estonia-be-the-model-for-secure-online-voting.html, 2020.

[15] A. L. Anita, P. Junaid, P. Talif, and P. Prathmesh, Blockchain technology-based e-voting system. ITM Web Conf. vol. 32, 2020 International Conference on Automation, Computing and Communication 2020 (ICACC-2020). https://doi.org/10.1051/itmconf/20203203001.

[16] S.H. Freya, G. Apostolos, N. A. Raja, M. Konstantinos, "An E-Voting Protocol with Decentralisation and Voter Privacy", 2018 IEEE International Conference on Internet of Things (iThings) and IEEE Green Computing and Communications (GreenCom) and IEEE Cyber, Physical and Social Computing (CPSCom) and IEEE Smart Data (SmartData). https://doi.org/10.1109/Cybermatics_2018.2018.00262.

[17] N. Shanthi, R. Suvitha, and R.C. Suganthe, "Blockchain based e-voting approach in P2P Network", Journal of Critical Reviews, vol 7, issue 9, 2020. http://www.jcreview.com/fulltext/197-1590993271.pdf.

[18] E. Febriyanto, Triyono, N. Rahayu, K. Pangaribuan, and P. A. Sunarya, "Using Blockchain Data Security Management for E-Voting Systems", 8th International Conference on Cyber and IT Service Management (CITSM), 2020, https://doi.org/10.1109/citsm50537.2020.9268847

[19] M. N. Neloy et al., "A remote and cost - optimized voting system using blockchain and smart contract", IET Blockchain. 2023, https://doi.org/10.1049/blc2.12021

[20] B. Yu et al., "Platform-independent secure blockchain-based voting system", In: Chen, L., anulis, Schneider, S. (eds.) ISC 2018. LNCS, vol. 11060, pp. 369–386.Springer, Cham 2018. https://doi.org/10.1007/978-3-319-99136-8 20

[21] H. Tsung-Chih, W. Zhen-Yu., L. Chia-Hui, and C.Yu-Fang, "An Electronic voting system for defending free will and resisting bribery and coercion based on ring anonymous signcryption scheme", Sage journals, vol. 9 issue. 1, 2017. http://dx.doi.org/10.1177/1687814016687194

[22] https://nvlpubs.nist.gov/nistpubs/SpecialPublications/NIST.SP.800-160v1r1.pdf, Accessed April 6, 2023

[23] https://www.owasp.org, Accessed April 6, 2023.

[24] ISO/IEC/IEEE 12207:2017(en) Systems and software engineering — Software life cycle processes, 2017.

[25] ISO/IEC/IEEE 42010:2022(en) Software, systems and enterprise — Architecture description, 2022.

[26] https://docs.decidim.org/en/develop/develop/guide_architecture, Accessed April 7, 2023.

[27] H. J. Scholl and M. C. Scholl, ''Smart governance: A roadmap for research and practice,'' in Proc. IConference, 2014, pp. 163–176, https://dcentproject.eu/wp-content/uploads/2014/03/D4.2-final_new1.pdf Accessed April 7, 2023.

[28] OWASP SAMM v2.pdf https://owaspsamm.org/, Accessed November 6, 2023.

[29] R. Geetanjali, I. Razi, O. Waqar, K. B. Ali, "On the Design and Implementation of a Blockchain Enabled E-Voting Application Within IoT-Oriented Smart Cities" IEEE Access, 9:34165-34176, 2021, doi: 10.1109/ACCESS.2021.3061411 Accessed November 6, 2023.

Forecasting Failure Risk in Early Mathematics and Physics Courses of a Bachelor's in Engineering Degree

Isaac Caicedo-Castro*†‡, Mario Macea-Anaya†‡§, Samir Castaño-Rivera*‡
*Socrates Research Team
†Research Team: Development, Education, and Healthcare
‡Faculty of Engineering
§CINTIA, Centre of INnovation in Technology of Information to support the Academia
University of Córdoba
Montería, Colombia
emails: {isacaic, mariomacea, sacastano}@correo.unicordoba.edu.co

***Abstract*—In this research, we study the functional mapping between university admission test scores and the risk of failing in initial mathematics and physics courses for students embarking on a Bachelor's degree in Systems Engineering. We assume that the admission test assesses students' competence and proficiency in natural sciences and mathematics, essential prerequisites for success in the foundational courses of this Systems Engineering program. A deficiency in these subjects might result in failure, leading to dropouts or an extended degree completion timeline. We harnessed machine learning techniques to probe this issue, focusing on the landscape of Colombian universities, specifically analysing the Systems Engineering program at the University of Córdoba. In this Colombian educational context, universities, including our case study institution, rely on the national standardized admission test known as Saber 11 to evaluate candidates for Bachelor's degree programs. By adopting machine learning methods to unveil underlying patterns that govern this functional mapping, we might proactively identify students at risk of struggling in the aforementioned courses based on their admission test scores. Early identification of these at-risk students opens the opportunity to pre-emptive measures, such as offering preparatory courses to fortify their prerequisites for success in these challenging subjects. Our research involved the examination of academic records from 56 anonymized students, using both 10-fold and 5-fold cross-validation. The outcomes from the 10-fold cross-validation reveal that the support vector machine method yields mean values of 71.33% for accuracy, 68.33% for precision, 60% for recall, and 62.05% for the harmonic mean (F_1). Therefore, we conclude that this method outperforms the others studied in this work.**

Keywords*—*machine learning; quantum machine learning; educational data mining; supervised learning; classification methods; failure forecasting.

I. INTRODUCTION

This study is part of a broader research project called Course Prophet, whose goal is to design and implement an intelligent system to predict the risk of undergraduate students failing or dropping a course in the area of scientific computing in systems engineering at the University of Córdoba in Colombia. Scientific computing involves the use of mathematical models and computer simulations to solve complex engineering problems, such as, e.g., numerical methods and linear (or non-linear) programming. Our focus in this study is on predicting whether students are at risk of failing the foundational first courses of mathematics and physics in scientific computing, which are critical for success in advanced courses. The forecasting is based on the student's admission test outcomes. Early identification of at-risk students by the Course Prophet system has the potential to improve retention rates and support targeted interventions that enhance student success.

We delve into the details of the problem addressed in this study in Section I-A, while we motive this work in Section I-B. The assumptions and limitations of this work are presented in Section I-C. Finally, we summarize our contributions and outline the remainder of this paper in Section I-D.

A. *Problem Statement*

It is assumed that the high school experience and education process prepare college students to succeed in the endeavour of attaining an undergraduate degree. Nevertheless, other factors might influence their success in university, such as, e.g., personal circumstances, study habits, motivation, and so forth. Having a strong foundation in mathematics and natural sciences, particularly physics, might increase a student's chances of success in pursuing a Bachelor's degree in Systems Engineering. Therefore, it is important for the admission test to assess these subjects for candidates applying to the Bachelor's degree in Engineering.

Since 1968, the Saber 11 has been the standardized test used in Colombia to assess the competencies of high school students who are about to graduate. This test has been designed to be the official admission test for pursuing a Bachelor's degree in Colombian universities [1]. The same way as the Scholastic Assessment Test (SAT) is used for the same purpose in the United States. This study is focused on Systems Engineering students at the University of Córdoba in Colombia. Under Article 17 of the student code, candidates are admitted to the University of Córdoba based on their Saber 11 test scores [2].

The test Saber 11 evaluates five subjects: (i) mathematics, (ii) natural science, (iii) critical reading, (iv) social sciences, and (v) English language. The Colombian education ministry assumes these subjects are the foundation that all high school students must have learnt properly to pursue a bachelor's degree.

Thus, students with the highest scores in mathematics and natural science are better suited for engineering and science undergraduate bachelor's programs. Proficiency in other subjects might also be beneficial for success at the university. For instance, students with good critical reading skills and proficiency in the English language may be better equipped to learn any topic and access a wider range of literature sources compared to students who have poor skills in these subjects.

Therefore, the research question to be addressed in this study is as follows: is it possible to forecast if a student is at risk of failing mathematics and physics courses in Bachelor's degree in Systems Engineering based on their scores in the admission test called Saber 11?

The reason to focus the study on the first courses in mathematics and physics is twofold. Firstly, these courses are typically more challenging than others in the Bachelor's degree in Systems Engineering. Secondly, these courses form the foundation of scientific computing, which is the primary focus of the project that this study is a part of. Dealing with other courses in natural sciences, such as chemistry or biology, is beyond the scope of this study, as these subjects are not included in the curriculum of the systems engineering major. In other words, the problem addressed in this study is finding the functional mapping between the student's risk of failing early mathematics and physics courses, which is the target variable, and the scores achieved by the student in each subject evaluated in the admission test, which are the independent variables or the student's features.

B. Motivation

Failing early courses in mathematics and physics causes several negative consequences, such as, e.g., students feeling demotivated to continue pursuing a Bachelor's degree in Systems Engineering, wasted financial resources, frustration, stress, or even losing student status due to a low overall grade, for instance, students at the University of Córdoba must maintain at least an overall grade point average (GPA) of 3.3, where is in the range of 0 to 5 in every Colombian university (see also the student's code [2]). This problem is commonly referred to as *student dropout*.

On the other hand, those students who dropout courses might take longer to fulfill the requirements to receive their Bachelor's degree. This problem is known as *long-term retention*.

Knowing in advance who are the students at risk of failure, allows the universities to take precautions to prevent those students from failing the first courses in mathematics and physics, which usually are the most challenging ones. For instance, those students at risk might attend preliminary courses to improve their proficiency in those subjects that are prerequisites to pass actual early university courses.

If the university helps the population at risk, eventually, students' dropout and long-term retention rates might decrease, considering that both problems are a serious concern in the higher education systems and for policy-making stakeholders at universities [3].

C. Key Assumptions and Limitations

In this study, we have considered the following key assumptions:

(i) We have assumed the Saber 11 test measures the knowledge and competencies required for pursuing a bachelor's degree, as stated in Article 17 of the University of Córdoba's student code, which states that admission is based on a candidate's Saber 11 global score [2].
(ii) We have assumed the student at academic risk fails one or more courses about mathematics or physics during the first term. The early courses about mathematics are Calculus I and Linear Algebra, while the Physics I is the first course about physical science. Failing courses will lower the student's overall grade and potentially affect their academic standing.
(iii) We have assumed the student at academic risk has an overall grade lower or equal to 3.3, which is the minimum requirement for maintaining the student status according to the student's code at University of Córdoba (cf., Article 16 in [2]). Bachelor's students at Colombian universities are graded in the range from 0 up to 5. If a student's overall grade falls between 3 and 3.3, they must improve it to at least 3.3 in the next semester, or risk being expelled, per Article 28. Any student who obtains an overall grade below 3 will be forced to withdraw from the University of Córdoba.
(iv) We have assumed that wrongly classifying students as being at risk when they are not (i.e., false positive) is just as problematic as failing at classifying students who are actually at risk (i.e., false negative). In the former case, both the students and the university might waste resources addressing an unfounded risk. In the latter case, students might not receive the support they need for succeeding in their studies, and the university might miss the opportunity to take the required precautions and help them stay on track.
(v) We assumed that each student is represented through a vector in a real-valued multidimensional euclidean space, where each entry of the vector corresponds to a Saber 11 score in a specific subject.

The limitations of this study are as follows:

(i) We did not aim at designing an artificial intelligent system that predicts the dropout rate nor the failure rate of a given course.
(ii) We did not consider additional input variables for the prediction, such as, e.g., gender, ethnicity or economic variables, because the students who took the survey are alike regarding these features. Figure 1 shows an evidence that most of the sampled students are male, do not consider themselves part of an ethnic group, belong to the first economical stratum, and more than half of the sample of the students' families earn less than two Colombian monthly minimum wages. Therefore, these features do not help to differentiate students, contributing little information to the forecasting process.

Furthermore, we are interested in studying the extent the admission test contributes to accurate forecasting.

D. Contributions and Paper Outline

The contributions of this research are as follows:

(i) A data set with 56 records, where each one contains the student's profile and academic history. These students have completed courses from their second to the ninth semester. Additionally, each record includes the student's score in every subject from the admission test.

(ii) The prototype of an intelligent system, written in Python, that forecasts if a recently admitted student might be at academic risk of failing any of the early courses in mathematics or physics, namely Linear Algebra, Calculus I, and Physics I.

(iii) An empirical study that reveals Support Vector Machine (SVMs) outperform the other evaluated classifiers in forecasting students' failure risk. During the evaluation through 10-fold cross-validation, SVMs achieved the mean values for accuracy, precision, recall, and harmonic mean (F_1) of 71.33%, 68.33%, 60%, and 62.05%, respectively.

The rest of this paper is organized as follows: in Section II, we review the literature and related work, whereas in Section III we describe the research methods adopted in this study. We present and discuss the results of this research in Section IV. Finally, we draw the conclusions and outline the directions for further research in Section V.

II. Prior Research

This study falls within the domain of educational data mining, which aims to apply machine learning methods to educational data sets to gain insights into students' learning behaviour. This includes the analysis of data, the exploration of pedagogical theories through data mining, understanding students' domain knowledge, and evaluating their engagement in learning tasks.

Related research endeavours have focused on predicting whether a student is at risk of failing or dropping out of a course based on their performance in prerequisite courses [4] [5] [6].

Prior research has used SAT scores to predict if students will withdraw from their bachelor's program [7] [8]. One approach to predict student withdrawals from bachelor's programs involves using SAT scores and first-year university performance as input data [7]. Unfortunately, predicting student withdrawals after the first year of university does not provide with insight into their long-term retention issues. Another similar approach also includes both demographic information and pre-university performance as input data in order to forecast student withdrawals [8]. While the previously-mentioned research studies share similarities with ours, our specific goal is to predict the risk of students failing their first courses in mathematics and physics based on their admission test scores.

Predicting the risk of bachelor's student withdrawal has also been based on factors such as the student's school performance [9] [10], cognitive abilities [9], and even measurements of emotional intelligence [11]. It is worth noting that the admission test has not been considered in the last two mentioned studies. In one study [9], forecasting accuracy is reported as unfeasible, while in another study [10], the prediction model is tailored to a specific context, making it non-reproducible in other contexts, such as Colombia.

In the Colombian context, a study has been conducted to predict bachelor's student withdrawal based on their academic and personal data [12]. This study focused on students enrolled in the bachelor's program of engineering at the University of Los Andes, majoring in systems engineering. Unfortunately, the results of this study cannot be reproduced because the collected data set is not publicly available. Forecasting the individual students' risk of withdrawal is more useful for decision-making and addressing at-risk students compared to simply predicting the overall withdrawal rate.

In another study conducted in the Colombian context, Saber 11 scores from four out of five subjects (excluding natural sciences) were used to predict the risk of withdrawal or long-term retention faced by recently admitted bachelor's students. The mean prediction accuracy was 72.5% based on a 10-fold cross-validation using a data set of 47 records collected from a survey of 86 systems engineering students at the University of Córdoba. For further details, please refer to [13].

To our knowledge, so far no prior research has aimed at predicting the student's risk of failing an early course of mathematics and physics given their outcomes in the admission test, which is the goal of our study.

III. Research Methods

The research methodology adopted in this study is quantitative. We collected a data set with 81 observations or records by conducting a survey using Google Forms. The survey was administered to students pursuing a Bachelor's degree in Systems Engineering at the University of Córdoba in Colombia during the second half of 2022. The participating students had completed courses from the second to the ninth semester. Detailed information about the data set is provided in Section III-A.

Once the data set has been collected, we applied machine learning methods to address the problem posed in this study, specifically classification methods, which are supervised learning algorithms. The evaluation of the classifiers used in this study is carried out with consideration that machine learning is an experimental discipline. We discuss these classification methods in Section III-B, and the evaluation approach is described in Section III-C.

A. Data set Description

Let $\mathcal{D}$ be the data set, defined as $\mathcal{D} = \{(\mathbf{x}_i, y_i) \mid \mathbf{x}_i \in \mathbb{Z}^D \wedge y_i \in 0, 1, \forall i = 1, \ldots, n\}$, where n and D represent the number of observations and independent variables, respectively. The resulting data set contains 56 observations out of the original 81 due to changes in the curriculum structure of the undergraduate program in 2018, i.e., $n = 56$. In this

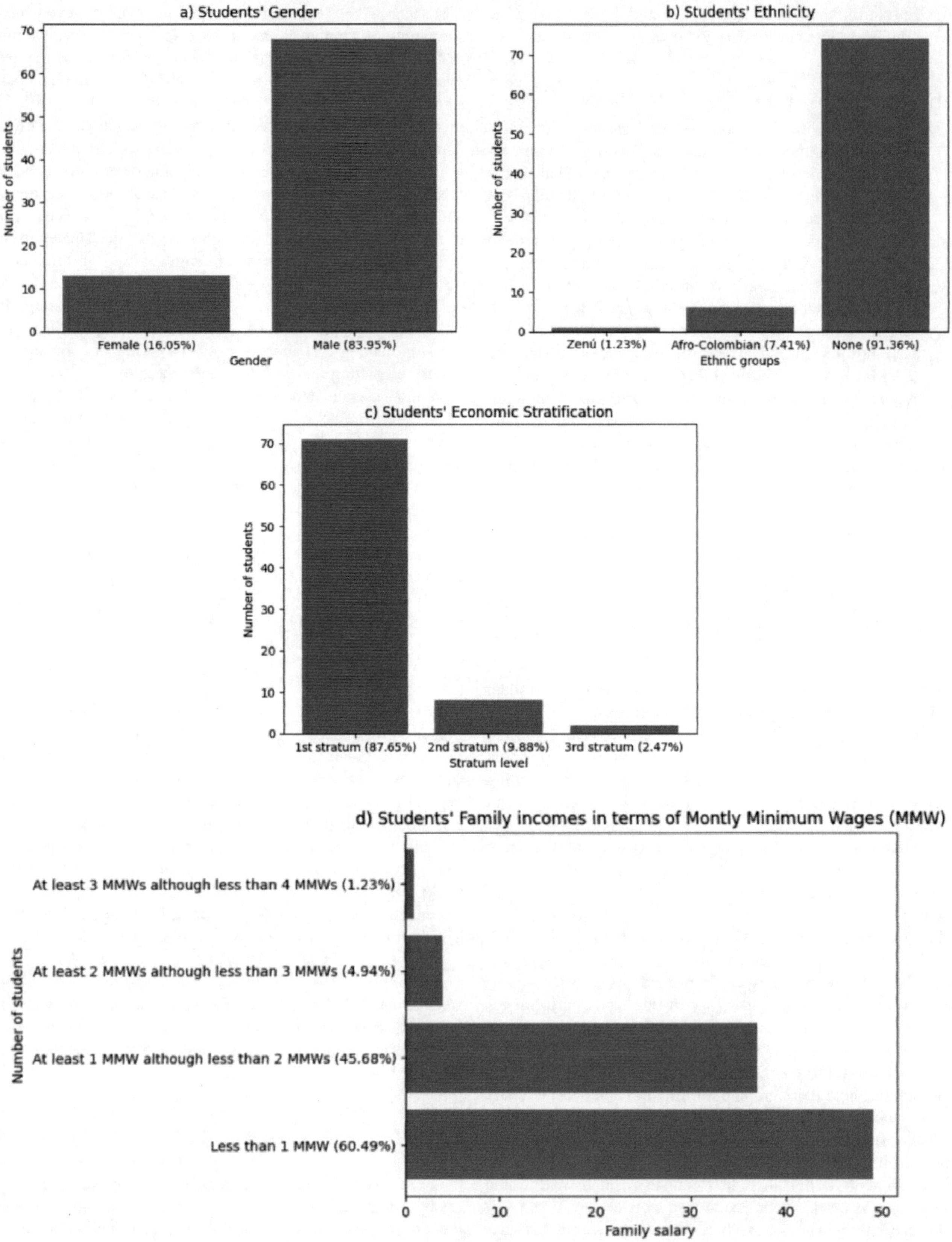

Figure 1. Sample distribution according to a) gender, b) ethnicity group, c) economical stratification, and d) family incomes.

context, the D-dimensional vector $\mathbf{x}_i$ represents the features or independent variables of the ith student, while y_i represents their corresponding target variable.

The target variable has one out of two possible values, i.e., $y_i = 1$ if the ith student has failed at least one of the early courses in mathematics or physics the first time the student enrolled them. These courses are calculus I, linear algebra, and physics I. In contrast, $y_i = 0$ otherwise.

On the other hand, there are five independent variables, where $D = 5$, representing the scores achieved by the ith student in each subject evaluated in the admission test. These scores range from 0 to 100. For a given ith student, the meaning of each component of their vector representation is explained as follows:

- x_{i1} is the score achieved by the ith student in the mathematics subject of the admission test.
- x_{i2} is the score achieved by the ith student in the natural science subject of the admission test.
- x_{i3} is the score achieved by the ith student in the social science subject of the admission test.
- x_{i4} is the score achieved by the ith student in the critical reading subject of the admission test.
- x_{i5} is the score achieved by the ith student in the social English proficiency evaluation of the admission test.

The proportion of classes is rather balanced in the data set, as it is illustrated in Figure 2.

The data set is available online to allow the reproduction of our study, and for further research [14].

B. Classification Methods

To find the functional mapping between the risk of failure and the performance in the admission test, we adopted supervised learning algorithms, specifically classification methods or classifiers. These algorithms identify patterns between students who have either failed or passed courses and their respective scores in every subject evaluated in the admission test. Formally, given the data set $\mathcal{D}$, the goal is to estimate the prediction function $g : \mathbb{R}^D \to \{0, 1\}$, such that $g(\mathbf{x}_i) \approx 1$ indicates that the function predicts the ith student is at risk, and $g(\mathbf{x}_i) \approx 0$ signifies otherwise.

To tackle the aforementioned problem, we used several classification methods, including Gaussian Process (GP). GP gets its name from the fact that it assumes the probability distribution of the target variable is Gaussian or normal [15] [16]. As a result, GP calculates the student's probability of failure risk, which is valuable for interpreting its forecasting outcome. One of the main advantages of GP is its ability to incorporate prior knowledge about the problem, improving forecasts even when the training data set is small. Another advantage is its suitability for solving non-linear classification problems. However, GP has the drawback of potentially high computational costs for fitting and forecasting, which can be problematic for large-scale data sets. In the context of this study, our data set is relatively small, so we chose to use this method, considering its advantages.

So far, Support Vector Machine (SVM) is considered one of the best theoretically motivated classification methods and amongst the most successful in the practice of modern machine learning [17, pg. 79]. Its objective function is convex, allowing for the discovery of a global maximum solution, which is its primary advantage. However, SVM is not particularly well-suited for interpretation in data mining, although it excels in training accurate intelligent systems. For a more comprehensive description of this algorithm, refer to the work by Cortes and Vapnik [18].

SVM is a linear classification method that assumes the input vector space is separable through a linear decision boundary or a hyperplane in multidimensional space. However, when this assumption is not satisfied, SVM can be used with kernel methods to handle non-linear decision boundaries. For further details, see Cortes and Vapnik [18].

In this study, we incorporated the Quantum Support Vector Machine (QSVM) method, which makes use of kernel methods. Our approach centres around the utilization of a quantum state space for the independent variables, as outlined in [19]. To achieve this, we employed the ZZ feature mapping, a well-implemented feature mapping in Qiskit, a prominent open-source software development kit. This mapping allows us to encode D input variables across D qubits. Qiskit provides a comprehensive toolkit with a wide range of quantum gates and circuits designed for various computational purposes [20]. For a deeper exploration of the ZZ feature mapping, we recommend consulting the documentation available on the Qiskit website [21]. In the context of qubit representation as normalized complex-value space vectors, we individually rescaled each variable, ensuring that the maximum value for each variable was standardized to 1.

We adopted the decision tree classifier, a commonly used model in data mining and knowledge discovery due to its tree-shaped hierarchical structure, which is easily interpreted and used for decision support. During training, a tree is created using the data set as input, with each internal node representing a test on an independent variable, branches representing the results of the test, and leaves representing estimated classes. The construction of the tree is carried out recursively, starting with the entire data set as the root node. At each iteration, the fitting algorithm selects the next attribute that best separates the data into different classes. The fitting algorithm can be stopped based on various criteria, such as when all the training data is classified or when the accuracy or performance of the classifier cannot be further improved.

The main drawback of decision trees arises from their fitting process, which relies on heuristic algorithms, such as greedy algorithms. These algorithms may lead to several local optimal solutions at each node, which is one of the reasons why there is no guarantee that the learning algorithm will converge to the most optimal solution. As a result, decision trees can exhibit different tree shapes due to small variations in the training data set. Breiman *et al.* introduced this method in 1984 [22]. Finally, we also adopted ensemble methods based on multiple decision trees such as, e.g., Adaboost (stands for adaptive

Figure 2. Distribution of students who have either failed or passed at least one of the early courses in Mathematics and Physics: calculus I, linear algebra, and physics I.

boosting) [23], Random forest [24], and XGBoost [25].

C. Evaluation Approach

We cannot determine in advance which machine learning method outperforms the others, as the *no free lunch theorem* states. Therefore, we need to conduct experiments to evaluate the quality of the machine learning methods, requiring multiple pairs of training and test data sets. To this end, we conducted experiments based on K-Fold Cross-Validation (KFCV), resulting in K pairs of training and test data sets derived from the original one. We selected values of $K = 10$ and $K = 5$, although K is typically set to 10 or 30. We opted for $K = 5$ in lieu of $K = 30$ due to the relatively small data set. Consequently, we tested each method K times using KFCV. Based on the test outcomes, we calculated the mean accuracy, mean precision, mean recall, and the average of the harmonic mean (F_1) to compare the learning methods and choose the best hyper-parameters for each of the previously mentioned methods.

IV. EVALUATION

In this section, we delve into the details of the test bed and results obtained through the evaluation of the aforementioned classification methods. The experimental setting is explained in Section IV-A and Section IV-B presents and discusses the results of the evaluation.

A. Experimental Setting

The evaluation is conducted through K-Fold Cross-Validation, where $K = 10$ and $K = 5$, as it was mentioned in Section III-C. This procedure is performed on a data set containing 56 records or examples, each having 5 independent variables and the corresponding target variable (as described in Section III-A)..

We adopted Python to write the source code of the test beds and experiments, moreover, we used Scikit-Learn library [26], Google Colaboratory [27], Qskit library, and the quantum computing simulator called Aer [20].

The best hyper-parameter setting resulting from applying 10-fold cross-validation to tune each method is presented as follows:

- Gaussian Process (GP) with the radial basis function kernel, where the best values for σ and γ are 16 and 19, respectively. Both hyper-parameters are part of the following equation $k_G(\mathbf{x}_i, \mathbf{x}_j) = \gamma \exp(-||\mathbf{x}_j - \mathbf{x}_i||^2/2\sigma^2)$.
- GP with the Matern kernel, where the best values for nu, σ and γ are 1.3, 4 and 3.8×10^{-6}, respectively. These hyper-parameters belongs to the following equation $k_M(\mathbf{x}_i, \mathbf{x}_j) = \gamma \frac{1}{\Gamma(\nu)2^{\nu-1}} \left(\frac{\sqrt{2\nu}||\mathbf{x}_j - \mathbf{x}_i||^2}{\sigma}\right)^{\nu} K_{\nu}\left(\frac{\sqrt{2\nu}||\mathbf{x}_j - \mathbf{x}_i||^2}{\sigma}\right)$, where $K_\nu(\cdot)$ and $\Gamma(\cdot)$ are the modified Bessel function and the gamma function, respectively.
- GP with the dot product kernel, which is defined as follows: $k_d(\mathbf{x}_i, \mathbf{x}_j) = 1 + \langle \mathbf{x}_i, \mathbf{x}_j \rangle$.
- GP with the rational quadratic kernel, where σ and α are 1.56×10^{-2} and 6.1×10^{-5}, respectively. The kernel is defined as follows: $k_r(\mathbf{x}_i, \mathbf{x}_j) = (1 + ||\mathbf{x}_j - \mathbf{x}_i||^2/(2\alpha\sigma^2))^{-\alpha}$
- Support Vector Machines (SVM) with the radial basis function kernel, where γ and C are 1.22×10^{-4} and 65536, respectively. In this case, the kernel is defined as follows: $k_G(\mathbf{x}_i, \mathbf{x}_j) = \exp(-\gamma||\mathbf{x}_j - \mathbf{x}_i||^2)$.
- SVM with the polynomial kernel, where d (degree) and C are 4 and 7.8×10^{-3}, respectively. The kernel is defined as follows: $k_p(\mathbf{x}_i, \mathbf{x}_j) = \langle \mathbf{x}_i, \mathbf{x}_j \rangle^d$.
- SVM with the sigmoid kernel, where γ and C are 1.22×10^{-4} and 16, respectively. The kernel is defined as follows: $k_s(\mathbf{x}_i, \mathbf{x}_j) = \tanh \gamma \langle \mathbf{x}_i, \mathbf{x}_j \rangle$.
- Quantum SVM, where C is 12 and we adopted the full entanglement strategy, i.e., the qubits are entangled to each other.
- The decision trees were fitted using both the Gini and entropy indexes. The parameters used were given by default in Scikit-Learn API.
- XGBoost algorithm was fitted with a learning rate,

TABLE I
TEN-FOLD CROSS-VALIDATION RESULTS

Machine learning method	*Mean Accuracy (%)*	*p-value*	*Mean Precision (%)*	*p-value*	*Mean Recall (%)*	*p-value*	*Mean* F_1 *(%)*	*p-value*
Support Vector Machines with the polynomial kernel (degree = 4)	**71.33**		68.33		60		**62.05**	
Support Vector Machines with the sigmoid kernel	62.67	0.26	56.67	0.51	38.33	0.14	42.67	0.16
Support Vector Machines with the radial basis function kernel	65.33	0.48	**70.17**	0.9	58.33	0.9	58.07	0.74
Quantum Support Vector Machines	62	0.78	55	0.64	56.67	0.84	53.38	0.93
Decision tree with entropy index	46.67	**0.003**†	38.17	0.05	46.67	0.39	38.1	0.07
Decision tree with gini index	57.33	**0.04**†	49	0.21	45	0.27	42.76	0.11
Gaussian Process with the rational quadratic kernel	64	0.23	46.67	0.23	30	**0.03**†	33.67	0.05
Gaussian Process with the dot product kernel	44	**0.01**†	28.33	**0.02**†	21.67	**0.01**†	23.33	**0.01**†
Gaussian Process with the Matern kernel	58.67	0.07	60	0.57	45	0.24	46.67	0.16
Gaussian Process with the radial basis function kernel	62	0.12	61.67	0.65	48.33	0.37	49	0.24
Random forest with the gini index	60	0.17	63.5	0.73	**61.67**	0.89	56.5	0.59
Adaboost with the entropy index	50.33	0.23	35.67	0.15	51.67	0.43	40.43	0.79
XGBoost	50.33	**0.03**†	44.83	0.18	38.33	0.14	37.33	0.07

†Student's paired t-test reveals the difference between means is statistically significant

maximum depth, and number of estimators equal to 6.25×10^{-2}, 6, and 50, respectively. Besides, we used the entropy index in the trees.

- Adaboost algorithm was fitted with a learning rate and number of estimators equal to 0.5 and 170, respectively. Besides, we used the entropy index in the trees.
- Random forest was fitted with 15 trees (with gini index), at least one sample per leaf, at most five samples per split, and a maximum depth of fifth levels.

The best hyper-parameter setting resulting from applying 5-fold cross-validation to tune each method is presented as follows:

- GP with the radial basis function kernel, where the best values for σ and γ are 4 and 1.52×10^{-5}, respectively.
- GP with the Matern kernel, where the best values for nu, σ and γ are 1.3, 4 and 3.8×10^{-6}, respectively.
- GP with the rational quadratic kernel, where σ and α are 1 and 1.22×10^{-4}, respectively.
- SVM with the radial basis function kernel, where γ and C are 1.22×10^{-4} and 16384, respectively.
- SVM with the polynomial kernel, where d (degree) and C are 4 and 3.9×10^{-3}, respectively.
- SVM with the sigmoid kernel, where γ and C are 6.1×10^{-5} and 64, respectively.
- Quantum SVM, where C is 8 and we adopted the full entanglement strategy.
- The decision trees were fitted using both the Gini and entropy indexes. The parameters used were given by default in Scikit-Learn API.
- XGBoost algorithm was fitted with a learning rate, maximum depth, and number of estimators equal to 0.5, 5, and 80, respectively. Besides, we used the entropy index in the trees.
- Adaboost algorithm was fitted with a learning rate and number of estimators equal to 0.5 and 170, respectively. Besides, we used the entropy index in the trees.
- Random forest was fitted with 15 trees (with gini index), at least two sample per leaf, at most five samples per split, and a maximum depth of eighth levels.

B. Results and Discussion

According to the evaluation conducted through K-Fold Cross-Validation (KFCV) with both K = 10 (10FCV) and K = 5 (5FCV), Support Vector Machines (SVMs) consistently

TABLE II
FIVE-FOLD CROSS-VALIDATION RESULTS

Machine learning method	*Mean Accuracy (%)*	*p-value*	*Mean Precision (%)*	*p-value*	*Mean Recall (%)*	*p-value*	*Mean* F_1 *(%)*	*p-value*
Support Vector Machines with the polynomial kernel (degree = 4)	**71.82**		65.33		**60**		**60.9**	
Support Vector Machines with the sigmoid kernel	58.94	0.26	52.29	0.29	56	0.85	53.56	0.67
Support Vector Machines with the radial basis function kernel	67.88	0.71	**69.67**	0.76	56	0.83	60.88	0.99
Quantum Support Vector Machines	65.91	0.96	65	0.84	56	0.99	59.80	0.91
Decision tree with entropy index	53.33	0.07	49.9	0.2	44	0.38	45.78	0.31
Decision tree with gini index	51.52	0.07	49.33	0.23	40	0.27	43.27	0.25
Gaussian Process with the rational quadratic kernel	62.58	0.32	38.43	0.19	40	0.42	38.67	0.32
Gaussian Process with the dot product kernel	46.67	0.05	40	0.23	20	0.05	26.03	0.07
Gaussian Process with the Matern kernel	60.91	0.31	55	0.46	44	0.45	47.88	0.47
Gaussian Process with the radial basis function kernel	62.58	0.37	57	0.52	52	0.69	53.77	0.68
Random forest with the gini index	55	0.12	56	0.55	44	0.37	47.23	0.37
Adaboost with the entropy index	51.52	0.06	48	0.17	48	0.53	46.47	0.35
XGBoost	55	0.12	56	0.55	44	0.37	47.23	0.37

†Student's paired t-test reveals the difference between means is statistically significant

outperformed the other machine learning methods in nearly every measure. In the case of 10FCV, SVMs with the polynomial kernel excelled in terms of accuracy and the harmonic mean (F_1), while SVMs with the radial basis function achieved the highest mean precision.

On the other hand, Random Forest (RF) achieved a better mean recall. However, SVM with the polynomial kernel attained the third-best mean recall, and RF achieved the third-best mean precision. This explains why the SVM with the polynomial kernel outperformed the others in the harmonic mean. Besides, it reached the second-best values in both mean precision and mean recall. The results obtained through 10FCV are presented in Table I.

Table II shows the results of the 5FCV, where SVM performs better than the other machine learning methods in every measured metric. The outcomes are consistent with those achieved through 10FCV because, in both kinds of experiments, the trend reveals that SVM outperforms the other evaluated methods. SVM with the radial basis function outperformed SVM with the polynomial kernel in terms of mean precision, although the latter method is better in the other metrics and obtains the second-best place in terms of mean precision.

TABLE III
CONFUSION MATRIX FOR SUPPORT VECTOR MACHINES WITH THE POLYNOMIAL KERNEL DURING K-FOLD CROSS-VALIDATION WITH K = 10 AND K = 5

	Predicted class		
True class	*Student without risk*	*Student at risk*	*Total*
Student without risk	25	6	31
Student at risk	10	15	25
Total	35	21	56

Based on the results of 10FCV, there is strong statistical evidence (p-value < 0.05) that SVM with the polynomial kernel is more accurate than decision trees, GP with the dot product kernel, and XGBoost, with an accuracy score of 71.33%. Additionally, the same results demonstrate strong statistical evidence that the precision and harmonic mean of SVM with the polynomial kernel are greater than those achieved through the predictions of GP with the dot product kernel. Furthermore, the results also indicate statistical evidence that the recall of SVM with the polynomial kernel is greater than that achieved through the predictions of GP with the rational

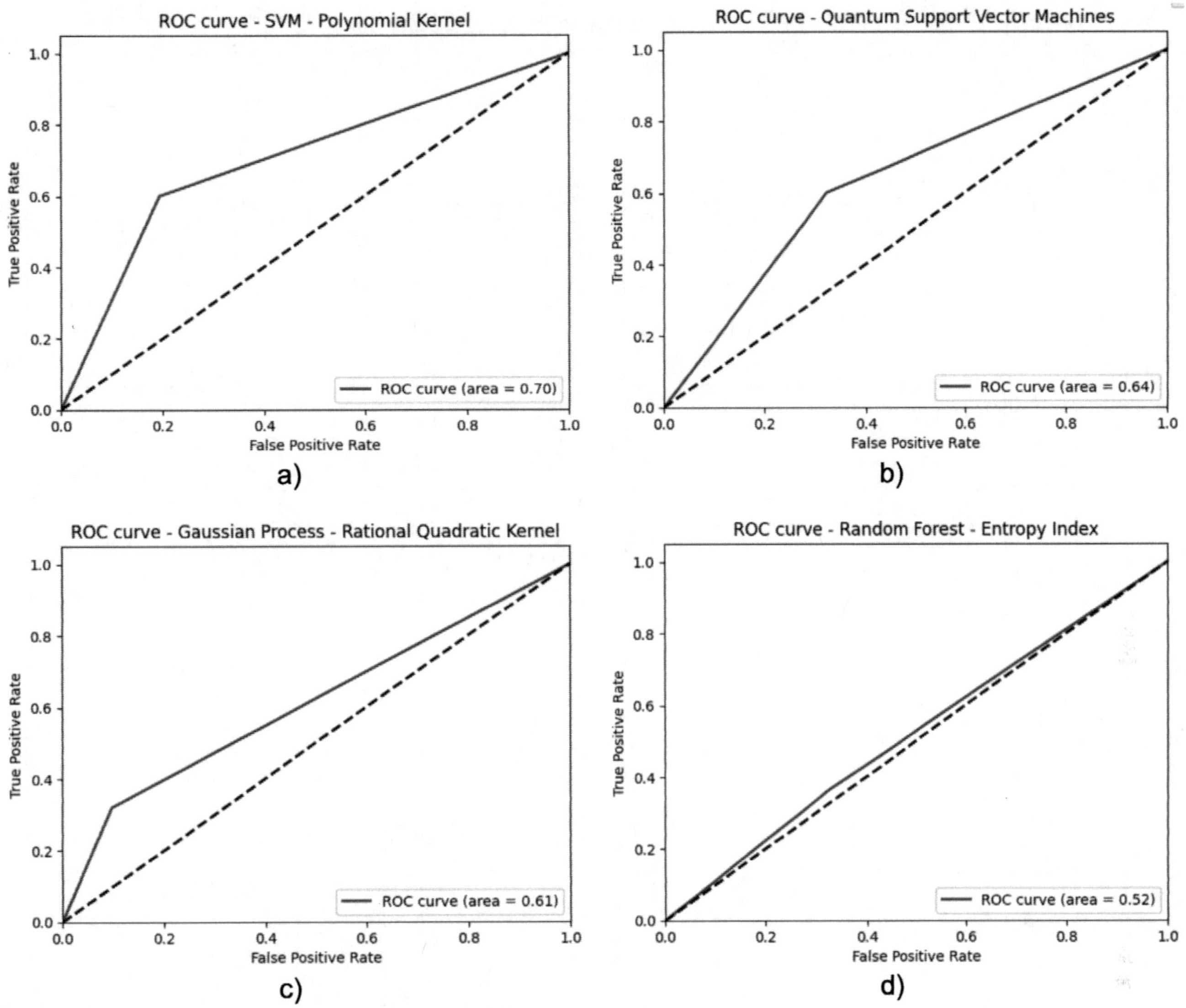

Figure 3. The highest ROC curve obtained from 10-Fold Cross-Validation for a) Support Vector Machine with the polynomial kernel, b) Quantum Support Vector Machine, c) Gaussian Process with the Rational Quadratic kernel, and d) Random forest

quadratic kernel. These results were obtained through a t-test comparing the performance of the classifiers, and the t-test results are reported in Table I. In contrast, the 5FCV results do not provide evidence of statistically significant differences between the classifiers' performance metrics.

Table III displays the confusion matrix obtained for both 10FCV and 5FCV, with the best-performing classifier being SVM with the polynomial kernel, as previously mentioned. The results obtained by this classifier align with the outcomes reported earlier, with 40 out of 56 students correctly classified, resulting in an accuracy of 71.42%. Only 6 out of 35 students at no risk were falsely identified as at risk, resulting in a false positive rate of 17%. Precision, which measures the proportion of correctly identified at-risk students out of all identified at-risk students, is a crucial metric in risk forecasting, as false positives can result in unnecessary expenditure of time and resources. In contrast, 10 out of 25 students at risk were not identified, resulting in a false negative rate of 40%. Recall, which measures the proportion of correctly identified at-risk students out of all at-risk students, is another important metric in risk forecasting, as false negatives can lead to students failing early courses in mathematics and physics. Both precision and recall exceed 60%, which is superior to random guessing.

Finally, the Receiver Operating Characteristic (ROC) curves shown in Figures 3 and 4 correspond to the classifiers with the highest areas under the ROC curves. Once again, these results reinforce that SVM outperforms the other methods. Besides, an area below the ROC curve of 0.7 is better than random guessing, although these classification methods were trained

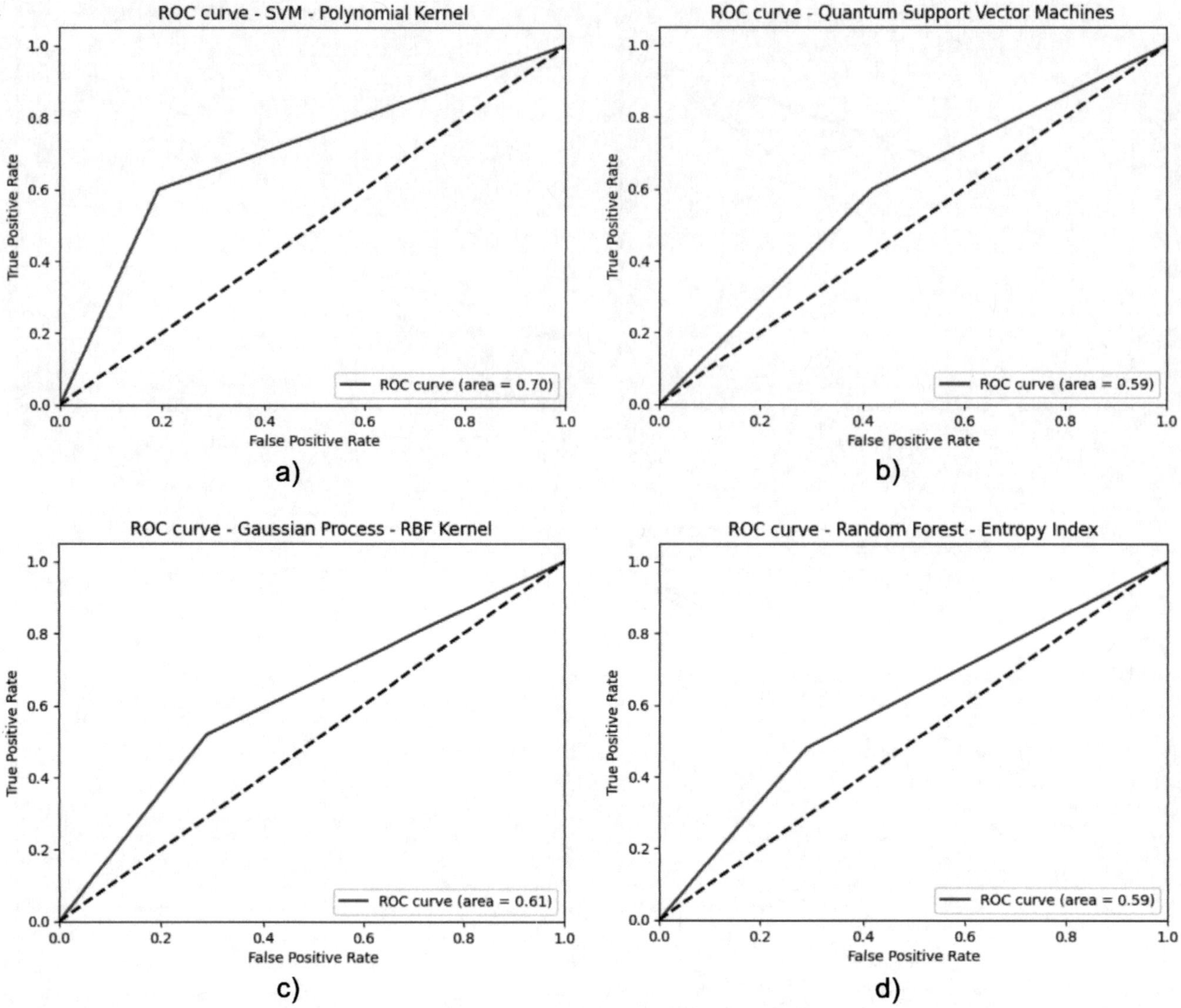

Figure 4. The highest ROC curve obtained from 5-Fold Cross-Validation for a) Support Vector Machine with the polynomial kernel, b) Quantum Support Vector Machine, c) Gaussian Process with the Radial Basis Function (RBF) kernel, and d) Random forest

on a small data set. Nevertheless, it is important to exercise caution when generalizing these results to larger data sets or different contexts, as classifier performance may vary. Further studies with larger and more diverse data sets are needed to confirm the robustness of these findings

V. Conclusions and Future Research

In this study, we explored the functional mapping between a student's risk of failing early courses in mathematics or physics and their performance on the admission test. Our contribution can be summarized in two parts: i) we have provided a data set for studying this relationship, and ii) we have developed a prototype intelligent system based on Support Vector Machine (SVM) that surpasses other machine learning methods, especially in terms of accuracy, as demonstrated by the conducted evaluation.

As a direction for further research, we shall collect more data to improve the accuracy, precision, recall, and harmonic mean of the intelligence system. Furthermore, with a greater data set, we shall evaluate models based on neural networks that tend to generalize well with large-scaled data sets.

Another research direction involves interpretable machine learning models that offer insights into the specific knowledge and skills that students need to succeed in these early courses. Such insights can be used to design courses that assist at-risk students in making a smooth transition from secondary school to the university. Moreover, we shall analyse the latent factors of the Saber 11 admission test to identify the most relevant factors contributing to success in these early mathematics and physics courses, as well as for visualization purposes.

Furthermore, we shall continue our research on Quantum Support Vector Machine (QSVM) by exploring the ZZ feature mapping across diverse domains. Additionally, in the domain of our study, we aim to evaluate the performance of QSVM with other circuits for feature mapping, such as, e.g., angle encoding and amplitude encoding.

Finally, we aim at extending this study to other majors in engineering, such as, e.g., mechanical, environmental, food, and industrial engineering at the University of Córdoba in Colombia. To this end, we will collect data from those departments that offer the Bachelor's degree in those majors.

ACKNOWLEDGEMENT

Caicedo-Castro thanks the Lord Jesus Christ for blessing this project. We thank Universidad de Córdoba in Colombia for supporting the Course Prophet Research Project (grant FI-01-22). Particularly, we would like to express our deepest appreciation to Dr. Jairo Torres-Oviedo and Dr. Deivis Lujan-Rhenals, who serve as the president and research vice-president of the University of Córdoba. We thank all students who collaborated with us, answering the survey conducted for collecting the data set used in our research. Finally, we thank the anonymous referees for their comments that contributed to improve the quality of this article.

REFERENCES

[1] Colombian Institute for Education Assesment - ICFES. National System of Standardized Evaluation of the Education - Guideline of the Saber 11 test. (2013) https://www.icfes.gov.co/ [retrieved: October, 2023].

[2] I. Pacheco-Arrieta *et al.* (2004) Agreement No. 004: Student's code at the University of Córdoba in Colombia. http://www.unicordoba.edu.co/wp-content/uploads/2018/12/reglamento-academico.pdf [retrieved: October, 2023]. University of Córdoba in Colombia.

[3] C. Demetriou and A. Schmitz-Sciborski, "Integration, Motivation, Strengths and Optimism : Retention Theories Past, Present and Future," in *Proceedings of the 7th National Symposium on Student Retention*. USA: The University of Oklahoma, 2011, pp. 300–312.

[4] I. Lykourentzou, I. Giannoukos, V. Nikolopoulos, G. Mpardis, and V. Loumos, "Dropout prediction in e-learning courses through the combination of machine learning techniques," *Computers and Education*, vol. 53, no. 3, pp. 950–965, 2009.

[5] J. Kabathova and M. Drlik, "Towards Predicting Student's Dropout in University Courses Using Different Machine Learning Techniques," *Applied Sciences*, vol. 11, p. 3130, 04 2021.

[6] J. Niyogisubizo, L. Liao, E. Nziyumva, E. Murwanashyaka, and P. C. Nshimyumukiza, "Predicting student's dropout in university classes using two-layer ensemble machine learning approach: A novel stacked generalization," *Computers and Education: Artificial Intelligence*, vol. 3, p. 100066, 2022.

[7] J. Lin, P. Imbrie, and K. Reid, "Student Retention Modelling: An Evaluation of Different Methods and their Impact on Prediction Results," in *Research in Engineering Education Symposium*. New York, USA: Curran Associates, Inc., 2009.

[8] L. Aulck, N. Velagapudi, J. Blumenstock, and J. West. (2016) Predicting Student Dropout in Higher Education. https://arxiv.org/abs/1606.06364 [retrieved: October, 2023]. arXiv.

[9] J. B. Berger and J. F. Milem, "The Role of Student Involvement and Perceptions of Integration in a Causal Model of Student Persistence," *Research in Higher Education*, vol. 40, no. 6, pp. 641–664, 1999.

[10] G. Dekker, M. Pechenizkiy, and J. Vleeshouwers, "Predicting Students Drop Out: A Case Study." *Computers, Environment and Urban Systems*, pp. 41–50, 01 2009.

[11] J. Parker, M. Hogan, J. Eastabroo, A. Oke, and L. Wood, "Emotional intelligence and student retention: Predicting the successful transition from high school to university," *Personality and Individual Differences*, vol. 41, pp. 1329–1336, 2006.

[12] B. Pérez, C. Castellanos, and D. Correal, *Predicting Student Drop-Out Rates Using Data Mining Techniques: A Case Study: First IEEE Colombian Conference, ColCACI 2018, Medellín, Colombia, May 16-18, 2018, Revised Selected Papers*. New York, USA: Institute of Electrical and Electronics Engineers, 05 2018, pp. 111–125.

[13] I. Caicedo-Castro, O. Velez-Langs, M. Macea-Anaya, S. Castaño-Rivera, and R. Catro-Púche, "Early Risk Detection of Bachelor's Student Withdrawal or Long-Term Retention," in *IARIA Congress 2022: International Conference on Technical Advances and Human Consequences*. Nice, France: International Academy, Research, and Industry Association, 2022, pp. 76–84.

[14] I. Caicedo-Castro. (2023) Dataset for Forecasting Failure Risk in Early Mathematics and Physical Science Courses in the Bachelor's Degree in Engineering. https://sites.google.com/correo.unicordoba.edu.co/isacaic/research [retrieved: October, 2023]. University of Córdoba in Colombia.

[15] C. Williams and C. Rasmussen, "Gaussian Processes for Regression," in *Advances in Neural Information Processing Systems*, D. Touretzky, M. Mozer, and M. Hasselmo, Eds., vol. 8. Cambridge, MA, USA: MIT Press, 1995, pp. 514–520.

[16] C. E. Rasmussen and C. K. I. Williams, *Gaussian Processes for Machine Learning*. Cambridge, MA, USA: MIT Press, 2006.

[17] M. Mohri, A. Rostamizadeh, and A. Talwalkar, *Foundations of Machine Learning*, 2nd ed. Cambridge, MA, USA: MIT Press, 2018.

[18] C. Cortes and V. Vapnik, "Support Vector Networks," *Machine Learning*, vol. 20, pp. 273–297, 1995.

[19] V. Havlíček, A. D. Córcoles, K. Temme, A. W. Harrow, A. Kandala, J. M. Chow, and J. M. Gambetta, "Supervised learning with quantum-enhanced feature spaces," *Nature*, vol. 567, no. 7747, pp. 209–212, 2019.

[20] Qiskit Development Team. (2017) Qskit Development Kit. [Online]. Available: https://qiskit.org/[retrieved:October,2023]

[21] ——. (2017) ZZ Feature Mapping Library Documentation. https://qiskit.org/documentation/stubs/qiskit.circuit.library.ZZFeatureMap.html [retrieved: October, 2023].

[22] L. Breiman, J. H. Friedman, R. A. Olshen, and C. J. Stone, *Classification and Regression Trees*. Monterey, CA: Wadsworth and Brooks, 1984.

[23] Y. Freund and R. E. Schapire, "Experiments with a new boosting algorithm," in *International Conference on Machine Learning*, vol. 96. Bari, Italy: Cambridge University Press, 1996, pp. 148–156.

[24] L. Breiman, "Random forests," in *Machine learning*, vol. 45, no. 1, Springer. USA: Springer, 2001, pp. 5–32.

[25] T. Chen and C. Guestrin, "Xgboost: A scalable tree boosting system," in *Proceedings of the 22nd acm sigkdd international conference on knowledge discovery and data mining*, ACM. New York, USA: Association for Computing Machinery, 2016, pp. 785–794.

[26] F. Pedregosa *et al.*, "Scikit-learn: Machine Learning in Python," *Journal of Machine Learning Research*, vol. 12, pp. 2825–2830, 2011.

[27] Colab. (2017) Google Colaboratory. https://colab.research.google.com/ [retrieved: October, 2023]. Google LLC.

An Exercise Recommendation System While Performing Daily Activities Based on Contextual Information

Mizuki Kobayashi
Grad. School of Bio-Functions and Systems Science
Tokyo University of Agriculture and Technology
Tokyo, Japan
email: crescent3033@gmail.com

Kaori Fujinami
Div. of Advanced Information Technology and Computer Science
Tokyo University of Agriculture and Technology
Tokyo Japan
email: fujinami@cc.tuat.ac.jp

***Abstract*—Although exercise has positive physical and mental effects, many people worldwide are inactive, and this trend has not improved over the years. One reason for not increasing opportunities for exercise is that people are busy with work and household chores. Thus, we propose incorporating light exercise into daily activities to help people develop exercise habits. In this study, we present an exercise recommendation method based on the contextual information of the user and environment. The results of the offline and online evaluations showed that the recommendation was successfully performed according to the given context and that more than 80 % of the participants judged the recommended exercises as appropriate.**

Keywords—recommendation system; context-awareness; wearable sensors; exercise; daily activities.

I. INTRODUCTION

Exercise has physical and mental benefits, preventing diseases such as heart disease, diabetes, and cancer, and delaying the onset of dementia. However, a survey conducted by the World Health Organization (WHO) in 2016 indicated that more than 1.4 billion people worldwide lead sedentary lifestyles–a trend unchanged since 2001 [1]. Moreover, a 2021 Sports Agency poll [2] revealed that the primary reason for not exercising is preoccupation with work or household chores. Notably, the percentage of respondents who answered that they exercised less frequently than they did one year ago exceeded those who answered that they exercised more frequently.

The high cost and the need to make time for gymnasium training are major hurdles to motivation for exercise. There are concerns that self-initiated training may increase the risk of injury owing to incorrect methods or excessive loads. Electrical Myo Simulation (EMS) belts, which stimulate muscles using electricity, have emerged in recent years and can be used even while performing other tasks, and their effectiveness in physical training has been demonstrated [3]. However, repeated use in the same area may cause muscle fatigue and risks muscle damage, without the user knowing. In addition, when used in conjunction with medical electrical devices such as pacemakers, EMS equipment may malfunction, resulting in severe physical damage [4].

To solve these challenges and make exercise a habit, it is desirable to incorporate it into daily life, which can be performed while working or doing housework. In this study, we focused on exercising while working [5] as an exercise method that satisfies this requirement. Exercise relies on muscular strength to obtain beneficial health effects, and exercising while working allows people without sufficient time for traditional exercise to incorporate it into their daily activities at an appropriate intensity with a low risk of injury.

Kobayashi et al. have developed a systematic exercise promotion system in an Internet of Things (IoT) environment, aiming to develop an infrastructure system that can handle various tasks and exercises using exercise recommendation and evaluation during desk work as a case study [6]. The exercise promotion system lowers barriers to exercise for people who do not normally exercise and encourages behavioral changes, such as spontaneously engaging in exercise. Appropriate recommendations that reflect the user's current task and the urgency and possibility of interruption, i.e., the context, are crucial for enabling exercise while working. This appropriate recommendation can be a solution for maintaining motivation. In this study, we added an exercise recommendation function based on user context to an existing exercise promotion system.

The remainder of this paper is organized as follows. Section II examines the related work. Section III presents the basic system configuration and describes the design of the exercise recommendation mechanism, followed by a detection method for user-related contextual information in Section IV. Offline and online experiments are described in Sections V and VI, respectively. Finally, Section VII concludes the paper. This research was conducted with the approval of the Tokyo University of Agriculture and Technology Ethics Review Committee.

II. RELATED WORK

A. Reducing the lack of exercise

Consolvo et al. [7] investigated the effectiveness of presenting information on underutilized cell phone background screens and screen savers to increase awareness of exercise in daily life. This study revealed that the abstract display of the user's own activity and physical information on the background screen of a cell phone increased the user's awareness and influenced their behavior. Another study by Klasnja et al. [8] described lessons learned from a study that developed and evaluated two systems aimed at promoting physical activity. These studies have revealed that it is possible to develop systems that effectively motivate behavior by providing support to sustain health maintenance goals, thereby encouraging various types of healthy behaviors and promoting social support. Although these studies can sustain motivation to exercise, actual exercise requires conscious time allocation. For non-regular exercisers, barriers to participation may be lower if they can exercise without conscious time allocation. In this study, the system supports exercise while the user is performing work; therefore, there is no need for conscious time allocation for exercise.

Certain studies encourage users to engage in physical activity while working at their desks. Shimizu et al. [9] proposed an exercise system that replaced computer keystrokes with body movements. The proposed system assigns keys to body movements (bending and stretching of knees and ankles) that are equivalent to walking and disables the keys assigned to the original keyboard. These movements can be performed naturally by disabling the keys assigned to the keyboard. Notably, their contribution is akin to our proposed system as users can exercise while performing key input operations. In this study, the proposed system enabled users to perform exercises while performing tasks other than keyboard inputs. Therefore, we aim to recommend appropriate exercises that consider the user's context.

B. *Exercise recommendations*

Lee et al. [10] proposed an exercise recommendation algorithm that utilizes information on personal tendencies such as eating habits and physical conditions. This algorithm enables the recommendation of highly efficient exercises suitable for everyone. However, before using the proposed algorithm, it is necessary to collect personal information, including sensitive information such as the user's height, weight, and medical history. The exercise events recommended in this study were of moderate intensity; therefore, they can be easily performed by anyone without the need to consider their physical conditions. In addition, the recommendations are remarkably practical because they can be formulated without requiring sensitive information.

Zhao et al. [11] proposed an exercise recommendation system that included gamification-based exercise promotion. This system can yield personalized exercise recommendations based on the information obtained from user questionnaires. However, the system recommends exercises during breaks, considering only the time and location of the user. In this study, we differentiated our system by recommending exercises that could be performed simultaneously without interfering with the user's work.

Yong et al. [12] designed an IoT-based fitness system. The system consists of equipment installed in gyms and wearable devices that measure and record the amount of exercise performed by fitness users using the equipment and other user activity data. The system can also calculate the cosine similarity between users based on the data of users' scores, indicating their level of interest in the equipment installed in the fitness club and can present recommendations to similar users. However, a user evaluation of the proposed system has not been conducted. Based on user evaluations, in addition to offline evaluations, the recommendation system can be evaluated more accurately.

III. Exercise facilitation system for exercising while working

A. *System Overview*

Figure 1 depicts the major system components. First, the system detects the user's state based on data obtained from the equipment and location (Figure 1 A). If the system detects that the user is performing a less urgent task that can be interrupted, an exercise recommendation process is invoked (Figure 1 B). The type of exercise, that is, item, is determined by referring to the rule using the contextual information obtained from the user and the environment, such as the objects being used and the places frequented by the user (Figure 1 C). The information to be presented to the user includes an image of the exercise category and the goal, ensuring that the necessary information is conveyed in a concise manner. Subsequently, the generated information is presented to the user via a push notification to their smartphone at a time that does not interrupt the current task (Figure 1 F). Once the user accepts and follows the recommendation, the duration and form of the exercise are evaluated based on the information collected on wearable sensors and the sensor-augmented objects (Figure 1 D). In accordance with the evaluation, a feedback message, including a chart of the exercise duration, is forwarded to the user's device through the same push-type mechanism as the recommendation process (Figure 1 E, F).

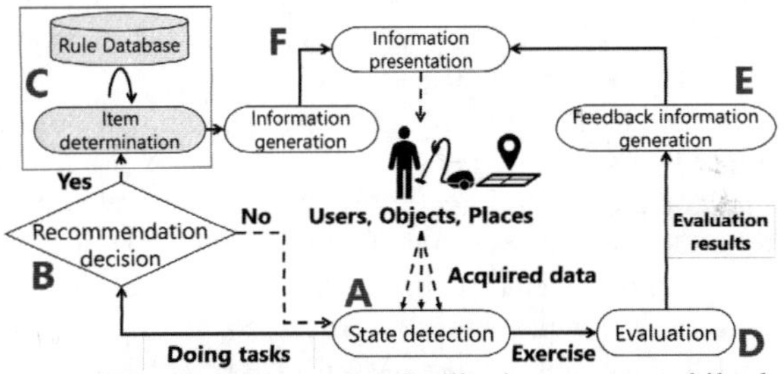

Figure 1. The flow of exercise facilitation system while doing daily activities.

In the event that objects or places are used and frequented by an unspecific number of people, a user identification function can be added to enable individual exercise recommendations, feedback, and management of the exercise results using the user's device. Even in the absence of a user identification function, the installation of a display device on or near objects enables on-the-spot exercise recommendations and feedback.

User context is used in two aspects: the determination of recommendation items and the timing of recommendations. In this study, we focused on the item selection aspect (Figure 1 C), which is described in detail in Sections III-B and IV. In contrast, context processing for timing determination is outside the scope of this study.

TABLE I: CATEGORIES OF CONTEXTUAL INFORMATION AND SPECIFIC VALUES OR EXAMPLES IN EACH SUB-CATEGORY, AND INFORMATION TO BE INFERRED FROM THE CONTEXTUAL INFORMATION.

Main-category	Sub-category	Elements in sub-category	Information to be inferred
User	Basic behavior	Sitting (SIT), Standing (STD), Walking (WLK), Lying (LYN)	Performable exercise
	Main working part	Upper body (UB), Lower body (LB)	Interruptibility to current task
Environment	Object in use	Fixed (FIX), e.g., chair, Portable (POT), e.g., vacuum cleaner	Performable exercise and interruptibility to current task
	Characteristics of place	Stay (STY), e.g., in front of a microwave, Travel (TRV), e.g., Corridor Wide (WID), e.g., Space to spread hands Narrow (NRW), e.g., Space to bump into things if spreading hands Public (PUB), e.g., Office, Private (PRI), e.g., User's home	Performable exercise and interruptibility to current task

B. Recommendation Method

1) Contextual Information: Table I summarizes the categorization of contextual information and the elements in the subcategories. The types of information inferred from these subcategories are also presented. Contextual information from the user side is further divided into *basic behavior* and *main working part* as subcategories. *Basic behavior* consists of four elements: sitting, standing, walking, and lying down, which are common in various daily activities. This information can be used to infer performable exercises. For example, knee lift abdominal exercises are easier to perform while a person is seated and not walking. The body part mainly used during a specific task represents the availability (or unavailability) of a certain exercise, specified as upper and lower body parts. Standing push-ups are difficult to perform when a user is using a smartphone, regardless of their behavior, because the exercise mainly involves the arms. We refer to this subcategory as the *main working part*. We assume that information on the basic behavior and the main working part is obtained by analyzing signals from wearable sensors, such as those in smartwatches and smartphones.

Contextual information from the environment is also categorized into two subcategories: *object in use* and *characteristics of place*. The state of use and information of the objects represent the current task of the user, such that a person sitting on an office chair is involved in a task related to desk work, as well as representing the social context, identity, and place [13]. Thus, information regarding the object in use can be used to infer performable exercises and interruptibility in a current exercise recommendation task. Two elements exist in this subcategory: fixed and portable. We assume that the information is obtained by sensors embedded in the object to determine if the object is being used as intended [14] and that a dedicated "object-use detector (OUD)" is provided. For example, more than two fixed objects can exist in a system with a one-to-one relationship between the objects and OUDs. Moreover, the location of a user contains meaningful information, as indicated by the fact that location information has been used for the longest period among the contextual information [15]. For example, a person in front of a microwave appears to wait for the heated food, which indicates an appropriate timing for recommending heel lift-up exercises. As another example, a person standing in front of a wall is recommended to perform push-ups. On the other hand, standing push-ups may be inappropriate when climbing stairs in the office but is acceptable at home. These examples suggest that information regarding the location of a user can be used as a cue to infer the performable exercise and interruptibility of the user. We divided the characteristics of a place into six elements: places for staying/traveling, wide/narrow areas, and public/private areas. Location Information can be obtained in various manners, such as motion sensors, distance sensors, and cameras, which are placed in a specific location and tagged. A Global Positioning System (GPS) can also be used for outdoor localization, where the label is obtained from the original geographic coordinates using a reverse geocoding service. Similar to OUDs, we assume that a dedicated "presence detector (PD)" is available and that more than two PDs in the same place characteristic may exist. The left section of Figure 2 depicts the relationship between the context sources, detectors, and contextual information. This information is used to determine the recommended items by referring to the rules stored in the database, as described in Section III-B2.

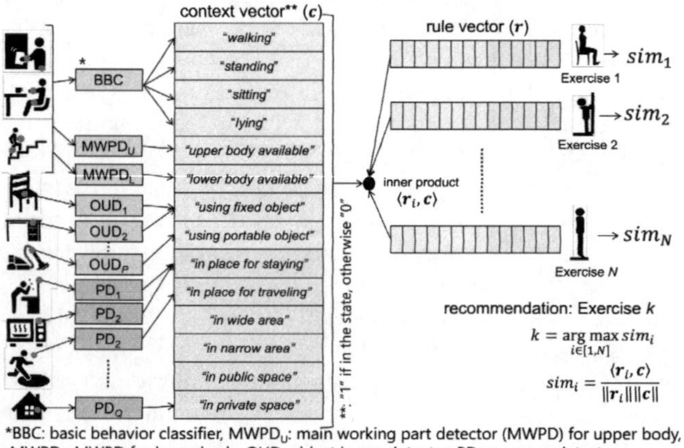

*BBC: basic behavior classifier, $MWPD_U$: main working part detector (MWPD) for upper body, $MWPD_L$: MWPD for lower body, OUD: object in use detector, PD: presence detector

Figure 2. The scheme of recommendation.

2) Recommendation algorithm: An exercise is recommended based on the similarity of context between the user and candidate exercises in the rule database. A rule for a specific exercise is represented by a tuple with binary values indicating the suitability of the element of context for the exercise, that is, 0 and 1 for unsuitable and suitable, respectively. Table II shows a rule for the knee-lift abdominal exercise with

14 elements, indicating that the exercise is suitable for people who are sitting, with the lower body available for exercise, and using a fixed object, for example, a chair; conversely, it is unsuitable for people who are standing, walking, lying, or performing upper-body work.

The context similarity was measured using the cosine similarity. Cosine similarity is a measure of the similarity between vectorized items. Let $\boldsymbol{r_i}$ be a rule vector as presented above, containing the suitability and unsuitability of each contextual element for exercise $i \in [1, N]$, and let $\boldsymbol{c}$ be a vector that represents the user's context. The method of obtaining the value of each element of the vector depends on the implementation of the system. Section IVdescribes the proposed implementation. The posterior probability for each class can be applied to the values in a classification-based method such as those in basic behavior identification, whereas a binary value, that is, 0 or 1, can be used for threshold-based detection, such as for main working part detection, object usage detection, and place detection. The similarity (sim_i) between these rules for exercise i and the user's context are expressed in (1), where $\langle \boldsymbol{a}, \boldsymbol{b} \rangle$ indicates the inner product of vectors $\boldsymbol{a}$ and $\boldsymbol{b}$, and $\|\boldsymbol{a}\|$ is the length of vector $\boldsymbol{a}$.

$$sim_i = \frac{\langle \boldsymbol{r_i}, \boldsymbol{c} \rangle}{\|\boldsymbol{r_i}\| \|\boldsymbol{c}\|} \quad (1)$$

We assumed that at least one wearable sensor was mandatory in the system, whereas sensors for the environmental context were optional. For example, if there is no sensor-augmented fixed object, the value is ignored in the calculation of proximity. Exercise k with the highest similarity for all exercises was recommended and selected by (2).

$$k = \arg\max_{i \in [1, N]} sim_i \quad (2)$$

The recommended items determined in this manner are passed to the information presentation (Figure 1 F), where a message is created with information such as the exercise method and the number of sets required. Figure 2 illustrates the recommendation scheme.

IV. Contextual Information from the User

As shown in Section III-B1, contextual information from the user and the environment is used to recommend exercises. The information obtained from the user's movement or posture using wearable sensors is generic compared to that obtained from the environment, such as the object in use and the user location. This section presents methods for obtaining user contextual information.

A. Basic behavior classification method

The behavioral context assumes three values: sitting, standing, and walking. Thus, various daily activities must be classified as one such behavior. One approach may be to recognize each activity first, for example, brushing teeth and vacuum cleaning, and then categorize them into one of three behaviors based on predefined rules, for example, "brushing teeth is usually performed while standing." However, this approach must handle an unlimited number of daily activities in its recognition task, which is computationally infeasible. Instead, we assumed a different approach wherein the input signal obtained during various activities is forcibly classified into one of three classes.

Two accelerometers were attached to the left wrist and right thigh, assuming a smart watch and a smartphone stored in a trouser pocket, respectively. A machine learning-based classification approach was used, featuring a random forest classifier. In total, 66 features were calculated from a window of 256 samples (50 Hz) with four axes, that is, x, y, z, and magnitude ($= \sqrt{x^2 + y^2 + z^2}$), with 50 % overlap, as summarized in Table III.

The information from the two sensor nodes is integrated to obtain the final result, as follows: First, each classifier independently classifies the input feature vector into one of the three classes with posterior probabilities. Subsequently, the result of the classifier with the highest posterior probability is chosen as the final answer. An advantage of classifier-level fusion over data-level fusion, which uses a feature vector consisting of features from sensor nodes, is that our approach does not always require users to wear both sensors. If the sensor on the thigh (wrist) is missing, the result from the sensor on the wrist (thigh) is selected. From the perspective of classification performance, we validated the superiority of the proposed approach over data-level fusion.

B. Main working part detection method

Various daily activities need to be supported in the system. Unlike basic behavior classification, it is not feasible to judge the main working parts via individual daily activity recognition using a predefined list. Instead, we assumed an approach based on the information that "the moving body part is currently in use." Thus, if the acceleration signal exceeds a certain threshold, the body part is considered in use for an activity; otherwise, it is not in use.

The threshold was specified as follows: First, a moving variance calculation was performed on the entire dataset of daily activities described in Section V-A [16], using a window of 256 samples (50 Hz) with a 50 % overlap. The median of the variance values was specified as the threshold value. The threshold is determined for each axis of the acceleration signal. A threshold judgment was formulated for each axis, given the time-series data during an activity. If the mean of the variance of four consecutive windows exceeded the threshold on all three axes, the body part was judged as unavailable for exercise because it was in use; otherwise, it was considered available. Detection was performed for each sensor node on the left wrist and right thigh. The value in the context vector (c) is represented as binary, that is, 0 and 1, for unavailable and available, respectively.

V. Offline Experiment

A. Daily activity dataset

We utilized a dataset previously collected by the authors' laboratory [16]. Data were collected from a Bluetooth-

TABLE II: A RULE FOR KNEE-LIFT ABS EXERCISE.

Basic behavior				Main working part		Object in use			Characteristics of place				
SIT	STD	WLK	LYN	UB	LB	FIX	POT	STY	TRV	WID	NRW	PUB	PRI
1	0	0	0	0	1	1	0	0	0	0	0	0	0

TABLE III: CLASSIFICATION FEATURES FOR BASIC BEHAVIOR CLASSIFICATION.

Signal domain	Feature
Time	mean, standard deviation, skewness, kurtosis, minimum first quartile, median, third quartile, maximum, inter-quartile range, correlation coefficient of two axes
Frequency	energy, entropy, average frequency, maximum amplitude frequency component at the maximum amplitude

based Inertial Measurement Unit (IMU) (ATR-Promotions Inc. TSND151 [17]), comprising three-axes acceleration data and three-axes angular velocity data of 23 daily life activities from seven positions on the bodies of 14 volunteers (five females and nine males in their 20s). Six of the seven sensor nodes were attached symmetrically to the upper arms, wrists, and thighs, whereas one node was placed on the chest.

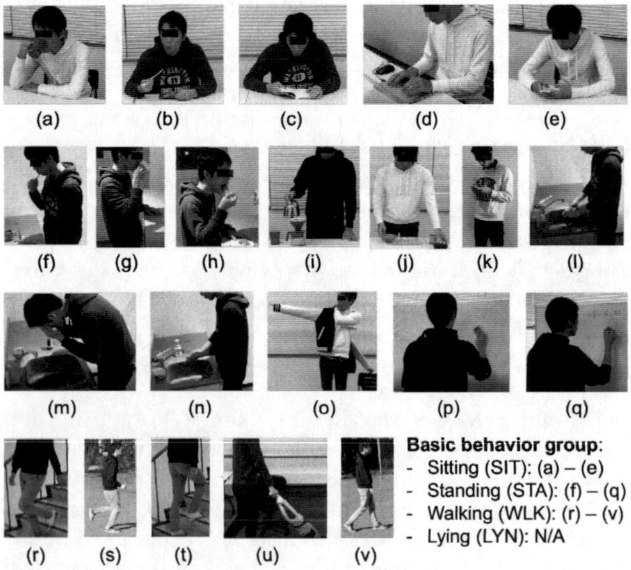

Figure 3. 22 daily activities and grouping into basic behaviors used in the evaluation: (a) having a drink while sitting down (DK_SIT), (b) eating food while sitting down (ET_SIT), (c) reading a book (RB), (d) using a computer while sitting down (UC), (e) using a smartphone while sitting down (SP_SIT), (f) brushing teeth (BT), (g) having a drink while standing (DK_STD), (h) eating food while standing (ET_STD), (i) making coffee (MC), (j) setting table (ST), (k) using a smartphone while standing (SP_STD), (l) washing dishes (WD), (m) washing face (WF), (n) washing hands (WH), (o) wearing and taking off the jacket (WJ), (p) erasing figures on a whiteboard (EW), (q) writing figures on a whiteboard (WW), (r) going down stairs (DS), (s) running (RN), (t) going up stairs (US), (u) vacuum cleaning (VC), and (v) walking (WK).

In the present study, we only used data from the sensors on the left wrist (LW) and right thigh (RT), assuming a smart watch on the wrist and a smartphone in the trouser pocket. Additionally, we removed the bicycle riding activity because it did not fit any basic behavior, and only signals from the three-axis accelerometer were used. The scenes of the activities are depicted in Figure 3, which also shows the grouping of basic behaviors as the ground truth for the basic behavior classification experiment described in the next section. Grouping (relabeling) was performed by judging the photographs shown in Figure 3.

B. *Evaluation on basic behavior classification*

1) Method: The performance of the basic behavior classification was evaluated. The basic behavior classifier was trained using data collected from 10 university students who were instructed to perform four basic behaviors. They were right-handed and attached to the same sensor nodes as those used in Section V-A on their LWs and RTs. The dataset described in Section V-A was used to test the classifier after we relabeled the original 22 activities with one of the four basic behaviors, as shown in the lower right of Figure 3. New labels were treated as the ground truth. Notably, no activity related to LYN exists in the dataset, and the results represent general classification performance because the participants in the training and test data collection were different.

2) Result and analysis: Figure 4 (a) presents the confusion matrix of basic behavior classification. For example, the numbers in the row of DK_SIT indicate that the instances of DK_SIT were judged 2718 times as "Sitting", 300 times as "Standing", 12 times as "Walking", and 903 times as "Lying".

The performance metrics are calculated and summarized in Table IV, where the recall, precision, and F-measure are defined by (3), (4), and (5), respectively. Suffix i indicates the basic behavior classes, and $N_{correct_i}$, N_{tested_i}, and N_{judged_i} represent the number of instances correctly classified as class i, the total number of instances in class i, and the number of instances judged as class i, respectively.

$$recall_i = N_{correct_i}/N_{tested_i} \quad (3)$$

$$precision_i = N_{correct_i}/N_{judged_i} \quad (4)$$

$$F-measure_i = \frac{2}{1/recall_i + 1/precision_i} \quad (5)$$

Table IV and Figure 4 (a) imply that the daily activities were mostly classified into the appropriate basic behaviors that the authors labeled, with some exceptions. Presumably, the sitting-related activities, i.e., DK_SIT, ET_SIT, RB, UC, and SP_IT, were judged as "Lying" because they involved minimal movement and the postures of the sensors were similar,

TABLE IV: SUMMARY OF BASIC BEHAVIOR CLASSIFICATION.

Basic behavior	Recall	Precision	F-measure
SIT	0.763	0.998	0.865
STD	0.940	0.937	0.939
WLK	0.867	0.902	0.884
LYN	N/A	N/A	N/A
Macro average	0.857	0.946	0.896

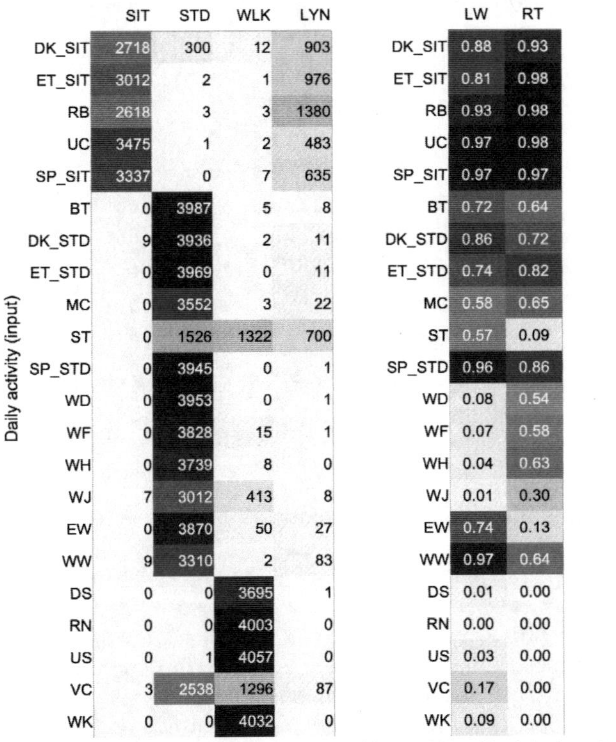

(a) Number of classified basic behavior (b) Availability of basic body parts

Figure 4. Offline experimental results.

particularly when the participants were lying on their backs. Vertical positioning must be considered to reduce misclassifications. Furthermore, the classification of ST (setting table) into "Walking" occurs because the activity includes occasional walking around the table during serving meals. Similarly, we consider that the judgment on VC (vacuum cleaning) was dichotomized into "Standing" and "Walking" because the vacuuming behavior is a mixture of standing and walking. Because we expect to use posterior probabilities rather than classification results (i.e., labels) for the elements of context vector (c), we do not consider these trends problematic for the recommendation in which multiple behaviors exist in a single activity.

C. Evaluation on main working part detection

1) Method: The appropriateness of the main working part detection was evaluated by counting the number of instances judged as "being used." The same dataset used to calculate the thresholds was used for testing.

2) Result and analysis: Figure 4 (b) shows the availability of each part by the ratios of "being not used" to the total number of instances per activity. The closer the value is to 0.0, the more cases are judged as "the body part is being used," while the closer it is to 1.0, the more cases are judged as "the body part is not being used." Note that the sum of the ratios of "Upper body part" and "Lower body part" is not equal to 1.0 because the judgment was performed independently.

From Figure 4 (b), it was judged that the availability of the wrist was lower than that of the thigh for hand-dominated movements such as washing dishes (WD) and washing faces (WF), and the value of the thigh was lower than that of the wrist for activities involving movement but minimal hand movement such as setting a table (ST), both of which were judged to be low when the arms and legs were moved together, such as walking (WK), climbing down stairs (WD), and vacuuming (VC). In these cases, the proposed method using threshold values functioned appropriately.

Misjudgment of the availability of activity that was assumed to use the dominant hand (i.e., the right hand without a sensor) was unavoidable, for example, DK_SIT (drinking while sitting). However, we found that even UC (using a computer while sitting) had high availability of the left wrist (0.97). In a UC, we can assume that the computer user uses both hands. Therefore, there is a possibility of misjudging the main working part of daily activities that use the fingertips, which does not occur in wrist movements. To solve this problem, a value corresponding to the confidence level of the judgment can be calculated instead of using a binary judgment of "being used" (unavailable). Furthermore, two types of exercises suitable for the upper and lower body can be recommended simultaneously such that the user can determine which exercise to perform if their confidence level is low. This may prevent mismatches between the recommended exercise and the user's situation, given that the final judgment is exercised by the user.

D. Evaluation on recommendation

1) Method: Similar to the previous evaluations, a simulation-based experiment was carried out using the dataset described in Section V-A in a situation where a user performs 22 daily activities, which determines one of the following six exercises based on context: knee pull-up abdominal exercise (KLA), leg-pushing exercise (LP), standing push-up (SPU), heel lift-up exercise (HL), breathing with a protruding belly (DI), and striding with a large belly and fast walking (FW). Table V lists the rule vectors (r) for the six exercises. As described in Section III-B2, the values '0' and '1' indicate that the element is unsuitable and suitable for the exercise, respectively.

Regarding information on the use of objects and halts in certain locations, the dataset did not gather such information when it was collected. Thus, we specified the values '1' by assuming that a sensor-augmented chair, e.g., [6], was used in the five activities categorized into "Sitting" and that an area in front of a microwave was occupied by a person who was preparing coffee (MC); otherwise, the values were set to '0'. These assumptions also imply 100 % complete detection.

2) Result and analysis: Figure 5 shows the results of the exercise recommendations for daily activities. The columns in the matrix represent the recommended exercises, whereas the rows represent the assumed daily activities. Note that normalized values are shown because the amount of data for each daily activity was different; thus, the number of recommendations varied. KLA and LP, which are exercises performed while sitting, are recommended more frequently for daily activities performed while sitting such as sitting and eating (ET_SIT) and reading a book (RB). When a user is in a sitting position, the user often performs tasks that use the upper body; therefore, LP, an exercise that uses the lower body, is recommended more often. For daily activities that require standing, such as preparing coffee (MC) and washing the face (WF), SPU and HL, which are exercises performed in the standing position, were recommended more often. However, DI was most frequently recommended for ST (Setting Table). Catering involves walking around a table, similar to walking. Therefore, exercises that can be performed during walking are recommended. In addition, DI and FW, which can be performed while walking, such as going downstairs (DS) and going upstairs (US), are often recommended. As the lower body is used while walking, DI, an exercise that uses the upper body, has been recommended in many cases.

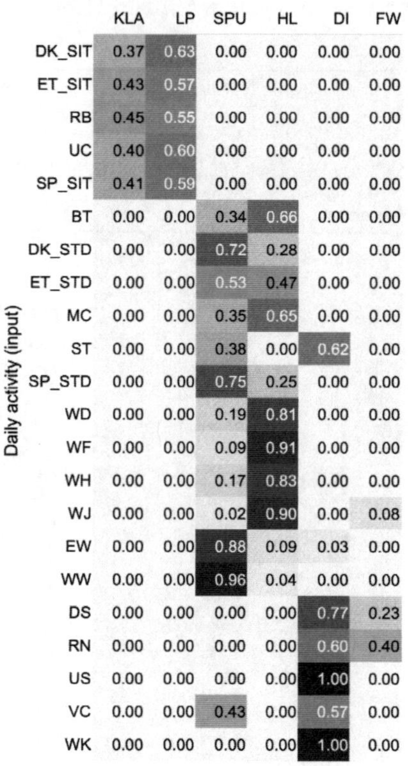

Figure 5. Recommendation results for exercise in daily activities.

VI. ONLINE USER EVALUATION

As elaborated in Section V, we validated the feasibility of the proposed exercise recommendations for daily activities through a simulation-based experiment. Subsequently, we conducted an online experiment with 15 participants to validate the recommendations based on the users' actual work context. Two conditions were specified: specified and free conditions. In the "specified" condition, the participants were instructed to perform three tasks in a laboratory room that corresponded to three basic behaviors, i.e., watching videos on a computer as SIT, waiting for their snacks to warm up in front of microwave as STD, and entering and leaving the room as WLK. In contrast, in the "free" condition, the participants performed freely in the same room for 10 minutes. To understand the effectiveness of each of the main-category of contextual information, i.e., "User" and "Environment" shown in Table I, recommendation in the following three cases were performed.

1) User: Basic behavior and main work part obtained by two accelerometers on the user's body.
2) Environment: The state of use of a chair from a sensor-augmented chair [6] and the presence of a microwave detected by a distance sensor placed on a shelf under the microwave.
3) All: All the contextual information and sensing devices above.

Under both conditions, the participants were provided with recommendations by the system while performing certain activities. A questionnaire survey was conducted for each recommendation to evaluate whether the recommended exercise was appropriate for the situation on five levels 5: appropriate, 4 = slightly appropriate; 3 = neither appropriate nor inappropriate; 2 = slightly inappropriate; and 1 = inappropriate.

Table VI summarizes the relative frequencies of the user evaluation scores for each experimental condition. Values in the row with a score of 5 indicate participants. As listed in the table, more than 80 % of participants in all conditions evaluated the recommended exercise as appropriate. The "All" conditions exhibited the highest ratios in both specified and free activity conditions. We assumed that the users always wore sensors on their bodies. The results show that the recommendation accuracy can be improved by combining information from the environment.

VII. CONCLUSION

In this study, we present an exercise recommendation method based on the contextual information of the user and the environment, which is a core part of an exercise facilitation system for performing other activities. Both offline and online experiments were conducted. An offline experiment was performed to simulate an already-collected dataset. The recommended items were deemed reasonable for each of the

TABLE V: RULE VECTORS (r_i) REPRESENTING THE RULES OF EXERCISE RECOMMENDATION WITH THE NAMES OF EXERCISE.

Exercise[a]	Basic behavior				Main working part		Object in use		Characteristics of place					
	SIT	STD	WLK	LYN	UB	LB	FIX	POT	STY	TRV	WID	NRW	PUB	PRI
KLA	1	0	0	0	0	1	1	0	0	0	0	0	0	0
LP	1	0	0	0	1	0	1	0	0	0	0	0	0	0
SPU	0	1	0	0	0	1	0	0	1	0	0	0	0	0
HL	0	1	0	0	1	0	0	0	1	0	0	0	0	0
DI	0	0	1	0	0	1	0	0	0	0	0	0	0	0
FW	0	0	1	0	1	0	0	0	0	0	0	0	0	0

[a] KLA: knee lift abdominal exercise, LP: leg-pushing exercise, SPU: standing push-up exercise, HL: heel lift-up exercise, DI: drawing-in exercise, and FW: striding with a large belly and fast walking.

TABLE VI: RELATIVE FREQUENCIES OF THE USER EVALUATION SCORES ON THE RECOMMENDED EXERCISES.

Score	Specified			Free		
	User	Environment	All	User	Environment	All
1	0.014	0.000	0.005	0.014	0.012	0.014
2	0.032	0.022	0.014	0.041	0.012	0.010
3	0.045	0.034	0.032	0.041	0.043	0.024
4	0.104	0.134	0.127	0.092	0.092	0.077
5	0.805	0.810	0.824	0.812	0.840	0.876
N_{rec}*	221	179	221	218	163	209

* Total number of recommendation

main activities of sitting, standing, and walking, as well as for the availability of the working part. An online experiment was conducted using a real-time system to obtain user feedback in real-world situations. The result showed that more than 80 % of the participants judged the recommended exercise as appropriate ones in their current situations.

In the current implementation, the association of the elements in the object in use and the characteristics of the place with specific objects and places were performed by the authors; however, numerous objects and places exist in real-world conditions. Considering this aspect, we recommend that extensibility and scalability in various operating environments should be considered in practical systems. Regarding the recommendation rule, the set of rules used in the experiment was created by the authors and was thus not optimized for individual users or a large population. In the future, we shall report a method for user-driven recommendation rule creation using an Interactive Genetic Algorithm (IGA), where the rules listed in Table V are considered as gene sequences and the user's subjective evaluation is applied as a fitness function to perform evolutionary processes, such as crossover and mutation, to generate the user's preferred rules.

REFERENCES

[1] R. Guthold, G. A. Stevens, L. M. Riley, and F. C. Bull, "Worldwide trends in insufficient physical activity from 2001 to 2016: a pooled analysis of 358 population-based surveys with 1·9 million participants," *The Lancet Global Health*, Vol. 6, No. 10, pp. e1077–e1086, 2018.

[2] Japan Sports Agency, "Public opinion poll on the status of sports implementation, etc.," https://www.mext.go.jp/sports/content/20220310-spt_kensport01-000020487_1.pdf (In Japanese. Last accessed: 20 August 2023).

[3] N. Maffiuletti et al., "The effects of electromyostimulation training and basketball practice on muscle strength and jumping ability," *International Journal of Sports Medicine*, Vol. 21, No. 6, pp. 437–443, 2000.

[4] The Japan Home-health Apparatus Industrial Association, "Voluntary standards for the safety of ems equipment for home use," https://www.hapi.or.jp/documentation/information/ems_20201009r.pdf (In Japanese. Last accessed: 20 August 2023).

[5] S. Nagano, "Get rid of your busy schedule and get some exercise! One-minute exercise diet," PHP Institute, 2003 (In Japanese).

[6] M. Kobayashi, A. Tsuji, and K. Fujinami, "An exercise-promoting system for exercising while doing desk work," In *Distributed, Ambient and Pervasive Interactions. Smart Living, Learning, Well-being and Health, Art and Creativity*, pp. 273–291, 2022.

[7] S. Consolvo et al., "Flowers or a robot army?: Encouraging awareness & activity with personal, mobile displays," In *Proceedings of the 10th International Conference on Ubiquitous Computing*, pp. 54–63, 2008.

[8] P. Klasnja, S. Consolvo, D. W. McDonald, J. A. Landay, and W. Pratt, "Using mobile & personal sensing technologies to support health behavior change in everyday life: lessons learned," *AMIA 2009 Symposium Proceedings*, pp. 338–342, 2009.

[9] Y. Shimizu, A. Ohnishi, T. Terada, and M. Tsukamoto, "DeskWalk: An Exercise System by Replacing Key Inputs with Body Movements," In *Proceedings of the 18th International Conference on Advances in Mobile Computing & Multimedia*, pp. 202–209, 2020.

[10] H. Lee and O. Jeong, "A personalized exercise recommendation system using dimension reduction algorithms," *Journal of The Korea Society of Computer and Information*, Vol. 26, No. 6, pp. 19–28, 2021.

[11] Z. Zhao, A. Arya, R. Orji, and G. Chan, "Physical Activity Recommendation for Exergame Player Modeling using Machine Learning Approach," In *Proceedings of the 2020 IEEE 8th International Conference on Serious Games and Applications for Health*, pp. 1–9, 2020.

[12] B. Yong et al., "IoT-based intelligent fitness system," *Journal of Parallel and Distributed Computing*, Vol. 118, pp. 14–21, 2018.

[13] K. Fujinami, "Interaction design issues in smart home environments," In *Proceedings of the 2010 5th International Conference on Future Information Technology*, pp. 1–8, 2010.

[14] K. Fujinami and T. Nakajima, "Sentient artefacts: Acquiring user's context through daily objects," In *Embedded and Ubiquitous Computing – EUC 2005 Workshops*, pp. 335–344, Berlin, Heidelberg, 2005. Springer Berlin Heidelberg.

[15] M. Addlesee et al., "Implementing a sentient computing system," *Computer*, Vol. 34, No. 8, pp. 50–56, 2001.

[16] S. Toyomasu, "A Study on a Semantic Zero-Shot Human Activity Recognition Based on Action Elements Content," Master Thesis, Tokyo University of Agriculture and Technology, 2020 (In Japanese).

[17] ATR-Promotions Inc., "Wireless sensors," http://www.atr-p.com/products/sensor.html (Last accessed: 20 August 2023).

The Triumvirate of Bespoke Diverse Hybridized Activation Functions, Adaptive Momentum, and Enhanced Entropic Wavelet Energy Spectrum Discernment for Higher Efficacy Detection of Artificial Intelligence-centric Attacks

Steve Chan
Decision Engineering Analysis Laboratory, VTIRL, VT
Orlando, USA
e-mail: schan@dengineering.org

***Abstract*—Artificial Intelligence-centric Attacks (AIA) involving False Data Injection and False Command Injection have become increasingly sophisticated and have also involved Metamorphic Malware (MM), which leverages numerous transformation techniques to avoid detection. Accordingly, the use of AI defender systems requires continuous learning so as to decrease the advantage held by the high cycles of adaptation of attackers. This paper explored Exponential Linear Unit (ELU) Mish as a hybridized activation function that could avoid the cessation of learning when a substantive portion of the Neural Network (NN) neurons output zero and weights are no longer updated. The involved Robust Convex Relaxation (RCR)-based Convolutional NN capitalized upon its architecture by utilizing a Nonlinear Conjugate Gradient and Nesterov's Accelerated Gradient approach to Adaptive Momentum (AdaM) so as to mitigate against oscillation, facilitate convergence, and achieve a more optimal global minimum. This more resilient foundational architecture could then better support a more accurate and expedient Entropic [Wavelet Energy Spectrum] Discernment (ED). Central to this was the use of Second-Order Cone Programming Relaxations to address certain nonconvex subproblems, which were inadvertently spawned via the utilized RCR framework. The described triumvirate approach constitutes the beginnings of a potential mitigation pathway, which exhibited some promise during the preliminary experimentation.**

Keywords-Artificial Intelligence Attack; Cyber; Smart Grid; Operational Technology; Adaptive Momentum; Second-Order Cone Programming Relaxations; Robust Convex Relaxations.

I. INTRODUCTION

Cyber Physical Power Systems (CPPS) are envisioned to enable Smart Grid (SG) technologies with more optimal monitoring and control. Numerous SG enablers have emerged at the convergence of Information Technology (IT) and Operational Technology (OT), and IT/OT engineers have increasingly utilized REpresentational State Transfer (REST) Application Programming Interfaces (APIs) to operationalize desired SG capabilities. However, the Open Worldwide Application Security Project (OWASP) notes the use of deprecated API versions as well as exposed debug endpoints (API9:2023) and potentially compromised third-party APIs (API10:2023). This attack surface area at the IT/OT nexus is of concern to many. Security firms have noted that while advisories often contain a patch to ameliorate the cited vulnerability, oftentimes, it is difficult to implement due to the downtime risk for the involved OT system. Contemporaneously, the World Economic Forum's (WEF) Global Risk Report notes that attacks on critical infrastructure operations (e.g., OT) are among the top five "currently manifesting risks" [1], and McKinsey & Company notes that these OT cyberattacks have particularly profound negative effects (e.g., outages, explosions, etc.) [2]. Among other attacks, polymorphic and Metamorphic Malware (MM) have beset CPPS, and advances in the area of mitigation have remained fairly nascent, particularly if patching is not an option. Yet, perhaps, of even greater concern for CPPS are Artificial Intelligence Attacks (AIA), which are designed to deceive AI-centric defense systems, such as via False Data Injection (FDI), False Command Injection (FCI), and other forms of insidious attack vectors.

While CPPS/SG defenders have increasingly looked to AI to defend at machine speed, these defending systems may be at a disadvantage due to the adversarial cycles of adaptation and may not yet be sufficiently robust against adversarial AIA. Contemporary defense research tends to center upon improving Machine Learning (ML) approaches to attain higher detection accuracy and computational performance, but efforts to mitigate against AIA remain fairly nascent. This paper delineates a potential mitigation pathway, and the paper is structured as follows. Section I provided a backdrop and introduces the problem space. Section II provides the background by way of describing the operating environment as well as the state of the challenge. Section III provides some theoretical foundations and the posited/utilized approach. Section IV delineates some preliminary experimental forays regarding the posited AIA mitigation approach. Section V concludes with some preliminary reflections, puts forth envisioned future work, and the acknowledgements close the paper.

II. BACKGROUND INFORMATION

MM mitigation efforts have already illuminated the sophistication of modern attack vectors. For example, crypters (i.e., a paradigm, wherein the use of obfuscation and/or encryption is at play) and protectors (i.e., a paradigm, wherein a hybridization of packing — self-extracting archives that unpack in memory upon execution — and encrypting is utilized) are becoming increasingly successful at obfuscating their malicious intent from detectors. Likewise, AIA endeavor to obscure their intent from

Endpoint Detection and Response (EDR) applications and CPPS/SG Detectors (CSD) alike by leveraging Generative Adversarial Networks (GANs), among other approaches, to spawn/facilitate FDI, FCI, and other attack vectors, which are difficult to discern in real-time by the EDR and CSD.

The literature tends to approach CSD by classifying the involved Machine Learning (ML) constructs as supervised, unsupervised, and Reinforcement Learning (RL) with the further nuance of conventional versus deep learning (e.g., via Convolutional NNs or CNNs). For sophisticated target attacks, wherein the perpetrator is already cognizant of the inherent weaknesses of AI/ML, such as the high number of false positives limiting supervised approaches, the high false negatives that beset unsupervised approaches, as well as the general strategy/approach taken by defensive AI/ML constructs amidst the current trend of Explainable Artificial Intelligence (XAI) and open AI, the perpetrator may bypass "Maginot Line" defenses and resort to a poisoning attack at the source (a.k.a., "poisoning the well"). In other words, AIA may seek to corrupt the source-derived training data used by the ML algorithm, thereby impacting the CSD's performance under specific circumstances. Unfortunately, the inherent constraints and blindspots of the underlying ML algorithms, in this regard, remain an ongoing issue, have yet to be resolved, and reside in a fairly nascent space.

Even when hybridized approaches are taken that combine the strengths of various ML approaches, the issue of numerical stability remains. Let us take the case of a particular CNN — a Constriction Factor (CF)-based Particle Swarm Optimization (PSO) Convex Relaxation (CR) Long Short-Term Memory (LSTM) Deep Learning NN (DLNN) construct. On the one hand, in terms of advantages, Khare and Bajaj have shown that CNNs tend to have a lower false positive rate [3], Osei-kwakye et al. have highlighted how CFs facilitate convergence stability [4], Zhao has highlighted how PSOs have fewer parameters to tune [5], Eltved has noted that CRs have been utilized with great efficacy for nonlinear optimizations [6] while [7] showed how Robust Convex Relaxations (RCR) may enhance efficacy. Also, Moradi et al. have described how LSTMs address the gradient vanishing issue (a consequence of the derivative of the activation function used for instantiation of the involved NN) [8], and Bai et al. have described how DLNNs enhance feature expression in terms of best-fit approximation [9]. On the other hand, in terms of disadvantages, You et al. and Zadiri et al. have noted how Adaptive Inertial Weighting (AIW) approaches may outperform CF approaches (when CF is used in isolation) [10]. Du et al. have noted how PSO is particularly prone to stagnation at local optima (e.g., if AIW is not utilized) [11], Song et al. have noted that CRs can segue to underestimations (e.g., if an approach for Robust CRs or RCRs are not adopted) [12]. Gong et al. have noted that the large model size issue for LSTMs impedes more prevalent deployments [13]. Shrestha and Mahmood have noted that the initial parameter selection for DLNNs have an "outsized influence" on how quickly the training converges [14]. Accordingly, regarding the referenced CF-PSO-CR-LSTM-DLNN (CPCLD) construct, while its bespoke design and implementation was intended to foster numerical stability, an AIA can indeed target and exploit the intricate intrinsic counterpoising at play.

III. THEORETICAL FOUNDATIONS

A. *Numerical Stability Challenges*

As an exemplar case study, the current version of PyTorch is at v2.0.1. However, CPPS/SG implementations often lag further behind the most recent version. For one specific case study, certain functions, while stable in v0.4.1, encountered stability issues as of v1.0.0, and some of these were only resolved as of 2020, as affirmed in Github (e.g., "Update the div formula for numerical stability #43627, as higher order gradients were returning Not a Number or NaN quite often") with an earlier partial resolution in 2019 (e.g., "Fix #11752: correct numerical issue with log_softmax #11866, as large inputs with small differences were producing numerical issues in the log_softmax"); there were also other issues (e.g., "nn.CrossEntropyLoss() yields wrong output for big logits #11752, as larger logits, which operate on the unscaled output of prior layers, were returning incorrect results") that are yet to be fully examined. To further the complexity, the well-known open-source ML framework/toolkit Convolutional Architecture for Fast Feature Embedding (Caffe2) repository was merged into the PyTorch repository on Github in 2018, and maintainers, core-developers, and users have noted that there may be incompatible elements (although Open NN Exchange or ONNX is intended to help resolve that). In the interim, AIA may exploit these incompatabilities.

As the numerical stability paradigm of the CPCLD is predicated upon a Deep Convolutional GAN (DCGAN) (which serves as a mitigator against mode failure/mode collapse — a paradigm wherein two competing NN being trained concurrently fail to converge or have an unusual convergence), CNN#1 (which serves as the key solver for the involved convex optimization problems), and CNN#2 (which serves as the key solver for the involved functions), it should be axiomatic that the aforementioned amalgam will likely (as is the case for prototypical DCGANs) exhibit a non-graceful degradation of performance even at imperceptible perturbation levels, which results in numerical instability. For the CPCLD, batch normalization (a.k.a., batchnorm) (a method of inducing stability into a NN, via normalization of the input layer and the layers of the NN), as one example, when selectively applied to the generator output layer and the discriminator input layer, avoids instability. However, if the AIA, such as via FCI Attack (FCIA), were able to induce application of batchnorm to all the layers of the involved NN, oscillation and instability would likely ensue. Alternatively, if the AIA were able to increase the learning rate of the NN, instability could ensue as well as an increased computational cost, which might trigger certain governor actions (that would be quite ironic, as it would be a contradictory unanticipated consequence) to reduce the utilization rate and energy consumption. Also, as previously discussed, the source of the training data is particularly vulnerable.

B. *Potential Mitigation Heuristics*

By way of pertinent context, as higher dimensional spaces are quite sparse, the substantive portion of the training data is constrained to the comparatively small manifold region. Hence, the training data can, potentially, be readily subject to manipulation (i.e., the previously referenced "poisoning of the well"); this may have an adverse impact on the NN being trained. While NN are, technically, nonlinear, a favored Activation Function (AF) is the Rectifier Linear Unit (ReLu) (due to its ease/speed of training and inherent stability), which is linear (a non-zero gradient) for inputs greater than zero and has the characteristic that it does not saturate (for positive values). In comparison, by way of example, the Sigmoid or Tanh AFs tend to saturate at high activations (with gradients very close to zero). Yet, ReLu is more vulnerable to adversarial attacks, as it is more readily skewed. Hence, prototypical AFs are limited with regards to their efficacy/resiliency, and the use of diverse hybridized AFs may be prudent to provide a modicum of enhanced resiliency against poisoning attacks, particularly from AIA.

Apart from AF, elongated training (with the notion that greater Volume and Variety — as well as Value, Velocity, and Veracity from the 5 Vs of Big Data — will assist the NN) for various NN architectures can actually degrade the performance [15]. Some architectures can be hindered by even a single hyperparameter (e.g., "epsilon") [16]. As discussed in Section IIIA, certain applied functions or even increased learning rates can induce oscillations. However, particularly in the adversarial case, the oscillations can indeed be dampened via Momentum, which is an additional weighting parameter (that chronicles and considers the gradient of prior steps, rather than simply rely upon the gradient of the current step, which can be readily skewed, as previously discussed) that can provide enhanced resiliency.

In cases, such as the CPCLD, the construct supports a Recurrent NN (RNN) to Feedforward NN (FNN) progression by facilitating an enhanced Entropic Wavelet Energy Spectrum (EWES) Discernment (a.k.a., ED) via a bespoke Nonnegative Matrix Factorization (NMF) to Multiresolution Matrix Factorization (MMF) to Continuous Wavelet Transform (CWT) Sequence of Transformations (SOT); this segues to ED accuracy, such as in the case of Indications and Warning (I&W) for MM. This mechanism (as a potential mitigation pathway), in particular, is referred to as MMED.

In essence, the use of the described triumvirate constitutes the beginnings of a potential mitigation pathway: (1) the use of diverse hybridized AFs, (2) the use of Momentum, particularly Adaptive Momentum (a.k.a., AdaM), to serve as an oscillation dampener; and (3) the use of the CPCLD construct to operationalize ED accuracy and expediency (via the application of Second-Order Cone Programming Relaxations or SOCPR to apropros subproblems spawned by the RCR). The issue of subproblems, such as nonconvex, by the CPCLD RCR is shown in Figure 1, which depicts the pathway of complete (a.k.a., exact) and incomplete (a.k.a., relaxed) verifiers. In essence, wherein exact verifiers are typically based upon a Mixed Integer Programming (MIP), such as that of Mixed Integer Non-Linear Programming (MINLP) progression, relaxed verifiers are Mixed Integer Linear Programming (MILP)-centric. While MILP segues to convex, MINLP can segue to either convex or nonconvex, and the SOCPR is intended to address the nonconvex subproblems that are spawned.

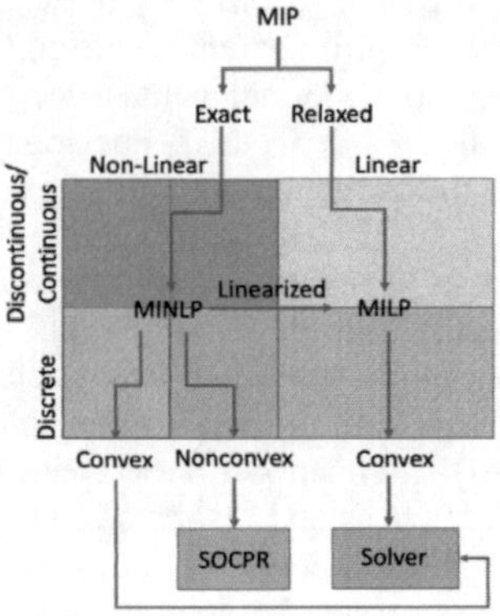

Figure 1. Exact and Relaxed Verifier Pathways with SOCPR Support.

As can be seen, convex problems can proceed directly to the utilized Solver. Hence, ideally, MINLP is linearized to MILP and convex along the way, but for some cases, wherein MINLP leads to nonconvex, SOCPR can be invaluable in facilitating the resolution of the potential problematic subproblems.

IV. EXPERIMENTATION

A. *Experimental Considerations*

First, the preliminary experimental forays in the area of diverse hybridized activation functions are extrapolated from the works of, among others: (1) Privietha and Raj, who combined softmax (which maps the input values to probabilities that sum to 1 — a requisite for multi-class classification problems) and sparsemax (which has an advantage over softmax in its ability to assign a probability of 0 so as to filter out noise, among other facets) in the last activation layer of the involved DLNN so as to achieve improved computational performance and higher accuracy [17], (2) Zhang et al., who utilized Mish AF, which seems to overcome the disadvantages of prototypical AF (which do not readily learn when the activation is 0) [18], and (3) Mercioni and Holban, who utilized Soft Clipping [Learnable] Mish (SCL Mish), which was inspired by Mish, and has a "learnable parameter" [19]. As [20] was very close to the venue of classification undertaken by Zhang et al., the datasets of CIFAR-10 and CIFAR-100 were utilized for calibration purposes. Then, MM samples were obtained by using krmaxwell/maltrieve and jstrosch/malware-samples (available via Github).

Second, preliminary experimental forays in the area of AdaM as an oscillation dampener (as well as facilitator for convergence and a more optimal global minimum) were derived from/built upon the notions put forth by: (1) Sun et al., who focused upon a more optimal AdaM approach rather than tuning a single Momentum hyperparameter (which, if set too high, can not only propel past the global minimum, but also segue to, ironically, oscillations or divergence during training) [21], (2) Hakimi et al., who noted that Momentum can exacerbate Gradient Staleness (GS) (thereby hindering convergence) and, therefore, concentrated on GS mitigation, via an approach called DANA (which undertakes the gradient calculation predicated upon the posited future position of the involved parameters) [22]; GS was further considered via Jelassi's and Li's unpacking of the matter [23], (3) Wang and Ye, who focused upon AdaM via the Nonlinear Conjugate Gradient (NCG) method (widely utilized for unconstrained optimization) [24], (4) Hu et al., who utilized an Iterative Soft-Thresholding Algorithm (ISTA), specifically an accelerated ISTA implementation referred to as Fast ISTA (FISTA), so as to explore the case studies of both convex and non-convex situations [25], (5) Amini and Faramarzi, who put forth a positive parameter requirement to control the condition number of the direction matrix and improve the efficiency of the algorithm (which fosters an expedited delineation of convex/non-convex) [26], as well as (6) Karimi and Vavasis, who leveraged Nesterov's Accelerated Gradient (NAG) (which has better complexity bounds compared to NCG) so as to undertake a hybridized approach of NCG and NAG (i.e., NCG steps are taken until the point, wherein insufficient progress is made, at which time NAG steps are taken and resorts back to NCG at a certain point) and explored the convex/non-convex demarcation [27]. Again, CIFAR-10, CIFAR-100 were utilized for level-setting purposes. Then, the same corpus of MM samples was utilized, as previously noted.

Third, experimental excursions with regards to EWES, built upon those described by Wojnowicz et al., who utilized wavelet transforms to derive a Suspiciously Structure Entropic Change Score (SSECS) [28], Gilbert et al., who used EWES with regards to CNNs and malware [29], and Ling et al, who applied NMF for the purposes of MMED [30]. Furthermore, this paper builds upon the MMED case delineated in [31]. In particular, the CPCLD leverages SOCPR so as to address nonconvex subproblems via various Semi-Definite Programming (SDP) algorithms, which were implemented on a modified GNU Octave platform (m-GNU-O) (a numerical computation platform, which is mostly compatible with the likes of MATLAB). Fuzzy logic packages were obtained, via Octave Forge, for use on the m-GNU-O. A Quadratically Constrained Quadratic Programming (QCQP) Step-Down Algorithm was used to compute the resultant QCQP special class convex optimization problem in polynomial time.

B. Experimental Design & Implementation

First, for a NN to learn ever-increasing complexity, a nonlinear function is needed, such as via the involved AF. Many consider the AF as a defining facet for the NN, as in the case of Artificial NN (ANNs). As the desire for quickly ascertaining the global minimum and convergence have become key metrics, variations of ReLU, such as Leaky ReLU (LReLU) have risen in popularity (to mitigate against the "dying ReLU" issue of outputting a value of 0, when the input is negative, by introducing a small slope *a*) and Parametric ReLU (PReLU), wherein *a* becomes a dynamic "learnable parameter" versus simply a static parameter [19]. Other variants include Softplus (which has inclination and gradient properties besides 0), Swish (an amalgam composite function of ReLU and Sigmoid), Mish (a composite function comprised of ReLu, Tanh, and Softplus), SCL Mish (a composite function similar to Mish, wherein *a* is learnable), etc. However, as ReLU can have relatively large outputs, it is typically not utilized for LSTMs, which is an intrinsic component of the CPCLD construct. Moreover, as previously noted, ReLU may be particularly susceptible to AIA. Consequently, a composite function that utilizes Exponential Linear Unit (ELU) (which can produce negative outputs but tends to saturate for very large negative values) as an alternative to ReLU was investigated and is referred to as ELU Mish (a composite function of ELU, Tanh, and Softplus). Some of these composite function AFs are shown in Figure 2.

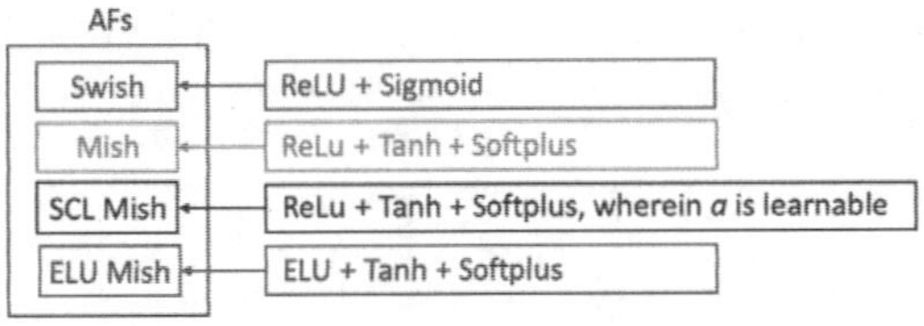

Figure 2. List of some Exemplar Composite Function AFs.

Second, as it was found that Momentum can generate a Momentum Gap (MG) (e.g., when the batch size increases, the gap between the Momentum and non-Momentum curves can dramatically increase), which needs to be constrained and decreased by approaches, such as DANA, so as to foster the desired fast convergence and accuracy (even on large clusters, thereby successfully mitigating again "gradient staleness"). In addition, the Fletcher-Reeves formula applied to Gradient Descent (FRGD) and Stochastic Gradient Descent (FRSGD) shows promise with regards to increased robustness against adversarial attacks (e.g., robustness under large learning rates) and the use of NCG for AdaM (wherein no training for a momentum hyperparameter is required), as well as the FRGD/FRSGD approach to accelerate GD/SGD was explored. The delineated approach seems to have the value-added proposition of having higher efficacy in cases wherein the optimization problem is ill-conditioned (i.e., wherein certain directions, construed as "narrow canyons," experience slower progress than others). Also, the technique of averaging over subsequent gradients can facilitate more stable directions of descent. Perhaps, for the overarching consideration, the sparse recovery consideration or "compressed sensing paradigm" for both convex and nonconvex situations is vital, as it should be remembered that with regards to nonconvex to convex transformations, the transformations themselves may spawn further nonconvex problems. Restated, the architected NN (e.g., CNN) may incorporate a variety of approachs for the resolving of a succession of convex optimization problems. However, even when the involved construct is specifically designed so as to segue to a convex paradigm, the resultant may still turn out to be nonconvex, thereby necessitating a further transformation to a convex optimization problem via certain relaxation techniques. Yet, the referenced transformation, in itself, may spawn yet further nonconvex optimization problems, thereby highlighting the advantage of utilizing a RCR framework, such as the CPCLD, along with SOCPR.

Third, in general, wavelet analysis predicated upon EWES can well delineate the complexity of the involved paradigm. In particular, ED can successfully ascertain potentially suspect patterns of entropic change across the code of an executable file. Moreover, as noted in [31], because NMF has the intrinsic constraint that the factorized matrices be comprised of non-negative (i.e., positive) elements, NMF can provide a better-fit interpretation of the original matrix data (given the more intuitive and logical structural representation by parts). It has been previously discussed in [31] that the sum of positive elements (e.g., "matrices, vectors, integers") is "more intuitive, logical, and naturalistic given the matrices of positive integers, and by capitalizing upon NMF's non-negative constraint, various high-level features are more readily discerned from the hidden layers of the involved NN." Also, the "less contrived NMF-based approach reduces the need for feature engineering (i.e., a coarser and less elegant approach of extraction)." The CPCLD architectural construct, which supports the aforementioned for the discussed NMF-related SOT, is particularly apropos for supporting the positive parameter requirement so as to shape the condition number of the direction matrix and the ensuing operationalization efficiency. Hence, for this case, the CPCLD would not only utilize a bespoke AF (i.e., ELU Mish), but also a bespoke NCG/NAG for AdaM in conjunction with an ED schema leveraging SOCPR for rate-limiting key subproblems.

C. *Experimental Results*

For benchmarking purposes, the Architectural Construct used was that of a CNN; specifically, the classic LeNet-5 CNN was utilized prior to experimentation on the CPCLD CNN. To level-set, epochs were set to 50, data samples from the previously discussed corpus were set to 50,000, and validation was performed on 10,000. The benchmarking can be seen in Table I below.

TABLE I. CNN EXPERIMENTAL RESULTS

Architectural Construct	**Activation Function**			
	ReLu	***Sigmoid***	***Tanh***	***Softplus***
CNN: LeNet-5/	64.32% [19]	58.12% [19]	56.83% [19]	61.43% [19]
	Swish	***Mish***	***SCL Mish***	***ELU***
CPCLD				***Mish***
	62.47% [19]	61.77% [19]	63.26% [19]	61.74%

It can be seen that while the highest value was achieved by ReLU, for an enhanced resiliency against AIA, the slightly lower performance by ELU Mish is still respectable and remains in the upper tier of the AF results. To further this, with regards to AdaM and SOCPR, this enhanced version was compared to a prior instantiation of [31].

TABLE II. CLASSIFICATION RESULTS OF VARIOUS ML METHODS

Methods	**Models**	**Accuracy (ACC)**
Prototypical ML methods	Random Forest (RF)	91.43-97.74% [32]
	k-Nearest Neighbor (KNN)	97.17% [33]
Prototypical DLNN methods	Convolutional NN (CNN)	96.96% [34]
	Recurrent NN (RNN)-Bidirectional (Bi)LSTM hybrid	98.2%-98.9% [35]
Posited bespoke CPCLD method	CF-PSO-CR-LSTM-DLNN (CPCLD)	97.9%-98.2% [31]
	CPCLD with Triumvirate (T) (CPCLD-T)	98.5%

It can be seen that the construct with the Triumvirate (T) was able to achieve a slightly higher value than without. By way of comparison, as a rudimentary baseline, Khammas cites the study of Zhang et al, which reported an accuracy of 91.43% using RF and himself attains even better results at 97.74% [32]. More in line with the experimentation herein, Roy experiments with KNN along with MCDM and TOPSIS and attains results at 97.17% [33]. Lad and Adamuthe experimented with various CNN instantations, and their specific implementation was able to achieve 96.96% [34]. For a RNN-BiLSTM hybrid, Samee et al. reported that 98.2%-98.9% was achieved for their application [35]. Experimentation based upon the aforementioned works was conducted. Preliminary experimentation for more rudimentary versions of the discussed CPCLD yielded results of 97.9%, as previously reported in [31], and the experimentation for this round attained similar results to that of the RNN-BiLSTM. However, when T was leveraged, 98.5% was attained. A comparative summary (using the lower bound figures) can be seen in Figure 3 below.

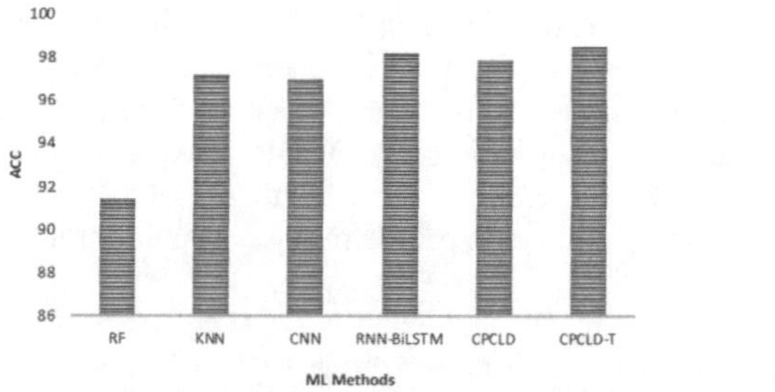

Figure 3. Comparative Summary by ACC for the Classification Results of Various ML Methods.

Although the CPCLD method did not achieve the 98.9% reported by Alam et al. [36], it is hoped that future iterations of the CPCLD will exhibit improvements in this regard.

V. CONCLUSION

In an era of MM and ChatGPT generating mutating malware [37], the potential lethality of AIA has become increasingly illuminated. Niazazari and Livani as well as others have affirmed adversarial capabilities, such as FDI Attacks, and the ensuing misclassification by CNN-based event cause analysis frameworks, among others [38]. In the case of this paper, the focus was on MM-centric AIA, particularly MM targeting Industrial Systems at the nexus of IT/OT, as this domain has been cited as among the top "currently manifesting risks" [1]. The nascent nature of mitigation pathways has been illuminated in [7] and [39], as contemporary research efforts have predominantly focused upon ML approaches for enhanced detection accuracy and computational performance while AIA mitigation pathways remain relatively unexplored and represent greenfield opportunities. Indeed, even defending constructs that operationalize MMED, such as the discussed CPCLD/CPCLD-T constructs, can be targeted by AIA to exploit intricate intrinsic mechanisms, such as the numerical stability paradigm. To buttress the CPCLD/CPCLD-T constructs, this paper explored the beginnings of a potential mitigation pathway. In particular, a bespoke AF (i.e., ELU Mish as a hybridized AF that avoids the cessation of learning so as to allow the AI defender system to be able to maintain continuous learning), NCG/NAG AdaM approach, and SOCPR-based ED (to assist with the RCR-based CPCLD construct) triumvirate was put forth. Future work will likely involve further exploration and experimentation in the area of defender NN stability issues amidst AIA.

ACKNOWLEDGMENT

This research is supported by the Decision Engineering Analysis Laboratory (DEAL), an Underwatch initiative of VTIRL, VT. This is part of an ongoing VTIRL technical series, on behalf of the Quality Assurance/Quality Control (QA/QC) unit, to advance the involved TRLs.

REFERENCES

[1] World Economic Forum, Marsh McLennan, and Zurich Insurance Group, "Global Risks Report 2023," World Economic Forum, January 11, 2023, Accessed on: July 28, 2023. [Online]. Available: https://www.weforum.org/reports/global-risks-report-2023/in-full/1-global-risks-2023-today-s-crisis/.

[2] McKinsey & Company, "How to Enhance the Cybersecurity of Operational Technology Environments," March 23, 2023, Accessed on: July 28, 2023. [Online]. Available: https://www.mckinsey.com/capabilities/risk-and-resilience/our-insights/cybersecurity/how-to-enhance-the-cybersecurity-of-operational-technology-environments.

[3] S. K. Khare and V. Bajaj, "Time–Frequency Representation and Convolutional Neural Network-Based Emotion Recognition," IEEE Transactions on Neural Networks and Learning Systems, vol. 32, pp. 2901-2909, July 2021, doi: 10.1109/TNNLS.2020.3008938.

[4] J. Osei-kwakye, F. Han, A. Amponsah, Q. Ling, and T. Abeo, "A Hybrid Optimization Method by Incorporating Adaptive Response Strategy for Feedforward Neural Network," Connection Science, vol. 34, pp. 578-607, Jan 2022, doi: 10.1080/09540091.2021.2025339.

[5] M. Zhao, H. Zhao, and M. Zhao, "Particle Swarm Optimization Algorithm With Adaptive Two-Population Strategy," IEEE Access, vol. 11, pp. 62242-62260, June 2023, doi: 10.1109/ACCESS.2023.3287859.

[6] A. Eltved, "Convex Relaxation Techniques for Nonlinear Optimization," Technical University of Denmark, 2021, Accessed on: September 17, 2023. [Online]. Available: https://backend.orbit.dtu.dk/ws/portalfiles/portal/257935519/Anders_Eltved.pdf.

[7] S. Chan and P. Nopphawan, "Bespoke Mitigation Framework for False Data Injection Attack-Induced Contingency Events," 2023 International Conference On Cyber Management and Engineering (CyMaEn), February 2023, pp. 492-499, doi: 10.1109/CyMaEn57228.2023.10050946.

[8] M. Moradi, S. Sadrossadat, and V. Derhami, "Long Short-Term Memory Neural Networks for Modeling Nonlinear Electronic Components," IEEE Transactions on Components, Packaging and Manufacturing Technology, vol. 11, pp. 840-847, May 2021, doi: 10.1109/TCPMT.2021.3071351.

[9] T. Bai et al., "Deep Learning for Change Detection in Remote Sensing: A Review," Geo-spatial Information Science, July 2022, doi: 10.1080/10095020.2022.2085633.

[10] S. Zdiri, J. Chrouta, and A. Zaafouri, "An Expanded Heterogeneous Particle Swarm Optimization Based on Adaptive Inertia Weight," Mathematical Problems in Engineering, vol. 2021, October 2021, pp. 1-24, doi: https://doi.org/10.1155/2021/4194263.

[11] S. Du, W. Fan, and Y. Liu, "A Novel Multi-Agent Simulation Based Particle Swarm Optimization Algorithm," PLoS One, vol. 17, October 2022, doi: 10.1371/journal.pone.0275849.

[12] Y. Song, H. Cao, C. Mehta, and K. Khan, "Bounding Convex Relaxations of Process Models from Below by Tractable Black-Box Sampling," Computers & Chemical Engineering, vol. 153, October 2021, doi: https://doi.org/10.1016/j.compchemeng.2021.107413.

[13] Y. Gong, M. Yin, L. Huang, C. Deng and B. Yuan, "Algorithm and Hardware Co-Design of Energy-Efficient LSTM Networks for Video Recognition With Hierarchical Tucker Tensor Decomposition," IEEE Transactions on Computers, vol. 71, pp. 3101-3114, December 2022, doi: 10.1109/TC.2022.3212642.

[14] A. Shrestha and A. Mahmood, "Review of Deep Learning Algorithms and Architectures," IEEE Access, vol. 7, pp. 53040-53065, April 2019, doi: 10.1109/ACCESS.2019.2912200.

[15] M. Advani, A. Saxe, and H. Sompolinsky, "High-dimensional Dynamics of Generalization Error in Neural Networks," Neural Networks, vol. 132, December 2020, pp. 428-446, doi: 10.1016/j.neunet.2020.08.022.

[16] Y. Ozaki, M. Yano, and M. Onishi, "Effective hyperparameter optimization using Nelder-Mead method in deep learning," IPSJ Transactions on Computer Vision and Applications, vol. 9, November 2017, doi: https://doi.org/10.1186/s41074-017-0030-7.

[17] P. Privietha and V. Raj, "Hybrid Activation Function in Deep Learning for Gait Analysis," 2022 International Virtual Conference on Power Engineering Computing and Control: Developments in Electric Vehicles and Energy Sector for Sustainable Future (PECCON), May 2022, pp. 1-7, doi: 10.1109/PECCON55017.2022.9851128.

[18] Z. H. Zhang, Z. Yang, Y. Sun, Y. Wu, and Y. Xing, "Lenet-5 Convolution Neural Network with Mish Activation Function and Fixed Memory Step Gradient Descent Method," 2019

16th International Computer Conference on Wavelet Active Media Technology and Information Processing, December 2019, pp. 196-199, doi: 10.1109/ICCWAMTIP47768.2019.9067661.

[19] M. Mercioni and S. Holban, "Soft Clipping Mish - A Novel Activation Function for Deep Learning," 2021 4th International Conference on Information and Computer Technologies (ICICT), March 2021, pp. 13-17, doi: 10.1109/ICICT52872.2021.00010.

[20] S. Chan, I. Oktavianti, and P. Nopphawan, "Optimal Convex Relaxation-based Wavelet Covariance Transform for More Robust AOD-PM Characterization and Tracer Tracking of Biomass Burning Over Land/Sea Boundary Regions," 2022 IEEE Ocean Engineering Technology and Innovation Conference: Management and Conservation for Sustainable and Resilient Marine and Coastal Resources (OETIC), December 2022, pp. 1-10, doi: 10.1109/OETIC57156.2022.10176215.

[21] T. Sun, H. Ling, Z. Shi, D. Li, and B. Wang, "Training Deep Neural Networks with Adaptive Momentum Inspired by the Quadratic Optimization," Oct 2021, doi: https://doi.org/10.48550/arXiv.2110.09057.

[22] I. Hakimi, S. Barkai, M. Gabel, and A. Schuster, "Taming Momentum in a Distributed Asynchronous Environment," October 2020, https://doi.org/10.48550/arXiv.1907.11612.

[23] S. Jelassi and Y. Li, "Towards Understanding How Momentum Improves Generalization in Deep Learning," Proceedings of the 39th International Conference on Machine Learning, 2022, Accessed on: July 28, 2023. [Online]. Available: https://proceedings.mlr.press/v162/jelassi22a/jelassi22a.pdf

[24] B. Wang and Q. Ye, "Stochastic Gradient Descent with Nonlinear Conjugate Gradient-Style Adaptive Momentum," December 2020, Accessed on: October 4, 2023. [Online]. Available: https://arxiv.org/abs/2012.02188.

[25] M. Hu et al., "Accelerated Sparse Recovery via Gradient Descent with Nonlinear Conjugate Gradient Momentum," April 2023, Accessed on: October 4, 2023. [Online]. Available: https://arxiv.org/abs/2208.12183.

[26] K. Amini and P. Faramarzi, "An Adaptive Modified Three-Term Conjuage Gradient Method with Global Convergence," Applied Numerical Mathematics, vol 190, August 2023, pp. 187-199.

[27] S. Karimi and S. Vavasis, "Nonlinear Conjugate Gradient for Smooth Convex Functions," Jan 2023, Accessed on: October 4, 2023. [Online]. Available: https://arxiv.org/abs/2111.11613

[28] M. Wojnowicz, G. Chisholm, M. Wolff, and X. Zhao, "Wavelet decomposition of software entropy reveals symptoms of malicious code," Journal of Innovation in Digital Ecosystems, vol. 3, pp. 130-140, doi: https://doi.org/10.1016/j.jides.2016.10.009.

[29] D. Gilbert, C. Mateu, J. Planes, and R. Vicens, "Classification of malware by using structural entropy on convolutional neural networks," Proceedings of the Thirty-Second AAAI Conference on Artificial Intelligence and Thirtieth Innovative Applications of Artificial Intelligence Conference and Eighth AAAI Symposium on Educational Advances in Artificial Intelligence, February 2018, pp. 7759-7764, doi: https://doi.org/10.5555/3504035.3504987.

[30] Y. Ling, N. Sani, M. Abdullah, and N. Hamid, "Nonnegative matrix factorization and metamorphic malware detection," J Comput Virol Hack Tech, vol. 15, April 2019, pp. 95–208, doi: https://doi.org/10.1007/s11416-019-00331-0.

[31] S. Chan, "Bespoke Sequence of Transformations for an Enhanced Entropic Wavelet Energy Spectrum Discernment for Higher Efficacy Detection of Metamorphic Malware," The Eighth International Conference on Cyber-Technologies and Cyber-Systems, September 2023, Accessed on: October 4, 2023. [Online]. Available: https://www.thinkmind.org/index.php?view=article&articleid=cyber_2023_1_80_80045

[32] B. Khammas, "Ransomware Detection Using Random Forest Technique," ICT Express, vol. 6, issue 4, pp. 325–331, Dec. 2020, Accessed on: October 4, 2023. [Online]. Available: https://www.researchgate.net/publication/346882787_Ransomware_Detection_using_Random_Forest_Technique

[33] A. Roy et al., "Comparative analysis of KNN and SVM in multicriteria inventory classification using TOPSIS," Int J. Inf. Technol, vol. 15, 2023, pp. 3613-3622, doi: https://doi.org/10.1007/s41870-023-01397-2.

[34] S. Lad and A. Adamuthe, "Malware Classification with Improved Convolutional Neural Network Model," I.J. Computer Network and Information Security, 2020, 6 30-43. doi: 10.5815/ijcnis.2020.06.03.

[35] N. Samee et al., "RNN and BiLSTM Fusion for Accurate Automatic Epileptic Seizure Diagnosis Using EEG Signals," Life (Basel), vol. 12, no. 12, 22 November 2022.

[36] S. Alam, I. Traore, and I. Sogukpinar, "Annotated Control Flow Graph for Metamorphic Malware Detection," The Computer Journal, vol. 58, no. 10, Oct. 2015, pp. 2608-2621, doi: 10.1093/comjnl/bxu148.

[37] S. Sharma, "ChatGPT creates mutating malware that evades detection by EDR," CIO, June 2023, Accessed on: July 28, 2023. [Online]. Available: https://www.csoonline.com/article/575487/chatgpt-creates-mutating-malware-that-evades-detection-by-edr.html#:~:text=ChatGPT%20creates%20mutating%20malware%20that%20evades%20detection%20by%20EDR,-News&text=Mutating%2C%20or%20polymorphic%2C%20malware%20can,and%20response%20(EDR)%20application.

[38] I. Niazazari and H. Livani, "Attack on Grid Event Cause Analysis: An Adversarial Machine Learning Approach," May 2020 IEEE Power & Energy Society Innovative Smart Grid Technologies Conference (ISGT), 2020, pp. 1-5, doi: 10.1109/ISGT45199.2020.9087649.

[39] S. Chan and P. Nopphawan, "Bespoke Weighting Schema and Sequence of Transformations for Enhanced Insight into Prospective False Command Injection Attacks," 2023 International Conference On Cyber Management And Engineering (CyMaEn), February 2023, pp. 230-239, doi: 10.1109/CyMaEn57228.2023.10051057.

Moment Generating Function Based Calculation of Average Bit Error Probability in an α-μ Fading Environment with Selection Diversity Receiver

Dragana Krstic
University of Nis, Faculty of Electronic Engineering
Nis, Serbia
Email: dragana.krstic@elfak.ni.ac.rs

Suad Suljovic
Academy of Applied Technical Studies Belgrade
Belgrade, Serbia
Email: ssuljovic@atssb.edu.rs

Devendra S. Gurjar
Department of Electronics and Communications Engineering, National Institute of Technology Silchar
Assam, India
Email: dsgurjar@ece.nits.ac.in

Suneel Yadav
Department of Electronics and Communication Engineering, Indian Institute of Information Technology
Allahabad
Email: suneel@iiita.ac.in

***Abstract*—In this paper, a wireless system in the presence of α-μ fading is analyzed. Also, there is Co-Channel Interference (CCI), i.e., crosstalk from two different radio transmitters using the same frequency channel. The CCI has the same distribution as the fading in the observed environment. To mitigate these adverse effects, a diversity receiver with Selection Combining (SC) is used. For such wireless system configuration, we calculated the Average Bit Error Probability (ABEP) based on the Moment Generating Function (MGF). Analytical results are presented graphically in order to highlight the influence of fading and CCI parameters.**

Keywords- α-μ fading; Average Bit Error Probability (ABEP); Co-Channel Interference (CCI); Moment Generating Function (MGF); Selection Combining (SC).

I. INTRODUCTION

One of the most critical disruptions to signal propagation in wireless channels is fading. A fading channel is a wireless communication channel that experiences fading [1]. Fading is modeled as a random variable with a certain statistical distribution. It is very important that this distribution describes the conditions in the wireless channel as closely as possible.

Recently, a lot of work has been done on the research of different distributions that satisfy these conditions. Thus, the α-μ distribution is introduced as a small-scale fading model. This model includes the nonlinearity of the propagation medium since the assumption of a homogeneous diffuse scattering field is only an approximation [2]. Actually, this is generalized Gamma distribution that encompasses some other distributions. Among them are: Gamma, with Erlang as its discrete versions and central Chi-squared, then Nakagami-*m* with its discrete version- Chi distribution, and also Weibull, Rayleigh, exponential, and One-sided Gaussian distributions. Therefore, α-μ distribution is suitable for a comprehensive analysis of the performance of wireless systems in the presence of the listed types of fading by reducing to special cases for certain values of parameters α and μ.

In addition to [2], there are not many papers in the literature considering this type of fading, despite its convenience. Nevertheless, we will mention some of them [3]-[8]. The authors in [3] evaluated the Moment Generating Function (MGF) for the Probability Density Function (PDF) that describes the α-μ wireless fading channel. The derived expression for MGF was utilized in obtaining the Bit Error Rate (BER) for different modulation techniques over this channel. An expression for the outage probability was also derived in the closed form. Both expressions can be reduced as special cases to those earlier obtained in the literature for known fading channel distributions such as Rayleigh, Nakagami-*m*, and Weibull.

The same authors worked with this fading even further, and in [4] they derived expressions for the amount of fading and the average channel capacity for this channel model. They confirmed once again the generality of this fading model as they reduced the expressions for the obtained performance metrics to other expressions for other channel models as special cases.

In [5], the authors proposed a novel MGF for α-μ fading distribution valid for all values of parameter α, as modification of the MGF from [3], where the MGF was valid only for non-integer values of α. Then, the closed-form expressions of BER for different modulation techniques such as Binary Phase-Shift Keying (BPSK), Binary Frequency Shift Keying (BFSK), Differential Quadrature PSF (DQPSK), Binary Differential PSK (BDPSK), and *M*-ary PSK (MPSK) over α-μ fading channels are determined.

In [6], the exact PDF of the square ratio of two multivariate exponentially correlated α-μ distributed variables is derived. Then, the expressions in the closed form are determined for the Cumulative Distribution Function (CDF) and PDF of the maximal and minimal square ratio of two multivariate exponentially correlated variables. These formulae are the base for Signal-to-Interference Ratio (SIR) based analysis of Selection Combining (SC) receiver through communication systems.

An enriched $\alpha-\mu$ distribution which may act as fading model is analyzed in [7]. The complex α-μ fading channel is observed in [8] with an Orthogonal Frequency-Division Multiplexing (OFDM) application.

The Co-Channel Interference (CCI) can occur in wireless systems beside fading. The most common reasons causing CCI are: bad weather condition and bad frequency planning. Its influence must be studied along with the influence of fading. In this paper, we performed a MGF-based calculation of the Average Bit Error Probability (ABEP) in an α-μ fading and CCI environment when SC diversity receiver was used to mitigate the influences of these disturbances. As far as we know, the derivation the MGF for the defined scenario has not been reported in the open literature.

Here, we choose discuss MGFs since, beside other reasons, they are useful in analysis of sums of Random Variables (RVs). Namely, the MGF of RV gives all moments of this RV, which is a fact that gives the name to the moment generating function. Second, the MGF (if it exists) uniquely determines the distribution. This means, if two RVs have the same MGF, then they must have the same distribution. Thus, if the MGF of an RV is found, its distribution is determined.

Our paper consists of four sections. After the introduction, in Section II, the SIR-based performance analysis at the output of SC receiver in the presence of α-μ fading and CCI is presented. In Section III, some graphs highlighting the parameters influence are plotted. At the end, a conclusion part is given. Finally, we conclude the paper in Section IV.

II. Performance Analysis Based on the SIR at the Output of the Receiver

In this section, we will derive the performance of a wireless system in the presence of α-μ fading and CCI. To mitigate the effects of fading and CCI, a SC diversity receiver with L branches, shown in Figure 1, is used. The SC receiver transmits to the user the signal from the input antenna whose value is the highest.

The input signals are x_i, i=1, 2, …, L; $L \geq 2$. The output signal is x. The CCI envelopes at the input are y_i, i=1, 2, …, L with output value y. We will derive the Signal-to-CCI ratio (SIR)-based system performance.

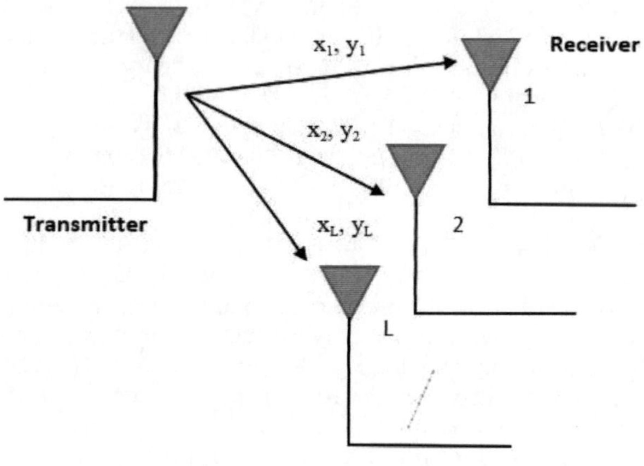

Figure 1. Model of a selection combining diversity receiver.

So, the input ratios of the useful signals and the CCIs are $z_i = x_i / y_i$, and the output SIR is denoted by z.

A. The PDF of the Output SIR

As mentioned, the transmitted signal has the α-μ distribution [2]:

$$p_{x_i}(x_i) = \frac{\alpha \mu_1^{\mu_1} x_i^{\alpha\mu_1 - 1}}{\Omega_i^{\mu_1} \Gamma(\mu_1)} e^{-\mu_1 \frac{x_i^\alpha}{\Omega_i}}, \qquad (1)$$

where parameter α characterizes the nonlinearity of the propagation environment; parameter μ_j shows the number of clusters in that environment, where j=1 for the signal, and j=2 for the CCI; Ω_i, i=1, 2, …, L, represents the mean values of the input signals powers, and $\Gamma(\cdot)$ marks the Gamma function.

The CCI is also under α-μ distribution:

$$p_{y_i}(y_i) = \frac{\alpha \mu_2^{\mu_2} y_i^{\alpha\mu_2 - 1}}{s_i^{\mu_2} \Gamma(\mu_2)} e^{-\mu_2 \frac{y_i^\alpha}{s_i}}, \qquad (2)$$

where s_i are the average powers of the CCI.

The PDFs of the SIRs z_i are mathematically given as [9]:

$$p_{z_i}(z_i) = \int_0^\infty y_i p_{x_i}(z_i y_i) p_{y_i}(y_i) dy_i, \qquad (3)$$

Substituting (1) and (2) into (3), we can obtain the PDFs for SIRs as:

$$p_{z_i}(z_i) = \frac{\alpha \mu_1^{\mu_1} \mu_2^{\mu_2} z_i^{\alpha\mu_1 - 1} \Omega_i^{\mu_2} s_i^{\mu_1} \Gamma(\mu_1 + \mu_2)}{\Gamma(\mu_2)\Gamma(\mu_1)\left(\Omega_i \mu_2 + \mu_1 s_i z_i^\alpha\right)^{\mu_1 + \mu_2}}. \qquad (4)$$

Let us derive the expression for CDF of z_i from the definition given in [9]:

$$F_{z_i}(z_i) = \int_0^{z_i} p_{z_i}(t) dt. \qquad (5)$$

Further, we can obtain the CDF of the SIR z_i after substituting (4) into (5):

$$F_{z_i}(z_i) = \frac{\alpha (\mu_1 s_i)^{\mu_1} (\mu_2 \Omega_i)^{\mu_2}}{\Gamma(\mu_2)} \cdot \frac{\Gamma(\mu_1 + \mu_2)}{\Gamma(\mu_1)} \times$$

$$\times \int_0^{z_i} \frac{z_i^{\alpha\mu_1 - 1}}{\left(\Omega_i \mu_2 + \mu_1 s_i z_i^\alpha\right)^{\mu_1 + \mu_2}} dt. \qquad (6)$$

The integral appearing in (6) will be solved using Beta function [10], as presented below:

$$\int_0^\lambda \frac{x^m}{(a + bx^n)^p} dx = \frac{a^{-p}}{n} \left(\frac{a}{b}\right)^{\frac{m+1}{n}} B_z\left(\frac{m+1}{n}, p - \frac{m+1}{n}\right)$$

$$z = \frac{b\lambda^n}{a + b\lambda^n}, a > 0, b > 0, n > 0, 0 < \frac{m+1}{n} < p. \qquad (7)$$

Now, the CDF of z_i is obtained in the form:

$$F_{z_i}(z_i)=\frac{\Gamma(\mu_1+\mu_2)}{\Gamma(\mu_2)\Gamma(\mu_1)}B_{\frac{\mu_1 s_i z_i^{\alpha}}{\Omega_i\mu_2+\mu_1 s_i z_i^{\alpha}}}(\mu_1,\mu_2)\cdot \tag{8}$$

The incomplete Beta function from (6) will be represented by [10, eq.8.391]:

$$B_x(p,q)=\int_0^x t^{p-1}(1-t)^{q-1}dt=\frac{x^p}{p}\,{}_2F_1(p,1-q;p+1;x)=$$

$$=\frac{x^p}{p}\,{}_2F_1(a,b;c;z)=\frac{x^p}{p}\sum_{j=0}^{\infty}\frac{a_j b_j}{c_j}\frac{z^j}{j!}, \tag{9}$$

where ${}_2F_1$ is the hyper geometric function of the second order. By some substitutions, the CDF can be written in the following form:

$$F_{z_i}(z_i)=\frac{\Gamma(\mu_1+\mu_2)}{\mu_1\Gamma(\mu_2)\Gamma(\mu_1)}\sum_{j=0}^{+\infty}\frac{(\mu_1)_j}{j!}\cdot$$

$$\cdot\frac{(1-\mu_2)_j}{(\mu_1+1)_j}\left(\frac{\mu_1 s_i z_i^{\alpha}}{\Omega_i\mu_2+\mu_1 s_i z_i^{\alpha}}\right)^{j+\mu_1}. \tag{10}$$

In SC, the received signal from the antenna that experiences the highest SIR (i.e., the strongest signal from L received signals) is chosen to be processed in the receiver (see Figure 1). Thus, the SIR z at the output of SC receiver with L branches is the maximum SIR of all the received signals:

$$z=\max(z_1,z_2,\ldots,z_L). \tag{11}$$

The PDF of the SIR z from SC receiver output is calculated using the formula [11]:

$$p_{z_i}(z)=Lp_{z_i}(z_i)\left(F_{z_i}(z_i)\right)^{L-1}. \tag{12}$$

By substitutions of (4) and (10) into (12), the PDF of the output SIR z becomes:

$$p_{z_i}(z)=\frac{L\alpha\mu_2^{\mu_2}}{\mu_1^{L-\mu_1-1}}\cdot\frac{z_i^{\alpha\mu_1-1}\Omega_i^{\mu_2}s_i^{\mu_1}}{\left(\Omega_i\mu_2+\mu_1 s_i z_i^{\alpha}\right)^{\mu_1+\mu_2}}\left(\frac{\Gamma(\mu_1+\mu_2)}{\Gamma(\mu_2)\Gamma(\mu_1)}\right)^{L}\times$$

$$\times\left(\sum_{j=0}^{+\infty}\frac{(\mu_1)_j(1-\mu_2)_j}{(\mu_1+1)_j\, j!}\left(\frac{\mu_1 s_i z_i^{\alpha}}{\Omega_i\mu_2+\mu_1 s_i z_i^{\alpha}}\right)^{j+\mu_1}\right)^{L-1}. \tag{13}$$

B. Moment Generating Function

The complicated PDF expression often limits the evaluation of performance measures of generalized fading channel models. The MGF is an important statistical function for each distribution. In the theory of probability and statistics, the MGF of a real RV is an alternate feature of its PDF.

The main formula for derivation the MGF is [12, eq. (6)]:

$$M_z(h)=\overline{e^{zh}}=\int_0^{\infty}e^{-zh}p_{z_i}(z)dz \tag{14}$$

By applying (4) into formula (14) for MGF, we obtain for our case:

$$M_z(h)=\frac{L\alpha\mu_2^{\mu_2}\Omega_i^{\mu_2}}{\mu_1^{L-1}\mu_1^{\mu_2}s_i^{\mu_2}}\cdot\left(\frac{\Gamma(\mu_1+\mu_2)}{\Gamma(\mu_2)\Gamma(\mu_1)}\right)^{L}\times$$

$$\times\left(\sum_{j=0}^{+\infty}\frac{(\mu_1)_j(1-\mu_2)_j}{(\mu_1+1)_j\, j!}\right)^{L-1}\times$$

$$\times\int_0^{\infty}\frac{z_i^{2\frac{\alpha jL-\alpha j+\alpha\mu_1 L}{2}-1}e^{-hz}}{\left(\left(\sqrt{\frac{\mu_2\Omega_i}{\mu_1 s_i}}\right)^2+\left(z_i^{\frac{\alpha}{2}}\right)^2\right)^{1-(j-jL-\mu_1 L-\mu_2+1)}}dz. \tag{15}$$

By using [10; 3.389]:

$$\int_0^{\infty}\frac{x^{2v-1}e^{-\mu x}}{\left(u^2+x^2\right)^{1-q}}dx=\frac{u^{2v+2q-2}}{2\sqrt{\pi}\,\Gamma(1-q)}G_{13}^{31}\left(\frac{\mu^2u^2}{4}\middle|\begin{matrix}1-v\\1-q-v,0,\frac{1}{2}\end{matrix}\right), \tag{16}$$

where G[·] is the Meijer's G-function [10; 9.301], and by replacing form of (16) into (15), the MGF for output SIR z becomes:

$$M_z(h)=\frac{L\alpha}{2\sqrt{\pi}\mu_1^{L-1}}\left(\frac{\Gamma(\mu_1+\mu_2)}{\Gamma(\mu_2)\Gamma(\mu_1)}\right)^{L}\left(\frac{\mu_2\Omega_i}{\mu_1 s_i}\right)^{\frac{\mu_1 L(\alpha-2)}{2}}\cdot$$

$$\times\left(\sum_{j=0}^{+\infty}\frac{(\mu_1)_j(1-\mu_2)_j}{(\mu_1+1)_j\, j!}\left(\frac{\mu_2\Omega_i}{\mu_1 s_i}\right)^{\frac{j(\alpha-2)}{2}}\right)^{L-1}\times$$

$$\times\frac{1}{\Gamma(jL-j+\mu_1 L+\mu_2)}\times$$

$$\times G_{13}^{31}\left(\frac{h^2\mu_2\Omega_i}{4\mu_1 s_i}\middle|\begin{matrix}1-\left(\frac{\alpha jL-\alpha j+\alpha\mu_1 L}{2}\right)\\\left(\frac{(2-\alpha)(jL-j+\mu_1 L)+2\mu_2}{2}\right),0,\frac{1}{2}\end{matrix}\right). \tag{17}$$

C. Average Bit Error Probability

The ABEP is among the performance that best describe the nature of the system's behavior, and that is why it is most often used to describe that behavior. So, determining the ABEP in the simplest possible way is of great importance. In reality, the difficulty in evaluating the ABEP is that the conditional BEP is a nonlinear function of the SNR or SIR. The nonlinearity is a consequence of the modulation/detection scheme. This is the reason for considering the MGF-based approach to determine ABEP.

Using the MGF-based approach, the ABEP for two modulations will be determined very efficiently, without numerical integrations. By utilizing the expression for MGF from (17), the ABEP for non-coherent BFSK and BDPSK modulations will be [1]:

$$P_{be}(\Omega_0)=0.5M_z(0.5), \quad \text{for BFSK,} \qquad (18)$$

$$P_{be}(\Omega_0)=0.5M_z(1), \quad \text{for BDPSK.} \qquad (19)$$

III. PERFORMANCE RESULTS

To examine the influence of fading and CCI severity on the ABEP, numerically obtained results are illustrated in the next two subsections. In the first subsection, the case of BFSK modulation is observed, and in the second one, the case of BDPSK modulation is shown. We used the programs Origin and Mathematica to plot graphs.

A. Binary Frequency Shift Keying Modulation

In Figures 2 and 3, we present the curves for ABEP versus SIR $w=\Omega/s$ at the output of the SC receiver with L branches, in the case when BFSK modulation was used. In these figures, we changed the values for one group of parameters, and kept the values for the other parameters.

So, in Figure 2, the ABEP is presented for BFSK modulation and dual branch SC receiver (L=2), with μ_2=1, while parameters α and μ_1 are changing. One can see from Figure 2 that the ABEP grows with an increasing in parameter α. This means that system performance gets worse. When the parameter μ_1 increases, the ABEP decreases and the system has better performance.

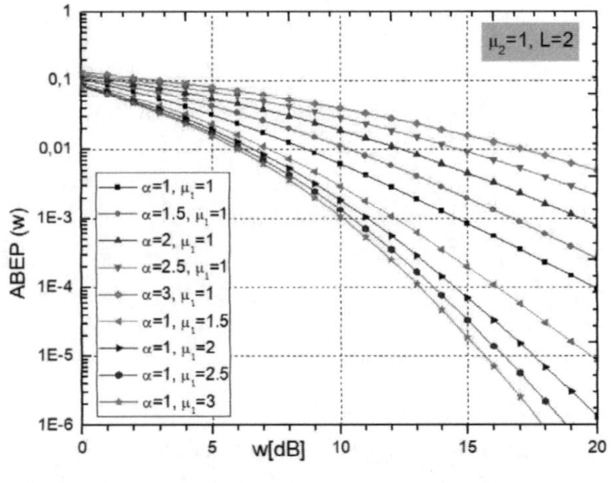

Figure 2. ABEP versus SIR for BFSK modulation when parameters α and μ_1 are changing.

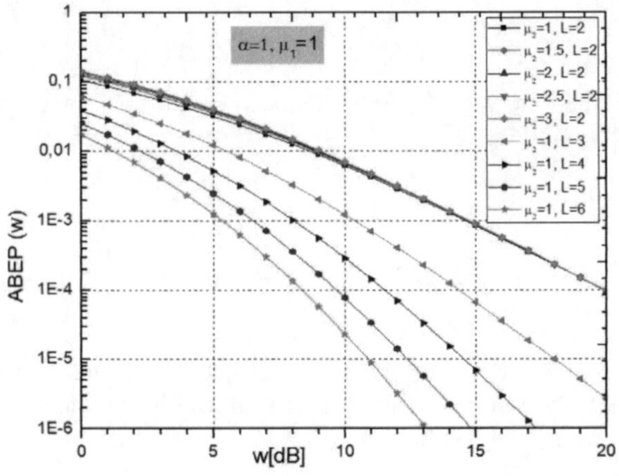

Figure 3. ABEP versus SIR for BFSK modulation with variable parameters μ_2 and L.

In Figure 3, the ABEP is plotted versus SIR for BFSK modulation with variable parameters μ_2 and L. In this figure, the parameters whose values are retained are: α=1, and μ_1=1, while parameters L and μ_2 are changing. From Figure 3, we can see that the increase in the parameter μ_2 has no effect on the ABEP, while with the increase in the number of branches L, the ABEP decreases significantly and the system has better performance.

B. Binary Differential Phase-Shift Keying Modulation

In Figures 4 and 5, the curves for ABEP versus SIR at the output of SC receiver with L branches are presented for BDPSK modulation. Figure 4 shows graphs for dual branch SC receiver (L=2). In this figure, μ_2=1 and parameters α and μ_1 took several values.

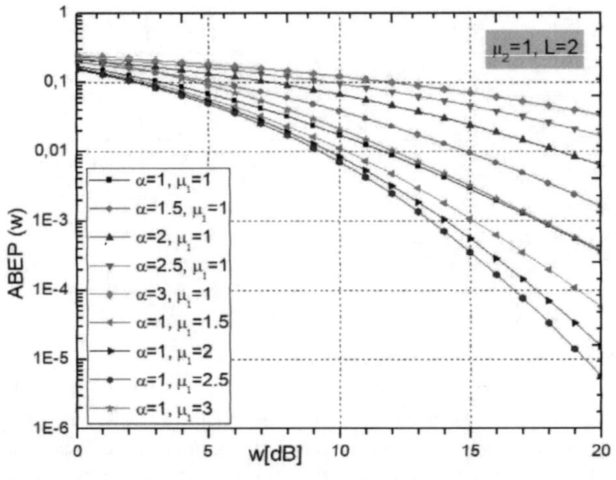

Figure 4. ABEP versus SIR for BDPSK modulation when parameters α and μ_1 are changing.

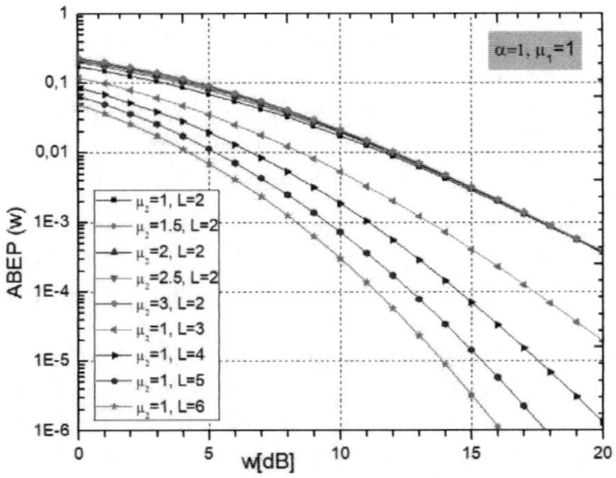

Figure 5. ABEP versus SIR for BDPSK modulation and variable parameters μ_2 and L.

It is visible from this figure that the ABEP grows when the parameter α increases. This spoils the system performance. When the parameter μ_1 increases, the ABEP decreases, improving the system performance.

In Figure 5, the ABEP is presented versus SIR for the BDPSK modulation with parameters μ_2 and L that are changing. In this figure, the parameters whose values are retained are: $\alpha=1$, $\mu_1=1$. From Figure 5, one can conclude that the increase in the parameter μ_2 is without significant impact on the ABEP, while with the increase in the number of branches L, the ABEP drops significantly. This leads to an improvement of the system performance and is in accordance with theoretical assumptions.

Comparing the results from these two figures, we can conclude that the system has better performance with smaller ABEP in the case of using BDPSK than BFSK modulation.

IV. CONCLUSION

In this work, a wireless system in an α-μ fading and CCI environment is analyzed. To improve the system performance by mitigating these harmful effects of CCI interference, SC diversity receiver is employed. The MGF-based ABEP is obtained for BFSK and BDPSK modulation types. The analytical results are presented graphically and the influence of parameters of fading and CCI is highlighted. Based on them, we concluded that in α-μ environments, it is more advantageous to use BDPSK than BFSK modulation.

One of the main contributions of our paper is that it can be used to determine the ABEP of wireless systems in the presence of other types of fading, namely for Rayleigh, Nakagami-*m*, Weibull, and One-sided Gaussian, in the presence of CCI, by setting certain values for parameters α and μ.

In our future work, we will consider correlated α-μ channels, since correlation between the faded channels also affects the PDF of SIR at the output of the SC or some other diversity system.

ACKNOWLEDGMENT

This paper has been performed under the auspices of the bilateral project "Development of Secure and Spectral Efficient Simultaneous Wireless Information and Power Transfer Systems for Large-Scale Wireless Networks" under Science and Technological Cooperation Projects (2022-2024) between the Republic of Serbia and the Republic of India.

REFERENCES

[1] M. K. Simon and M. S. Alouini, Digital Communication over Fading Channels, 2nd ed. Hoboken, NJ, USA: Wiley-IEEE, 2004.

[2] M. D. Yacoub, "The α-μ distribution: a physical fading model for the Stacy distribution", IEEE Transactions on Vehicular Technology, vol. 56, no. 1, pp-27-34, Jan. 2007. DOI: 10.1109/TVT.2006.883753

[3] A. Magableh and M. Matalgah,"Moment generating function of the generalized α-μ distribution with applications", IEEE Communications Letters, vol. 13, issue 6, pp. 411–413, June 2009. DOI:10.1109/lcomm.2009.090339

[4] A. M. Magableh and M. M. Matalgah, "Channel characteristics of the generalized alpha-mu multipath fading model", Proceedings of the 7th International Wireless Communications and Mobile Computing Conference, IWCMC 2011, Istanbul, Turkey, 4-8 July, 2011, pp. 1535-1538. DOI: 10.1109/IWCMC.2011.5982766

[5] S. P. Singh, M. Jadon, R. Kumar, and S. Kumar "BER analysis over alpha-mu fading channel using proposed novel MGF", International Journal of Wireless and Mobile Computing, vol.10, no.2, pp.174 – 182, 2016. DOI: 10.1504/IJWMC.2016.076162

[6] G. Milovanović, M. Stefanović, S. Panić, J. Anastasov, and D. Krstić, „Statistical analysis of the square ratio of two multivariate exponentially correlated α-μ distributions and its application in telecommunications", Mathematical and Computer Modelling, vol. 54, no. 1-2, pp. 152–159, July 2011. DOI:10.1016/j.mcm.2011.01.046

[7] W. H. M. Freitas, R. C. D. V. Bomfin, R. A. A. de Souza, and M. D. Yacoub, "The complex α-μ fading channel with OFDM application", International Journal of Antennas and Propagation, vol. 2017, 2017. https://doi.org/10.1155/2017/2143541

[8] J. T. Ferreira, A. Bekker, F. Marques, and M. Laidlaw, "An enriched α − μ model as fading candidate", Mathematical Problems in Engineering, vol. 2020, 2020. https://doi.org/10.1155/2020/5879413

[9] S. Suljović, D. Krstić, D. Bandjur, S. Veljković, and M. Stefanović, "Level crossing rate of macro-diversity system in the presence of fading and co-channel interference", Revue Roumaine des Sciences Techniques, Publisher: Romanian Academy, vol. 64, pp. 63–68, 2019.

[10] I. S. Gradshteyn and I. M. Ryzhik, Tables of Integrals, Series and Products Academic. New York: 1980.

[11] M. Savic, M. Smilic, and B. Jaksic, "Analysis of Shannon capacity for SC and MRC diversity system in α-k-μ fading channel", University Thought, Publication in Natural Sciences, vol.8, no.2, pp. 61-66, 2018. DOI: https://doi.org/10.5937/univtho8-19491

[12] N. C. Sagias and G. K. Karagiannidis, "Gaussian class multivariate Weibull distributions: Theory and applications in fading channels", IEEE Transactions on Information Theory, vol. 51, issue 10, pp. 3608–3619, 2005. DOI: 10.1109/TIT.2005.855598

Estimating Text Similarity based on Semantic Concept Embeddings

Tim vor der Brück
School of Computer Science and Information Technology
Lucerne University of Applied Sciences and Arts (HSLU)
Rotkreuz, Switzerland
tim.vorderbrueck@ffhs.ch

Marc Pouly
School of Computer Science and Information Technology
Lucerne University of Applied Sciences and Arts (HSLU)
Rotkreuz, Switzerland
marc.pouly@hslu.ch

***Abstract*—Due to their ease of use and high accuracy, Word2Vec (W2V) word embeddings enjoy great success in the semantic representation of words, sentences, and whole documents as well as for semantic similarity estimation. However, they have the shortcoming that they are directly extracted from a surface representation, which does not adequately represent human thought processes and also performs poorly for highly ambiguous words. Therefore, we propose Semantic Concept Embeddings (CE) based on the MultiNet Semantic Network (SN) formalism, which addresses both shortcomings. The evaluation on a marketing target group distribution task showed that the accuracy of predicted target groups can be increased by combining traditional word embeddings with semantic CE.**

***Index Terms*—Concepts, MultiNet, concept embeddings, semantic similarity estimation.**

I. Introduction

Word2Vec (W2V) word embeddings became a popular method for creating semantic representations of words, sentences, and whole documents as well as their semantic similarity estimation. Their key success factors are ease of use, scalability, and performance. However, there are also important downsides. Consider, for example, a word just in front of an embedded sub-clause. Potentially, the words just succeeding this sub-clause might constitute a more characteristic word context than the words actually occurring inside this sub-clause despite being farther apart. So, in some situations, considering only the word context based on the surface structure may not be the optimal choice. Hence, we hereby introduce semantic Concept Embeddings (CEs) that consider the neighborhood in a semantic network (SN). We expect a meaning-oriented structure such as an SN to provide a much more adequate description of neighborhood since it is oriented on human thought processes. The SNs are automatically constructed from arbitrary surface texts by the Wocadi parser [1], which combines manual word function-oriented rules with statistical disambiguation methods. In a pre-study, Wocadi obtained superior results than the only state-of-the-art semantic role labeling parser supporting German out-of-the-box, which is AMR-Eager-Multilingual [2] (AMR stands for Abstract Meaning Representation), a Deep Learning based approach. The SNs as generated by Wocadi are much more comprehensive than, for example, WordNet [3] or GermaNet [4], since they can represent the semantics of arbitrary texts and not only ontologies.

The CEs obtained from these SNs are then employed in the task of assigning participants of an online contest to certain marketing target groups, called youth milieus, by analyzing short text snippets provided by these participants.

Finally, we applied our estimate to the scenario of distributing participants of an online contest into several target groups called youth milieus by exploiting short text snippets they were asked to provide. The evaluation revealed that our novel estimators performed superior to several baseline methods for this scenario.

The remainder of the paper is organized as follows. In the next section, we look into several state-of-the-art methods for estimating semantic similarity. Sect. III introduces the MultiNet semantic network formalism. In Sect. IV, we describe in detail how these networks can be used for estimating semantic similarity between two texts. Our application scenario for our proposed semantic similarity estimates is given in Sect. V. Sect. VI describes the conducted evaluation, in which we compare our approach with several baseline methods. The results of the evaluation are discussed in Sect. VI. Finally, this paper concludes with Sect. VII, which summarizes the obtained results.

II. Related Work

The main application area of knowledge graph embeddings is link prediction [5]. They are very rarely used to estimate the semantic similarity of texts, confer as an example for the latter the approach of Goikoetxea et al. [6]. They generate random walks on WordNet to extract sequences of words, where the lexicalization is randomly chosen for the associated synset nodes. These sequences are then fed into the ordinary W2V to create (ontology) embedding vectors. They evaluated several possibilities to combine such vectors with ordinary word embeddings obtained from large corpora like averaging or concatenating them. Another embeddings extraction method for WordNet synsets is proposed by Kutuzov et al. [7]. They obtained superior results to random walks by obtaining the embedding vectors as a result of an optimization problem that ensures local (graph neighbor) and global (user annotations) consistency. Note that WordNet is much smaller than Wikipedia, which we use as a basis for our approach. Furthermore, MultiNet concepts have some advantages over MultiNet synsets, since in some cases word senses cannot be fully captured by synsets.

An approach to obtain CEs from ordinary surface texts is proposed by Mencia et al. [8]. In particular, they generate CE by counting co-occurrences of *concepts* akin to obtaining

GloVe [9] word embeddings. A similar approach was introduced by Beam et al. [10] that directly uses GloVe to obtain the semantic concept vectors. However, both approaches do not employ a proper Word Sense Disambiguation to obtain their concept representation. Instead, they restrict their embeddings vocabulary to certain medical terms, which are usually specific enough to represent only unique word senses.

After their extraction, word or concept embeddings can be used to estimate document similarity as follows:

1) The embeddings (often weighted by the tf-idf coefficients of the associated words [11]) are looked up in a hashtable for all the words in the two documents to compare. These embeddings are determined beforehand on a very large corpus typically using either the skip-gram or the continuous bag of words variant of the W2V model [12]. The skip-gram method aims to predict the textual surroundings of a given word by means of an artificial neural network. The influential weights of the one-hot-encoded input word to the nodes of the hidden layer constitute the embedding vector. For the so-called *continuous bag of words* method, it is just the opposite, i.e., the center word is predicted by the words in its surroundings.
2) The centroid over all word embeddings belonging to the same document is calculated to obtain its vector representation.

Alternatives to W2V are GloVe [9], which is based on aggregated global word co-occurrence statistics and the Explicit Semantic Analysis (or shortly ESA) [13], in which each word is represented by the column vector in the tf-idf matrix over Wikipedia.

The idea of W2V can be transferred to the level of sentences as well. In particular, the so-called Skip Thought Vector (STV) model [14] derives a vector representation of the current sentence by predicting the surrounding sentences.

If vector representations of the two documents to compare were successfully established, a similarity estimate can be obtained by applying the cosine measure to the two vectors. [15] propose an alternative approach for ESA word embeddings that establishes a bipartite graph consisting of the best matching vector components by solving a linear optimization problem. The similarity estimate for the documents is then given by the global optimum of the objective function. However, this method is only useful for sparse vector representations. In the case of dense vectors, [16] suggests applying the Frobenius kernel to the embedding matrices, which contain the embedding vectors for all document components (usually either sentences or words, cf. also [17]). However, crucial limitations are that the Frobenius kernel is only applicable if the number of words (sentences respectively) in the compared documents coincide and that a word from the first document is only compared with its counterpart from the second document. Thus, an optimal matching has to be established already beforehand.

Word embeddings as described so far are represented by a fixed word-vector mapping, which means that these word vectors do not vary depending on the current word context. This is different for Elmo [18] and Bert [19], [20] embeddings that take this context into account basically realizing a kind of word sense disambiguation.

Before going into more details of our method, we first want to introduce the MultiNet SN formalism.

III. SNs BASED ON THE MULTINET FORMALISM

In contrast to other popular knowledge graphs or SNs like WordNet [3], OdeNet [21] or Yago [22] that represent ontologies, MultiNet is designed to grasp the entire semantics of natural language. Therefore, MultiNet embeddings can be trained on much larger data sets than the formerly mentioned knowledge graphs, in case of this paper on the entire German Wikipedia. SNs of the MultiNet (Multilayered Extended SNs) formalism [23] allow to homogeneously represent the semantics of single words, phrases, sentences, texts, or text collections.

An SN node represents a concept, while an SN arc expresses a relation between two concepts. A concept *lemma.x.y* is represented by a lemma, and two numbers, where the first (x) denotes the homograph and the second (y) the polyseme. In addition, each node is semantically classified by a *sort* from a hierarchy of 45 sorts organized in a taxonomy.

Furthermore, a node has an inner structure (depending on its sort) containing *layer features* like CARD (cardinality) and REFER (referential determinacy).

The Wocadi parser can construct SNs of the MultiNet formalism for German phrases, sentences, or texts. During this process, SNs and syntactic dependency structures are built.

An important component of this deep syntactico-semantic analysis of natural language is HaGenLex, a semantically based computer lexicon [24]. This lexicon not only lists verb valencies, but also their syntactic and semantic types. Consider, for example, the German verb *essen* (*'eat'*). Sentences like *Die Birne isst den Apfel.* (*'The pear eats the apple.'*) are rejected because semantic selectional restrictions are violated. Besides this comprehensive lexicon with around 28,000 entries, a shallow lexicon, many name lexicons, and a sophisticated compound analysis is applied to achieve the parser coverage required for natural language processing applications.

Disambiguation is realized by specialized modules which work with symbolic rules and disambiguation statistics derived from annotated corpora. Currently, such modules exist for (intrasentential and intersentential) coreference resolution, the attachment of prepositional phrases, and the interpretation of prepositional phrases.

The following MultiNet relations and functions are relevant to this paper [23]:

- AGT: Definition: In its standard interpretation, the expression (e AGT o) characterizes the relation between an event e or, to be specific, an action e and a conceptual object o which actively causes e (i.e. o is originating/sustaining/giving rise to e). In other words, o is the active object (the agent or carrier of the action).

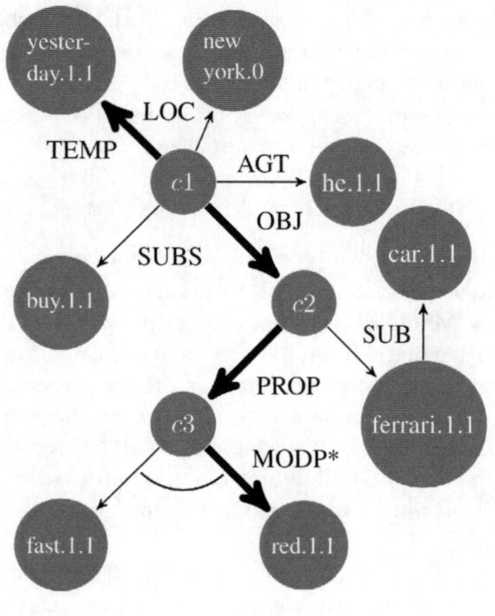

Fig. 1. Example for a random walk (yesterday.1.1 TEMP^{-1} OBJ PROP MODP* red.1.1) in the SN.

- CHEA: The statement (e CHEA a) expresses the connection between an event e (usually a verb) and an abstract concept a (usually a noun) which agree, at least partially, in their meaning. Concepts connected by CHEA correspond to each other in a systematic way. Example: (inform.1.1 CHEA information.1.1)
- CHPA: The statement (p CHPA c) establishes a connection between a property p (usually adjective) and an abstract concept (usually a noun) c which is semantically close to p and whose meaning is systematically related to p. Example: (cold.1.1 CHPA coldness.1.1).
- SUB: The expression (o_1 SUB o_2) specifies that the individual or generic concept o_1 is subordinate (a hyponym) to the generic concept o_2, i.e. everything derivable for o_2 is also valid for o_1.

An example for an SN following the MultiNet formalism is given in Figure 1.

IV. Using semantic CEs for estimating semantic similarity

A. Procedure

To better understand why a representation as an SN can be beneficial, let us consider the following example sentence: *The car he bought yesterday in New York is a fast red Ferrari.* This sentence contains the embedded relative clause *he bought yesterday in New York*. Actually, the noun phrase *fast red Ferrari* is much more characteristic for the word car than the subclause *he bought yesterday in New York* despite being farther away from that word. The representation of this sentence as an SN on MultiNet is shown in Figure 1. The main node representing the entire sentence is c1, which is a specific buying operation expressed by the relation SUBS. The relation LOC specifies the location of the event, in this case *New York.*

TABLE I
COSINE MEASURE APPLIED TO WORD AND CONCEPT VECTORS.

Wort 1 / Concept 1	Word 2 / Concept 2	Example for Concept 2	Cosine
Lok (locomotive)	Zug (move(ment)/train)		0.428
lok.1.1	zug.1.1	Der Zug nach London fährt ab. (The train to London is departing.)	0.633
lok.1.1	zug.1.2	Zug der Vögel (bird migration (movement))	0.321

The trailing .0 at the concept name denotes the fact that the concept is identified by a proper name. The agent (relation: AGT) of the event is *he.1.1*, which can potentially be resolved by an anaphora resolution and replaced by its antecedent. The Ferrari that is bought is identified by the concept c2, connected to c1 by an object (OBJ) relation. The red Ferrari is also fast, which is expressed by a modifier (MODP*) combined with a property relation (PROP).

Now let us consider a second example given by the following two sentences: *Pete kauft einen neuen roten Ferrari.* (*Pete buys a new red Ferrari.*) und *Ein neuer roter Ferrari wird von Pete gekauft.* (*A new red Ferrari is bought by Pete.*) Both sentences express the same meaning but the surface structure is different. The representation in passive voice contains the additional word (*wird* (English: *was*)), which is in German a function word that can also express future tense, i.e., this word is ambiguous and can therefore add additional noise to the word vectors. The SNs of both sentences however coincide, which results in more exact embedding vectors.

Let us consider as a third example the word *space*, which can either denote a certain geographical area or the universe. Actually, the word vector of *space* integrates all possible word senses. Thus, the cosine distance between the word vectors of *space* and *planet* should be smaller than for *universe* and *planet*. However, if it is known from the word context that *space* means *universe* in a certain text, then *space* and *planet* should be similarily semantically related as *universe* and *planet*. Using our SN-based approach, we no longer generate vectors for surface words but for word senses instead, which solves this issue. A concrete German example comprises the two German words *Lok* (locomotive) and *Zug* (move(ment) / train) and is given in Table I. It demonstrates that the concept *lok.1.1* (locomotive.1.1) has a higher cosine similarity to the word sense of *Zug* denoting *train* (*zug.1.1*) than to the word sense *zug.1.2* denoting move(ment), and this cosine similarity also exceeds the one between the word vectors of *Zug* and *Lok*.

Our workflow to create semantic CEs is as follows:

- Parse the German Wikipedia by means of Wocadi to create SNs
- Create random walks on these SNs

- Feed the random walks into W2V to create CEs

Note that we obtained already a fully parsed Wikipedia from Sempria GmbH, a spin-off of the Distance University of Hagen. Once the CEs are generated, they can be exploited to estimate semantic text similarity in the following way:

- Apply a Word Sense Disambiguation to both texts to obtain MultiNet concepts.
- Create CEs for both concept representations.
- Determine the two CEs centroids.
- Estimate the semantic similarity between two texts using the cosine measure.

There are several approaches to obtaining embeddings from knowledge graphs and SN like RotatE [25], TransE [26], or TorusE [27]. We decided to train W2V on random walks over the MultiNet-SNs, which has the advantage that hereby word embeddings and CEs are better comparable since both are obtained using the same method, namely W2V. To generate such a random walk, one first picks an initial node from an SN randomly. Afterwards, one randomly chooses a neighboring node and repeats this process using the newly picked node. Additionally, one generates in each step a continuous random number between 0 and 1 and terminates the random walk, if this number assumes a value below a certain (small) threshold. Note that in contrast to a path, edges can appear several times in a certain random walk and one can also move back and forth on the same edge. The random walk representation is then given by an interleaving sequence of nodes and edges. If an edge is followed against the arc direction, we note down the inverse of the relation associated with the arc. Let us consider as an example the SN shown in Figure 1, in which the following possible random walk is already highlighted:

yesterday.1.1 TEMP^{-1} c1 OBJ c2 PROP c3 MODP* red.1.1

Since the inner nodes like c1 and c2 are named arbitrarily without expressing any sort of meaning, we remove such nodes from the random walk. Thus, our modified random walk becomes:

yesterday.1.1 TEMP^{-1} OBJ PROP MODP* red.1.1

In case of symmetric relations Rel with $Rel = Rel^{-1}$, we only consider the non-inverted relations in the random walk. In our example, the random walk does not contain any symmetric relations so it stays unchanged.

To estimate the semantic similarity between two texts using CEs, one first has to map the words appearing in these texts to concepts, which boils down to applying a Word Sense Disambiguation. One possibility to accomplish this task is to parse both texts using Wocadi, which generates for each text an SN and also establishes a mapping from each word to the associated concept. However, note that Wocadi is not freely available but requires a license from Sempria GmbH. Therefore, we use a different approach based on so-called word-concept embeddings. As the name insinuates, word-concept embeddings denote concept vectors, which are based on a surface oriented approach. In particular, we obtain a word-concept vector of some concept c by averaging the word vector centroids of all sentences, where c occurs in the associated SN. We then chose the word sense c of a word w occurring in a certain sentence s, where the word-concept vector of c is most similar to the centroid of s.

V. Application Scenario: Market Segmentation

Market segmentation is one of the key tasks of a marketer. Usually, it is accomplished by clustering over behaviors as well as demographic, geographic, and psychographic variables [28]. In this paper, we will describe an alternative approach based on unsupervised natural language processing. In particular, our business partner operates a commercial youth platform for the Swiss market, where registered members get access to third-party offers such as discounts and special events like concerts or castings. Actually, several hundred online contests per year are launched over this platform sponsored by other firms, an increasing number of them require the members to write short free-text snippets, e.g. to elaborate on a perfect holiday at a destination of their choice in case of a contest sponsored by a travel agency. Based on the results of a broad survey, the platform provider's marketers assume five different target groups (called *youth milieus*) being present among the platform members: *progressive postmodern youth* (people primarily interested in culture and arts), *young performers* (people striving for a high salary with a strong affinity to luxury goods), *freestyle action sportsmen*, *hedonists* (rather poorly educated people who enjoy partying and disco music) and *conservative youth* (traditional people with a strong concern for security). A sixth milieu called *special groups* comprises all those who cannot be assigned to one of the upper five milieus. For each milieu (with the exception of *special groups*) a keyword list was manually created by describing its main characteristics. For triggering marketing campaigns by marketers, an algorithm shall be developed that automatically assigns each contest answer to the most likely target group: we propose the youth milieu as best match for a contest answer, for which the estimated semantic similarity between the associated keyword list and user answer is maximal. In case the highest similarity estimate falls below the 10 percent quantile for the distribution of highest estimates, the special groups milieu is selected (cf. also [29]).

Since the keyword list typically consists of nouns (in the German language capitalized) and the user contest answers might contain a lot of adjectives and verbs as well, which do not match very well to nouns in the W2V vector representation, we actually conduct two comparisons for our W2V based measures, one with the unchanged user contest answers and one by capitalizing every word beforehand. The final similarity estimate is then given as the maximum value of both individual estimates.

The same procedure does not work with CEs, since concepts are always written lower case in MultiNet. To identify corresponding nouns for adjectives and verbs, we use the MultiNet relations CHEA and CHPEA. For instance, (inform.1.1 CHEA information.1.1) or (cold.1.1 CHPA coldness.1.1). These lexical relations are directly stored in the semantic lexicon named HaGenLex. Note that for better illustration, we gave English examples although we investigated German texts.

TABLE II
MINIMUM AND MAXIMUM AVERAGE INTER-ANNOTATOR AGREEMENTS (COHEN'S KAPPA).

Method	Contest		
	1	2	3
Min kappa	0.123	0.295/0.030	0.110/0.101
Max. kappa	0.178	0.345/0.149	0.114/0.209
# Entries	1544	100	100

TABLE III
ACC. VALUES FOR SEVERAL ESTIMATES. RW: METHOD OF [6] APPLIED TO ODENET, CE=SEMANTIC CONCEPT EMBEDDINGS, STV=SKIP THOUGHT VECTORS, CE+W2V: WEIGHTED AVERAGING COSINE OVER WORD AND CES.

Method	1	2	3	Total
Random	0.152	0.090	0.167	0.146
Jaccard	0.150	0.194	0.045	0.142
GloVe	0.203	0.254	0.303	0.222
RW	0.294	0.254	0.227	0.281
W2V	0.299	**0.313**	0.258	0.296
STV	0.241	0.194	**0.348**	0.249
Elmo	0.150	0.224	0.258	0.173
Bert	0.221	0.209	0.212	0.218
CE	0.274	0.299	0.258	0.275
CE+W2V	**0.305**	0.299	0.303	**0.304**

VI. EVALUATION

For evaluation of the marketing group segmentation task, we selected three online contests (language: German), where people elaborated on their favorite travel destination (contest 1), speculated about potential experiences with a pair of fancy sneakers (contest 2), and explained why they emotionally prefer a certain product out of four available candidates. To provide a gold standard, three professional marketers from different youth marketing companies annotated independently the best matching youth milieus for every contest answer. We determined for each annotator individually his/her average inter-annotator agreement with the others (Cohen's kappa). The minimum and maximum of these average agreement values are given in Table II. Since for contest 2 and contest 3, some of the annotators annotated only the first 50 entries (last 50 entries respectively), we specified min/max average kappa values for both parts. We further compared the youth milieus proposed by our unsupervised matching algorithm with the majority votes over the human experts' answers (see Table III) and computed its average inter-annotator agreement with the human annotators (see again Table II).

We evaluated both, our similarity estimate based on CEs alone and its weighted mean with W2V (weight for CE: 0.2, weight for W2V: 0.8).

The W2V, CEs, and Skip Thought Vectors (STV) were trained on the German Wikipedia. The actual document similarity estimation for STVs is accomplished by the usual centroid approach. An issue we are faced with for our evaluation scenario of market segmentation (see Sect. V) is that STVs are not bag-of-word models but actually take the sequence of the words into account and therefore the obtained similarity estimate between the milieu keyword list and contest answer would depend on the keyword ordering. However, this order could have arbitrarily been chosen by the marketers and might be completely random. A possible solution is to compare the contest answers with all possible permutations of keywords and determine the maximum value over all those comparisons. However, such an approach would be infeasible already for medium keyword list sizes. Therefore, we apply for this scenario a beam search to extend the keyword list iteratively while keeping only the n-best performing permutations.

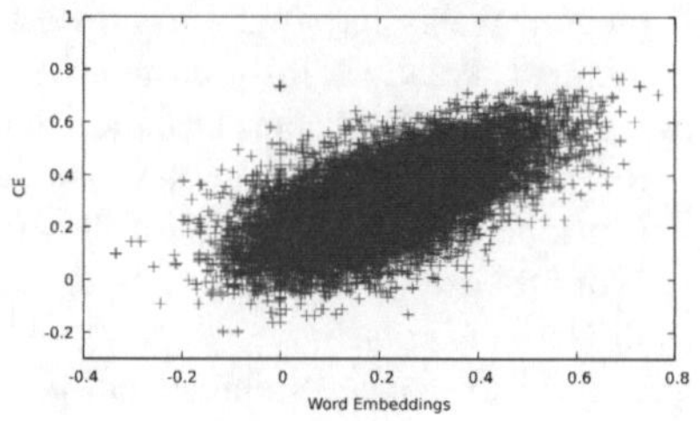

Fig. 2. Scatterplot between similarity estimate based on word embeddings (x-axis) and semantic CEs (y-axis).

We also applied the approach of Goikoetxea et al. [6], another embeddings approach based on a linguistic network. Originally, the embeddings have been created by applying random walks on WordNet choosing randomly lexicalizations for the synset nodes. Since WordNet is not available for German and we failed to obtain an academic license for the largest German-based linguistic network GermaNet, we applied their approach to the freely available German linguistic ontology OdeNet [21]. Goikoetxea et al. proposed several combination methods of ordinary W2V and their linguistic network-based word vectors, where the concatenation of both performed best. This is also the approach we evaluated in this paper.

Note that we did not conduct a hyperparameter search on our input parameters like the random walk sentence restart threshold or the 10% quantil for selecting the Special Groups milieu. Instead we selected values based on experience that gave good results in practice. The window size for the embeddings has been chosen with seven rather large to obtain a reasonable number of concepts in the window.

Consider the annotations provided by the marketing experts, the evaluation showed that the inter-annotator agreement values vary strongly for contest 2 part 2 (minimum average annotator agreement according to Cohen's kappa of 0.03 while the maximum is 0.149, see Table II). In general, the kappa values, which estimate inter-annotator agreement are rather small, which insinuates that the manual labeling of the contests and therefore also the automatic labeling process proved to be quite challenging.

In combination with word embeddings, semantic CEs outperforms on our three contests word embeddings alone as well as the approach of Goikoetxea et al. as well as several deep learning based approaches like German Bert model, multilingual Elmo model, and Skip Thought Vectors. Still, semantic CEs alone perform currently worse than ordinary word embeddings. Sources of errors are the word sense disambiguation (especially the word sense disambiguation of Wocadi) and the lemmatizer LemmaGen, which is currently trained on Wiktionary which provides a good coverage of generic nouns but falls short in terms of named entities. Additionally, Wocadi proved to be quite vulnerable in case of misspelled words or highly complex syntactic structures. In such cases it often only produces a chunk part or the parsing process fails altogether. Figure 2 shows a scatterplot, where we compare the similarity estimate based on word embeddings (x-axis) with its counterpart based on CEs (y-axis). The figure shows that there is a considerable correlation between both estimates. One advantage of our method over using Bert and Elmo embeddings is that the marketer can directly specify the intended word senses as key words for the youth milieus. This is especially important if the keyword list is small and contains not enough textual contexts for Bert and Elmo embeddings to perform well.

VII. Conclusion and Further Work

We proposed a novel semantic similarity measure based on semantic CEs. These embeddings were extracted from an SN using random walks on them. All the SNs were automatically generated from Wikipedia using the Wocadi parser. The evaluation showed that semantic CEs outperformed W2V embeddings when used in combination with the latter on the task of assigning participants to the best matching marketing target group. There is still space for further improvement. For instance, inner nodes are currently eliminated from the random walk and therefore not used at all. Instead one could replace them with their associated ontological sort (see Section III).

Currently, our system depends on the Wocadi parser, which is not freely available. Therefore, we aim to test, whether similar results can be obtained, if one uses freely available semantic role labeling parsers instead of Wocadi. A concept representation of each word could hereby be obtained by determining the WordNet / OdeNet / GermNet synset group that best fits to the given context as obtained by a Word Sense Disambiguation.

Acknowledgement

Hereby we want to thank Sven Hartrumpf and Sempria GmbH for providing us with semantic network parses from the entire Wikipedia.

References

[1] S. Hartrumpf, "Hybrid disambiguation in natural language analysis," Ph.D. dissertation, FernUniversität in Hagen, 2002.

[2] M. Damonte, S. B. Cohen, and G. Satta, "An incremental parser for abstract meaning representation," in *Proceedings of EACL (2017)*, Valencia, Spain, 2017, pp. 536–546.

[3] C. Fellbaum, *WordNet: An Electronic Lexical Database*. Cambridge: MIT Press, 1998.

[4] B. Hamp and H. Feldweg, "GermaNet - a lexical-semantic net for German," in *Proceedings of the ACL workshop Automatic Information Extraction and Building of Lexical Semantic Resources for NLP Applications*, 1997, pp. 9–15.

[5] T. Trouillon, J. Welbl, S. Riedel, E. Gaussier, and G. Bochard, "Complex embeddings for simple link prediction," in *Proceedings of the 33rd International Conference on Machine Learning*, 2016, pp. 2071–2080.

[6] J. Goikoetxea, E. Agirre, and A. Soroa, "Single or multiple? Combining word representations independently learned from text and WordNet," in *Proceedings of the AAAI Conference on Artificial Intelligence*, Phoenix, Arizona, USA, 2016, pp. 2608–2614.

[7] A. Kutuzov, A. Panchenko, S. Kohail, M. Dorgham, O. Oliynyk, and C. Biemann, "Learning graph embeddings from wordnet-based similarity measures," *CoRR*, vol. abs/1808.05611, 2018. [Online]. Available: http://arxiv.org/abs/1808.05611

[8] E. L. Mencía, G. de Melo, and J. Nam, "Medical concept embeddings via labeled background corpora," in *Proceedings of the Tenth International Conference on Language Resources and Evaluation (LREC'16)*. Portorož, Slovenia: European Language Resources Association (ELRA), May 2016, pp. 4629–4636. [Online]. Available: https://www.aclweb.org/anthology/L16-1733

[9] J. Pennington, R. Socher, and C. D. Manning, "Glove: Global vectors for word representation," in *Proceedings of the Conference on Empirical Methods in Natural Language Processing (EMNLP)*, Doha, Katar, 2014.

[10] A. L. Beam *et al.*, "Clinical concept embeddings learned from massive sources of multimodal medical data," in *Proceeding of the Pacific Symposium of Biocomputing*, 2020, pp. 295–306.

[11] G.-I. Brokos, Prodromos, and I. Androutsopoulos, "Using centroids of word embeddings and word mover's distance for biomedical document retrieval in question answering," in *Proceedings of the 15th Workshop on Biomedical Natural Language Processing*, Berlin, Germany, 2016, pp. 114–118.

[12] T. Mikolov, I. Sutskever, C. Ilya, G. Corrado, and J. Dean, "Distributed representations of words and phrases and their compositionality," in *Proceedings of the Conference on Neural Information Processing Systems (NIPS)*, Lake Tahoe, Nevada, USA, 2013, pp. 3111–3119.

[13] E. Gabrilovic and S. Markovitch, "Wikipedia-based semantic interpretation for natural language processing," *Journal of Artificial Intelligence Research*, vol. 34, 2009.

[14] R. Kiros, Y. Zhu, R. Salakhudinov, R. S. Zemel, A. Torralba, R. Urtasun, and S. Fiedler, "Skip-thought vectors," in *Proceedings of the Conference on Neural Information Processing Systems (NIPS)*, Montréal, Canada, 2015, pp. 3294–3302.

[15] Y. Song and D. Roth, "Unsupervised sparse vector densification for short text similarity," in *Proceedings of the Conference of the North American Chapter of the Association for Computational Linguistics (NAACL)*, Denver, Colorado, USA, 2015, pp. 1275–1280.

[16] V. Mijangos, G. Sierra, and A. Montes, "Sentence level matrix representation for document spectral clustering," *Pattern Recognition Letters*, vol. 85, 2017.

[17] K.-J. Hong, G.-H. Lee, and H.-J. Kom, "Enhanced document clustering using wikipedia-based document representation," in *Proceedings of the 2015 International Conference on Applied System Innovation (ICASI)*, 2015, pp. 183–186.

[18] M. E. Peters, M. Neumann, M. Iyyer, M. Gardner, C. C. K. Lee, and L. Zettlemoyer, "Deep contextualized word representations," in *Proc. of NAACL*, New Orleans, Louisiana, USA, 2018, pp. 2227—2237.

[19] J. Devlin, M.-W. Chang, K. Lee, and K. Toutanova, "Bert: Pre-training of deep bidirectional transformers for language understanding," in *Proceedings of NAACL*, 2019, pp. 4176–4186.

[20] E. Alsentzer *et al.*, "Publicly available clinical bert embeddings," 2019.

[21] M. Siegel and F. Bond, "OdeNet: Compiling a germanwordnet from other resources," in *Global WordNet Conference*, 2021. [Online]. Available: https://api.semanticscholar.org/CorpusID:232021541

[22] F. Mahdisoltani, J. Biega, and F. M. Suchanek, "YAGO3: A knowledge base from multilingual wikipedias," in *Proceedings of the 7th Biennial Conference on Innovative Data Systems Research (CIDR 2015)*, Asilomar, California, USA, 2015.

[23] H. Helbig, *Knowledge Representation and the Semantics of Natural Language*. Berlin, Germany: Springer, 2006.

[24] S. Hartrumpf, H. Helbig, and R. Osswald, "The semantically based computer lexicon HaGenLex – Structure and technological environment," *Traitement automatique des langues*, vol. 44, no. 2, pp. 81–105, 2003.

[25] Z. Sun, Z.-H. Deng, J.-Y. Nie, and J. Tang, "RotatE: Knowledge graph embedding by relational rotatoin in complex space," in *Proceedings of ICLR*, 2019.

[26] A. Bordes, N. Usunier, A. Garcia-Duran, J. Weston, and O. Yahnenko, "Translating embeddings for modeling multi-relational data," in *Advances in neural information processing systems*, 2013, pp. 2787–2795.

[27] T. Ebisu and R. Ichise, "TorusE: Knowledge graph embedding on a lie group," in *Proceedings of the 32nd AAAI Conference on Artificial Intelligence*. AAAI Press, 2018, pp. 1819–1826.

[28] M. Lynn, "Segmenting and targeting your market: Strategies and limitations," Cornell University, Tech. Rep., 2011, online: http://scholorship.sha.cornell.edu/articles/243.

[29] T. vor der Brück and M. Pouly, "Text similarity estimation based on word embeddings and matrix norms for targeted marketing," in *Proceedings of NAACL*, 2019, pp. 1827–1836.

Database Technology Evolution II: Graph Database Language

Malcolm Crowe
Emeritus Professor, Computing Science
University of the West of Scotland
Paisley, United Kingdom
Email: Malcolm.Crowe@uws.ac.uk

Fritz Laux
Emeritus Professor, Business Computing
Reutlingen University
Reutlingen, Germany
Email: Fritz.Laux@reutlingen-university.de

Abstract— **This paper reviews the changes in database technology represented by the incorporation of property graphs and associated language in the International Standards Organization (ISO) standard 9075 (Database Languages – Standard Query Language SQL) and the current development of the draft international standard ISO 39075 (Database Languages – Graph Query Language GQL), and presents an implementation of the resulting combined technology in a single relational database management system. These developments continue a trend towards integrating conceptual modeling design into the physical database.**

Keywords—typed graph model; graph schema; relational database; implementation; information integration.

I. INTRODUCTION

For many years, the process of database implementation has included a conceptual data modeling phase, and this has often been supported by declarative structures using annotations or attributes, as reported in our previous contribution [1]. Graph models have become popular for this purpose, originally in relation to social networks, and numerous graphical database products such as Neo4j have applied these in many domains.

The growth in the use of graph models has led to the development of standards including the publication of ISO 9075-16: Property Graph Queries [2], and the imminent emergence of a draft international standard for GQL [3], [4]. These developments draw on experience with commercial graph database products and envisage a clear convergence at the conceptual level between graph-based and relational database management, while GQL remains a separate standard.

Our previous work has recommended the use of a Typed Graph Model (TGM) for conceptual modeling [5], with the help of additional data types in the Relational Database Management System (RDBMS) specified using metadata. In this paper we present an open-source RDBMS implementation that is able to perform graph creation and pattern matching including repeating patterns and also aligns well with the draft international GQL standard.

The plan of this paper is to review the new implementation details in Section II. Section III presents an illustrative example, and Section IV provides some conclusions.

II. IMPLEMENTATION IN THE RELATIONAL DATABASE SCHEMA

The implementation of a typed graph modelling system can build on the user-defined type mechanism of an RDBMS. Node and edge types can have special columns for leaving and arriving properties, which should have additional automated support from the RDBMS. It should be possible to convert between standard types and node/edge types and rearrange subtype relationships. These tables can be equipped with indexes, constraints, and triggers in the normal ways.

Then, if every node type or edge type corresponds to a single base table containing the instances of that type, one way to build a graph is to insert rows in these tables. But a satisfactory implementation needs to simplify the tasks of graph definition and searching. Most implementations add CREATE and MATCH statements, which we describe next, and indicate how they can be implemented in the RDBMS.

A. Graph-oriented syntax added to SQL

The typical syntax for CREATE sketches nodes and edges using additional arrow-like tokens, for example:

```
[CREATE (:Person {name:'Fred Smith'})<-[:Child]-
(a:Person {name:'Peter Smith'}),
(a)-[:Child]->(b:Person {name:'Mary Smith'})
-[:Child]->(:Person {name:'Lee Smith'}),
(b)-[:Child]->(:Person {name:'Bill Smith'})]
```

Without any further declarations, this builds a graph with nodes for Person and edges for Child, as in Figure 2(b). There is already a standard syntax for this in [2]. But an RDBMS engine can and should without further declaration also build base tables for Person and Child with columns sufficient to represent the specified properties, and indexes to support the edge structure.

The MATCH query can contain unbound identifiers for nodes and edges, their labels and/or their properties, which are bound by searching the database. This also has a standard syntax in [2], but in this section we indicate how it can be integrated into the SQL data manipulation language DML:

MatchStatement = MATCH Match {',' Match} [WhereClause] [Statement] [THEN Statements END].
Match = (MatchMode [id '='] MatchNode) {'|' Match}.

In this syntax, Statement(s) and WhereClause are as in ordinary SQL. The first part of the MATCH clause has an optional MatchMode (see below) and one or more graph expressions, which in simple cases appear to have the same form as in the CREATE statement.

MatchNode = '(' MatchItem ')' {(MatchEdge|MatchPath) MatchNode}.
MatchEdge = '-[' MatchItem '->' | '<-' MatchItem ']-' .
MatchItem = [id | *Node*_Value] [GraphLabel] [Document | WhereClause] .

In all cases, the execution of the MATCH proceeds directly on the tables, without needing auxiliary SQL statements. The MATCH algorithm proceeds along the node expressions, matching more and more of its nodes and edges with those in the database by assigning values to the unbound identifiers. If we cannot progress to the next part of the MATCH clause, we backtrack by undoing the last binding and taking an alternative value. If the processing reaches the end of the MATCH statement, the set of bindings contributes a row in the default result, subject to the optional WHERE condition.

In this way, the MATCH statement can be used (a) as in Prolog, to verify that a particular graph fragment exists in the database, (b) to display the bindings resulting from the process of matching a set of fragments with the database, (c) to display a set of values computed from such a list of bindings, or (d) to perform a sequence of actions for each binding found. In case (d) no results are displayed, as the MATCH statement has been employed for its side effects. These could include further CREATE, MATCH or other SQL statements, or assignment statements updating fields referenced in the current bindings.

Following the forthcoming GQL standard, repeating patterns are supported by the MATCH statement (see [8]):

MatchPath = '[' Match ']' MatchQuantifier .
MatchQuantifier = '?' | '*' | '+' | '{' int , [int] '}' .
MatchMode = [TRAIL|ACYCLIC| SIMPLE] [SHORTEST |ALL|ANY] .

MatchMode controls how repetitions of path patterns are managed in the graph matching mechanism. A MatchPath creates lists of values of bound identifiers in its Match. By default, binding rows that have already occurred in the match are ignored, and paths that have already been listed in a quantified graph are not followed. The MatchMode modifies this default behaviour: TRAIL omits paths where an edge occurs more than once, ACYCLIC omits paths where a node occurs more than once, SIMPLE looks for a simple cycle. The last three options apply to MatchStatements that do not use the comma operator, and select the shortest match, all matches or an arbitrary match.

The implementation of the matching algorithm uses continuations to control the backtracking behavior. Continuations are constructed as the match proceeds and represent the rest of the matching expression.

The MATCH statement can be used in two ways. The first is make the dependent Statement a RETURN statement that contributes a row to a result set for each successful binding of the unbound identifiers in the MATCH, for example,

```
MATCH ({name:'Peter Smith'}) [()-[:Child]->()]+
(x) RETURN x.name
```

will yield a list of the descendants of Peter Smith. (See Figure 2(a).)

Without using RETURN or any dependent statements, the result of a MATCH statement is the list of bindings. The following example has two columns, one for each of the unbound identifiers p and x, but p will be an array with an element for each iteration of the pattern.

```
MATCH ({name:'Peter Smith'}) [(p)-[:Child]->()]+
({name:x})
```

The results are shown in Figure 2(a), which also shows all of the statements needed to build and display this small example, including two lines for authentication for browser access to the database, and two for replacing the default primary key ID. A feature of the implementation described in this paper is the lack of structural clutter.

B. Graph versus Relation

The nodes and edges contained in the database combine to form a set of disjoint graphs that is initially empty. Adding a node to the database adds a new entry to this set. When an edge is added, either the two endpoints are in the same graph, or else the edge will connect two previously disjoint graphs. If each graph in the set is identified by a representative node (such as the one with the lowest uid) and maintains a list of the nodes and edges it contains, it is easy to manage the set of graphs as data is added to the database.

If an edge is removed, the graph containing it might now be in at most two pieces: the simplest algorithm removes it from the set and adds its nodes and edges back in.

The database with its added graph information can be used directly in ordinary database application processing, with the advantage of being able to perform graph-oriented querying and graph-oriented stored procedures. The normal processing of the database engine naturally enforces the type requirements of the model, and also enforces any constraints specified in graph-oriented metadata. The nodes and edges are rows in ordinary tables that can be accessed and refined using normal SQL statements. In particular, using the usual dotted syntax, properties can be SET and updated, and can be removed by being set to NULL.

C. Database Design by Example

From the above description of the CREATE statement, we can see that this mechanism allows first versions of types and instances to be developed together, with minimal schema indications. The MATCH statement allows extension of the design by retrieving instances and creating related nodes and edges.

If example nodes and edges are created, the DBMS creates suitable node and edge types, modifying these if additional properties receive values in later examples. Since transactions are supported, tentative examples can be explored and rolled back or committed. Alter statements can change names, enhance property types and modify subtype relationships, and the SQL Cast function can be used to parse the string representation of a structure value. The usual restrict/cascade actions are available, and node and edge types can have additional constraints, triggers, and methods. As each node and edge type has an associated base table in the database, the result of this process is a relational database that is immediately usable.

As the TGM is developed and merged with other graphical data, conflicts will be detected and diagnostics will help to identify any obstacles to integrating a new part of the model, so that the model as developed to that point can be refined. The SQL ALTER TABLE and ALTER TYPE statements, together with a metadata syntax, allow changes to the model to be performed automatically, e.g., to enforce expectations on the data.

An extreme case of this occurs where a graph has been created using the server's autokey mechanism for primary keys, and the analyst has identified a more suitable numeric or string-valued key. A single ALTER TABLE statement can install this as the new primary key and the change automatically propagates to the edge types that attach to the node type in question. The previous primary key remains as a unique key but can later be dropped without losing any information. See Figure 2 and Figure 3 below.

Other restructuring of node types can be performed with the help of the CAST function, which can be used to parse complex types from strings, array and set constructors, and UNNEST. Node and edge manipulations can also be performed by triggers and stored procedures.

The points covered in the above section already go a long way towards an integrated DBMS product that supports the TGM. The resulting TGM implementation inherits aspects such as transacted behavior, constraints, triggers, and stored procedures from the relational mechanisms, since Match and Create statements are implemented as Procedure Statements. The security model in the underlying RDBMS, with its users, roles, and grants of privileges also applies to the base tables and hence to the graphs. Node and edge types emerge as a special kind of structured type. It is thus a relatively simple matter to support view-mediated remote access and object-oriented entity management. Nodes and edges are entities and the same access and Multiple Version Concurrency Control (MVCC) models in our previous work [11] transfer with little trouble into the new features.

Our database server implementation has for years generated classes for C#, Python or Java applications corresponding to versioned database objects. This leads to object-oriented application programming, where node and edge types correspond to classes whose instances are nodes and edges (see Figure 2(c) for a C# example). The Match and Create statements can be used (a) for SQL clients in commands and prepared statements, (b) in the generated C#, Java or Python and the widely used database connection methods ExecuteReader and ExecuteNonQuery, or (c) in JavaScript posted to the web service interface of the database server.

The normal processing of the database engine naturally enforces the type requirements of the model, and also enforces a range of constraints specified in graph-oriented metadata. In particular, using the usual dotted syntax, properties can be SET and updated, and can be removed by being set to NULL.

As the TGM is developed and merged with other graphical data, conflicts will be detected and diagnostics will help to identify any obstacles to integrating a new part of the model, so that the model as developed to that point can be refined.

It is natural to expect a user interface that displays a graphical version of the property graph. Figure 3 shows that Pyrrho's HTTP service can draw a picture of a portion of a graph starting at a given node.

III. AN EXAMPLE

Examples for a graph structure usually choose social networks. We want to show that the TGM is equally suitable for Enterprise Resource Planning (ERP) and other business systems. As a non-trivial example, we have chosen a commercial enterprise, which buys parts and products, resells the purchased products or assembles products from purchased parts and sells these value-added products. It does not develop and construct products from raw material but adds some value to parts or assembles some products to form systems.

The data model is suitable for a customer-supplier ordering system and comprises 3 company divisions or departments: sales (green), stock (blue), and procurement (red). These are framed in Figure 1(a) with a green dashed line for sales data, with blue for stock data, and red for procurement or purchase. The graph schema is visualized using UML notation, which allows specifying the cardinality of the edges. The correspondence between Typed Graph elements and the UML is shown in Table I.

The sales division consists of Customer nodes with properties CustNo, Name and Address. The Name and Address might as well be structured data types for first- and last name resp. street, ZIP code, and city. The CustOrder node mainly comprises OrdNo, the (redundant) CustNo, order date Date and the order total Sum in Euros. The CustOrder contains 1 to many order detail lines of OrderPos, which consist at least of the order quantity as property. According to the semantics of the TGM the edge arrows signify the reading direction of the edge type. In the case of "belongs_to" the reading direction is from OrderPos to CustOrder.

All other necessary properties for an order line (e.g., partNo, PartName, UnitPrice) could be determined by following the edges of the model to the Part, Stock, and CustOrder node. In Figure 1 (a), only the nodes Customer and CustOrder are showing exemplified properties. More properties are maintained in a real situation, e.g., planned delivery, shipping date, etc. for a customer order. The same applies to all other nodes, e.g., unit and quantity discount for parts.

The procurement division mirrors the sales model structurally and comprises supplier, the purchases (SupplOrd, PurchPos) and the supplier catalogue. Purchase- and Sales divisions have connections to the stock management.

The central node of the stock model is the Part node who distinguishes between purchased parts (PurchasedParts) and in-house products (InHouseProduct) modelled as subtypes of Part. We have a BOM structurally represented as a recursive edge "part_of" on the part nodes. The BOM forms a tree structure with the product at the top. The product is made up recursively of components (composed parts) and finally of single parts. The stock itself is represented as a node with properties like number of parts, reservations, and commissions. A stock node is linked to a part and a storage location. This allows knowing exactly which part is located at a certain location in the warehouse.

Figure 1 (b) gives a high-level view of the scenario. Such abstractions are important for complex graphs in order to keep the model manageable. CASE tools that support zoom-in and zoom-out functions would be beneficial to assist the graph modelling.

The syntax of the above presented example ERP model will be presented in the following subsection. Multiline statements are enclosed in square brackets.

A. *Syntax of the ERP example*

First, we start with the sales graph (green schema), followed by the supplier (red schema) and stock division (blue schema), and finally the three divisions are linked by the edge types "serves", "supplies", "canSupply", "orders", and "from".

```
// sales division
[CREATE
(a:Customer {CustNo:1001, Name:'Adam', Address:'122, Nutley Terrace, London, ST 7UR, GB'} ), // Customer
// …
(f:Customer {CustNo:1006, Name:'Eddy', Address:'72, Ibrox Street, Glasgow, G51 1AA, UK'} ), // customer without order
 (o1:CustOrder {OrdNo:2001, CustNo:1001, Datum:DATE'2023-03-22', SummE:211.00} ), // CustOrder
// …
(o8:CustOrder {OrdNo:2008, CustNo:1002, Datum:DATE'2023-04-24', SummE:808.00} ),
(op1:OrderPos {Quantity:4, Unit:'piece'} ), // OrdPos
// …
(op18:OrderPos {Quantity:10, Unit:'piece'} ),
(a)<-[:ORDERED_BY]-(o1), // each order was ordered by exactly 1 customer
(a)<-[:ORDERED_BY]-(o6),(a)<-[:ORDERED_BY]-(o7),
(b)<-[:ORDERED_BY]-(o2),
//…
(o1)<-[:BELONGS_TO]-(op1), // each orderPos belongs to exactly 1 order
// …
(o8)<-[:BELONGS_TO]-(op9), // and an order has at least 1 orderPos
// …
(o8)<-[:BELONGS_TO]-(op18)]
```

```
// supplier division
[ CREATE
(a:Supplier {SupplNo:101, Name:'Rawside Furniture', Address:'58 City Rd, London , EC1Y 2AL, UK'} ),
// …
// SupplOrd
(o1:SupplOrd {OrdNo:2001, SupplNo:101, Datum:DATE'2023-01-11', "Sum€":260.00} ),
// …
// OrdPos purchase details
```

```
(op1:PurchOrd {PosNo:1, Quantity:4, Unit:'piece'} ),
// …
// (Supplier)<-[:SUPPLIED_BY]-(SupplOrd)
(a)<-[:SUPPLIED_BY]-(o1), // each order was ordered by exactly 1 Supplier
// …
// (SupplOrd)<-[:IS_POS_OF]-(OrdPos)
(o1)<-[:IS_POS_OF]-(op1), // each PurchPos belongs to exactly 1 order
// …
```

```
(o1)<-[:IS_POS_OF]-(op7), // and an order has at least 1 PurchPos
//…
// SupplCatalog
(sc11:SupplCatalog {SupplNo:101, SPartNo:'sp1', description:'Hammer handle, Wood (ash), Weight:100 g', unit:'piece', unitPrice:2.00}), //P15
//P16
// …
(sc46:SupplCatalog {SupplNo:104, SPartNo:'sp6', description:'Shelf spruce, Color: white, Weight:6 kg, Size:60w x180h cm', unit:'piece', unitPrice:20}),
// (Supplier)-[:HAS]->(SupplCatalog)
(a)-[:HAS]->(sc11), (a)-[:HAS]->(sc12), (a)-[:HAS]->(sc13), (a)-[:HAS]->(sc14), (a)-[:HAS]->(sc15), (a)-[:HAS]->(sc16),
(b)-[:HAS]->(sc21), (b)-[:HAS]->(sc22), (b)-[:HAS]->(sc23), (b)-[:HAS]->(sc24), (b)-[:HAS]->(sc25)]
```

```
// stock division
// create Part types
create type Part as (PartID char ,Designation char, Color char, Weight char, Size char) nodetype
// PurchasedPart
create type PurchasedPart under Part as (PreferredSupplNo int, sumOrderedThisYear currency, discountPrice currency)
// InHouseProduct
create type InHouseProduct under Part as (ProductionPlan char, producedThisYear int, manufacturingCosts currency)
[CREATE
(a1:Location {LocationNo:10011, Aisle:1, Shelf:'left A', Rack: 'A1'} ), // Location
// …
(l:Location {LocationNo:10111, Aisle:2, Shelf:'left A', Rack: 'A1'} ), // Location without parts
//Part will be filled implicitly
// PurchasedPart
(p1:PurchasedPart {PartID:'P01', Designation:'Wallplug',Material:'Fiber', Color:'grey', Weight:'6 g', Size:'12 cm', PreferredSupplNo:103, sumOrderedThisYear:2000, discountPrice:'0.04 €' }), //p1 Wallplug
(p5:PurchasedPart {PartID:'P05' ,Designation:'Metal nail', Material:'Metal', Color:'grey', Weight:'2 g', Size:'A 50 x2.2 mm', PreferredSupplNo:102, sumOrderedThisYear:10000, discountPrice:'0.005 €'}), //p5 Metal nail
// …
(p30:PurchasedPart {PartID:'P30' ,Designation:'Degreasing liquid', Material:'benzine', Color:'clear', Weight:'100 g', Size:'100 ml bottle' ,
    PreferredSupplNo:101, sumOrderedThisYear:150, discountPrice:'1.80 €'}), //p30 Degreasing liquid
// InHouseProduct
(p2:InHouseProduct {PartID:'P02' ,Designation:'Power plug', Color:'white', Weight:'30 g', Size:'dia 5 cm
',
ProductionPlan:'P02 Power plug', producedThisYear:1000, manufacturingCosts:'2.50 €'}),
// …
(p28:InHouseProduct {PartID:'P28' ,Designation:'Tableleg', Material:'Metal',Color:'Silver', Weight:'1 kg',Size:'80w x120l cm', ProductionPlan:'P28 Tableleg', producedThisYear:160, manufacturingCosts:'7.00 €'}),
// Stock
(s1:Stock {PartID:'P02', LocationNo:10011, available:55, commissioned:20, reserved_until:DATE'2023-09-22'} ),
```

```
// ...
(s34:Stock {PartID:'P30', LocationNo:10101,
available:30, commissioned:5,
reserved_until:DATE'2024-09-21'} ),
 //BOM
(p2)<-[:IS_Part_OF {no_of_components:2}]-(p12)<-
[:IS_Part_OF {no_of_components:1}]-(p13),
(p3)<-[:IS_Part_OF {no_of_components:1}]-(p14),
// ...
(p26)<-[:IS_Part_OF {no_of_components:1}]-(p23),
// Links: Parts<-Stock->Location
(p1)<-[:stocked]-(s33)-[:at]->(i3),
),
// ...
(p30)<-[:stocked]-(s34)-[:at]->(k)]
```

```
// linking together the 3 divisions
// links between Customer and Stock
// (OrderPos)-[:ORDERS]->(Part) (4)
[ match (o1:CustOrder {OrdNo:2001})<-[:BELONGS_TO]-
(op1:OrderPos {Pos:1} ), (p2:Part {PartID:'P02'})
 create (op1)-[:ORDERS]->(p2) ]  // P02 Power plug
[ match (o2:CustOrder {OrdNo:2002})<-[:BELONGS_TO]-
(op2:OrderPos {Pos:1} ), (p10:Part {PartID:'P10'})
create (op2)-[:ORDERS]->(p10) ] // Rubber glue
// ...
// (OrderPos)-[:FROM_]->(Stock) (5)
[ match (o1:CustOrder {OrdNo:2001})<-[:BELONGS_TO]-
(op1:OrderPos {Pos:1} ),   (s1:Stock {PartID:'P02',
LocationNo:10011})
 create (op1)-[:FROM_]->(s1) ] // Power plug
[ match (o2:CustOrder {OrdNo:2002})<-[:BELONGS_TO]-
(op2:OrderPos {Pos:1} ), (s30:Stock {PartID:'P10',
LocationNo:10083})
create (op2)-[:FROM_]->(s30) ] // Rubber glue
// ...
// links between Supplier and Stock
// (PurchPos)-[:SUPPLIES]->(PurchasePart) (2)
[ match (o1:SupplOrd {OrdNo:2001} )<-[:IS_POS_OF]-
(pp1:PurchPos     {PosNo:1}     ),     (p18:PurchasePart
{PartID:'P18'}),
 create (pp1)-[:SUPPLIES]->(p18) ] // P18 Splint pin
[ match (o2:SupplOrd {OrdNo:2002} )<-[:IS_POS_OF]-
(pp2:PurchPos     {PosNo:1}     ),     (p10:PurchasePart
{PartID:'P10'}),
 create (pp2)-[:SUPPLIES]->(p10) ] // P10 Rubber Glue
// ...
// (SupplCatalog)-[:CAN_SUPPLY]->(PurchasePart) (3)
[     match     (sc11:SupplCatalog     {SupplNo:101,
SPartNo:'sp1'}), (p15:PurchasePart {PartID:'P15'}),
create (sc11)-[:CAN_SUPPLY]->(p15) ]  //P15 Hammer
handle
[              match               (sc12:SupplCatalog
{SupplNo:101,SPartNo:'sp2'}),         (p16:PurchasePart
{PartID:'P16'}),
 create (sc12)-[:CAN_SUPPLY]->(p16) ] //P16 Table top
// ...
// links between Supplier and Customer
// (PurchPos)-[:SERVES]->(OrderPos) (1)
```

```
[ match (so1:SupplOrd {OrdNo:2001, SupplNo:101}) <-
[:IS_POS_OF]-(pp1:PurchPos {PosNo:1}), (o1:CustOrder
{OrdNo:2001})<-[:BELONGS_TO]-(op1:OrderPos {Pos:1})
create (pp1)-[:SERVES]->(op1) ] //P16 Table Top
[ match (so1:SupplOrd {OrdNo:2001, SupplNo:101}) <-
[:IS_POS_OF]-(pp7:PurchPos {PosNo:2}), (o2:CustOrder
{OrdNo:2002})<-[:BELONGS_TO]-(op12:OrderPos {Pos:2})
29.     create (pp7)-[:SERVES]->(op12) ] // P17 Table
Frame
// ..
```

There are opportunities here to alter some of these types to implement some of the comments in the model. Table I summarizes the schema objects (node and edge types) of the ERP graph schema and Figure 1 presents the TGS in graphical form using UML notation.

IV. CONCLUSIONS AND FUTURE WORK

The purpose of this paper was to report on a successful mechanism for graph modeling, creation, and pattern-matching in an RDMS. The software is available on Github [8] for free download and use and is not covered by any patent or other restrictions.

The current "alpha" state of the software implements all of the above ideas. The test suite includes simple cases that demonstrate the integration of the relational and typed graph model concepts in Pyrrho DBMS.

Future work will include meeting the requirements of successive drafts of the GQL standard and enhancing the typed modeling features.

REFERENCES

[1] M. Crowe and F. Laux, "Database Technology Evolution", IARIA International Journal on Advances in Software, vol. 15 numbers 3 and 4, 2022, pp. 224-234, ISSN: 1942-2628

[2] ISO 9075-16 Property Graph Queries (SQL/PGQ), International Standards Organisation, 2023.

[3] N. Francis et al., A Researcher's Digest of GQL. 26th International Conference on Database Theory (ICDT 2023), Mar 2023, Ioannina, Greece, doi:10.4230/LIPIcs.ICDT.2023.1, pp. 1-22. https://hal.science/hal-04094449 [retrieved: 18 October 2023]

[4] https://www.GQLStandards.org, October 4, 2023 – GQL status update [retrieved 18 October 2023].

[5] F. Laux and M. Crowe, "Information Integration using the Typed Graph Model", DBKDA 2021: The Thirteenth International Conference on Advances in Databases, Knowledge, and Data Applications, IARIA, May 2021, pp. 7-14, ISSN: 2308-4332, ISBN: 978-1-61208-857-0

[6] M. Crowe and F. Laux, "Graph Data Models and Relational Databe Technology", DBKDA 2023: The Fifteenth International Conference on Advances in Databases, Knowledge, and Data Applications, IARIA, March 2023, pp. 33-37, ISSN: 2308-4332, ISBN: 978-1-68558-056-8

[7] M. Crowe, PyrrhoV7alpha, https://github.com/MalcolmCrowe/ShareableDataStructures [retrieved: Sept 2023]

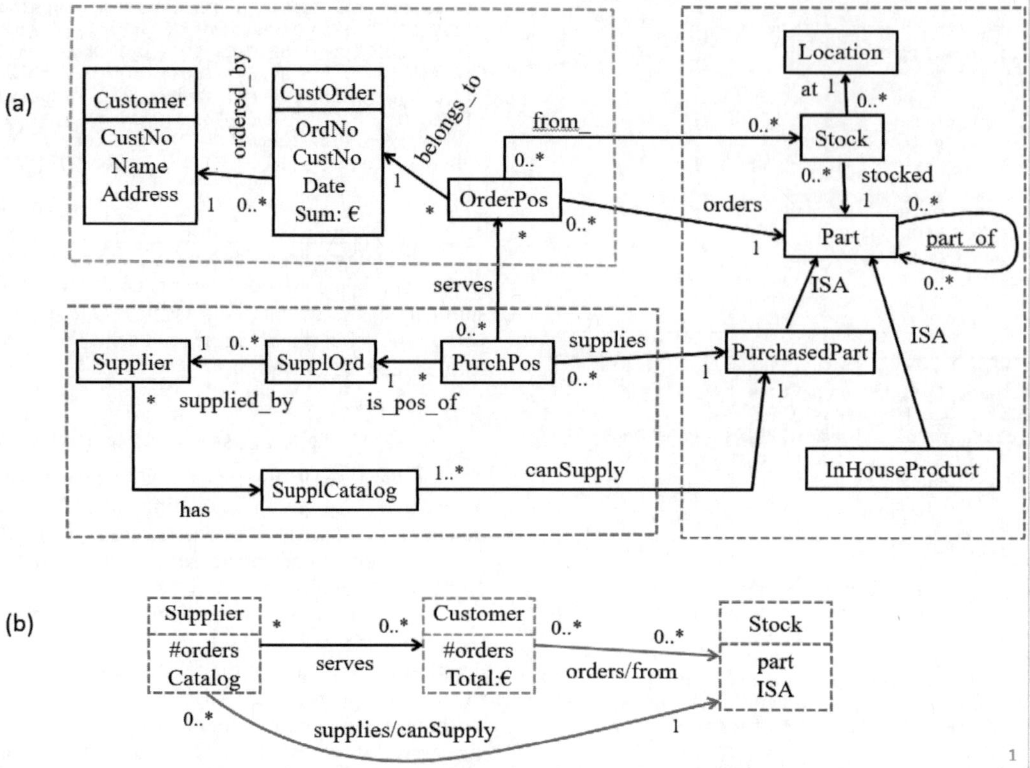

Figure 1. Example TGM of a commercial enterprise showing two levels of detail

TABLE I. NODE AND EDGE TYPES IN AN EXAMPLE DATABASE (RELATIONAL DESCRIPTION)

Type name	Informal Description	SuperType
Customer	(CustNo, Name, Address)	
CustOrder	(CustNo, Datum, OrdNo, Summ€)	
OrderPos	(Id, Quantity, Unit)	
Location	(LocationNo, Reihe, Shelf, Rack)	
PurchasePart	(PartID, Designation, Material, Color, Weight, Size)	Part
InHouseProduct	(PartID, Designation, Material, Color, Weight, Size)	Part
Stock	(PartID, LocationNo, Available, Commissioned, Reserved_Until)	
Supplier	(SupplNo, Name, Address)	
SupplOrd	(OrdNo, SupplNo, Datum, Sum€)	
PurchPos	(PosNo, Quantity, Unit)	
SupplCatalog	(SupplNo, SPartNo, Desription, Weight, Unit, unitPrice)	

Type name	Leaving	Arriving	Other properties
Ordered_by	CustOrder	Customer	
Belongs_to	OrderPos	CustOrder	
Is_Part_Of	Part	Part	No_of_components
Stocked	Stocked	Part	
At	Part	Location	
Supplied_by	SupplOrd	Supplier	
Is_Pos_of	PurchPos	SupplOrd	
Has	Sypplier	SupplCatalog	
Orders	OrderPos	Part	
From_	OrderPos	Stock	
Supplied	PurchPos	ParchasePart	
Can_Spply	SupplCatalog	PurchasePart	
Serves	PurchPos	OrderPos	

```
E:\PyrrhoDB70\Pyrrho>pyrrhocmd ps
SQL> [CREATE (:Person {name:'Fred Smith'})<-[:Child]-(a:Person {name:'Peter Smith'}),
> (a)-[:Child]->(b:Person {name:'Mary Smith'})
> -[:Child]->(:Person {name:'Lee Smith'}),
> (b)-[:Child]->(:Person {name:'Bill Smith'})]
SQL> MATCH ({name:'Peter Smith'}) [()-[:Child]->()]+ (x) RETURN x.name
|----------|
|NAME      |
|----------|
|Fred Smith|
|Lee Smith |
|Bill Smith|
|Mary Smith|
|----------|
SQL> MATCH ({name:'Peter Smith'}) [(p)-[:Child]->()]+ ({name:x})
|----------------------------------------------------------------------|----------|
|P                                                                     |X         |
|----------------------------------------------------------------------|----------|
|ARRAY[PERSON(ID=2,NAME=Peter Smith)]                                  |Fred Smith|
|ARRAY[PERSON(ID=2,NAME=Peter Smith),PERSON(ID=3,NAME=Mary Smith)]|Lee Smith |
|ARRAY[PERSON(ID=2,NAME=Peter Smith),PERSON(ID=3,NAME=Mary Smith)]|Bill Smith|
|ARRAY[PERSON(ID=2,NAME=Peter Smith)]                                  |Mary Smith|
|----------------------------------------------------------------------|----------|
SQL> alter table person add primary key(name)
SQL> alter table child to childof
SQL> alter table childof alter leaving to parent
SQL> alter table childof alter arriving to child
SQL> create role ps
SQL> grant PS to
SQL> |
```

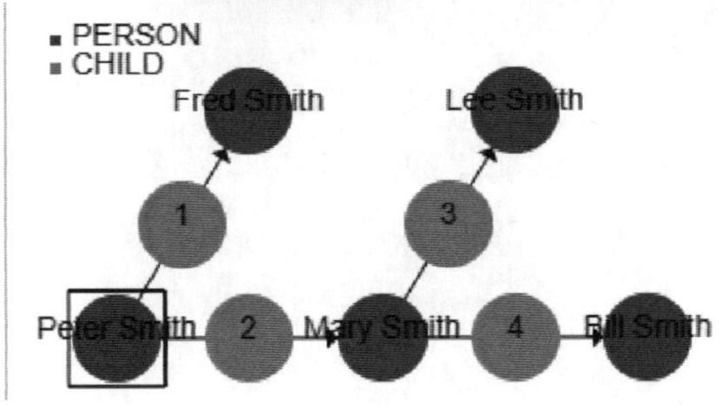


```csharp
public class CHILDOF : Versioned
{
    [Identity]
    [Field(PyrrhoDbType.Integer)]
    [AutoKey]
    public Int64? ID;
    [Leaving]
    [Field(PyrrhoDbType.String)]
    public String? PARENT;
    [Arriving]
    [Field(PyrrhoDbType.String)]
    public String? CHILD;
    0 references
    public PERSON? PARENTis => conn?.FindOne<PERSON>(("NAME", PARENT));
    1 reference
    public PERSON? CHILDis => conn?.FindOne<PERSON>(("NAME", CHILD));
}
0 references
public class Demo
{
    static PyrrhoConnect? conn = null;
    2 references
    static List<PERSON> Descendants(PERSON p)
    {
        var ds = new List<PERSON>();
        if (p.ofPARENTs is CHILDOF[] ca)
            foreach (var c in ca)
                if (c.CHILDis is PERSON d)
                {
                    ds.Add(d);
                    ds.AddRange(Descendants(d));
                }
        return ds;
    }
    0 references
    static void Main()
    {
        conn = new PyrrhoConnect("Files=ps;Role=PS");
        conn.Open();
        try
        {
            // Get a list of all descendants of Pete Smith
            var pa = conn.FindWith<PERSON>(("NAME","Peter Smith"));
            if (pa.Length == 1)
                foreach (var c in Descendants(pa[0]))
                    Console.WriteLine(c.NAME);
        }
        catch (Exception ex)
        {
```

Figure 2. A simple repeating pattern (a) Command line SQL interaction to build and display a simple database (b) Browser display of the graph: http://localhost:8180/ps/PS/PERSON/NAME='Peter Smith'?NODE (c) An extract from a C# client program to list Peter Smith's descendants showing PyrrhoDB's Versioned API

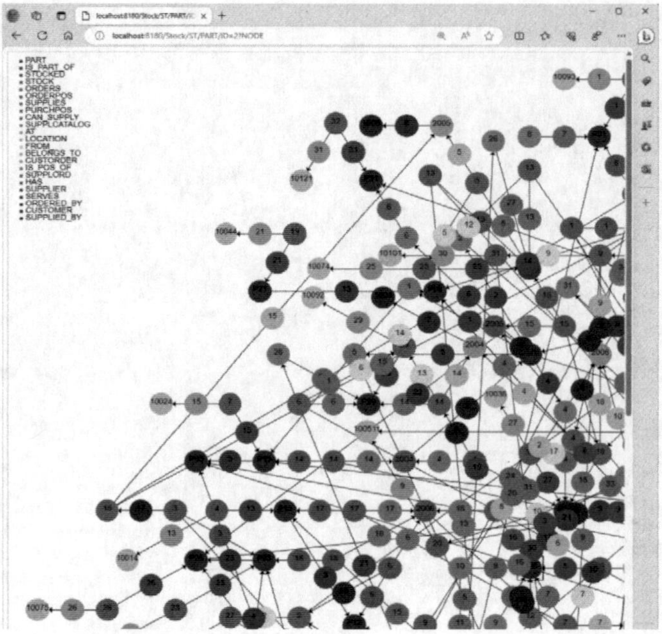

Figure 3. A part of the ERP example graph, after similar changes to primary keys (e.g., PART now has key PartID).

International Academy, Research, and Industry Association (IARIA)
412 Derby Way
Wilmington, DE 19810

CURRAN ASSOCIATES INC.
proceedings.com

ISBN 978-1-7138-8128-5
9 781713 881285

Fall Technical Meeting of the Western States Section of the Combustion Institute (WSS/CI 2017 Fall Meeting)

Laramie, Wyoming, USA
2 – 3 October 2017

WSSCI
Western States Section Combustion Institute